Caroline County Virginia

Bureau of Vital Statistics Death Records

1853-1896

Herbert Ridgeway Collins

HERITAGE BOOKS
2007

HERITAGE BOOKS
AN IMPRINT OF HERITAGE BOOKS, INC.

Books, CDs, and more—Worldwide

For our listing of thousands of titles see our website
at
www.HeritageBooks.com

Published 2007 by
HERITAGE BOOKS, INC.
Publishing Division
65 East Main Street
Westminster, Maryland 21157-5026

Copyright © 1999 Herbert Ridgeway Collins

Other books by the author:

Caroline County, Virginia Death Records (1919-1994) from The Caroline Progress,
A Weekly Newspaper Published in Bowling Green, Virginia

Cemeteries of Caroline County, Virginia, Volume 1: Public Cemeteries

Cemeteries of Caroline County, Virginia, Volume 2: Private Cemeteries

Cemeteries of Caroline County, Virginia, Volume 3: Private Cemeteries

All rights reserved. No part of this book may be reproduced or transmitted in any form or by any means, electronic or mechanical, including photocopying, recording or by any information storage and retrieval system without written permission from the author, except for the inclusion of brief quotations in a review.

International Standard Book Number: 978-0-7884-1291-2

TABLE OF CONTENTS

INTRODUCTION v
DISEASES AND CAUSES OF DEATH ix
COMMISSIONERS OF CAROLINE xiii
CAROLINE DEATH REGISTER 1
1853 1
1854 5
1855 10
1856 13
1857 17
1858 35
1959 40
1860 46
1861 53
1862 61
1863 73
1864 73
1865 76
1866 81
1867 85
1868 89
1869 92
1870 92
1871 92
1872 92
1873 95
1874 98
1875 101
1876 104
1877 107
1878 111
1879 114
1880 117
1881 120
1882 125
1883 127
1884 131
1885 134
1886 139
1887 142
1888 146
1889 151
1890 154
1891 157

1892	160
1893	163
1894	166
1895	169
1896	171
INDEX	175

INTRODUCTION

Blood, sweat, tears and lots of swearing can best sum up this undertaking. It all began several years ago. When I first examined the records in their entirety, I thought this publication would be impossible. I first went through and copied just the names of the deceased so that I could access the feasibily of the project and also to acquint myself with the names. After that, I hand copied the actual records, then fed them into my computer.
By act of the General Assembly in 1853, the State of Virginia Bureau of Vital Statistics required localities to keep birth, marriage and death records. In 1897, the Bureau ceased this practice and, from that time to 1912, no records were kept either on the local or State level. After 1912, the records begin again on the State level and continue today. These are only available from the Bureau of Vital Statistics in Richmond.

The handwriting is beyond belief, the spelling awful, the abbreviations make no sense, and carelessness in filling in the information made this job almost impossible. Some of the pages are faded beyond recognition. Others appear to have suffered water damage, and still others have portions of the pages missing completely. Aside from that, the information for the years 1863, 1869, 1870, and 1871 are all missing from the files in The Library of Virginia. In addition, I have discovered that some files in the remaining years are also missing. For instance, for the year 1895, there is only one district of Caroline in the files. It is difficult to determine how many more are missing, since the division of the county differed from year to year in this endeavor. Because of this situation, individuals using this reference should not assume that their ancestor did not die during this time or died in another county just because they are not listed here. In many cases I have consulted other sources, such as marriage records, census records, county histories, family histories and other sources to get a clue as to what the names and dates could be, then returned to the original record. In this way, one can read into the record and figure it out. It was very helpful that I had already recorded so many of the cemeteries of Caroline County and could identify the deaths with the places of residence and burial. The fact that I have studied the history and records of Caroline County my entire life also helped in figuring out the data. Because of the difficulty in reading this record, I would warn my readers to double check the information both against the original, when in doubt, or against their own family data. I have done my level best to produce as accurate an interpretation as possible, but I am sure there are mistakes, which I hope are minimal. One thing is for sure, and that is, the longer one waits to publish this information, the more of it will be lost due to the fading of the ink which continues year by year.

I have used one format throughout the book, although several were followed in the original. This format includes: Name of deceased/race/owner of slave where listed/sex/date of death/place of death if other than Caroline County/cause of death/age at death/name of parents/occupation if listed/place of birth if listed/name of person reporting death and their relationship to the deceased. I have only listed places of birth and death if they were outside Caroline County or if postoffices within Caroline County are listed. In a few instances, farm and plantation names are listed. Those appear in quotation to avoid confusion.

In some cases, the masters are listed as young masters for slave entries. In those cases, I have used a dash mark to separate the the name, since "young" could be taken for a proper name, for example: "John Hamilton - Young Master".

For the most part, I have tried to leave the spellings as they appear in the original. I have inserted information in brackets, which is additional information or my own interpretation. There are few recorded occupations of the deceased and when there are, I have recorded them, otherwise I have not left the usual two spaces __ for them. Also the commissioner recorded the occupation of the parent. To avoid confusion, that information follows the parents' names at the end of the entry, for example: "father & mechanic". The names of the slaves were recorded by the commissioner the way they sounded since they were seldom written before. There are no records available to double check their spellings and I am sure some are wrong, but I have done my best to record them as accurately as possible. If they sound unusual to us today, they probably were right then. Where the information is missing completely, I have used two underlines __ to show that the information was not included. If the information is there but cannot be read, I have used [illeg]. Some information printed here is sketchy, but any that is legible is given however little it may be.

This publication records 7,642 deaths in Caroline County during the period 1853-1896. These are broken down as follows in the records: 1853-171, 1854-230, 1855-327, 1856-185, 1857-772, 1858-234, 1859-277, 1860-310, 1861-332, 1862-558, 1863-missing, 1864-107, 1865-230, 1866-125, 1867-168, 1868-117, 1869-missing, 1870-missing, 1871-missing, 1872-105, 1873-106, 1874-124, 1875-142, 1876-152, 1877-160, 1878-132, 1879-136, 1880-100, 1881-202, 1882-73, 1883-163, 1884-136, 1885-200, 1886-140, 1887-191, 1888-197, 1889-124, 1890-132, 1891-157, 1892-125, 1893-138, 1894-116, 1895-74, 1896-174. Four years are missing completely as indicated above. There are some years not all the districts in Caroline are represented in the records. For instance, 1895 only reflects the Bowling Green District. There is a lot of inconsistency in the division of the County by districts. However, if one looks at the number of deaths for the given years, you will see that there must be missing districts. The year 1857 lists 772 deaths which is unrealistic. Within that year there seems to be a mix-up of the years 1856 and 1857. At the top of the pages, in large contemporary handwriting is 1857, however in the name listings, the dates jump back and forth between 1856 and 1857. For fear, I would only more confuse the reader, I have chosen to stick with the information at the top of the pages. Therefore, if in doubt as to whether it is 1857 or 1856, one should check the original.

The view on longevity at this time makes little sense. The commissioner records many persons as dying of old age, sometimes as young as 60 years of age. In contrast, many persons lived in their 80's, 90's, and a good representation reached the century mark. At least two are recorded to have lived to the age of 110 years. The mortality rate was the highest among children, since there were no known cures for many childhood diseases such as diptheria and typhoid fever, which would wipe out entire families. One wonders how the couple recorded as losing their three children all on the same day could have coped with such tragedy. There seems to have been a sufficient number of physicians in Caroline County at the time. At the beginning of the 1850s when the death register began, there were 32 practicing physicians in Caroline County. This may seem like a lot; however, distances and bad roads, coupled with the slow transportation of horse and buggy, account for the need for such a large number. As a matter of interest, there is only one recorded divorce during this period and that was in 1886 for one Joe [sic] Seal, a female who was 30 years of age.

This publication supplements my earlier publications, three books on the cemeteries of Caroline County and one on deaths recorded in the Caroline County newspaper. I will do another book on deaths recorded in miscellanous sources, such as church records, newspapers, county histories, etc. Also, to complete the death records will be the Bible records of Caroline County, which I hope to complete by the Spring of 1999.

Herbert R. Collins
"Green Falls"
Caroline County,
Virginia

DISEASES AND CAUSES OF DEATH

Affliction of Brain
Abscess Liver
Absyss of Stomach
Abyscess
Ague
Albuminusia
Anasmea
Angina Pectoris
Anthrax
Anurmia
Aphonia
Apoplexy
Arthragra
Aspentry
Asthma
Anthrophy
Aunfuler
Barber's Itch
Battle Wound
Bed Fever
Bilious
Bilious Diarreah
Billious Fever
Billious Liver
Bilious Pluericy
Black Tongue
Blackwater Fever
Bleed to Death
Bleeding of Navel
Blood Poison
Blow from Falling
Brain Fever
Brain Inflamation
Brights Disease
Brights Kidney
Bronchitis
Buboes
Burnt to Death
Burnt Chills
Bursting Blood Vein
By Fall of a Cart Body

Camp Fever
Cancer
Cancer of the Bowels
Cancer of Womb
Canine Madness
Carbuncle
Catalepsey
Catank
Catank Fever
Cerebis Spira Mening
Cerebritis
Child Bed
Child Birth
Childblains
Chills
Choked
Cholera Infantum
Cholera Infection
Cholera Inflamation
Cholera Morbus
Cold
Colic
Congestion of the Brain
Congestion of Lungs
Congestive Chill
Congestive Liver
Consumption
Continued Fever
Convulsions
Corruption
Costive
Cramp
Cramp Cholic
Cronic Croup
Cronic Diarrhea
Cronic Disease
Cronic Thrush
Croup
Cynanche Lorsillius
Dasbough
Deformity

Delirious Tremors
Dentition
Denlitio
Diapepsia
Diarrhea
Died on the Roadside
Diptheria
Disease of Head
Disease of Heart
Disease of Kidneys
Diseased Liver
Disease of Spine
Disease of Throat
Dropsy
Dropsy of Brain
Dropsy in Chest
Drowning
Dysentery
Dyspepsia
Eating Cherries
Eating Dirt
Embolism
Embolism
Enysipelia
Epilipsy
Erysipelas
Erysifulas Metart
Eurycephsious
Erysephilous
Exposure
Falling Sickness
Falling Tree
Fell from a Mule
Fits
Flux
Fothergill's Pain
French Pox
General Debility
Gravel
Grappe or LaGrippe
Gun Shot
Hanged
Hemorrhage
Hemorrhage of Bowels
Hestick Fever
Hickups
Hives
Humid Tetter

Hydrocephalus
Hydrophobia
Indigestion
Inexperience of Doctor
Infantile Fits
Inflammatory Rheumatism
Inflamation of Bowels
Inflamation of Sore
Inflamation of Stomach
Influenza
Irrespeles
Intemperance
Intermittant
Intermitting Fever
Interuption of Bowel
Intoxication
Jail Fever (Typhus Fever)
Kicked by horse
Killed Accidently
Killed by a Cow
Killed by Falling Tree
Killed by Railroad Car
Killed by a Street Car
Killed in Battle
Killed in Saw Mill
Killed in Well
Killed on Railroad
La Grippe (Grippe)
Larfula
Lead Colic
Lenfulos
Lenofula
Lock Jaw
Lung Fever
Malaria
Marasmus
Malarial Fever
Measles
Membraneous Cough
Membrane Croup
Meningitis
Metastatic Abyscess
Milk Crust
Mortification
Murdered
Nemberry
Neglect
Nephritis

Neuralgia
Neuralgia of Head
Newvas Typhoid
Old Age
Over heated
Overlaid
Palpitation of Heart
Palsy
Paralysis
Paregoric
Parson's Disease
Pellagra
Pericarditis
Perilyphlitis
Poisoned
Rheumatic Neurolgia
Phletalis
Phthisis Pulmonalis
Phthisis Pulmonal
Physical Infirmity
Piles
Plurisy
Pneulogy
Pneumonia
Pneumonia Typhoides
Poisoned
Premature Birth
Prostrate Cancer
Puerperal Fever
Puerperal Peutonila
Pusspinal Fever
Putrid Fever
Putrid Throat
Quinsy
Remitting Fever
Rheumatism
Rickets
Rising on Head
Rneupera Fever
Rubeola
Run Round
Rupture
St. Anthony's Fire
St. Vitus' Dance
Sawmill Explosion
Scalded
Scarlet Fever
Screws

Scrofula
Scurvy
Shingles
Ship's Fever
Sinking Chill
Slow Fever
Small Pox
Smothered
Softening of Brain
Sore Throat
Spasms
Spinal Disease
Spinal Meningitas
Spotted Fever
Spleen
Stebismus
Strangled
Stricture of Bladder
Stillborn
Stone Fever
Strangled
Strangury
Steam Explosion
Struck by Lightning
Structure of Bowels
Suffocation
Summer Compliant
Summer Disease
Sun Fever
Teething
Tetanus
Thrush
Theuselism of Heart
Tic Douloureux
Tobacco Heart
Tonsilitis
Tsemus
Tumor
Tumor in Bowels
Typho Malina
Typhoid Fever
Typhoid Flux
Typhoid Pneumonia
Typhus Fever
Ulser in Heart
Water on Brain
White Rising
Whooping Cough

Winter Fever
Worms
Worm Fever
Yellow Fever

COMMISSIONERS OF REVENUE FOR CAROLINE COUNTY APPOINTED TO RECORD VITAL STATISTICS AS REPORTED IN THE DEATH REGISTER

1853 - William J. Murray
1854 - Joseph M. Seay
1855 - Joseph M. Seay
1856 - Joseph M. Seay
    William J. Murray
1857 - William J. Murray
1858 - John Shepherd
    William J. Murray
1859 - William J. Murray
1860 - William J. Murray
    John Shepherd
1861 - John Shepherd
1862 - John Shepherd
1863 - No records exist
1864 - John Shepherd
1865 - William J. Murray
1866 - John Shepherd
1867 - William J. Murray
1868 - F.S. Talkey
    Geo. W. Marshall
1869 - No records exist
1870 - No records exist
1871 - No records exist
1872 - James B. Wood
    Thos W. Gouldin - Port Royal District
    A.G. Goodwin - Reedy Church District
    William J. Murray - Bowling Green District
    Walter J. Anderson - Bowling Green District
1873 - Thos H. Blanton - Madison District
    P.W. Gouldin - Port Royal District
    A.G. Goodwin - Reedy Church District
    William J. Murray - Bowling Green District
    Walter J. Anderson - Bowling Green District
1874 - Walter J. Anderson - Bowling Green District
    A.G. Goodwin - Reedy Church District
    P.W. Gouldin - Port Royal District
1875 - Walter J. Anderson - Bowling Green District
    Thomas W. Gouldin - Port Royal District
    A.G. Woodin
1876 - Walter J. Anderson
1877 - Walter J. Anderson

A.G. Goodwin
1878 - A.G. Goodwin
Walter J. Anderson
1879 - E.R. Coghill
Walter J. Anderson
1880 - E.R. Coghill
Walter J. Anderson
1881 - E.R. Coghill
Walter J. Anderson
1882 - E.R. Coghill
Walter J. Anderson
1883 - Walter J. Anderson - Bowling Green District
Thos H. Blanton - 2nd District (formerly Reedy Church)
1884 - Walter J. Anderson - Bowling Green District
Thos H. Blanton - 2nd District
1885 - Walter J. Anderson - Bowling Green District
Thos H. Blanton - 2nd District
1886 - Walter J. Anderson - Bowling Green District
Thos H. Blanton - 2nd District
1887 - Walter J. Anderson - Bowling Green District
Thos H. Blanton - Second District
1888 - Thos H. Blanton - Second District
Walter J. Anderson - Bowling Green District
1889 - Walter J. Anderson - Bowling Green District
Thos H. Blanton - Second District
1890 - Thos H. Blanton - Second District
Walter J. Anderson - Bowling Green District
1891 - Thos H. Blanton - Second District
Walter J. Anderson - Bowling Green District
1892 - Robert S. Gravatt - No One District (Bowling Green)
Thos H. Blanton - Second District
1893 - Robert S. Gravatt - No One District
Thos H. Blanton - Second District
1894 - Robert S. Gravatt - No One District
Thos H. Blanton - Second District
1895 - Robert S. Gravatt - No One District
No other districts represented
1896 - Robert S. Gravatt - First District
Thos H. Blanton - Second District
Walter J. Anderson

CAROLINE COUNTY DEATH REGISTER
1853-1896

Act for Registration of Deaths, Marriages and Births passed April 11, 1853

Key: Name/Race/Owner of Slave where applicable/Sex/Date of Death/Place of Death/
Cause of Death/Age/Parents of Deceased/Place of Birth/Occupation/Spouse/Person Reporting Death

[Note: I have not left two spaces for Place of Death, Place of Birth, Occupation, and Spouse since they are not usually given, but have included them when it is given.
The two spaces means nothing was inserted by the Commissioner. If it is given and I cannot read it, then I insert "illeg" for illegible in brackets]

1853

Fanny Pitts/W/F/Nov/__/65y/__/Wm S. Anderson
Ellen Ellenora Allen/W/F/July/__/2y 7m/Wm & Elizth Allen/Wm L. Allen
Sarah C. Bruce/W/F/Aug/__/1y/Wm S. & Mary H. Bruce/Wm S. Bruce
Nancy Samuel/W/F/Oct/__/40y/__/Nancy Bird
Caty Puller/W/F/Dec/__/60y/__/Jas Barlow
Walker/S/Wm D. Bates/M/July/__/__/Nancy/Wm D. Bates Master
Bettie/S/Jas S. Barbee/F/Aug/__/__/Eliza/Jas S. Barbee Master
No Name/S/Jno H. Bernard/F/Aug/__/__/Charlotte/John H. Bernard Master
Sallie Brooks/W/F/Dec 28/__/47y/Thos & __ Coghill/b.Essex Co/H.B. Brooks
No Name/S/Gray Boulware/F/Dec 28/__/__/Ann/Gray Boulware Master
No Name/S/Wm A. Buckner/F/Nov/__/2y 7m/Phillis/Wm A. Buckner Master
No Name/S/Wm A. Buckner/F/Feb/__/__/Nancy/Wm A. Buckner Master
Scott/S/Wm S. Broaddus/M/July/__/2y 9m/Jane/Wm S. Broaddus Master
Lucy A. Cox/W/F/Sept/__/60y/__/b.Spotsylvania/Jeff M. Bullock
Nancy Loven/W/F/Sept/__/70y/__/Isaac Cecil
Saml Chenault Jr/W/M/Sept/__/3y/Saml & Mary Chenault/Saml Chenault
Nancy Noel/W/F/Dec/__/67y/__/b.Essex County/Jas Carneal
Hiram Carter/Free/M/Aug/__/__/Eliza Carter/Eliza Carter
Maria/S/John Conway/F/__/50y/__/John Conway Master
Reuben/S/Wm Collawn/M/Oct/__/60y/__/Wm Collawn Master
Vilett/S/Ro. Chapman/F/Sept/__/63y/__/Ro Chapman Master
Edward/S/Wm S. Chandler/M/July/__/45y/__/Wm S. Chandler Master
Philip/S/Lucy A. Dew/M/July 4/__/__/Judy/Jno Purke
Bob/S/Lucy A. Dew/M/Sept/__/__/Amey/Lucy A. Dew Mistress
No Name/S/Lucy A. Dew/F/Dec/__/__/Sallie/Lucy A. Dew Mistress
Steven/S/D.C. DeJarnette/M/Oct/__/60y/__/D.C. DeJarnette Master
No Name/S/J.M. Dillard/F/Oct/__/28y/__/Jane/Jas M. Dillard Master
George/S/J.W. Gouldin/M/Nov/__/__/Sydney/John W. Gouldin Master
Harriett S. Estes/W/F/Nov/__/52y/__/Franl. Fitzhugh

Agnes/S/Saml Gordon/F/Dec/__/7y/Mary/Saml Gordon Master
Vilett/S/John Gouldin/F/Sept/__/__/__/John Gouldin Master
Harry/S/John Gouldin/M/Sept/__/62y/__/John Gouldin Master
Rina/S/R. Broaddus Est/F/Oct/__/73y/__/Mary Harrison
Matilda/S/M.B. Harrison/F/Nov/__/__/M.B. Harrison
Bettie/S/A.L. Holloway/F/Nov/__/__/__/A.L. Holloway Master
William/S/A.L. Holloway/M/Nov/__/70y/Lettie/A.L. Holloway Master
Rose/S/Ro Hudgin/F/Dec/__/70y/__/Ro Hudgin Master
Lepnober/S/Wm E. Jones/M/Dec/__/15y/__/Wm E. Jones Master
Lewis/S/Wm E. Jones/M/Dec/__/12y/__/Wm E. Jones Master
Mary/S/L.M. Jeter/F/Oct/__/__/Mary/Lawr H. Jeter Master
No Name/S/L.M. Jeter/F/July/__/__/Rebecca/Lawr H. Jeter Master
Mildred C. Kay/W/F/Sept/Consumption/26y/Phil & Eliza Green/Wm Kay
Sallie Loven/W/F/Sept/__/70y/__/Willis Loven
Rebecca Rouse/W/F/Nov/__/80y/Edwd & R. Clarke/Lewis D. Longest
Caroline/S/Thos Motley/F/Nov/__/__/__/Thos Motley Master
Ginney/S/Thos Motley/F/Nov/__/__/__/Thos Motley Master
Paty/S/Wm G. Maury/F/Aug/__/__/Patsy/Wm G. Maury Master
Mary Marinor/W/F/Sept/__/__/__/Sophia Marinor
Susan Minter/W/F/Nov/__/21y/Jos Minter/Jos Minter
No Name/S/M.R. Micou/F/July/__/__/Margarett/Monger R. Micou
Jos F. Powers/W/M/Aug/__/32y/Marshall & Eliza Rollins/Jos F. Powers
Stafford/S/Eliza Powers/M/Sept/__/Derangement/__/40y/__/Jos F. Powers
Ada/S/S.J. Peyton/F/Dec/__/12y/__/Randolph Peyton Master
Amy/Free/F/Apr/__/14y/Frances Hudson/Dandridge Pitts
Sarah E. Puller/W/F/Nov/Fitts/15y/Jno B. & Elizth Puller/John B. Puller
Elizabeth/S/R.B. Richerson/F/Nov/Consumption/47/__/R.B. Richerson Master
Almeda/S/R.B. Richerson/F/Nov/Consumption/__/__/R.B. Richerson Master
Thos C. Rixey/W/M/Nov/Consumption/49y/__/b.Culpepper County/John P. Downing Adm
Charles/S/Wm W. Roper/M/July/__/__/Frances/Wm W. Roper Master
No Name/S/Wm W. Roper/F/July/__/__/Jane/Wm W. Roper Master
No Name/S/Wm W. Roper/F/Dec/__/__/Fanny/Wm W. Roper Master
Abram/S/R.T. Roane/M/Sept/__/__/Rose/Judy M. Dillard Master
Jane/S/Garl Samuel/F/Sept/__/__/__/Garl Samuel Master
Baughm/S/P.S. Spindle/M/Sept/__/__/Polly/P.S. Spindle Master
Edmond/S/Phil Samuel/M/July/__/__/__/Phil Samuel Master
Wm Sylva/W/M/Aug/__/__/Wm & __ Sylva/Phil Samuel
Lucy E. Sylva/W/F/Aug/__/__/Wm & __ Sylva/Wm Sylva Son
Pierce Sylva/W/M/Aug/__/__/Wm & __ Sylva/Wm Sylva Son
Kitty/S/Thos R. Sale/F/July/__/__/Judy/Thos B. Sale Master
No Name/S/J.A.L. Shaddock/F/Dec/__/Saley/J.A.L. Shaddock Master
Caroline/S/Geo R. Samuel/F/Aug/__/__/__/F. Leacock Master
Tulip/S/J.B. Skinker/F/July/__/__/Caty/J.B. Skinker Master
Malinda Saunders/W/F/Sept/__/__/__/Hay B.___[Battaile?]
Martha Taylor/W/F/Nov/__/2m/Thos T. & J.F. Taylor/Thos T. Taylor
Mary Taylor/W/F/Nov/__/2m/Thos T. & J.F. Taylor/Thos T. Taylor
Virginia S. Trible/W/F/Sept/__/Thos J. & A.E. Trible/Thos J. Trible
Sallie/S/Wm E. Thornton/F/Aug/__/__/Mary/Elijah Kelly

Jno/S/Wm E. Thornton/M/Aug/__/__/Charlotte/Elijah Kelly
Bassett/S/P.R. Thornton/M/July/__/__/Ann/P.R. Thornton Master
No Name/S/Geo W. Trice/F/Oct/__/6m/Esther/Geo W. Trice Master
Virginia White/W/F/July 27/__/__/Muscoe & E. Boulware/J.S.R. White - Husband
Columbia Weasner/W/F/July/__/2y 5m/Peter & Ann Weasner/Peter Weasner Father
George/S/Edmd P. White/M/Oct/__/__/Amanda/E.P. White - Master
Cath. Brooks/W/F/Nov/__/__/__/Saml Wright Son-In-Law
Maria/S/H.B. White/F/July/__/__/Agnes/H.B. White - Master
Jacob/S/J.D. Withers/M/July/__/__/Nicey/J.D. Withers Master
No Name/S/J.D. Withers/F/July/__/__/Jane/J.D. Withers Master
Amanda/S/R.[euben]B. Yates/F/Dec/__/__/__/R.B. Yates Master
James/S/Robt Dickinson/M/Aug 12/Pneumonia/1y 11m/Frances/Robt Dickinson Master
Allah/S/Thos T. Chandler/F/Dec 27/Child Bed/32y/Unknown/Thos T. Chandler Master
Edwina Chandler/W/F/July 1/Disentary/55y 10d/Dabney & Lucy Williamson/b.Hanover
 County/Thos T. Chandler Husband
Sarah T. Hackett/W/F/Aug 21/Inflamation of Stomach/56y 5m 25d/Wilson & Polly
 Quarles/Thos C. Hackett Husband
Wm L. Southworth/W/M/Dec 5/Shingles/1m/John D. & Louisa D. Southworth/John D.
 Southworth
Mary L. Bendell/W/F/Dec 7/Consumption/71y 8m 7d/John & Sarah White/James Bendell
 Husband/Alexander H. Bendell
Eliza Winston/W/F/Oct 9/Tumor in the Bowels/47y/Matthew & Ann Winston/
 Unmarried/Matthew Winston
Clem Cooper/S/Wm T. Quarles/F/Sept 2/Tumor on Bowels/88y/Unknown/Wm T.
 Quarles Master
Anna/S/Buckner T. Trevilian/F/Aug 9/Heart Disease/53y/Unknown/Buckner T. Trevilian
Billy/S/Winston Haley/M/July 5/Disentary/3y/Hannah/Wilson Haley
Fanny/S/Ann Coleman/F/July 25/Croup/8m/Frances/Wm A. Dick
Lucy/S/Chas W. Coleman/F/Sept 21/Disentary/1y 3m/Phillis/Wm A. Dick
Anthony/S/Woodford Garnett/M/Oct 30/Influensay/2m 10d/Mary/Woodford Garnett Master
Henry B. Hackett/W/M/Sept 9/Liver disease/56y 8d/Garrett & Sophia Hackett/Jas W. Hackett
Aureliius Garland/S/Sarah T. Wortham/M/Aug 12/Whooping Cough/10m 10d/Martha Hill/Sarah T.
 Wortham
Amanda/S/Elliott P. Campbell/F/July 15/Disentary/3y/Clemy/Manasseh Campbell
John Sutton/W/M/July 30/Disentary/8m/Richard & Mary Sutton/Richard Sutton
No Name/S/Lucy Peatross/M/Sept 15/Born dead/Judy Ann/Geo W. Peatross
Mary Moren/W/F/Oct 1/Disentary/5y/James & Ann Moren/James Moren
Nehemiah Lambert/S/Horace A. Richards/F/Oct 6/Burnt Chills/6y 7m/David & Frances
 Lambert/David Lambert
Randal/S/Horace A. Richards/M/July 10/Inflamation of throut/32y/Unknown/Horace
 A. Richards Master
Betsy/S/Ryland Jeter/F/Aug 1/Dropsy/23/Unknown/Ryland Jeter Master
James T. Carnal/W/M/Nov/Scarlet Fever/1y 1m/Archille & Matilda M.Carneal/Archille T. Carnall
Harriett/S/Sally Wood/F/Dec 17/Smothered in bed/3m 17d/Charlotte/Sally Wood Mistress
William/S/Henry Hill/M/Nov 3/Diarrah/50y/Sookey/b.King & Queen Co/Henry Hill Master
No Name/W/F/July 4/Fitts/3m/Nancy/Reuben Farmer
Juda/S/John S. Blanton/F/Oct 12/Old Age/70y Milly/John S. Blanton Master
No Name/S/Geo B. Pollard/F/Sept 22/Disease Not Known/7d/Louisa Myers/Geo B. Pollard Master

No Name/W/M/Sept 17/Disease Not Known/2d/Jas B. & Elizth Southworth/Jas B. Southworth
Louisa/S/Lyttleton Goodwin/F/Dec 15/Pneumonia/19y/Caty/Harriett Goodwin
Millard F. Burruss/W/M/July/Inflamation of Stomach/18d/John & Eliz P. Burruss/John Burruss
Sarah Ann/S/Wm Hancock/F/July 1/Disentary/1y 6m/Ellen/Wm Hancock Master
Andrew Broaddus/S/Wm J. Hancock/M/July 6/Disentary/5m/Rainy/Wm Hancock Master
Jane R. Smith/W/F/Sept 5/Billious Fever/80y/Betsy Rogers/Rice Smith Husband
Gardener/S/Amelia J. Farish/M/Nov 15/__/7m/Frances/Robert S. Farish
No Name/S/Fleming Bibb/M/Apr 15/Typhoid Fever/15y 2m/Lucy Ann/Fleming Bibb Master
Jane Dabney/S/Fleming Bibb/F/Apr 20/Typhoid Fever/16y/Evelina/Fleming Bibb Master
Edward/S/Benjamin Coleman/M/Aug 15/Disentary/9m/Martha/Elizth D. Coleman
Isaac Anderson/S/Est of J.E. Burruss/M/Sept 1/Disentary/3y/Nancy/Jacob Burruss
Oscar/S/Richard Blanton/M/July 25/Whooping Cough/1y/Adena/ Richard Blanton Master
Elijah M. Bell/W/M/July 2/Disentary/2y 1m 2d/Joseph H. & Lucy A. Bell/Jos H. Bell
Ann W. Samuel/W/F/Aug 14/Consumption/19y/Thos & Jane Samuel/Jane F. Samuel
Tom/S/Steven Oliver/M/Aug 15/Disentary/35y/Charity/Steven Oliver Master
Philip A. Samuel/W/M/July 29/Disentary/5y 4m 1d/Philip & Sarah W. Samuel/Philip Samuel
Maria/S/Philip Samuel/F/Sept 15/Disentary/1y 2d/Mary/Philip Samuel Master
Robert E. Coleman/W/M/Dec 15/Colic/2y 9m/Geo F. & Ann W. Coleman/Ann W. Coleman
Oteria A. Campbell/W/F/Oct 20/Child Bed/35/D.W. & Judith M.Kimbrough/b.Hanover
  County/S.E.H. Campbell Husband
Littleton/S/Ira E. Dickinson/M/July 20/Inflamation of bowels/1y/Sally/Ira E. Dickinson Master
Mary/S/Ira E. Dickinson/F/July 23/By a fall/7m/Maria/Ira E. Dickinson Master
No Name/W/M/Sept 18/Not Known/3d/Henry & Ann Taylor/Henry T. Taylor
Lindsey/S/George Tyler/M/Dec 5/Disentary/1y/Lucy/George Tyler Master
Sarah/S/Nancy Washington/F/Aug 1/Croup/1y 6m/Emily/Geo Washington
Rice W. Schooler/W/M/Nov 20/__/57y/Saml & Ann Schooler/b.Spotsylvania Cty/Mary A. Schooler
  Wife
Delphia/S/James Stewart/F/July 25/Disentary/26y/__/b.Spotsylvania Co/Robt S. Luck
Mary/S/John Chandler/F/Dec 15/By fall of a cart body/3y/Grace/John Chandler Master
Comadore/S/Geo W. Madison/M/Nov 15/ulser on w pipe/35y/Nancy/Geo W. Madison Master
Patrick Washington/S/Chas J. Fox/M/July 20/Thrash/4m 14d/Jane Burke/Chas J. Fox Master
Jinney/S/Wm W. Dickinson/F/Dec 18/Billious pneumonia/68y/Sarah/ Wm W. Dickinson Master
Hartsey/S/Wm W. Dickinson/F/Dec18/Billious Pneumonia/6y/Emeline/Wm W. Dickinson Master
Richard J. Clarke/W/M/July 1/Disentary/1y 5m 26d/Andrew J. & Mary F.Clarke/Mary F. Clarke
Frances Wright/W/F/Aug 7/Chronic Diah/84y/James & Rebecca Wright/Wm Wright
  Husband/Elizabeth Burruss
Mary/S/Dr Jos A. Flippo/F/Nov 1/__/50y/Unknown/Dr Jos A. Flippo Master
Polly/S/Dabney W. Waller/F/Aug 30/Hestick Fever/42y/Dinah/Dabney W. Waller Master
Polly/S/Dabney W. Waller/F/Dec 16/Hestick Fever/5m 14d/Polly/Dabney W. Waller Master
Lucy Young/W/F/July 27/Breast Compliant/49y/Lawrence & Catharine Young/b.Louisa
  County/Unmarried/Catharine Young
Frank/S/Aquilla Goodloe/M/July 2/Disentary/1y/Lucy/Aquilla Goodloe Master
Bettie/S/Jesse Winn/F/July 15/Worms/1y/Lucy/Jesse Winn
Samuel W. Luck/W/M/July 11/Disordered bowels/11m/Wm F. & Mary S. Luck/Mary S. Luck
William/S/Albert G. Ware/M/Aug 5/Smothered in bed/4m/Julia Ann/Albert G. Ware
Davy/S/Henry Wright/M/July 6/Disease of Lungs/35y/Unknown/Clement M. Harris
Jim/S/Emily T. Morris/M/July 3/Consumption/21y/Unknown/Edmund T. Morris
Jemima/S/Luther Wright/F/July/25y/Disentary/16y/Lucy/Luther Wright Master

Maria/S/Luther Wright/F/Nov 11/Child fever/__/Etta/Luther Wright Master
No Name/S/Woods. Wright/F/Sept 27/Not Known/62y 7d/Mary/Woodson Wright Master
Sela/S/Woods. Wright/F/Oct 24/Dropsy/62/Unknown/Frances A. Goodwin
No Name/S/Robt C. Sutton/M/Aug 1/Diarea/4m/Ritta/Robert C. Sutton Master
Jerry/S/Henry M. George/M/Aug 15/Pheumatic/50y/Sela/Henry M. George Master
No Name/S/Henry M. George/F/Aug 17/Lock Jaw/4d/Delila/Henry M. George Master

1854

Thomas/S/Edwin Andrews/M/Apr 16/Bil. Fever/50y/b.Essex Co/Edwin Andrews Master
Eugen[e] Broaddus/W/M/Dec 25/Typd Fever/10y/__/Silas J. Broaddus Father
William/S/Silas J. Broaddus/Aug/Fever/12y/Lucy/S.J. Broaddus Master
No Name/S/Betsey Broaddus/M/Nov/Fever/20d/Caroline/Jas J. Broaddus Master
Etta/S/Jno D. Butler/Nov 1/Fever/5y/Julia/Jno D. Butler Master
John/S/Mark S. Boulware/M/Apr/Fever/60y/__/Mark Boulware Master
Lucy/S/Mark S. Boulware/F/Apr/Fever/50y/__/Mark Boulware Master
Mark Boulware/W/M/Feb 17/Fever/5y/Mark Boulware/Mark Boulware
Jerry/S/Elizth Boulware/M/July/Fever/40y/E. Boulware Mistress
Lucy/S/Elizth Boulware/F/Aug/Fever/50y/E. Boulware Mistress
Jackson/S/Jno T. Boutwell/M/Feb/__/40y/__/Jno T. Boutwell Master
William/S/Jno T. Boutwell/M/Apr/__/15y/Jno T. Boutwell Master
Mary/S/Jno T. Boutwell/F/May/__/40y/Jno T. Boutwell Master
William/S/J.H. Burnard[Bernard]/M/Jan/Steam explosion/35y/__/J.H. Burnard Master
Beverley/S/J.H. Burnard[Bernard]/M/Jan/Steam explosion/40y/__/J.H. Burnard Master
No Name/S/Jno Broaddus/M/Nov/Bed Fever/6m/Jane/Jno Broaddus Master
Eli/S/Thos Broaddus/M/Oct/Fever/5y/Martha/Thos Broaddus Master
Judy/S/Wm D. Boulware/F/Mar/Fever/10y/Margarett/Wm D. Boulware Master
No Name/S/Jno R. Baylor/F/Mar/Fever/10d/Frances/Jno R. Baylor Master
Andrew/S/Jno R. Baylor/M/Mar 30/Fever/15y/Frances Jr[sic]/Jno R. Baylor Master
Richard/S/Jno R. Baylor/M/Sept/Fever/35y/__/Jno R. Baylor Master
Adam/S/Jas S. Barbee/M/Jan/Fever/55y/__/Jas S. Barbee Master
No Name/S/E. Bell/F/Aug/Fever/6m/Emily/Elizabeth Bell Mistress
No Name/S/E. Bell/F/Aug/Fever/5m/Jane/Elizabeth Bell Mistress
Henry/S/Wm D. Bates/M/Dec/Fever/1m/Margaret/Wm D. Bates Master
No Name/S/Wm A. Buckner/M/Feb/Fever/9m/Phillis/Wm A Buckner Master
No Name/S/Wm A. Buckner/F/Mar/Fever/6m/Sally/Wm A. Buckner Master
Bettie E. Cronie/W/F/Apr 16/__/4y 1m/__/Henry R. Cronie Father
Jas Anderson/W/M/Aug 17/Fever/40y/__/Jas Carneal Father-in-Law
Thomas/S/Jas S. Cole/M/Dec 25/d.Louisa Co/Typd Fever/20y/__/ Jas S. Cole Master
Thomas/S/Thos C.__/M/Aug/Typd Fever/30y/__/Alex W. Carter Overseer
No Name/W/M/Apr 17/Typd Fever/15d/__/Ro R. Chapman Father
Jno Grimes/Free/M/Aug 22/__/40y/__/Jas S. Catlett
No Name/S/Wm F. Catlett/F/Oct/Typd Fever/20d/Lucinda/Wm F. Catlett Master
Eliza/S/Thos C. Chandler/F/Dec/Typd Fever/30y/__/Thos C. Chandler Master
Joseph/S/Wm Collawn/M/__/Typd Fever/7y/Judy/Richd Collawn
Granville/S/Wm A. Collawn/M/Typd Fever/5y/Susan/Wm A. Collawn Master
Sally/S/Jno P. Downing/F/Dec 7/Typd Fever/30y/__/Jno R. Downing Master
Geo Duval/W/M/Sept/Consumption/43y/__/Mechanic/Saml P. Farmer Neighbor

Polly Estes/W/F/Sept 1/__/60y/__/Arron Estes Husband/Edmd M. Estes Son
Geo W. Monday/W/M/Nov/__/25y/R.T. Monday/Day Laborer/ Unmarried/P.S. Farmer Bro-in-Law
Polly/S/Dade Fountloe/F/June/__/50y/__/Dade Fountloe Master
Geo H. Green/W/M/Nov 18/__/24y/Phil Green/Teacher/Unmarried/Phil Green Father
Robt/S/Phil R. Garnett/M/Aug/__/__/Mary/Phil R. Garnett Master
Major Tinsley/W/M/Feb 15/Burned to death/65y/__/Richd Gouldman Neighbor
Letty/S/Bazil Gordon/F/Sept/__/6m/Mary/Bazil Gordon Master
No Name/S/Bazil Gordon/F/Sept/__/1y/Susan/Bazil Gordon Master
Henry/S/Bazil Gordon/M/Sept/__/9m/Mary/Bazil Gordon Master
Virginia/S/Bazil Gordon/F/Sept/__/12y/__/Bazil Gordon Master
Wm Cowen/Free/M/May/__/50y/__/Day Laborer/Geo W. Gouldman Neighbor
Strother/S/Jno Gouldin/M/Dec/__/50y/__/Jno Gouldin Master
No Name/S/Jno Gouldin/__/Dec/__/__/Ann/Jno Gouldin Master
Keziah/S/Jno Goodwin/F/Aug/__/__/Agnes/Jno Goodwin Master
Bristoe/S/Richd Green/M/Dec/Fever/60y/__/Richd Green Master
Sarah/S/A.M. Glassell/F/Apr/Fever/2m/__/A.M. Glassell Master
Adeline/S/A.M. Glassell/F/Apr/Fever/__/__/A.M. Glassell Master
Louisa/S/John T. Harrison/F/Dec/Fever/__/__/Thos H. Howard Employer
Fanny/S/Ro G. Holloway Est/F/June/Fever/__/Ann/Thos Holloway son of sd Decedent
George/S/Ro G. Holloway Est/M/June/Fever/5y/Ellen/Thos Holloway son of sd Decedent
Harriett/S/Conduit's Est/F/Sept/Fever/30y/__/Thos D. Jones Employer
No Name/S/Lawr H. Jeter/M/__/Fever/6d/Rebecca/Lawr H. Jeter Master
Lucy/S/Ro Jesse/F/Jan/Fever/__/Ann/Ro Jesse Master
Henry & Mary/S/Ro Jesse/1M 1F/Apr/Fever/___/Mary/Ro Jesse Master
John/S/Wm E. Jones/M/Jan/Fever/2y/Arin/Wm E. Jones Master
Walker/Son/B.A. Jordan/M/Jul/Fever/__/Jane/B.A. Jordon Master
Geo S. Jones/W/M/Aug 15/Fever/4y/Wm J. Jones/Father
Mary/S/Wm J. Jones/F/Aug 30/Fever/5y/Maria/Wm J. Jones Master
No Name/S/Sally Keeser/F/Jan/Fever/__/Eliza/Sally Keeser Mistress
Nicey/S/Sally Keeser/F/Aug/__/__/__/Sally Keeser Mistress
Wm Kidd/W/M/Feb/Appoplexy/60y/__/Farmer/Wm Kidd Jr Child of Decedent
Rebecca/S/Phil Lightfoot/F/Sept/__/35y/__/Phil Lightfoot Master
Soloman/S/Garrett's Est/M/__/__/50y/__/Thos Motley Neighbor
Elizth Murrow/W/F/Dec 24/__/60y/__/Jas Murrow Husband/David Murrow Chd of Decedent
Mira/S/Geo Mahon/F/Feb 5/__/__/Emily/Geo Mahon Master
H.B. McChesney/W/M/Oct 20/__/2y/A.N. McChesney/A.N. McChesney Father
No Name/W/M/Mar/__/5d/Jos H. Pavy/Jos H. Pavy Father
Chas Harrey/S/Wm Page/M/Dec/__/__/Maria/Wm Page Master
Jno H. Pittman/W/M/Dec 30/Consumption/60y/__/Farmer/Wm H. Pittman Ch of decedent
Horace/S/Richerson's Est/M/Aug/d.Hanover Co/__/40y/Susan/Polly Richerson wife of decedent
Susan/S/R.T. Roane/F/Sept/__/25y/__/R.T. Roane Master
S. Jane Self/W/F/Oct/__/2y/Job Self/Job Self Father
Wm Southworth/W/M/Oct/__/65y/__/Leroy H. Kemp Neighbour
Matilda/S/J.A.L. Shaddock/F/Dec/__/40y/J.A.L. Shaddock Master
No Name/W/F/Apr/__/__/Wm H. Taylor/Mechanic/Wm A. Taylor Father
Jarod/S/Edmond T. Thornton/M/Oct 5/__/35y/__/Edmd T. Thornton Master
No Name/S/Edmd Thornton's Est/F/Dec/__/__/Maria/Edmd Thornton's Est Master

No Name/S/A. Thornton/F/Apr/__/10d/Peggy/Ann Thornton Mistress
No Name/S/Jno Taylor/F/Aug/__/__/Lucy/Jno Taylor Master
Frances Trible/W/F/Dec/__/__/Thos J. Trible/Overseer/Thos J. Trible Father
Richard B. Wright/W/M/June/[white rising]/[9y]/Ro M. Wright/Ro M. Wright Father
Betty Weasner/W/F/Apr/__/11m/Peter Weasner/Peter Weasner Father
Anthony/S/H.B. White/M/Mar/__/__/Milly/H.B. White - Master
George/S/Wm J. Dickinson/M/Mar/__/54y/__/Wm J. Dickinson Master
Clemenza/S/Wm J. Dickinson/F/Mar/__/60y/__/Wm J. Dickinson Master
Nancy Satterwhite/W/F/Aug 6/Hart Disease/64y/Pleasant & Ann Carnal/Edmd
  Satterwhite Husband
Jerry/S/Richard Hutcheson/M/Oct 14/__/80y/John W. Hutcheson
Humphrey Mills/S/Dr Thos B. Anderson/M/Apr/Inflamation of brain/60y/Aggy Mills/Dr Thos B.
  Anderson Master
Lizza/S/E.W. Burruss/F/Nov 8/Teething/1y 4m/Aggy/Elliott W. Burruss
No Name/W/M/Aug 7/__/1d/E.W. & Clement C. Burruss/Elliott W. Burruss
Edmond/S/Richd C. Wortham/M/Mar 1/Inflamation of chest/5y/Charlotte/Benson M. Wright
Chana/S/Richd H. Woolfolk/F/Mar 20/Dropsy/__/Richd H. Woolfolk Master
No Name/S/Lewis M. George/M/June/Tsesmus/6d/Clara/Lewis M. George Master
Patsey/S/Virginia [illeg]/F/Aug/affection of brain/5m/Daphnay/Lewis M. George
No Name/S/Hy H. George/F/Dec 19/Tsesmus/7d/Delila/Hy H. George Master
Benjamin Mason/W/M/Nov 24/Dropsy/65y/__/Labourer/John B. Chandler
Thomas G. Lambert/W/M/Sept 19/Inflamation of brain/12y 2m 9d/ David & Frances
  Lambert/Frances Lambert
Wm T. Winston/W/M/Mar 12/Inflamation of bowels/2y 7m 18d/Ro B. & Eugenia P.
  Winston/b.Louisa County/Ro B. Winston
Rachel Anderson/W/F/Jan/Diapepsia/60y/John & Sally Walden/b.James City/Benjm Anderson
  Husband
Marsha/S/Saml P. Luck/F/July/Scroffola/15y/Martha/Saml P. Luck Master
John P. Hackett/W/M/Oct 12/Nervous affection/43y/Garrett & Sophia Hackett/Jas W. Hackett
Mary Louisa/S/Jos W. Terrell/F/July 22/Consumption/3y/Sarah/Jos W. Terrell Master
Wm K. Terrell/W/M/Jan 11/Inflamation of brain/11y 2m/Jos W. & Mary E. Terrell/Jos W. Terrell
Maria E. Campbell/W/F/Nov 20/Consumption/19y 2m/John G. & Betsy Coleman/Richd P.[arr]
  II.[oomes] Campbell Husband/John G. Coleman
Julia/S/Saml Coleman/F/Aug/incaration of lungs/2m/Molly/Samuel Coleman Master
Maria/S/Richardson Turner/F/__/__/__/Polly/John R. Turner
Sarah/S/Rachael S. White/F/July/Inflamation/__/Eliza/Horace A. Richards
Richard Hutcheson/W/M/Nov 5/__/62y 8m/John & Sarah Hutcheson/ Mary Hutcheson Wife/John W.
  Hutcheson
Sam/S/Fleming Bibb/M/Oct/Scarlet Fever/2y/Sally/Fleming Bibb Master
Elizth West/W/F/Mar 7/Palsy/78y/Edmd & Mary West/Edmund West
James T. Stevens/W/M/Mar 15/Erysipelas/26y 11m 27d/Elijah L. & Lucy Stevens/Elijah L. Stevens
Polly/S/Robt Dickinson/F/Aug 23/Child bed Fever/25y/Rachel/Robt Dickinson Master
Coleman/S/Robert Dickinson/M/Aug 20/Consumption/14y/Frances/Robt Dickinson Master
No Name/S/Ro G. Hill/F/Nov/Spasms/8d/Sarah/Robt G. Hill Master
Fanny/S/A.S. Hundley/F/Jan 3/Worms/1y 1m/Adaline/Albert S. Hundley Master
Mary P. Bowers/W/F/Dec 23/Scarlet Fever/3y 1m 6d/John E. & Mary F. Bowers/John E. Bowers
Mickaelborough Young/W/M/May 24/Old Age/79y/Wm & Jane Young/b.Middlesex Cty/Farmer/
  Ann Young Wife/Wm R. Young

Anna/S/M. Young/F/July/Cancer of womb/35y/__/Wm R. Young Master
Mary/S/A. Ware's Est/F/Mar/Disease of Bowels/2m 15d/Susan/Ann G. Ware
Andrew Jackson/S/A. Ware's Est/M/Dec/Smothered in bed/20d/ Martha/Ann G. Ware
Edmund/S/A. Ware's Est/M/Mar/Reumatism/65y/Not Known/Ann G. Ware
Alexander/S/Ro T. Cobbs/M/Nov/Smothered in bed/3m/Sally/Ro T. Cobbs Master
Wm Mallory/W/M/Dec 13/Consumption/68y/Jas W. & [illeg] Mallory/b.Hanover/
  Pametia Mallory wife
James/S/Jos C. Luck/M/Aug 22/Not Known/__/Susan/Jos C. Luck Master
John F. Lewcord/W/M/Aug/Consumption/39y/[illeg] & Sally Lewcord/b.King Wm Co/Mary Lewcord
  wife
Mary E. Thompson/W/F/Oct/Teething/1y 1m/Geo W. & Mary A. Thompson/Geo W.
  Thompson
Garland/S/Susan Wyatt/M/Sept/Not Known/55y/Jenny/Susan Wyatt Mistress
John/S/Geo M. McLaughlin/M/Oct 25/InflamatoryRheumatism/18y 4m/Martha/ b.Hanover
  Cty/Geo M. McLaughlin Master
Georgeanna Atkinson/W/F/June/Disentary/1y/Chas & Mary Atkinson/Chas Atkinson
Willis/S/John J. Blanton/M/Oct/Burns/2y/Jane/John J. Blanton Master
Johnathan Estis/W/M/Feb 12/Pneumonia/87y 11m 24d/Phillip & Polly Estis/Samuel Estis
Richd Yarbrough/W/M/May 28/Paralysis/58y 2m/Joel & Agnes Yarbrough/Farmer/
  Maria Yarbrough wife
Caroline/S/Wesley Wright/F/Croup/18d/Lucinda/Wesley Wright Master
Emily/S/Wesley Wright/F/Skin disease/6m/Sally/Wesley Wright Master
Lee/S/Woodford Garnett/M/Sept/Teething/6m/Courtney/Woodford Garnett Master
Anthony/S/Woodford Garnett/M/Mar/Cold/10m/Mary/Woodford Garnett Master
Sally Yarbrough/W/F/Dec 18/Chills/80y/Not Known/Joel Yarbrough Husband/Ambrose Bayhan
Henry T. Barlow/W/M/Nov/Typhoid Fever/21y/Lorenzo & Elizth Barlow/Carpenter/Jas B. Southworth
Not Named/S/Geo B. Pollard/F/Feb or Mar/Not Known/9d/Louisa/Mrs Frances Pollard
Not Named/S/Geo B. Pollard/M/Nov/Inflamation of bowels/4y/Sally/Mrs Frances Pollard
Becky/S/Nicholas Mills/F/Nov/Consumption/44y/Ailsey/Wm S. Young
Maria/S/Nicholas Mills/F/Apr/Old Age/80y/Not Known/Wm S. Young
Silva/S/Wm P. Napier's Est/F/Nov/Consumption/14y/Polly/Harriett Napier
Jos R. Mason/W/M/Mar 13/Consumption/50y/Joel & Virginia Mason/Mary Mason wife
No Named/W/M.June 25/Trichinosis/10d/John & Adaline Baughan/John Baughan
Sarah Dyson [Long]/W/F/June 27/Dropsy/40y/Maynor & Elizth Dyson/Ellis Long Husband
John M. Thomas/W/M/Aug/Diapepsia/14y/Wm T. & Susan H. Thomas/Wm F. Thomas
Mary G. Thomas/W/F/Oct 28/Inflamatory Rheumatism/52y/John & Hannah Morgan/
  b.Pottersville, Pa/Ira L. Thomas Husband
Lucinda Kelley/W/F/Apr 17/Inward Cancer/46y/Jas & Sarah West/ Sarah A. Twisdale
Lucy A. Stevens/W/F/June/Diarreah/1m 12d/John B. & A.A. Stevens/Jas W. Dyson
Not Named/S/Sarah K. Dyson/F/Apr/Diarreah/1m/Nancy/Sarah K. Dyson Mistress
Sarah A. Dyson/W/F/July 20/Chronick Thrash/3m 10d/Jas W. & Margaret Dyson/Jas W. Dyson
Sam/S/Peter Quarles/M/May/Scroffola/18y/Amanda/Peter Quarles
Ann Fortune/S/Emily T. Morris/F/Oct 5/Disease of Lungs/73y/__/Emily T. Morris
Ella/S/Emily T. Morris/F/Nov 27/Liver disease/70y/__/Emily T. Morris Mistress
James/S/Edmd T. Morris/M/Oct 27/Not Known/3m 13d/Maria Braxton/Edmd T. Morris Master
No Name/S/William Carter/F/Oct/Not Known/1m/Betsey/Wm Carter Master
Richard/S/William Carter/M/Mar/Not Known/1y/Elizabeth/Wm Carter Master
John/S/William Carter/M/Aug/Fever/2y 2m/Polly/Wm Carter Master

William/S/William Carter/M/Aug/Fever/4y/Polly/Wm Carter Master
Wm Henry/S/William Carter/M/July/Fever/1y/Lucy Mills/Wm Carter Master
Not Named/S/William Carter/F/Oct/Fever/2m/Lucy/Wm Carter Master
Fanny/S/John Smith/F/Mar/Inflamation of brain/1y/Salena/John Smith Master
Charles/S/John V. Kean/M/Nov/Cholic/2y 6m/Fanny/John V. Kean Master
Not Named/S/John V. Kean/M/May/Tsesmus/2d/Betsey/John V. Kean Master
Siras/S/Martha T. Ball/M/Apr/Old Age/76y/Not Known/Martha T. Ball Mistress
Wm/S/Richd B. White/M/Dec 27/Not Known/36y/Polly/Clara E. Dickinson
Henry/S/Stephen Blaydes/M/Feb/Pneumonia/23y/Lydia/__
John R. Morris/W/M/Oct 2/Sore Throat/11y 1m/Robt & Barbary Morris/Barbara Morris
Joe/S/Wm Hancock/M/Apr/Pneumonia/35y/__/Wm Hancock Master
John G. Richerson/W/M/Sept 22/Consumption/17y/John & Mary B. Richerson/John Richerson
Charlott/S/Jas Hunter/F/Sept 13/Typhoyd/12y/Elvira/Jas Hunter Master
Delia/S/Barton W. Morris/F/May or June/__/10y/Hannah/Barton W. Morris Master
Mary Smith/W/F/July/Not Known/79y/Christopher Smith/unmarried/John Goldsberry [Goldsby]
Palace/S/Ryland Jeter/F/Aug/Cholic/62y/Litty/R. Jeter Master
Not Named/S//Ryland Jeter/F/June/Not Known/2m/ Mary/R. Jeter Master
Salina/S/Hugh Chandler/F/June/Teething/6m/Jemima/Hugh Chandler Master
Jim/S/Wm W. Dickinson/M/Oct/Not Known/6y/Mildred/Wm W. Dickinson Master
Lucy/S/Wm W. Dickinson/F/Nov/Not Known/16y/Lucy Ann/Wm W. Dickinson Master
Elizabeth Campbell/W/F/Feb 4/Disentary/65y/Elliott P. Campbell Husband/Manasseh Campbell
Washington/S/Jas C. DeJarnette/M/Oct/Hernia/38y/Kesiah/Jas C. DeJarnette Master
Dennis/S/Judith A. Swann/M/Nov/Thphoyd/__/Anna/Judith Swann Mistress
Not Named/S/[illeg]Wiglesworth/M/Sept/Bleeding of Navel/7d/Silva/Mrs Wiglesworth
Cornelia/S/Robt S. Luck/F/Aug/From a fall/23y/Lucy Ann/Ro S. Luck Master
Not Known/S/Tavenor Winn/F/Nov 19/Not Known/14d/Any/Tavenor Winn Master
John/S/Jesse Winn/M/Feb/Inflamation from sore/50y/Nancy/Jesse Winn Master
Angelo/S/George Thompkins/F/Dec/Child bed/44y/Esther/Ira E. Dickinson
Reuben/S/Ira E. Dickinson/M/Aug/Typhoyd Fever/60y/Not Known/Ira E. Dickinson Master
Susan/S/Ira E. Dickinson/F/Aug/Typhoyd Fever/12y/Maria/Ira E. Dickinson Master
Jane Dickinson/W/F/Aug/Typhyd Fever/50y/Matthew & Polly Campbell/Ira E. Dickinson Husband
Phillis/S/Timberlake's Est/F/Feb 28/Old Age/85y/__/Thos Mitchell
Tony/S/Ann Washington/M/Apr/Rhuematism/70y/Phillis/Ann Washington Mistress
Milly/S/Geo Washington/F/Mar/Hemerage of Lungs/65y/Phillis/Ann Washington
Thomas/S/Geo Washington/M/June/Diaria/28y/Lucinda/Albert R. Flippo
Not Named/S/Elizth Coleman/__/Aug 10/Not Known/1d/Elenor/John B. Coates
Manuel/S/Jno B. Coates/M/July/Typhyd/23y/Kitty/John B. Coates Master
Randal/S/Est of E. Coates/M/June/Not Known/65y/Not Known/__
Wm C. Burruss/W/M/Feb 2/Disentary/2y 6m/Wm H. & Elizth Burruss/Wm H. Burruss Father
Jas A. Burruss/W/M/Jan 25/Disentary/1y/Wm H. & Elizth Burruss/Wm H. Burruss Father
Ann M. Quarles/W/F/June 16/Inflamation of Bowels/28y/John & Rebecca Smith/Wm H. Burruss
Elizth A. Cobbs/W/F/Aug 25/inflamation of Stomach/20y/Steven & Lucinda Oliver/
  Jesse L. Cobbs
Wm White/W/M/July 22/Parralasis/89y/John & Frances White/Hugh R. White
Henry/S/Woodson Wright/M/Nov/Not Known/2m/Mary/Woodson Wright Master
Billy/S/Mildred E. Wright/M/May 8/disease of Lungs/38y/__/Wm H.N. Burruss
Thos Marshall/W/M/June 27/Not Known/78y/Jno & Margarett Marshall/Francis Marshall
Not Named/S/Mary D. & F. Marshall/F/July/Trismas/14d/Isabella/Frances Marshall

Wm D. Schooler/W/M/Oct 2/disease of brain/23y/Rice W. & Mary Schooler/Mary Schooler
[illeg]Nelson/W/M/Oct 3/__/__/__/Peter & Ann Nelson/Mary Schooler
Amelia/S/Geo F. Coleman/F/June/disease of heart/45y/Sally/Ann M. Coleman
Not Named/S/Pleasant Carnall/M/Oct/__/__/Sally/Pleasant Carnall
George/S/Jane F. Smith/M/Feb/Dropsy in Chest/65y/Sophia/Jane F. Samuel Mistress
Not Named/S/Miss B. Quesenberry/__/Nov/__/15d/Not Known/Geo Tyler
Elizth Tyler/W/F/Oct 29/Chronic Coloria/1y 2m/Geo & Jane Tyler/Geo Tyler
Susan/S/Geo W. Burke/F/Nov/Consumption/18y/Betty/Wm Taliaferro
Robert/S/Geo W. Burke/M/Nov/Fits/11m/Mary Jane/Wm Taliaferro
Celia/S/Francis A. Goodwin/F/Oct/Dropsy/63y/Not Known/Chas Woolfolk
Mary Hughes/W/F/May 27/Child Bed Fever/33y/Geo & Mary Smith/John Hughes
Jas A. Hughes/W/M/June 23/Not Known/2m/Geo & Mary Smith/John Hughes
James/S/Sarah A. Saunders/M/Aug/Colora Infantum/4m/Arrena/Sarah A. Saunders Mistress
Ellis G. Saunders/W/M/Apr 23/Pneumonia/51y/Richard & Leanna Saunders/Sarah A. Saunders wife
Allice/S/Ann J. Wright/F/Dec/Croup/3y/Harriett/Ann J. Wright Mistress

1855

Not Named/S/Jos F. Robinson/F/Feb/__/__/Malinda/Jos F. Robinson Master
Lewis/S/Lucy Peatross/M/June/Consumption/25y/Polly/Geo W. Peatross
James/S/Lucy Peatross/M/July/Teething/8m/Juda Ann/Geo W. Peatross
Humphrey/S/Warner M. Mason/M/July 4/Old Age/77y/Not Known/Wm M. Mason
Not Named/S/Ryland Jeter/M/Oct/__/__/__/Ryland Jeter Master
Betsy Fox/S/Henry Doggett/F/Aug/Disentary/55y/Anna/Henry Doggett Master
John Washington/S/Lucy Hundley/M/Apr/Smothered/4m/Amanda/Lucy Hundley Mistress
Lydia Goodwin/S/Lucy Hundley/F/Nov/Smothered/2m/Harriet/Lucy Hundley Mistress
Spencer/S/Virginia L. George/M/Oct/Inflamation of Bowels/7y/Lucy/H.H. George
Not Named/W/M/June 5/dis not known/23d/H.H. & Ellen W. George/H.H. George
George Anna/S/Richd H. Woolfolk/F/Mar/Bronchitis/6m/Patsy/Sarah Wood
Milly/S/Sarah Wood/F/Mar/Consumption/43y/Sarah/Sarah Wood Mistress
Not Named/S/Wm F. Burruss/M/Oct/Fit/10d/Minova/Wm F. Burruss Master
Not Named/W/M/June/Not Known/20d/Mary T. Long/A.B. Long
Not Named/W/F/June/Not Known/4d/Mary T. Long/A.B. Long
Elisha Grubbs/W/M/Feb/Disease/84y?/__/R.J. Madison
[no name]/S/H. Chandler/M/Oct/Disease/1y 2m/Eliza/H. Chandler Master
Mary Shenault/W/F/Feb 15/Not Known/24y/Not Known/George W. Blanton
John W. Abraham/W/M/Aug 27/Congestion of Brain/54y/Mordecai Abraham/George W. Blanton
Barnett/S/No Owner/M/Oct 12/Old Age/90y/Not Known/George W. Blanton
Minerva P. Long/W/F/Jan 14/Child bed/25y/Stephen & Sarah Carnal/J.M. Long
Jesse/S/L. Redd/M/Apr/Consumption/55y/Sukey/L. Redd
James Stevens/Free/M/May/Inf of brain/6y/Lucy Stevens/W.J. Anderson
Virginia A. Gatewood/W/F/Apr 23/Consumption/26y/Wm B. & Peggy W. Gatewood/
  Wm B. Gatewood
Sarah J. Lowry/W/F/May 26/Intermitting Fever/34y/Hasting & Ann T. Watkins/H. Watkins
Wyatt Durrett/W/M/Sept/Dirpepsia/74y/Claiborn & Eliz Durrett/Fanny Newton
Albert/S/Saml P. Luck/M/Dec 10/Worms/4y 3m/Ellen/S.P. Luck Master
Eveline/S/Fleming Bibb/F/Mar/Scrofula/39y/Milly/F. Bibb
Emma/S/Lynch Cobbs/F/July 4/Not Known/6d/Emily/L. Cobbs Master

Ella/S/Lynch Cobbs/F/July 20/Not Known/22d/Emily/L. Cobbs Master
Pleasant/S/Mary Cobbs/M/Jan 15/Scarlet Fever/5y/Mary/Mary Cobbs Mistress
Dick/S/Jno Hackett/M/Sept/Not Known/52y/Betty/Jno Hackett Master
Polly/S/Jno Hackett/F/Sept/Old Age/96y/Not Known/Jno Hackett Master
Ben/S/Robt C. Garnett/1m/Jan/__/__/__/Ann Baughan
Not Named/S/Mary Wright/M/Nov/__/9d/Liza/Ann Baughan
John/S/Mary Wright/M/Dec 18/Chills/3y/Liza/W.B. Chandler
Not Named/S/N.A. Chandler/M/Sept/Not Known/1d/Patsy/W.B. Chandler
Not Named/W/F/Jan/Not Known/18d/Wm & [illeg] Carneal/Wm Carneal
Malinda/S/Garland Hargrave/F/Sept/Inf Stomach/27y/Not Known/Garland Hargrave Master
Lucy/S/B. Robinson's Est/F/Nov 7/Old Age/100y/Not Known/Garland Hargrave
Lucy A. Hargrave/W/F/Dec 7/Cong Brain/58y/David & Molly Bibb/Garland Hargrave Husband
Kitty/S/Mildred/F/July/Inf brain/1y/Caroline/Rebecca Burruss
Winney/S/Francis W. Battaile/F/Jan/Consumption/50y/Not Known/F.W. Battaile Master
Not Named/S/Francis W. Battaile/M/Jan/Not Known/2y/Kitty/F.W. Battaile Master
Not Named/S/Samuel C. Gatewood/M/Jan/__/2m/Martha Ann/S.C. Gatewood Master
Not Named/S/Thos L. Catlett/M/Sept/Not Known/4d/Fanny/Thos L. Catlett Master
Not Named/S/R. White/M/May/Not Known/8d/Eliza/H.A. Richards
Mordecai Loving/W/M/May/Fits/21y/Pittman & Mary Loving/Wade H. Loving
Edmund/S/R.E. Sutton/M/July/Disentary/10d/Kitty/Robt C. Sutton
Henry/S/Wesley Wright/M/Mar 31/Pneumonia/32y/Sarah/Wesley Wright Master
Ann A.G. Wright/F/July 9/Congestive Chill/38y 10m 8d/Jas & Elizabeth White/Wesley Wright
Martha Freeman/Free/F/Oct/Consumption/3y/Sally/Willis Freeman
Albert/S/Wm O. Doggett/M/Aug 9/Disentary/2y/Dinah/Wm O. Doggett Master
Thomas/S/Geo McLaughlin/M/May/Flux/3y/Fanny/G.M. McLaughlin
Claiborne Harris/W/M/July 11/Paralisis/76y/Wm & Ann Harris/John Newton
Jane Harris/W/F/Oct/Not Known/60y/Jno & Rachel Harris/John Newton
James/S/Overton Burruss/M/Aug/Cong of brain/8y/Maria/Clarissa Burruss [wife of owner]
Eliza Satterwhite/W/F/Apr 17/Scarlet Fever/16y/Sophia Satterwhite/Ed Satterwhite
Narcissis Moore/W/F/Feb/Scarlet Fever/25y/Ed & Nancy Satter white/Lunsford Moore
Eldred Moore/W/M/Feb/Scarlet Fever/12m/Lunsford Moore/Lunsford Moore
Not Named/S/Jos A. Flippo/M/Dec/Scarlet Fever/3d/Ellen/J.A. Flippo Master
Not Named/S/Jos A. Flippo/M/Dec/Scarlet Fever/3d/Ellen/Jos A. Flippo Master
Daniel/S/Geo F. Swann/M/Aug/Congestive Fever/28y/Malincea/Geo F. Swann Master
James C. Madison/W/M/Jan/Scarlet Fever/5y/R. Madison/Thos Madison
Sandy/S/Layton Harris/M/Dec/Not Known/70y/Betty/Layton Harris Master
Joel B. Winn/W/M/Aug 3/Influenza/1y 7m/Tav & Lucinda Winn/Tav Winn
Randal/S/Tavenor Winn/M/Apr 12/Consumption/41y/Nancy/Tav Winn Master
Warner/S/Geo Tompkins/M/Dec/Consumption/21y/Angela/Geo Tompkins Master
Maria/S/Geo Tompkins/F/Sept/Not Known/16y/Patty/Geo Tompkins Master
William/S/Jacob C. Burruss/M/June 1/Yellow Fever/10y/Nancy/J.C. Burruss Master
Angelina/S/F.W. Scott/F/Dec 15/Consumption/15y/Amelia/F.W. Scott Master
Linder/S/Emily Scott/F/Aug/Burnt/90y/Not Known/F.W. Scott
Vira/S/Jas Hunter/F/Dec/Consumption/55y/__/Jas Hunter Master
Not Named/W/F/Dec/Not Known/21d/O.D. & S.C. Harris/O.D. Harris Father
Elizabeth/S/Jas Duval/F/Nov/Smothered/1m/Silva Anna/Jas Duval Master
Not Named/W/M/Nov 13/__/__/Wm H. & Ellen Wright/Wm H. Wright Father
Emily/S/Albert L. Hundley/F/Nov/Teething/1y 8m/Adaline/A.L. Hundley Master

Tom/S/Wm W. Dickinson/M/Mar 12/Not Known/3d/Nancy/W.W. Dickinson Master
Not Named/S/W.W. Dickinson/F/Mar 17/Whooping Cough/6m/Martha/W.W. Dickinson Master
Not Named/S/W.W. Dickinson/F/June/__/2m/Cassandra/W.W. Dickinson Master
Not Named/S/W.W. Dickinson/F/June/__/28d/Sally Jane/W.W. Dickinson Master
Roderick/S/Richd E. Boulware/M/July/__/43y/Not Known/R.E. Boulware Master
Lewis M. Cobbs/W/M/Mar 21/Spasms/7d/L.V. & O.E. Cobbs/Lewis V. Cobbs Father
James Cobbs/W/M/__/__/3y/L.V. & O.E. Cobbs/Lewis V. Cobbs Father
Robt Yarbrough/W/M/July 3/__/12y/Richd & Maria Yarbrough/ Maria Yarbrough Mother
Sarah Yarbrough/W/F/__/__/__/Richd & Maria Yarbrough/Maria Yarbrough Mother
Patrick H. Yarbrough/W/M/Mar 15/Slow Fever/9d/Richd & Maria Yarbrough/Maria Yarbrough Mother
Milly/S/Mary L. Newton/F/Mar 26/Not Known/45y/Fanny/Mary L. Newton Mistress
Elizabeth/S/Ann M. Coleman/F/Cancer/62y/Amelia/Ann M. Coleman
Wesley/S/Ann M. Coleman/M/__/__/__/Elizabeth/Ann M. Coleman Mistress
Not Named/S/Thos Goodwin/M/Nov 1/Not Known/1m/Maria/Thos Goodwin Master
Victoria/S/Jas D. Coleman/F/Dec 11/Not Known/4m/Nancy/Jas D. Coleman Master
Martha/S/Chas Collins Est/F/May/Not Known/20y/Lucy/Cath. Collins [wife of owner]
Not Named/W/M/Nov/Not Known/1d/Jas & Ann Donahoe/Jas Donahoe
Dick/S/Oliver Beazley/M/May/Not Known/45y/Milly/Oliver Beazley Master
Mary/S/Oliver Beazley/F/Oct/Whooping Cough/9m/Nelly/Cath. Collins
Louisa/S/Emily Scott/F/Oct/Bilious/24y/Milly/Annie G. Ware
Jane/S/Jas J. Jerrold/F/Apr/Dropsy/35y/Patty/Jas J. Jerrold Master
Bob/S/Geo B. Pollard/M/Dec/Pneumonia/70y/Not Known/Geo B. Pollard Master
Caty/S/Geo B. Pollard/M/Dec/Asthma/100y/Not Known/Geo B. Pollard Master
Not Named/S/Geo Pollard/F/Apr/bled to death/2d/Keziah/Geo B. Pollard Owner
Lucy Southworth/W/F/June/Diapepsia/65y/Chas Southworth/Miss Southworth
Nancy/S/Mary C. Corbin heirs/F/Apr/Bilious Pluricy/60y/Not Known/Wm J. Young
Camilla/S/Mary C. Corbin heirs/F/June/Consumption/12y/Mary Jane/Wm J. Young
Frances/S/Mary C. Corbin heirs/F/Oct/Consumption/10y/Mary Jane/Wm Young
Jane R. West/W/F/Nov/Congestive Liver/52y/Joel & Jane Mason/Ed West
John/S/Ed & Chas Berkley/M/July/Diarrhea/70y/Not Known/Temple C. Moore Overseer
Abram/S/Ed & Chas Berkley/M/Aug/Measles/50y/Not Known/Temple C. Moore Overseer
Jonny/S/Ed & Chas Berkley/M/Aug/Measles/22y/Not Known/Temple C. Moore Overseer
Randal/S/Ed & Chas Berkley/M/Aug/Measles/19y/Charity/Temple C. Moore Overseer
Robert/S/Ed & Chas Berkley/M/Aug/Measles/12y/Delphy/Temple C. Moore Overseer
Rose/S/Ed & Chas Berkley/F/Aug/Diarrhea/70y/Not Known/Temple C. Moore Overseer
Hannah/S/Ed & Chas Berkley/F/Aug/Measles/18y/Delphy/Temple C. Moore Overseer
Clara/S/Ed & Chas Berkley/F/Aug/Measles/2y/Lydie/Temple C. Moore Overseer
Maria/S/Ed & Chas Berkley/F/Oct/Measles/2y/Winny/Temple C. Moore Overseer
Henry/S/Jas Thomas Est/M/Aug/Measles/26y/Effeshe/Ira L. Edwards
Elizth Wood/W/F/May 1/Consumption/55y/Jas & Rachel Graves/Jos Wood Husband/
  Henry M. Wood
Alfred Dyson/W/M/June 21/Diarrhea/49y/Maynard & Betsey Dyson/Sarah A. Dyson wife/
  S.A. Dyson
Henry E. Chiles/W/M/Apr/Dis of brain/29y/Ed C. & Lucy A. Chiles/E.C. Chiles Father
Amy/S/Lucy Taliaferro/F/Nov/Not Known/3m/Amanda/Wm T. Taliaferro
Not Named/W/F/Aug/Not Known/2d/Woodford & Elizabeth Long/__
Frankey/S/John John/F/Aug/Old Age/83y/Not Known/John Long Master
Micklh. Yarbrough/W/M/__/Not Known/__/Joel & Agnes Yarbrough/Wilmore A. Yarbrough

Not Named/S/Thos Hurt/M/July/__/1d/Hannah/Thos Hurt Master
George F. Terrell/W/M/Feb/37y 8m/Saml & Eliza Terrell/Alfred Rix [Ricks]
Walker/S/John T. Goodwin/M/__/Not Known/70y/Juda/John T. Goodwin Master
Bartlett/S/Luther Wright/M/Nov/Not Known/5y/__/Amey/Luther Wright Master
Clara/S/Luther Wright/F/Sept/__/78y/Ann/Luther Wright Master
Not Named/W/M/__/Unknown/__/Jennett A. Carnal/Jennett A. Coghill[sic]
Robt Wright/W/M/__/__/__/Jno & Eliza Wright/Woodson Wright
Not Named/S/Eliza Burruss/F/July/Whooping cough/2m/Jane/Pleasant Burruss
Jane/S/Geo Washington/M/Sept/Killed by cow/87y/Winney/G. Washington Master
Lucy Covington/W/F/Aug/Typhoid/16y/Leroy & Sally Covington/Nelson Beazley
John W. Burke/W/M/Nov 8/Croup/Geo W. & Eliza Burke/Geo W. Burke Father
Jim/S/S.[amuel]E.[lliott]H.[ugh] Campbell/M/June/eating dirt/2y/Sarah/S.E.H. Campbell Master
Sally/S/Dr L. George/F/Mar 4/Consumption/33/Malissa/Dr L.M. George Master
Not Named/S/Eldred Turner/F/Oct/Not Known/8d/Susan/Eldred Turner Master
Arin/S/Eldred Turner/F/Sept/Chronic Brain/55y/__/Eldred Turner Master
Sam/S/Jas Hunter/M/Oct/affection Lungs/17y/__/Jas Hunter Master
Richd A. Woolfolk/W/M/June/Spinal affection/1m/Chs & Ann E. Woolfolk/Chas Woolfolk Father
Not Named/S/A.L. Coleman/M/Oct/Not Known/1y 10m/Maria/A.L. Coleman Master
Not Named/W/M/June/Col. Infantum/1y 4m/Wm B. & Mary A. Tompkins/Wm B.Tompkins Father
Elizabeth G. Seay/W/F/July 30/Chronick Bronchitis/52y 11m 16d/Thomas & Anne Adams/Jos M. Seay Husband

1856

Louisa/S/Sophia Allen/F/July/__/4y__/Sophia Allen Mistress
William/S/Sophia Allen/M/July/1y/__/Sophia Allen Mistress
No Name/S/Sophia Allen/F/__/__/5d/Frances/Sophia Allen Mistress
No Name/S/Sophia Allen/M/__/__/__/Milly/Sophia Allen Mistress
Henry/S/Wm Thornley/M/__/__/1y 10m/Mary/Wm Thornley Master
William/S/Bazil Gordon/M/Mar/Scarlet Fever/7y/Betsy/Bazil Gordon Master
Lucy/S/Bazil Gordon/F/Mar/Scarlet Fever/4y/Betsy/Bazil Gordon Master
Hellen/S/Bazil Gordon/F/Mar/Scarlet Fever/1y/Lucy/Bazil Gordon Master
Matilda/S/Bazil Gordon/F/Mar/Scarlet Fever/35y/Lucy/Bazil Gordon Master
Jas Pare/Free/M/Aug/Scarlet Fever/40y/__/Ditcher/Bazil Gordon
Jane I. Dickinson/W/F/Aug/Scarlet Fever/7m/Jas E. & E.C. Dickinson/Jas E. Dickinson Father
Selina/S/Walker Washington/F/Aug/Bil Fever/2y/Lelia/Walker Washington Master
Arthur/S/Wm S. White/M/Aug/Bil Fever/1y/Adeline/Wm J. White Master
No Name/S/Wm J. Dickinson/M/__/__/1y/Elizabeth/Wm J. Dickinson Master
Jack/S/Ro B. Walker/M/__/C/F/55y/__/Ro B. Walker Master
Lison Terrell/W/Oct/Not Known/54y/__/Hatter [occupation]/unmarried/Wm Young Brother-in-Law
Claiborne/S/Thos C. Chandler/M/Oct/Liver Dis/21y/Clarey/Thos C. Chandler Master
Willis/S/Thos C. Chandler/M/__/__/Not Known/30y/Frankey/Thos C. Chandler Master
Gabriel/S/Thos C. Chandler/M/Not Known/65y/Judy/Thos C. Chandler Master
Peter/S/Thos C. Chandler/M/Not Known/100y/__/Thos C. Chandler Master
Susan/S/Thos C. Chandler/F/__/Congestive Fever/16y/Mary/Thos C. Chandler Master

Lucinda/S/Thos C. Chandler/F/__/Congestive Fever/16y/Mary/Thos C. Chandler Master
Mary/S/E.S. Motley/F/__/Old Age/85y/Mary/E.S. Motley Master
Chas/S/Wm C. Pratt/M/Sept/Scarlet Fever/16y/Mary/Wm C. Pratt Master
James/S/Wm C. Pratt/M/Nov/Scarlet Fever/8y/Eliza/Wm C. Pratt Master
Eve/S/Wm C. Pratt/F/Sept/__/75y/Eve/Wm C. Pratt Master
Jno Pratt/W/M/Oct 20/Cancer/66y/Wm Pratt/Wm C. Pratt Son
Jno Pratt Jr/W/M/Jan 18/__/36y/Jno Pratt/Wm C. Pratt Brother
No Name/S/Wm A. Buckner/M/__/__/6m/Lucy/Wm A. Buckner Master
Moses/S/Wm A. Buckner/M/__/__/26y/Sarah/Wm A. Buckner Master
Richd Satterwhite/W/M/__/Old Age/90y?/__/unmarried/Milly Rollins Relative
Jno/S/Ro G. Holloway/M/Aug/__/4y/__/Ro G. Holloway Master
Patience/S/E.D. Holloway/F/June/Diarrhea/18y/Sarah/E.D. Holloway Mistress
William/S/R.G. Jones/M/June/Scarlet Fever/2y/Mahala/Richd G. Jones Master
Emma/S/M.F. Thornton/F/Aug 1/__/1y 6m/Sarah/Maria F. Thornton Mistress
Jane/S/Ro Hudgin/F/Mar/Dropsy/18y/Mary/Ro Hudgin Master
Ellen/S/Elizth Green/F/Apr/S. Fever/15y/Sarah/Richd Green Brother {of owner}
Letitia/S/Eunice Green/F/Apr/S. Fever/9y/Harriett/Richd Green Brother [of owner]
Albert/S/Eunice Green/M/Apr/S. Fever/11y/Lucy/Richd Green Brother [of owner]
William/S/Richd Green/M/Apr/S. Fever/11y/Susan/Richd Green Master
Stephen/S/Geo Mahon/M/Nov/Old Age/75y/__/[Elizabeth]Mahon Mistress
Louisa/S/Franky Boulware/F/May/__/1y/Jane/Franky Boulware Mistress
Cornelius/S/__/M/May/__/1y/Chas Price/Jane Prior Mother
James/S/__/M/May/__/__/Jno Smith/Elizth Smith Mother
No Name/S/Edmd Sale/F/__/__/Eliza/Edmd Sale Master
Polly/S/Wm P. Taylor/F/Oct/__/16y/__/Edmd Sale Overseer
Chancy/S/J.B. Skinker/F/Nov/Dropsy/3y/Lydia/J.B. Skinker Master
Penny/S/Wm B. Taylor/F/__/Old Age/80y/__/Wm B. Taylor Master
Cathl/S/Wm B. Taylor/F/__/__/2y/Clary/Wm B. Taylor Master
Matthew/S/Wm B. Taylor/F/__/__/1y/Clary/Wm B. Taylor Master
Humphrey/S/Phil Dew's Est/M/__/__/2m 2d/Elizabeth/John Purkes Master
Ann/S/Phil Dew's Est/F/__/2m 2d/Eliza/Jno Purkes Master
Cornelius/S/Jas P. Corbin/M/__/1y 6m/Eliz/Jas P. Corbin Master
Dosha Wilson/W/F/Oct/Old Age/65y/Thos Wilson/Jno T. Holt son-in-Law
No Name/S/Jos Jesse/M/__/__/6d/Susan/Jos Jesse Master
No Name/S/Elizth Gray/M/__/7d/Phillis/Elizth Gray Mistress
Archie/S/Henry McChalley/M/___/40y/__/Henry McChalley Master
Saml/S/P.R. Thornton/M/__/Old Age/72y/P.R. Thornton Master
No Name/S/Jas J. White/__/__/__/20d/Emeline/Jas J. White Master
Henry B. White/W/M/__/__/5y/Henry B. & Ann E. White/H.B. White - Father
M.E. Thornton/W/F/Mar/Consumption/18y/E.T. & C.E. Thornton/Edmd T. Thornton Father
Nelly/S/Anthony Thornton/F/July/Old Age/75y/__/Anthony Thornton Master
No Name/S/Anthony Thornton/F/July/__/8d/Catharine/Anthony Thornton Master
No Name/Phebe Lafoe/F/May/__/8d/Mary/Anthony Thornton/Friend & C [of owner]
Wm Collawn/W/M/Mar/__/82y/Jane Collawn/Farmer/Jno W. J. Collawn son
Harriett/S/R.T. Roane/F/__/__/1y/Ellen/R.T. Roane Master
Jno/S/R.T. Roane/M/Aug/Scarlet Fever/25y/Aberilla/R.T. Roane Master
Hillyard/S/R.T. Roane/M/Aug/Scarlet Fever/[illeg]/Rose/R.T. Roane Master
Louisa/S/R.T. Roane/F/Aug/Scarlet Fever/10y/Mary Ann/R.T. Roane Master

George/S/Keeling Rowe/M/Aug/Scarlet Fever/1y 1m/Milly/Keeling Rowe Master
Thomas/S/Keeling Rowe/M/Aug/Scarlet Fever/4m/Milly/Keeling Rowe Master
Daniel/S/Keeling Rowe/M/Aug/Scarlet Fever/3m/Sally/Keeling Rowe Master
Caty/S/Keeling Rowe/F/Aug/Scarlet/1y 1m/Henrietta/Keeling Rowe Master
Abraham/S/Richd Buckner/M/Apr/Typd Fever/10y/Mima/Richd Buckner Master
No Name/S/Elizth Collawn/M/__/__/__/Julia Ann/Richd Collawn Son [of owner]
George/S/John Burnard [Bernard]/M/Oct/Intoxication/65y/__/Jno H. Burnard Master
Paul/S/John H. Burnard [Bernard]/M/__/Mortification/45y/__/John H. Burnard Master
Louisa/S/John H. Burnard[Bernard]/F/__/Consumption/16y/Sarah/John H. Burnard Master
John/S/John H. Burnard [Bernard]/M/Mortification/4y/Sarah/John H. Burnard Master
William/S/John H. Burnard [Bernard]/M/__/__/Sarah/John H. Burnard Master
Wm/S/Jno T. Boutwell/M/Desp./55y/__/Jno T. Boutwell Master
Polly Murrow/W/F/__/__/3y/Hiram & Kitty Murrow/Hiram Murrow Father
J[John?]/Noel/W/M/May 4/__/44y/Saml Noel/Farmer/H.B. Brooke Neighbor & C
Terissa/S/Susan Noel/F/__/Measles/34y/Eliza/H.B. Brooke Neighbor
Patsy/S/Susan Noel/F/__/Measles/35y/__/H.B. Brooke Neighbor
Wm Mason/W/M/__/Old/60y/Jno Mason/Printer/Richd Mason Brother
W.M. Gayle/W/M/Feb/__/70y/Ellen Gayle/Farmer/Jno Gayle Son
Margarett/S/Alfd Terrell/F/Feb/__/__/Mary/Alfd Terrell Master
No Name/S/P. Woolfolk/F/__/__/__/Susan/P. Woolfolk Master
No Name/S/P. Woolfolk/M/__/__/__/Cilla/P. Woolfolk Master
Anney Collins/W/F/Old Age/70/__/Rivingston Collins Son
Wm D. Glassell/W/M/__/Convulsions/3y/And. M. & T.A. Glassell/And M. Glassell Father
No Name/S/And. M. Glassell/F/__/7d/Nancy/And M. Glassell Master
F. Coleman/W/M/__/__/1y 6m/R.H. & F.C. Coleman/Richd H. Coleman Father
Thomas Jeter/W/M/Dec 19/Bilious Colic/50y/__/Overseer/Mary Jeter wife
Jno Norment/W/M/Nov/Old Age/70y/__/Farmer/Willis Pitts Friend & C
Larkin Litchfield/W/M/May__/60y/__/[b.Matthews Co]/Geo Todd Father-in-Law
Sam/S/Jno Taylor Jr/M/June/Killed/45y/Mary/Jno Taylor Jr Master
Lucy/S/Elizth Collawn/F/__/__/35y/__/Jno Taylor Jr. Friend & C
Albert/S/C.W. Jones/M/__/__/60y/Milly/C.W. Jones Master
Phillis/S/Chas Phillips/F/Old Age/73y/Frances/Chas Phillips Master
Thos/S/R.L. Harrison/M/__/Hooping Cough/6y/Maria/A.L. Harrison Mistress
Walker/S/Wm D. Quisenberry/M/__/__/50y/__/Jno W. Blake Friend & C
Margt Martin/W/F/Bills. Fever/1y/Wm P. & M.N. Martin/Wm P. Martin Father
Phebe Chenault/W/F/Consumption/25y/Jno Cecil/Atwell Chenault Husband
Robt Marshall/W/M/Scarlet Fever/8y/Geo & T. Marshall/Geo Marshall Father
Madison/S/Geo Marshall/M/__/Dropsy/23y/__/Geo Marshall Master
Lucy/S/Geo Marshall/__/__/Scrofula/37y/Lucy/Geo Marshall Master
Maria/S/Geo Marshall/F/__/Scarlet Fever/__/Lucy/Geo Marshall Master
No Name/S/Geo Marshall/F/__/Scarlet Fever/10d/Mary/Geo Marshall Master
Harry/S/J.H. Broaddus/M/Oct/Old Age/70y/__/J.H. Broaddus Master
Mary/S/J.H. Broaddus/F/Aug/ 20y/Cintha/J.H. Broaddus Master
Maria/S/Phil R. Garnett/F/__/__/32y/Lucy/P.R. Garnett Master
Winney/S/Phil Green/F/__/Old Age/75y/__/Phil Green Master
Henrietta Cole/W/F/Jan 2/Scarlet Fever/6y/Jas J. & Elizth Cole/Jas J. Cole Father
Wallis/S/A.G. Broaddus/F/May/Scarlet Fever/3y 9m/Fanny/A.G. Broaddus Master
Geo/S/Jos A. Broaddus/M/Feb/Scarlet Fever/9y/Elizabeth/Jos A. Broaddus Master

Rachel/S/Thos B. Sale/F/Aug/__/1y 6m/Jane/Thos B. Sale Master
Jas/S/Jas J. Broaddus/M/Apr/Scarlet Fever/3y/Susan/Jas J. Broaddus Master
Patrick/S/Jno Broaddus/M/Feb/Scarlet Fever/2y/Louisa/Jno Broaddus Master
Jno/S/Ro R. Sale/M/Dec/Brain Fever/2y 9m/Martha/Ro R. Sale Master
George/S/Jno C. Gravatt/M/June/Scarlet Fever/4m/Mary/Jno C. Gravatt Master
Cintha/S/Caty White/F/Oct/__/35y/Betsy/Caty White Mistress
Lucy Didlake/W/F/Jan 19/__/64y/__/Caty White Sister
And. Cecil/W/M/June/Typd Fever/1y 10 m/Isaac & Betsey Cecil/ Isaac Cecil Father
Sally/S/Richd F. Streshley/F/Aug/__/1y/Polly/Richd Streshley Master
Wm Cowen/Free/M/Apr/Consumption/45y/Geo F. Gouldman Friend & C
George/S/Wm A. Saunders/M/__/10m/Lilly/Wm A. Saunders Master
C.N.H. Goodwin/W/M/June 30/Consumption/15y/C.H.P. Goodwin/Littleton Goodwin Brother
Judy/S/C.H.A. Goodwin/F/June 15/Consumption/70y/__/C.H.A. Goodwin Mistress
E.C. Cronie/W/F/Dec 1/Scarlet Fever/3m/H.R. & E. Cronie/Henry R. Cronie Father
S.B. Wright/W/M/Mar 20/Gravel/5d/Ro B. & L.A. Wright/Ro B. Wright Father
W.[illeg] Broaddus/W/M/Aug 15/Chro Diarrhea/1y 3m/Cors [Cornelius] & A.L.
   Broaddus/Cors Broaddus Father
Matthew/S/Thos Broaddus/M/Dec/__/10y/Amanda/Thos Broaddus Master
No Name/S/Ed McKenny/F/Mar/__/__/Martha/Edgar McKenny Master
S.M. Beazley/W/F/Apr 15/__/4y/Thos & E. Beazley/Thos Beazley Father
Sally M. Bagby/W/F/Apr 15/__/4y 4m/Travis & M.E. Bagby/Mary E. Bagby Mother
Lucy/S/Ro B. Tunstall/F/Nov/Parls/42y/__/Robt Tunstall Master
Jesse/S/Ro B. Tunstall/M/Dec/Heart Dis/20y/__/Robt Tunstall Master
Jno Tennant/W/M/Apr 10/__/56y/__/Chas H. Tennant Son
Susan/S/N.L. Battaile/F/Sept/Scarlet Fever/2y/Phillis/N.L. Battaile Master
George/S/B.R. Clarke/M/Oct/Hooping Cough/3y/Maria/B.R. Clarke Master
Maria/S/B.R. Clarke/F/Oct/Hooping Cough/1y/Jane/B.R. Clarke Master
Walton/S/B.R. Clarke/M/Oct/Hooping Cough/2y 6m/Lucy/B.R. Clarke Master
N.M. Thomas/W/F/July 17/__/56y/Mary Toombs/Catlett Thomas Husband
Lewis/S/B.R. Clarke/M/Oct/Hooping Cough/5y6m/Mary/B.R. Clarke Master
Jane Chapman/W/F/Nov 11/Typhoid Fever/64y/John C. Chapman/Wm B. Gravatt Son-in-Law
No Name/S/Jno Noel's Est/M/June/__/1y/__/[illeg]
No Name/S/Jno Woolfolk/M/June/__/1m/__/Benjm P. Coleman Overseer
Jolly/S/Wm G. Maury/M/Sept/Fever/18y/Eliz/Wm G. Maury Master
Mary Brown/W/F/Feb/Old Age/98y/__/Wm Wright Son-in-Law
George/S/El Green/W/Apr/__/3d/Polly/Eldred Green Master
Clary/S/Lucy Kidd/F/Apr 23/__/30y/Peggy/Lucy Kidd Mistress
Caro. Covington/W/F/Oct/__/2y 6m/Wm N. & N.J. Covington/Wm N. Covington Father
Danl Covington/W/M/__/1y 6m/Wm N. & N.J. Covington/Wm N. Covington Father
Henry/S/C.S. Richerson Est/M/Aug/Dropsy/35y/Mary/Polly Richerson Mistress
Ida Coghill/W/F/Aug/__/4m/S.A. & A.S. Coghill/Sam A. Coghill Father
Burtie/S/__/F/Apr/__/4y/Mary/Bettie Stern Mistress
James/S/Ellis Gravatt/M/Oct/Pneumonia/60y/__/Ellis Gravatt Master
Susan/S/Ellis Gravatt/F/Feb/__/60y/__/Ellis Gravatt Master
J.M. Fields/W/M/Nov/__/1m/Jno M. & Mary Fields/Jno M. Fields Father
Jno Morton/Free/M/Dec/__/9y/Jno & Caty Morton/Jno Morton Father
Lucy Catlett/W/F/Dec/__/65y/__/Colin B. Catlett Son
Jas Samuel/W/M/Mar/__/19y/Frances Samuel/Frances Samuel Mother

Willis/S/Jno O. Sale/M/__/__/53y/__/Jno O. Sale Master
Harry/S/R.G.R. Catlett/M/Nov/Dropsy/70y/__/Ro G.R. Catlett Master
M.A. Roberts/W/F/Jan 8/__/38y/[illeg]/S. Roberts Husband
C.G. Thornton/W/M/Sept 2/Bil Fever/8y/C.L. Thornton Father
No Name/W/M/Aug/__/4m/[illeg]
No Name/S/Jno B. Lightfoot/F/Aug/2d/[illeg]/Jno B. Lightfoot Master
No Name/S/M.M. Case/M/Sept/__/3y/[illeg]/Margaret M. Case Mistress
Eliza/S/Chas Urquhart/F/Apr/Hemor of Brain/30/[illeg]/Chas Urquhart Master
Geo/S/Chas Urquhart/M/Apr/Consumption/2m/[illeg]/Chas Urquhart Master
Julia Whiticoe/W/F/Oct/Scarlet Fever/2y/[illeg] Whiticoe Father
Adam/S/Jas J. Barbee/M/Apr/__/70y/[illeg]/Jas J. Barbee Master
James/S/Cors [Corneluis] Campbell/M/May/Consumption/19y/Mary/Cors Campbell Master
Sally/S/Cors [Cornelius] Campbell/F/Apr/__/35y/Milly/Cors Campbell Master
Mary/S/Jno P. Downing/F/July 29/__/7y/Ursley/Jno P. Downing Master
Ginay/S/Jno P. Downing/F/May/__/46y/Aggy/Jno P. Downing Master
Lucy/S/Frances Downing/F/June/___/3m/Melvina/Jno P. Downing Master
Thomas/S/Frances Downing/M/July/__/70y/Jane/Jno P. Downing Master
No Name/S/Frances Downing/M/Feb/__/1y 2m/__/Jno P. Downing Master
J.J. Donahoe/W/M/Jan/Old Age/70y/__/Jno L. Donahoe Son
Caroline/S/Wm W. Roper/F/Oct/__/1y 6m/Rachel/Wm W. Roper Master
Jno L. Cooper/Free/M/Sept/5y/Jno L.& Jane Cooper/Jno L. Cooper Father
Amy/S/Ira White/F/Oct/Typhoid Fever/21y/[illeg]/Smith R. White
Milly/S/Ira White/F/Nov/Typhoid Fever/23y/[illeg]/Smith R. White
Wm W. Carter/W/M/Aug/Apoplexy/60y/__/Wm W. Carter Jr

1857

James/S/Ira E. Dickinson/M/Dec 4/Plurisy/68y/Not Known/Ira E. Dickinson Master
Lucy/S/Catharine Collins/F/Mar/Paralisis/64y/Not Known/Catharine Collins Mistress
Not Named/S/Jesse Cobbs/M/Feb/Cold/21d/Frances/Jesse Cobbs Master
Not Named/S/Jesse Cobbs/F/Sept 1/Consumption/81y/Hannah/Jesse Cobbs Master
William/S/John D. Wright/M/Sept/Diariah/1y/Alfrances/John D. Wright Master
Temple/S/Henrietta Goodwin/M/Oct 31/Hart Disease/45y/Hannah/Henrietta Goodwin Mistress
Lydia/S/Richard Blanton/F/Apr/Hart Disease/42y/Milly/Richd Blanton Master
Andrew/S/Richard Blanton/M/Aug/Scrofula/9y/Lydia/Rich Blanton Master
Betty Ayres/W/F/Nov/Congestion of brain/27y/Not Known/Geo W. Blanton Superintendent Poor House
Nancy Brooks/W/F/Dec 17/Old Age/90y/Not Known/Geo W. Blanton Superintendent Poor House
Newton/S/Jas R. Garnett Est/F/Dec 20/Asthma/75y/Not Known/Hugh Chandler Friend
Not Named/S/Wesley Wright/F/Dec/Overlaid/10d/Fanny/Wesley Wright Master
Aley/S/Wesley Wright/F/__/Not Known/28y/Martha/Wesley Wright Master
Not Named/S/Wesley Wright/F/Spasms/1m 20d/Lucy/Wesley Wright Master
Not Named/S/Wesley Wright/M/   /born dead/Isbel/Wesley Wright Master
Not Named/S/Jesse Winn/F/Dec/Not Known/10d/Lucy/Jesse Winn Master
Frances/S/Tavenor Winn/F/June/Hooping Cough/3y/Nancy/Tavenor Winn Master
James T. Cobbs/W/M/Nov/Hart Disease/23y/David T. & Ann Cobbs/David T. Cobbs Father
Phebe/S/Elliott Wright/F/June 20/Brain Fever/54y/Nancy/Elliott Wright Master
Winston/S/Sarah P. Kelley/M/__/Scrofula/7y/Rachael/Wm M. Kelley Son of Sarah Kelley

George T. Madison/W/M/Apr 3/Consumption/30y/Henry W. & Frances Ann Madison/Wm J. Madison Brother

Major/S/Obey Burruss/M/Aug/Hooping Cough/2y/Emaline/Obey Burruss Master

Not Named/S/Obey Burruss/M/Sept/Hooping Cough/1y/Malinda/Obey Burruss Master

William/S/Obey Burruss/M/Nov/Typhoid Fever/5y/Kesiah/Obey Burruss Master

Sarah/S/Elliott Wortham/Feb/Dec 12/Bilious Cholic/50y/Dellia/Elliott Wortham Master

Mary/S/Wm T. Noel/F/July/Hooping Cough/4m/Mary Jane/Wm T. Noel Master

Martha/S/Wm T. Noel/F/Nov/Pneumonia/8m/Mary/Wm T. Noel Master

Mary/S/Henry H. George/F/Nov/Hooping Cough/12y/Mary/Wm T. Noel hired master of H.H. George

Reuben/S/Ann G. Ware/M/Nov/Typhoid Fever/4y/Martha/John H. Ware - Young Master

Not Named/S/Geo B. Pollard/F/Dec 3/Overlaid/__/Louisa/Geo B. Pollard Master

Not Named/S/Jno W. Scott/M/Nov/30y/Still born/Lucinda/John W. Scott Master

Wm Francis Scott/W/M/Sept 29/Billious Pneumonia/8m 8d/John W. & [illeg] H. Scott/John W. Scott Father

Not Named/S/Nicholas Mills/M/May 10/Lock Jaw/7m/Sally/Wm J. Young Overseer

Not Named/S/Nicholas Mills/F/Sept 1/Not Known/3m/Elizabeth/Wm J. Young Overseer

Elizabeth/S/Nicholas Mills/F/Dec 1/Consumption/38y/Nancy/Wm J. Young Overseer

Emily Frances Thomas/W/F/Aug/Dropsy/24y/Wm F. & Susan H. Thomas/Wm F. Thomas Father

Cupid/S/Ira L. Thomas/M/Nov/Spasms/30y/Sally/Ira L. Thomas Master

Matthew P. Dimmue/W/M/Dec 4/Pneumonia/45y/John & Nancy Dimmue/Frances Dimmue wife

Tom/S/John Long/M/Nov/Cold/45y/Betty/John Long Master

Not Named/S/Elijah L. Stevens/F/Sept 17/Not Known/6m/Mariah/E.L. Stevens Master

Susan/S/James G. White/F/Jan 16/Scrofula/2y/Harriett/James G. White - Master

Not Names/S/James G. White/M/May 8/Still born/Elijah/Jas G. White - Master

Alace Willis/W/F/Nov 26/Scarlet Fever/4y/Rich & Delileh W. Southworth/Richard Southworth Father

Nancy Hughes/W/F/Sept 1/Cold/54y/Not Known/Jno Hughes Husband

Alice W. Richards/W/F/Nov 24/Scarlet Fever/5y 10d/Horace A. & Louise T. Richards/ Horace A. Richards Father

Not Names/S/Wm R. Young/Apr/Not Known/__/Nancy/Wm R. Young Master

Ellen Elizabeth Osgood/W/F/Dec 31/Brain Fever/5m/Franklin H. & Martha L. Osgood/John Trainham Uncle

Not Named/F/Aug/Brain Fever/__/Wm V. & Mary Jane Dickins/John Trainham Uncle

Ann/S/Julia Samuel/F/Dec 6/Smothered/9m/Patsy/Henry H. George hired Master

Thomas Jordan/S/John Pare [Parr]/W/Jan/Spasms/1m/Harriett/John Pare Master

Patsy/S/Elizabeth Burruss/F/Aug/Cold/11m/Jane/Elizabeth Burruss Mistress

Delia/S/Elizabeth Burruss/F/June/Consumption/28y/Judy/Elizabeth Burruss Mistress

Not Named/W/F/Aug/Cholera Infantum/3m/Wm H.N. & Rebecca Burruss/Wm H.N. Burruss Father

Aquilla Goodloe/W/M/Nov 15/Old Age/82y/George & __/b.Spotsylvania/Betsy L. Goodloe Wife/James L. Goodloe Son

Not Named/S/Aquilla Goodloe/M/July/Hooping Cough/8m/Hullah/James L. Goodloe - Young Master

Not Named/S/John D. Longdon/M/Dec/Lock Jaw/7m/Melinda/John D. Longdon Master

Petro/S/Phil J. Reynolds/M/Jan 1/Pneumonia/62y/Not Known/b.Essex/Phil J. Reynolds Master

Not Named/W/M/July 25/Not Known/2d/Christopher & Tabitha Collins/Christopher Collins Father

Caroline/S/Warner M. Mason/F/Oct/Scarlet Fever/11y/Rhoda/Warner M. Mason Master

Esther/S/Warner M. Mason/F/Nov/Scarlet Fever/18y/Patsy/Warner M. Mason Master

Dolly/S/Warner M. Mason/F/Nov/Not Known/55y/Judy/Warner M. Mason Master

Caroline L. Christian/W/F/June 15/Congestion of bowels/23y 2m/Ernest & Barbary Shuman/
 b.Baltimore Md/Edmund Christian Husband
Not Named/2W/2M/Aug/Still born/Wm T. & Caroline L. Taliaferro/Wm T. Taliaferro Father
Lucy Peatross/W/F/Dec/Constant Fever/82y/__ & Lucy Peatross/Geo W. Peatross Son
Martha J. Carter/W/F/Dec 21/Dropsy/16y 6m/Horace & Nancy Carter/Horace Carter Father
Mary/S/John Chandler/F/Sept 1/Thrash/1y 2d/Elizabeth/John Chandler Master
Thomas Kemp/S/John Chandler/M/July/Spasms/1y 1m/Martha/John Chandler Master
Sam/S/Robert T. Wortham/M/Jan/Consumption/36y/Martha/Robert T. Wortham Master
Peggy Adams/W/F/Oct/Old Age/80y/__/Robert T. Wortham Physician
Not Named/S/Henry Doggett/M/Sept/Lock Jaw/17m/Martha/Henry Doggett Master
Martha T. Doggett/W/F/Apr 7/Cronic Liver/46y/John & Mary White/Henry Doggett Husband
James H.L. Yarbrough/W/M/Dec 8/Dropsy/25y/Mickleberry & Willworth Yarbrough/
 Mickleberry Yarbrough Father
William/S/Louisa Turner/M/Aug 25/Summer Compliant/8y 14d/Dinah/b.King & Queen/John O.
 Hutcheson Hired by his mother
Lucy/S/L.M. George/F/May/Spasms/1y 11m/Mariah/L.M. George Master
Nancy/S/Phil Samuel/F/June/Spasms/50y/Daphney/Phil Samuel Master
Not Named/S/S.W. Allen/M/Nov/Not Known/__/Betsy/Silas W. Allen Master
Woodford Garnett/W/M/Apr 12/Influenza/62y/James & Catharine Garnett/b.King & Queen/Caroline
 Garnett wife/Wm R. Young Bro-in-Law
Jordan/S/Woodford Garnett/M/Apr 6/Pneumonia/[illeg]/__/Wm R. Young
Sarah Hundley/W/F/Nov 13/Dropsy in Chest/__/Frank R. & D. Hundley/Saml D. Peatross relative
Billy/S/Geo T. Collins/M/Apr/Spasms/10y/Not Known/b.Gloucester/Geo T. Collins Master
Ellis/S/Wm C. Gatewood/M/Apr/Not Known/4d/Josie/Wm C. Gatewood Master
Not Named/S/[illeg] O. Coleman/F/Sept/__/14m/Melanda/ O. Coleman - Young Master
Martin/S/Jos Flippo/M/May/__/22y/__/Joseph A. Flippo Master
Not Known/S/Buckner Trainham/M/July/[illeg]/[illeg]/__/Buckner Trainham Master
Jane/S/Emily T. Morris/F/July/[illeg]/[illeg]/Martha/Emily T. Morris Mistress
Charles/S/Emily T. Morris/M/[illeg]/[illeg]/[illeg]/Martha/Emily T. Morris Mistress
[illeg]/S/Emily T. Morris/M/[illeg]/[illeg]/[illeg]/Martha/Emily T. Morris Mistress
Tulip/S/Jame Hunter/F/Apr/Erysipelas/68y/__/James Hunter Master
Jane T. Samuel/W/F/Mar 8/Brain Fever/6y/Philip & Sarah W. Samuel/Philip Samuel Sr Father
Not Named/W/F/Oct/Spasms/3d/Henderson & Subbrina E. Carneal/Henderson Carneal Father
Harry/S/Wm Carnal/F/June/Measles/2y 1m/Caroline/Wm Carnal Master
Wm Boulware/W/M/July 11/Old Age/88y 11m 15d/John & __/Richard E. Boulware Son
Elliott/S/Rich E. Boulware/M/Dec/Cronic disease/27y/Clary/Richard E. Boulware Master
Melvina/S/Wm Boulware/F/Dec/__/6y/Charlott/Richard E. Boulware - Young Master
China/S/Wm Boulware/F/Dec/__/6y/Mary/Richard Boulware - Young Master
Matilda/S/Wm Boulware/F/Nov/__/6y/Emaline/Richard Boulware - Young Master
Wm B. Grimes/W/M/May 28/Not Known/49y/Wm & Susan Grimes/James Grimes Son
Elizabeth Cobbs/W/F/Mar 10/Pneumonia/53y/Garnett & Elizabeth Woolfolk/Henry P. Martin
 Neighbor
Risey/S/Jno V. Kean/F/June/Consumption/50y/Sucky/John V. Kean Master
L.W. Allen Jr/W/M/Dec 5/Scarlet Fever/7y 3m/L.W. & Ann M. Allen/L.W. Allen Sr Father
Caroline Swann/W/F/Dec 12/Paralysis of Stomach/62y/Richd & Elizabeth Lowery/Saml A. Swann
 Husband/Saml A. Swann Jr Son
Elizabeth E. Swann/W/F/Sept 8/Dispepsia/31y/Saml A. & Caroline Swann/Saml A. Swann Brother
Jno W[illeg] Wright/W/M/July/Inflamation of brain/4m/Geo & Mary E. Wright/George V. Wright

Father
Not Named/S/A.G. Goodwin/F/Feb/Not Known/2d/Sarah/A.G. Goodwin Master
Alexander/S/A.G. Goodwin/M/May 10/Measles/4y/Patsy/Louisa Co/A.G. Goodwin Master
Jefferson/S/Saml Coleman/M/Nov 19/Bronchitus/9m/[illeg]/Saml Coleman Master
Mary D. Coleman/W/F/Nov 22/Disentary/55y/Edward & Polly Withers/Saml Coleman Husband
John R. Turner/W/M/Oct 11/Stricture of bladder/67y 10m 22d/James & Mary Turner/Richardson
 Turner son
Roger Pleasant Lumpkin/W/M/Oct 1/Brain Fever/6m 22d/Thos & Frances E. Lumpkin/Thos Lumpkin
 Father
Isabella/S/Thos Lumpkin/F/Mar 20/Inflamation bowels/82y/Susannah/Thos Lumpkin Father
Not Named/S/Robert Woolfolk/M/Sept 15/Spasms/7d/Mary/Robert Woolfolk Master
Frances Gravatt/W/F/Nov 17/Inflamation of Stomach/94y/David & ___/b.Essex/Wm Gravatt Husband
Julia/S/Saml E.H. Campbell/F/Sept 15/Typhoid Fever/12y/Rhody/Saml E.H. Campbell
Ben/S/Clara H. Goodwin/Nov 28/Paralisis/63y/Daphney/Jno T. Goodwin Brother to owner
James/S/George W. Burk/M/Feb/Asthma/65y/Not Known/George W. Burk Master
Lucy/S/Hugh R. White/F/June 8/Quinsy/72y/Not Known/b.Spotsylvania/Hugh R. White Master
Jane Tyler/W/F/Feb 25/Puspinal Fever/26y 3m/Wm & Elizabeth Quisenberry/George Tyler Husband
Patsy Stevens/W/F/Mar 11/Consumption/80y/[illeg] & Betsy [illeg]/Geo Stevens Husband/Henry
 Stevens Son
Caroline/S/Jefferson Flippo/F/Apr/Bowel Compliant/2y 6m/Frances/Jefferson Flippo Master
William/S/Jefferson Flippo/M/Sept/Bowel Complaint/1y/Frances/Jefferson Flippo Master
Walker/S/Ann Washington/M/Nov 27/Dropsy/52y/[illeg]/Ann Washington Mistress
Elizth/S/J.D. Coleman/F/Mar/Pneumonia/65y/Hannah/Jas D. Coleman Master
Sukey/S/Joseph Flippo/F/__/Not Known/65y/Sally/Joseph Flippo Master
[illeg]/W/F/Dec 5/Pneumonia/69y/Jos & Mary Ann Flippo/[illeg] Husband
[illeg]/S/Susan Wyatt/F/Oct/Summer Compliant/[illeg]/Not Known/Susan Wyatt Mistress
[illeg]/W/M/Dec 7/Croup/5m/Wm H. & Virginia Dickinson/Sarah L. C[illeg]
[illeg]/S/Elissa Wright/M/Not Known/1y 3m/Frankey/Elissa Wright Mistress
[illeg]/S/Elissa Wright/M/Sept/Not Known/3d/Frankey/Elissa Wright Mistress
[illeg]/S/M/__/Dropsy/45y/__/Horace Wright Master
[illeg]/S/M/Feb/Not Known/69y/__/Horace Wright Master
Martha/S/Ro Wright's Est/F/Nov/Dropsy/33y/S[illeg]/Horace Wright - Young Master
Not Named/S/Woodson Wright/F/Feb 1/Smothered/2m/Ann/Horace Wright Manager
Jemima Durrett/W/F/Dec/Consumption/44y/Pleasant & Jane Winston/John Durrett Husband
Not Named/S/John Samuel/F/July/Overlaid/3m/Betsy/Philip Samuel Bro of owner
Patsy/S/Jos B. Flippo/F/Sept/Worms/3y/Dinah/Jos B. Flippo Master
William/S/Saml Schooler/M/Oct/Not Known/2y/Suckey/Saml Schooler Master
James/S/Saml Schooler/M/__/Not Known/1y 6m/Suckey/Saml Schooler Master
Betty/S/Dabney B. Waller/F/Sept 14/Not Known/38y/Cloe/b.Spotsylvania/D.W. Waller Master
Lewis/S/Albert Durrett/M/Oct/Croup/44y/Frankey/Albert Durrett Master
Marcus/S/Ruffin H. Coleman/M/Sept/Overlaid/1m/Hardenia/Ruffin H. Coleman Master
Judy/S/Robert S. Luck/F/Dec 28/Old Age/69y/Not Known/Ro Sam Luck Master
Litty Durrett/W/F/Oct 20/Pneumonia/64y/Tavenor & Nancy Winn/Ro A. Durrett Son
Anne B. Harris/W/F/Nov 7/Typhoid Fever/39y/Layton & Elizabeth Harris/Layton Harris Father
Not Named/S/Saml E. Swann/F/June 1/Not Known/__/Frankey/Saml E. Swann Master
Not Named/S/Rob Farish/F/May 15/Not Known/Lucy Ann/Rob Farish Master
Lucy Ann/S/Rob Farish/F/May 17/Child Birth/25y/Suckey/b.Culpepper/Rob Farish Master
Not Named/S/Clementina Dickinson/F/Nov/Not Known/10d/Ann George/Judson Dickinson -

Young Master
Not Named/S/Clemintina Dickinson/M/__/Not Known/8y/Harriett/Judson Dickinson - Young Master
Benjamin F. Madison/W/M/Mar/Consumption/21y/George W. & Lucy Madison/Richd J. Madison
   Brother
Elizabeth Atkins/W/F/__/Fits/__/b.Orange/Philip B. Atkins Son
Rudy/S/Eldred Turner/F/Dec/Mashed/6m/Frances/Eldred Turner Master
Not Named/S/Eldred Turner/F/Sept 30/Not Known/__/Aggy/Eldred Turner Master
Mary Baughn/W/F/Apr 27/Erysipelas/66y/__ & Mary Kersy/b.Hanover/James Baughn Husband/
   James Baughn Son
Nancy W. Chandler/W/F/July 8/Pneumonia/73y 2m 23d/Thos & Susanna Travillian/ Thos T. Chandler
   Son
Not Named/W/M/June/Not Known/1d/Stephen & Sarah Jane Terry/Stephen Terry Father
Taylor/S/Daniel Turner/M/Nov 30/Whooping Cough/19y/Pheby/b.Goochland/Daniel Turner Master
Sam/S/Lewis W. Coleman/M/Nov/Whooping Cough/5m/Rose/Wm B. Wittakire O Seer
Precilla [illeg]/W/F/Feb/Old Age/80y/Henry & [illeg] Mallory/b.Hanover/Hastings Watkins Son-in-Law
George/S/John Burruss Sr/M/Feb/__/85y/Not Known/b.Hanover/Jno Burruss Sr Master
Robert Hackney/W/M/June/Dropsy/30y/Durrett & Elizabeth Hackney/Claiborne Durrett Friend
Ned/S/Josephus Gatewood/M/Mar/Hectic Fever/35y/Not Known/b.Spotsylvania/ Josephus Gatewood
   Master
Not Named/S/F/__/Not Known/15d/Esther/William Carter Master
Not Named/S/F/__/Not Known/1y 5m/Lucy/William Carter Master
Not Named/S/F/__/Not Known/1m/Judy/William Carter Master
Not Named/S/M/Not Known/1y 6m/Judy/William Carter Master
Not Named/S/William Carter/F/__/__/__/Fanny/William Carter Master
Joe/S/William Carter/M/__/Consumption/15y/__/William Carter Master
Sarah/S/William Carter/F/__/Consumption/27y/__/William Carter Master
Milly/S/William Carter/F/__/Consumption/25y/__/William Carter Master
Billy/S/William Carter/M/__/Bowel Compliant/56y/__/William Carter Master
Molly/S/William Carter/F/__/Bowel Compliant/60y/__/William Carter Master
Dick/S/Wm Carter/M/__/Bowel Compliant/38y/__/Wm Carter Master
Rachel/S/Wm Carter/F/__/Bowel Compliant/28y/__/Wm Carter Master
Nathan/S/Wm Carter/M/__/Bowel Complaint/36y/__/Wm Carter Master
Jerry/S/George Todd/M/June/Dropsy/50y/Not Known/George Todd Master
John Henry/S/Mrs. Ann Gatewood/M/Sept/Consumption/51y/Mary/Wm C. Moncure/Grandson of
   owner
Adrianna/S/Peter Quarles/F/Nov 21/Croup/4m/Milly/Peter Quarles Master
Isabella/S/Rhody N. Reynolds/F/June 12/Heart Disease/50y/Not Known/Rhody N. Reynolds Mistress
Mariah/S/Louisana Redd/F/July/Smothered/1m 14d/Lucy/Mrs. L. Redd Mistress
Anna/S/Louisana Redd/F/Dec 8/Paralysis/70y/Anna/Mrs L. Redd Mistress
Not Named/S/Elizabeth Redd/M/July/Not Known/__/Kesiah/Mrs. E. Redd Mistress
Sazelson/S/Jno G. Dickinson/M/Oct 28/Burn/2y 6m/Ann/Jno G. Dickinson Master
Silva/S/Thos B. Anderson/F/July/Dropsy Chest/76y/Not Known/Thos B. Anderson Master
Not Named/S/Thos N. Welch/M/July/Not Known/1d/Fanny/b.Madison/Thos N. Welch Master
Not Named/S/Jas C. DeJarnette/M/Jan/Smothered/25d/Ellen/Jas C. DeJarnette Master
Not Named/S/Thos Hurt/M/Jan/Not Known/7d/Hannah/Thos Hurt Master
Not Named/S/Eliz B. Coleman/F/__/Smothered/4d/Jane/Elizth B. Coleman Mistress
Not Named/S/Wm W. Dickinson/M/Aug/Not Known/__/Judy/Jas L. Sizer Overseer
Thos Rock/Free/Dec/Old Age/81y/Not Known/Wm C. Moncure Friend

No Name/W/F/June/__/2d/Owen C. & R.E. Tuck/Owen C. Tuck Father
Burton/S/Ira E. White/M/Aug/__/2y/Harriett/Ira E. White - Master
Phinella Green/W/F/Aug 29/Bra Fever/24y/Phil Green/Phil Green Father
Virginia W. Taylor/W/F/Sept 26/Hooping Cough/3y 3m/Geo K. & R.L. Taylor/Geo K. Taylor Father
Patsy Garrett/W/F/Apr 25/Heart Dis/62y/Jas Garrett/Ed Garrett Son
Emma T. Coghill/W/F/Apr 2/Disy/9y/L.A. & A.E. Coghill/Law A. Coghill Father
Nancy/S/Ross Broaddus/F/June/Heart Dis/30/Eddy/Ross Broaddus Master
Mabel Broaddus/W/F/Nov 26/Scarlet Fever/9m/And & J. Broaddus/And Broaddus Father
Alice/S/A. Broaddus/F/Nov 3/Scrofula/__/Frances/And Broaddus Master
Elizth Ayres/W/F/Dec/Scrafula/30y/Susan Ayres/[illeg]
Jesse Taylor/W/F/Aug/Consumption/40y/Fanny Reynolds/[illeg]Taylor Husband
No Name/W/F/Oct 15/__/1m 15d/Wm & Mary Self/Wm Self Father
Mary Houston/W/F/July/Child Bed/2y/Betsy Houston/Atwell Houston Father
No Name/W/F/July__/1m/Ellis A. & Mary Beazley/Ellis A. Beazley Father
Matilda Norment/Free/F/Dec/Scarlet Fever/40y/Milly Norment/Ellis Norment Brother
M[illeg]/S/Garl Samuel/M/May/Old Age/70y/__/Garld Samuel Master
Kinsford Baldwin/W/M/Aug/Scarlet Fever/1y 2m/Nancy A. Baldwin/Geo Baldwin Father
No Name/W/M/Apr/__/14m/Thos & Nancy Eubank/Thos Eubank Father
Keziah/S/Thos R. Dew/F/July/Disy/60y/__/Ed Sale Overseer
William/S/Ro B. Tunstall/M/Feb/__/60y/__/Ro B. Tunstall Master
Robt/S/Thos R. Dew/M/Mar/Dis of the Lungs/6y/Lizie/Ed Sale Overseer
Ron Garnett/W/M/July/Disy/1y 6m/R.B. & R.A. Garnett/Reu B. Garnett Father
Augustine Pugh/W/M/Jan 19/__/19y/Henry & Ivania Pugh/Henry Pugh Father
Lewis/S/Theop F. Green/M/Sept/__/12m/Milly/Theop F. Green Master
Nancy Beazley/W/F/Apr 3/__/15y/Spencer & Mary Beazley/Spencer Beazley Father
Maria/S/Wm Chapman/F/__/d.Richmond/__/25y/Louisa/Wm Chapman Master
Robt/S/Wm Chapman/M/June/Consumption/20y/Betty/Wm Chapman Master
Dinah/S/Thos Broaddus/F/Jan/Old Age/65y/__/Thos Broaddus Master
Alexander/S/Thos Broaddus/M/Jul/__/5y/Charity/Thos Broaddus Master
Z.T. Warwick/W/M/Aug/Hooping Cough/2y/Wm & Margt Warwick/Cors [Cornelius] R. Rose Uncle
No Name/S/Jno Woolfolk Est/F/__/__/1y/Betsy/B.F. Coleman Manager
Courtney Picardett/W/F/May 15/Child Bed/3y/Patsy Brooks/Rufus Travis Uncle
No Name/S/B.A. Jordan/F/__/__/5y/Lavenia/B.A. Jordan Master
G.G. Jeter/W/F/Apr 21/Lock Jaw/30y/Wm & J. Chapman/Law Jeter Husband
Francis Howard/W/F/June/Hooping Cough/5y/M.W. & Virg Howard/Mor W. Howard Father
Flora Howard/W/F/Oct/Hooping Cough/8y/M.W. & Virg Howard/Mor W. Howard Father
M.S. Traynham/W/F/Jul/__/18y/L. & E. Traynham/Larkin Traynham Father
Harry/S/Sophia Allen/M/July/__/55y/__/Sophia Allen Mistress
Anthony/S/Sophia Allen/M/July/__/60y/__/Sophia Allen Mistress
No Name/S/Wm G. Maury/F/Aug/__/1m/Louisa/Wm G. Maury Master
Clara B. Cranie/W/F/Sept/__/10m/H.R. & M.A. Cranie/Henry R. Cranie Father
Maria/S/Thos Motley/F/__/Consumption/35y/Milly/Thos Motley Master
Thos Jones/W/M/Nov 8/Old Age/65y/Robin Jones/Allen J. Rose Nephew
Fielding Pittis/W/M/Dec 6/Old Age/70y/Jno & F. Pittis/Farmer/Jos Wright Bro-in-Law
Ed Donahoe/W/M/Nov 7/__/40y/Lucy Donahoe/Jno L. Donahoe Brother
Nancy Donahoe/W/F/Nov 7/__/60y/Thos Donahoe/Jno L. Donahoe Brother
Cath Pugh/W/F/Sept/__/50y/Patsy Donahoe/Jno L. Donahoe Brother
Jack/S/Jno H. DeJarnette/M/June/__/40y/__/Jno H. DeJarnette Master

Nissa/S/Jno H. DeJarnette/M/__/__/60y/__/Jno H. DeJarnette Master
Matilda/S/Jno H. DeJarnette/F/__/__/80y/__/Jno H. Dejarnette Master
Sarah Loven/W/F/Dec/__/45y/Betsy Loven/Brookin Loven Husband
No Name/S/R.F. Streshley/M/__/__/10m/Polly/R.F. Streshley Master
Thos Boulware/W/M/Oct/Rubeola/46y/Sally Boulware/Betsy Boulware Wife
No Name/Free/F/July/__/__/Adeline Freeman/Geo Freeman Uncle
Jno L. Beazley/W/M/Aug/Disy/2y/Jno P. & M.F. Beazley/Jno P. Beazley Father
Reu Beazley/W/M/Aug/Diahr/35y/Phil Beazley/Jno Beazley Jr[sic] Bro
Geo L. Phillips/W/M/Aug/[illeg]/35y/Chas Phillips/Chas Phillips Father
Toler Vaughan/W/M/Aug/Stabbed/23y/Corbin Vaughan/Wm P. Martin Uncle
Harriett/S/Ro G. Holloway Est/F/Sept/[illeg]/6y/Eliza/Thos R. Holloway - Young Master
Ro Farinholt/W/M/Aug 10/__/5m/Wm H. & S.E. Farinholt/Wm H. Farinholt Father
Mary Owen/W/F/July 2/__/1m 15d/Wm P. & M.F. Owen/Wm P. Owen Father
Jno Walker/Free/M/Aug/__/1m/M. & Jane Walker/Mishick Walker Father
Jane Walker/Free/F/July/Child Bed/24y/Sophia Grimes/Mishick Walker Uncle
Jno Lumpkin/W/M/Nov 19/Old Age/72y/Isaac Lumpkin/Thos D. Lumpkin Son
Jack Warwick/W/M/Sept/__/5y/Mary Warwick/C.C. Rose Uncle
Patsy Scrange/Free/F/Sept/Womb Dis/25y/Jane Smith/Richd Scrange Husband
Geo Scrange/Free/M/__/__/3y/Fanny Scrange/Richd Scrange Uncle
Sally/S/Jno B. Lightfoot/F/Sept/__/35y/Fanny/Jno B. Lightfoot Master
Chaney/S/Jno B. Lightfoot/F/__/__/2y/Susan/Jno B.Lightfoot Master
Bankhead/S/Jno B. Lightfoot/M/Oct/__/65y/__/Jno B. Lightfoot Master
Scott/S/Jno B. Lightfoot/M/Jan/Lock Jaw/20y/Emily/Jno B. Lightfoot Master
No Name/S/Richd A. Puller/F/__/__/5y/Letty/R.A. Puller Master
Lucy C. Kidd/W/F/__/Disy/1y/Henry & Mary Kidd/Henry Kidd Father
Jas L. Southworth/W/Mar/Croup/20y/A. & C.M. Southworth/Archilles Southworth Father
Isabella Southworth/W/F/Oct/__/16y/A. & C.M. Southworth/Archilles Southworth Father
Harriett/S/Thos R. Dew/F/Feb/__/45y/Sallie/Thos R. Dew Master
Maria/S/V.L. Harrison/F/Feb/__/26y/__/V.L. Harrison Mistress
No Name/S/Jas H. Garnett/__/3m/Cecily/Jas H. Garnett Master
Sarah A. Dew/W/F/__/__/79y/And & Hart Dew/And Dew Father
Maria/S/Jno Broaddus/F/__/__/60y/Susan/Jno Broaddus Master
Rhoda/S/Geo T. Burruss/F/Feb/__/40y/Fanny/G.T. Burruss Master
Edward/S/Geo T. Burruss/M/Jan/__/18y/Hannah/G.T. Burruss Master
Danl/S/Geo T. Burrus/M/Oct/__/19y/Mary/G.T. Burruss Master
Robt Wright/W/M/Nov 9/__/47y/Ro & Mary [Margt] Wright/Margt B. Crump Sister
John/S/B.B. Wright Est/M/Mar/[illeg]60y/__/Margt B. Crump Mistress [sister to B.B.Wright]
Jesse/S/Ro E. DeJarnette/M/Mar/[illeg]/[illeg]/Louisa/Ro E. DeJarnette Master
Judy/S/Jor [Jourdan] Woolfolk/F/Oct/__/__/Maria/Jor Woolfolk Master
Fanny/S/Jor [Jourdan] Woolfolk/F/Oct/Maria/Jor Woolfolk Master
Judith/S/Jor [Jourdan] Woolfolk/F/__/__/75y/__/Jor Woolfolk Master
Billy/S/Jor [Jourdan] Woolfolk/M/__/__/50y/Bettie/Jor Woolfolk Master
No Name/Free/__/__/__/9m/Geo & Amey Norment/Geo Norment Father
Caty Pugh/W/F/May/__/50y/Gouldin Pugh/Cath Donahoe Mother
Tulip/S/Arch B. Samuel/F/Mar/56y/__/Arch B. Samuel Master
Jno Anderson/W/M/Feb 10/Consumption/52y/Jno & Mary Anderson/ Sidney B. Anderson Widow
Jane/S/Arthur Lewis/F/July/__/1y 4m/Sophia/Arthur Lewis Master
No Name/S/C.H. Boutwell/__/__/__/1d/Betsy/C.H. Boutwell Mistress

Robt Calliss/W/M/Nov 24/d.Essex Co/Brain Fever/51y/Ro & G. Callis/Peggy J. Calliss Widow
Jas T. Garnett/W/M/Aug 25/d.Essex Co/__/33y/Phil & Ann Garnett/Phil R. Garnett Father
Martin/S/Thos C. Rixey Est/M/__/__/65y/__/And M. Glassell Overseer
Harriett/S/Thos C. Rixey Est/F/__/__/30y/__/And M. Glassell Overseer
Milly/S/Thos C. Rixey Est/F/__/[illeg]/__/__/And M. Glassell Overseer
L. Latham/W/F/July 7/Croup/16y/D. & Milly Latham/Ayt H. Conway Cousin
Matilda/S/Geo W. Trice/F/__/Consumption/16y/Betty/Geo W. Trice Master
Caty Murrow/W/F/Apr 19/__/70y/Benj Murrow/Saml Gray Neighbor
Thos E. Morris/W/M/Apr/Diap/32y/__/Jno G. Pavy Father-in-Law
No Name/S/Jno C. Bowie's Est/M/__/__/6y/Bettie/Jno A. Miller Admr
Turner/S/Jos W. Kay/M/Apr/Fits/25y/Delphia/Jos W. Kay Master
Olive/S/E.P. White's Est/F/Mar/Croup/3y/Cresee/Wm Dishays Overseer
James/S/Ed P. White's Est/M/Feb/__/45y/__/Wm Dishays Overseer
Lucy/S/Jno J. Gravatt/F/July/Disy/2y/Mary/Jno J. Gravatt Master
E. Lunsford/S/J.H. Bernard/F/July/__/20y/Jackie/Wm R. Bernard - Y Master
No Name/S/F/Oct 31/__/__/Sarah/Wm R. Bernard - Yg Master
Reu Toombs/Free/M/Apr/__/65y/__/Jas Bird Neighbor
Tulip/S/Jos E. Penney/F/Oct/__/82y/Franky/Jos E. Penney Master
No Name/S/J.A.L. Shaddock/F/Oct/__/15d/Cathl/J.A.L. Shaddock Master
Lewis/S/Peter R. Thornton/M/Jan/__/62y/Judith/P.R. Thornton Master
J. Walker/Free/F/Feb/__/30y/Sophia Walker/S. Grimes Neighbor
No Name/Free/F/__/__/__/Sophia Grimes/Sophia Grimes Mother
Heskiah Walker/Free/M/Mar/__/__/__/S. Grimes Neighbor
Frank/S/M.L. Boulware/M/__/__/7m/Sally/M.L. Boulware Mistress
Caty/S/Rich Collawn/F/Mar/Pneumonia/50y/Rich Collawn Master
Walter/S/Wm D. Boulware/M/Aug/__/1y/Matilda/Wm D. Boulware Master
No Name/S/Thos W. Gouldin/F/__/__/2m/Lucy/Thos W. Gouldin Master
Anthony/S/Wm H. Farish/M/Aug/Dropsy of Brain/22y/Eliza/Wm H. Farish Master
No Name/S/S.C. Jones/F/__/__/3d/Hannah/S.C. Jones Master
[illeg]/S/Thos W. Gouldin/F/Sept/Disy/75y/__/Thos W. Gouldin Physician
Sarah/S/Thos W. Gouldin/F/__/Dis of Lungs/[illeg]/Mary/Thos W. Gouldin Physician
Milly Taylor/W/F/__/[illeg]/1y 6m/Jas & C[illeg] Taylor/Jas Taylor Father
[illeg] Taylor/W/F/__/__/__/Jas & C. Taylor/Jas Taylor Father
[illeg]/S/Ed L. Holloway/M/__/[illeg]/[illeg]/__/Ed L. Holloway Master
S.A. Carneal/W/F/Feb/Consumption/32y/Jno & Elizth Jeter/Geo T. Carneal Husband
No Name/S/Gray Boulware/__/__/__/__/Emeline/Gray Boulware Master
Sallie H. Boulware/W/F/Oct 20/Disy/1y 20d/Gray & Milly Boulware/Gray Boulware Father
Blanch Gouldin/W/F/Sept/Brain Fever/1y 15m/Geo F. & M. Gouldin/Geo F. Gouldin Father
Lewis/S/Jos Jesse/M/Jan/__/2d 6m/Caty/Jos Jesse Master
No Name/S/P. Woolfolk/__/__/__/9d/Mary/P. Woolfolk Master
Caroline/S/Wm Thornley/F/__/__/1y/Mary/Wm Thornley Master
Wm Thornton/W/M/Feb/Consumption/13y/Ed T. & E. Thornton/Ed T. Thornton Father
Reana/S/Henry McCalley/F/__/__/__/Sallie/Henry McCalley Master
Amey/S/M.E. Thornton/F/Mar/__/10y/__/M.E. Thornton Mistress
Charlotte/S/M.E. Thornton/F/__/__/12y 6m/Charlotte/M.E. Thornton Mistress
Charlotte/S/Wm F. Catlett/F/May/__/12y/Emily/Wm F. Catlett Master
Louis/S/Thos C. Chandler/F/__/__/10y/Phillis/Thos C. Chandler Master
Mary/S/Ed S. Motley/F/__/__/70y/Manl/Ed S. Motley Master

Hannah/S/Jno Conway/F/Sept/Pneumonia/23y/Nancy/Jno Conway Master
William/S/Jno Conway/M/June/__/75y/__/Jno Conway Master
No Name/S/Ro B. Walker/F/__/__/7d/Rebecca/Ro B. Walker Master
Reuben/S/Law Battaile/M/July 30/Pneumonia/30y/Daphney/Law Battaile Master
Bettie/S/Ro & R Jesse/F/Oct/__/85y/__/Ro [Robert] & R. [Richard] Jesse Master
No Name/S/Ro & R Jesse/F/Feb 4/Consumption/40y/__/Ro & R. Jesse Master
Mary D. Jesse/W/F/Feb 2/__/40y/Ann H. Thornton/Robt Jesse Husband
Lucy/S/Est of Jno H. Pittman/F/Feb/__/4y/Lavenia/Wm H. Pittman - Yg Master
D.S. Pittman/W/F/Jan/__/74y/Jno H. Pittman/Wm W. Pittman Son
Jno F. Pittman/W/M/Jan/76y/Jno H. Pittman/Wm W. Pittman Nephew
Peggy/S/Est of Jno Pittman/F/Feb/__/60y/__/Wm W. Pittman - Yg Master
Virginia/S/Est of Jno Pittman/F/Dec/__/80y/__/Wm W. Pittman - Yg Master
William/S/Wm A. Buckner/M/__/__/17y/Louisa/Wm A. Buckner Master
No Name/S/Wm A. Buckner/F/__/__/12y/Louisa/Wm A. Buckner Master
No Name/S/Wm A. Buckner/M/__/__/3y/Caty/Wm A. Buckner Master
Betty/S/H.F. Thornton/F/June/__/5y/Rose/H.F. Thornton Master
John/S/H.F. Thornton/Mar/__/2y/Catharine/H.F. Thornton Master
No Name/S/Wm P. Taylor/__/__/__/__/Daphney/Wm P. Taylor Master
Saml Skinner/W/M/July 23/Scarlet Fever/3y/Jas & Susannna Skinner/Jas Skinner Father
Wellford Skinner/W/M/July 4/Scarlet Fever/3y/Jas & Susanna Skinner/Jas Skinner Father
Fannie/S/Jas P. Corbin/F/__/Pneumonia/25y/__/Richd Corbin - Yg Master
Esaw/S/Jas P. Corbin/M/__/Heart Dis/55y/__/Richd Corbin - Yg Master
Peter/S/Keeling Rowe/M/[illeg]/8y/Betty/Keeling Rowe Master
Charlotte/S/Keeling Rowe/F/__/[illeg]/[illeg]/Eliza/Keeling Rowe Master
[illeg]/S/Sophia Allen/F/__/Lock Jaw/[illeg]/__/Sophia Allen Mistress
[illeg]/S/Sophia Allen/M/__/[illeg[/[illeg]/__/Sophia Allen Mistress
James Crowley/W/M/[illeg[/[illeg]/Elizth Crowley/Jos M. Seay
[illeg] Donahoe/W/M/__/__/17y/Sallie Donahoe/Jno F. Donahoe Brother
[illeg] Freeman/Free/M/[illeg]/[illeg]/Wm Freeman/Wm Freeman Father
[illeg] Freeman/Free/M/__/__/__/Wm Freeman/Wm Freeman Father
Americus/S/Jno D. Butler/M/Scarlet Fever/5y/Franky/Jno D. Butler Master
Seldon Anderson/W/M/Sept 10/__/20d/Wm L. & Alice Anderson/Wm L. Anderson Father
Patsy Loven/W/F/May 22/Spinal Dis/__/Geo & Lavenia Loven/Jno Loving Husband
Adeline/S/Willis Kidd Est/F/Nov/Pneumonia/13y/Eliza/W.A. Kidd Mistress
Leland Houston/W/M/Sept 8/Murdered/17y/Mor & Anna Houston/Geo W. Houston Brother
Jane/S/Martha Brown/F/July 25/Consumption/55y/Malinda/Martha Brown Mistress
Georganna/S/E.D. Allen/F/June 14/__/12d/Emily/E.D. Allen Mistress
Jno/S/Martha Brown/M/Mar/__/1y 6m/Jane/Martha Brown Mistress
Amelia/S/Jas Clarke/F/Sept/Hemmorage/25y/__/Shff
Prince/S/Ira E. Dickinson/M/May/d."Poplar Inn"/Old Age/90y/Ira E. Dickinson Master
Atking Madison/W/M/Apr/d.near "Poplar Inn"/Throat [illeg]/5y/Amelia Madison/ b.near "Poplar Inn"/Elliott Madison Grandfather
Peter/S/F.W. Scott/M/Jan 24/d."Hard Bargain"/Old Age & Cold/75y/__/Jno W. Scott Friend & Head of a family
Jacob/S/Woodford Garnett/M/Jan 18/d."Burnetts"/Heart Disease/ 75y/__/Woodford Garnett Master
Henry/S/Robert Dickinson/M/__/d."Roseville"/Pneumonia/40y/__/Robert Dickinson Master
Not Named/S/Lewis M. George/M/June/d."Fairford"/Trismus/6d/Courtney/b."Fairford"/ Lewis M. George Master

Not Named/S/Lewis M. George/F/Jan 5/d."Fairford"/Trismus/8d/Rhoda/b."Fairford"/ Lewis M. George Master
Not Named/S/Lewis M. George/Jan/d."Fairford"/Trismus/1/2m/Mariah/Lewis M. George Master
Not Named/S/Lewis M. George/__/Jan/Unknown/6d/Caroline/Lewis M. George Master
Not Named/W/M/Dec/Unknown/22d/Wm E. & Mary A. Claytor/Wm Claytor Father
Mary A. Claytor/W/F/Dec 31/Disease of Womb/24y/Lewis & Peggy Madison/Wm E. Claytor Husband
Petro/S/Philip J. Reynolds/Jan/d."Union" [Union Tavern]/Fever/__/__/b.Essex/ Philip J. Reynolds Master
Harriett/S/Geo T. Todd/F/__/d."Hickory Grove"/Consumption/22y/Geo T. Todd Master
Polly/S/Geo T. Todd/F/__/d."Hickory Grove"/Consumption/8y/Delphy/Geo T. Todd Master
Martha/S/Geo T. Todd/F/__/Consumption/3y/Delphy/Geo T. Todd Master
Maria/S/Geo T. Todd/F/__/d."Hickory Grove"/__/2y/Harriett/Geo T. Todd Master
Mary W[illeg] Wright/F/Dec/d."Marl Hill"/Croup/8d/Jos & Ottawa Wright/b."Marl Hill"/James C. Wright
James Watkins Turner/W/M/Aug 2/d."Pine Hill"/Unknown/31y 7m/John A. & Elizth Turner/b.King George/Farmer/Jno R. Turner
Sampson/S/Thos Lumpkin/M/__/d."Cedar Lane"/Broncitis/8m/Catharine/b."Cedar Lane"/Thos Lumpkin Master
Ann Elizabeth Carter/W/F/July 8/Diarrhea/7m/Jas J. & Martha Carter/Jas J. Carter
Betty/S/Ann Young/F/May 5/d."White Chimneys"/Spinal Disease/45y/__/Wm R. Young Friend
Thomas/S/Wm R. Young/M/Aug/d."White Chimneys"/Consumption/35y/__/Wm R.Young Master
Henry M. Kelley/W/M/Nov 5/Chronic Thrash/15m/Wm M. & Martha Kelley/Wm M. Kelley Father
Martha Kelley/W/F/July 12/d.[Campbell's]"Old Tavern"/Accidently Shot/22y/Seth & Susanna Campbell/Wm M. Kelley Husband
Fanny/S/James J. Jerrell/F/June 1/d."Mount View"/Diarrah/1y/Betsy/Jas J. Jerrell Master
W.H.[illeg]/S/Eldred Turner/M/Aug/Unknown/1y/Aggy/Eldred Turner Master
[illeg]/S/Eldred Turner/F/Sept/Summer Complaint/1y/Frances/Eldred Turner Master
Agnes A. Samuel/W/F/July/d."Locust[illeg]"/Consumption/37y/John P. & Sarah A. Samuel/Philip Samuel Jr. Husband
Sarah Samuel/W/F/Mar/d."Clifton"/Disease of brain/1y 4m/Philip P. & Agnes A. Samuel/Philip Samuel Jr. Father
[illeg]Elizabeth Hughes/W/F/Dec/Not Known/2y 1m/Richd & P[illeg] Hughes/b.King Wm/Richard Baughn Friend
Nancy/S/Edmund S. Motley/F/__/Consumption/55y/__/Temple C. Moore Overseer
George/S/Edmund S. Motley/M/__/Not Known/7y/Melinda/Temple C. Moore Overseer
Catharine/S/Edmund S. Motley/F/__/Not Known/5y/Winny/Temple C. Moore Overseer
[illeg/S/Edmund S. Motley/F/__/__/10m/[illeg/Temple C. Moore Overseer
Archibald Thomas/W/M/Aug/d.Williamsburg/Diarrah/19y/Jno & Mary L. Thomas/Jno Thomas Father
Nancy/S/James Munday/F/Aug/[illeg]/10y/Sally & Moses/James Munday Master
Susannah/S/Henry M. Young/F/__/2y/Charlotte/Henry M. Young Master
Robert Yarbrough/W/M/Sept/__/__/Mickleberry & Wilma Yarbrough/Wilmouth Yarbrough Wife
Not Named/W/M/[illeg]/[illeg]/[lleg/Wm & Martha Turner/Wm Turner Father
[illeg] Saunders/W/M/[illeg]/[illeg]/[illeg]/[illeg]Saunders/__ Saunders Mother
Molly/S/Henry Hill/F/[illeg]/[illeg]/[illeg]/Eliza/Henry Hill Master
Amos/S/Nicholas Mills/M/May/d."Reeds"/Spinal/58y/__/b."Reeds"/Wm G. Young Overseer
Joseph/S/Nicholas Mills/M/July/d."Reeds"/Unknown/2y 6m/__/b."Reeds"/Wm G. Young Overseer
Leland/S/Nicholas Mills/M/Dec/Typhoid Fever/18y/__/b."Reeds"/Wm G. Young Overseer
__/S/Robert G. Hill/M/Sept/d."Grove"/Not Known/10d/John & Fanny/b."Reeds"/ Robt G. Hill

Master

Lewis Scott Wortham/W/M/June/d."Grove"/Catank/9m/Robt T. & Mary T. Wortham/b."Grove"/Robt T. Wortham Father

__/S/Robt T. Wortham/M/Oct/d."Grove"/Unknown/3d/James &Hannah/b."Grove"/ Robt T. Wortham Physician

Lucy/S/William Carter/F/Oct/d."North Wales"/Cronic Typhoid/10y/Patty/b."North Wales"/William Carter Master

Joe/S/William Carter/M/Oct/d."North Wales"/Cronic Typhoid/8y/Franky/b."North Wales"/William Carter Master

Peggy/S/William Carter/F/Nov/d."North Wales"/Cronic Typhoid/12y/Nancy/William Carter Master

Jerry/S/John Freeman/M/June/Diarrah/7y 6m/Darcus/John Freeman Master

Charles Robert Baughn/W/M/Dec 24/Tonsilitus/1y 8m 9d/Saml & Agness E. Baughn/Saml Baughn Father

Philis/S/Jas C. Luck/F/Dec 15/Scrofula/45y/Mariah/Jas C. Luck Master

Warner/S/Obediah Atkinson/M/Dec 23/Scrofula/5y/Philis/Obediah Atkinson Master

Jas B. Atkinson/W/M/Oct 12/Spasms/1y 6m/Obediah & Margaret Atkinson/Obediah Atkinson Father

Eve/S/Thomas Hurt/F/July/d."Locust Grove"/Cholera Infantum/1y/Ellen/Thos Hurt Master

Polly/S/Addison G. Goodwin/F/Dec/d."Locust Hill"/Unknown/3y/Sarah Ann/b.Louisa/Addison G. Goodwin Master

Sally B[Brinter?] Tennant/W/F/July 30/d."Oak Grove"/Unknown/1y 6m/Wm W. & R.A. Tennant /b.Bowling Green/Wm W. Tennant Father

Anna Woolfolk/W/F/Feb/Congestion of brain/1y 2m/Robert & Virginia Woolfolk/ Robert Woolfolk Father

Alfred/S/George Tyler/M/Aug/d."Blenheim"/Whooping Cough/1y/Milly/George Tyler Master

Ann/S/George Tyler/F/Aug/d."Blenheim"/Whooping Cough/3y/Judith/George Tyler Master

Caroline/S/George Tyler/F/Aug/d."Blenheim"/Whooping Cough/3y/[illeg]/George Tyler Master

Adaline/S/George Tyler/F/Sept/d."Blenheim"/Whooping Cough/2y/__/George Tyler Master

Joseph/S/George Tyler/M/Sept/d."Blenheim"/Whooping Cough/4m/Lucy/George Tyler Master

Dallas/S/Geo W. Burke/M/Oct 20/d."Bromsfield"/Teething/2y/Susan/b."Bromsfield"/Geo W. Burke Master

Sally/S/Hugh F. Blaydes/F/May/d."Poplar Plain"/Pneumonia/1y/Dabney & Silby/b."Poplar Plain"/ Hugh F. Blaydes Master

Anna/S/F/Aug/d."Chalk Level"/Disentery/6m/John & Eliza/b."Chalk Level"/John Burruss Overseer

Not Named/S/F/Aug/d."Chalk Level"/Disentery/6m/Emaline/b.Richmond/John Burruss Overseer

Not Named/W/F/Nov/d."Flat Field"/Irreseples/3m/Robert F. & Sarah C. Evans/b."Flat Field"/ Robert K. Evans Father

Elliott/S/M/Dec 12/d."Solitude"/Not Known/5y/Henry & Caroline/Albert G. Ware Master

Margarett/S/Lucy R. Temple/F/Apr/Brain Fever/7y/John & Mary Ann/Lucy R. Temple Mistress

Robert Samuel Swann/W/M/Mar/Brain Fever/3y/Benjm & Mary Swann/Benjamin Swann Father

William Knote/W/M/Sept/d."River Edge"/Paralasis/75y/Robert & ElizabethKnote/Hanover/ Married/Susannah Knot[sic] Widow

Frances Madison/W/F/Oct/Consumption/65y/James & Elizabeth Kelly/Robert Madison Son

Not Named/S/Elliott Wortham/M/Sept 18/d."Poplar Level"/Not Known/3m/Julia/ b."Poplar Level"/Elliott Wortham Master

Marshall/S/Peter Quarles/M/Nov/d."Mount Pleasant"/Dropsy/22y/Saml & Amanda/b."Mount Pleasant"/Peter Quarles Master

Lavenia/S/Benjamin Anderson/F/Oct 28/Scrofula/4y 6m/[illeg]/Benjamin Anderson Master

Cary/S/Benjamin Anderson/M/Aug 27/[illeg]/2y/Camilla/Benjamin Anderson Master

Adison/S/John DeLongan/M/July/[illeg]/3y/Attaway/b.Hanover/John DeLongan Master
Winney/S/John DeLongan/F/Feb/__/25y/Charlotte/b.Orange/John DeLongan Master
John Thomas/S/Wm T. Noel/M/Oct/__/4m/Mary Jane/Wm T. Noel Master
Eliza W. Pare [Parr]/W//F/[illeg]/[illeg]/[illeg]/[illeg]/Not Married/John Pare Father
James & Milly/S/John Pare/1M 1F/[illeg]/[illeg]/[illeg]/Matilda/John Pare Master
Nancy/S/Oliver Beazley/F/[illeg]/[illeg]/[illeg]/Milly/Oliver Beazley Master
Martha/S/Oliver Beazley/F/[illeg]/[illeg]/[illeg]/[illeg]/Oliver Beazley Master
Anna/S/Oliver Beazley/F/Aug/Consumption/50y/Not Known/Oliver Beazley Master
Roburta/S/Jas T. Henderson/F/Aug/Hooping Cough/3y/Sally/Jas T. Henderson Master
Not Named/S/Mary L. Henderson/F/Apr/d."Green Hill"/Not Known/__/Anna/ b."Green Hill"/
   Mary L. Henderson Mistress
Sally Hill Clark/W/F/May 15/d.Spottsylvania/Not Known/3m/Jackson & Mary F.Clark/
   b.Spottsylvania/Jackson Clark Father
Ginny/S/John P. Samuel Sr/F/June 17/Hooping Cough/7y/Susan/John P. Samuel Sr Master
Albert Thomas Madison/W/M/Apr 14/d.Culpepper/Croup/1y 2m/Archibald & Sarah Ann
   Madison/b.Culpepper/Archibald Madison Father
James/S/Albert G. McKenney/M/Oct/d."Poplar Hill"/Typhoid Fever/14y/Kesiah/Albert G.
   McKenney Master
Sarah Jane Dickinson/W/F/Aug 15/Flux/6y/Robert & Emily Dickinson/Miss Carneal Aunt
Lucy/S/Wm H. Wright/F/Feb 10/Consumption/54y/Alley/Wm H. Wright Master
Minova/S/Ruffin H. Coleman/F/July/Typhoid Flux/6y/Betsy/Ruffin H. Coleman Master
Major/S/Ruffin H. Coleman/M/July/Typhoid Flux/4y/Eliza/Ruffin H. Coleman Master
Nancy Newton/W/F/Oct/Fits/79y/Saml & Agnes Newton/b.Hanover/Claiborne Durrett Brother-in-Law
Tom/S/Jos T. Collins/M/June 1/Pneumonia/50y/Not Known/Jos T. Collins Master
Henry/S/Jos T. Collins/M/Apr/Pneumonia/19y/Tom & Mary/b.Stafford/Jos T. Collins Master
James/S/Jos T. Collins/M/May/Pneumonia/1y 6m/Robert & Polly/Jos T. Collins Master
Virginia Ann Fox/W/F/Feb 27/d.Essex/Not Known/34y/Jerry & Ann Fox/b.King William/Elias
   C. Fox Husband
Not Named/S/Richard Woolfolk/F/Aug 30/Not Known/1d/Elijah/Richard Woolfolk Master
Richard A. Woolfolk/W/M/June 2/Spinal/7y/Charles & Ann C. Woolfolk Father
Adaline/S/Wesley Wright/F/Mar 11/Consumption/32y/Franky/b.Goochland/Wesley Wright Master
Louisa/S/Wesley Wright/F/July/Measles/3y 2m/Lucy/Wesley Wright Master
Joseph/S/Wesley Wright/M/July/Measles/1y/Lucy/Wesley Wright Master
Elmore/S/Wesley Wright/M/July/Measles/6y/Adaline/Wesley Wright Master
Sarah/S/Wesley Wright/F/July/Measles/1y/Hilda/Wesley Wright Master
Lewis/S/F.W. Scott/M/Dec 21/Old Age/80y/Not Known/b.Hanover/Francis W. Scott Master
Peter/S/F.W. Scott/M/Dec 1/Old Age/87y/Not Known/Francis W. Scott Master
George Washington/S/Geo M. McLocline [McLaughlin]/M/July 19/Flux/2y 1m/Fanny/
   George M. McLocline Master
Not Named/S/Geo M. McLockland [McLaughlin]/M/Dec/Not Known/___/Franky/ George M.
   McLockline Master
Judy/S/John T. Goodwin/F/Apr/Pneumonia/29y/Hannah/John T. Goodwin Master
Walker/S/John T. Goodwin/M/May/Not Known/4m/Judy/John T. Goodwin Master
Not Named/S/Betty G. Lewis/F/June/Overlaid/1m 24d/Lucy/Betty G. Lewis Mistress
Nelly/S/Betty G. Lewis/F/June/Not Known/2y/Charlott/Betty G. Lewis Mistress
Joe/S/Jefferson Flippo/M/Feb/Pneumonia/9m/Jane/Jefferson Flippo Master
Sally/S/George Washington/F/Apr/Small Pox/4y/Peggy/George Washington Master
William/S/Saml Schooler/M/Oct/Not Known/3y/Franky/Timothy Young Overseer

William/S/Patrick R. Catlett/M/Oct/Not Known/3y/Emily/Patrick R. Catlett Master
Jesse/S/John N. Gatewood/M/Oct 4/Croup/22y/Rachael/ Woodford Miller Overseer
Not Named/W/M/May 9/Spasms/8d/Geo & Ann J. Collins/Geo T. Collins Father
Not Named/S/Geo T. Collins/F/Feb/Not Known/3m/Susan/Geo T. Collins Master
Not Named/S/Thos C. Catlett/F/Apr/[illeg]/[illeg]/Julia/Thos C. Catlett Master
Anderson/S/Thos T. Goodwin/M/May/[illeg]/Betsy/Thos T. Goodwin Master
Milly/S/Dabney Waller/F/Sept/[illeg]/Dabney Waller Master
Joe/S/George F. Swann/M/Feb/[illeg]/Milly/George F. Swann Physician
Not Named/S/Jesse Winn/F/Sept/[illeg]/Lucy/Jesse Winn Master
Elijah/S/Tavenor Winn/F/Oct 13/Not Known/49y/Not Known/b.Albemarle/Tavenor Winn Master
Letty Jane/S/Tavenor Winn/F/June 28/Cold/10m/Amey/Tavenor Winn Master
Silas/S/Elizabeth Dick/M/Feb 26/Consumption/21y/Betty/Elizabeth Dick Mistress
Warner/S/George Tompkins/M/Jan/Not Known/22y/Sarah/George Tompkins Master
Not Named/W/M/Dec/Not Known/3d/James H. & J[illeg] Watkins/Jas H. Watkins Father
Not Named/S/Pleasant Carneal/M/Sept/Not Known/1m/Sophia/Pleasant Carneal Master
Lucy Carnal/W/F/Aug 14/Sinking Chill/63y/Patrick & Betsy Carnal/George England Husband
Ethelvin H. England/W/M/Oct 6/Flux/14y/George & Martha England/Geo England Father
Jefferson/S/Lynch Cobbs/M/Feb 7/Bronchitis/21y/John & Emily/Lynch Cobbs Master
George/S/John Burruss/M/Dec 31/Burnt/55y/Not Known/b.Hanover/John Burruss Master
Cornelia H. Smith/W/F/Jan/Consumption/40y/Saml P. & Sarah Luck/Robert P. Smith Husband
Anna/S/Robert P. Smith/F/June/Pneumonia/2y/Judy/Robert P. Smith Master
Pricilla Blunt/W/F/Dec 17/Not Known/85y 10m/Thomas & Ann Mallory/b.Hanover/John Blunt
  Husband/Hastings Watkins Friend
Mary/S/Richd B. White/F/Nov/Cancer/35y/Maria/Elijah Partlow Friend
Richard B. White/W/M/Nov 3/Paraletic/70y/Wm & Catharine White/Elijah Partlow Friend
Ida/S/Richd B. White Estate/F/Mar/Not Known/8m/Martha Ann/Elijah Partlow Friend
Lucy/S.Richd B. White Estate/F/Apr/Paraletic/4y/Louisa/Elijah Partlow Friend
Wm Hancock/W/M/Nov 17/Stricture of Bowels/17y/Wm & Nancy Hancock/b.Hanover/
  Wm Hancock Cousin & Son-in-Law
Lizzy/S/__ Allen/F/Mar/Smothered/9m/Jane/[illeg] Allen Master
Not Named/S/John V. Kean/M/Aug 15/__/__/Catharine/John V. Kean Master
John Martin/W/M/Jan 24/Not Known/83y/Names Not Known/Henry T. Martin Son
Lydia/S/Richd F. Blanton/May/Not Known/45y/Milly/Richd F. Blanton Master
Adalade/S/Woodson Wright/F/Nov/Smothered/3m/Roxy/Woodson Wright Master
Judy/S/Ro J. Luck/F/Dec 21/Consumption/11y/Martha Ann/Robert J. Luck Master
Not Named/S/Seth Campbell/M/Apr/Not Known/__/Mary/Seth Campbell Master
Davy/S/James Hunter/M/May/Consumption/30y/Anna/b.Essex/James Hunter Master
Burton Oliver/W/M/May/Not Known/24y/Saml B. & Martha Oliver/James Oliver Brother
Not Named/W/F/July 21/Cold/8d/James B. & Elizabeth Eubank/James B. Eubank Father
Wm W. Dickinson/W/M/Sept 1/Cold/7d/__/Judson Dickinson Son
Robert Wood/W/M/Nov 13/Bilious Fever/83y 5m/Robert & [Lydia?] Wood/Robert Wood Father
Not Named/S/Benjamin Anderson/M/Sept/Not Known/__/Mary/Benjamin Anderson Master
Tomasia Redd/W/F/May/Rheumatic/5y/James T. & Thomasia [sic] Redd/James T. Redd Father
Henry/S/Jas D. Coleman/M/Jan/Not Known/36y/__/Jas D. Coleman Master
Joe/S/Jas D. Coleman/Aug/Dropsy/3y/__/Jas D. Coleman Master
Victoria/S/Jas D. Coleman/F/Apr/Tetanus/1m/__/Jas D. Coleman Master
Frances H. Sale/W/F/Oct 8/Bra Fever/77y/Gray Samuel/Robt R. Sale Son
Mary E. Sale/W/F/Apr 20/Consumption/18y 10m/Robt R. Sale/Robt Sale Father

Silas B. Sale/W/M/Dec 3/Bil Colic/22y/Robt R. Sale/Robt R. Sale Father
Jane Martin/W/F/Dec/Consumption/83y/Obey Martin/Robt Martin Jr Nephew
Phil W. Pitts/W/M/Feb/Hooping Cough/3m/And J. Pitts/ And J. Pitts Father
Mary/S/Charles W. Jones/F/Aug/Hooping Cough/6y/Milly/Chas W. Jones Master
Taliaferro/S/Charles W. Jones/M/Aug/Hooping Cough/3y//Milly/Chas W. Jones Master
Milly/S/Jas S. Carter/F/Nov/Hooping Cough/50y/__/Jas S. Carter Master
Andrew Cecil/W/M/June/Scarlet Fever/1y 6m/Isaac & Betty Cecil/Isaac Cecil Father
Kitt/S/Jas H. Broaddus/M/June/Old Age/70y/__/Jas H. Broaddus Master
Lewis/S/Wm Page/M/July/Hooping Cough/3m/Maria/Wm Page Master
Francis/S/Saml Noel/F/July/Hooping Cough/8y/Eliza/Hiram A. Brooks Manager
Milly/S/Jno W. Gouldin/F/Sept/Scarlet Fever/25y/Nelly/Jno W. Gouldin Master
Jas Pitts/W/M/Oct/Old Age/82y/Ann Pitts/Willis Pitts Nephew
Molly/S/Sally Keezer [Keesce or more likely Kelso, one Walker Kelso married Sally Chapman in
    1803]/F/Oct/Liver Compliant/10y/Charlotte/Sallie Keezer Mistress
Betsy/S/Rich Thomas/F/__/Liver Compliant/35y/__/Richd Thomas Master
Robt Goode/W/M/__/d.King Wm Co/Poisoned/24y/Phil & Sallie Goode/Phil Goode Father
Ambrose Alexander/W/M/Sept 20/Old Age/60y/__/Arch Alexander Son
Nancy Saunders/W/F/Sept/__/25y/Elizth Gayle/Elizth Gayle Mother
Wm A. Saunders/W/M/July/Consumption/46y/Wm Saunders/Edgar Saunders Son
Margarett/S/Mary E. Saunders/F/__/Consumption/11m/Virginia/Mary E. Saunders Mistress
Lewis Martin/W/M/Aug 29/Dropsy/6y/Malissa Martin/L.W. Edmondson Grandfather
No Name/S/Jas J. Broaddus/M/May 25/__/7d/Mary Jane/Jas J. Broaddus Master
No Name/S/Jas J. Broaddus/M/Aug 20/7d/Caroline/Jas J. Broaddus Master
Hart [Harriett] Houston/W/F/Dec/Dropsy/12y/Cath Houston/Redd Houston Father
No Name/S/Nathl C. Motley/F/Aug/__/1m/Malinda/Nathl Motley Master
No Name/S/Nathl C. Motley/F/__/__/1m/Caroline/Nathl Motley Master
Winney/S/Nathl C. Motley/F/Apr/__/48y/__/Nathl Motley Master
No Name/S/Jno L. Motley/F/Apr/Scarlet Fever/1m 10d/Emma/Jno L. Motley Master
Wm Covington/W/M/Apr 21/Apoplexy/73y/__/Farmer/Mary Covington Widow
Robt Wright/W/M/Dec 10/Consumption/53y/Margt Wright/M.J. Wright Widow
Etta/S/M.R. Broaddus/F/Feb 1/__/1y 6m/Maria/M.R. Broaddus Master
Lucius/S/Mary Harrisison/M/Apr/Hooping Cough/2d/Courtney/Robt J. Pitts Manager
Reuben/S/Mary Harrison/M/Nov/Old Age/90y/__/Robt J. Pitts Manager
No Name/W/F/__/__/7d/Wm L. & E. Allen/Wm L. Allen Father
Lewis/S/B.F. Smoot/M/__/Fitts/16y/Milly/B.F. Smoot Master
Jno Ambrose/W/M/__/Bi Fever/50y/__/Mechanic/B.F. Smoot Employer
Chas/S/Ro B. Tunstall/M/Jan 1/[illeg]/[illeg]/Lucy/Ro B. Tunstall Master
Wilton Howard/W/M/June/Dis/[illeg]/__ Howard/Mich Howard Jr Father
Frances Howard/W/F/Oct/[illeg]/__ Howard/Mich Howard Jr Father
Lucinda/S/Festus [illeg]/F/Sept/[illeg]/[illeg]/[illeg]/Chas B. Burruss Manager
M.H. Puller/W/M/July/[illeg]/[illeg]/Ed R. Puller Father
Amey/S/Jno B. Puller/F/Oct/[illeg]/[illeg]/[illeg]/Jno P. Puller Master
Sarah T. Conway/W/F/Dec/[illeg]/Aylett H. Conway Brother
Alfred/S/Aylett H. Conway/M/Aug/[illeg]/[illeg]/Aylett H. Conway Master
[illeg] Thornton/W/F/[illeg]/[illeg]/Ed T. Thornton
Nancy/S/Wm S. Royston/F/Dec 4/Old Age/80y/__/Wm S. Royston Master
Jolly/S/Wm G. Maury/M/Aug/Typhoid Fever/17y/Jno H.D. - Master
Lucy/S/Jno H. DeJarnette/F/Jan/__/15y/Amanda/Jno H. DeJarnette Master

Henry/S/Phil Gatewood/M/Dec/Scarlet Fever/11y/Caroline/Phil Gatewood Master
Goldsby Poats [sic]/W/M/July/__/10m/S.L. Poates/Wm L. Poates Father
Polly/S/Wm Kidd's Est/F/July 15/Spasms/5y/Jenny/Burton Kidd - Young Master
Jordan/S/Wm Kidd's Est/M/July/Dis/1y/__/Burton Kidd - Young Master
Benjamin/S/Ro [Robert] M. [Moseley] Wright/M/Mar/6m/Elvira/Ro M. Wright Master
Walker/S/B. [Burton] B. [Boutwell] Wright Est/S/Sept 18/Dis Lungs/46y/Milly/Burton Wright - Young Master [& son]
M.[Mildred] A.E. Crump/W/F/May 8/Consumption/24y/Margt B. [Bell Wright] Crump/ Margt B. Crump Mother
Hiram Wharton/W/M/Sept/Dis T/3m/Juliett Wharton/Jno W. Wharton Father
M.A.S. Wharton/W/F/Sept/Dis T/2y/Juliett Wharton/Jno W. Wharton Father
S.S. Sirls/W/F/July/Hooping Cough/3y/Mary Sirls/Wm L. Sirls Father
Hausey/S/Thos R. Dew/F/Feb/Pneumonia/2y 6m/Dinnah/Thos R. Dew Master
No Name/S/R.B. Richerson/F/Dec/Pneumonia/1m/Amey/R.B. Richerson Master
George/S/Sarah Andrews/M/Oct/Killed Accidently/24y/Aisley/Jas B. Andrews - Young Master
Washington/S/Sarah Andrews/Nov/Hooping Cough/6m/Mary/Jas B. Andrews - Young Master
Washington/S/Sarah Andrews/Nov/Hooping Cough/6m/Mary/Jas B. Andrews - Young Master
No Name/W/F/Oct/Hooping Cough/2m/Sophia Beazley/Reuben Beazley Father
Cornelius Covington/W/M/Aug 13/Dis/2y/Mary Covington/Wm N. Covington Father & Mechanic
Danl Covington/W/M/July 30/Dis/1y 6m/Mary Covington/Wm N. Covington Father & Mechanic
Adam/S/Jos W. Kay/M/Dec/__/70y/__/Jos W. Kay Master
Walker/S/Jno T. Boutwell/M/Jane/Typhoid Fever/16y/Maria/Jno T. Boutwell Master
Elzer/S/Jno T. Boutwell/M/July/Typhoid Fever/10y/Jenney/Jno T. Boutwell Master
Phillis/S/Jno T. Boutwell/F/July/Typhoid Fever/26y/Jinney/Jno T. Boutwell Master
Rebecca/S/Jno T. Boutwell/F/June/Typhoid Fever/13y/Maria/Jno T. Boutwell Master
Mary S. Boutwell/W/F/Sept/Typhoid Fever/30y/Cath E. Smith/Jno T. Boutwell Husband
Birkenhead Boutwell/W/M/Dec/Typhoid Fever/35y/Cath H. Boutwell/C.H.B. Mother
Blanch Boutwell/W/F/Mar/Typhoid Fever/5y/Cath E. Boutwell/C.H. Boutwell Grand Mother
Cath Boutwell/W/F/Mar/Typhoid Fever/7d/Cath E. Boutwell/C.H. Boutwell Grand Mother
Robert/S/Apollos Boutwell/M/Aug/Pneumonia/29y/Sallie/A. Boutwell Master
Peter/S/C.H. Boutwell/M/Dec/Pneumonia/50y/__/C.H. Boutwell Master
Jim/S/Wm C. Pratt/M/Mar/Hooping Cough/3y/Kitty/Wm C. Pratt Master
Robt B. Farinholt/W/M/Dec 25/Hooping Cough/23y/Maria/John R. Farinholt Brother
George/S/Chas Urguhart/M/Aug/Consumption/1m/Mary/Chas Urguhart Master
Lucy/Jno C. Gibbs/F/Aug/d.Richmond County/Inflam of Brain/1m/Anna/John C. Gibbs Master
Lucy Gravatt/W/F/Jul 17/Dis T/64y/__/Jno J. Gravatt Son
Sallie/S/Phil Lightfoot/F/Dec/Burnt/55y/Anna/Phil Lightfoot Master
Chaney/S/Jno B. Lightfoot/F/May/Hooping Cough/6m/Not Known/Jno B. Lightfoot Master
Joe/S/Jno B. Lightfoot/M/May/Hooping Cough/2y/[illeg]/Jno B. Lightfoot Master
Deliliah/S/Jno B. Lightfoot/F/June/Hooping Cough/8m/[illeg]/Jno B. Lightfoot Master
William/S/Jno B. Lightfoot/M/July/Hooping Cough/3y/[illeg]/Jno B. Lightfoot Master
No Name/S/Jno B. Lightfoot/F/June/Hooping Cough/6m/[illeg]/Jno B. Lightfoot Master
Harriett/S/Jno B. Lightfoot/F/Aug/Hooping Cough/3y/[illeg]/Jno B. Lightfoot Master
Bernice/S/Jno B. Lightfoot/F/Aug/Hooping Cough/1y 5m/[illeg]/Jno B. Lightfoot Master
No Name/S/Richd Royston/F/Oct/Hooping Cough/1y 6m/[illeg]/Richd Royston Master
No Name/Free/F/Nov/Hooping Cough/[illeg]/[illeg]/[illeg]/__
Margt Bander/W/F/July 19/Dis T/1y 4m/J.C. Bander/Ezra Bander Father & Teacher
Elizth Gray/W/F/Aug/Dis T/65y/Susan Rowe/Wm P.H. Gray Son

Missey/S/R.G.R. Catlett/F/Sept/Asthma/50y/Esther/R.G.R. Catlett Master
Julia Buruss/W/F/July/Dis T/15y/Thos O. Burruss/Thos O. Burruss Father & Mechanic
Terror/S/Elizabeth Peyton/F/Nov/Dis T/62y/___/Randolph Peyton -Young Master
Michel/S//Robt G. Holloway Est/M/Jan/Consumption/23y/Esther/Thos R. Holloway - Young Master
Andrew/S/Robt G. Holloway Est/M/Jan/Consumption/25y/Sarah/Thos R. Holloway - Young Master
Susan/S/M.L. Boulware/F/May/Child Bed/42y/__/M.L. Boulware Master
Mark/S/M.L. Boulware/M/Mar/__/2m 15d/Sallie/M.L. Boulware Master
Malinda/S/Misses Boulware/F/Oct/Fitts/25y/Fannie/Elizth Boulware Mistress
Lucy C. Kidd/W/F/Feb/__/11m/Mary Kidd/Henry Kidd Father
Eliza/S/Wm L. Harrison/F/Oct/Child Bed/42y/Fanny/Robt B. Duling Overseer
William/S/Wm L. Harrison/M/Aug/Murdered/40y/__/Robt B. Duling Overseer
Robin/S/Wm L. Harrison/M/Dec/Bil Fever/16y/Amey/Robt B. Duling Overseer
Dennis/S/Geo W. Gatewood/M/Jan/Consumption/70y/__/Geo W. Gatewood Master
Phebe/S/Silas J. Broaddus/F/Jan/Old Age/75/__/S.J. Broaddus Master
Courtney/S/B. [Burton] B. Wright Est/F/Sept/Disarrangement/65y/__/B.B. Wright Jr - Young Master
Jordan/S/Jordan [Jourdan] Woolfolk/M/Aug/Consumption/85y/Milly/Jor Woolfolk Master
Moses/S/Jordan [Jourdan] Woolfolk/M/Feb/Old Age/80y/__/Jor Woolfolk Master
Wm P. Napier/W/M/Oct/Diarh/6y/E.C. Napier/John P. Napier Father
Ryland G. Gravatt/W/M/July 16/Diarh/5y/Mary Jane Gravatt/Wm B. Gravatt Father
Cor [Cornelius] A.J. Houston/W/M/Aug 12/Diarh/4y/Elizth Houston/J.R.P. Houston Father
Cynthia/S/Jno Woolfolk Est/F/July/Old Age/75y/__/B.F. Coleman Overseer
Alfred/S/B.F. Coleman/M/Mar/__/6d/Sarah/B.F. Coleman Master
No Name/S/Thos C. Rixey Est/M/__/Hooping Cough/7y/Cosley/And M. Glassel Admr
No Name/S/Thos C. Rixey Est/M/__/Hooping Cough/3y/Louisa/And M. Glassel Admr
No Name/S/And M. Glassell/F/__/Hooping Cough/2y/Louisa/And M. Glassel Master
No Name/S/And M. Glassell/M/__/Hooping Cough/3y/Sallie/And M. Glassell Master
No Name/S/And M. Glassell/F/__/Hooping Cough/1y/Susan/And M. Glassell Master
No Mame/S/And M. Glassell/M/__/Hooping Cough/3d/Nancy/And M. Glassell Master
No Name/S/And M. Glassell/M/__/Hooping Cough/8d/Nancy/And M. Glassell Master
Hezekiah/S/Henry B. White/F/June/Bills Fever/1y/Agnes/H.B. White - Master
Edward Kay/W/M/Feb 10/Apoplexy/60y/__/Wm W. Kay Son
Ellerson/Free/M/Feb/__/50y/__/Jas Thomas Employer
Edy/S/Frances Downing/F/Feb/Rheumatism/60y/__/F. Downing Mistress
No Name/Free/F/Feb/Hooping Cough/7y/Mary Dollins/Rivingston Dollins Father
Danl Duval/W/M/Feb/Old Age/87y/Wm A. Allport Son-in-Law
Sally/S/M.E. Thornton/F/Sept/Old Age/90y/__/M.E. Thornton Mistress
L.E. Thornton/W/F/Sept/__/27y?/[illeg]/M.E. Thornton Mother
Charlotte/S/Jas J. White/F/Sept/Burnt/10y/__/Jas J. White - Master
Alpheus/S/Jas J. White/M/Sept/[illeg]/[illeg]/Jas J. White - Master
No Name/S/Jas J. White/F/Sept/[illeg]/[illeg]/Jas J. White - Master
Wm Taylor/W/M/Sept/[illeg]/[illeg]/[illeg]/[illeg]Taylor Father
[illeg]Long?/W/F/Sept/[illeg]/[illeg]/[illeg]Long?
Eliza/S/B.A. Jordan/F/__/__/2y/Maria/B.A. Jordan Master
No Name/S/B.A. Jordan/M/__/__/1y 15d/Lavenia/B.A. Jordan Master
Sally/S/Cors [Cornelius] Campbell/F/__/Appolexy/40y/__/Cor L. Campbell Master
Rebecca/S/Jas Barbee/F/Old Age/__/Old Age/70y/__/Jas Barbee Master
True Love/S/Thos C. Rixey Est/F/12m/Sophia/A.M. Glassell Adm
Arthur/S/Cath Anderson/M/Disy/4y/Obedine/Jno H. Anderson - Young Master

Wm B. Smither/W/M/Killed accidently/30y/Lucy Smither/Brock Peyton Employer
Fanny/S/Abraham Wilson/F/__/__/12y/Lavenia/Wm W. Pitman Comm for Wilson
William/S/Abraham Wilson/M/__/Disy/10y/Lavenia/Wm W. Pitman Comm for Wilson
Henry/S/Dorithan Pitman/M/__/Disy/5y/Lavenia/Wm W. Pitman - Young Master
Sanford/S/Dorithan Pitman/M/__/Disy/3y/Lavenia/Wm W. Pitman - Young Master
Robt Samuel/W/M/White Rising/17y/Cathy Samuel/Chas Samuel Father
Ira White/W/F/Apr 31/Consumption/62y/Ambrose White/Ira E. White Son
Anna/S/E.G. Andrews/F/Aug/Typhoid Fever/23y/Affeah/E.G. Andrews Master
William/S/E.G. Andrews/M/Aug/Typhoid Fever/15y/Ellen/E.G. Andrews Master
George/S/E.G. Andrews/M/Aug/Thphoid Fever/10y/Anna/E.G. Andrews Master
No Name/S/E.G. Andrews/M/Aug/Typhoid Fever/2d/Anna/E.G. Andrews Master
Richd H. Andrews/W/M/Aug/Typhoid Fever/17y/Hortinese Andrews/E.S. Andrews Father
Paulina Chinault/W/F/Mar 31/Typhoid Fever/10d/Hannah Chinault/Cath Murrow Sister-in-Law
Ann Howard/W/F/April/White Rising/17y/Matilda Howard/Wm Howard Father
Wm G. Richerson/W/M/Mar/__/25y/Anelina Richerson/Geo Richerson Father
Peter/S/Jno H. Bernard/M/Aug/__/60y/Jno H. Bernard Master
Jim/S/Jno H. Bernard/M/Aug/__/20y/Milly/Jno H. Bernard Master
Hannah/S/Jno H. Bernard/F/Aug/Hooping Cough/5y/Milly/Jno H. Bernard Master
Maria/S/Jno H. Bernard/F/Aug/Hooping Cough/5y/Milly/Jno H. Bernard Master
Chas/S/Jno H. Bernard/M/Aug/Hooping Cough/1y/Kitty/Jno H. Bernard Master
Richard/S/Jno H. Bernard/M/Aug/Hooping Cough/1m/Milly/Jno H. Bernard Master
Martha/S/Jno H. Bernard/F/Aug/Hooping Cough/__/Sarah/Jno H. Bernard Master
Jno Purks/W/M/Sept/Consumption/43y/__/Lucy Purks Wife
Mary W. Reeves/Free/F/Sept/Hooping Cough/10y/Sarah L. Reeves/Jos Reeves Father
Sara Reeves/Free/F/Sept/Hooping Cough/3y/Sara L. Reeves/Jos Reeves Father
Jos H. Reeves/Free/M/Sept/Hooping Cough/1y/Sara L. Reeves/Jos Reeves Father
Martha Taylor/Free/F/Sept/__/__/Jas Taylor/Jas Taylor Father
Elizth Taylor/Free/F/Sept/Hooping Cough/2d/Jas Taylor/Jas Taylor Father
Alfred/S/Wm A. Buckner/M/__/Hooping Cough/7d/__/Wm A. Buckner Master
Jane/S/Wm A. Buckner/F/__/Hooping Cough/__/__/Wm A. Buckner Master
Jno/S/Wm A. Buckner/M/__/Hooping Cough/__/__/Wm A. Buckner Master
No Name/S/Wm J. Broaddus/M/__/__/__/Wm J. Broaddus Master
Philip/S/Jno Gouldin/M/Mar/Consumption/__/Jno Gouldin Master
Sara L./S/Jno Gouldin/F/Jan/__/__/__/Jno Gouldin Master
Sam/S/Jno Gouldin/M/Jan/__/__/__/Jno Gouldin Master
Thos/W/Jno Gouldin/M/Aug/__/__/__/Jno Gouldin Master
Emelina/S/Jno Gouldin/F/[illeg]/__/__/__/Jno Gouldin Master
No Name/S/Jno Gouldin/F/Jan/__/__/__/Jno Gouldin Master
Fanny/S/Lovel P. Tod/F/__/__/__/Lovel P. Tod Master
Lewis/S/Wm J. Boulware/M/__/__/__/Wm J. Boulware Master
Richard/Rich D. Collawn/M/Aug/Disy/2y/Lavinia/Richd Collawn Master
Frances Griffin/W/F/Jan/__/[illeg]/Molly Barbee/Elijah Griffin Husband
No Name/S/K.L. Battaile/F/Sept/Scarlet Fever/2y 6m/Phillis/K.L. Battaile Master
Richd/S/Henry McCalley/M/Jan/Disy/6y 8m/Louisa/Henry McCalley Master
Susan/S/Thos C. Chandler/F/Mar/Consumption/30y/Louisa/Thos C. Chandler Master
No Name/S/Thos C. Chandler/F/Mar/Pneumonia/2y/Susan/Thos C. Chandler Master
Louisa/S/Thos C. Chandler/F/May/Pneumonia/2y 6m/Sarah/Thos C. Chandler Master
Lewis/S/Thos C. Chandler/M/May/Consumption/30y/Caty/Thos C. Chandler Master

Gabriel/S/Thos C. Chandler/M/Feb/Dropsy/70y/__/__/Thos C. Chandler Master
Agness/S/Thos C. Chandler/F/May/Hooping Cough/3y/Eliza/Thos C. Chandler Master
Lewis/S/Thos C. Chandler/M/May/Hooping Cough/6m/Polly/Thos C. Chandler Master
Milly/S/Thos C. Chandler/F/May/Hooping Cough/6m/Mary/Thos C. Chandler Master
Beverley/S/Thos C. Chandler/M/May/Hooping Cough/2y/Mary/Thos C. Chandler Master
No Name/S/Law Battaile/M/Jan/Consumption/25y/Jenny/Law Battaile Master
Amy M. Battaile/W/F/Dec/__/55y/Ann Fitzhugh/Law Battaile Husband
Festus/S/Ro & Rich Jesse/M/Feb/Old Age/90y/Judith/Ro & Rich Jesse Masters
Agnes/S/Wm P. Taylor/F/Aug/Scarlet Fever/2y/Sallie/Wm P. Taylor Master
Philicia/S/Wm P. Taylor/F/Aug/Scarlet Fever/2y/Betsy/Wm P. Taylor Master
Shakespear/S/Saml Gordon/M/Aug/Scarlet Fever/5y/Betsy/Saml Gordon Master
Sarah/S/Saml Gordon/F/Aug/Scarlet Fever/2y/Elizth/Saml Gordon Master
Sallie/S/Jno Goodwin/F/Dec/Old Age/88y/Jno Goodwin Master
Fanny/S/Jas P. Corbin/F/Dec 1/Scarlet Fever/5y/Betty/James P. Corbin Master
Jas/S/Jas P. Corbin/M/Dec/Scarlet Fever/2y/Elizth/James P. Corbin Master
Jno/S/Ed Sale/M/July/Scarlet Fever/5y/Eliza/Ed Sale Master
Charlotte/S/Lucy A. Dew/F/Dec/Pneumonia/54y/__/Lucy A. Dew Overseer
No Name/S/S.C. Jones/M/Mar/__/6m/Hannah/S.C. Jones Master
No Name/S/Gray Boulware/M/Dec/Lock Jaw/6d/Matilda/G.B. Jr. - Young Master
Jno P. Downing/W/M/Sep/Typhoid Fever/30y/Frances Downing/Robert Hudgin Father- in-Law
Thos Charlton/W/M/Nov 24/Typhoid Fever/40y/Susan Charlton/Susan Charlton Wife
Gustavus Pugh/W/M/Dec/Typhoid Fever/19y/__/Wm Cox Uncle
No Name/S/Jno Y. Martin/F/Aug/Typhoid Fever/1y/Nancy/Jno Y. Martin Master
Malinda/S/Ellis Gravatt/F/Oct/Scarlet Fever/2y/Sylvia/Ellis Gravatt Master
No Name/S/Jas L. Powers/M/Nov/Typhoid Fever/10d/Lucy/Jas L. Powers Master
No Name/S/Jas L. Powers/F/Nov/Typhoid Fever/2m//Jenny/Jas L. Powers Master
Mary Ann/S/Jas L. Powers/F/Sept/Typhoid Fever/__/Lucy/Jas L. Powers Master
Alexander/S/C.C. Broaddus/M/Sept/Typhoid Fever/2m/Phillis/C.C. Broaddus Master
Saburnah Wright/W/F/Mar 20/Typhoid Fever/5y/Louise A. Wright/Ro B. Wright Father
Alberta Wright/W/F/Sept 12/Typhoid Fever/3y/Louise A. Wright/Ro B. Wright Father
B.R. Clarke/W/M/Aug/Killed accidently/68y/Virginia Clark/Virginia E. Clark Wife
Ed P. White/W/M/Aug/Typhoid Fever/55y/__/Ann Champ White Wife
Wm L. McKenney/W/M/Aug/Brain Fever/27y/[illeg]/__ Pendleton
Cheadle Chiles/W/M/Feb/__/__/[illeg]/Eldred Chiles Brother
Vivian Reeves/Free/M/Mar/[illeg]/[illeg]/[illeg]
Frances/S/Jas E. Dickinson/F/Oct 13/[illeg]/[illeg]
Samuel Skinner/W/M/Jul/[illeg]/[Illeg]___
Wellford __/W/M/June/[illeg]/[illeg]___
__ Thomas/W/M/Aug/[illeg]/[illeg]_____
Sam/S/Peter R. Thornton/M/Feb/Hooping Cough/5y/Emily/P.R. Thornton Master
Mattie/S/Peter R. Thornton/F/Feb/Hooping Cough/5m/Nancy/P.R. Thornton Master
Alice/S/Peter R. Thornton/F/Feb/Hooping Cough/1m/Julia/P.R. Thornton Master
William/S/Peter R. Thornton/M/Feb/Hooping Cough/1m/Annie/P.R. Thornton Master
Colin B. Catlett/W/M/Aug 23/Consumption/47y/Lucy Catlett/Wm A. Buckner Relative
Patsy/S/Susan Noel/F/Feb/Measles/[illeg]/Winney/Susan Noel Mistress
Christine/S/Susan Noel/F/Sept/Measles/14y/Eliza/Susan Noel Mistress
Margarett/S/Susan Noel/F/Sept/Measles/[illeg]/Mary/Susan Noel Mistress
Martha Noel/W/F/Aug/__/20y/Nancy Noel/Susan Noel Sister

Ro W. Farmer/W/M/July 22/Brain Fever/1y 6m/__/Thos Farmer Father
Mary A. Clarke/W/F/May/Disy/4y/Elie Clarke/Planny Clarke Father
Thos Whitticoe/W/M/Feb 11/Disy/5y/__/Reuben Whittacoe Father
No Name/W/M/Apr/__/2d/S.A. Rouse/Wm Rouse Father
Isabella Atkins/Free/F/June 15/Murdered/30y/Thos S. Clarke Employer
M.J. Wright/W/F/Sept/15m/Elizth Wright/Elizth Wright Mother
Thomas/S/M/Aug 30/Liver Complication/50y/__/Chas Phillips Master
Phillis/S/F/May/Old Age/70y/__/Chas Phillips Master
Jno Seal/W/M/Dec 15/Apoplexy/67y/__/Ira D. Seal Son

1858

John B. Mobile/W/M/Sept 2/Consumption/5y/Joseph & __/b.King George/Mary Mobile Wife
Mary Cooper/Free/F/May 22/Smothered/4m/Mariah Cooper/Mariah Cooper Mother
Not Named/W/F/June 9/[illeg]/11d/John & Mary E. Shackleford/John Shackleford Father
John/S/Chastine Dickinson/M/Oct 1/Not Known/18y/Milly/Judson Dickinson - Young Master
William/S/Lewis M. George/M/Apr 1/Overlaid/3m 2d/[illeg]/Lewis M. George Master
Selah/S/Nicholas Mills/F/July 30/Neuralgia/64y/Diannah/Wm J. Young Overseer
Jerry/S/Nicholas Mills/M/Sep/Consumption/46y/Cissey/Wm J. Young Overseer
Mariah Page/S/Nicholas Mills/F/Sept 1/Not Known/2m 1d/[illeg]/Wm J. Young Overseer
Martha/S/Edward P. Wood/F/July Cholery Infection/1y/[illeg]/b.Louisa Co/Edward P. Wood Master
James W. Dyson/W/M/Feb 3/Lung Fever/8m/Jos W. & Mary Ann Dyson/Jos W. Dyson Father
Sam/S/Edward Mickelberry/M/Aug/Pneumonia/7y/Lydia/Temple C. Moor Overseer
Not Named/S/Henry George/M/Dec/Triconas/5d/Betsy/H.H. George Master
Not Named/W/__/Aug 30/Thrash/14d/John H. & __ Cox/John H. Cox Father
Not Named/S/Richardson Turner/F/Oct/Spasms/21d/Polly Richardson Turner Mistress
Not Named/S/Geo K. Taylor/M/Aug/Not Known/1m/Harriett/Jas W. Coleman Physician
Caroline/S/Saml Coleman/F/Aug/Typhoid Fever/2y 6m/Mariah/Saml Coleman Master
Bumerage/S/Saml Coleman/F/Apr/Consumption/[illeg]Kathy/Saml Coleman Master
Ann G. Ware/W/F/Apr 23/Measles/68y/John & Patsy Scott/Nathaniel Ware Husband/
  John H. Ware Son
Samuel W. Ware/W/M/June 10/Summer Compliant/1y 6m/John & Mary J. Ware/John H. Ware Father
Not Named/S/Wm R. Young/M/Oct/Smothered/3m/Nancy/Wm R. Young Master
Robinson/S/Woodford Garnett/M/Oct/Old Age/72y/Not Known/Wm R. Young Friend
Patsy/S/Woodford Garnett/F/Nov/Old Age/110y/Not Known/Wm R. Young Friend
Martha/S/John Chandler/F/Oct 1/Hickups/38y/Not Known/John Chandler Master
Not Named/Jno Chandler/F/Aug/Not Known/1m/Elizabeth/John Chandler Master
Lewis/S/Horace A. Richards/M/Jan/Scarlet Fever/9m/[illeg]/Horace A. Richards Master
Dolly/S/Robt Wortham/F/May/Apoplexy/45y/[illeg]/Robert T. Wortham Master
Charlotte/S/W.R.B. Wyatt/F/Aug 1/Not Known/65y/Not Known/b.New Kent Co/W.R.B. Wyatt
  Master
Not Named/S/W.R.B. Wyatt/F/Dec 2/Not Known/1d/Sophia/W.R.B. Wyatt Master
Jane/S/Francis Norment/F/Dec 22/Consumption/35y/Lucy/Francis Norment Master
Not Named/S/Julia Samuel/M/Dec/Overlaid/1m/Patsy/Phillip Samuel Jr [illeg]
Not Named/S/Wm L.N. Burruss/F/Jan/Spasms/8d/Louisa/Wm L.N. Burruss Master
Not Named/W/F/June/Not Known/11m/Richard & Martha James/M.R. James Mother
Fleming/S/Robt Samuel/M/July/Cholera Inflamation/11m/Lucy/Robt Samuel Master
Randal/S/John B. Flippo/M/Oct/Not Known/1y 6m/Cleopatria/John B. Flippo Master

Adelina/S/Betty G. Lewis/F/Oct 5/Not Known/1y 1m/Jane/John T. Goodwin Agent
Adam/S/Richd Washington/M/Aug/Inflamation of [illeg]/[illeg]/Richd Washington Master
Not Named/S/Geo W. Burnett/M/Feb/Not Known/3d/[illeg]Geo. W. Burnett Master
Sarah Jane/S/Geo W. Burnett/F/Dec 25/[illeg]/3y/Susan/Geo W. Burnett Master
Robt Thomas/W/M/May/Dropsy on brain/6m 18d/John & Sarah Jane Thomas/John Thomas Father
[illeg]/S/Jno W. Scott/M/Nov/Old Age/95y/Unknown/Jno W. Scott Master
Not Known/S/Thos Lumpkin/M/Nov/Not Known/14d/[illeg]/Thos Lumpkin Master
Charity/S/Wm A. Dickinson/F/Jan 26/Old Age/90y/Lizzie/Wm Carneal [illeg]
Delpey/S/Geo T. Todd/F/Apr/[illeg]/22y/Larkin Litchfield - Young Master
Chaplis/S/Geo T. Todd/M/Brain Fever/9y/Elizabeth Larkin Litchfield - Young Master
Martha/S/Barton Harris/F/Nov/Hooping Cough/5y/Barton Harris Master
Jane/S/Barton W. Morris/F/June/Cholora Infantum/1y 6m/Adaline/Barton W. Morris Master
Schnook/S/Barton W. Morris/M/Nov 1/Stated?/26y/Charlotte/Barton W. Morris Master
Sarah Moren/W/F/June 10/Cold/40y/Geo & Polly Smith/James Moran Husband
James Thos Freeman/W/M/June/Disease of Lungs/1y 6m/Jas & Mary E. Freeman/J.W. Freeman
  Father
Not Named/W/M/Oct 31/Spasms/4d/Eldred & Mary Blanton/Eldred Blanton Father
Not Named/S/Eldred Blanton/F/Nov 6/Spasms/8d/Matilda/Eldred Blanton Master
Rosa Goldberry/W/M/May 10/Old Age/77y/Thos T. Morris/Geo Goldberry Son
Arthur Pleasant Coats/W/M/May/d.Spot Co/[illeg]/3m/John & Elizabeth Jane Coats/b.Hanover
  Co/John B. Coats Father
Nancy/S/John B. Coats/F/May/Typhoid Fever/52y/Nelly/John B. Coats Master
Rosetta/S/Geo T. Collins/F/Nov/Not Known/8d/Adaline/Geo T. Collins Master
Not Named/S/Wesley Wright/M/Aug/Diprah/__ 2m/Lucy/Wesley Wright Master
James Hunter Flagg/W/M/Mar 2/Croup/4m 17d/E.F. & Annette Flagg/E.F. Flagg Father
Harriett/S/Richard Wortham Est/F/Mar/Scrofula/23y/Charlotte/John Burruss Overseer
Jane Tyree/Free/F/Dec 26/Consumption/18y/Lindsey & Betsey Tyree/Leroy Evans Friend
Not Named/Free/F/July/Not Known/1d/Lucy Bazell Mother
John Thos Henderson/W/M/Sept 7/Chronic [illeg]//18y/Jas & [illeg] R. Madison/ b.Richmond Va/
  Jas Henderson Father
Anna/S/Geo Allen/F/Feb/Scarlet Fever/6y/Ellen/Geo Allen Master
Rosa/S/Geo Allen/F/Feb/Scarlet Fever/6y/Ellen/Geo Allen Master
Jane/S/Geo Allen/F/Feb/Scarlet Fever/3m/Ellen/Geo Allen Master
[illeg]/S/Geo Allen/F/Feb/Not Known/1y/Mary/Geo Allen Master
Catherine Blunt/W/F/June 2/Consumption/98y/Wm & Ann Tiller/John Blunt Husband
Not Known/W/M/June/Not Known/6d/Stephen & Sarah Jane Terry/Stephen Terry Father
Not Named/W/M/Aug/Not Known/__/Wm A. & [illeg] Moor/Turner Moor Grandfather
Not Named/W/F/June 15/Measles/[illeg]/__/Wm & [illeg] Carneal/Wm Carneal Father
Isaac/S/Wm T. Quarles/M/Oct 26/Stomach Fever/30y/Not Known/b.Spot Co/Wm T. Quarles Master
James E. Estes/W/M/Nov/Pneumonia/22y/Samuel & Mary J. Estes/Samuel Estes Father
Charlotte/S/Richd E. Boulware/F/Nov/Dropsey/[illeg]/Rosanna/Richd E. Boulware Master
David/S/Claiborne Harris Est/M/Nov/Killed/52y/[illeg]/John Newton Lawyer
Not Named/W/F/Jan 30/d.Orange/Pleurisy/40y/Thos & Frances Thacker/b.Culpepper Co/Thos T.
  Thacker Father
Harry/S/Ruffin H. Coleman/M/Apr 30/Pleurisy/40y/Not Known/d.Culpepper/Ruffin H. Coleman Master
[illeg]/S/Thomas N. Welsh/M/May/[illeg]/1y/Anna/b.Louisa C.H./Thos N. Welsh Master
[illeg]/S/Jas D. Coleman/Nov/tumor in stomach/65y/Mariah/b.Spot Co/Jas D. Coleman Master
George/S/Jas D. Coleman/M/June/Measles/16y/Nancy/Jas D. Coleman Master

John/S/Jas D. Coleman/M/June/Measles/3y/Mariah/Jas D. Coleman Master
Albert/S/Jas D. Coleman/M/June/Measles/2y/Charlotte/Jas D. Coleman Master
John Tyree/Free/M/Nov/Consumption/22y/[illeg]/Jas D. Coleman Friend
Caroline/S/Richd Wright/F/Apr/d.Richmond/Measles/6m/Jenny/b.Richmond/Richd Wright Master
George Goodloe/W/M/Oct 8/Croup/3y/Wm H. & [illeg]Goodloe/Wm H. Goodloe Father
Dabney/S/James L. Coleman/M/Nov/Disease of Stomach/56y/[illeg]James L. Coleman Master
Reuben/S/Henrietta Winn/M/Feb 25/Old Age/95y/Not Known/Geo T. Swann Physician
Wm Minor/S/Blueford Durrett/M/Apr/Scarlet Fever/1y/b.Louisa/Blueford Durrett Master
Abraham/S/Blueford Durrett/M/Apr/Not Known/[illeg]/[illeg]/Blueford Durrett Master
Jeter George/S/Blueford Durrett/M/Feb/20y/Not Known/1m/Anna/Blueford Durrett Master
John Thomas/S/Thos L. Scott/M/__/Hurt/[illeg]/Lucy/Thos L. Scott Master
Joseph May/W/M/Feb 26/Dropsy/64y/Moses & Martha May/James May Son
Frances Carnal/W/F/Mar 4/Dropsy/40y/Archilles & Mary Carnal/Cath Carnal Sister
Harriett Coor/W/F/July/Disabled/65y/John & [illeg] Stevens/b.King Wm/John Cor[sic]
Lorane/S/Saml Schooler/F/July 15/Old Age/70y/Not Known/Saml Schooler Master
Julia/S/Saml Schooler/F/Apr 7/Croup/Not Known/Saml Schooler Master
Nelson/S/Thos L. Catlett/M/Feb/Pneumonia/75y/Lilly/Thos L. Catlett Master
Mary Ann/S/Saml C. Gatewood/F/May/Not Known/50y/Not Known/Saml C. Gatewood Master
Not Named/S/Saml C. Gatewood/F/July/__/__/Philis/Saml C. Gatewood Master
Not Named/S/Thos C. Catlett/F/Oct/Smothered/1m/Elijah/Thos C. Catlett Master
Not Named/S/Reuben Coghill Est/F/Apr 24/Not Known/4d/Lucy/Mrs Coghill Mistress
Not Named/S/Franklin Cannon/M/Oct/Not Known/__/Eliza/Mrs. Coghill Neighbor
Amy Blyth Battaile/W/F/July 19/Typhoid Fever/14y/Francis W. & Ellen H. Battaile/Francis W.
  Battaile Father
Franky/S/Hy W. Newton Est/F/May/Dropsy/70y/Not Known/b.Hanover/Ann Newton Mistress
Matilda Ann/S/Hy W. Newton Est/F/Nov/Burnt/4y 2m/Martha/Ann Newton Mistress
Lewis/S/Ro J. Luck/M/June/Pneumonia/1y/Eliza/Ro J. Luck Master
Sulky/S/John R. Young/F/Sept 10/[illeg]/45y/Lucy/b.Louisa Co/Jno R. Young Master
Eliza/S/Jesse Winn/F/Feb 15/Typhoid Fever/45y/Nancy/Jesse Winn Master
John/S/Jesse Winn/M/Apr 1/Measles/17y/Kesiah/Jesse Winn Master
Fred/S/Josephus Gatewood/M/Apr/Consumption/23y/Not Known/Spott Co/Jas Gatewood Master
Elliott/S/John Burruss Sr/M/May 17/Measles/12y/Elton/John Buruss Sr Master
Kilate/S/Lewis W. & Ro L. Coleman/F/Aug/Old Age/74y/Not Known/Miacel D. Johnson Overseer
Jos E. Durvin/W/M/Jan 15/Drowned/9y 10m 23d/Jos & Eliza Durvin/b.Louisa Co/Jas Durvin Father
Cornelia/S/C.H. Newton/F/July 12/Puralitt[illeg]/48y/Milly/Cath H. Newton Mistress
Charles Woolfolk/W/M/Dec 1/Liver Disease/54y 9m 27d/Spillsby & Sally Woolfolk/Ann Cath
  Woolfolk Widow
Alfred Ricks/W/M/Mar 8/Diptheria/59y/Richd & Julia Ricks/b.Southampton Co/Mary A. Ricks
  Wife/Richd Ricks Son
Caroline/S/Henry Doggett/F/Se[t/Disentery/1y/Ellen/Henry Doggett Master
Not Named/S/Henry Doggett/F/June/Lock Jaw/1m/Martha/Henry Doggett Master
Ellen/S/Richd W. Hutcheson/F/Mar/Burnt/1y/Mary/Richd W. Hutcheson Master
Mary Jane/S/A.G. Ware/F/Nov 13/Inf Consumption/4y/Mary/Albert G. Ware Master
Lewis/S/John G. Dickinson/M/Nov 24/[illeg]/10y/__/Jno G. Dickinson Master
Not Named/S/John G. Dickinson/F/__/Spasms/1y/Emaline/John G. Dickinson Master
Not Named/S/John G. Dickinson/M/Oct/Not Known/6d/Emaline/John G. Dickinson Master
Not Named/S/John G. Dickinson/M/Oct/Not Known/25y/Grace/John G. Dickinson Master
Lucinda/S/Thos Hurt/F/Mar/Not Known/2d/Not Known/Thos Hurt Master

Walker/S/Thos Hurt/M/Apr/Not Known/1y/Lucinda/Thos Hurt Master
Not Named/S/Thos Hurt/F/June/Not Known/2d/Jane/Thos Hurt Master
Frances/S/Geo Tyler/F/Apr/Putrid Fever/19y/Nancy/Geo Tyler Master
Lucy/S/Geo Tyler/F/Apr/Dropsy/11y/Milly/Geo Tyler Master
William/S/Geo Tyler/M/June/Heart Disease/35y/Allace/Geo Tyler Master
Frank/S/Geo Tyler/M/Sept/[illeg]/__/Fanney/Geo Tyler Master
Susan Carnal/W/F/Sept/Brain Fever/3m/Archibald & Mildred M. Carnal/Archibald P. Carnal Father
Ella/S/John V. Krass/F/Apr/Scarlet Fever/2y/Hortense/John V. Krass Master
Alfred/S/John V. Krass/M/Apr/Scarlet Fever/4y/Fanny/John V. Krass Master
Clement/S/John V. Krass/F/Sept/Typhoid Fever/[illeg]/Betsy/John V. Krass Master
Louisa/S/John V. Krass/F/Sept/Typhoid Fever/13y/Betsy/John V. Krass Master
Virginia/S/John V. Krass/F/Sept/Typhoid Fever/[illeg]/Betsy/John V. Krass Master
Kennie/S/Walker Terrell/M/May 23/Cold/1y 6m/Jane/Walker Terrell Master
Martha/S/Mary Cobbs/F/Dec 8/Not Known/10y 6m/Mary/Mary Cobbs Mistress
Mary/S/Thos B. Anderson/F/Aug/[illeg]chest/45y/Nancy/Thos B. Anderson Master
Elizabeth Redd/W/F/Nov 5/Not Known/83y/Ed & Ann Taylor/b.Hanover Co/Saml Redd
  Husband/Jas T. Redd Son
Tom/S/Jas T. Butler/M/Apr/Consumption 19y/Molly/Wm O. Doggett Agent
Geo J. Duvall/W/Aug 4/Effect of [illeg]/43y/Jas & Elizth Duvall/Wm O. Doggett Son-in-Law
Courtney/S/Seth Campbell/F/Apr 30/Smothered/6m/Adeline/Seth Campbell Master
Sarah Tiller/W/F/Apr 9/Measles/56y/Nathan & Mary Winston/Jos Tiller Husband
Thos H. Bell/W/M/__/Consumption/76y/__/Jas F. Campbell Neighbor
Sallie/S/Jas Wright/F/Sept/Pneumonia/16y/Jane/Jas Wright Master
Purity/S/Jno Broaddus/F/__/Burnt/16y/Not Known/Jno Broaddus Master
Edmund/S/Wm T. Broaddus/M/Nov/Old Age/65y/Not Known/Wm T. Broaddus Master
Daniel/S/Jno J. Andrews/M/Nov/Scarlet Fever/1y 6m/Milly/Jno J. Andrews Master
Robt Upshaw/W/M/Aug/Lock Jaw/2y/M.E. Upshaw/Ro H. Upshaw Father
No Name/S/Richd A. Puller/F/July/__/__/Letty/Rich A. Puller Master
Sallie J. Gray/W/F/May/Brain Fever/6m/Elizabeth A. Gray/Geo W. Gray Father
No Name/W/F/Apr/__/__/Ro S. & E. Broaddus/Ro S. Broaddus Father
Moses/S/Ro S. Broaddus/M/June/Not Known/2y/Margt/Ro S. Broaddus Master
No Name/S/Ro S. Broaddus/F/Feb/Scarlet Fever/5m/Margt/Ro S. Broaddus Master
Jos W. Pavy/W/M/Aug/Scarlet Fever/__/Jos H. & S.A. Pavy/Jos H. Pavy Father
L. Southworth/W/M/Mar/__/19y/A. & C. Southworth/A. Southworth Father
Abraham/S/Jno Gouldin/M/Mar/Scarlet Fever/35y/[illeg]/Jno Gouldin Master
Lewis/S/Jno Gouldin/M/mar/Scarlet Fever/24y/Jno Gouldin Master
No Name/S/Thos E. Dew/M/Dec/Scarlet Fever/__/Judith/Ed Sale Overseer
Mary [illeg]/S/Cor [Cornelius] L. Campbell/F/Dec/Scarlet Fever/1m 10d/Susan/C. Campbell
  Master
Bettie C. Sale/W/F/June/Scarlet Fever/11y/Thos B. & E. Sale/Thos Bell Sale Father
Hart Sale/W/F/June/Scarlet Fever/__/Thos B. & E. Sale/Thos Bell Sale Father
No Name/S/Ira E. White/M/June/Scarlet/3d/Harriett/Ira E. White - Master
No Name/S/Jno L. Cox/M/Dec/Scarlet Fever/21d/Hannah/Jno L. Cox Master
No Name/S/Thos Broaddus/M/__/Scarlet Fever/__/Martha/Thos Broaddus Master
No Name/S/Thos Motley/M/Nov/Scarlet Fever/21d/Matilda/Thos Motley Master
Bob/S/Wm Chapman/M/__/Scarlet Fever/12y/Betsy/Wm Chapman Master
Maria/S/Wm Chapman/F/__/21y/b.Louisa/Wm Chapman Master
Phebe Pittis/W/F/Aug/__/50y/J. Pittis/Jos Pittis Son

Lacy/S/Ed Lunsford/F/Nov/__/58y/__/Ed Lunsford Master
A.E. Broaddus/W/F/Sept 26/__/35y/Agnes Boulware/J.H. Broaddus Husband
Ellen/S/Jas H. Broaddus/F/Sept__/35y/Esther/Jas H. Broaddus Master
S.E. Gatewood/W/F/Dec 8/Consumption/42y/Elizth Gatewood/Jas R.P. Houston Bro-in-Law
Lucy/S/S.B. Anderson/F/Apr/__/60y/__/E.D. Anderson - Young Master
Frances? Vaughan/W/F/Feb 1/Old Age/98y/__/Thos Vaughan Son
Preston B. Gibbs/W/M/July 8/__/1m 10d/Hart [Harriett] A. Gibbs/Jno C. Gibbs Father
Kitty/S/Geo Taylor/F/July/__/2y/Kitty/Jas T. Gouldin Manager
Phil/S/Geo Taylor/M/Sept/__/1y 6m/Kitty/Jno T. Gouldin Manager
John H. Bernard/W/M/Apr/__/69y/J.P. & Wm Bernard/Wm K? Bernard Son
Caty Samuel/W/F/Apr/Consumption/65y/[illeg]Parker/Ro H. Parker Relative
Wm E. Toombs/W/M/Aug/[illeg]/8m/Wm H. & M.E. Toombs/Wm H. Toombs Father
No Name/S/__/F/Dec/__/5d/Emily/Wm H. Toombs
John/S/Phil Lightfoot/M/Jan/Old Age/80y/__/P. Lightfoot Master
No Name/S/Jno B. Lightfoot/F/Jan/__/11m/Susan/Jno B. Lightfoot Master
No Name/S/Jno B. Lightfoot/F/__/__/__/Peggy/Jno B. Lightfoot Master
Wm H. Farinholt Jr/W/M/Oct 15/__/__/Wm & S.E. Farinholt/Wm H. Farinholt Father
Betsy/S/Agnes Taylor/F/Sept/__/50y/__/Jas N. Shaddock Master Pro Temp
Anna Marie?/S/C.H. Boutwell/F/Mar/Betsy/C.H. Boutwell Mistress
Mary A. Lewis/W/F/Dec 27/__/__/__/Jno Y. Martin Son-in-Law
Ellen/S/Thos R. Dew/F/Sept/Old Age/70y/Thos R. Dew Master
Jim/S/H.M. Kidd/M/May/Pneumonia/40y/Esther/Harry M. Kidd Mistress
Rachel/S/H.M. Kidd/F/July/Disy/9m/Jane/Harr M. Kidd Mistress
No Name/S/B.B. Kidd/F/May/Disy/13d/Martha/Bur B. Kidd Master
No Name/S/B.B. Wright Est/F/June/__/__/Eliza/Ann Wright Mistress
Ciley/S/R. [Robert] M. [Mosley] Wright/F/May/Old Age/80y/__/Dolly Wright Mistress
   [at "Green Falls"]
Nelly/S/Theo T. Green/F/May/Consumption/50y/Rose/Theo T. Green Master
Emily/S/A.G. Broaddus/F/July/21d/Sarah/A.G. Broaddus Master
Sarah/S/A.G. Broaddus/F/June/22m/Fanny/A.G. Broaddus Master
No Name/S/J.H. Garnett/F/Dec/__/__/Marsella/J.H. Garnett Master
Robin/S/J.H. Garnett/M/Mar/__/3m/Jane/J.H. Garnett Master
Jim/S/J.H. Garnett/M/Dec/__/7m/America/J H Garnett Master
Thos/S/J.H. Garnett/M/Nov/11m/Judith/J.H. Garnett Master
Delpha/S/Jno R. Monday/F/Apr/Old Age/70y/__/J.H. Garnett Master
No Name/S/Mary A. Beazley/F/Jan/__/12y/Mahala/Mary A. Beazley Mistress
No Name/W/M/Jan/__/7d/A.B. & Sally Duling/A.B. Duling Father
No Name/W/F/Dec/__/7y/J. & S. Southworth/Jordan Southworth Father
Martha E. Puller/W/F/Dec/Consumption/22y/Mary A. Puller/M.A. Puller Mother
No Name/S/Jor [Jourdan] Woolfolk/M/__/__/9d/Mary/Jor Woolfook Master
Woofd Carter/W/M/__/__/50y/[illeg]/L. & Nancy Carter/ Elizabeth P. Carter Wife
Judy/S/Francis Fitzhugh/F/Mar 15/Dropsy/35y/Susan/F. Fitzhugh Master
Jane/S/Nancy Parker/F/Feb/Old Age/80y/Nancy Parker Mistress
V.H. Gouldman/W/F/July 8/Hoop Cough/3m/Richd & Ann Gouldman/ Richd Gouldman Father
No Name/S/Wm C. Pratt/F/Jan 1/__/7d/Eliza/Wm C. Pratt Master
Lucy/S/Geo Fitzhugh/F/__/__/70y/__/Geo Fitzhugh Master
George/S/Henry Kidd/M/__/Old Age/76y/__/Henry Kidd Master
Nancy Taylor/W/F/Sept 26/Old Age/75y/__/Theo Taylor Son

Afferiah?/S/R.G. Holloway Est/F/Feb/__/3m/Rachel/Thos Holloway Master
Sophia/S/Richd Royston/F/Apr/__/7d/Matilda/Richd Royston Master
Eliz/S/Wm D. Boulware/F/__/Consumption/56y/__/Wm D. Boulware Master
Not Named/S/Gray Boulware/F/__/1y 4m 10d/Milly/Gray Boulware Master
__ G. Puller/W/F/June 12/Jas T. & M.L. Puller/Jas T. Puller Father
Not Named/S/Elixa Boulware/F/July 10/[illeg]/[illeg]/E. Boulware Mistress
Minor/S/Eliza Boulware/M/June 18/Dropsy/17y/Caroline/Eliza Boulware Mistress
Jos Beazley/W/M/Jan/[illeg]/[illeg]/Albert & Anna Beazley/Albert Beazley Father
Eliza Gray/W/F/June/__/11m/Leml & Frances Gray/Leml Gray Father
___ Pickett?/W/F/May/Old Age/70y/Lucy Atkins/Leml Gray Son-in-Law
Patsy Loven/W/F/Sept/__/23y/Sally Loven/Lindsay Loven Brother
No Name/S/Jas L. Shaddock/F/Oct/[illeg]/[illeg]/[illeg]/J.A.L. Shaddock Master
[illeg]S/Jno T. Boutwell/M/Dec/__/1y/Matilda/Jno T. Boutwell Master
Ro C. Bruce/W/M/June 26/[illeg]/[illeg]/Wm & Maria Bruce/Eliza Bruce Wife
[illeg] Braynham/W/F/Aug/[illeg]/[illeg]/Marshall Oliver/Larkin Braynham Husband
__ Norment/W/M/Dec/1y/Geo & Emma Norment/Al Carter Uncle
Mary/S/P. [Pichegru] Woolfolk/F/Dec/Typhoid Fever/[illeg]/Eliza P. Woolfolk Master
No Name/S/Wm Thornley/M/Sept/__/__/Mary/Wm Thornley Master
No Name/S/Wm Thornley/F/Aug/__/__/Frances/Wm Thornley Master

1859

Jackson/S/John B. Coats/M/Feb 15/Typhoid Fever/37y/Kitty/John B. Coats/Master
Rachel/S/John B. Coats/F/Dec 26/Not Known/4m 5d/Eliza/John B. Coats Master
Nancy/S/R.K. Chandler/F/June/Teething/2y/Victoria/John B. Chandler Master
Peter Quarles/W/M/Apr 28/Paralisis/63y/Minor & Mary Quarles/Farmer/Jas W. Quarles Son
Paul & Silas/2S/Overton Burruss/2M/June Diariah/6m/Emaline/Overton Burruss Master James Henry
Miller/W/M/Nov/Consultions/8d/Woodford & Margarett Ann Miller/Woodford Miller Father
Not Named/S/James C. DeJarnett/M/Dec/Not Known/__/Aggy/James C. DeJarnett Master
Temple Miller/W/M/Dec 12/Not Known Known/69y/Larkin & Frances Miller/Jas A. Miller Son
Not Named/W/F/May/Not Known/21d/Christopher & Carmelia Collins/Christopher Collins Father
Not Named/W/F/May 12/__/21d/Christopher & Carmilia Collins/Christopher Collins Father
Not Named/S/Richard H. Burruss/M/Sept 22/Croop/7d/Alace Minor/Richard H. Burruss Master
Pamela H. Mallory/W/F/June 28/Liver Disease/57y/___/Richard H. Burruss Relation
Not Named/W/M/May/born dead/George W. & Eliza Burke/George W. Burke Father
Not Named/S/George W. Burke/Feb/Jan 1/Not Known/10d/Susan/George W. Burke Master
Thomas/S/George Tyler/M/May 30/Hurt/5m/Lucy Page/Thos Proctor Overseer
Sam/S/Catharine Collins/M/Apr/Old Age/90y/Not Known/Catharine Collins Mistress
Not Named/S/Jesse L. Cobbs/M/Nov 15/Not Known/__/Malinda/Jesse L. Cobbs Master
Amanda/S/Philip Samuel/F/Apr/Spasms/1y/Mary/Philip Samuel Master
Paul/S/Thomas B. Coghill/M/Apr/Bowel Compliant/10m/Aggy/Thos P. Coghill Master
Maria Bet/S/Thomas B. Coghill/F/Feb/Smothered/2m/Susan/Thos B. Coghill Master
Overton/S/Thomas B. Coghill/M/Oct/Dropsy/54y/Not Known/b.Louisa/Thos B. Coghill Master
Not Named/S/Richard H. Woolfolk/M/Jan 2/Not Known/__/Eliza/Richard H. Woolfolk Master
Lucy/S/Stephen Oliver/F/Feb 4/Heart Disease/37y/Ginney/b.N. Carolina/Stephen Oliver Master
Mariah/S/Rachel B. Dabney/F/Mar/Burnt/40y/Sally/b.Louisa/Jas B. Dabney Son of Rachel Dabney
Anna/S/Ruffin H. Coleman/F/Apr/Dropsy/4y/Judy/b.Spottsylvania/R.H. Coleman Master
Robert William Wright/W/M/July 25/Dropsy in Brain/8m 5d/Wm H. & Ellen V.Wright/Wm H.

Wright Father
Not Named/S/Joseph Flippo/M/Aug/__/__/Jesse/Albert R. Flippo - Young Master
Elizabeth C. Catlett/W/F/May/Scrofula of Stomach/[illeg]/Lawrence & Elizabeth Catlett/Thomas Catlett Brother
Tom/S/Nancy Gibson/M/July/d.Spottsylvania/Not Known/60y/Tinah/b.Spottsylvania/Mrs Coghill Friend
Peggy/S/Thos N. Welch/F/Nov/Disease of Stomach/65y/Not Known/b.Hanover/Thomas N. Welch Master
Rose/S/Thos N. Welch/F/Dec/Child Birth/41y/Hannah/b.King & Queen/Thomas N. Welch Master
Achiles/S/Ann Washington/M/Dec/Croop/6m/Eliza/Ann Washington Mistress
Not Named/2S/Ann Washington/2M/Feb/Smothered/3m/Susan/Ann Washington Mistress
Lucinda/S/George Washington/F/Aug/Typhoid Fever/35y/Lilly/George Washington Master
Elvira/S/George Washington/F/Oct/Typhoid Fever/10y/Precilla/George Washington Master
Clarah/S/Richard E. Boulware/F/May 30/Consumption/50y/Daphney/Richd E. Boulware Master
Major/S/Richd E. Boulware/M/July/Consumption/19y/Clarah/Richd E. Boulware Master
Ellen/S/George Allen/F/Aug/Consumption/30y/Caroline/George Allen Master
Joseph T. Collins/W/M/Oct 14/Paralisis/59y/James & Clary Collins/Farmer/Mrs. Collins Wife
Thomas Bradley/W/M/Feb/Old Age/80y/Not Known/James Carlton Jr Friend
Charles Heywood Hancock/W/M/July 4/Cholera Infantum/6m/Wm J. & Margarett Ann Hancock/Wm J. Hancock Father
Not Named/W/F/July/Not Known/1d/Henry & Lucy Gatewood/Henry W. Gatewood Father
Winston/S/George Tompkins/M/March/Consumption/25y/Angelina/George Tompkins Master
Betsy/S/Geo Tompkins/F/Mar/Cold or Bronchitis/12y/Easter/Geo Tompkins Master
Peter/S/Elizth G. Bibb/M/Apr/Consumption/35y/Lucy Ann/Elizth G. Bibb Mistress
Frances B. Richerson/W/M/June 23/Diapeptia/50y/R[illeg]/ & Ann [illeg]/Wm R. Richerson Son
Wm Joseph Long/W/M/Sept 11/Heart disease/5d/John M. & Adeline Long/John M. Long Father
Martha Ann/S/Charles E. Farish/F/Sept/Fever/25y/Mary Ann/Charles E. Farish Master
Not Named/S/Beatty Peatross/F/Oct 1/Smothered/3m/Sarah Ann/John C. Long Friend of Owner
Nancy/S/Joseph A. Flippo/F/May/Trismus/6d/Kiah/Jos A. Flippo Master
Not Named/S/Jos A. Flippo/F/June/Pneumonia/3d/Harriett/Jos A. Flippo Master
Not Named/W/F/Sept 4/Still born/Jas J. & Betty Blanton/Geo W. Blanton Uncle
Shakespear/S/Richard Blanton/M/Nov 30/Typhoid Fever/2y/Susan/Richd Blanton Master
Not Named/S/Agness Terrell/M/Oct 1/Cold/15d/Anna/Granville A. Sizer Friend
Polly/S/Richd B. White's Est/F/Apr 15/Cholora Infantum/60y/Ginney/Elijah J. Partlow Friend
Ellett/S/Ro P. Smith/M/Jan 19/Lock Jaw/16y/Martha/Robt P. Smith Master
Martha/S/Ro T. Coleman/F/Aug 18/Consumption/30y/Lucy Woodson/M.D. Johnson Overseer
Not Named/S/Richd B. White's Est/F/Oct 17/Not Known/7d/Martha Ann/W.J. Anderson Friend
Humphrey/S/Saml Lee/M/Dec 15/Scrofula/20y/Not Known/b.Spottsylvania/Leroy B. Gatewood Friend
Hannah/S/Wm B. Harris/F/June/Old Age/76y/Not Known/b.King William/Wm B. Harris Master
Albert/S/Hy H. George/M/Apr/Pneumonia/13y/Tinah/Hy H. George Master
Ben/S/Hy H. George/M/June/Measles/21y/Esther/Hy H. George Master
John/S/Hy H. George/M/June/Measles/1y 1m/Littia Ann/Hy H. George Master
William/S/Hy H. George/M/July/Measles/1y 6m/Maria/Hy H. George Master
Not Named/S/Wm Gravatt/F/July/Not Known/5d/Matilda/Robt Scott Friend
Not Named/S/Thos Hurt/M/July/Not Known/3d/Hannah/Thos Hurt Master
Henry Hill/W.M.May 8/Diarriah/76y 11m 20d/Robert & Hannah Hill/b.King & Queen/James Hill Son

Tom/S/Hy Hill's Est/M/Nov/Erysipelas/46y/Jacob & Fanny/James Hill - Young Master
Wm Allen/S/John Chandler/M/June 12/Spasms/1y 6m/Martha/John Chandler Master
Robert Edmund/S/John Chandler/M/Sept/Typhoid Fever/21y 1m 4d/Martha/John Chandler Master
Nancy/S/John Chandler/F/Sept 26/Typhoid Fever/12y 2m 26d/Martha/John Chandler Master
Not Named/John Chandler/F/Aug/Not Known/2m/Elizabeth/John Chandler Master
John/S/Robert S. Hill/M/Dec 26/Hurt/35y/Catharine/Ro G. Hill Master
Not Named/S/R.S. White/M/June/Not Known/1y/Eliza/Horace A. Richards Friend
Mary Frances Peatross/F/June 11/Child bed/31y 4m/Richd & Mary M. Peatross/ William R. Peatross Husband
Mary Johnston Peatross/W/F/June 15/Diarriah/18d/Wm R. & Mary Frances Peatross/Wm R. Peatross Father
Not Named/W/F/Sept 16/Not Known/1y/Leonidus & Margaret E.[Kidd] Pollard/L.C. Pollard Father
John Courtney/Free/Apr/Deep Cold/65y/Not Known/Brick Layer/Sinah Courtney Wife
Betsy Brown/Free/F/May/Not Known/70y/Dolly K[illeg]/Sinah Courtney Sister
Not Named/S/Ryland Jeter/F/July/Diariah/1m/Mary/Ryland Jeter Master
Not Named/S/Jos W. Dyson/M/July 25/Not Known/5d/Mary/Jos W. Dyson Master
Joseph/S/Luther Wright/M/June/Thrash/11m/Rose/Luther Wright Master
Wm Mitchell/W/M/Dec 20/Typhoid Fever/21y 4m 12d/Pascal & Delilah Mitchell/Pascal Mitchell Father
[illeg]/S/James D. Coleman/M/Aug/Hooping Cough/5m/Mariah/James D. Coleman Master
Molly/S/James D. Coleman/F/Sept/Hooping Cough/8m/__/James D. Coleman Master
[illeg]/S/W/F/__/Hooping Cough/12y 4m 12d/Jas D. & Huldah C. Coleman/James D. Coleman Father
[illeg]/S/John R. Young/F/[illeg]/[illeg]/[illeg]/Lucy/b.Louisa/Jno R. Young Master
Lucy F. Winn/W/F/[illeg]/[illeg]/[illeg]/John Franklin Durrett/Jesse Winn Husband
[illeg]/S/[illeg]/[illeg]/[illeg]/Lucy/Jesse Winn Master
[illeg]/S/[illeg]/[illeg]/[illeg]/Joel T. Luck Master
Betsy Southworth/W/F/Mar 17/Consumption/76y/John & Lucy Mason/Walker Southworth Husband
Betty/S/Louisana Redd/F/Aug/Smothered/1m 14d/Patsy/Louisana Redd Mistress
Sarah Taylor/W/F/Mar/Consumption/60y/Saml & Betsy Taylor/Reuben Taylor Husband
Winston/S/R[illeg] Wigglesworth/M/Apr/Old Age/90y/Not Known/Thos H. Blanton Overseer
George/S/Lydia A. Swann/M/May 8/Not Known/1m/Catharine/Saml A. Swann Brother to owner
Mary Ann/S/Thos J. Tribble/F/Sept/Spasms in Bowels/22y/Darcas/b.Spottsylvania/Thos J. Tribble Master
George/S/Ed & Chas Burkley/M/Aug/Brain/1y/Celah/Temple C. Moor Overseer
Not Named/Ed & Chas Burkley/M/Sept/Not Known/__/Mihala/Temple C. Moor Overseer
Not Named/S/John S. Blanton/F/June 27/Spasms/7d/Amanda/John S. Blanton Master
Mariah E. Young/W/F/Feb 30[sic]/Child Bed/22y/Richard & Lucinda Kelly/Joseph W. Young Husband
William/S/Nicholas Mills/F/Mar/Hooping Cough/20d/Dinah/Wm J. Young Overseer
Not Named/S/Nicholas Mills/F/Mar/Hooping Cough/6m/Henretta/Wm J. Young Overseer
B[illeg] Wright/W/M/July 26/Heart Disease/52y/Robert & Agnes C. Wright/Farmer/Woodson Wright Brother
Clemmy/S/Robt Wright Est/F/June/Spasms/37y/Martha/Woodson Wright
Peter/S/Fleming Wood/M/Mar 3/Disease of Bladder/51y/Not Known/Fleming Wood Master
Not Named/S/John V. Kean/M/Nov/Lock Jaw/3d/Catharine/John V. Kean Master
Aggy/S/Thos B. Anderson/F/Apr 7/Inflamation of Bowels/41y/Nancy/Thos B. Anderson Master
Eliza/S/Wm T. Quarles/F/Jan/d.Richmond/Spasms/55y/Not Known/b.King Wm/Wm T. Quarles

Master
Horace Carter/W/M/Oct/Dropsy/59y/John Carter Jr./Farmer/Wm F. Carter Son
Not Named/S/Geo B. Pollard/M/Sept/Tetanus/21d/Betty/Geo B. Pollard Master
John Robertson/S/Wm A. Doggett/M/Aug/Disentary/1y/Dinah/Wm A. Doggett Master
Tabitia/S/Chas Woolfolk/F/June/Liver Disease/68y/Patsy/Chas Woolfolk Master
John Miller/S/James C. Luck/M/Dec/Dropsy/70y/Not Known/b.Hanover/Jas C. Luck Master
Not Named/S/James C. Luck/M/May 15/Not Known/__/Polly/Jas C. Luck Master
Hannah/S/Seth Campbell/F/Jan/Pneumonia/45y/Hannah/Seth Campbell Master
Philip/S/Seth Campbell/M/June/Pneumonia/4y/Adeline/Seth Campbell Master
Fanny/S/Augustine Taliaferro/F/June/Cholic/65y/Not Known/George Abraham Friend
William Chandler/W/M/Aug 9/Pneumonia/2m 24d/Thos T. & Eugenia M. Chandler/ Thos T.
  Chandler Father
Wm J. Richardson[sic]/W/M[sic]/Dec 24/Bronchitis/50y/John & __ Young/William Richardson
  Husband[sic]
Milly/S/Geo T. Collins/F/July/Scrofula/20y/Mary/Geo T. Collins Master
Juliett/S/Thos Lumpkin/F/Dec/Not Known/14d/b.Louisa/Thos Lumpkin Master
Frances/S/Rufus K. Chandler/F/July/Disentary/1y 2m/Victoria/Rufus K. Chandler Master
Not Named/S/Wesley Wright/M/Apr/__/__/Dolly/Wesley Wright Master
Not Named/S/Wesley Wright/M/Apr/__/__/Martha/Wesley Wright Master
Lucy Ann/S/John G. Coleman/Feb/Dec 26/Not Known/2y/Dolly/John Geo Coleman Master
Not Known/S/William Carter/[illeg]/__d."North Wales"/ Hooping Cough/4y/Not Known/b."North
  Wales"/William Carter Master
Not Known/S/William Carter/[illeg]/__d."North Wales"/Want to breath/27y/Not Known/b."North
  Wales"/William Carter Master
George/S/D.C. Dejarnette/M/Aug/2y 6m/Matilda/Owen C. Tuck Overseer
Jos/S/D.C. Dejarnett/M/Oct/Cold Fever/9m/Lucy/Owen C. Tuck Overseer
No Name/S/D.C. DeJarnette/M/Feb/Cold Fever/7d/Eliza/Owen C. Tuck Overseer
No Name/S/Littleton Goodwin/F/Nov/Cold Fever/2m/Caroline/Littleton Goodwin Master
No Name/W/F/Apr 15/Cold Fever/2m/Richd F. & Eliza Broaddus/Richd F. Broaddus Father
John/S/Thos Broaddus/M/Sept/Consumption/1m/Milly/Thos Broaddus Master
Jenny/S/Jos Wright/F/Aug/Consumption/38y/__/Jos Wright Master
Cor Vaughan/W/M/July 19/Consumption/9y/Ross & Eliz T. Vaughan/Ross Vaughan Father
No Name/W/M/Sept/__/5m/Geo W. & P.M. Marshall/Geo W. Marshall Father
No Name/S/Jno B. Puller/F/__/Consumption/__/Susan/Jno B. Puller Master
Mor [Mordecai] R. Broaddus/W/M/June/Consumption/__/Mor & P. Broaddus/Jno P. Broaddus Son
No Name/S/Jos Andrews/F/Nov/Heart Dis/50y/Emeline/Jos Andrews Master
Courtney Picardatte/W/F/June/__/2d/Lewis & Marg Picardatte/L.C. Picardatte Bro
Henry/S/Francis Boulware/W/Aug/__/57y/Caroline/Jas Broaddus Overseer
No Name/S/Ed Shaddock/M/Aug/__/26y/Sallie/Jno T. Lewis Overseer
No Name/S/Mary E. Saunders/F/Aug/__/7d/Milly/Wm A. Saunders Overseer
Robinson/S/O.M. Harris/M/Aug/__/3m/Sophia/O.M. Harris Master
Lewis Ware/W/M/Aug/Inf Bowels/2y 6m/Archl Ware/Jo Cecil Bro-in-Law
M.C. Shackleford/F/Nov 16/Dis of Kidneys/47y/B.C. & M.G. Shackleford/B.C. Shackleford Father
Sarah/S/Jas M. Carneal/F/Sept/[illeg]/7d/Agnes/Jas M. Carneal Master
Benjamin/S/Jno Woolfolk/M/Apr/Dropsy/50y/Agnes/Richd W. Green Overseer
Richard/S/Jno Woolfolk/M/Dec/__/70y/Agnes/Richd W. Green Overseer
No Name/S/Richd H. Coleman/M/Dec/__/60y/Hannah/R.H. Coleman Master
R.L. Taylor/W/F/Jan 11/1y 5m/Saml & M.D. Coleman/Wm Y. Williamson Neighbor

Milton/S/Jno L. Motley/M/Jan/Heart Dis/2y/Emma/Jno L. Motley Master
R.M. Gouldin/W/F/July/Consumption/31y/Jas J. & Eliza Broaddus/Wm J. Broaddus Brother
Rachel Johnson/Free/F/June/__/10m/Elijah & E. Johnson/Elijah Johnson Father
Harriett/S/Ira E. White/F/Dec/Pneumonia/35y/__/Ira E. White - Master
Willy Howard/Free/M/Aug/Dropsy/18y/Patsy Howard/Jas Carneal Neighbor
Eliz Carter/Free/F/July/Consumption/28y/Thos & Betsy Fortune/Thos Fortune Father
Mary/S/S.A. Anderson/F/July/__/4m/Jane/S.A. Anderson Master
James/S/Phil Green/M/July/Typhoid Fever/24y/Winney/Phil Green Master
I[sabella] G. Turner/W/F/Apr/Heart Dis/57y/Thos & I.G. Magruder/Geo P. Turner Husband
Mary Berry/W/F/Feb/Liver/65y/Jos & Nancy Berry/Benj Merryman Bro-in-Law
Howard/S/Arthur Lewis/M/July/1y 1m/Sophia/A. Lewis Master
Virginia/S/Clem Farish/F/July/Old Age/75y/__/Clem Farish Mistress
Frances/S/R.A. Gravatt/F/Feb/__/35y/Caroline/Ro A. Gravatt Master
Mary A. Jordan/W/F/Oct/Pneumonia/2y 3m 11d/Wm H. & M.F. Jordan/Wm H. Jordan Father
Not Named/S/L.H. Jeter/M/Oct/__/12d/Eliza/L.H. Jeter Master
Not Named/S/Nathl Motley/F/Oct/[illeg]/7d/Malinda/Nathl Motley Master
[illeg]/S/Jno Y. Martin/F/[illeg]/Child Bed/40y/Jno Y. Martin Master
[illeg]/S/Wm H. Allen/F/[illeg]/[illeg]/[illeg]/Sallie/Wm H. Allen - Yg Master
[illeg]S/Ro Maury/F/__/__/7m/Anna/Ro Maury Master
[Elizabeth]/C/F/[illeg]/[illeg]/[illeg]/[illeg]/John Clarke Husband
[illeg] Rose/W/[illeg]/[illeg]/[illeg]/Cors [Cornelius] C. & S.A. Rose/Cors C. Rose Father
[illeg]/S/Cors [Cornelius] Campbell/[illeg]/[illeg]/[illeg]/Lung/Cors Campbell Master
Phil/S/Frans Downing/M/Apr/Old Age/70y/__/Jas Acors Overseer
Rosetta/W/Wm J. Jones/F/Dec/Child Bed/20y/Jane/Wm J. Jones Master
Judith Jones/W/F/Dec 26/Consumption/74y/__/S.C. Jones Son
Jos Southworth/W/M/Sept/__/9m/P. & Jane Southworth/Pichigru Southworth Father
No Name/W/M/Sept/__/10d/F.D. & J.A. Campbell/F.D. Campbell Father
No Name/S/Chas T. Jesse/__/__/9d/Harriett/Chas T. Jesse Master
No Name/S/Chas T. Jesse/__/__/9m/Mary/Chas T. Jesse Master
Maria/S/And M. Glassell/M/__/Kill by the [illeg]/11y/Amey/A.M. Glassell Master
No Name/S/Ro B. Tunstall/M/__/10d/Lavania/Ro B. Tunstall Master
Bettie Parish/W/F/__/__/11y/Jno G. & Bettie Parish/Jno G. Parish Father
No Name/S/Jno W. Woolfolk/F/__/2d/Eliza/Jno W. Woolfolk Master
No Name/S/Thos R. Dew/F/Jan/__/8d/Emily/Thos R. Dew Master
Mary Taylor/W/F/Dec/Consumption/54y/Milly Ball/Wm T. Taylor Son
No Name/W/M/__/__/__/Wm A. & Marie Brooks/Wm A. Brooks Father
Austin/S/Ed J. Motley/M/Sept/Asthma/75y/Dinah/Ed J. Motley Master
No Name/S/Wm W. Broaddus/F/Apr/__/15y/Ellen/Wm W. Broaddus Master
Daniel/S/B.R. Clarke Est/M/Aug/Pneumonia/9y/Maria/S.E. Clark Mistress
Lydia/S/Jas H. Broaddus/F/Apr/Consumption/22y/Mary/Jas H. Broaddus Master
Nancy Boulware/W/F/Feb/__/80y/__/Pauper/Jas H. Broaddus Overseer P.[Poor]
Jo Chandler/W/M/July/__/75y/__/Pauper/Wm W. Broaddus Neighbor
Jane Frazier/W/F/Feb/__/90y/__/Pauper/Wm W. Broaddus Overseer P.[Poor]
B.E. Taylor/W/F/Sept/__/6y/Thos & S. Taylor/Thos Taylor Father
J.C. Grimes/W/M/Oct/__/40y/__/Jno Grimes Brother
Jno F. Thornton/W/M/July/__/70y/H.F. & A.R. Thornton/And Thornton Bro-in-Law
Henry Kidd/W/M/July/Typhoid Fever/60y/Joel & Sally Kidd/Farmer/Wm J. Kidd Son
No Name/S/Richd Royston/F/May/Lock Jaw/5d/Matilda/Richd Royston Master

Lewis/S/R.E. Thornton/M/Feb/__/6y/Pink/Peter R. Thornton Master
Ginny/S/Wm D. Boulware/F/Feb/__/__/Lucy/Wm D. Boulware Master
No Name/S/Wm D. Boulware/M/__/__/__/Sally/Wm D. Boulware Master
No Name/S/Frances Powers/F/May/__/__/Polly/Frances Powers Mistress
Mary/S/M.L. Boulware/F/Jan/Dropsy/70y/__/M.L. Boulware Master
Mary A. T[illeg]/W/F/Sept/B. Fever/1y 7m/Jas & Eliza T[illeg]/Jas T[illeg] Father
No Name/S/B. [Burton] B. [Boutwell] Wright Est/M/__/__/2m/Ellen/B.B. Wright Est by Chas Wright [son]
Louisa/S/B.B. Wright Est/F/Jan/Burnt/8m/Elvira/Jno F. Green Overseer
Katy/S/Theo F. Green/F/Jan/__/6m/Symtha/Theo F. Green Master
Jas H. Garnett/W/M/Apr 9/__/37y/Eliz Garnett/Grif T. Garnett Brother
Judith/S/Jas H. Garnett Est/F/__/__/12y/Jane/Grif T. Garnett Admr
Eliza/S/Mary H. Conway/F/Apr/Bronchitis/58y/Frances/Ay [Aylett] H. Conway - Yg Master
James/S/Mary H. Conway/M/__/__/9m/Fanny/Ay H. Conway - Yg Master
[illeg] Roane/W/F/__/Old Age/91y/__/Reu T. Roane Son
[illeg]/S/Reu T. Roane/M/__/[illeg]/70y/Dinah/Reu T. Roane Master
[illeg]/S/Younger Martin/__/__/__/7m/Anna/Younger Martin Master
[illeg]/S/Wm J. White/__/__/__/4m/Adeline/Wm J. White Master
[illeg]/S/Geo W. Catlett/__/__/__/__/Mary/Geo W. Catlett Master
[illeg]/S/Chas E. Gibbs/__/__/__/__/Alberta/Chas E. Gibbs Master
[illeg]/S/J.A.L. Shaddock/__/__/__/__/Not Known/J.A.L. Shaddock Master
Ann Wright/W/F/Dec/__/40 or 90?y/__/__/__
Jno A. Samuel/W/M/July 3/Teething/2m/Thos L. Samuel Father
Thos Vaughan/W/M/Sept/60y 1m 15d/__/Leml Gray Neighbor
Hannah/S/D.C. DeJarnette/F/Sept/Old Age/65y 1d/__/Geo P. Luck Overseer
No Name/W/F/Mar/Fever/38?/Reu & Mary E. Garnett/Reu Garnett Father
Lucy/S/Geo Fitzhugh/F/Sept/Fever/70y/__/Geo Fitzhugh Master
Mary/S/R.G.R. Catlett/F/Feb/Palsy/59y/Esther/R.G.R. Catlett Master
William/S/A.G. Gouldman/M/Feb/Penumonia/12y/__/Jas T. Gouldin Hirer
Sarah/S/Geo Taylor/F/Sept/Child Bed/20y/Eliz/Jas T. Gouldin Overseer
Harry/S/Geo Taylor/M/Mar/Pneumonia/27y/Eliza/Jas T. Gouldin Overseer
No Name/S/Geo Taylor/F/Mar/__/3m 10d/Sarah/Jas T. Gouldin Overseer
Jno Malin/S/M/Apr/Dropsy/55y/__/R.G.R. Catlett Overseer Poor
Mary Warwick/S/F/Jan/Suicide/52y/__/R.G.R. Catlett Overseer Poor
Jas H. Johnson/Free/M/July/[illeg]/35y/Felicia Johnson/Jas Jeter Neighbor
Jno P. Napier/W/M/July 26/Congestive Brain/46y/Ro G. Holloway Bro-in-Law
Jno/S/Jno Washington/F/Jan/Consumption/67?/Sally/Albert Lourie Overseer
Rose/S/Martha Smith/F/__/__/3m 2d/b.Louisa/M.S. Smith Mistress
Susan/S/Thos C. Chandler/F/Dec/__/40y/Fannie/Thos C. Chandler Master
Simon/S/Law [Lawrence] Battaile/__/Typhoid Pneumonia/[illeg]/Peggy/Law Battaile Master
Spencer/S/Law Battaile/M/__/Spinal Inf/21y/Kitty/Law Battaile Master
Washington/S/Law Battaile/Hart Dis/29y/Jane/Law Battaile Master
No Name/S/Ro Jesse/M/__/D___/8d/Nancy/Ro Jesse Master
Alice Farmer/W/F/__/Robt & Nancy Farmer/Ro Farmer Father
Henretta/S/Jas M. Dillard/F/__/__/35y/Hannah/Jas M. Dillard Master
Rebecca Hailstock/Free/F/__/Bronchitis/30y/Jno & __ Hailstock/Jas M. Dillard Neighbour
No Name/S/Wm Thornley/F/__/__/5d/Catherine/Wm Thornley Master
Peter/S/Jor [Jourdan] Woolfolk/M/__/Paralysis/60y/Jor Woolfolk Master

Gregory/S/Jor [Jourdan] Woolfolk/M/Heart Dis/70y/__/Jor Woolfolk Master
Frank/S/Jor [Jourdan] Woolfolk/M/__/Pneumonia/22y/Polly/Jor Woolfolk Master
Mary/S/Jor [Jourdan] Woolfolk/F/__/Consumption/30y/Nancy/Jor Woolfolk Master
Eliz/S/Jor [Jourdan] Woolfolk/F/__/Burnt/10y/Amey/Jor Woolfolk Master
Lewis Farmer/W/M/Sept/Cancer/70y/__/Thos Motley Overseer Poor
Susan Chenault/W/F/Dec/Burnt/60y/__/Geo Chinault Husband
No Name/S/P. [Pichegru] Woolfolk/F/__/__/1m/Kitty/P. Woolfolk Master
No Name/Wal [Walker] Washington/M/__/__/65y/Wal Washington Master
Jerry/S/Bazil Gordon/M/__/__/70y/__/Bazil Gordon Master
Charlotte/S/Wm P. Taylor/F/__/1m 15d/Sally/Wm P. Taylor Master
No Name/S/Rich Corbin/F/__/__/1d/Clary/Rich Corbin Master
George/S/Thos R. Dew/M/__/Consumption/35y/Caroline/Thos H Peregory Overseer
Eliza/S/Keeling Rowe/F/__/[illeg]/25y/Caty/Keeling Rowe Master
Emily/S/Keeling Rowe/F/__/[illeg]/[illeg]/Dinnah/Keeling Rowe Master
[illeg]/S/Jno Gouldin/F/__/[illeg]/[illeg]/[illeg]/Jno Gouldin Master
[Note: Next three entries are illegible. These are three slaves belonging to Jno B. Lightfoot]
Soloman/S/Benjamin Anderson/M/__/__/50y/Fanny/Benj Anderson Master
Jas Barlow/W/M/Sept/Suicide/52y/Overseer/Robt Broaddus Admr
Cloe/S/Thos W. Baylor/F/Oct/Old Age/60y/__/Thos W. Baylor Master
Jno P. Beazley/W/M/Apr/__/45y/Miller [by trade]/J.R.P. Houston Bro-in-Law
Jos Sorrell/W/M/Mar/Pneumonia/47y/Jno & Ann Sorrell/Farmer/__ Sorrell Son
No Name/S/Reu B. Richerson/F/Nov/2d/Malinda/R.B. Richerson Master
No Name/W/F/July/2y/Jas & Susan Chinault/Jas Chinault Father
Phillis/S/Jno Broaddus/F/July/Asthma/65y/Jane/Jno Broaddus Master
Fannie Houston/W/M/Sept/[illeg]/65y/Thornton & __ Seal/Jordan Houston Son
Pollux?/S/Jno T. Boutwell/M/Sept/Drowned/17y/Kitty/Jno T. Boutwell Master
Mary/S/Wm C. Pratt/F/Mar/__/10y/Judy/Wm Humphries Overseer
Judith/S/Wm C. Partt/F/Apr/__/60y/__/Wm Humphries Overseer
Ann/S/Martha J. Wright/F/Apr/__/2y/Eliza/M.J. Wright Mistress

1860

Mary Beazley/Free/F/July/Consumption/57y/[illeg]/Ed Whiticoe Son-in-Law
No Name/S//D.C. DeJarnette/F/Feb/Consumption/15d/Lucy/Owen C. Tuck Overseer
Nancy Sale/S/D.C. DeJarnette/F/Oct/7d/Eliz/Owen C. Tuck Overseer
__/W/F/July/Consumption/70y/Jas & Ann Puller/b.Spotsylvania/Jas J. Puller Nephew
No Name/S/Theo F. Green/M/July/__/1m/Id/Theo F. Green Master
Cordelia Gray/W/F/July/__/2y/Thos & Ellen Gray/Oswald Beazley Grandfather
H.C. Brooks/W/F/Mar 28/11m/H.A. & H.B. Brooks/Hiram A. Brooks Father
__/S/R.S. Broaddus/F/Aug/__/1y/Martha/Ro S. Broaddus Master
Davey/S/Wiley Wright/M/Nov/Old Age/90y/__/Wiley Wright Master
Peter Loven/W/M/Dec/__/20y/Phebe Loven/Unmarried/Carter Loven Rejected Brother
Pattie/S/M.R. Broaddus Est/F/June/Dis/63y/Jno P. Broaddus Admr
Overton Baker/Free/M/May/Heart Dis/90y/Jas S. Cole Neighbour
Bettie/S/Eiza Hill/F/July/1y/Agnes/Thos H. Richerson Agt
Temple/S/Louise T. Turner/F/July/Brain Fever/3y/__/Ira E. Seal Neighbour
Esther/S/M. Marmaduke/F/July/Old Age/85y/__/M. Marmaduke Master
Dennis/S/H.M. Alsop/M/June/d.Richmond/Brain Fever/15y/Candice/H.M. Alsop Master

No Name/W/M/June/__/__/Jas T. & M.S. Moore/M.S. Moore Mother
Wm T. Gouldin/W/M/Sept/1y 1m/Ro L. & Martha Gouldin/Ro L. Gouldin Father
Silas/S/Simon Gouldin/M/Nov/Typhoid Fever/11y/Betsy/Simon Gouldin Master
Susan/S/J.H. Garrett Est/F/Dec/Burnt/1y 6m/Amanda/Thos B. Garrett Admr
Grif J. Garrett/W/M/Dec/Dis/42y/Thos & Cath Garrett/Thos B. Garrett Brother
Vilett/S/Wm F. Catlett/F/Jan/__/60y/[illeg]/Wm F. Catlett Master
Marg E. James/W/F/Aug/Consumption/22y/Albert & Mary James Fountton [Fountain?] Uncle
S.R. Ball/W/M/Apr/Typhoid Fever/8y/Jno P. & M.A. Ball/Jno Ball Father
No Name/S/Saml H. Jeter/M/Oct/5m/Mary/Saml H. Jeter Master
Edy/S/Rob Andrew/F/June/Dropsy/70y/__/Rob Andrew Master
Jack/S/Rob Andrew/M/Sept/__/99y/Matilda/Rob Andrews Master
Daniel/S/M.B. Brooks/M/June/__/23y/M.B. Brooks Master
Jane/S/Jas S. Barbee/F/Apr/Killed by Lightning/89y/Diane/Jas S. Barbee Master
Eliza/S/Jas S. Barbee/F/Apr/Killed by Lightning/25y/Jane/Jas S. Barbee Master
Humphrey/S/Geo T. Burruss/M/Aug/__/60y/__/Geo T. Burruss Master
No Name/W/M/June/__/1m/Jas & Patsy Cecil/Jas Cecil Father
Eliz Houston/W/F/Feb/__/28y/Jack & Sally Cecil/A. Houston Husband
George/S/Jas W. Carneal/M/Sept/__/__/Jas W. Carneal Master
__/W/F/June/d.Spotsylvania/8d/J.H. & J.A. Bullock/b.Spotsylvania/J.H. Bullock Father
Temple/S/Louisa Turner/M/Aug/__/2y 6m/Malinda/Louisa Turner Mistress
Charlott/S/R.[Robert] M.[Mosley] Wright/F/__/28y/Matilda/Ro M. Wright Est Master
No Name/S/R.[Robert] M.[Moseley Wright]/F/__/__/2m/Matilda/Ro M. Wright Est Master
__/W/F/Sept/__/4y/Paul & Lucy Self/Paul Self Father
__/S/Reu B. Richerson/M/__/__/2m/Maline/R.B/ Richerson Master
Salena/S/Reu B. Richerson/F/May/[illeg]/[illeg]/Dinah/R.B. Richerson Master
Maria/S/Silas J. Broaddus/F/Aug/[illeg]/[illeg]/__/Silas J. Broaddus Master
Eliza? Chenault/W/M/Apr/[illeg]/[illeg]/[illeg]/__
Infant Dollins/Free/M/__/Consumption/__/Nannie Dollins/Rivington Dollins Brother
Cath Puller/W/F/June 6/Heart Dis/63/Wm & __ Puller/R.A. Puller Son
Chas McMullin/W/M/Dec/d.Richmond City/__/9m/Chas & Milly McMullin/Chas McMullin Father
__/S/D.C. DeJarnette/F/__/__/8d/Jane/Owen C. Tuck Overseer
Not Known/W/M/Aug/__/5m/And J. & M.B. Gravatt/b.King George Co/And J. Gravatt Father
Jas/S/Jno T. Boutwell/M/Aug/Consumption/37y/__/Jno T. Boutwell Master
No Name/S/P.H. Pendleton/F/May/__/3y/Ellen/P.H. Pendleton Master
No Name/W/F/Mar 19/__/4d/Reu & Mary E. Garrett/ Reu Garrett Father
Danl Fitzhugh/W/M/Oct 9/__/40y/Danl & Eliz Fitzhugh/Ann E. Fitzhugh Wife
M[illeg] A.B. Fitzhugh/W/F/Oct 24/__/18y/Danl & A.E. Fitzhugh/Ann E. Fitzhugh Mother
[illeg] Kay/Free/M/Mar/__/55y/Ann Kay/Mildred Kay Wife
Abram/S/Phil Lightfoot/M/Nov/__/70y/Nancy/Phil Lightfoot Master
Henry/S/Phil Lightfoot/M/Mar/Pneumonia/16y/Jane/Phil Lightfoot Master
Jane/S/Phil Lightfoot/F/June/40y/__/Phil Lightfoot Master
No Name/W/F/Feb 27/__/4d/Wm A. & Ellen C. Gray/Wm Gray Father
Chany/S/Jno B. Lightfoot/F/__/__/55y/__/John B. Lightfoot Master
Joe/S/Jno B. Lightfoot/M/__/__/60y/__/John B. Lightfoot Master
Steven/S/Jno B. Lightfoot/M/__/__/75y/__/John B. Lightfoot Master
No Name/S/Jno B. Lightfoot/M/__/__/89d/Eliza/John B. Lightfoot Master

No Name/2S/F/__/__/__/Marg/John B. Lightfoot Master
Rich Serinage/Free/M/__/__/53y/Nancy Serinage/Rich Seringe Jr. Son
Arthur [illeg]/Free/M/__/__/40y/__/John C. Gibbs Neighbor
Lucy/S/Geo W. Catlett/F/Mar/Brain Fever/8y/Jane/Geo W. Catlett Master
[illeg] Loven/W/F/Dec/__/8m/Sidney & Eliz A. Loven/Sidney Loven Father
__/S/Sarah A. Bowie/M/__/__/2d/Betsy/Allen B. Bowie Master
Thomas/S/Wm R. Roper/M/May/Inf dis/1y 6m/Rachel/Wm R. Roper Master
Geo/S/Jor [Jourdan] Woolfolk/M/__/__/2m/Ann/Jor Woolfolk Master
Mary Hardiman/Free/F/Oct/__/40y/Patty Johnson/Wm Hardiman Neighbor
Maria/S/Smith J.R. White/F/Jan/Pneumonia/16y/Louise/Smith J.R. White - Master
Ed L. Clarke/W/M/June/__/37y/Ed & Sallie Clarke/Jas W. Anderson Nephew
Thos Farmer/W/M/Jan/__/70y/Thos & Susan Farmer/Susan Farmer Mother
John L. Motley Jr/W/M/[illeg]/__/5d/Jno L. & M.L. Motley/Jno L. Motley Father
Peter/S/Jno L. Motley/M/July/__/6d/Emma/Jno L. Motley Master
Lucy/S/Cor [Cornelius] Campbell/F/Feb/Consumption/10y/Pollie/ Cor Campbell Master
John/S/Thos Broaddus/M/Mar/Not Known/__/Kitty/Thos Broaddus Master
Lucy/S/Phil R. Garnett/F/__/Hooping Cough/1y/Martha/Phil R. Garnett Master
[illeg] Crowley/M/__/__/1y 11d/Lewis & Jane Crowley/H. Crowley Father
[illeg] Pickett/W/M/[illeg]/[illeg]/[illeg]/Geo Pickett Brother
[illeg] Royston/[illeg]/__/__/__ Royston/Jas Marshall Neighbor
[illeg]/S/[illeg]/__/__/__/Mary E. Saunders Mistress
[illeg]/[illeg_____]/L. Gouldman Father
[Note: 2 more entries at bottom of page, faded beyond recognition]
Mor P. Samuel/W/M/Aug/Teething/1y 2m/Thos & Sarah F. Samuel/Thos Samuel Father
Millgard/S/Thos S. Samuel/M/Aug/Teething/1y 2m/Mary/Thos S. Samuel Master
__/S/Jos Jesse/F/__/__/1m/[illeg]/Jos Jesse Master
Phillis/S/Jos Jesse/F/Aug/__/1m/[illeg]/Jos Jesse Master
Abraham/S/Jos Jesse/M/Aug/Dis/1y/Mary Ann/Jos Jesse Master
Willy J. Carter/W/F/Oct/Dis/2y/Hiram & G.G. Carter/Hiram Carter Father
__/S/Bird A. Jordan/F/July/1y/Ellen/B.A. Jordan Master
Humphrey/S/Jas S. Davis/M/Sept/__/70y/__/Jas S. Davis Master
Oliver/S/Ro B. Tunstall/M/Aug/Pneumonia/22d/[illeg]/Ro B. Tunstall Master
Louisa/S/Jas J. White/F/June/Dropsy/8y/Betsy/Jas J. White - Master
Mary/S/Julia A. Anderson/F/Dec/__/3m/Jane/J.A. Anderson Mistress
Susan/S/Geo Farish's Est/F/__/__/90y/Jane/Wm P. Farish - Young Master
Mary/S/Geo Farish's Est/F/__/__/90y/__/Wm P. Farish - Young Master
Elliott/S/Thos C. Chandler/M/Mar/Pneumonia/25y/__/Thos C. Chandler Master
Susan/S/Thos C. Chandler/F/May/Paralysis/40y/Fannie/Thos C. Chandler Master
Richard/S/Thos C. Chandler/M/June/__/4d/Fannie/Thos C. Chandler Master
Sallie/S/Ed J. Motley/F/Dec/Smothered/6m/Maria/Ed J. Motley Master
Moses/S/Wm C. Pratt/M/Oct/Pneumonia/25y/__/Wm C. Pratt Master
Moses/S/Wm C. Pratt/M/Feb/__/17y/Sallie/Wm C. Pratt Master
Robt/S/Ed P. White's Est/M/May/Dropsy/45y/Caty/Jno White - Young Master
Geo/S/Ed P. White's Est/M/Mar/__/40y/__/Jno White - Young Master
John/S/Jno A. Miller/M/Apr/Pneumonia/65y/__/Jno A. Miller Master
Edmund/S/Jno A. Miller/M/Apr/Pneumonia/12y/Dolly/Jno A. Miller Master
Wm S. Martin/W/M/Apr/Pneumonia/18/Jno & Mary Martin/John Y. Martin Guardian
Pleasant/S/S. Downing/F/__/__/__/Rose/And M. Glassell Neighbour

James/S/__/M/Pneumonia/__/Frances/And M. Glassell Neighbour
W.J. Sale/W/M/May 9/Pneumonia/43y/Jno & Frances Sale/Farmer/Wm J. Murray Neighbour
__/S/Lovel P. Todd/M/__/__/3m/Isabella/Lovel P. Todd Master
Eliza/A/Wm P. Baylor/F/Dec/Diapesia/60y/__/Wm P. Baylor Master
Andrew/S/Cath Corbin/M/__/__/9y/Mahala/Rich Corbin Neighbour
Nancy/S/Saml Gordon/F/June/Heart Dis/51y/__/Henry Gordon - Yg Master
__/S/John Conway/F/__/__/3m/Pollie/John Conway Master
Washington/S/Wm J. Dickinson/M/Apr/Hernia/22y/[illeg]/Wm J. Dickinson Master
Sam/S/Wm J. Dickinson/M/__/Argue/72y/__/Wm J. Dickinson Master
Bettie/S/Wm J. Dickinson/F/__/Consumption/56/Florah/Wm J. Dickinson Master
Phil/S/Wm J. Dickinson/M/__/__/8m/Fannie/Wm J. Dickinson Master
No Name/S/Wm J. Dickinson/M/__/__/__/Selina/Wm J. Dickinson Master
No Name/S/Wm J. Dickinson/M/__/__/__/Roberta/Wm J. Dickinson Master
Rosetta Taylor/W/F/Dec/Old Age/75y/__/Joardan Toombs Neighbor
John/S/Rich Buckner/M/__/Dropsy/85y/Betsy/R.H.W. Buckner - Yg Master
Rosetta/S/Wm J. Jones/F/Dec/Child Bed/23y/Jane/Wm J. Jones Master
No Name/W/F/May/__/6d/__/Gutridge/[illeg] Guthridge Father
Robt/S/Jno DeJarnettte/M/__/[illeg]/[illeg]/Jno DeJarnette Master
Columbia Broaddus/W/F/Dec/Diptheria/11y 7m/And & Jane Broaddus/And Broaddus Father & Minister
No Name/S/John Coalter/F/__/Fits/Rhoda/ Jno Coalter Master
No Name/S/John Gouldin/M/__/__/15d/Susan/John Gouldin Master
No Name/S/Ed Sale/M/__/__/1m/Eliza/Ed Sale Master
Lucinda/S/Wm Carrick/F/July/__/30y/__/Wm Carrick Master
Thos R. Holloway/W/M/Sept 11/Typhoid Fever/43y/[illeg] G. & Joanna Holloway/Robt G. Holloway Brother
E.G. Massie/W/F/June/Typhoid Fever/37y/[illeg] G. & Joanna Holloway/Robt G. Holloway Brother
Richard/S/Ro G. Holloway Est/M/Aug/Consumption/70y/Rachel/Ro G. Holloway - Yg Master
Emenual/S/Ro G. Holloway Est/M/Sept/Typhoid Fever/16y/Nannie/Ro G. Holloway - Yg Master
Danl/S/Jno H. Bernard/M/Aug/Dropsy/65y/Eliziah/Wm R. Bernard - Yg Master
Cyrus/S/Jno H. Bernard/M/Sept/Dropsy/27y/Susan/Wm R. Bernard - Yg Master
Name Not Known/S/Ellis Gravatt/F/__/__/1y 6m/Rebecca/Ellis Gravatt Master
Sarah/Wm A. Buckner/F/Aug/Diptheria/50y/Mahala/Wm A. Buckner Master
Grace/S/Wm A. Buckner/F/Sept/Old Age/75y/Phillis/Wm A. Buckner Master
__/S/Jas A.L. Shaddock/M/Apr/__/3m/Cathl/Jas A.L. Shaddock Master
Abram/S/Jas A.L. Shaddock/M/Nov/Fits/65y/__/Jas A.L. Shaddock Master
Thos Chenault/W/M/May/Dis/45y/__/Geo F. Carneal Neighbour
Mark J. Boulware/W/M/June/Murdered/23y/M. & Susan Boulware/Geo W. Price Father-in-Law
Walter Crowley/W/M/June/__/1y/Humphrey? & Jane Crowley/Humpy Crowley Father
Wm G. Maury/W/M/__/Old Age/72y/__/Jas J. White Son-in-Law
Nancy Acors/W/F/Apr 10/Not Known/65y/Richard & Mary Harris/Thomas A. Acors Husband
Not Named/W/F/June 30/Not Known/__/Richard D. & Sarah Arnold/Rich D. Arnold Father
Not Named/W/M/July 3/Not Known/4d/Richard D. & Sarah Arnold/Richard D. Arnold Father
Andrew/S/L.W. Allen/M/Jan 2/Whooping Cough/1y 3m/Jane/L.W. Allen Owner
Not Named/S/James O. Allen/M/Apr 27/Not Known/7m/Maria/James O. Allen Owner
Not Named/S/Obidiah Atkinson/F/Not Known/Mary Susan/Obidiah Atkinson Owner
James M. Atkins/W/M/Apr/Consumption/23y/James & Elizabeth Atkins/Not Married/

Philip B. Atkins Brother
Abner Bullard/M/W/Oct 20/Not Known/4m/William & Virginia Bullard/Wm Bullard Father
Virginia Bullard/W/F/Jul 2/Dropsy/28y 9m/George & Mary [illeg]/William Bullard Husband
No Named/W/F/Sept 10/Not Known/__/Richard & [illeg] Baughn/Richard Baughn Father
Peter/S/Elizabeth G. Bibbs/M/Mar 30/Consumption/19/Lucy/Elizabeth G. Bibbs Mistress
William/S/Elizabeth G. Bibbs/M/May 1/Lock Jaw/8y/Dolly/Elizabeth G. Bibbs Mistress
York/S/Elizabeth G. Bibbs/M/May 8/Pneumonia/60y/Vicy/Elizabeth G. Bibbs Mistress
William M. Blaydes/W/M/Sept 24/Whooping Cough/__/Hugh & Mary E. Blaydes/Hugh F.
  Blaydes Father
Not Named/S/Richard Blanton/M/Jan 28/Not Known/8d/Susan/Richard Blanton Owner
James S. Blanton/W/M/Jan 13/Consumption/29y/Richard & Mary Blanton/Richard Blanton
  Father
Adam/S/John R.Young/M/July/Erysipelas/30y/Lucy/William Blanton Friend
Clarah/S/Rich E. Boulware/F/Apr/Consumption/50y/Dapney/Richard E. Boulware Master
Major/S/Rich E. Boulware/M/May/Pneumonia/19y/Clarah/Richard E. Boulware Master
Sally/S/Richard W/ Burruss/F/July/Cold/59y/Not Known/Richard W. Burruss Master
Not Named/S/Edward & P. Buckley/F/Oct/Not Known/3d/Ginney/Temple C. Moor Overseer
John/S/Edward & P. Buckley/M/Aug/Typhoid Fever/15y/Delphy/Temple C. Moor Overseer
Not Known/S/Mrs. R.B. Burruss/F/July/Not Known/__/Lavinia/Rebecca B. Burruss Mistress
Lewis Burruss/W/M/July 26/Not Known/6m 16d/Wm? & Rebecca Burruss/Rebecca B. Burruss
  Mother
[illeg]/S/Overton Burruss/M/Nov 1/Not Known/1y 6m/Delia/Clarisa J. Burruss Mistress
No Named/S/Overton Burruss/F/May 10/Brain dead/__/Kisiah/Clarissa J. Burruss Mistress
Nancy/S/William Carter/F/Dec/Not Known/9m/Milly/Wm Carter Master
Peter/S/William Carter/M/Nov/Consumption/70y/Emily/William Carter Master
Not Named/S/Lydia A. Swann/F/June 23/Not Known/2d/Kitty/Cyrus Carson Friend
Not Named/W/M/Apr/Still born/[illeg] & Emily Carlton/[illeg] Carlton Father
Not Named/S/John B. Coats/F/Aug 6/Not Known/1y//Mary/John B. Coats Master
Alexander/S/George T. Collins/M/July/Whooping Cough/10m/Henrietta/George T. Collins Master
Lucy/S/George T. Collins/F/July/Whooping Cough/__/Emily/George T. Collins Master
M[illeg] Cobbs/W/F/May 14/Consumption/78y 1m/Thompson & Elizabeth Cobbs/Lynch Cobbs
  Brother
William/S/Lynch Cobbs/M/Mar 30/Bronchitis/20y 2m/Emily/Lynch Cobbs Master
Mary/S/Jesse L. Cobbs/F/Jan 1/Croup//1y 7m/Malinda/Jesse Cobbs Master
Not Named/S/Jno Chandler/F/May/[illeg]/8d/William & Lucy/John Chandler Master
Elizabeth Dickins/W/F/Dec 5/Consumption/65y/Wm & Lucy Southworth/Paul J. Dickins Son
Not Named/S/Robert Dickinson/M/May/Still born/Betty/Robert Dickinson Master
No Name/Robert Dickinson/F/__/Still Born/Caroline/Robert Dickinson Master
[illeg]/S/Jno G. Dickinson/F/__/__/__/Hannah/Jno G. Dickinson Master
__Durrett/__/__/__/[illeg] & Elizabeth Durett/Farmer/[illeg] Durrett Son
[Note: Last listed death on this page is illegible]
Henry/S/Frances B. Durrett/M/Mar/Spasms/3y/Jane/Bleuford Durrett Friend
Winfred Eubank/W/F/July/1y 8d/James B. & Elizabeth Eubank/Jas B. Eubank Father
Ellen/S/Samuel Estes/F/Mar/Burnt/3y/Sarah/Samuel Estes Master
Not Named/S/Chas T. Farish/M/Oct/Spasms/2d/Lucy/Chas T. Farish Master
Thomas/S/Lewis M. George/M/May/Mumps/11m/Maria/Lewis M. George Master
Charlott/S/Lewis M. George/F/June/Mumps/8m/Phillis/Lewis M. George Master
Not Named/Clarah H. Goodwin/M/May 14/Not Known/Mary/John T. Goodwin Brother to owner

Jarrett/S/John T. Goodwin/M/July/Not Known/1m/Sarah/John T. Goodwin Master
Not Named/S/Betty G. Lewis/M/Nov/Not Known/1m/Lucy/John T. Goodwin Agt for owner
John T. Goodwin/W/M/Aug 5/Diarea/11m/John T. & Ann E. Goodwin/John T. Goodwin Father
Michael E. Goldbery [Goldsby]/W/M/June/Spasms/2y 6m/Caleb & Martha Ann Goldsbery [Goldsby]/Caleb Goldsbery Father
Not Named/W/F/July 14/Spasms/11d/William J. & Margarett Hancock/Wm J. Hancock Father
Oteria/S/Garret Hackett Est/F/Mar/Consumption/18y/Judy/James W. Hackett - Young Master
Frances/S/Garret Hackett Est/F/July/Not Known/3m/Jane/James W. Hackett - Young Master
Betsy/S/Garret Hackett Est/F/Aug/Stomach Affection/1m/Martha/James W. Hackett - Young Master
Henry Davis/S/Garret Hackett Est/M/Apr/Cold or Consumption/3m/June/James W. Hackett - Young Master
Leyton Harris/W/M/Oct 20/Gravel/83y/Wm & Ann Harris/Farmer/Widower/Tarlton Harris Grand Son
Frances Harris/W/F/July 14/[illeg]/52y/Baily & Nancy Tompkins/Wm B. Harris Husband
Pleasant/S/Thos C. Hackett/M/Sept/Paraletic/68y/Hannah/Thomas C. Hackett Master
Edmund/S/James Hill/M/May 15/Typhoid Fever/60y/[illeg]/James Hill Master
Fanny/S/James Hill/F/Dec 8/Typhoid Fever/__/Betty/James Hill Master
Agnes/S/James Hill/F/Dec 28/Pneumonia/8y/Ellen/James Hill Master
Sarah Hutcheson/W/F/Dec 8/Croupe/1m 14d/John & Parthenia Hutcheson/John W. Hutcheson Father
Samuel Jones/W/M/Nov 26/Spinal Affection/1y 6m/Thos & Elizabeth Jane Jones/ Thomas Jones Father
Margt Agnes Luck/W/F/June/__/9m/Wm F. & Mary S. Luck/Wm F. Luck Father
Sarah Ann Luck/W/F/June 19/Consumption/46y/Samuel & Sarah Luck/Saml P. Luck Brother
Abraham/S/Sarah Ann Luck/M/Oct 15/[illeg]/15y/Martha/Saml P. Luck Manager
Elizabeth Southworth/W/F/Nov 8/Heart Disease/74y/__ Alport/Widow/John M. Long Son-in-Law
Not Named/W/F/Oct 4/Croup/28d/Henry H. & Silida? Martin/Henry H. Martin Father
Martha J. McKenney/W/F/Sept 20/Typhoid Fever/10y/Charles & Melinda Beazley/A.G. McKenney Husband
Emily Jane Mitchell/W/F/Aug 11/Consumption/20y 11m/James & Emily Mitchell/Single/Emily Mitchell Mother
Not Named/W/F/Feb 12/Still born/Henry & Sarah Miller/Henry Miller Father
James Morr/W/M/Dec/Consumption/__/[illeg] Morr/John Morr Relation
Wilson/S/Henry W. Newton/M/Sept/Not Known/9y/Ann/Mary L. Newton Mistress
Randolph/S/Barton W. Morris/W/Sept/Cholera Infantum/__/Patsy/Barton W. Morris Owner
[illeg] Newton/W/F/Sept 12/Typhoid Fever/23y/C[illeg] & Jane Newton/John Newton Husband
Not Named/S/Lucy J. Harris/M/Dec 18/Not Known/8m/Mary/Jos Newton Manager
[illeg]/S/R.[Richard] Norment Est/M/Nov/Old Age/[illeg]/Not Known/Frances D. Norment Mistress
Lewis/S/R.[Richard] Norment Est/M/[illeg]/[illeg]/80y/Not Known/Frances D. Norment Mistress
Robert Noel/W/M/[illeg]/[illeg]/34y?/Edward & Sarah Noel/[illeg] Noel Father
Mark 'Livia Peatross/W/F/June/2y/Henry C. & Frances Ann Peatross/Henry C. Peatross Father
[illeg] Penney/W/M/[illeg]/[illeg]/9d/Ed M.C. & Sophia J. Penney/E.M.C. Penney Father
[Note: The last two entries, one a slave belonging to Geo B. Pollard and another whose owner is illegible, the rest of the text is faded beyond recognition]
Not Named/S/Philip Samuel Jr/F/Apr/Theuaelism/3d/Betty/Philip Samuel Jr Owner
Araminta Samuel/W/F/Apr 17/Consumption/25y/Reuben & Frances Saunders/Jno P. Samuel Jr Husband

John P. Samuel/W/M/May 15/Not Known/1m 8d/Jno P. & Araminta S. Samuel/John P. Samuel Jr Father
Simon/S/Ro G. Samuel/M/Dec 10/Pneumonia/75y/Not Known/Ro G. Samuel Owner
John/S/Ro G. Samuel/M/Dec 30/Consumption/30y/Eliza/Ro G. Samuel Owner
Allen/S/Philip Samuel Jr/M/Aug/Not Known/1m/Mary/Philip Samuel Owner
Sinah/S/John Samuel Jr/F/May/Scrofula/22y/Selah/John P. Samuel Owner
Mary Elizabeth Samuel/W/M/Apr/Diarriah/19y/John P. & Sarah P. Samuel/John P. Samuel Father
Sally Sacra/W/F/Apr/Typhoid Fever/7y/Benjamin & Maria Sacra/Benjamin Sacra Father
Thomas Sacra/W/M/Oct/Poison/30y/John & Elizabeth Sacra/Benjamin Sacra Father
Sandy/S/Robert Scott/M/Oct 29/Croup/2m/Malinda/Robert Scott Owner
Allen Durwood Scott/W/M/Jan 11/Not Known/1d/Jno & Ellen H. Scott/Jno M. Scott Brother
William M. Ship/W/M/July 8/Not Known/63y/Thomas & Mary Ship/John M. Ship Son
Alfred/S/Reuben M. Sizer/M/Aug 26/Pneumonia/20y/Not Known/Reuben M. Sizer Master
Jane Spicer/W/F/Dec 5/Consumption/41y/John & Lucy Grannell/b.Louisa/Thos H. Spicer Husband
William Peyton Stevens/W/M/Nov 21/Croup/3y/Theoderick & Louisa J. Stevens/Theoderick Stevens Father
Ann Hatton/W/F/July 1/Dropsy/37y/Thomas & Catherine Hatton/Geo T. Swann Physician
[illeg Theodore F] Jones/W/M/Apr/Appoplexy/24y/Thomas & Mary L. Jones/Geo T. Swann Physician
Not Named/W/F/Oct 19/Still born/Geo T. & Mary E. Swann/Geo T. Swann Father
Mary E. Swann/W/F/Oct 24/Jandice/5y/Dabney W. & Caroline Waller [sic]/Dabney W. Waller Husband [sic]
Sally [Sarah] B. Terrell/W/F/Sept 23/Consumption/65y/[illeg] Mother not recollected/Wm P. Terrell Son
Mary Eliza Clore/Free/F/Mar 28/Fever/6y/Reu & Jane Cloe/Wm P. Terrell Friend
Leanna/S/George Washington/F/Feb 11/Strangled/2m/Peggy/George Washington Owner
Jack/S/Geo Washington/M/Apr/Pneumonia/30y/Nelly/George Washington Owner
Julia/S/Geo Washington/F/July/Teething/8m/Lucinda/George Washington Owner
Gay/S/Dabney M. Waller/M.May 28/Not Known/6y/Pamela/Dabney M. Waller Owner
Not Named/S/Richard B. White/M.Apr/Not Known/4m/Emily/Jno W. Watkins Neighbor
Not Named/S/Edmund West/M/Apr 25/Deformed/1m/Jane/Joseph E. West - Young Master
Not Named/S/Tavenor Winn/F/Nov/Not Known/2m/Lucy/Tavenor Winn Owner
Edmund/S/Rich H. Woolfolk/M/Oct 26/Whooping Cough/1y 3m/Eliza/Rich H. Woolfolk Owner
Anderson/S/Rich H. Woolfolk/M/Dec/Pneumonia/23y/Anna/Rich H. Woolfolk Owner
Mary Ann/S/Rich H. Woolfolk/F/Oct/Whooping Cough/7m/Ellen/Rich H. Woolfolk Owner
Ben/S/Edmund P. Wood or Hord?/M/Aug/Pneumonia/38y/Judy/E.P. Wood or Hord?
Clemy/S/Robert Wright Est/F/June/Not Known/38y/Matilda/Woodson Wright - Young Master
Harriett/S/Robert Wright Est/F/Aug/Cholic/6y 6m/Louisa/Woodson Wright - Young Master
Louisa/S/Wm R.B. Wyatt/F/Dec 31/Congestion of Brain/1y 6m/Gloria/Wm R.B. Wyatt Master
John Blunt/W/M/May 13/Consumption/8y/James P. Blunt M[other] Not Known/Widower/ William M. Blunt Son
[illeg]/W/M/June 25/[illeg]/63y/Not Known/Not Married/Henry T. Doggett Neighbor
[illeg] Carter/W/F/July 5/Whooping Cough/6m 7d/[illeg]/[illeg]Carter Father
Polly Cash/Free/F/Feb/Measles/62y/Not Known/John Cash Husband
[Note: Last 3 entries faded beyond reading]
William/S/Robert D. Coleman/M/Sept/Whooping Cough/6y/Martha/Mr Waldress Overseer
Martha/S/Robert D. Coleman/F/Aug/Typhoid Fever/30y/Lucy/Mr Waldress Overseer
Lucy/S/Robert D. Coleman/F/Aug/Typhoid Fever/33y/Not Known/Mr. Waldress Overseer

Henry/S/Robert D. Coleman/M/Nov/Not Known/6m/Mary Eliza/Mr Waldross Overseer
Lucinda/S/James T. Redd/F/Mar/Not Known/16y/Catharine/James T. Redd Master
Not Named/S/Sarah R. Kelly/F/Sept 1/Not Known/7d/Rachael/Sarah R. Kelly Mistress
Edmund C. Chiles/W/M/Nov 5/Consumption/63y/Wm & Sarah Chiles/Lucy Ann Chiles Wife
Ellen/S/John E. Bowers/F/July/Typhoid Fever/24y/Jane/John E. Bowers Owner
Not Named/W/F/Mar/Croup/7d/Leonidas C. & Margarett E. [Kidd] Pollard/L.C. Pollard Father
Not Named/W/F/June/Croup/21d/Richard & Ellen Moren/Richard Moren Father
Lucy Blanton/W/F/Jan 2/Natural Debility/65y/James & Betsy Southworth/John B. Blanton Husband
Not Named/S/Jno S. Blanton/F/July 8/Not Known/4d/Amanda/Jno B. Blanton Owner
Silas/S/Wm P.C. Ramsey/M/Jan 1/Croup/7m/Sally/Wm P.C. Ramsey Owner
Maria/S/H. Jones/F/June/Dropsy/64y/Phebe/George Acors Friend
Harry/S/Jno M. Gatewood/M/Apr 26/Dropsy/50y/Not Known/Saml Gatewood nearest Brother [to owner]
Name Not Recollected/S/Jno M. Gatewood/M/May/Sore Throat/6y/Caroline/Saml Gatewood nearest Brother [to owner]
Name Not Recollected/S/James M. Gatewood/M/May/Sore Throat/4y/Caroline/Saml Gatewood nearest Brother [to owner]
Ann/S/Peter R. Catlett/F/Mar/Pneumonia/35y/Milly/Peter R. Catlett Owner
Eliza/S/Peter R. Catlett/F/Nov/Diptheria/34y/Ann/Peter R. Catlett Owner
John Catlett/W/M/Nov/Diptheria/11y/Peter R. & Elizabeth Catlett/Peter R. Catlett Father
Margarett Catlett/W/F/Nov 9/Diptheria/9y/Peter R. & Elizabeth Catlett/Peter R. Catlett Father
Not Named/S/Saml Schooler/M/June/Still born/Marg/Saml Schooler Owner
[illeg]/S/Saml Schooler/F/Sept/Pneumonia/69y/Grace/Saml Schooler Owner
Wm E. Flippo/W/M/Jan 11/Hemorage/68y/John & Elizabeth Flippo/Elizabeth Flippo Widow
Joseph Flippo/W/M/Apr/Heart Disease/66y/John & Elizabeth Flippo/Widower/A.R. Flippo Son
Ben/S/Hugh Chandler/M/June/Cl Inflamation/6m/Ann/Hugh Chandler Master
William A. Coghill/W/M/Nov 29/[illeg]/42y 5m/Willy[Coghill]/Sally Coghill Widow
Mildred Ann/S/A.G. Goodwin/F/July/Whooping Cough/3y/Mary Ellen/A.G. Goodwin Owner
Thomas/S/A.G. Goodwin/M/July/Whooping Cough/__/Patsy/A.G. Goodwin Owner

1861

June/No Name/S/Wm Chapman/F/Overlaid/25d/Wally/Wm Chapman Master
Jordan Pittis/W/M/Dec/Pneumonia/22y/__/Jos Wright Neighbour
G.A. Richeson/W/F/Nov/Consumption/20y/Lucy A. Fitzhugh/Jos M. Richeson Husband
Ceophas/S/Richard Gouldman/M/July/Typhoid Fever/25y/Dianna/Richard Gouldman Master
Mary A. Spindle/W.F.Aug/Bilious Fever/57y/Jas & Mary Bagby/John W. Spindle Neighbour
Fletah/S/Gray Boulware/F/Jan/Burnt/22y/__/Gray Boulware Master
Hetta/S/Gray Boulware/F/June/Lock Jaw/26y/__/Gray Boulware Master
William/S/Gray Boulware/M/Aug/Scrofula/36y/__/Gray Boulware Master
Julia/S/Cor [Corneluis] Campbell/F/Dec/__/12y/Erelina/Cor Campbell Master
Sallie Cecil/W/F/Sept/Diptheria/13y/Eliza Cecil/Isaac Cecil Father
Lucy H. Broaddus/W/F/Dec/Diptheria/5y/Virginia M. Broaddus/Richd F. Broaddus Father
Not Known/S/Richd F. Broaddus/M/Dec/__/__/Priscilla/Richd F. Broaddus Master
Danl Johnson/Free/M/Dec/Dropsy/80y/Judy Johnson/Danl Johnson Jr Son
Chl Samuel/W/M/Sept/__/65y/Jos & R. Samuel/R.H. Parker Son-in-Law
No Name/W/F/July/__/1m/Leo & Mary F. Guthridge/Leo Guthridge Father

William/S/Geo W. Marshall/M/July/__/1y/Susan/Geo W. Marshall Master
Abraham/S/Chas Phillips/M/Jan/__/75y/Fanny/Chas Phillips Master
No Name/W/M/Sept 23/__/4d/Lindsey C. & Ann Pitts/L.C. Pitts Father
Virginia A. Taylor/W/F/Sept 23/Putred S Throat/10y/Jos & Cath Taylor/Cath Taylor Mother
Nancy Taylor/W/F/Dec 20/Old Age/72y/Thos Hutcherson/Cath Taylor Daughter-in-Law
Nannie Martin/W/F/Dec 15/Old Age/65y/Sam & L. Chenault/L.C. Pitts Neighbour
Jas B. Dun[n]/W/M/Sept/Dis Lungs/25y/And & Harrt Dun/Harriett Dun Mother
William Taylor/W/M/Nov/__/2y/P.G. & Polly Taylor/Polly Taylor Mother
Mildred Gates/W/F/Oct/Heart Dis/60y/__/Chas W. Jones Son-in-Law
Milly/S/Chas W. Jones/F/Oct/Dis of Lungs/35y/__/Chas W. Jones Master
Dinah/S/Louise Turner/F/Oct/__/1y 6m/Dolly/L.T. Turner Mistress
Robin/S/R. [Robert] M. [Moseley] Wright Est/M/June/Dropsy/50y/__/Wife of R.M. Wright Mistress
No Name/S/Theo F. Green/M/June/__/1m/[illeg]/Theo F. Green Master
Mary Ann/S/Maria L. Kidd/F/June/Measles/19y/Pattie/Maria L. Kidd Mistress
Allen/S/Maria L. Kidd/M/June/__/5m/Mary Ann/Maria L. Kidd Mistress
R.H. Kidd/W/M/May 13/__/28y/Wm & Hart [Harriett] M. Kidd/Hart M. Kidd Mother
Samuel/S/Thos H. Richerson/M/Nov/Stricture/60y/Thos H. Richerson Master
Rose/S/Thos H. Richerson/F/Nov/Pneumonia/20y/Melinda/Thos H. Richerson Master
No Name/S/Rev R. Richerson/F/Mar/__/7d/Virginia/Rev R. Richerson Master
R.W. Cole Jr/W/M/Nov/Diptheria/6y/R. & Lucy B. Cole/R.W. Cole Father
B.F. Sale/W/F/Apr 3/Consumption/41y/James J. & Eliza Broaddus/Thos B. Sale Husband
Randolph/S/Mary W. Jones/M/Jan 3/Pneumonia/17y/Clary/Wm P. Jones - Yg Master
Ann/S/Mary W. Jones/F/Jan 19/Pneumonia/26y/Clary/Wm P. Jones - Yg Master
Albert/S/Geo Mahon/M/Feb/__/6m/Betty/Geo Mahon Master
__/S/Geo Taylor/F/__/__/15d/Judy/Ben Merryman Overseer
Wm Pavey/W/M/Sept/Old Age/85y/__/Jno G. Pavy Son
Bettie/S/Edgar McKenney/F/Oct/__/9y/Margt/Edgar McKenney Master
Sarah Lunsford/W/F/July 28/Consumption/61y/John & Mary Anderson/Ed Lunsford Husband
Jim/S/Ed Lunsford/M/June/Dis of Throat/35y/__/Ed Lunsford Master
McKensie C. Gouldman/W/F/June/Brain Fever/7m/Geo F. & Mary T. Gouldman/Geo F. Gouldman
  Father
No Name/W/F/June/__/__/Ed & Rebecca Whiticoe/Ed Whiticoe Father
No Name/S/Lunsf Fitzhugh/F/Nov/__/1m/Hannah/Lunsfd Fitzhugh Master
No Name/S/John Coatter/F/Dec/__/14d/Rhoda/Jas W. Garret Manager
__/S/Sarah A. Bowie/M/__/__/__/Betty/Allen Bowie - Yg Master
William/S/John C. Bowie Est/M/May/Pneumonia/35y/Aggy/Allen Bowie - Yg Master
Henry T. Gouldin/W/M/July/Fits/4m/Ross & Martha A. Gouldin/Ross Gouldin Father
No Name/S/S.C. Jones/F/Dec/__/21d/Cillah/S.C. Jones Master
Henry G. Allen/W/M/Aug/Dysentary/1y 6m 9d/R.G. & Molly D. Allen/R.G. Allen Father
Mary F. Kidd/W/F/Apr/Diptheria/35y/Henry & Caty Whitie/Henry Kidd Husband
No Name/S/R.G. Allen/M/Sept/Fits/7d/Fannie/R.G. Allen Master
L.A. Taylor/W/F/Nov 24/__/30d/Jno C. & L.M. Taylor/F.B. Taylor Neighbour
Humphy Brooks/W/M/Sept 22/Consumption/25y/Jos F. & Frances Brooks/Nancy Brooks Wife
Julia Brooks/W/F/__/__/3m/Humpy & Nancy Brooks/Nancy Brooks Mother
Martha/S/Phil Gatewood/F/Jan/__/1y 2m/Caroline/Phil Gatewood Master
Polly Self/W/F/Sept/Apolexy/66y/Jno F. & __ Alport/John Self Husband
Isaac/S/Jno R. Baylor/M/Nov/Dropsy/35y/Jno R. Baylor Master
Polly/S/Jno R. Baylor/F/__/Consumption/20y/Winney/Jno R. Baylor Master

Milly/S/Jno R. Baylor/__/__/3y/Mirah/Jno R. Baylor Master
Robert/S/Jno R. Baylor/M/__/__/1m 15d/Kitty/Jno R. Baylor Master
Not Known/S/Jno R. Baylor/__/__/__/1m 15d/Polly/Jno R. Baylor Master
[illeg]/S/Joe Jesse's Est/__/__/__/2m/Jenny/B.B. Wright [son-in-law] Adm
[illeg]/S/Joe Jesse's Est/__/__/__/__/Caty/B.B. Wright Adm
Thomas/S/Eliza Gray/M/Oct/Typhoid Fever/30y/__/B.B. Wright Adm
Joe Jesse/W/M/Nov/Pneumonia/55y/__/B.B. Wright Son-in-Law
[illeg]/S/R.B. Dapree/__/__/1y 3m/Peggy/Jos M. Lyall Head of Family
[illeg] Norment/W/M/Dec/Brain Fever/31y/__ & Milly Norment/Ellis Norment Brother
__ Riddle/W/F/__/d.Stafford Co/Pneumonia/55y/John & V. Riddle/Jno Riddle Brother
Lelia Sale/W/F/Oct/Dis/2y/Wade H. & S.S. Sale/Wade Sale Father
No Name/W/M/Apr/__/7d/Jas L. & C.P. Barlow/Jas L. Barlow
Virgl P. Barlow/W/F/Ocxt/Thrash/2y/Jas L. & C.P. Barlow/Jas L. Barlow
Ben/S/Jno P. Downing's Est/M/Oct/Brain Fever/1y 2m/Melvina/Hess R. Corse Overseer
Thomas/S/Thos Broaddus/__/__/11m/Milly/Thos Broaddus Master
Chas/S/Thos Broaddus/M/__/__/10m/Adeline/Thos Broaddus Master
Milly/S/Thos Broaddus/F/__/__/__/Adeline/Thos Broaddus Master
Davey/S/Jas S. Barbee/__/3m/Sarah/Jas S. Barbee Master
Caroline/S/Frances Boulware/F/Aug/Consumption/45y/Lucy/Frances Boulware Mistress
Eliza Boulware/W/F/May/Consumption/60y/Mark & Molly Boulware/Frances Boulware Sister
Mary/S/M.S.Wright/F/Dec/Scarlet Fever/17y/Sarah/Martha S. Wright Mistress
Harriett/S/M.S. Wright/F/Oct/__/55y/__/Martha S. Wright Mistress
John/S/M.S. Wright/M/June/__/10m/Kitty/Martha S. Wright Mistress
Martha Wright/W/F/July/__/35y/Turner Clayton/Lund Gray Neighbour
Delia Vessells/Free/F/__/Lunatic/26y/Davey Vessells/Davey V. Vessells Father
Temple Bird/Free/M/Dec/Consumption/30y/__/Robt Parker Neighbour
Virgl L. Frazier/W/F/__/Child Bed/45y/Wm & Martha Harrison/A.M. Frazier Husband
Sarah Jones/W/F/Feb 6/Tu of Lungs/45y/Coleman & Sally Wharton/W.T. Jones Husband
Not Known/S/Wm J. Jones/__/__/1y/Maria/Wm T. Jones Master
Susan Collawn/W/F/Mar 28/Pneumonia/37y/R. & J.A. Holloway/Wm A. Collawn Husband
Eustus S. Barlow/W/M/Sept/P.S. Throut/4y/Wm & J.A. Barlow/Wm Barlow Father
Bennette/S/Thos W. Gouldin/M/July/__/22y/Betsy/Thos W. Gouldin Master
Charlotte/S/Thos W. Gouldin/F/Oct/Pnuemonia/48y/__/Thos W. Gouldin Master
McKensie/S/Thos L. Broaddus/M/June/__/55y/Matelon/Wm J. Broaddus Grad Master
Not Known/S/Jno D. Butler/M/__/__/2y/__/Jno D. Butler Master
A.L. Houston/W/M/June/__/2y/A.L. & Martha Houston/A.L. Houston Father
Martha/S/Wm Thornley/F/__/__/36y/Maria/Wm Thornley Master
Bettie/S/Wm Thornley/F/__/__/2y/Martha/Wm Thornley Master
Joe/S/Wm Thornley/M/__/__/1y/Amanda/Wm Thornley Master
Oliver/S/Joe J. White/M/Jan/Dropsy/62y/__/Joe J. White - Master
Chas/S/A.M. Boulware/M/__/__/__/Minnie/A.M. Boulware Master
Sally/S/Clem Farish/F/Aug/__/1y 1m/Margaret/C. Farish Mistress
Mary/S/Wm S. Dickinson/F/__/Measles/20y/Ann/Wm S. Dickinson Master
Louise/S/Wm S. Dickinson/F/__/__/6m/Mary/Wm S. Dickinson Master
Sam/S/Wm S. Dickinson/M/__/Dropsy/70y/__/Wm S. Dickinson Master
John/S/Wm S. Dickinson/M/__/Measles/2y/Minnie/Wm S. Dickinson Master
Tunstall/S/Wm S. Dickinson/M/__/Measles/6m/Minnie/Wm S. Dickinson Master
Betty/S/Wm S. Dickinson/F/__/__/60y/__/Wm S. Dickinson Master

Patsy/S/Jno Conway/F/__/__/4m/Jane/Jno L. Conway Master
Lucy/S/Benjm Anderson/F/__/Consumption/40y/Lucy/Benjm Anderson Master
L.F. Chandler/W/F/__/Grad Consumption/7y/R.T. & J.C. Chandler/R.T. Chandler Father
Wm Pruett Jr/W/M/Oct/Diptheria/24y/Wm & Mary Pruett/Wm Pruett Father
Martha E. Pruett/W/F/Oct/Diptheria/18y/Wm & Mary Pruett/Wm Pruett Father
Virg Pruett/W/F/Oct/Diptheria/17y/Wm & Mary Pruett/Wm Pruett Father
Elijah Pruett/W/M/Oct/Diptheria/7y/Wm & Mary Pruett/Wm Pruett Father
Caroline Pruett/W/F/Oct/Diptheria/12y/Wm & Mary Pruett/Wm Pruett Father
E.P. Pruett/W/F/Oct/Diptheria/2y/Wm & Mary Pruett/Wm Pruett Father
John/S/Travis Bagby's Est/M/Oct/Typhoid Fever/10y/Lucinda/R.H. Upshaw Overseer
Lucy/S/John W. White/F/__/__/45y/__/Henry Kidd Overseer
Geo/S/John W. White/M/__/__/23y/Cyndy/Henry Kidd Overseer
__/S/C.H. Boutwell/M/__/__/8m/Eliza/C.H. Boutwell Mistress
Isaac/S/Jno T. Boutwell/M/Aug/__/55y/Betty/M.B. Smith Mistress
Peter/S/Jno T. Boutwell/M/__/__/75y/__/M.B. Smith Mistress
Emanuell/S/M.B. Smith/M/__/Consumption/50y/__/M.B. Smith Mistress
Jim/S/Jno J. Gravatt/M/__/Consumption/20y/Maria/John J. Gravatt Master
Margt/S/Jno J. Gravatt/F/__/Consumption/20y/__/John J. Gravatt Master
Soloman/S/Chas Urguhart/M/Jan/Dropsy/7y/__/Chas Urguhart Master
Polly/S/Chas Urguhart/F/Dec/Pneumonia/62y/__/Chas Urughart Master
Millard W. Shaddock/W/M.July 10/__/1y 3m/J.A.L. & Ann Shaddock/Jos A.L. Shaddock Father
Virg A. Krauss/W/F/June/__/1y 1m/Geo W. & Lucinda Krauss/Lucinda Krauss Mother
Malinda/S/Wm H. Toombs/F/Sept/__/75y/__/Marietta Toombs Mistress
Eva/S/Mat Boulware/F/__/__/21y/Lucy/Edgar Richerson Manager
Robert/S/Peter R. Thornton/M/__/6y/Nancy/Peter R. Thornton Master
Willis/S/Peter R. Thornton/M/__/__/4y/Nancy/Peter R. Thornton Master
Rose/S/Peter R. Thornton/F/__/__/2y/Nancy/Peter R. Thornton Master
Jos H. Acors/W/M/__/__/2y/Henry & Sarah J. Acors/Henry Acors Father
No Name/S/Bird A. Jordan/F/__/__/1m/Fanny/B.A. Jordan Master
Not Known/S/Fanny Downing/F/__/__/__/Rose/Jas Acors Overseer
Not Known/S/Fanny Downing/M/__/__/__/Fannie/Jas Acors Overseer
William/S/Richd Corbin/M/__/Pneumonia/31y/Maria/Richd Corbin Master
Walker/S/O.M. Harris/M/__/Consumption/12y/Daphia/O.M. Harris Master
Delphia/S/M.T. Campbell/F/__/Scarlet Fever/4y/Rose/M.T. Campbell Master
Roberta/S/M.T. Campbell/F/__/Scarlet Fever/4y/Edith/M.T. Campbell Master
George/S/M.T. Campbell/M/__/Scarlet Fever/6y/Rose/M.T. Campbell Master
N.S. Lourie/W/F/__/Scarlet Fever/2y/Albert & Mary Lourie/John Washington Neighbour
Aaron/S/Thos C. Chandler/M/__/Scarlet Fever/50y/Lucy/Thos C. Chandler Master
Albert/S/Thos C. Chandler/M/__/Scarlet Fever/2y/Lucy/Thos C. Chandler Master
Thornton/S/Thos C. Chandler/M/__/Scarlet Fever/8y/Eliza/Thos C. Chandler Master
William/S/Thos C. Chandler/M/__/Scarlet Fever/3y/Rachel/Thos C. Chandler Master
L.C. Chandler/W/F/Mar/Scarlet Fever/5y/Thos C. & Mary L. Chandler/Thos C. Chandler Father
Henry/S/Thos K. Chandler/M/__/Scarlet Fever/6y/Harriett/Thos K. Chandler Master
Isabella/S/Thos K. Chandler/F/__/Scarlet Fever/2y/Harriett/Thos K. Chandler Master
Washington/S/Wm S. Royston/M/__/Cramp Col/49y/__/Wm S. Royston Master
Albert Taylor/W/M/Oct/Consumption/30y/Major & Clary Taylor/Sarah Taylor Sister
Sally/S/Ed S. Motley/F/__/__/7m/Maria/Ed S. Motley Master
Betsey/S/R.O. Jesse/F/__/Chrs Rheu/45y/__/R.O. Jesse Master

Huldah DeJarnette/W/F/Oct/__/60y/Danl & H. DeJarnett/J.H. DeJarnette Son
John Norment/W/M/__/__/63y/__/Wm R. Jeter Son-in-Law
John H. Pitts/W/M/Pneumonia/27y/Willis & Mahala Pitts/Willis Pitts Father
John B. Vaughan/W/M/__/30y/John Vaughan/Ed Vaughan Brother
Evelina/S/Willis Pitts/F/__/__/45y/__/Willis Pitts Master
No Name/W/F/Apr 27/__/1m/R.H. & F.B. Garrett/Richd H. Garrett Father
Mary/S/F. Fitzhugh Est/F/__/__/15y/Judith/Mary Fitzhugh Mistress
Matilda/S/Richd Buckner/F/__/Diptheria/3m/Polly/Richd Buckner Master
Jim/S/Richd Buckner/M/__/Dptheria/7m/Polly/Richd Buckner Master
John/S/Richd Buckner/M/__/Diptheria/52y/Betty/Richd Buckner Master
Peter/S/Jno Gouldin/M/__/__/1y 6m/Susan/Amey B. Gouldin Mistress
Lucy/S/Mary J. Saunders/F/__/__/1y 5m/Lucy/Mary B. Saunders Mistress
Major Samuel/W/M/__/Typhoid Fever/20y/Jas & Phebe Samuell/Landon Samuell Bro
William Oliver/W/M/July/Brain Fever/9m/Oscar Oliver & Mary Ann Oliver/Jos B.
  Southworth Grand Father
Oscar Oliver/W/M/Dec/Consumption/24y 6m/Saml & Martha Oliver/Mary Ann Oliver Wife/
  Jas B. Southworth Father-in-Law
Stephen/S/Geo W. Burk/M/Oct 20/Consumption/25y/Winney/William Taliaferro Friend
Reuben/S/Saml C. Schooler/M/Nov 20/Atrophy/8y/Nancy/Saml C. Schooler Owner
Zacariah/S/Saml C. Schooler/M/Aug 25/Colic/2y 3m/Ann/John F. Duke Overseer
Brutus/S/James D. Coleman/M/June/Heart Disease/75y/__/James D. Coleman Owner
Harry/S/James D. Coleman/M/Dec/Burn/1y/Mary Susan/James D. Coleman Owner
Garland/S/Elliott Wortham/M/June 20/Consumption/24y/Sarah/E. Wortham Owner
Mary Louisa/S/Elliott Wortham/F/June 2/Typhoid Fever/13y 8m/Margarette/E. Wortham Owner
Harriett/S/Elliott Wortham/F/Aug/Pneumonia/1y/Ellen/E. Wortham Owner
Isaac/S/Thos B. Anderson/M/July 18/Damaged Liver/60y/__/Thos B. Anderson Owner
Not Named/Free/M/Dec/Cold/18d/Sarah Jane Fox/Geo M. McLaughlin Friend
Aley Minor/S/Richd Burruss/F/Oct 1/Consumption/22y/Sally/Rich Burruss Owner
William/S/Francis W. Scott/M/Aug/Congestive Chill/45y/Dolly/W. Scott Owner
Phillip/S/Francis W. Scott/M/Mar/Pneumonia/55y/Bucky/F.W. Scott Owner
John/S/Francis W. Scott/M/Dec/Consumption/35y/Franky/F.W. Scott Owner
Walter/S/Chas B. Stuart/M/Nov/Croup/1y 6m/Jane/F.W. Scott Owner
Ephraim/S/Mary L. Henderson/M/June/Not Known/22y/Ann/B.M. Wright Son-in-Law [of owner]
Not Named/S/Rebecca B. Burruss/F/Aug/Not Known/1d/Lavinia/Manasseh Campbell Friend
McKessigal Jackson/W/M/Oct 6/Paraletic/62y/Robert & Sarah Jackson/Martha Jackson Wife
Gus/S/John H. Scott/M/Aug/Teething/1y/Levinia/John W. Scott Owner
Cornelius C. Penney/W/M/Oct 19/Pneumonia/1y 8m/Edward M.L. & Sophia Jane Penney/E.M.L.
  Penney Father
Not Named/S/Rebecca B. Burruss/F/Mar/Born Dead/Sarah/R.B. Burruss Owner
Joshua Turner/W/M/Sept 1/Camp Fever/20y 11m 2d/Daniel & Mary Turner/Danl Turner Father
Elizabeth Southworth/W/F/Nov 18/Typhoid Fever/18y/John D. & Mary Southworth/John D.
  Southworth Father
James/S/Henry H. George/M/June/Teething/1y/Malinda/Henry H. George Owner
Matty/S/Saml C. Goodwin/F/Oct 1/Dropsy/55y/__/Saml C. Goodwin Owner
Dorethea Cloe/Free/F/Mar/Not Known/12y/Molly Cloe/Cora England Neighbour
Woodson/S/Thos L. Catlett/M/May/Hooping Cough/3y/Dina/Thos L. Catlett Owner
Horace/S/Thos L. Catlett/M/May/Hooping Cough/4y/Fanny/Thos L. Cattlett Owner
Not Named/S/Thos L. Catlett/M/May/Hooping Cough/6m/Nancy/Thos L. Catlett Owner

Henirietta Carpenter/W/F/Aug/Rupture of Skin/11m/Wm & Elizabeth Carpenter/Wm Carpenter Father
Elizabeth Terrell/W/F/July 6/Inf Brain/5m/Robert L. & Rachael T. Terrell/R.S. Terrell Father
Not Named/W/F/Feb 6/Not Known/1y/Churchill G. & Mary Ann Carter/C.G. Carter Father
Not Named/W/M/Nov 22/Not Known/2m/John R. & Elizabeth N. Napier/John P. Napier Father
Not Named/S/Wm T. Chandler/M/Sept/Not Known/2d/__/Wm T. Chandler Owner
Lamah/S/Philip Samuel Sr/F/Feb 14/Pneumonia/12y/__/Philip Samuel Jr Owner
Judson/S/John P. Samuel/M/June/Consumption/2y/Dinah/John P. Samuel Owner
Mary T. Samuel/W/F/May 13/Consumption/25y 3m 13d/John P. & Sarah T. Samuel/John P. Samuel Father
Sally/S/Geo F. Coleman/F/Oct/Bronchitis/23y/Amelia/Ann W. Coleman Owner
Philip/S/Geo F. Coleman Est/M/Dec/Bronchitis/9m/Ginny/Ann W. Coleman Owner
Sibrena/S/Gideon Flippo/F/Dec/Not Known/24d/Kitty/Gideon Flippo Owner
Brutus/S/Gideon Flippo/M/Nov 29/Not Known/12d/Kitty/Gideon Flippo Owner
Richard/S/G. Flippo/M/July 22/Not Known/18m/Ann/Gideon Flippo Owner
Robert/S/Albert R. Flippo/M/Sept 30/Diptheria/7m/Frances/Albert R. Flippo Owner
William Porter Carter/W/M/Nov/Not Known/23d/Melzor & Marguil Carter/Malzor Carter Father
Dinah/S/Dabney W. Waller/F/Apr 26/Old Age/85y/__/Dabney W. Waller Owner
Adam/S/John R. Young Est/M/Nov 20/Lock Jaw/34y/__/Henry Martin Friend
Not Named/S/Richd White's Est/F/July/__/__/Louise/P.T. Partlow Friend
Gabriel/S/Joel T. Luck/M/Oct 21/Congestive Fever/21y/Dinah/Joel T. Luck Owner
Not Named/W/M/Aug 23/__/__/Geo W. & Lucy J. Southworth/Geo W. Southworth Father
George T. Evans/W/M/Nov 7/Consumption/27y 5m 28d/Leroy & Frances Evans/Leroy Evans Father
Sampson/S/Elizabeth D. Coleman/M/Oct/Cancer/70y/__/Addison L. Coleman - Young Master
Josephine Johnson/W/F/Nov/Consumption/21y/Allen J. & Dorcus Ann Thomas/Wm A. Johnson Husband/Allen Thomas Father
Not Named/S/Nicholas Mills/F/July/Not Known/1y/Williamina/Wm J. Young Overseer
Not Named/S/Edward & Norbourne Burkley/F/Dec 20/Born Dead/Celia/Temple C. Moor Overseer
Henry/S/Ira L. Thomas/M/Dec/Lock Jaw/9y 6m/Margarett/Ira L. Thomas Overseer
Richard Dyson/W/M/Sept 15/Typhoid Fever/30y/James & Sarah Dyson/Virginia A. Dyson Widow
Jack Ware/S/Henry M. Young's Est/M/Dec 30/Congestion of Brain/20y/Charlotte/H.M. Young Overseer
Not Named/S/Henry M. Young's Est/M/Dec 20/Smothered/15d/Aggy/Henry M. Young Overseer
Aggy/S/Wm R. Young's Est/F/Nov 1/Congestion of Brain//20y/Betsy/H.M. Young Adm of W.R.Y.
Catherine/S/Wm R. Young's Est/F/Nov 7/Congestion of Brain/13y/Milly/H.M. Young Adm of W.R.Y.
John F. Lewcord/W/M/Oct 30/Typhoid Fever/21y 8m/John F. & Mary Lewcord/Mary Hart Mother
Delilah Southworth/W/F/July 15/Consumption/48y/John & Betty Mason/Richard Southworth Husband/Levi W. Southworth Son
Richard Southworth/W/M/July 22/Deranged/55y/John & __ Southworth/Delilah Southworth Wife/ Levi Southworth Son
Eliz Ann/S/Robert Hudgins/F/Aug/Not Known/3m/Ann/Mary Mabile Friend
Anna/S/Jasper L. Cobbs/F/Aug/Inf Bowels/1y/Lucy/Jasper L. Cobbs Owner
No Named/S/Charles T. Farish/M/Oct 23/Not Known/__Lucy/Charles T. Farish Owner
Not Named/S/Charles T. Farish/F/Dec 20/Born Dead/Judy/Charles T. Farish Owner
Not Named/S/Jefferson Flippo/F/Mar 8/Smothered/2m/Matilda/Jefferson Flippo Owner
Not Named/S/Thos N. Welch/M/Apr 15/Not Known/15d/Fanny/Wm A. Pritchett Overseer
Not Named/S/Ruffin H. Coleman/F/Dec/Born Dead/Rose/R.H. Coleman Owner

Not Named/S/Ed Robert Dickinson/F/Mar/Not Known/__/Molly/Robert Dickinson Owner
James W. Terrell/W/M/Nov 2/Typhoid Fever/29y/James S. & Rachael Terrell/Unmarried/James S.
  Terrell Father
Not Named/S/Sarah R. Diggs/F/Jan/Born Dead/Charlotte/Sarah E. Diggs Owner
Not Named/S/Sarah R. Diggs/M/Jan/Not Known/1d/Charlotte/Sarah E. Diggs Owner
Not Named/S/Sarah R. Diggs/F/Jan/Not Known/2d/Charlotte/Sarah E. Diggs Owner
Mary/S/Sarah R. Diggs/F/Apr/Pneumonia/10y/Dinah/Sarah R. Diggs Owner
Henry/S/E.B. Coleman/M/Jan 10/Consumption/10y/Catherine/Elizabeth B. Coleman Owner
Lucy M. Moncure/W/F/Sept/Typhoid Fever/11y/William A. & __/Ledger Moncure Brother
Catherine S. Allen/W/F/Oct 20/Typhoid Fever/21y/Stephen & Jane Farish/Silas W. Allen Husband
Catherine/S/George Allen/F/Oct 20/Typhoid Fever/69y/Ruby/George Allen Owner
Robert/S/George Allen/M/June 28/Not Known/2m/Mary/George Allen Owner
Silby/S/Jno V. Keane/F/July/Deformed/10m/Catherine/Jno V. Keane Owner
Elizabeth/S/Albert G. Ware/F/Nov 14/Typhoid Fever/27y/Mary/A.G. Ware Owner
Francis C. Ware/W/M/Dec 10/Typhoid Fever/10y/Albert G. & Judith Ware/A.G. Ware Father
Buckner/S/Jos T. Collins Est/F/Oct/Typhoid Fever/15y/Mary/Jos T. Collins - Young Master
Jacob/S/Jos T. Collins Est/M/Jan 1/Croop/1y/Betty/Jos T. Collins - Young Master
Mary/S/Lucy R. Temple/F/June/Nervous Croup/32y/Betty/Curtis W. Durrett Friend
Simon/S/Lucy R. Temple/M/Sept/Drowned/23y/Betty/Curtis W. Durrett Friend
Maria/S/Wm F. Luck/F/Jan 23/Cold/2y/Charlotte/Wm F. Luck Owner
Ginny Richards James/W/F/June/__/1y 10m 18d/N. Richards & Martha L. James/N. Richards James
  Father
Not Named/S/Rachael Harris/F/June/Summer Complaint/2y/Harriett/W.W. Smith Friend
Amanda/S/Wm H. Farish/F/Oct/Typhoid Fever/22y/Clarah/Jane Farish Gdn for Son
Robert S. Farish/W/M/Oct 19/Typhoid Fever/26y 4m/Stephen & Jane Farish/Jane Farish Mother
Davy/S/Lindsey L. Terrell/M/Mar 22/Not Known/45y/Pauline/L.L. Terrell Master
Joseph/S/Napoleon P. Luck/M/Feb 22/Smothered/2m/Amanda/N.P. Luck Owner
Lucy/S/Napoleon P. Luck/F/Sept/Smothered/2y/Rose/N.P. Luck Owner
William/S/James P. Cobbs/M/Sept/Not Known/21d/Julia/James P. Cobbs Owner
John Wm/S/William B. Wiltshire/M/Aug/Not Known/10m/Martha Jane/Wm B. Wiltshire Owner
Samuel Coleman/W/M/Dec 3/Inf Bowels/82y/Samuel & __ Coleman/Mary Coleman Wife/James W.
  Coleman Son
William/S/Winston Atkinson/M/Oct 1/Typhoid Fever/15y/Charity/W. Atkinson Owner
Francis Austin Dyson/W/M/Dec 22/Typhoid Fever/25y/Alfred & Sarah Dyson/Unmarried/Sarah
  Dyson Mother
Burwell Hart/W/M/Apr 16/Rheumatism/62y/Peter & Susan Hart/Rachael Hart Widow
Not Named/S/John Chandler/M/June 3/Not Known/1d/Ginny/John Chandler Owner
Rosena/S/William Carter/F/Nov 1/Not Known/1m 1d/Patsy/William Carter Owner
Franky/S/William Carter/F/Sept/Old Age/60y/__/Wm Carter Owner
Paster/S/William Carter/F/Nov/Consumption/20y/Molly/Wm Carter Owner
Billy/S/William Carter/M/Aug/Abscess/23y/Nancy/Wm Carter Owner
Tinah/S/William Carter/F/Nov/Dysintery/60y/__/Wm Carter Owner
Hannah/S/William Carter/F/Sept/Typhoid Fever/11y/Fanny/Wm Carter Owner
John Thomas Hughes/W/M/June 11/Not Known/1y/John & Mary E. Hughes/Mary E. Hughes
  Mother
Henry Southworth/W/M/Feb 1/7y/Jos & Emily Southworth/Jos Southworth Father
Lucy Carey Ramsey/W/F/June/Not Known/2y/Wm P.C. & Fanny Ramsey/Wm P.C. Ramsey Father
Moses/Wm P.C. Ramsey/M/June/Pneumonia/55y/__/Wm P.C. Ramsey Owner

Silvia/S/Wm P.C. Ramsey/F/Apr/Not Known/6m/Dolly/Wm P.C. Ramsey Owner
Lamer/S/E.C. Chiles Est/S/Dec 21/Rheumatism/60y/__/E.C. Chiles Est Friend
William/S/Albert S. Hundley/M/May/Not Known/5y/Lucy/A.S. Hundley Owner
Philip/S/Albert S. Hundley/M/Aug 20/Measles/19y/Adaline/A.S. Hundley Owner
Wilton/S/Edmund West/M/July/__/2y/June/E. West Owner
Jerry/S/Geo B. Pollard/M/Jan/Pneumonia/1y 6m/Louise/Geo B. Pollard Owner
Not Named/S/James Duvall/M/Dec 20/Spasms/11m 15d/Jane/James Duvall Owner
Nimrod/S/Warner M. Mason/M/Sept/Typhoid Fever/53y/Patsy/W.M. Mason Owner
Abraham/S/Warner M. Mason/M/Sept/Typhoid Fever/48y/Winny/W.M. Mason Owner
Evelena/S/Warner M. Mason/F/Sept/Typhoid Fever/45y/Winny/W.M. Mason Owner
Not Named/S/Robert S. Luck/M/Jan/Thrash/5d/Malinda/R.S. Luck Owner
Not Named/S/Robert S. Luck/F/Jan/Thrash/8d/Malinda/R.S. Luck Owner
Not Named/S/Robert S. Luck/F/Thrash/12d/Melinda/Malinda/R.S. Luck Owner
Frances/S/Jno B. Cootes/F/Aug/Fits/35y/Matilda/R.S. Terrell Overseer
Sandy/S/Jno B. Cootes/M/Nov/Typhoid Fever/5y/Delia/R.S. Terrell Overseer
Betty Ann Coghill/W/F/Dec 23/Consumption/22y/Oliver & Martha Beazley/Thos B. Coghill Husband
Jerry/S/Obey Burruss/M/Feb 13/Bronchitis/2y/Mary Jane/O. Burruss Owner
Claibourne/S/Richd H. Woolfolk/M/July 12/Dropsy/55y/Rose/R.H. Woolfolk Owner
Robert/S/William C. Peatross/M/Mar/Spasms/12y/Judith/Wm C. Peatross Owner
Not Named/S/Wesley Wright/M/June 7/Known Known/5d/Jane/W. Wright Owner
Dick Clayton/S/Wesley Wright/M/June 18/Consumption/82y/__/W. Wright Owner
Aggy/S/Wesley Wright/F/July/Old Age/76/Judy/W. Wright Owner
Margarett/S/Wesley Wright/F/Sept/Not Known/1y 4m/Martha/W. Wright Owner
Willis/S/Ellett Wright/M/May/Not Known/61y/Violet/E. Wright Owner
Mary/S/Margaret & Sarah Dick/F/June 3/Consumption/25y/Maria/Margarett Dick Owner
George/S/Blueford Durrett/M/Sept/Whooping Cough/6y/Louise/B. Durrett Owner
Joe/S/Martha T. Ball/M/June/Cholera Infection/2y/Emily/Martha T. Ball Owner
Not Named/S/Edward P. Wood/M/Mar/Born Dead/Lucinda/E.P. Wood Owner
Not Named/S/Geo P. Luck/M/Dec 27/Not Known/__/Pudorah/Geo P. Luck Owner
Aaron/S/Garland Hargrave/M/Mar 1/__/__/Amy Maria/G. Hargrave Owner
Not Named/S/William Carter/M/Nov/Not Known/7d/Hannah/Wm Carter Owner
James/S/William Carter/M/June/Not Known/3m/Easter/Wm Carter Owner
Not Named/S/William Carter/F/Sept/Born Dead/Susan/Wm Carter Owner
Not Named/William Carter/M/Dec/Not Known/1m/Dorothy/Wm Carter Owner
Not Named/W/F/Feb 20/Not Known/2d/Wm A. & Mary E. Sutton/Jno Shepherd Friend
Not Named/S/Seth Campbell/F/July/Not Named/7d/Adeline/Seth Campbell Owner
Susanna Campbell/W/F/Aug 27/Not Known/66y/__/Seth Campbell Husband
Kissy/S/O.W. Sutton/F/May/Abscess/19y/Celina/O.W. Sutton Owner
Not Named/W/F/Sept 22/Born Dead/Wesley & Jane Wright/Wesley Wright Father
Edward Coleman/W/M/Oct/Typhoid Fever/20y/Saml & Mary Coleman/Unmarried/J.W. Coleman Brother
Elizabeth H. Sutton/W/F/Aug/Not Known/27y/Clayton & Elizabeth Coleman/Henry C. Sutton Husband
Not Named/W/M/July 2/Not Known/15d/Henry C. & Elizabeth H. Sutton/H.C. Sutton Father
John J. Baughn/W/M/Sept/d.Fredericksburg/Consumption/25y/John Baughn/Unmarried/ H.C. Sutton Friend
Eldred Baughn/W/M/Nov/d.Fredericksburg/Typhoid Fever/19y/John Baughn/Unmarried/

H.C. Sutton Friend

1862

James/S/Richard F. Broaddus/M/Dec/Diptheria/2y/Henritte/Richard F. Broaddus Master
Wesley? Vaughan/W/M/Diptheria/11y/Richd & Sarah Vaughan/Richd Vaughan Father
Not Known/S/M/__/Diptheria/2m/Rebecca/Ro W. Cole Guardian
Not Known/S/F/__/__/1m 10d/Caroline/Ro W. Cole Guardian
No Name/S/M/__/__/6d/Sally/Ro W. Cole Guardian
No Name/S/Robt Broaddus/F/__/1m 1d/Rachel/Robt Broaddus Master
Eugene L. Broaddus/W/M/Apr 25/__/__/Robt & Letitia E. Broaddus/Practitiour of M.D./
  Unmarried/Robt Broaddus Father
H.L. Whitel/W/F/Sept/Diptheria/1y 6m/Jno E. & Sophia Whitel/Jno E. Whitel Father
William/S/Jno E. Whitel/M/Sept/Diptheria/7y/Lavinia/Jno E. Whitel Master
Catharine/S/Jno E. Whitel/F/Sept/Diptheria/6m/Mary/Jno E. Whitel Master
Sept/No Name/S/Jno E. Whitel/Sept/Diptheria/4m/Mary/Jno E. Whitel Master
Evelina/S/Ro H. Upshaw/Dec/Hooping Cough/4y 1m 1d/Louisa/Ro H. Upshaw Master
Kitty/S/Thos Broaddus/__/F/__/2y 1m 1d/Margarett/Thos Broaddus Master
Dicey Martin/W/F/Oct/__/72y/Jos & Dicey Loren/LeRoy Martin Husband
Thos L. Martin/W/M/Oct/__/28y/LeRoy & Dicey Martin/Farmer/LeRoy Martin Father
Malinda/S/Corl C. Broaddus/F/__/Burnt to Death/Jane/Corl C. Broaddus Master
No Name/S/S. Fitzhugh/F/__/__/1d 3m/Hannah/S. Fitzhugh Master
Rachel/S/Wm B. Gravatt/F/Jan/__/90y/__/Wm B. Gravatt Master
Frances E. Lyall/W/F/Apr/Child Bed Fever/27y/Jas & Eliza Watkins/Jas. M. Lyall Husband
Emily/S/Jno L. Motley/Dec/Chro Dis/4y 5m/__/Jno L. Motley Master
Jim/S/Molly Boulware/M/Dec/Scarlet Fever/15y/Fanny/Molly Boulware Mistress
Virginia Southworth/W/F/Nov/Diptheria/10y/Woodfd & Margt Southworth/Woodfd
  Southworth Father
Frances Southworth/W/F/Oct/Diptheria/12y/Woodfd & Margt Southworth/Woodfd
  Southworth Father
Samuel Southworth/W/M/Aug/Diptheria/9y/Woodfd & Margt Southworth/Woodfd
  Southworth Father
Bettie Southworth/W/F/Aug/Diptheria/7y/Woodfd & Margt Southworth/Woodfd
  Southworth Father
No Name/S/And Broaddus/F/Sept/__/__/Bettie/And Broaddus Master
Thos Marshall/W/M/Sept 17/Killed at Sharpsburg/18y/Geo & [illeg] Marshall/Geo Marshall Father
Jane Houston/W/M/Feb/Consumption/58y/Jas & Mary Houston/J.R.P. Houston Brother
Walker/S/O.W. Harris/M/Feb/Consumption/12y/Sophia/O.W. Harris Master
Battaillel/S/Phil Green/M/Dec/Diptheria/2y/Frances/Phil Green Master
Dallas/S/Phil Green/M/Jan/Diptheria/5y/Sally/Phil Green Master
Jas E. Ennis/W/M/Apr/Hooping Cough/11m/Jas & Columbia Ennis/Jas E. Ennis Father
Hugh Allen/W/M/Nov 22/__/2d/C. E. & Ann M. Allen/Mechanic/Chris L. Allen Father
Thomas/S/Jos W. Ray/M/Dec/__/90y/__/Jos W. Ray - Young Master
Littleton Goodwin/W/M/Oct/Pneumonia/24y/Farmer/Little & C.A.M. Goodwin/Elrd Chiles
  Father-in-Law
No Name/S/Julia A.S. Andrews/M/Jul/__/1m/Jane/Julia A.S. Andrews Mistress
Charity/S/F.H. Broaddus/F/Jan/Diptheria/5y/Lydia/F.H. Broaddus Master
Annie/S/F.H. Broaddus/F/Jan/Diptheria/6y/Sarah/F.H. Broaddus Master

Maria/S/Wm Andrews/F/Jan/Diptheria/16y/Molley/Wm Andrews Master
Emanuel Gurst/W/M/Feb/Pneumonia/9m/Henry & Bettie Gurst/Henry Gurst Father
Hannah B. Brooks/W/F/Apr 2/__/__/Robt & Cathd Brooks/Hiram A. Brooks Husband
No Name/W/F/Dec/Heart Dis/43y/Bur [Burton] B. & Ellen W. Wright/Farmer/Bur B. Wright Father
E.C. Roper/W/F/Sept/Inf Brain/2m/Wm & E.C. Roper/b. Green Co/Wm W. Roper Father and Practitinur of M.D.
Lewis Dollins/W/M/Mar/Typhoid Fever/30y/Yelvin & Peggy Dollins/Farmer/Mrs. Chandler Mother-in-Law
Aunice Jones/W/F/Sept/__/8y/Jos T. & Nancy Jones/Jos T. Jones Father and Shoemaker
Walker/S/B.R. Clark Est/M/Sept/Diptheria/10y/Jane/Virgl A. Clark - Young Mistress
Martha/S/B.R. Clark Est/F/Sept/Diptheria/5y/Jane/Virgl Clark - Young Mistress
Adison/S/B.A. Clark Est/__/Sept.Diptheria/2y/Jane/Virgl Clark - Young Mistress
George-Anna/S/Geo Mahon/F/July/Diptheria/__/Betty/Geo Mahon Master
Albert/S/Geo Mahon/M/Feb/Measles/__/Betty/Geo Mahon Master
Burton/S/Geo Mahon/M/Aug/Diptheria/__/Betty/Geo Mahon Master
No Name/S/Geo Mahon/M/Aug/Diptheria/__/Courtney/Geo Mahon Master
Jordan Houston/W/M/July 24/Typhoid Fever/32y/Henry & FrancesHouston/Farmer/Mary J.E. Houston Sister
Jas D. Carter/W/M/Sept 17/d.Maryland/Killed at Sharpsburg/22y/Rd & Jane Carter/Farmer/ Mrs. Carter Mother
Richd Carter/W/M/Jan/Pneumonia/48y/__/Mrs. Carter Mother
Sarah Taylor/W/M/Nov/__/11y/Robt & Armaginda Taylor/Robt Taylor Father
No Name/S/Thos L. Jones/F/Apr/__/3m/Sally/Thos L. Jones Master
John G. Carter/W/M/Dec/Typhoid Fever/25y/Wash & Martha Carter/Martha Carter Mother
David/S/Franky Boulware/M/July/__/11y/Martha/Franky Boulware Mistress
Ellen/S/Wm T. Jenkins/F/Aug/__/__/Lucy/Mrs. Jenkins Mistress
Archie/S/Geo W. Trice/F/__/Diptheria/8y/Judy/Geo W. Trice Master
Charlotte/S/Geo W. Trice/F/__/Diptheria/1y/Julia/Geo W. Trice Master
Lucy/S/Geo W. Trice/F/__/Hooping Cough/10y/Sallie/Geo W. Trice Master
Lucy Ann/S/Geo W. Trice/F/__/__/1y/Bettie/Geo W. Trice Master
Sally/S/Frances Powers/F/Feb/Child Bed/26y/Minnie/Frances Powers Mistress
David Sternes/W/M/July 17/__/18y/F.G. & Eliz Sternes/Farmer/F.G. Sternes Father
No Name/W/F/Mar/__/28d/Leo & Mary Guthright/d.Port Royal/Leo Guthright Father
Wm W. Humphries/W/M/Aug 10/Diptheria/24y/Ro W. & Susan H. Humphries/b.Port Royal/ Overseer/Ro W. Humphries Father
Wm H. Loven/W/M/__/__/9m/Lindsey & E.A. Loven/Lindsay Loven Father
George/S/Chas Loven Est/M/__/__/5y/Caroline/Solomon Loving Neighbor
Saberna Dollins/Free B/F/__/Scarlet Fever/14y/Remington & Mary Dollins/ Remington Dollins Father and Shoemaker
Edward Powers/W/M/__/__/20y/Thomas & Frances Powers/Frances Powers Mother [Edward S. Powers, born 1842, was killed in battle 1862, Co E, 47th Regt, Va Vol, C.S.A.]
Chas Powers/W/M/__/[killed in battle with brother Edward]/25y/Thomas & Frances Powers/ Frances Powers Mother
Lucinda/S/Shaddock [illeg]/F/__/__/__/Chas W. Jones Neighbor
Martha/S/Phil Gatewood/F/__/__/2y/Caroline/Phil Gatewood Master
Loury S. Elliott/W/M/__/__/23y/Berryman & Caroline Elliott/Farmer/Berryman Elliott Father
Fanny Elliott/W/F/__/__/10y/Berryman & Caroline Elliott/Berryman Elliott Father

Oliver/S/Thos C. Rixey's Est/M/__/__/6m/Eliza/Thos E. Rixey's Est Mistress
Edgar Mahon/W/M/Aug/__/2y/Alex & Kitty Mahon/Alex Mahon Father
Ann/S/Keeling Rowe/F/Jan/Consumption/40y/Joyce/Keeling Rowe Master
Thos A. Green/W/M/Apr/Liver Dis/68y/Geo & Bettie Green/Farmer/Jno F. Green Son
Gabriel/S/Edward S. Motley/M/Jan/109y/__/Edward J.[sic] Motley Master
Thornton/S/Thos F. Green Est/M/Sept/__/1y/Milly/Jno F. Green - Y Master
Sally/S/Thos F. Green Est/F/Sept/__/1y/__/Jno F. Green - Y Master
Bettie Chapman/W/F/Dec/Scarlet Fever/3y 6m/Jas & Ann E. Chapman/Jas Chapman Father
Wm C. Samuel/W/M/Aug/Diptheria/8y/Thos L. & Frances A. Samuel/Thos L. Samuel Father
Carter Johnson/Free B/M/Feb.Diptheria/8y/Danl & Polly Johnson/Daniel Johnson Father
Jane Johnson/Free B/F/Feb/Diptheria/4y/Danl & Polly Johnson/Daniel Johnson Father
Martha Whiticoe/W/F/May/Diptheria/3y/Edm & Rebecca Whiticoe/Edm Whiticoe Father
No Name/W/F/May/Diptheria/1d/Edm & Rebecca Whiticoe/Edm Whiticoe Father
Battaillel Loven/W/M/Jul/Measles/28y/John & Patsy Loven/John Loven Father
Polly Wright/W/F/Jan/__/60y/John & Maley Wright/John Wright Son
Soloman Loven Jr/W/M/__/__/30y/__/John Wright Neighbor
Brookin Taylor/W/M/Mar/Shott/72y/Wm & Rebecca Taylor/Temple H. Taylor Son
Sally Sale/W/F/__/__/19y/__/John B. Puller Son-in-Law
Andrew/S/Henry M. Alsop/__/Diptheria/20y/Milly/Henry M. Alsop Master
Elizabeth/S/Henry M. Alsop/F/__/Diptheria/13y/Rose/Henry M. Alsop Master
Not Known/S/Henry M. Alsop/F/__/Diptheria/5y/Martha/Henry M. Alsop Master
Ursley/S/Henry M. Alsop/F/__/Diptheria/15y/Rosey/Henry M. Alsop Master
Thornton/S/Henry M. Alsop/M/__/Small Pox40y/Ursley/Henry M. Alsop Master
No Name/S/Henry M. Alsop/F/__/__/2y/America/Henry M. Alsop Master
William/S/Bandridge Lumpkin/M/__/__/70y/__/Jno B. Pullen Neighbor
Not Known/S/Bandridge Lumpkin/F/__/__/27y/Phoebe/Jno B. Pullen Neighbor
Patsy Lumpkin/W/F/__/__/70y/__/Jno B. Pullen Neighbor
Lucy/S/Richd A. Pullen/F/__/__/4m/Louisa/Richd A. Pullen Master
Edwd Green/W/M/Nov 9/Consumption/67y/Geo & Eliz Green/Farmer/Ro G. Green Son
Emma/S/Ed Green Est/__/Typhoid Fever/6y/Polly/Ro G. Green - Y Master
John/S/Mary E. Wright/M/__/__/3m/__/Mary E. Wright Mistress
Jim/S/Richd Buckner/M/__/Diptheria/7y/Mary/Richd Buckner Master
Matilda/S/Richd Buckner/F/__/Diptheria/9y/Polly/Richd Buckner Master
Not Known/S/Richd Buckner/M/__/Diptheria/2y/Emily/Richd Buckner Master
Not Known/S/Richd Buckner/F/__/Diptheria/2y/Louisa/Richd Buckner Master
Thos King/W/M/Sept/Diptheria/4m/Thos S & Eliz King/Thos S. King Father
Ellen/S/Ro B. Walker/F/Sept/__/__/Rebecca/Ro B. Walker Master
Lucy/S/Ro B. Walker/F/__/__/__/Nancy/Ro B. Walker Master
Martha/S/Eugene Baker/F/Sept/__/8d/Phebe/Eugene Baker Master
Maria/S/John Conway/F/__/Scarlet Fever/6y/Hannah/John Conway Master
Geo/S/John Conway/M/__/Scarlet Fever/4y/Hannah/John Conway Master
Saml P. Farmer/W/M/Dec/Scrofula/4y/Wm P.(mechanic) & Sarah Farmer/Saml P. Farmer
  Gr Father
Lewis/S/Lawr Battaile Est/M/__/Scrofula/2y/Louisa/Robt Jesse Neighbor
Winston/S/Lawr Battaile/M/__/__/2m/Huldah/Robt Jesse Neighbor
Anna/S/Lawr Battaile/F/__/__/__/Susan/Robt Jesse Neighbor
Willie/S/Ro Jesse/M/__/Scarlet Fever/3y/Catherine/Robt Jesse Master
Billy/S/Ro Jesse/M/__/Scarlet Fever/2y/Dolly/Robt Jesse Master

James/S/Ro Jesse/M/__/Pneumonia/2y/Nancy/Robt Jesse Master
Warren/S/Jno R. Baylor/M/__/__/32y/Mary/Jno R. Baylor Master
William/S/Jno R. Baylor/M/__/Hooping Cough/4y/Mary/Jno R. Baylor Master
William Self/W/M/Sept 17/d.Maryland/Killed in Battle/37y/Vincent Self/Farmer/Mrs. Self Widow
Kerle Farinholt/W/M/Dec/Diptheria/27y/William & Maria Farinholt/Clerkship/Robt Farinholt Brother
Waller/S/Jno Woolfolk/M/__/__/__/Isabella/Jno Woolfolk Master
Randolph/S/Jno Woolfolk/M/__/__/__/Charlotte/Jno Woolfolk Master
Dunmore/S/Jno Woolfolk/M/__/__/__/Sally/Jno Woolfolk Master
Chas/S/Jno Woolfolk/M/__/__/__/Martha/Jno Woolfolk Master
Thornton/S/Jno Woolfolk/M/__/__/__/Lucinda/Jno Woolfolk Master
Pichegru Woolfolk/W/M/Jan/Heart Disease/67y/Chas H. & Fanney/Mrs. Woolfolk Widow
McKensie/S/Thos M. Kidd/M/__/__/22y/Eve/Thos M. Kidd Master
Edward Houston/W/M/__/__/19y/Sears & Lucy Houston/Sears Houston Father
Wahala/S/Edmd Salie/F/__/Diptheria/13y/Harriett/Judson Salie - Y Master
Walinda/S/Jno Gouldin/F/__/__/__/Mary/Jas P. Gouldin - Y Master
Peter/S/Jno Gouldin/M/__/Diptheria/__/Leagie/Jas P. Gouldin - Y Master
Not Known/S/Jno Gouldin/F/__/__/__/Jane/Jas P. Gouldin - Y Master
Emily/S/Peter R. Thornton/F/__/Heart Disease/35y/Betsy/P.R. Thornton Master
Gricie/S/Peter R. Thornton/F/__/__/75y/__/P.R. Thornton Master
Piney/S/Peter R. Thornton/F/__/Diptheria/__/__/P.R. Thornton Master
Walker/S/Peter R. Thornton/M/__/Diptheria/__/__/P.R. Thornton Master
Robt/S/Peter R. Thornton/M/__/Diptheria/__/Emily/P.R. Thronton Master
Willis/S/P.R. Thornton/M/__/Diptheria/__/Nancy/P.R. Thornton Master
Not Known/S/P.R. Thornton/__/__/__/__/Nancy/P.R. Thornton Master
Not Known/S/Jas A. Shaddock/M/__/__/3m/Ann/Jas A. Shaddock Master
Geo/S/Jas A. Shaddock/M/__/Typhoid Fever/38y 3m/Jane/Jas A. Shaddock Master
Larcellus P. Turner/W/M/__/Typhoid Fever/18y/John W. & Mary Turner/Jno W. Turner Father
Thos Marshall/W/M/Feb/Diptheria/8y/Jas & Mary Marshall/Jas Marshall Father
No Name/S/Judith Coghill/M/__/__/5d/Sarah/Mrs. Boulware Neighbor
Eda/S/Mrs. Boulware/F/__/__/28y/Lucy/Mrs. Boulware Mistress
Harriett/S/Richd H. Garrett/F/__/Pneumonia/60y//Judith/R. H. Garrett Master
Ro H. Parker/W/M/June 28/Measles/25y/Ro P. & Sarah Parker/Mrs. Parker Widow
Sarah C. Parker/W/F/June 26/Measles/11m/Ro H & Martha Parker/Mrs. Parker Mother
Bettie/S/Ro H. Parker/F/__/Measles/4y/Mary/Mrs. Parker Mistress
Eslie Anderson/W/F/__/__/20y/Sydney B. Anderson/Smith R.F. Whitel Neighbor
Henry/S/Sydney B. Anderson/M/Aug/Diptheria/2y/Emily/S.B. Anderson Mistress
Samuel/S/Smith R.F. Whitel/M/Apr/__/42y/S & R Whitel Master
Billy/S/Thos Motley/M/Jan/__/2m/Mary/Hannah Motley Mistress
Alfred/S/Ann W. Thornton/M/__/__/10y/Lucy/Mrs. Thornton Mistress
Hellen/S/Ann W. Thornton/F/__/__/6y/Lucy/Mrs. Thornton Mistress
No Name/S/Ann W. Thornton/M/__/__/15d/Lucy/Mrs. Thornton Mistress
Chas F. Hicks/W/M/__/Scarlet Fever/15y/B.H. & Sarah A. Hicks/Benj H. Hicks Father & Miller
Virginia E. Hicks/W/F/__/Scarlet Fever/7y/B.H. & Sarah A. Hicks/Benj H. Hicks Father
Chas H. Hicks/W/M/__/Scarlet Fever/3y/B.H. & Sarah A. Hicks/Benj H. Hicks Father
Coleman/S/H.B. Whitel/M/__/__/__/Agnes/H.B. Whitel Master
Willis/S/Harvey B. Whitel/M/__/__/__/Jane/H.B. Whitel Master

Chas/S/Harvey B. Whitel/M/__/__/__/__/H.B. Whitel Master
Eliza/S/Harvey B. Whitel/F/__/__/__/Eliza/H.B. Whitel Master
Emma V. Whitel/W/F/__/Brain Fever/4y/H.B. & Ann E. Whitel/H.B. Whitel Father
Jas H. Loury/W/M/__/Brain Fever/8y/Albert & Sarah A. Loury/Albert Loury Father
Nannie D. Loury/W/F/__/Scarlet Fever/6y/Albert & Mary F. Loury/Albert Loury Father
Ro Anderson/W/M/__/d.Washington City/Brain Fever/25y/Benj & Martha B. Anderson/
  Benj Anderson Father
No Name/S/Jos A. Chandler/F/__/Scarlet Fever/1m/Pleasants/Jos A. Chandler Master
Charles/S/Jos A. Chandler/M/__/Scarlet Fever/5y/Pleasants/ Jos A. Chandler Master
Charles/S/Jos A. Chandler/M/__/Scarlet Fever/__/Fannie/Jos A. Chandler Master
Not Known/S/__/__/__/__/Hannah/Law A. Coghill Neighbor
Louisa/S/Geo K. Taylor/F/__/__/__/Jane/Geo K. Taylor Master
Eliza/S/Geo K. Taylor/F/__/__/__/Jane/Geo K. Taylor Master
Wm H. Carneal/W/M/Dec 20/Pneumonia/27y/Tillman & Sarah Carneal/Tillman Carneal Father
Adeline/S/Ro B. Tunstall/F/__/Scarlet Fever/Sarah/Ro B. Tunstall Master
Hillgard/S/Wm Dickinson/M/__/__/16y/__/Wm Dickinson Master
Bonie/S/Wm Dickinson/F/__/__/1y 1m/Sarah/Wm Dickinson Master
Richd Saunders/W/M/Jul/__/25y/Not Known/R.C. Yates Neighbor
Robt/S/M.T. Campbell/Jan/Pneumonia/25y/Alice/M.T. Campbell Master
Not Known/S/C.H. Boutwell/M/__/__/__/Margt/C.H. Boutwell Mistress
Not Known/S/C.H. Boutwell/F/__/__/__/Patsy/C.H. Boutwell Mistress
Not Known/S/C.H. Boutwell/M/__/__/__/Milly/C.H. Boutwell Mistress
No Name/S/Wm Page Est/F/__/__/__/Caroline/Wm Page Jr - Y Master
Simon Gouldin/W/M/June/Camp Fever/40y/Richd & Nancy Gouldin/Julia Gouldin Sister
Delia/S/G. Samuel/F/__/__/__/Fanny/G. Samuel Master
Oscar Beazley/W/M/Sept 17/d. Sharpsburg/Killed in Battle/22y/Wm & Nancy Beazley/Wm
  Beazley Father
Sophia/S/Susan Noel/F/__/Consumption/70y/__/Susan Noel Mistress
Jane Noel/W/F/Aug/Diptheria/12y/John & Susan Noel/Susan Noel Mother
Thos Farmer/W/M/Aug/Dropsey/50y/Lewis & Susan Farmer/Farmer[by occupation]/
  Rem A. Farmer Son
Geo/S/Ernest Harvey/M/__/__/3m/Martha/Jno G. Martin Guardian
Not Known/S/M.A.C. Junny/__/__/__/Patsy/Mrs. Gray Neighbor
Margaretta/S/Eliz Peyton/F/__/__/22y/Winney/Rand Peyton - Y Master
Louisa/S/John A. Miller/F/__/__/__/Rebecca/Jno A. Miller Master
Ellen/S/John A. Miller/F/__/__/__/Rebecca/Jno A. Miller Master
Mary/S/John A. Miller/F/__/__/__/Rebecca/Jno A. Miller Master
Peter/S/Jno T. Boutwell/M/__/__/8d/Ellen/Jno T. Boutwell Master
Isaac/S/Jno T. Boutwell/M/__/__/70y/__/Jno T. Boutwell Master
Bobby/S/Jno T. Boutwell/M/__/__/55y/Betsy/Jno T. Boutwell Master
Not Known/S/Jno T. Boutwell/F/__/__/4m/Lavina/Jno T. Boutwell Master
John/S/Apolo Boutwell/M/__/__/14d/Lavina/Apolo Boutwell Master
Not Known/S/Apolo Boutwell/F/__/__/2d/Mary/Apolo Boutwell Master
Polly/S/E.G. Andrews/F/__/Burnt/10y/Jane/Mrs. Andrews Mistress
Jas Carneal/W/M/Apr/Suicide/63y/__/John Riddle Neighbor
Emily/S/Silas G/ Garrett/__/Typhoid Fever/21y/Hannah/Silas G. Garrett Master
John McDaniel/W/M/__/__/25y/__/Wm F. McDaniel
Washington/S/Dan Pitts/M/__/Diptheria/12y/Rachel/Dan Pitts Owner

Ann/S/Jas Jones Est/F/__/Pneumonia/25y/Clary/Thos Jones - Y Master
Randolph/S/Jas Jones Est/M/__/__/15y/Clary/Thos Jones - Y Master
Ned/S/Jas Jones Est/M/__/Disentary/5y/Ann/Thos Jones - Y Master
Susan/S/Sam Gordon/F/__/__/__/Mary Ann/Sam Gordon Master
Fitzhugh/S/Sam Gordon/M/__/__/__/Elizabeth/Sam Gordon Master
No Name/S/Sam Gordon/F/__/__/__/Emiline/Sam Gordon Master
Fred/S/Sam Gordon/M/__/__/__/Fanny/Sam Gordon Master
Bob/S/Wm P. Taylor/M/__/Pneumonia/70y/Phillis/Wm P. Taylor Master
Henry/S/Wm P. Taylor/M/__/Heart Disease/45y/Nancy/Wm P. Taylor Master
John/S/Wm P. Taylor/M/__/Pneumonia/50y/Lucy/Wm P. Taylor Master
Gabriel/S/Ro G. Holloway Est/M/__/__/7m/Eliza/Ro G. Holloway Master
Barnett/S/Ro G. Holloway Est/M/__/__/__/Sally/R.G. Holloway Master
Louise Farinholt/W/F/July 6/__/__/Wm H. & S.E. Farinholt/Wm H. Farinholt Father
Frank/S/Jas S. Barbee/M/__/__/25y/Jane/Jas S. Barbee Master
Not Known/S/Wm R. Bernard/M/__/__/50y/__/Wm R. Bernard Master
James Edwards/W/M/Sept/__/50y/E. & Merril Edwards/Phil Gatewood Neighbor
Edmd Garrett/W/M/Sept/Typhoid Fever/25y/Thos & Patsy Garrett/H.A. Brooks Neighbor
Royal Eubanks/W/M/Oct/Typhoid Fever/30y/James & Nancy Eubanks/Mary Eubanks Widow
Rufus Ennis/W/M/May/Typhoid Fever/ 35y/Wm & Sally Ennis/Mrs. Self Neighbor
B.T. Barlow/W/M/__/Typhoid Fever/25y/Wm & Mary Barlow/Wm Barlow Father
David/Free B/M/__/__/50y/W. Washington/Servant [informant]
Atway/Free B/M/__/__/15y/W. Washington/Servant [informant]
Richd L. Carneal/W/M/May/d.Hanover Co/Camp Fever/25y/James Carneal/Jas Carneal Father
John Carneal/W/M/May/d.Hanover Co/Camp Fever/23y/James Carneal/Jas Carneal Father
Wm Houston/W/M/__/__/20y/Richd & Nancy Houston/Richd Houston Father
Not Known/S/Mary E. Saunders/M/__/__/__/Sally/Mary E. Saunders Mistress
No Name/S/Wm W. Broaddus/M/__/__/__/Ellen/Wm W. Broaddus Master
Peyton Rollins/W/M/__/__/70y/__/Henry McCally Neighbor
Peter Fortune/Free B/M/__/__/25y/__/__
McKensie Gray/W/M/__/d.Winchester/__/50y/__
Woodfd Gray/W/M/May/d.Hanover Co/__/23y/McKensie & Polly Gray/Polly Gray Mother
Riley Gouldman/W/M/June/__/50y/__/Edw Gouldman Son
Robt Gouldman/W/M/May/Camp Fever/20y/Riley Gouldman/Edw Gouldman Brother
Wilbon W. Pitts/W/M/Sept/Camp Fever/22y/Willis & Matilda Pitts/Willis Pitts Father
Evelina/S/Willis Pitts/F/__/45y/__/Willis Pitts Master
No Name/W/M/Apr 27/__/9m/R.H. & F.B. Garrett/R.H. Garrett Father
Mary Jane/S/F. Fitzhugh Est/F/__/__/__/Judith/Mrs. Fitzhugh Mistress
Matilda/S/Richd Buckner/F/__/Diptheria/9y/Polly/R. Buckner Master
Jim/S/Richd Buckner/M/__/Diptheria/7y/Nancy/Richd Buckner Master
John/S/Richd Buckner/M/__/Diptheria/18y/Betty/Richd Buckner Master
Peter/S/John Gouldin/M/__/__/1m 6d/__/Jno F. Gouldin - Y Master
Lucy/S/Mary E. Saunders/F/__/__/__/Lucy/M.E. Saunders Mistress
Major Samuel/W/M/__/Camp Fever/19y/James & Phebe Samuel/Phebe Samuel Mother
Wm W. Taylor/W/M/__/Camp Fever/46y/Thos & Ann Taylor/Nancy Taylor Wife
W.T. Taylor/W/M/__/Camp Fever/25y/Benj Taylor/Mrs. Greenstreet Mother-in-Law
John W. Puller/W/M/Sept 17/d.Maryland/Killed in Battle/23y/Jas & M.A. Puller/Mary A. Puller Mother
Geo W. Gravatt/W/M/__/Camp Fever/24y/John & Nancy Gravatt/John Gravatt Father

Jeff Richerson/Free/M/__/__/27y/Caty/Thos Richerson Bro
Eld R. Sorrell/W/M/__/Consumption/30y/John & Ann Sorrell/A.R. Monday Neighbor
Wm A. Saunders/W/M/__/d.Maryland/Killed in Battle/27y/Wm A. & M.E. Saunders/ Mary E. Saunders Mother
Richd Savage/Free/M/May/__/22y/Richard Savage/Rand. Peyton Neighbor
Jas M. Shaddock/W/M/May/Camp Fever/30y/__/Jas A.L. Saunders Neighbor
Wm Seamer/W/M/__/__/22y/__/Lew W. Garrett Neighbor
Mor [Mordecai] E. Taylor/W/M/June/d.Richmond/Died of Wound/ 27y/Major & Nancy Taylor/Mary F. Taylor Widow
Eliza A. Taylor/W/M/June/Consumption/60y/__/Geo K. Taylor Son
Arthur Welch/Free/M/__/22y/Lang Welch/Lewis W. Garrett Neighbor
John Carter/Free/M/__/__/24y/Billy Carter/Lewis W. Garrett Neighbor
Levi W. Edmondson/W/M/May/__/70y/__/Major Taylor Neighbor
Not Known/S/D.C. DeJarnett/__/__/__/Louisa/D.C. DeJarnett Master
Phill/S/D.C. DeJarnett/M/__/__/__/Martha/D.C. DeJarnett Master
Jim/S/D.C. DeJarnett/M/__/__/__/__/Martha/D.C. DeJarnett Master
Ann/S/Geo T. Burruss/F/Apr/__/19y/Ann/Geo T. Burruss Master
Cath/S/Geo T. Burruss/F/Sept/__/21y/Ann/Geo T. Burruss Master
Beverly/S/Geo T. Burruss/M/__/__/2m/Ann/Geo T. Burruss Master
Wilson/S/Geo T. Burruss/M/__/__/8d/Catherine/Geo T. Burruss Master
No Name/S/Lucy A. Garrett/__/__/Diptheria/3y/Nancy/Lucy A. Garrett Mistress
Maria/S/Jas H. Garrett/F/__/Diptheria/5m/Marcella/Mrs Garrett Mistress
Elmira/S/Jas H. Garrett/F/__/Diptheria/12d/Esther/Mrs Garrett Mistress
Not Known/S/Thos R. Dew/F/__/__/2d/Charlotte/Thos R. Dew Master
No Name/S/Gray Boulware/M/__/__/9m/Roberta/Gray Boulware Master
Lucy/S/Gray Boulware/F/__/__/__/Sally/Gray Boulware Master
Griffin/S/Gray Boulware/M/May 4/__/22y/Harriett/Gray Boulware Master
Lucy/S/Gray Boulware/F/__/Scarlet Fever/4m/Sarah/Gray Boulware Master
Hattie/S/Gray Boulware/F/Dec/__/29y/Lucy/Gray Boulware Master
William/S/Gray Boulware/M/July/__/2y/Sarah/Gray Boulware Master
Andrew L. Beazley/W/M/June/d.Henrico/Camp Fever/30y/E.J. & S.A. Beazley/Robt Gatewood Neighbor
Ruffin/S/Jno D. Butler/M/Feb/Dropsy/40y/Clary/John D. Butler Master
Cynthia/S/Jno D. Butler/F/Feb/Consumption/60y/__/John D. Butler Master
Rebecca/S/Jno D. Butler/F/Feb/__/18y/Pauley/John D. Butler Master
Titus/S/Lucy Kidd/M/Nov/Typhoid Fever/22y/Eliza/Lucy Kidd Mistress
John Sorrell/W/M/__/Camp Fever/25y/Jas Sorrell/Mrs Dew Neighbor
Jacobs/S/Anne Samuel/M/Sept/d.Richmond/Typhoid Fever/30y/Cynthia/Ann Samuel Mistress
James/S/R.F. Streshley/M/Jan/Worm Fever/3y/Polly/Richd F. Streshley Master
Lawson/S/R.F. Streshley/M/Jan/Worm Fever/3y/Alice/Richard F. Streshley Master
Major Thomas/W/M/Aug/Camp Fever/27y/Richd & Matilda Thomas/Richard F. Streshley Neighbor
Benjamin Thomas/W/M/July/Camp Fever/20y/Richd & Matilda Thomas/Richard F. Streshley Neighbor
Sampson/S/Salley Kingsly/M/Apr/__/40y/Phebe/Richard F. Streshley
Richd Carneal/W/M/June/d.Ashland/Measles/27y/Jas & Polly Carneal/Jas Carneal Father
John Carneal/W/M/June/d.Ashland/__/19y/Jas & Polly Carneal/Jas Carneal Father
Aley/S/Jesse L. Cobb/F/Feb/Old Age/70y/Jesse L. Cobb Master

Judy/S/Mary C. Corbin Est/F/Apr/Consumption/30y/Sally/Wm F. Young Overseer
Clementine/S/Mary C. Corbin Est/F/Aug/Not Known/2y/Willianna/Wm S. Young Overseer
Not Named/S/Mary C. Corbin Est/M/June/Cholera Infantum/10d/Louisa/Wm S. Young Overseer
Not Named/S/Mary C. Corbin Est/F/Sept/Cholera Infantum/2d/Isabella/Wm S. Young Overseer
[illeg]age/S/Mary C. Corbin Est/M/Oct/Typhoid Fever/6y/Catherine/Wm S. Young Overseer
[illeg]iz/S/John Chandler/M/Dec 1/Not Known/2d/Lucy/John Chandler Master
Wesley/S/Ruffin H. Coleman/M/May/Dropsy/1y/Ellen/Ruffin H. Coleman Master
Maria Carr/W/F/Jan/Gutrid Sore Throat/15y/John & Martha Carr/John Carr Father
Lizzy/S/Fitzhugh Catlett/F/Dec/Congestive Chill/2y/Fitzhugh Catlett Master
Patsy/S/Fitzhugh Catlett/F/June/Typhoid Fever/6y/Louise/Fitzhugh Catlett Master
Arthur/S/Catharine Collins/M/June/Pneumonia/1y/Jane/Catharine Collins Mistress
[illeg]M. Bougard Carter/W/M/July 13/Scarlet Fever/6y 6m/N. Hay & Emily Carter/N. Hay
  Carter Father
George/S/Mary Coghill/M/Jan 15/Typhoid Fever/28y/Maria/Mary Coghill Mistress
[John] B. Cox/W/M/Dec 6/d.Near Fredericksburg/Shot in Battle/40y/James & Catherine
  Cox/Wheel Wright[occupation]/Louisa S. Cox Wife
Not Named/S/Hugh Chandler/M/July/Brain Dead/__/Fanny/Hugh Chandler Master
[Cor]delia Collins/W/F/Sept 20/Typhoid Fever/26y/Lewis & Peggy Madison/Christopher Collins
  Husband
[Joan]na Chiles/W/F/July 20/Consumption/23y/John & Mary Peatross/James Chiles, dec'd
  [Husband]/Richard W. Peatross
Abraham/S/John B. Coats/M/Dec 20/Heart Disease/50y/Not Known/Jno B. Coats Master
Amanda/S/John B. Coats/F/Oct/Whooping Cough/3y/Eliza/Jno B. Coats Master
Horace/S/John B. Coats/M/Aug/Not Known/1y 6m/Eliza/Jno B. Coats Master
Mary Susan Cobb/W/F/July 6/Typhoid Fever/16y/Liston T. & Ann Thomas Cobb/Liston T.
  Cobb Father
[Ann] Thomas Cobb/W/F/Sept 18/Typhoid Fever/52y/Samuel & Rebecca Terrell/Liston T. Cobb
  Husband
Wesley Carneal/W/M/Feb/Scarlet Fever/1y/William J. & Mary A. Carneal/William J. Carneal Father
Ginny/S/James D. Coleman/F/Nov/Consumption/22y/Mary/James D. Coleman Master
Phillip/S/James D. Coleman/M/Aug/Inf Bowels/12y/__/James D. Coleman Master
Porter/S/Elizabeth D. Coleman/F/Nov/Typhoid Fever/52y/__/Elizabeth D. Coleman Mistress
Henry/S/Elizabeth D. Coleman/M/Nov/Scarlet Fever/4y/Rachel/Elizabeth D. Coleman Mistress
Mary Ann/S/Elizabeth D. Coleman/F/Dec/Scarlet Fever/1y 6m/Ginny/Elizabeth D. Coleman
  Mistress
George/S/Elizabeth D. Coleman/M/Dec/Typhoid Fever/30y/Porter/Elizabeth D. Coleman Mistress
Not Named/W/M/Mar 23/Liver Disease/1m 15d/Jesse L. & Margaret L. Cobb/Jesse L. Cobb Father
James F.Dustin/W/M/May 13/d.Richmond/Typhoid Fever/47y/Wm & Elizabeth Dustin/b.Louisa/
  Elizabeth E. Dustin Mother
Ginny/S/Bluford Durrett/F/June 22/Dropsy/65y/Nicy/Bluford Durrett Master
Mary Frances/S/Maynard Dyson/F/Dec 23/Burnt/5y/Aggy/Maynard Dyson Master
Lewis/S/Virginia A. Dyson/M/June/Paralized/40y/Philis/Virginia A. Dyson Mistress
Not Named/S/Lucy A. Dew/F/June/Not Known/3m/Sarah/Thos K. Welch Overseer
Harriett/S/Thos B. Anderson/F/Aug/Scarlet Fever/9y/Jane/John McLaughlin Anderson
Franklin/S/Thos B. Anderson/M/July/Not Known/1y 6m/Milly/John McLaughlin Anderson
Not Named/S/James O. Allen/M/June/Cholic/7d/Maria/James O. Allen Master
Reuben/S/George Allen Estate/M/Mar/Dropsy/56y/__/Maria Allen
George Allen/W/M/June 3/Not Known/68y/James & Martha Bain Allen/Maria Allen Wife

Bob/S/L.W. Allen/M/July 10/d.Hospital in Richmond/TyphoidFever/20y/Margarett/b. James City/ L.W. Allen Master

Maria/S/Richard M. Bridges/F/Apr/d.Richmond/Typhoid Fever/11y/Rhoda/b.Orange Co/R.M. Bridges Master

Landon/S/Richard M. Bridges/M/Aug/d.Richmond/Typhoid Fever/4y/Rhoda/b.Orange Co/Richd M. Bridges Master

Joe Minor/S/Richard H. Burruss/M/Oct 15/Not Known/1y 6m/Aleg Minor/Richard H. Burruss Master

Jeter Blanton/W/M/Oct 25/Diptheria/4y 5m/John T. & Martha Blanton/John T. Blanton Father

Ginney/S/George W. Burke/F/Mar 1/Consumption/27y/Not Known/George W. Burke Master

Sally/S/George W. Burke/F/Apr/Dropsy/65y/Hannah/George W. Burke Master

Tom/S/George W. Burke/M/July/Drownd/25y/Catherine/George W. Burke Master

Garland Burruss/W/M/May 5/Scarlet Fever/3y 5m 11d/__/John & Eliza P. Burruss/John Burruss

[Thomas] P. Burruss/W/M/June 27/d.Gaine's Mill/Shot at Gaine's Mill/21y 9m/John & Eliza P. Burruss/John Burruss Father

Violet/S/Rebecca B. Burruss/F/Oct/Old Age/85y/Caroline/Rebecca B. Burruss Mistress

Soloman/S/Edwin & Norbourne Bundy/M/Sept/Cold/18y/Lucy/Temple C. Moor Overseer

Frederick/S/Edwin & Norbourne Bundy/M/Sept/Smothd/2y/Harriett/Temple C. Moor Overseer

[Georgia]na F. Burruss/W/F/Mar 20/Typhoid Fever/16y 2m 30d/Elliott W. & C.B. Burruss/ Elliott W. Burruss Father

Cornelius/S/Fleming Bibb/M/Mar/Not Known/1y/Charlotte/Fleming Bibb Master

[Thom]as W. Blunt/W/M/Oct 17/d.Sharpsburg, Md/Shot in Battle/26y/John & Catharine Blunt/ Thos B. Blunt

Molly/S/James T. Butler/F/Aug/Pneumonia/60y/b.Spottsylvania/James T. Butler Master

[John] H. Campbell/W/M/Oct 28/d.Richmond/Wounded at Sharpsburg Md/20y/Seth & Susanna Campbell/Seth Campbell Father

[Jam]es Carlton Jr/W/M/July/d.Near Richmond/Camp Fever/25y/Philip & Dorothea Carlton/ James Carlton Sr

Betsy/S/William Carter/F/Aug/Not Known/20y/Delah/William Carter Master

Franky/S/William Carter/F/June/Old Age/75y/Unknown/William Carter Master

[illeg]/S/William Carter/F/Dec/Bowel Complaint/10y/Beth/William Carter Master

John Guash/S/William Carter/M/Mar 1/Consumption/10y/Beth/William Carter Master

John James/S/William Carter/M/Mar/Not Known/__/Becky/William Carter Master

Hannah/S/William Carter/F/Apr/Bowel Compliant/11y/Elizabeth/William Carter Master

Kannaki/S/William Carter/F/May/Dropsy/11y/Fanny/William Carter Master

Not Named/S/William Carter/M/May/Not Known/1y/Susan/William Carter Master

Richard/S/William Carter/M/June/Dropsy/4y/Elizah/William Carter Master

[illeg]is Floyd Coleman/W/M/July 2/Inf Bowels/10m/James W. & [illeg]Coleman/b.Spotsylvania/ James W. Coleman Father

Not Named/S/George T. Collins/M/July 2/Measles/10y/1m/ Henrietta/George T. Collins Master

Thomas/S/George T. Collins/M/Nov/Diarrhea/20y/Maria/George T. Collins Master

Jane/S/Sarah F. Diggs/F/June 5/Appoplexy/2y 9m 13d/Charlotte/b.Nelson Co/Sarah A. Diggs Mistress

Lucy R. Doggett/W/F/Oct 16/Consumption/28y/James & Elizabeth Duvall/Wm O. Doggett Husband

Caroline/S/Robert Dickinson/F/Nov/d.Richmond/Small pox/25y/Frances/Robert Dickinson Master

Parneat Donahoe/W/M/Nov/fever/4y/James & Ann J. Donahoe/James Donahoe Father

William/S/Henry Doggett/M/Sept/Typhoid Fever/8y/Judy/Henry Doggett Master

[illeg]vira Temple Dickinson/W/F/Mar 17/Scarlet Fever/1y 8m 15d/Saml T. & Betty Ann Dickinson/Betty Ann Dickinson Mother
James/S/Samuel T. Dickinson/M/Mar 1/Scarlet Fever/4y/Martha/Samuel T. Dickinson Master
[illeg]icy Durrett/W/F/Dec 10/Jaundice/60y/Samuel Newton & __/Claibourne Durrett, dec'd Husband/Mary Durrett
John M. Dyson/W/M/March/Congestive Chill/__/Alfred & Sarah Ann Dyson/W.M. Mason
Ellen/S/John C. Dickinson/F/July/Affective Brain/6y/Harriett/John C. Dickinson Master
Spencer/S/John C. Dickinson/M/Sept/Spasms/2y/__/John C. Dickinson Master
[Ja]mes B. Eubank/W/M/Aug 20/Typhoid Fever/28y/James & Lucy Eubank/Elizabeth Eubank Wife/Charles Atkinson
[illeg]cy Evans/W/F/Dec 28/Old Age/95y/Thomas & Elizabeth Evans/Leroy Evans
Belfield/S/Jos A. Flippo/M/July 20/Consumption/23y/Unknown/Joseph A. Flippo Master
Cost[illeg]/S/John B. Flippo/F/Nov/Dropsy/25y/Anna/John B. Flippo Master
Not Named/S/Albert R. Flippo/M/June/Not Known/2d/Frances/Albert R. Flippo Master
Agnes/S/Littleton Flippo/F/Dec 20/Not Known/10y/Eleanor/Littleton Flippo Master
Edmund Gant/W/M/June 15/Paralized/76y/Susan Gant/Wm T. Carlton
Henry H. Goodloe/W/M/June 18/Pneumonia/17y 12d/William H. & Virginia C. Goodloe/Archibald G. Goodloe
Malissa/S/Lewis M. George/F/Nov/Pneumonia/68y/Dolly/Lewis M. George Master
John/S/Henry H. George/M/Aug/Lightning/48y/Not Known/Henry H. George Master
Esteller/S/Henry H. George/F/Sept/Diptheria/9y/Celia/Henry H. George Master
Joe/S/Henry H. George/M/Nov/Congestion/18y/Sarah/Henry H. George Master
Mariah/S/Rachael Harris/F/Typhoid Fever/11y 6m/Harriett/Rachael Harris Mistress
Margarett/S/Rachael Harris/F/Mar 12/Burnt/17y/May/Rachael Harris Mistress
Isaac/S/Albert S. Hundley/M/May 1/Pneumonia/24y/Becky/Albert S. Hundley Master
Not Named/S/Albert S. Hundley/M/Dec 25/Not Known/__/Ellen/Albert S. Hundley Master
Rose/S/Albert S. Hundley/F/May/Whooping Cough/4y/Lucy/Albert S. Hundley Master
Willyann/S/Albert S. Hundley/F/May/Whooping Cough/10m/Lucy/Albert S. Hundley Master
Peter/S/__ Hacket Est/M/Feb/Plurisy/25y/Ellen/James W. Hackett
Sally/S/Thomas Hurt/F/Apr/Whooping Cough/1y 6m/Clara/Thomas Hurt Master
Cornelius/S/Thomas Hurt/M/June/Whooping Cough/7m/Rachael/Thomas Hurt Master
Laberta/S/Thomas Hurt/F/June/Whooping Cough/5m/Betsy/Thomas Hurt Master
Lucinda/S/Thomas Hurt/F/June 30/Old Age/81y/Hannah/Thomas Hurt Master
William Philip Jackson/W/M/June 1/d.Richmond Hospital/Typhoid Fever/22y3m/McKenzee & Elizabeth Jackson/Elizabeth Jackson Mother
William Robert Jackson/W/M/Aug 30/d.Manassas/Shot in Battle/23y 3m/McKenzie & Elizabeth Jackson/Elizabeth Jackson Mother
William/S/Sarah P. Kelley/M/Apr 10/Brain fever/7y/Rachel/Sarah P. Kelley Mistress
Miltin/S/Sarah P. Kelley/M/Sept/Whooping Cough/1y 6m 10d/Judy Ann/Sarah P. Kelley Mistress
James T. Kelley/W/M/Oct 29/d.Near Manchester/Shot/27y 11m 2d/Richard & Mary E. Kelly/Mary Ellen Kelley Mother
Willy Ann/S/John V. Keane/F/Nov/Whooping Cough/6y/Judy/John V. Keane Master
Thornton/S/John V. Keane/M/Nov/Whooping Cough/1y/Judy/Jno V. Keane Master
Bennett/S/John V. Keane/M/Nov/Whooping Cough/2y 2m/Judy/Jno V. Keane Master
Emma/S/John V. Keane/S/Nov/Whooping Cough/6m/Catherine/Jno V. Keane Master
William/S/William F. Luck/M/Mar/Not Known/6m/Catherine/William F. Luck Master
Rosey Lee/S/Thomas Lumpkin/F/Sept/Bronchitis/5m/Catherine/Thos Lumpkin Master
Mary/S/Thomas Lumpkin/F/July/Whooping Cough/2m/Sally/Thos Lumpkin Master

Argyle/S/Thomas Lumpkin/M/Aug/Whooping Cough/1y/Ann/Thos Lumpkin Master
Preston/S/Betty G. Lewis/M/Mar/Pleurisy/7y/Jane/Betty G. Lewis Mistress
Camillus A. Mason/W/M/Sept 17/d.Sharpsburg Md/Shot in Battle/25y/Warner W. Mason & Mary
  Ann F. Mason/Warner Mason Father
Francis M. Mason/W/M/Nov 1/from Wounds laid at Sharpsburg/20y/Warner M. & M.F. Mason/
  Warner M. Mason Father
Sarah Luck/W/F/Aug 28/Dropsy/63y/John & Sarah Hutcheson/James C. Luck Husband
Barton W. Morris/W/M/Dec 11/Congestive fever/44y/Charles & Emily T. Morris/Annie F. Morris
  Wife/Edmund F. Morris
Ben/S/Emily T. Morris/M/June 14/M/Typhoid Fever/57y/[illeg]/Edmund F. Morris
Maria May/W/F/Nov 26/Consumption/68y/Larkin & Frances Miller/ Jos May dec'd Husband/
  Frances May
Milly/S/Catharine Newton/F/Aug 13/Abortion/23y/Catherine/Catharine Newton Mistress
Isaac/S/John Newton/M/Aug/Not Known/4y/Jane/John Newton Master
William F. Norment/W/M/Nov 15/Consumption/26y 4m/Richard & Charlotte Norment/
  Not Married/Francis A. Norment
[Li]ttleton C. Noel/W/M/March 5/d.Stafford Co/Congestive Chills/17y/Wm T. & Barbara G. Noel/
  Wm T. Noel Father
Jerry/S/George B. Pollard/M/Jan/Spasms/1y 6m/Louise/Geo B. Pollard Master
Willaim W. Quarles/W/M/Mar 20/Consumption/32y/William & Lucy Quarles/Sarah J. QuarlesWife/
  Garland Hargrave
John W. Quarles/W/M/May 11/d.Goldsboro N.C./Congestion of Lungs/31y 1m 14d/Wilson & Mary
  Susan Quarles/William T. Quarles
John Richeson/W/M/Mar 22/Consumption/63y/John & Mary Richeson/Mary Richeson Wife/
  Mary J. Richeson
John W. Richeson/W/M/Sept 12/d.Richmond/Typhoid fever/21y/John & Mary Richeson/Mary J.
  Richeson
William J. Richeson/W/M/Aug 8/d.Cedar Run/Shot/20y 5m 5d/William & Nancy Richeson/William
  Richeson Father
Marion Sutton/W/M/Aug/Paralysis/4y 1m 7d/Henry & Elizabeth Sutton/Jno Shepherd Uncle
Lillyann/S/Joseph M. Seay/F/May/Not Known/1y 6m/Emily/Joseph M. Seay Master
Elizabeth Seay/W/F/Apr 5/Old Age/81y/Richard & Sally Peatross/Fluray? Seay dec'd Husband/
  Jos M. Seay
Henry/S/Ellen Scott/M/May 1/Not Known/3y/Patsy/Ellen Scott Mistress
Lindsey/S/George F. Swann/M/Apr/Consumption/9y/[illeg]/Geo F. Swann Master
Martha/S/George F. Swann/F/Sept/Consumption/30y/Betsey/Geo F. Swann Master
George Smith/W/M/[illeg]/32y 11m/Rice & Jane Smith/Virginia Smith Sister
Henry/S/Thomas B. Smith/M/Dec/Pluerisy/6y 6m/[illeg]/Thos C. Smith Master
Nancy/S/Francis T. Samuel/F/Dec 23/Measles/1y 2m/Josephine/Francis T. Samuel Master
Venice/S/Francis W. Scott/F/Sept/Uterine affection/56y/Not Known/b.Essex Co/Francis W. Scott
  Master
John/S/Francis W. Scott/M/Apr/Consumption/40y/Franky/Francis W. Scott Master
Not Named/S/Francis W. Scott/F/July/__/__/Sophia/Francis W. Scott Master
Julia/S/Francis W. Scott/F/Aug/Congestive Chill/5y/Jane/Francis W. Scott Master
William Robert Sutton/W/M/July 5/d.Richmond/Poison/2y 6m/William O. & Mary Ellen Sutton/
  b.Hanover/William O. Sutton Father
Oscar Sutton/W/M/Dec/Croup/4m/William O. & Mary Ellen Sutton/b.Hanover Co/William O. Sutton
  Father

Beverly/S/Pilaski Dutton/M/June/Whooping Cough/1y 6m/Isabella/b.King Wm Co/Virginia A. Dyson
William T. Turner/W/M/Sept 1/d.Sharpsburg Md/Shot in Battle/25y/Daniel & Mary Turner/
  Daniel Turner Father
Agnes Tyree/Free/F/June 25/Typhoid Fever/48y/Mary Carter/Liston T. Cobb
Mary Eliza Tribble/W/F/Feb 25/Diptheria/7y/Thos J. & Lithiana Tribble/Thos J. Tribble Father
Elizabeth Thos Tribble/W/F/Mar 12/Diptheria/12y/Thos J. & Lithiana Tribble/Thos J. Tribble Father
Nancy Henerson Tribble/W/F/Apr 17/Diptheria/1y 6m/Thos J. & Lithiana Tribble/Thos J. Tribble
  Father
Not Named/S/George Tyler/M/May/Not Known/2d/Molly/George Tyler Master
Elizabeth Turner/W/F/Jan 13/Paralized/72y 3m/Richard & Frances Turner/Jno R. Turner dec'd
  Husband/Richardson Turner
Susan Thomas/W/F/May 27/Consumption/55y/Robert & Martha Rowe/b.King Wm/William F.
  Thomas Husband
Henrietta/S/Richard C. Tunstall/F/July/Dropsy/5y/Sally/Richard C. Tunstall Master
Richard H. Tompkins/W/M/Sept 17/d.Sharpsburg Md/Shot in Battle/29y 1m 8d/Augustus & Nancy
  Tompkins/Augustus Tompkins Father
Benjamin Tompkins/W/M/Sept 17/d.Sharpsburg Md/Shot in Battle/19y 2m/Robert W. & Jane
  Tompkins/Augustus Tompkins Uncle
Robert P. Tompkins/W/M/Mar 10/Diptheria/22y 2m/Robert W. & Jane Tompkins/Maria D. Marshall
  Aunt
Andrew/S/Mayland Terrell/M/Sept 26/Scarlet Fever/8y/Margarett/Edward M.C. Penny Friend
Edmund West/W/M/July 7/Rheumatism/70y/Edmund & __/b.Louisa Co/Jane K. West dec'd
  Wife/W.M. Mason Bro-in-Law
Joseph E. West/W/M/Apr 6/d.Richmond/Rheumatism/82y/Edmund & Jane K. West/Agness N. West
  Wife/Warner M. Mason Uncle
Bob/S/Elliott Wortham/M/Feb 22/Consumption/24y 7m/Margarette/Elliott Wortham Master
Sam/S/Elliott Wortham/M/May 1/Not Known/72y/Not Known/Elliott Wortham Master
Ellar/S/Elliott Wortham/F/July 2/Consumption/[illeg]Sarah/Elliott Wortham Master
Joseph/S/Susan Wyatt/M/Mar 7/Not Known/15d/Nancy/Susan Wyatt Mistress
Not Named/S/Susan Wyatt/F/Nov/Not Known/__/Dolly/Susan Wyatt Mistress
Not Named/S/Susan Wyatt/F/Dec/Born dead/Dana/Susan Wyatt Mistress
Susan/S/Susan Wyatt/F/Dec 20/Typhoid Fever/23y/Mary/Susan Wyatt Mistress
Adam/S/Tavinor Winn/M/May/Affective Lungs/10y/Amey/Tavinor Winn Master
Archie/S/Fleming Wood/M/Sept/Inf Bowels/11y 6m/Henrietta/Fleming Wood Master
Richard Wood/W/M/July 3/Old Age/96y/H[illeg] Wood/b.Maryland/Tabatha Wood Wife/Edmund R.
  Wood
Richard H. Woolfolk/W/M/May 27/Liver disease/62y/Archilles & Mary Woolfolk/Elizabeth T.
  Woolfolk Wife
Not Named/Richd H. Woolfolk/F/Aug 1/Not Known/28d/Sarah/Elizabeth T. Woolfolk Mistress
Not Named/S/Richd H. Woolfolk/M/July 20/Born dead/Eliza/Elizabeth T. Woolfolk Mistress
Not Named/Wesley Wright/F/July 5/Not Known/8d/Jane/Wesley Wright Master
Sam/S/Wesley Wright/M/Dec/Smothered/6m/Betty/Wesley Wright Master
Worter/S/Wesley Wright/M/Sept/Teething/1y 3m/Sally/Wesley Wright Master
Lucinda/S/Wesley Wright/F/Oct 22/Child Bed/28y/Lucy/Wesley Wright Master
Marcellus/S/Wesley Wright/M/Apr/Fitts/2y 3m/Sally/Wesley Wright Master
Norman/S/Wesley Wright/M/Jan/Croup/4y/Eliza/Wesley Wright Master
Isabella/S/Bennett Wright/F/Apr 14/Diptheria/4y/Mary/Jno W. Wright
Not Named/S/Geo B. Washington/F/May 20/Born dead/Margarett/Geo B. Washington Master

Delphy/S/Geo B. Washington/F/Feb 23/Typhoid Fever/18y/Charlotte/Geo B. Washington Master
Walker/S/Geo B. Washington/M/Apr 1/Measles/2y/Lucy/Geo Washington Master
Joe/S/Geo B. Washington/M/July 20/d.Near Richmond/Camp Fever/25y/Peggy/Geo B. Washington Owner
John Minor/S/Albert G. Ware/M/Mar/Inf Brain/1y/Eliza/Albert G. Ware Master
Vina/S/Henry M. Young/F/Sept 27/Typhoid Fever/16y/[illeg]/Henry M. Young Master
Martha/S/Henry M. Young/F/Sept 27/Thrash/1y 6m/Charlott/Henry M. Young Master
James Henry Yarbrough/W/M/July 8/Typhoid Pneumonia/32y 8m/John & Lucy A. Yarbrough/ Not Married/Lucy A. Yarbrough Mother
William Jesse Yarbrough/W/M/Nov 14/Typhoid Fever/15y 5m/Richard & Maria Yarbrough/Maria Yarbrough Mother
Not Named/W/M/Sept/Born dead/Arthur & Mildred Beazley/Betty H. Sutton
Not Named/W/F/Sept/Not Known/6d/Arthur & Mildred Beazley/Betty H. Sutton
Walter T. Luck/W/M/Sept 17/d.Sharpsburg Md/Shot in Battle/19y/Joel T. & Nicey Luck/Joel T. Luck Father
James Long/W/M/Aug/Rose Ola/4y/Woodford P. & Eliza Jane Long/Woodford Long Father
Cornelius Gravatt/W/M/Aug 26/Typhoid Fever/27y/John & Kitty Gravatt/b.King George Co/Wm Gravatt
Caroline/S/Thomas C. Smith/F/Nov/Not Known/6y/Rena/Thos C. Smith Master
Lewis George Goldsbury [Goldsby?, who some references say was killed in Sharpsburg, Md September 17, 1862?]/W/M/June 27/d.Gaine's Mill, Henrico/Shot/21y 2m/John & Eliza Goldsbury/John Goldsbury Father
Not Named/W/M/July 6/Not Known/2d/George P. & Sophia J. Luck/George P. Luck Father
Charles Lewis Acres/W/M/July 13/Scarlet Fever/7y/Thomas & Almira Acres/Thomas Acres Father
Jane Norment [Mount]/W/F/Aug/Typhoid fever/9y 9m/Giles & Elizabeth Mount/Giles Mount Father
Alace/S/Betty G. Lovis/F/Sept/Bilious Typhoid/6y/Lucy/Betty G. Lovis Mistress
Esculapius A. Durrett/W/M/Sept 17/d.Sharpsburg Md/Shot in Battle/24y 14d/Bluford & Frances Durrett/Bluford Durrett Father
Clarence L. Goodwin/W/M/Nov 4/d.Barbins X Road/Fauquier Va/Killed in Battle/19y 2m 4d/John T. & Ann P. Goodwin/John T. Goodwin Father
Kisiah/S/Orville W. Sutton/F/Aug/Abscess/20y/Mary/O.W. Sutton Master
John Carter/Free/M/Aug/Not Known/23y/Not Known/Timothy Courtney Employer
William A. Moncure/W/M/__/Pneumonia/53y/__/Eustace Moncure Son

1863

[Note: Original records for the year 1863 are missing in The Library of Virginia]

1864

Not Named/W/F/October/Spasms/__/Wm H. & Ellen V. Wright/ William H. Wright Father
Edward/C/Stephen Oliver/M/Aug/Consumption/27y/Lucy/Robert B. Oliver - Young Master
Francis/C/Luther Wright Sr/M/Oct/Cold/1y/Jane/Luther Wright Master
Margarett/C/Phillip Samuel Sr/F/May/Not Known/2d/Mary/Phillip Samuel Sr Master
Tarlton/C/Phillip Samuel Sr/M/July/Measles/17y/Maria/Phillip Samuel Sr Master
Ann Oliver/W/F/Jan 20/Pneumonia/30y/Not Known/Thos B. Grubbs Friend
Woodford Miller/W/M/Dec 15/Pneumonia/46y/Temple & Peggy Miller/Farmer/Sarah Miller Wife

Elizabeth Britzin/W/F/Old Age/60y/Not Known/Sarah Miller Friend
Elizabeth Pare [Parr]/W/F/Aug 10/Whooping Cough/4y/Robt S. & Catharine Pare/Ro S. Pare Father
Ginney/C/Thos Lumpkin/F/June/Not Known/75y/__/Thomas Lumpkin Master
Elizabeth Donahoe/W/F/Mar 12/Old Age/70y/Wm & Jane Covington/Reuben Donahoe Husband/ Reuben Donahoe Son
Henry Fries/Free/M/Sept/Congestive Fever/7y/Lucinda Fries/Fleming Wood Friend
James Fries/Free/M/Sept/Congestive Fever/5y/Lucinda Fries/Fleming Wood Friend
James L. Goodloe/W/M/July/d.Spottsylvania/Shot in leg at Wilderness/44y/Aquilla & Elizabeth Goodloe/William Goodloe Brother
John Wesley Mitchell/W/M/Jan 24/Typhoid Fever/19y/Pascal & Delilah Mitchell/Pascal Mitchell Father
Jesse Winn/W/M/June 18/General Debility/75y/Tavener & Ann Winn/Jesse W. Winn Son
Margaret/C/Taviner Winn/F/May/Not Known/1y/Judy/Taviner Winn Master
Luther W. Jerrall/W/M/Sept 30/Wounded/20y/Jas S. & Rachael Jerrell/Jas S. Jerrell Father
Margarett Ann Dyson/W/F/Jan/Congestive Chill/22y/Nathl & Sarah Ann Young/Jas F. Dyson Husband
Cook/C/Ira L. Thomas/M/June/Summer Compliant/90y/Not Known/Ira L. Thomas Master
Braxton/C/Ira L. Thomas/M/Dec/Summer Compliant/6y/Eliz & Charles/Ira L. Thomas Master
Frank/C/Ira L. Thomas/M/Dec/Summer Compliant/2y/Eliz & Charles/Ira L. Thomas Master
Nancy/C/Chas & Norbourne Buckley/F/Jan/Consumption/65y/Ginny/ Chas & Norbourne Buckley Masters
Winny/C/Chas & Norbourne Buckley/F/Feb/Not Known/25y/Mary/Chas & Norbourne Buckley Masters
Simon/C/Chas & Norbourne Buckley/M/Feb/Consumption/25y/Patsy/Chas & Norbourne Buckley Masters
Dinah/C/Chas & Norbourne Buckley/F/Feb/General Debility/74y/__/Chas & Norbourne Buckley Masters
Harriett/C/Chas & Norbourne Buckley/F/Feb/Cold/25y/__/Chas & Norbourne Buckley Masters
Becky/C/Chas & Norbourne Buckley/F/May/Cold/12y/Lizzie/Chas & Norbourne Buckley Masters
Elizabeth Woolard/W.F.Nov 1/General Debility/75y/Reuben & Judy Johnson/Thos Woolard Son
Not Named/W/F/Apr/Not Known/7d/Edwd & Martha Ellen Chrisian/Edward Christian Father
Lydia Ann Luck/W/F/Disease of Throat/2y/N.P. & Eliz N. Luck/N.P. Luck Father
Jessie Bennett/W/F/Sept/Diarrhea/2y/Andrew & Caroline Bennett/Reuben Turner Friend
John/C/Lewis Stevens/M/Sept/Cold/2y/Nancy/Reuben Turner Friend
Patsy/C/Ryland Jeter/F/Apr/Consumption/30y/Ryland Jeter Master
John B. Stevens/W/M/Dec 10/Killed near Dahlgren/22y/Elijah & Lucy Stevens/Elijah Stevens Father
Elijah S. Stevens/W/M/Jan/Carbuncle/24y/Elijah & Lucy Stevens/Elijah Stevens Father
Grace/S/John Chandler/F/Aug/Hemorhage/72y/__/Geo Goldberry Friend
Martha Ellen Goldsberry [Goldsby]/W/F/Aug/Thrash/1m 7d/C. & M.A. Goldsberry/Caleb Goldsberry Father
Not Named/W/M/Aug 10/Thrash/1m 14d/Wm P.C. & Fanny E. Ramsey/Wm P.C. Ramsey Father
Nancy/S/Thos Hurt/F/June/Consumption/21y/Rose/Thos Hurt Master
George Carter/S/Thos Hurt/M/Dec/Bronchitis/13y/Nancy/Thos Hurt Master
Fanny/S/Thos Hurt/F/Feb/Congestion Brain/5y/Betsy/Thos Hurt Master
Horace/S/Thos Hurt/M/June/Chicken Pox/3m/Betsy/Thos Hurt Master
Mary/S/Sarah P. Kelley/F/May/Pneumonia/1m/Lucy Ann/Sarah P. Kelley Mistress
Hannah/S/Sarah P. Kelley/F/May/Cold/1m/Harriett/Sarah P. Kelley Mistress
Mehala/S/Sarah P. Kelley/F/May/Hemorhage/60y/Fanny/Sarah P. Kelley Mistress

Baceni/S/Ann Young/M/Feb/Liver Disease/17y/__/Ann Young Mistress
Elizabeth Dick/W/F/Apr/Old Age/80y/Bally Dick Husband/A.G. Ware Son-in-Law
Jordan P. Ware/W/M/Oct 1/d.near Petersburg/Killed near Petersburg/26y/A.G. & Judith Ware/A.G. Ware Father
Lucy/S/A.G. Ware/F/Mar/Inf'n Bladder/12y/Winny/Albert G. Ware Master
Not recollected/S/A.G. Ware/F/Nov/Not Known/1y 3m/Susan/A.G. Ware Master
Not Named/S/A.G. Ware/M/Nov/Not Known/__/Susan/Albert G. Ware Master
James S. Smith/W/M/May 16/d.Near Drewry's Bluff/Killed Near Drewry's Bluff/26y/Robt P. & Cornelia Smith/Robt Smith Father
Abba/S/Edward P. Wood/F/Oct/Typhoid Fever/22y/Judy/Edward P. Wood Master
Etter/S/Edward P. Wood/S/Dec/Typhoid Fever/16y/Amey/Edward P. Wood Master
Charles/S/Stanfield Wright/M/Dec/Paralysis/64y/__/Stanfield Wright Master
John Chandler/W/M/May 27/Pneumonia/63y/Timothy & Lucy Chandler/Lucy Ann Chandler Wife/Burton A. Chandler Son
Robert T. Tompkins/W/M/May 27/Typhoid Pneumonia/15y/Christopher Tompkins Father
Milly/S/Leroy B. Gatewood/F/Apr/Scrofula/22y/__/Leroy B. Gatewood Master
William O. Smith/W/M/June 16/Typhoid Fever/27y/Jas D. & Martha L. Smith/James D. Smith Father
Lewis Cannon/W/M/Mar/Diptheria/10y/Robt & Martha Ann Cannon/Robert Cannon Father
Alace/S/Ro S. Peatross/F/Mar/Cold/1y/Rose/Robert S. Peatross Master
John Kane/C/M/Feb/Pleurisy/25y/Vicy Trusdale & Nancy F. [Kane]/Maynard Dyson Friend
Not Named/S/Richd Blanton/__/Dec/Not Known/6m/[illeg]/Richd Blanton Master
Alfarria/S/James D. Wright/F/May/Typhoid Fever/23y/Louisa/James D. Wright Master
Maria/S/Lucy A. Moncure/F/Apr/40y/__/Lucy A. Moncure Mistress
Archy/S/Lucy A. Moncure/M/Dec/Cold 1y 6m/Ginny/Lucy A. Moncure Mistress
Mary Jane Hart/W/F/Aug 19/Diptheria/34y/Geo & Maria Allen/Andrew Hart Husband
Not Named/S/Andrew Hart/F/Apr/Cold/6y/Mary/Andrew Hart Master
Not Named/S/Andrew Hart/F/May/Cold/5y/Jane/Andrew Hart Master
George Washington Durvine/W/M/June 25/Cholic Infection/13y/Benj F. & Susanna Durvine/Susanna Durvine Mother
Lethia Redd/W/F/Oct/Croop/5y/Jas T. & Tomasia Redd/Jas T. Redd Father
Mary L. Taylor/W/F/May 27/Not Known/4m/Wm L. & Tomasia Taylor/Wm L. Taylor Father
James Henry Hill/W/M/Sept 27/Congestive Chill/23y/Robt G. & Rebecca Hill/Robt G. Hill Father
Ann Campbell/W/F/June/Not Known/1y 6m/S.E.H. & Rebecca Campbell/S.E.H. Campbell Father
Not Named/S/S.E.H. Campbell/F/Aug/Not Known/6m/Lianna/S.E.H. Campbell Master
Margarett/S/Elliott Wortham/F/June/Consumption/45y/Patty/Elliott Wortham Master
Georgia/S/Elliott Wortham/F/Apr/Consumption/2y/Margarett/Elliott Wortham Master
Lucy Satterwhite/W/F/July/Not Known/6y/Franklin & Frances C. Satterwhite/Franklin Satterwhite Father
John Harper/W/M/Aug/Shot/46y/Jesse & Sally Harper/Sally Harper Wife
Lewellen Redd/W/M/Apr/d.Near Spottsylvania C.H./Wounded/23y/James T. & Tomasia Redd/Jas T. Redd Father
John/S/Jos T. Collins/M/Sept/Consumption/19y/Caroline/Jos T. Collins - Young Master
Charles Farish/W/M/July 13/Typhoid Fever/25y/Stephen & Jane Farish/Fleming Farish Brother
Pendleton/S/A.B. Hundley/M/May/Cold/1y 6m/Lucy/Albert B. Hundley Master
Adeline/S/A.B. Hundley/F/Aug/Disease of Heart/40y/__/Albert B. Hundley Master
Catharine Dyson/W/F/May 30/Summer Compliant/2y/Maynard & Emaline Dyson/Maynard Dyson Father

Not Named/S/John S. Blanton/F/May 15/Summer Compliant/1y/__/John S. Blanton Master
Octavia Thacker/W/F/May/Diarrhea/3y/Elijah & Mildred Thacker/Thos T. Thacker Gd father
James/S/Nery Burruss/M/Oct 14/Gen Debility/75/__/Pinkney C. Burruss - Young Master
Gen'l Stuart/S/Wm G. Quarles/M/July/Brain Affection/__/Marcella/Wm G. Quarles Master
Jane/S/Horace A. Richards/F/Dec/Not Known/1m/Lavinia/Horace A. Richards Master
James/S/Horace A. Richards/M/Nov/Soft Brain/8y/Eliza/Horace A. Richards Master
Morgan Long/W/M/May/Spasms/6m/Woodford E. & Eliza J. Long/Woodford E. Long Father
Josiah Thornton Johnson/W/M/June/Brain Affection/2y/Wm & Mary Elizabeth Johnson/Wm
 Johnson Father
Robert Eugene Sutton/W/M/June 23/d.Richmond/Shot/__/Henry C. & Elizabeth C. Sutton/
 Henry C. Sutton Father
Wm T. Bendall/W/M/June 3/d.Henrico/Shot in Henrico/22y/Albert & Lucy Ann Bendall/Henry
 C. Sutton Friend
Not Named/__/__/June/Not Known/__/Charles L. & Elizabeth Flippo/Charles L. Flippo Father

1865

George Southworth/W/M/Oct/Fits/10m/George & Eliza Southworth/Farmer/William Pitts Grd Father
Not Named/C/F/__/__/6m/Bettie/Mor Shaddock Neighbour
Robert/C/F/June/Killed By Lightning/25y/Hanah/Jno C. Gravatt Neighbour
George W. Gravatt/W/M/June/Killed by Lightning/22y/Jno C. & Amanda Gravatt/Jno C. Gravatt
 Father
John C. Cole/W/M/Oct/Paralized/70y/__/Charles W. Jones Son-in-Law
Anna Mahon/W/F/July/Diptheria/2y/Alex & Cathr Mahon/Alex Mahon Father
Not Known/C/F/__/Diptheria/13y/Mahala/Wm L. Andrews Neighbour
No Name/C/F/June/Diptheria/6d/Mary/Thos B. Sale Neighbour
Mary/C/F/May/Parilized/67y/Not Known/George Marshall Employer
Henry/C/F/Nov/__/60y/Davy and Lelia/Ro Gatewood Employer
Hardee/C/M/Feb/__/7y/Susan/Ro Gatewood Employer
H.W. Brooks/W/M/__/__/26y/Wm & Patsy Brooks/Ro Gatewood Neighbour
Ro S. Brooks/W/M/__/__/22y/Wm & Patsy Brooks/Ro Gatewood Neighbour
Harry/C/M/Dec/__/70y/Not Known/Jno T. Lewis Neighbour
Amanda/C/F/__/__/11y/__/Jno B. Puller Neighbour
Jno Chenault/W/M/Aug/d.Hanover/Chro Dis/47y/Tom & Betsy Chenault/Arthur Chenault Son
Jno Martin/W/M/Mar/Chor Dis/43y/Thos & Maria Martin/George Martin Brother
James H. Sorrell/W/M/Mar/Chor Dis/25y/Thos & C. Sorrell/Wm J. Sorrell Brother
Reu T. Broaddus/W/M/May/Died in [Union] Prison/Chor Dis/24y/Jno & Hart. [Harriett]
 Broaddus/Jno Broaddus Father
Chas L. Andrews/W/M/__/__/22y/Robt & Sarah Andrews/James Andrews Brother
Robert S. Gouldin/W/M/__/__/30y/Richd & __ Gouldin/Gray Chenault Neighbour
Margaret Seal/W/F/Dec/Pneumonia/60y/Wm & Joanna Edmundson/Archilles Southworth Son-in-Law
No Name/W/M/June/__/2y/John & M. Cecil/John Cecil Father
Wm Hargrave/W/M/__/Diptheria/25y/Caleb & Lucy Hargrave/John Cecil Bro-in-Law
John Hargrave/W/M/July/d.Pensyl/Killed at Gettysburg/30y/Caleb & Lucy Hargrave/John Cecil
 Bro-in-Law
Thomas Hargrave/W/M/Dec/__/22y/Caleb & Lucy Hargrave/John Cecil Bro-in-Law
Robt O. Broaddus/W/M/__/__/2y/H.O. & J.A. Broaddus/H.O. Broaddus Father
John L. Houston/W/M/__/Diptheria/2y/Wm T. & Sarah A. Houston/Wm T. Houston Father

Laticia A. Houston/W/F/__/Diptheria/11m/Wm T. & Sarah A. Houston/Wm T. Houston Father
James M. Rouse/W/M/__/__/25y/Wm & Matilda Rouse/Wm Rouse Father
Carter Lovin/W/M/__/Old Age/67y/Lewis & __ Lovin/Jno Lovin Relative
Pinckney Taylor/W/M/__/__/2y/Thos & Sallie Taylor/Thos Taylor Father
Frank Self/W/M/__/__/21y/Muscoe & Lucy Self/Muscoe Self Father
John L. Purkes/M/W/__/__/25y/John & Judith Purkes/Presley Purkes Brother
Jno Broaddus/C/M/Sept/Consumption/74y/Mary & __ Broaddus/R.S. Broaddus Neighbour
J.J. Broaddus/W/F/Apr/Drowned/22y/R.S. & L.E. Broaddus/R.S. Broaddus Father
R.A. Jordan/W/M/Feb/Bil Fever/19y/Ro & Mat Jordan/Ro Jordan Father
Hanah/C/F/July/Old Age/90y/Not Known/E.R. Page Neighbour
Laura Garnett/C/F/Apr/Broncitis/[illeg]/Ben & L. Garnett/R.A. Puller Neighbour
Anna [illeg]/C/F/Nov/Heart Dis/55y/Not Known/R.A. Puller Neighbour
Nancy Dishago?/W/F/May/Consumption/67y/Not Known/S.J. Broaddus Neighbour
Wm Barlow/W/M/May/Heart Dis/64y/John & Milly Barlow/Robt Barlow Son
Therisa Dollins/W/F/June/Scarlet Fever/42y?/Not Known/Dr Gouldin
Hiram A. Brooks/W/M/__/Typhoid Fever/48y/Not Known/Dr Gouldin
John Self Sr/W/M/__/[illeg]/__/75y/__/Dr Gouldin
Peter Letany/C/M/__/Old Age/__/__/Dr Gouldin
Francis Houston/W/M/__/[illeg]/__/__/Dr Gouldin
[illeg] Broaddus/W/M/__/[illeg]/[illeg]/__/Dr Gouldin
George H. Gouldin/W/M/Feb/d.Richmond/Pneumonia/32y/Henry & Betsy Gouldin/Mechanic/
  Dr Gouldin
Thos L. Broaddus/W/M/Jan/d.Richmond/Pneumonia/23y/James J. & R.J. Broaddus/Farmer/
  Dr Gouldin
Louise Cole/W/F/Jan/Typhoid Fever/16y/R.W. & Lucy Cole/Dr Gouldin
Vick R. Gouldin/W/F/Apr/Scarlet Fever/25y/Nathl & Lucy Motley/Dr Gouldin
Elizabeth Gray/W/F/__/Dropsy/28y/McKensey & Elizth Gray/Dr Gouldin
Elizabeth G[illeg]/W/F/Typhoid Fever/60y/McKensey & Elizth Gray/Dr Gouldin
Jos H. Pavy/W/M/Jan/Paralized/40y/Wm & Nancy Pavy/Dr Gouldin
Oliver/C/F/Sept/Old Age/60y/Not Known/Dr Gouldin
Preston Broaddus/W/M/Apr/d.Dinwiddie/From around Richmond/25y/M.R. & S.A.
  Broaddus/Dr Gouldin
R.H. Callis/W/M/Apr/Dinwiddie/Killed in Battle/20y/Thos H. & M.J. Callis/H.N. Broaddus Friend
Sam'l J. Pitts/W/M/d.Manchester/Killed in Battle/21y/Willis & Maha Pitts/H.N. Broaddus Friend
Eugene Saunders [Richerson?]/W/M/Mar/1d/Spots/Killed in Battle/21y/R.B. & Susan
  Richerson/H.N. Broaddus Friend
F.B. Richerson/W/M/Feb/Consumption/29y/R.B. & Susan Richerson/H.N. Broaddus Friend
Wm A. Richerson/W/M/Sept/d.Pens/Killed at Gettysburg/24y/Not Known/Dr Gouldin
Mefrow Garnett/W/M/June/Old Age/70y/Not Known/Dr Gouldin
Lewis Washington/C/M/Nov/Liver Disease/50y/Not Known/Dr Gouldin
Ella Quisenberry/W/F/Aug/__/27y/Jas & Mary Thomas/H.N. Broaddus Relation
Robert Smith/C/M/Jan/Hoop Cough/6y/Leland & Ann Smithy/Dr Gouldin
Jerry A. Roots/C/M/Aug/Smothered/1y/Jerry & Fannie Roots/Dr Gouldin
No Name/C/F/June/__/1d/Harry & Silla/Dr Gouldin
Ella Shepherd/W/F/Mar/Typhoid Fever/16y/Jno W. & Sarah Shepherd/Dr Butler
No Name/C/F/Mar/__/14d/George & Isabella/Former Owner
Mary Johnson/C/F/Feb/Typhoid Fever/65y/Former Owner
No Name/C/M/Jan/Typhoid Fever/1m 12d/Henry & Nancy/John Kay Neighbour

Anne E. Andrews/W/F/Nov/Typhoid Fever/54y/Thos & Sally Puller/James Andrews Husband
Not Known/C/M/Dec/Typhoid Fever/1y/Jno & Betsy/James Andrews Neighbour
E.C. Tuck/W/F/Mar/Diptheria/4y/O. [Owen] C. & F.E. Tuck/O.C. Tuck Father
Reu T. Jeter/W/M/Mar/Consumption/27y/Thos & Matilda Martin/Mary Jeter Wife
A.H. Martin/W/M/Mar/Pneu/30y/Thos & Matilda Martin/H.P. Martin Wife
Wade Parker/C/M/Jan/__/15y/Taliaferro & M. Parker/Taliaferro Parker Father
Lew Washington/C/M/June/__/1y/Lewis & L. Washington/L. Washington Father
Matthew Rollins/C/M/Oct/__/2y/S. & A. Rollins/Soloman Rollins Father
Manitta Meyers/C/F/Sept/__/3y/G. & M. Myers/Geo Myers Father
Jno Brown/C/M/Aug/Dropsy/6y/Lewis & Judy Brown/Lewis Brown Father
Eliz Heywood/W/F/Mar/Pneu/40y/Jas & Cath Garnett/Jas Fields Neighbour
Ottis Carter/C/M/Mar/Pneu/50y/Susan Garnett/Jas Field Neighbour
Henry Parker/S/M/Mar/Pneu/60y/Not Known/Jas Fields Neighbour
Chas H. Munday/W/M/Jan/__/15y/Jno R. & Martha Munday/Jno R. Munday Father
Judith/C/F/Jan/Heart Dis/65y/Not Known/Jno R. Bursley Friend
Nancy/C/F/Jane/Old Age/70y/Not Known/Ro H. Upshaw Neighbour
Geo Pendleton/C/M/__/20y/Not Known/R.H. Upshaw Father[sic]
Olivia Upshaw/W/F/July/Diptheria/8y/Robt & C.M. Upshaw/Ro H. Upshaw Father
Richard F. Streshley/W/M/Oct/Typhoid Fever/64y/Not Known/Henry Rowzie Friend
Lewis Alsop/C/M/Aug/Typhoid Fever/18y/Not Known/Henry Rowzie Neighbour
Polley Garnett/C/F/Sept/Typhoid Fever/20y/Not Known/Henry Rowzie Neighbour
Eliza Morton/C/F/Oct/Typhoid Fever/30y/Not Known/Henry Rowzie Neighbour
Archilles/C/M/Nov/Typhoid Fever/64y/Not Known/Henry Rowzie Neighbour
Sally Garnett/C/F/Nov/Typhoid Fever/11y/Not Known/Henry Rowzie Neighbour
Joanna Alsop/C/F/Nov/Typhoid Fever/11y/Not Known/Henry Rowzie Neighbour
No Name/C/F/Nov/Typhoid Fever/15d/Not Known/Henry Rowzie Neighbour
Hattie Samuel/W/F/Nov/Typhoid Fever/7y/Jos & Anna Samuel/Jos Samuel Brother
No Name/C/M/Feb/__/1d/Maynard & Mary Bird/Maynard Bird Father
Leon Fortune/C/M/Feb/__/1y/Sally Fortune/Sally Fortune Mother
Mary A. Long/W/F/Oct/__/4y/Corl & Eliza Long/Cor [Cornelius] Long Father
Thos Carter/W/M/May/__/9y/Thos & Mary Carter/Thos Carter Father
[illeg] Bird/C/M/Oct/__/__/__ & Nancy Bird/Lilia Bird Wife
Thos Carter/W.M.May/__/9y/Not Known Willis Pitts Neighbour
Edith __/C/F/[illeg]/__/__/Richard Green Neighbour
Dan Covington/__/__/__/Wm N. & Mary Covington/Wm N. Covington Father
Larry Ray/C/M/June/Scrofula/1y/A[illeg] & Maria/Richard Green Neighbour
No Name/W/M/Mar/__/5d/Jas & Jane McCally/Jas McCally Father
Maria J. Trice/W/F/Aug/Bil Fever/7y/Geo W. & Jane Trice/Geo W. Trice Father
June Taylor/W/F/July/Conges Fever/4y/Thos & __ Taylor/Thos Taylor Father
No Name/C/F/Sept/__/3d/Ned & Eliza Morton/Ned Morton Father
Eliza Morton/C/F/Sept/Typhoid Fever/24y/Ned & Eliza Morton/Kingsford Thomas Father[sic]
Eliz A. Puller/W/F/Aug/__/47y/Ro & Sally Puller/Jno B. Puller Husband
Nancy Jones/W/F/June/Heart Dis/44y/Jno & Billy Farmer/Jno Farmer Father
No Name/C/M/May/__/2y/Jos & Frances/Jno Farmer Neighbour
S.H. Rowe/W/M/Oct/Old Age/91y/C. & E. Rowe/Mong's R. Micou Nephew
Wm Reynolds/W/M/June/Diptheria/4y/Wm E. & Cor [Cornelius] Reynolds/Wm E. Reynolds Father
Eliza Rose/W/F/Sept/Bil Fever/55y/Henry & Cathr Rowe/Henry Rowe Father
Maria T. Buckner/W/F/July/Typhoid Fever/32y/Reu & Ric Slaughter/R.H.W. Buckner Husband

Jno H. Kidd/W/M/Nov/Typhoid Fever/36d/Henry & Maria Kidd/Maria Kidd Mother
Thos Wright/W/M/Jane/__/60y/Not Known/Dr Broaddus Neighbour
Reubin Gouldin/W/M/Sept/Bil Fever/1y/Jno W. & Anna Gouldin/Jno W. Gouldin Father
Jno Morris/C/M/Sept/Old Age/75y/Not Known/__
Mary Johnson/C/F/Nov/Apoplexy/66y/Not Known/__
Peter Gallory/C/M/June/Lung Dis/1y/Not Known/__
No Name/W/F/Feb/__/1d/P.S. & Hellen Robb/Phil S. Robb Father
George Wright/W/M/Aug/__/18d/Geo & Va Wright/Geo Wright Father
No Name/W/M/Sept/__/1d/Geo & F. Haiden [Hayden]/Geo Haiden Father
George Baylor/C/M/July/Scarlet Fever/__/Not Known/Mrs. Rixey Neighbour
Frances Taylor/W/F/July/__/50y/Not Known/Henry Taylor Nephew
Mary Taylor/W/F/July/__/40y/Lee Roy & Fannie Taylor/F.H. Conway Son
Jno Conway/W/M/Mar/__/78y/Francis & Elizth Conway/F.H. Conway Son
Mary Lovin/W/F/Dec/Consumption/28y/Henry H. & Jane Alsop/Robert S. Lovin Jr Husband
Abraham? Long/C/M/Feb/Old Age/76y/Not Known/Geo Long Neighbour
Peter Alsop/C/M/Jan/Typhoid Fever/24y/Judith & Lewis/Geo Long Neighbour
Mary Ann/C/F/__/__/2y/Gabriella/Geo R. Taylor Neighbour
Not Known/C/M/__/37y/Betty/Geo R. Taylor Neighbour
Wm P. Taylor/W/M/June/__/74y/Jno & Lucy Taylor/Jas Taylor Nephew
Not Known/C/F/__/__/11y/Louisa/Jas Taylor Neighbour
Charleton Rowe/W/M/Aug/d.Richmond/Wounded in Battle/27y/Keeling & Frances Rowe/Jas C. Rowe Brother
James Watts/C/M/Nov/70y/Not Known/Jas C. Rowe Neighbour
Nancy Beazley/W/F/May/Typhoid Fever/46y/Thos & Patsy Parker/William Beazley Husband
Nancy Gatewood/W/F/Mar/Arth/73y/Mor [Mordecai] & Martha Broaddus/Phil Gatewood Husband
Jerry Chapman/C/M/Dec/Typhoid Fever/45y/Not Known/Wm B. Gravatte Neighbour
Phil Lightfoot/W/M/Dec/__/76y/Not Known/H.N. Broaddus Friend
Jno M. Barlow/W/M/Dec/__/26y/Wm & __ Barlow/Robert Barlow Brother
Jno M. Wright/W/M/Dec/__/27y/Robert H. Wright/Robert Wright Father
Richard T. Brooke/W/M/Dec/Brain Fever/11y/Thos H. & E. Brooke/Thos H. Brooke Father
M.B. Brooke/W/F/__/Typhoid Fever/8y/Thos H. & E. Brooke/Thos H. Brooke Father
Maria Acors/W/F/Nov 17/Liver Disease/40y/Chatel & Patsy Chiles/Geo W. Acors Husband
George W. Allen/W/M/Apr 6/Killed at Sailor's [Saylor's] Creek in Amelia/Killed in Battle/27y/ John & Nancy Allen/Farmer/Unmarried/Jno A. Allen Father
Ann/C/F/Nov/Consumption/28y/__Ennis/Unmarried/Henry Doggett Former Master
Josephine Bennett/W/F/Sept 16/Diptheria/7y/Wm S. & Elizabeth Bennett/Wm S. Bennett Father
Benjamin/C/M/__/Continued Fever/62y/Franky/John L. Blanton Former Master
Magg B. Blunt/W/F/Aug/Hooping Cough/2y 6m/Wm B. & Ellen E. Blunt/Wm B. Blunt Father
Netta Blunt/W/F/Aug/Hooping Cough/1y 6m/Wm B. & Ellen B. Blunt/Wm B. Blunt Father
Atwell Elberry Blunt/W/M/__/Continued Fever/7m/Atwell & Ellen S. Burruss/Atwell Burruss Father
Susan Louisa Burke/W/F/June 9/Disentary/6y 8m/Geo W. & Elizabeth Burke/Geo W. Burke Father
Eliza Carneal/W/F/June/Paralitics/55y/David & Nancy Haines/John Carneal Husband
Thomas C. Catlett/W/M.July 11/Inflamation of Stomach/56y/Lawrence & Elizabeth Catlett/ Farmer/Unmarried/Edwin C. Catlett Brother
Mary Ann Carneal/W/F/Dec 24/Pneumonia/61y/Larkin & Nancy Robinson/Patrick R. Carneal

Husband
James Collins/W/M/__/Typhoid Fever/20y/Charles & Catharine Collins/Farmer/Unmarried/ Catharine Collins Mother
Charlotte/C/F/Sept/Diareah/2y/Charlotte/Jno W. Flippo Former Owner
Luellen Chiles/C/F/Feb/Summer Compliant/1y/Ben & Christiana Chiles/Ben Chiles Father
Not Named/C/F/Aug 6/Summer Complaint/9m/John & Mary Coate/Jno Coate Father
George Washington Durvin/W/M/July 29/Summer Compliant/1y 1m 11d/Benjamin F. & Susan E. Durvin/Benjamin F. Durvin Father
Gideon Flippo/W/M/June 9/Gravel/70y/Joseph & __ Flippo/Farmer/John W. Flippo Son
Not Named/W/F/June 21/Not Known/1d/Charles L. & Elizabeth Flippo/Charles L. Flippo Father
Frank/C/M/May/Not Known/9m/Ann/Henry Doggett Former Master
Gimima Green/C/F/Sept/Dropsy/36y/John & Peggy Green/Richard Green Husband
Not Named/C/F/__/Not Known/__/Allen & Mary Ann Gatewood/Allen Gatewood Father
Ann Green/C/F/Sept/Bilious Colic/16y/Edward & Patsy Green/E.F. Flagg Former Master
Lucy Garnette/C/F/Dec 24/Typhoid Fever/23y/James & Eliza Garnette/E.F. Flagg Former Master
Nancy Haines/W/F/__/Not Known/1y 2m/James & Mary M. Haines/John Carneal Grand Father
Mary Hutcheson/W/F/Dec 15/Bronkitus/69y/William & Sarah Chiles/Richard Hutcheson Husband/John W. Hutcheson Son
Lucy Virginia Hays/W/F/Nov/7y/d.Richmond/Summer Compliant/2y/John & Julia Ann Hayes/ John Hayes Father
Not Named/W/F/Oct/Not Known/1d/John & Sally Hill/Philip Samuel Sr Grand Father
Mary Caterine Hancocke/W/F/Aug 22/Typhoid Fever/24y 6m 11d/John R. & Sarah K. Luck/ Wm W. Hancocke Husband
Henry/C/M/Oct 9/Pneumonia/50y/Not Known/James E. Cobb Former Master
Holmes/C/M/Oct 18/Pneumonia/56y/Philis/James E. Cobb Former Master
Mary Jane Hart/W/F/June 21/Consumption/32y/Philip & Dorothea Carter/Lewis M. Hart Husband
Not Named/C/F/Aug 10/Not Known/1m/Mary Jane Hall/Jas E. Cobb Former Owner
Patrick Henry Jackson/C/M/Aug 29/Not Known/1y/Andrew & Sophia Jackson/Andrew Jackson Father
Joe/C/M/Mar/Consumption/55y/Rose/Ruffin H. Coleman Former Owner
Jack/C/M/June/Scrofula/7y/Jane/R.H. Coleman Former Owner
Isam/C/M/Feb/Dropsy/65y/Not Known/John Newton Former Owner
Jack/C/M/Oct/Consumption/7y/Jesse Lewis/Jesse Lewis Father
Nancy Madison/C/F/Apr/Old Age/60y/Jack & Jane Lewis/Jack Lewis Father
Edmond T. Morris/W/M/Sept 12/d.Orange Co/Consumption/44y/__ & Emily Morris/Mary Ann Morris Widow
Wm Governor Moor/C/M/__/Not Known/1m/Babrella Moor/Jack Moor Uncle
George Mount/C/M/Mar/Not Known/7m/Gates & Elizabeth Mount/Gates Mount Father
Not Named/C/F/June/Spasms/__/Milly Jackson/Francis D. Battaile Former Master
Not Named/C/F/June/Measles/1m 3d/Ainetta/Edward Trice Former Owner
Not Named/C/M/Oct/Spasms/4m 7d/Isabella/F.D. Marshall Former Mistress
Not Named/C/F/Sept/Spasms/8d/Alford & Roannia Moor/Alfred Moor Father
Not Named/C/F/Mar/Not Known/__/Richard & Frances Mines/Richard Mines Father
Not Named/C/F/Dec 15/Not Known/__/Henry & Catharine Fox/Henry Fox Father
Not Named/C/F/Nov 7/Not Known/6d/Wm H. & Jane Sterns/Wm H. Sterns Father
Elizabeth Penny/W/F/Feb 27/Cancer/80y/Wm & __ Penny/Wm Penny Husband/Ann E. Taylor daughter
John F. Pemberton/W/M.Apr 15/Wounded at 5 forks/33y/Reuben & Elizabeth Pemberton/

Unmarried/Reuben A. Pemberton Brother
Pendleton/C/M/Aug/Consumption/20y/__ & Caroline/Jos T. Collins Former Master
Patsy/C/F/Mar/Scrofula/40y/Not Known/R.H. Coleman Former Master
Nancy Patterson/W/F/June 26/Disease of Lungs/79y/Thompson & Elizabeth Mills/R.R. Evans Neighbour
William Redd Sr/W/M/Aug 16/Congestion of Brain/3m 20d/Edmond & Elizabeth Redd/Edmond Redd Father
John S. Robinson/W/M/Sept 8/Teething/1y 7m/Jos & Mary C. Robinson/Jos Robinson Father
Clemantina Rock/C/F/May 4/Not Known/1y/John & Louisa Rock/John Rock Father
Sarah Robinson/C/F/__/Typhoid Fever/18y/Bristoe & Betty Robinson/Bristoe Robinson Father
Ellen Stevens/C/F/Jan/Bronkitus/25y/Lewis & Mannoa Miner/E.F. Flagg Former Master
John W. Ship/W/M/Dec 9/Consumption/22y/William & Lucy Ship/Richard Moren Neighbour
Eliza Thompson/C/F/__/Consumption/50y/__ & Dicy/Richard Green Cousin
John J. Tate/W/M/Mar 16/Heart Disease/55y/John & Mildred Tate/Farmer/Susan Tate Wife
Henry Taylor/W/M/Feb 18/Typhoid Fever/69y/Henry & Catharine Taylor/Ann E. Taylor Wife
Frances Ellen Tarapence/W/F/Mar/Typhoid Fever/20y/George & Martha Walker/Wm Tarapence Husband/George Walker Father
Branton/C/M/Feb/Diptheria/7y/Eliza/Ira L. Thomas Former Master
Frank/C/M/Feb/Diptheria/3y/Eliza/Ira L. Thomas Former Master
Cabriella Walker/W/F/Mar/Typhoid Fever/14d/George & Martha Walker/George Walker Father
Tompkins Walker/C/M/Dec/Dropsy/62y/Mily/Elliott Wright Former Master
George Waller/C/M/Aug 16/Thrash/4y/Ellen Turner/Hy M. Young Former Master
Sisy/C/F/Sept/Chronic Diarreh/4y/China/Hy M. Young Former Master
Winney/C/F/Sept/Old Age/90y/Not Known/Ro A. Durrett Former Master
Richard S. White/W/M/Sept/Old Age/74y/Ambrose & Ann White/Horace A. Richards Nephew
Minor/C/F/Sept/Typhoid Fever/22y/Pluby/Elliott Wright Former Owner
Not Named/C/M/Nov/Overlaid/2m/Judy/Tavenor Winn Former Master
Not Named/C/F/Dec/Not Known/2m/Lucy/Tavenor Winn Former Master
Thomas Adams/W/M/July 12/Old Age/87y/Samuel & Sally Adams/b.Maryland/Sally Adams daughter
Ellen Carter/W/F/Apr/Not Known/65y/Not Known/Henry Carter Husband
James/C/M/Sept/Diptheria/8y/Keter & Malinda/Jos M. Seay Former Master
Emma [L.?] Southworth/W/F/Dec/Not Known/18y 5m/Pitchigraw & V. Southworth/ Pitchigraw Southworth Father
Thomas Allen Still/W/M/Aug 29/Not Known/1m/Allen & Frances Still/Frances Still Mother
Not Known/C/M/June 14/Not Known/1m/Henry & Catharine Fose/Henry Fise[sic] Father
Not Known/W/M/Oct 12/Hooping Cough/1m/Wm J. & Sarah F. Madison/Wm S. Madison Father
[illeg]/W/F/Jan 25/Dropsy/27y/Samuel & Rebecca Terrell/Joel T. Luck Neighbour
Not Known/C/__/__/[illeg]/Not Known/5y/Wilson & Ann Walker/Henry Sizer Former Master
[illeg]/C/__/__/__/9y/Jas & Ellen Fox/James Fox Father
[illeg]/Satterwhite/W/__/__/__/1y/Ben & Angelina Satterwhite/Ben Satterwhite Father
Mary Scott/W/F/June 30/Summer Compliant/4m/Thos L. & Ann E. Scott/Thos L. Scott Father
Elijah J. Stevens/W/M/Mar/Carbuncle/37y/Elijah J. & Lucy Stevens/Elijah Stevens Father

1866

Not Named/W/M/Oct 10/Not Known/2d/John C. & Betty G. Allen/John C. Allen Father
Cotes Blanton/W/F/Sept 10/Cold/1y 6m/Richard F. & Jane D. Blanton/Richard F. Blanton Father

Ambrose Baynham/W/M/Oct/Rupture/70y/Ambrose & Lucy Baynham/Farmer/Lavina Baynham Wife/Armistead S. Baynham Son

Edward Bowers/W/M/Nov 7/Spasms/11d/Wm S. & Emily Bowers/Wm S. Bowers Father

Richard Banks/C/M/Mar 23/Cough/84y/John & Delphy/Labourer/Fanny Banks Wife/Albert T. Banks Son

Addison Corr/W/M/Apr/Drowned/18y/John & Martha Corr/Farmer/Not Married/John Corr Father

Mary A. Cobbs/W/F/June 9/Typhoid Fever/65y/John & Mary Humphreys/Nelson Cobb Husband/Jas E. Cobb Son

William Chandler/C/M/July/Chronic Disease/1y/Henry & Milly Chandler/Richard E. Boulware Friend

Beulah Carter/C/F/Aug/Not Known/1y/Buckner & Nancy Carter/Buckner Carter Father

Kitty Carter/C/F/Jan 1/Consumption/40y/Ginny/Ro Carter Husband/Henry Carter Son

Not Named/C/M/Nov/Born Dead/Andy & Jane Chiles/Andy Chiles Father

Ginny Coleman/C/F/Nov/Consumption/70y/Williby & Milly Weaver/Wm Coleman Husband

Not Named/C/M/Aug/Not Known/Born Dead/William & Matilda Coleman/Wm Coleman Father

Harriett Ann Conner/C/F/Dec 20/Hooping Cough/5m 6d/Frank & Patsy Conner/Frank Conner Father

Richard Crenshaw/C/M/May/Liver Compliant/7y/Robert & Maria Crenshaw/Robert Crenshaw Father

Elizabeth Cooper/C/F/Sept/Not Known/8m/Jordan & Jane Cooper/Jordan Cooper Father

Lewis Coleman/C/F/Aug/Running in head/1y 8m/Courtney Coleman/Ro Coleman Grand Father

Not Named/C/M/June 16/Not Known/8d/Remus & Courtney Coleman/Remus Coleman Father

Not Named/W/F/Oct 1/Not Known/13d/Richd H. & Sally Dunn/Richd H. Dunn Father

Carroll Hansford Flagg/W/M/Feb 11/Killed by the fall of a Tree/6y 11m/E.F. & Amanda Flagg/E.F. Flagg Father

John Truman/W/M.Sept 8/Old Age/80y/Jas Truman Mother Not Known/Farmer/John Truman Son

Not Named/C/F/Feb/Not Known/6m/John & Lucy Ann Frazier/John Frazier Father

Louisa Julia Farrington/W/F/July/Sore Throut/4m/William & Priscilla Farrington/William Farrington Father

Not Named/C/M/June/Not Known/__/Richard & Josephine Gallery/Richard Gallery Father

James Green/C/M/July/Over heat/8y/Simon & Molly Green/Simon Green Father

Judy Johnson/C/F/Aug/Consumption/41y/Willis & Polly Johnson/Cyrus Johnson Husband/Henry Doggett Employer

James Johnson/C/M/July/Hooping Cough/4y/Cyrus & Judy Johnson/Henry Doggett Employer

Ottaway Johnson/C/F/July/Hooping Cough/1y/Cyrus & Judy Johnson/Henry Doggett Employer

Martha Ellen Jones/C/F/Apr/Not Known/2y/James Jones & Not Known/James Jamison Cousin

Gilbert King/C/M/Dec 20/Not Known/__/Rufus & Siby King/Rufus King Father

Wm Henry Lawson/C/M/Apr/Bronkitus/8m/Henry & Charlotte Lawson/Henry Lawson Father

Margarett Mitler/W/F/Feb/Inf Stomach/70y/W. & Mrs Mitler/Temple Mitler/James A. Mitler Son

Maria Miner/C/F/Feb/Typhoid Fever/16y/Nelson & Pamelia Minor/Nelson Minor Father

John Minor/C/M/Oct/Typhoid Fever/18y/Nelson & Pamelia Minor/Nelson Minor Father

Milly Minor/C/F/Feb/Consumption/20y/Winston & Sarah Chiles/Silas Minor Husband

George Mount/C/M/Mar/Not Known/9m/Giles & Eliaz Mount/Giles Mount Father

Willy Pleasants/C/M/Feb 14/Not Known/1y 1m/Jesse & Harriett Pleasants/Jesse Pleasants Father

Lucy Morris/W/F/July/Consumption/2y/Richd & Martha Morris/Angelina W. Peatross Grand Mother

Nathaniel Pope/C/M/__/Paralized/22y/James & Ann Pope/Robert Minor Brother

Hiter Purks/W/M/Sept/Dropsy/9y/Henry & Sarah Purks/Henry Purks Father

Betty K. Redd/W/F/Nov 17/Typhoid Fever/24y/E. & [illeg] Sanford/b.Hanover/Edmond T. Redd Husband

Susan Tomasia Redd/W/F/Aug 20/Spasms/11m/E.T. & Susan B.A. Redd/Edmond T. Redd Father
Not Named/C/F/Sept/Spasms/7m/Wm & Paty Reynolds/Horace Reynolds Grand Father
Not Named/C/M/July/Brain Infl/__/Wm & Patty Reynolds/Wm Reynolds Father
No Name/C/M/[illeg]/__/__/__/Richard Rollins
Not Named/C/F/Mar 11/Not Known/2m/Richard & Emily Rollins/Richard Rollins Father
Not Named/C/M/Nov/Not Known/2m/Sally/E. Trice O.[older?] Sister
Molly Robinson/C/F/Feb/Not Known/1d/Wm & Maria Robinson/Robert Minor Grand Father
Not Named/W/F/Oct 18/Not Known/1d/John & Elizabeth Stanley/John Stanley Father
Wm T. Spicer/W/M/Dec 4/d.Hanover/Ran over by car/23y/Thomas H. & Lavinia Spicer/b.Louisa/
  Workman on Rail Road/Unmarried/Thos H. Spicer Father
James Taylor/C/M/Mar 30/Cough/2m/Samuel & Emily Taylor/Samuel Taylor Father
Edward Lee Taylor/W/M/Apr 9/Hooping Cough/2y 6m/Wm F. & Rebecca Taylor/Wm Taylor Father
Artimus Campbell Taylor/W/M/Apr 10/Hooping Cough/5y/Wm F. & Rebecca Taylor/Wm F. Taylor
  Father
Charles Thompson/C/M/Feb/Not Known/5m/Emily Thompson/Richd Thompson Grand Father
Nornah Thompson/C/F/June/Not Known/Mary Thompson/Richd Thompson Grand Father
Not Named Thompson/C/M/Feb/Born Dead/Major & Mary Thompson/Major Thompson Father
Caroline Thornton/C/F/Feb 23/Not Known/6m/Theodore & Ginny Thornton/Theodore Thornton
  Father
Not Named Thomas/C/M/Sept/__/1d/Not Known/Ro Henry & Milly Thomas/Ro Henry Thomas
  Father
Polly Tibbs/C/F/Aug/Dropsy/55y/Not Known/Lewis Tibbs Husband/Richd F. Blanton
Flossie Trice/W/F/Feb 4/Not Known/6y 8m/Edward & Mary Trice/Edward Trice Father
William Thomas Tribble/W/M/Mar/Spinal Affection/8m/Thos J. & Atkinston Tribble/Thos J.
  Tribble Father
Wm W. Trainham/W/M/Aug/Consumption/__/Thos C. & Mary Claytor/Larking Trainham Brother
Franky Terrell/C/F/June 6/Diariah/26y/John & Ann Quash/Armistead Terrell Husband
Lucy West/C/F/Aug/Not Known/4y/Davy & Milly Minor/Nelson White Husband[sic]
Anna White/M/F/Dec/Scrafula/40y/Wilton E. & Mary Eliza White/Wilton E. Wright [sic] Father
Not Named/W/M/Jan/Not Known/1m/Wilton E. & Mary Eliza White/ Wilton E. Wright
 [sic] Father
Stanfield Wright/W/M/Apr 10/Paralysis/61y/Richd & Rebecca Wright/Farmer/Martha W. Wright
  Wife
Isabella West/C/F/July/Child Bed/30y/Not Known/Henry West Cousin
Jefferson Winston/C/M/Nov/Cold/1y 1m/Robt & Judy Ann Winston/Robert Winston Father
Ann Jane Wright/C/F/June/Worms/1y 6m/Agnes Wright/James O. Allen kin
James Waller/C/M/Sept/Typhoid Fever/22y/Not Known/Ira L. Thomas Friend
Ann White/C/F/Dec/Asthma/40y/Not Known/Wm N. Samuel Friend
Caty Wyatt/C/F/May 6/Old Age/80y/Tom & Phebe/Henry Carter Cousin
Not Named/C/M/Nov 29/Not Known/11m/Wm & Sarah Brown/Wm Brown Father
Grant Matty Cannon/W/M/Nov/Cold/8m/Judy Cannon/Henry C. Peatross Overseer of Poor
Not Named/C/F/Oct/Not Known/1 hour/Wm H. & Saly Cauthorn/Anna F. Morris Friend
Not Named/C/M/Aug/Not Known/7d/Claibourne & Susan Cauthorn/Anna F. Morris Friend
Matilda James/W/F/Aug/Not Known/__/Parents Not Known/Henry C. Peatross Overseer of Poor
Mary Long/W/F/Feb 18/Liver Disease/70y/Andrew Long/Lindsey Young Friend
Wm/C/M/July 18/Dropsy/40y/Not Known/Henry C. Peatross Overseer of Poor
Pine Henry Baylor/C/M/Aug/Bronkites/10m/Walker & Nancy Baylor/Walker Baylor Father
Emma S. Andrews/W/F/Mar/__/1m/Jno & Emma Andrews/John J. Andrews Father

Emma Andrews/W/F/May/Consumption/28y/James J. & Jane Broaddus/John J. Andrews Husband
Peter J. Barlow/W/M/Aug/__/9y/Jas & E.E. Barlow/Jas Barlow Father
No Name/W/F/Apr 10/__/5m/Mora A. & Mary Beazley/Mora A. Beazley Father
Jas W. Broaddus/W/M/Aug/__/2y/O.H. & Julia Broaddus/O.H. Broaddus Father
Thos B. Sale/W/M/July/Typhoid Fever/40y/Thos & Hart [Harriett] Sale/Farmer/C.C. Broaddus Admr
Martha E. Jackson/C/F/July/Consumption/10y/Achilly & Emily Jackson/Jas Clarke Neighbor
Mary Covington/W/F/Sept/__/2m/Wm N. & M.J. Covington/Wm N. Covington Father
Eliza Covington/W/F/Dec/5m/Wm N. & M.J. Covington/Wm N. Covington Father
Patsy Beazley/W/F/Aug/__/70y/Chris Beazley/Seth Claytor Son-in-Law
Gray Chenault/W/M/Aug/d.Richmond Va/__/22y/Gray & Martha Chenault/Gray Chenault Father
No Name/W/M/__/__/1d/F.D. & Judith Campbell/F.D. Campbell Father
Willis Coleman Jr/C/M/Feb/2y/Willis T. & Margt Coleman/Willis Coleman Father
Maria Coleman/C/F/__/__/50y/Not Known/Eugene DeJarnett Neighbour
Alford E. Brown/C/M/Sept/Congestive Chill/11y/__ & Sarah Brown/George Edwards Neighbour
Not Known/C/F/__/__/__/Leo & Fanny Brown/And J. Greenstreet Neighbour
Not Named/C/M/Apr/__/1m/Chs & Susan Gallery/Chas Gallery Father
Lucy Monroe/C/F/Mar/Consumption/42y/__ & Hagor Monroe/P. Gatewood Neighbour
Jno F. Green/W/M/Dec 15/__/25y/Theo F. & Patsy E. Green/Thos W. Green Brother
M. Ella Green/W/F/July/Consumption/35y/Silas & Ann E. Conduit/Thops W. Green Bro-in-Law
Lewis W. Garnett/W/M/Jan/Consumption/60y/__ Garnett/Wm R.W. Garnett Son
Lewis Jones/W/M/__/Pneumonia/65y/__/Wm J. Jones Relation
Emily Jackson/C/F/Comsumption/18y/Archilles & Emily Jackson/Archs Jackson Father
Not Known/F/F/__/__/7y/Chas & Sally Jackson/Chas Jackson Father
Leonard Johnson/C/M/Oct/__/10y/Simon & Sarah Johnson/Simon Johnson Father
James Landrum/W/M/Oct/Consumption/45y//Not Known/Jno F. Lafoe Neighbour
Thos Loven/W/M/Dec/Old Age/75y/Mor [Mordecai] V. Loven/Thos Loven Son
Willis James/W/M/Apr/__/56y 7d/__/Jos A. Chandler Neighbour
No Name/W/F/June/__/__/Jas & Jane M. McCalley/James McCalley Father
A.J. Motley/W/M/Sept/__/24y/E. & E.J. Motley/E. Motley Father
Sally D. Napier/W/F/Oct/__/5y/Jno R. & Bettie Napier/Jno R. Napier Father
Martha Sale/W/F/__/__/17y/Saml & Rachel Sale/Saml Sale Father
Wm W. Roper/W/M/Aug 15/Infla Bowels/46y/George & Maria O. Roper/Doctor/b.Richmond Va/
Jou [Jourdan] Woolfolk Father-in-Law
Eliz Sirles/W/F/Nov/Consumption/30y/Not Known/Jas Sirles Husband
Eliza J. Swift/W/F/June/21d/R.G. & Judia Swift/R.G. Swift Father
Not Named/W/F/Aug/1m/Jos M. & Esther A. Sirle/Jos M. Sirle Father
Martha Taliaferro/C/F/Aug/__/18y/Nath & Lucy Taliaferro/Nath Taliaferro Father
Ann B. Thornton/W/F/June/__/6y/W.A. & C.W. Thornton/Wase A. Thornton Husband
__ Thornton/W/F/July/Consumption/66y/Jno & __ Conway/Anthony Thornton Husband
Chas Rapaport/W/M/June/50y/Not Known/Doctor/M.M. Care Mother
Wm Vessells/C/M/Mar/__/16y/Chas & Lucy Vessells/Charles Vessells Father
Sally Ware/W/C/[sic]F/__/__/__/Henry McCalley Neighbour
Wm G. White/W/__/M/__/Typhoid Fever/2y/[illeg]Jas T. White Father & Merchant
[illeg entry]/C/M/__
No Name/W/M/July/__/2m/R.W. & E.F. Smoot/R.W. Smoot Father
No Name/W/F/Nov/__/6m/R.W. & E.F. Smoot/R.W. Smoot Father
Geo Jeter/C/M/Oct/Typhoid Fever/20y/Jas & Eliz Jeter/Jas Jeter Father
Not Named/C/F/__/__/7d/A.C. & Eliza Allen/Susan Stewart Neighbour

1867

No Name/W/F/Oct/Not Known/7m/Jas & Mary Andrews/Jas B. Andrews Father
Janis Jane Alsop/W/F/July 15/Typhoid Fever/25y/Wm & Nancy Garnett/Henry M. Alsop Husband
Jack Catlett/C/M/Old Age/100y/__/J.E. Anderson Neighbour
No Name/C/F/__/__/2m/Maria/J.E. Anderson Neighbour
Jno H. Anderson/W/M/May 16/d.Essex County/Pneumonia/31y/Henry & Julia Anderson/Farmer/ Julia A.S. Anderson Mother
Champ Thornton/C/M/Dec/Not Known/10m/Not Known/H.T. Stevens Neighbour
[Three persons of color, 1 male age 70, 1 female age 10, 1 female age 8 and not further information, all reported by H.T. Stevens Neighbour]
Not Known/C/M/Nov/__/__/Danl & Susan Banks/R.B. Richerson Neighbour
Not Known/C/F/Nov/Typhoid Fever/__/And [Andrew] & Betsy Moore/And Moore Father
Ellen Beazley/C/F/Jan/__/3y/Jos & Letitia Beazley/Jos Beazley Father
Dolly Boulware/W/F/Oct 23/Old Age/82y/Mark & __ Boulware/Jas Boulware Nephew
Not Known/C/F/__/__/__/Allen & Nancy Flood/Unmarried/R.H.W. Buckner Neighbor
Not Known/W/F/Jan/[illeg]/[illeg]/Ro & Jane Chapman/Robt Wright Neighbor
Wm Chapman/W/M/Sept/__/20y/Not Known/Robt Wright Neighbor
Frances & Mary Christian/2C/2F/Feb/7m/Richd & Lucy Christian/Richard Christian Father
Jno Dunnarant/W/M/Mar/7y/Jno & Lucy Dunnarant/John H. Dunnarant Father
No Name/W/M/F[sic]/Sept/__/__/And [Andrew] J. & Julia F. Dunn/And J. Dunn Father
Clarence L.Ennis/W/M/Apr/__/1y/R.L. & Sallie Ennis/Richard L. Ennis Father
No Name/W/M/May/__/6m/Reu & Mary Farmer/Reu Farmer Father
Adeline Farmer/W/F/Dec/Child's etc/20y/Wm & Susan Farmer/Wm Farmer Father
Jas Farmer/W.M.Dec/__/16y/Frans & Ann Farmer/Frans Farmer Father
Sally Graves/W/F/May/Old Age/70y/Wm & __ Farmer/Wm Graves Husband
Not Named/C/F/__/__/1d/Abram Garnett/Henry Gordon Neighbor
Kate Gouldin/W/F/Aug/Typhoid Fever/5y/J.F. & Victoria Gouldin/Jas F. Gouldin Father
Benton Guthridge/W/M/Aug/Not Known/5y/Jas J. & Susan Guthridge/Jas J. Guthridge Father
McKensie Gouldman/W/M/Feb/Dropsy/1y/G.F. & M.F. Gouldman/George F. Gouldman Father
Benjm Garnett Jr/C/M/__/Chills etc/1y/Ben & Mary Garnett/Benjm Garnett Father
Maria B. Gravatt/W/F/July/Bloody [illeg]/32y/Geo & Theresa Marshall/And J. Gravatt Husband
Edmonia Hill/C/F/Aug/Not Known/16y/Reu & A. Hill/Reu Hill Father
Mary Haiden [Hayden]/W/F/Sept/Not Known/__/Miles & Mary Haiden Father
Susan Jackson/C/F/Heart Disease/__/Ed & __ Jackson/Robert Jackson Son
No Name/C/F/__/__/__/Phil & Lucy Johnson/Phil Johnson Father
No Name/C/F/__/__/__/John & Julie Johnson/John Johnson Father
Jno Kay/W/M/July/__/__/Richd & __ Kay/Lucy Kay Wife
Rebecca/C/F/__/Typhoid Fever/__/__/Dolly Wright Neighbor
Lucy Loving/W/F/__/Pneumonia/__/__/Lindsey Loving Husband
Billie Loving/W/M/Nov/Not Known/Ro & Sarah Living/Robt Loving Father
Jas Monday/W/M/Sept/Not Known/__/J.R. & M.W. Monday/Jas R. Monday Father
Nathaniel Motley/W/M/Feb/Pneumonia/__/Henry & Lucy A. Motley/Jno L. Motley Son
Bettie A. Clarke/W/F/__/__/__/Jos E. & Lucy Penny/Jos E. Penny Father
No Name/C/M/__/__/__/Lucy/Jos E. Penny Neighbor
Emma Pavy/W/F/June/__/__/Jos & Sarah Pavy/Jos J. Pavy Father & Mechanic
[illeg]/C/M/__/__/__/__/Jos R. Kay Neighbor

Wm A. Richerson/W/M/May/Dropsy/36y/Alvin & M.L. Richerson/Farmer/Mary L. Richerson
  Mother
Susanna/C/F/__/Brain Fever/6y/Ann/Mary L. Richerson Neighbor
Martha Sale/C/F/__/__/2y/Spencer & Celia Sale/Spencer Sale Father
Emma Stevens/W/F/July/Diariah/3m/H.T. & Hattie Stevens/H.T. Stevens Father
Maria/C/F/__/Old Age/70y/__/D.C. DeJarnette Neighbor
Frances/C/F/__/__/10y/Rachel/D.C. DeJarnette Neighbor
Agnes Taliaferro/C/F/__/__/10y/Mathw & Agnes Taliaferro/Mattw Taliaferro Father
Jno L. Thornton/W/M/Oct 4/Lock Jaw/19y/H.F. & M.S. Thornton/H.F. Thornton Father
Mary H. Thornton/W/F/July/Consumption/45y/G.B. & M.H. Conway/E.T. Thornton Husband
Not Known/C/M.__/Chills/3y/Geo & Kitty Washington/Wm M. Kelly informant
Not Known/C/F/__/__/1m/Jno & Sarah Miller/Jno T. Boutwell Informant
No Name/W/F/Nov/__/4m/B.A. & Martha Wharton/B.A. Wharton Father
Lucy Wharton/W/F/Nov/__/55y/__/Festus Wharton Nephew
Hesta Wharton/W/F/__/__/1y/B. & H. Wharton/Bird Wharton Father
Ox Wharton/W/F/Feb 17/__/4y/Otway & Martha E. Wharton/Informant Father
__/W/F/Oct/__/__/1m/B. & H. Wharton/Informant Father
Anna Washington/W/F/Oct/10m/Walk [Walker] & Mary Washington/Walk Washington Father &
  Physician
Not Known/W/F/__/__/__/P & Eliza Washington/John T. Boutwell Neighbor
Annie Washington/W/F/Sept/2y/J. & R. Washington/Jno Washington Father
Henry Saunders/W/M/__/__/60y/Not Known/Ro B. Wright Neighbor
Anna Maria Jones/W/F/Dec 16/Consumption/65y/Charles & Mary Jarvis/b.Hanover/Patrick Henry
  Jones Husband
Not Named/C/M/Sept/Consumption/16d/Isaac & Jane Johnson/Isaac Johnson Father
Henry O. Kelly/W/M/Aug 11/Consumption/28y/Richard & Mary Kelly/Farmer/Mildred Kelly
  Wife/Richard Kelly Father
Not Named/C/F/Sept/Not Known/9d/Zachariah & Harriett Lewis/Zachariah Lewis Father
Lucy/C/F/Feb/Not Known/80y/Not Named/E. Trice Friend
Sarah Minor/C/F/Aug/Consumption/27y/Lewis & Minera Minor/Lewis Minor Father
Maria Miner/C/F/Aug/Not Known/6m/Peter & Eliza Minor/Peter Minor Father
Martha Miner/C/F/Jan 4/Abcess/4y/Moses & Maria Miner/Moses Miner Father
Melinda Miner/C/F/Sept/Consumption/60y/Anna & Moses Wyatt/Moses Miner Son
Walker Miner/C/M/Nov/Diptheria/76y/C. & Rose Miner/Moses Miner Son
Josephine Miner/C/F/Jan 5/Not Known/1y 6m/Not Known & Betty Miner/Moses Miner Uncle
Not Named Myers/C/F/Sept/Not Known/6d/Jerry & __ Myers/Jerry Myers Father
Huldah Pendleton/W/F/May 17/Cholera Infection/6m/Wm M. & Sarah Pendleton/Wm M.
  Pendleton Father
Not Named Pendleton/C/M/Jan/Spasms/9d/Jesse & Ann Pendleton/ Jesse Pendleton Father
Priscilla/C/F/__/Asthma/80y/Not Known/George B. Pollard Friend
Not Named/W/M/July 12/Spasms/9d/Joseph B. & Mary C. Robinson/Joseph B. Robinson Father
Edmund Satterwhite/W/M/April 7/Consumption/76y/Robert & Catherine Satterwhite/Farmer/
  Nancy Satterwhite Wife/Franklin Satterwhite Son
Not Named Southworth/W/F/Nov 1/Not Known/James B. & Mary Frances Southworth/James B.
  Southworth Father
Frances Still/W/F/Dec/Consumption/60y/Not Known/Allen Still Husband/John E. Seal Son-in-Law
Aubrey Edward Swann/W/M/Apr/Hooping Cough/8m/Saml E. & Milly Swann/Samuel E. Swann
  Father

William James Taylor/C/M/Feb/d.Hanover/Cold/6m/James & Penny Taylor/b.Hanover/James Taylor Father
Not Named Terry/W/M/Mar 20/Not Known/4d/Thomas & Catharine Terry/Thomas Terry Father
[Note: Entries 77-82 in original are faded beyond recognition]
Rose Fell/W/F/[illeg]/[illeg]/[illeg]/Joe & Rose Fell/Benjamin Jackson Brother to Rose
__ Turner/W/F/July/Congestion/John & Mary Lipscomb/Richison [Richerson] Turner Husband
[illeg]/C/M/Sept/[illeg]/8y/Not Known/R.A. Durrett Friend
__ Weathers/C/F/Aug/Congestion/6y/Not Known/James Weathers Father
[illeg]6y/[rest is illeg]
Not Known/C/M/[illeg]/Stephen Minor Son-in-Law
[illeg]/C/F/Apr/d.Hanover/Pneumonia/6y/Alice & Hazel Yates/Alice[sic] Yates Father
Nancy [illeg]/W/F/Feb/Plurisy/68y/Davy B[illeg] & Not Known/Willis Jones Friend
Nancy [illeg]/C/F/Mar 3/Not Known/80y/Not Known/James Wright Friend
[illeg]/C/M/Feb 11/Consumption/28y/Not Known/b.Albemarle/Charles Minor Friend
Not Known Burkins/C/F/May 30/Fitts/1m/Not Known & Margaret Burkins/[illeg]Midwife
Caroline Coleman/C/F/Jan/Bronkitas/80y/Not Known & Sally Coleman/Joel T. Luck Friend
Henry Carater/C/M/Dec 20/Not Known/70y/Not Known/Albert S. Hundley Friend
Sarah B. Dabney/W/F/Sept 17/Bilious Fever/20y/Robt S. & Rebecca Hill/James Dabney Husband/ Robert S. Hill Father
[illeg]/C/F/Sept/Consumption/68y/Frederick & Sarah Martin/John Rock Friend
__Minor/C/F/Dec/Pneumonia/21y/Fanny Minor/Frederick Stevens Friend
__ Newton/W/F/Mar/Not Known/__/Thomas & Nancy Dickinson/Farmer/Johnson Newton Husband/John K. Sizer Son
[illeg]/C/F/Apr 10/__/__/Simon & Ginny/W.R.B. Wyatt Friend
Not Named/C/M/Aug/Spasms/8d/Martha/Edward Trice Friend
Jefferson [illeg]/C/M/Sept/Pneumonia/40y/Not Known/R. Turner Friend
Not Known/C/F/Nov/[illeg]/[illeg]/Not Known & Sally [illeg]/Edmund Trice Friend
Nancy Allen/W/F/Feb 4/Cancer/60y/Caleb & Betty Butts/b.Louisa/John A. Allen Husband
Not Named/W/F/May 22/Not Known/1m 21d/Richard D. & Sarah E. Arnall/Richard D. Arnall Father
Not Named/W/F/May 29/Not Named/1m 28d/Richard D. & Sarah Arnall/Richard D. Arnall Father
Sarah E. Arnall/W/F/June 12/Chronic Thrash/35y/Briscoe & Deliah Mitchell/Richard D. Arnall Husband
John Lewis Atkinson/W/M/Apr 24/Lung Fever/1y 2m/Obediah & Margarett Atkinson/Obediah Atkinson Father
Not Named/C/F/Nov/Not Known/2d/Not Known & Jane Beazley/Richard E. Boulware Friend
Fannie L. Blanton/W/F/Aug/Not Known/1y/Eldred & Mary F. Blanton/Eldred Blanton Father
Thomas & Etta Blunt/2W/1M/1F/May 17/Not Known/4m 15d/William & Ellen Blunt/Wm Blunt Father
Overton Burruss/W/M/Nov/Rheumatism/59y/Jacob & Mary Burruss/Farmer/Clarisy Burruss/ Jas W. Burruss Son
Caroline Buckner/C/F/July 20/Not Known/22y/James & Betsy Taylor/Spencer Buckner
John Bullock/W/M/Apr/Heart Disease/82y/James & Patsy Bullock/b.Spotsylvania County /Henrietta Bullock Wife/Wm K. Bullock Son-in Law
Janette Carneal/W/M[sic]/Sept 1/Not Known/2d/Archibald T. & Mildred M. Carneal/Archibald T. Carneal Father
Esther Carneal/W/F/Sept/Not Known/11m/John W. & Nancy Carneal/John W. Carneal Father
William Henry Carter/C/M/Nov/Dropsy/3m 1d/Henry & Agnes Ann Carter/Henry Carter Father

Benjamin Carter/C/M/July/Bronkites/1y 6m/James & Elizabeth Carter/James Carter Father
Butch Burton Canady/C/M/Oct/Not Known/2y/Jack & Malinda Canady/Jack Canady Father
Not Named Carrison/C/M/Feb/Not Known/1d/Richard & Susan Carrison/Richard Carrison Father
Not Named/C/F/June/Cold/11d/Andrew & Jane Chiles/Andrew Chiles Father
James E. Coleman/W/M/Sept 20/Brain Fever/22y/Ruffin H. & Bettie B. Coleman/Married/Ruffin H. Coleman Father
Addison Corr/W/M/May 6/Drowned/16y/John & Martha Corr/John Corr Father
Robert Cobb/W/M/Oct/Old Age/82y/Not Known/Miller [occupation]/ George S. Cobb Son
Not Named/C/F/Sept/Not Known/2d/Melville & Judy Cooper/Melville Cooper Father
Thomas Armistead Courtney/C/M/Apr/Not Known/11d/Timothy & Jane Courtney/Timothy F. Courtney Father
William Minor Conner/C/M/July/Cold/4y/Sarah & Patsy Conner [sic]/Frank Conner Father
Willis Cooper/C/M/Apr/Cold or Fits/21d/Jordan & Jane Cooper/Jordan Cooper Father
Richard Coleman/C/M/Aug/Typhoid Fever/14y/Resmus & Martha Coleman/Resmus Coleman Father
Not Named/C/F/Aug/Cold/28y/Robert & Martha Crenshaw/Robert Crenshaw Father
Charles/C/M/Aug/Not Known/22y/__/b.Washington/Wm A. Dickens Friend
John Douglace/W/M/Mar 28/Not Known/23d/John & Mary Jane Douglace/John Douglace Father
Charlotte DeJarnett/C/F/May 1/Consumption/29y/Robert & Maria Coats/John Coats Father
Allen Ferguson/C/M/Aug/Not Known/2y 7m/Andrew & Catharine Ferguson/Andrew Ferguson Father
Not Named/C/M/Feb/Not Known/__/Joseph & Harriett Flippo/Jos Flippo Father
Not Named/C/M/Aug 3/Not Known/1d/Thomas & Lydia Fose/Thomas Fose Father
Elizabeth Josephine Galery/C/F/July/Heart Disease/11m/Richard & Elizabeth Galery/Richd Galery Father
Harriett Galery/C/F/Aug/Heart Disease/2y 1m/Richard & Elizabeth Galery/Richd Galery Father
Sarah Goldsby/W/F/Aug/Typhoid Fever/18y/John & Eliza Goldsby/ John Goldsby Father
William James Gravatt/C/M/Sept/inf Bowels/11m/Henry & Catharine Gravatt/Henry Gravatt Father
Aaron Gregory/C/M/Jan/Not Known/1y 11m/Paul & Maria Gregory/Paul Gregory Father
Robert William Grimes/C/M/July/Typhoid Fever/10m/John F. & Louisa Grimes/John F. Grimes Father
Not Named Grimes/C/M/Oct 16/Not Known/1d/John F. & Louisa Grimes/John F. Grimes Father
William Thomas Haywood/W/M/Sept 3/Teething/10m/Jno R. & Emilene Heywood/Thos R. Heywood Father
Julia Marshall Harris/W/M[sic]/__/d.Spottsylvania/Clorera Infection/9y 6m/Octevus D. & Susan M. Harris/O.D. Harris Father
Pricilla Harris/C/F/Jan/Not Known/Croup/74y/Charlie & Litty Asko/Johnson Harris Son
Elizabeth Harris/C/F/Nov/Not Known/5m/Thomas & Rebecca Harris/ John A. Harris Uncle
Molley Holmes/C/F/__/Brain Fever/1y 4m/George [illeg] Holmes/Cornelius Holmes Uncle
Aley Henderson/C/F/Sept/Dropsy/70y/Daniel & Amey Lewis/Thomas Cash Friend
Horace/C/M/Feb/Dropsy/30y/Not Known/Charles W. Blanton Friend
Mary Eliza/C/F/Feb/Tsemus/12y/Becky/Thomas Hurt Friend
Dolly Hailstock/C/F/Apr/Liver Compliant/49y/[illeg]/Frank Cannor Friend
Selia Holmes/C/F/June/Consumption/60y/[illeg]James James [sic] Husband
Nancy James/C/F/June/[illeg]/[illeg]/James James Father
James Fleming/[illeg]/C/M/__/__/__/James Butler Friend

1868

Lucy Ann Turner/W/F/Apr 7/Dropsy/23y/Peter & Emily Wyatt/Wm Turner Husband
Not Named/C/F/June/Not Known/14d/George & Mary Jane Turner/G. Turner Father
Jackson Winn/C/M/Penumonia/65y/Not Known/Not Married/Joel T. Luck Friend
George Todd Wright/W/M/Dec 3/Diptheria/4y/Charles & Elizabeth Wright/Chas Wright Father
Robert Ridgeway Wright/W/M/Dec 3/Diptheria/2y/Charles & Elizabeth Wright/Chas Wright Father
Norville Wingfield/C/M/Sept/Spasms/14y/John & Aggy Wingfield/John Wingfield Father
Caleb Wingfield/C/M/Dec/d.Danville/Typhoid Fever/18y/John & Aggy Wingfield/John Wingfield Father
Mary T. Wright/W/F/Sept/Cholra Infection/1y/Philip M. & Julia A. Wright/Philip M. Wright Father
Anna Wyatt/C/F/Old Age/110y/Not Known/A. Dodson Friend
Not Named Young/W/F/Dec 5/Not Known/18d/Timothy & Lucy Young/Timothy Young Father
James M. Young/W/M/June 27/Consumption/67y/Wm & Ann Young/Sarah Young Widow
Wm F. Burnett/W/M/July/Dropsy/60y/Not Known/Henry C. Peatross Friend
Caroline/C/F/Feb/Old Age/85y/Litty/Joel T. Luck Friend
Anitia Dandridge/C/F/Mar 1/Not Known/55y/Not Known/Benj Stevens Friend
Benjamin Anderson/W/M/Feb 29/Old Age/99y/Thomas Anderson Mother Not Known/Farmer/ Married/Wm J. Anderson Son
Elmora Anderson/W/F/Sept 15/Cronic Congestion/44y 7m/Wm McGee & Eliza McGee/Thos B. Anderson Husband
Selia Allen/W/F/Mar 14/Not Known/6m/R.T. Allen/R.T. Allen Father
Sally Alexander/C/F/Sept 20/Not Known/1y 6m/Thornton & Sophia Alexander/ Washington D.C./ Thornton Alexander Father
Sally Bland/W/F/Jan 1/Consumption/70y/Not Known/Ambrose Bland Husband
Mary Catharine Blunt/W/F/July/Consumption/20y/Wm B. & Sarah E. Blunt/Not Married/Wm B. Blunt Father
Mary Ann Boulware/C/F/Dec 4/Disentary/1y 2d/Winston & Mary Boulware/Winston Boulware Father
Ann Brooks/W/F/Aug 14/Typhoid Fever/6y 6m/James P. & Angelicia Brooks/James P. Brooks Father
Henrietta Bullock/W/F/Oct 12/Old Age/79y/Stephen & Mary Lacost/b.Fredericksburg/Wm K. Bullock Husband/Wm K. Bullock Son
James A. Carter/C/M/Jan 8/Diptheria/10m/Henry & Aggy Carter/Not Married/Henry Carter Father
Nancy Carter/C/F/Dec/Dropsy/16y/Wm & Betty Carter/b.Washington/Wm Carter Father
Polly Ann Claytor/W/F/Apr 12/Child Bed/30y/Major & Elizabeth Taylor/Wm E. Taylor Husband
Emma Coats/C/F/Apr 1/Not Known/7m 7d/Benj & Kitty Carter/Wm Coleman Grandfather
Henry Fox/C/M/Dec 29/Hectic Fever/45y/Amey Pettis/b.Spotsylvania/Henry Fox Husband
Not Named/W/F/Feb 27/Not Known/__/Jas W. & Mary Elizabeth Freeman/James W. Freeman Father
Francis Alexander/C/M/Aug 7/Cholera Infantum/15m/Nelson & Betty Ann Freeman/Nelson Freeman Father
Margarett Luella Fox/W/F/July 10/Congestive Chill/8y/Richard A. & Margarett A. Fox/b.King William/Richard A. Fox Father
Not Named/C/M/Jan/Not Known/__/Dick & Harriett Coleman/Dick Coleman Father
Robert Gibbs/C/M/July/Croup/3m 10d/Anthony & Nancy Gibbs/Anthony Gibbs Father
Silvia Freeman/C/F/Feb/Scrofula/25y/Lucy West/Larry Mat Ellis Friend
George Grundy/C/M/Feb/Old Age/72y/Not Known/b.King William/Henry C. Peatross Friend

Mary Temple Harris/W/F/July 11/Bilious Fever/2y 2m/Charles M. & Mary Etta Harris/Charles M. Harris Father
Winston Harris/C/M/Sept/Ague & Fever/6m/Polly Harris/Johnson Harris Grandfather
Julia Hunter/C/F/Sept/Cold/7m/Robinson & Nancy Hunter/Robinson Hunter Father
Syrus Johnson/C/M/Feb 5/Consumption/9y 6m/Syrus & Judy Johnson/Syrus Johnson Father
Polly Johnson/C/F/Feb 2/Cold/35y/Ralph & Betty Johnson/Syrus Johnson Brother
Not Named/C/M/Jan/__/__/Polly Johnson/Syrus Johnson Uncle
Richard Kelley/W/M/Nov 14/Liver Disease/70y/James & Elizabeth Kelley/Farmer/Mary Ann Kelley Widow
John Franklin Kelley/W/M/Aug 25/Ireeseples/6y 6m/Thos & Betty Ann Kelley/Thomas Kelley Father
Thomas Lacy/C/M/Nov 28/Worms/2y 6m/Thomas & Elenor Lacy/Thomas Lacy Father
Not Named/C/M/Apr/Spasms/__/Fanny Lewis/F.W. Scott Friend
Margarett Madison/W/F/May 29/Not Known/66y/Anna Jones/Wm Madison Husband
Ann Maria Minor/C/F/June/Liver Disease/34y/__/James Minor Husband
Mary Minor/C/F/May/Not Known/2y/John & Eliza Minor/John Minor Father
Benjamin Franklin Moore/W/M/Aug/Heart Disease/15y/Sanford & Maria Moore/Benjamin F. Satterwhite Uncle
Mary Mildred Oliver/W/F/Mar/Consumption/55y/Marsha M. Oliver/Eldred Blanton Friend
Mary Page/C/F/Oct/Consumption/25y/Reuben & A. Page/Reuben Page Father
Sally Burton Robinson/C/F/May/Not Known/3y 1m/Burton & Sally Robinson/Burton Robinson Father
Ann Dishman Robinson/C/F/Aug/Typhoid Fever/16y/James & Margaret Robinson/James Robinson Father
Eldred Satterwhite/W/M/Aug 25/Consumption/55y/Edmond & Nancy Satterwhite/Farmer/Wm T. Satterwhite Son
Mary Ellen Satterwhite/W/F/July/Not Known/3m/Franklin & Mary Ellen Satterwhite/Franklin Satterwhite Father
Lucy Stanley/W/F/June/d.Spotsylvania/Old Age/96y/Wm & Mary Stanley/b.Spotsylvania/Louisa Hagan Grand Child
Humphrey Sales/C/M/Dec 1/Pneumonia/53y/__/Farm hand/___/Patsy Sales Widow
Not Named/C/F/Oct 19/Lock Jaw/21d/John & Lucinda Smith/John Smith Father
Not Named/C/F/May/Not Known/7d/Robert & Eliza Sugar/Robert Sugar Father
Walter Spindle/C/M/May/Spasms/2d/Lizzie Spindle/Winston Spindle Grand Father
Sally Taylor/C/F/Aug/Hectic Fever/14y 2m/John & Olivia Taylor/John Taylor Father
Wm Henry Taylor/C/M/May 1/Pneumonia/__/Sigh & Machelle Taylor/Sigh Taylor Father
Carter Taliaferro/C/M/May 17/__/__/__/Nancy Taliaferro Widow
No Name/C/__/Mar 20/5d/Alfred & Mary Allen/Alfred Allen Father
Lucy Houston/W/F/Dec 15/Heart Disease/65y/Not Known/Broaddus Allport Relation
No Name/W/F/Sept/10d/Jas & Mary Andrews/Jas Andrews Father
Alice Brown/C/F/Sept/__/5y/Robt & Mary Brown/Robt Brown Father
Wm J. Boulware Jr/W/M/Oct 27/Not Known/8y/Wm J. & A.E. Boulware/Wm J. Boulware Father
Sallie L. Baylor/C/F/__/Child Bed/35y/__/John Baylor Husband
Laura Baldwin/W/F/Sept 27/d.King & Queen Co/Not Known/5y/Geo B. & Nancy Baldwin/Geo B. Baldwin Father
Leland Baldwin/W/M/Sept 11/d.King & Queen Co/Not Known/3y/Geo B. & Nancy Baldwin/Geo B. Baldwin Father
No Name/W/F/Aug/Not Known/10d/Jos S. & Martha Davies/Jos S. Davies Father
No Name/W/F/Feb/Not Known/5d/Richd T. & Mary Chandler/Richd T. Chandler Father

Not Name/C/F/Feb/Not Known/15d/Richd & Mary Cooke/Richard Cooke Father
Nelson Coghill Jr/C/M/Aug/Not Known/20d/Nelson & Mary Coghill/Nelson Coghill Father
Frank H. Carter/W/M/Sept 15/Heart Disease/19y/Jas S. & Emiline Carter/Jas S. Carter Father
No Name/W/F/Oct/Not Named/5m/Wm P. & S.A. Chewning/Wm P. Chewning Father
Jas S. Catlett/W/M/July 18/Not Known/56y/Robt & Mary Catlett/Jas Catlett Brother
Cornl [Cornelius] Campbell/W/M/June 12/Heart Disease/65y/Cornl & Rosa Campbell/Emily Campbell Wife
Robt W. Cole/W/M/April/Heart Disease/52y/Jno G. & Nancy Cole/Lucy F. Cole Wife
Hyter Carter/C/M/May/Not Known/7y/Jno & Eliza Carter/John Carter Father
Lucy Haynes/W/F/__/Cor Diapepsia/60y/Stephen & Nancy Chinault/Lewis Haynes Husband
Francis Gouldin/W/M/June 10/Not Known/6y/J. Fran & E. Gouldin/Jas F. Gouldin Father
Patsy Gordan/W/F/Feb 20/Consumption/60y/__ and __ Fitzhugh/Henry Gordan Relation
[illeg] M. Gatewood/W/M/June 20/Cancer/60y/Chaney & Elizabeth Gatewood/America Gatewood Consort
Thomas Gray/W/M/Dec/Consumption/70y/Geo & __ Gray/Allen Gray Son
Not Known/C/F/__/Not Known/50y/__/Wm [illeg] Neighbour
Clementine Farish/W/F/Mar/Chronic Dyariah/67y/Geo & Clem Farish/Wm P.T. Farish Brother
Mary Jones/W/F/Apr/Not Known/25y/Wm & Ellen Jones/Wm Jones Father
Morton Jefferson/C/M/__/Not Known/26y/M. & J. Jefferson/Morton Jefferson Father
Mary Jones/C/F/Mar/Not Known/30y/Wm & Mary Jones/Wm Jones Father
No Name/C/F/Feb/__/12m/Henry & Eliza Turner/Henry Turner Father
Wm H. Kelley/W/M/Spasms/6y/Wm M. & Betty Kelley/Wm M. Kelley Father
Willis Lovin/W/M/July 15/Not Known/80y/J. & Betsy Lovin/Willis Pitts Neighbour
Emma Lovin/W/F/__/Not Known/2m/Brooking & Cam Lovin/Brooking Loving [sic] Father
James Lindsay/C/M/__/Not Known/40y/Not Known/Wm W. White Neighbour
No Name/W/M/Not Known/1m/Jno H. & Maria Lee/J.H. Lee Father
Thomas B. Lumpkin/W/M/Aug/Not Known/45y/Jno & Phebe Lumpkin/Joe B. Lumpkin Son
No Name/W/F/__/Not Known/2m/Jno & Margt Martin/Jno Martin Father
Jane A. Pavey/W/F/Sept 28/Appoplexy/50y/Thos & __ Madison/Jno G. Pavey Husband
Mary Pruett/W/F/__/Pneumonia/2y/Wm & Mary Pruett/Wm Pruett Father
Richard A. Puller/W/M/__/Pneumonia/42y/Wm & Caty Puller/Sarah A. Puller Consort
Rand Peyton/W/M/Apr 19/Not Known/40y/Brok & Eliz Peyton/Eliz Peyton Mother
John Richards/W/M/__/Brain Fever/12y/Richd & Alice Richards/Richard Richards Father
Courtney Robinosn/W/F/__/Typhoid Fever/40y/Stephen & Court Robinson/Stephen Robinson Father
Geo Richerson Jr/W/M/Not Known/5y/Geo & Eliza Richerson/Geo Richerson Father
Madison Southworth/W/M/__/Not Known/60y/__/Jno D. Southworth Relation
No Name/W/F/__/Not Known/2y/Geo W. & Eliz Sirls/Geo W. Sirls Father
David Sterne/W/M/__/__/10y/F.G. & Eliz Sterne/F.G. Sterne Father
Robt Saunders/C/M/__/__/40y/__/Jas R. Dishman Neighbour
Wm H. Allen/W/M/__/Consumption/50y/__/Ro B. Tunstall Bro-in-Law
Geo W. Trice/W/M/Feb/Pneumonia/62y/Not Known/Albert Carter Neighbour
Saburnah Vaughan/W/F/Consumption/37y/Wm & Polly Vaughan/Ro S. Vaughan Relation
John Wright/W/M/__/__/7m/__/Jas Wright Father
Jourdan Woolfolk/W/M/Sept/__/72y/Jno G. & Elizabeth Woolfolk/Jno W. Woolfolk Son

1869

[Note: Original records are missing in the files of The Library of Virginia]

1870

[Note: Original records are missing in the files of The Library of Virginia]

1871

[Note: Original records are missing in the files of The Library of Virginia]

1872

Cary Lee Allen/W/M/July 5/d.Golansville, Car Co/Brain Fever/1y 6m/R.T. & KateAllen/b.Golansville/
R.T. Allen Father

__ Alsop/C/F/Dec 7/d/ "Aspen Level"/Hooping Cough/17d/Joshua & Elisa Alsop/ b."Aspen Level"/
Joshua Alsop Father

Sarah Claiborne/C/F/Apr 9/d."Ellerslie"/Typhoid Fever"/3y 1m 9d/Joseph Claiborne/b.Mangohick
[King Wm Co]/Jos Claiborne Father

Liston Cobb/W/M/May 9/d."Eastern View"/Old Age/77y/__/b.Cedar Fork [Caroline Co]/Farmer/
Widower/S.T. Dickinson Physician

__ Coats/C/M/Dec 13/d."Green Hills"/Thrash/8d/John & Mary Coats/b."Green Hills"/John Coats
Father

__ Carneal/W/F/Jan 18/d."Liberty Grove"/Unknown/7d/J.A. & Anna B. Carneal/ b."Liberty Grove"/
J.A. Carneal Father

Samuel Carneal/W/M/July 23/d.Wright's Chapel [Caroline Co]/Fell From a Mule/12y 3m/Wm &
Tomasia Carneal/b.Near Bull Church [Caroline Co]/Wm Carneal Father

Charles Collins/W/M/July 27/d."Edge Hill"/Pneumonia/35y/Charles & Catharine Collins/Farmer/
Ro. E. Collins Brother

__Chiles/C/F/Jan 8/d."Colemans"/Unknown/3d/Rufus & Georganna Chiles/b."Colemans/Rufus Chiles
Father

Elizabeth Coleman/C/F/Aug 1/d."Burke's"/Scrofula/22y/Richard & Susan Coleman/Cook/Susan
Coleman Mother

Annie L. Carneal/W/F/Aug 3/d."DeJarnette's"/Chills/9y/Ira & Fannie Carneal/b."Cobbs"/Ira Carneal
Father

Mary R. Dorsey/W/F/July 1/d."South Garden"/Cholera Infantum/1y 7m/C.R. & Cattie Dorsey/Cattie
Dorsey Mother

Harriett Fox/C/F/May 9/d."Pleasant Hill"/Congestion of Brain/15y/Wm & Jane Fox/b."Pleasant Hill"/
Wm Fox Father

Matilda Fox/C/F/July 19/d."Wrights"/Child Bed/37y/Wm & Ann Fox/B."Green Hill"/Cook/Single/
__ Fox Son

John B. Flippo/W/M/Dec 18/d."Rose Plains"/Pneumonia/78y/__ & [illeg] Flippo/b."Sycamore Hill"/
Farmer/Sally Flippo wife/S.W. Flippo Son

__ Gray/W/M/Dec 11/d."Gravatt's"/Unknown/12d/Jas T. & V.D. Gray/b."Gravatt's"/Jas T. Gray
Father

__ Glascoe/C/__/June 30/d."Flippo's"/Unknown/24d/Warner & Matilda Glascoe/b."Flippo's"/Warner

Glascoe Father
Lucy J. Hailstock/C/F/July 7/d."Blanton's"/Cramp Cholic/8y/Josh & Sallie Hailstock/b."Blanton's"/Josh Hailstock Father
Mildred King/C/F/Feb 13/d."Blanton's"/Burned by Accident/5y/Wm & Rita King/Wm King Father
Samuel P. Luck/W/M/July 19/d.[on]Roadside/Old Age/77y/K.V. Luck/Farmer/Widower/S.A. Luck Grandson
Dilsey Minor/C/F/June 19/d."Taylor's"/Consumption/50y/James & Charice Minor/Widow/James Minor Son
__ Minor/C/F/Aug 30/d. "Johnson's"/Meazles/58y/James & Charice Minor/James Minor
__ Month/C/F/Nov 19/d."Bethel"/Unknown/8d/John & Mildred Month/b."Bethel"/John Month Father
Emma Reynolds/C/F/Aug 2/d."Flippo's"/Meazles/6y/Tom & Bettie Reynolds/b."Flippo's"/Tom Reynolds Father
Cornelius Scott/C/M/Apr 3/d."Gravatts"/Not Known/3y/Frank & Matilda Scott/b."Gravatts"/Frank Scott Father
Simon Tompkins Jr/C/M/Apr 26/d."Landora"/Hooping Cough/__/Simon & Mary Tompkins/"Landora"/ Simon Tompkins Father
Parthenia Wright/C/F/June 1/d."Wright's"/Consumption/24y/Louisa Rock/Louisa Rock Mother
__ Woolfolk/C/F/Aug 21/d."North Point"/__/8d/Wm & Louisa Woolfolk/b."North Point"/Wm Woolfolk Father
Infant Osborn/C/M/May 10/d."Windsor"/Unknown/1/2d/__/b."Windsor"/Harriett Osborn Grand Mother
Robert Parr/W/M/Apr/d.Port Royal/Unknown/22y/Henry H. Parr/C.C. Gibbs Bro-in-Law
Columbia Pendleton/C/F/July/d."Hazelwood"/Measles/1m 6d/Essex & Nancy Pendleton/Sally Payne/ Grand Mother
Moses Pierson/C/M/Mar 20/d."Wimbles"/Burnt/5y/Sally Pierson/b."Wimbles"/Sally Pierson Mother
Alexr Pugh Jr/W/M/Oct 12/d."Midway"/Measles/1y 5m/Alexr & Eliz Pugh/b."Midway"/Alexr Pugh Sr.
Starke Purkes Sr/W/M/July/Old Age/80y/__/Farmer/Widower/A.C. Purkes Son
Louise Raines/W/F/Dec 19/Measles & Pneumonia/18y/Isaac & Jane Raines/Geo. J. Raines Brother
James Redd/C/M/Apr/Unknown/2m/James & Nancy Redd/Geo Roberson Grand Father
Julia Roberson/C/F/May 27/d."Yew Springs"/Unknown/22y/Jennie Homes/b.Essex County/Larorer/ Isaac Roberson Husband
Sally Bet Sale/W/F/Feb 2/d."Cottage"/Pneumonia/20y/Edmd. & Martha Sale/Martha Sale Mother
Edmonia Saturwhite/C.F/Sept 10/Fever & Agrue/7y/Julia E. Saturwhite/Sally Fortune Aunt
Geo Henry Scott/C/M/June 21/d.Rapph Academy [Caroline Co]/ Unknown/1y 1m/Isaac & Milly Scott/b.Rapph Academy/Nat Jones Grand Father
Caty Scott/C/F/Sept 4/Measles/3y/Dabney & Malinda Scott/Dabney Scott Father
Infant Taliaferro/C/M/Aug/d."Spring Garden"/Unknown/10d/M. & Eliza Taliaferro/b."Spring Garden"/ M. Taliaferro Father
Mary E. Taylor/C/F/Aug/Fever & Argue/5y/Sally A. Taylor/Sally Fortune Aunt
Infant Toombs/2W/1M/1F/Mar/d. W.J. Jones'/Unknown/5d/Wm Toombs Uncle
Andrew Ward/C/M/June 20/Eating Cherries/14d/Peter & Ann Ward/Peter Ward Father
Alice Bowie/W/F/Jan/d.Port Royal/Pneumonia/5m/A.B. & B.L. Bowie/b.Port Royal/A.B. Bowie Father
Infant Battailes/2C/1M/1F/Sept 23/Unknown/1/2d/Spencer & Milly Battaile/S. Battaile Father
Lucy E. Bowers/C/F/June/Unknown/8m/Anderson & Lucy Bowers/An Bowers Father
Infant Baylor/C/M/Oct/Unknown/6d/Jno & Nancy Baylor/Jno Baylor Father
Infant Catlett/C/F/Dec 10/d."Mill Hill"/Unknown/6d/Wash [Washington] & Mary Catlett/b."Mill Hill"/Wash Catlett Father
Infant Campbell/C/M/June 16/d.Port Royal/6d/Geo & Lucy Campbell/b.Port Royal/Geo Campbell Father

Elizabeth Ennis/C/F/June/Consumption/45y/__/Laborer/Widow/Maria Jackson Sister
Emma Farinholt/W/F/Nov 20/d.Port Royal/Consumption/16y/Wm & Sarah Farinhold/ b.Port Royal/ Teacher/Jno R. Farinholt Uncle
Ida Fortune/C/F/Nov/d."Hazel Hill"/Pneumonia/3y/Cam & B. Fortune/d."Hazel Hill"/Cam Fortune Father
Aaron Fortune/C/M/Dec/d."Hazel Hill"/Pneumonia/2y/Cam & B. Fortune/d."Hazel Hill"/Cam Fortune Father
Jno Gibbs/W/M/May 10/d.Port Royal/Consumption/48y/Jno & T.A. Gibbs/b.Richmond Co/Shoe Maker/Harriett Gibbs wife/C.E. Gibbs Brother
Harriett Gibbs/W/F/Jan 18/d.Port Royal/Suicide/40y/Henry H. Parr/Jno Gibbs husband/C.E. Gibbs Bro-in-Law
Russell W. Gouldin/W/M/Feb 10/Fever/1y/Jno G. & Va G. Gouldin/Farmer/Jno G. Gouldin Father
George Hayden/W/M.Oct 10/d.Summit [Post Office]/Old Age/84y/b.Ireland/Widower/Miles Hayden Son
Adeline Homes/C/F/Aug 25/d."Windsor"/Consumption/23y/Rachel Homes/b.Essex Co/Laborer/Tom Homes Step Father
Mattie Holloway/W/F/Dec 16/Measles & Pneumonia/6d/Jno & Betty Holloway/Jno W. Holloway Father
Betty Holloway/W/F/Dec 17/Measles & Pneumonia/8y/Jno & Betty Holloway/Jno W. Holloway Father
Joannah Holloway/W/F/Dec 26/Pneumonia/82y/Royston/Widow/Dr R.G. Holloway Son
Eliza Hopkins/C/F/__/Dropsy/12y/Jim & Frances Hopkins/Jim Hopkiins Father
Hannah Hunter/C/F/Sept/d."Hayfield"/Cancer/50y/__/Jno Hunter Husband
Hannah Jackson/C/F/Oct/Old Age/80y/__/Oliver Jackson Husband
Mac Johnson/C/M/July 28/d."Hazelwood"/Measles/8y 6m/Danl & Sally Johnson/Sally Johnson Mother
Molly Jones/W/F/Oct/Old Age/80y/__/Widow/W.E. Jones Son
Saml Lomax/C/M/Apr/d."Mt Zephyr"/Measles/7y/Wm & Cora Lomax/b."Mt Zephyr"/W. Lomax Father
Patsy Lomax/C/F/Oct 1/Cancer/30y/__/Geo Lomax Husband
Judy Lockley/C/F/Nov 11/Burnt/62y/__/Geo Lockley Husband
Isaac Morton/C/M/Oct 29/d.Port Royal/Killed/45y/Merchant/Cath. Morton Wife
Infant Norman/C/M/Dec 20/d."White Hall"/Unknown/6y/Littleton & Sally Norman/L. Norman Father
Ella Robinson/W/F/March/Congestion of brain/23y/[illeg]/Tho Robinson husband/F. Robinson Friend
Robt Rawlings/C/M/Not Known/Unknown/16y/Carson & Nelly Rawlings/C. Rawlings Father
Jno Shepherd/W/M/Apr 5/Heart Disease/15y/Jno & J.A. Shepherd/ Jno Shepherd Father
Landon Southworth/W/M/June/Not Known/10y/P. & Virginia Southworth/Pichegru Southworth
Orville W. Sutton/W/M/Nov 5/Spinal affection/48y/Robt & __ Sutton/Farmer/J. Sutton Son
Aaron Sutton/C/M/Not Known/Old Age/80y/Not Known/Pauper/Single/Jno Gray Friend
Wm Sutton/C/M/June/Brain fever/8y/Nelson & Maria Sutton/Nelson Sutton Father
Mary Green/W/F/Apr 25/Dropsy/37y/__/Edward Green Husband
Sarah L. Terry/W/F/July 3/Dropsy/44y/Ben & Patsy Moore/Stephen Terry Husband
Clarence W. Taylor/W/M/July 3/Spotted Fever/7m/J. & Sarah Taylor/Jno Taylor Father
Henry Taylor/C/M/Not Known/Pneumonia/32y/Not Known/Laborer/Married/A. Allen Friend
Daisy Thompson/C/F/Not Known/Old Age/100y/__/Reuben Thompson Husband/Benj Thompson Friend
Maria Tunstall/W/F/Nov 15/Consumption/37y/R.G. & J.J. Tunstall/R.G. Tunstall Father
May Wortham/W/F/May 2/Old Age/72y/Widow/R.T. Wortham Son

Jno G. Blanton/W/M/Oct/Old Age/80y/Farmer/Widower/G.W. Blanton Son
Cassandra Bendall/W/F/July 2/Brain Fever/2y/A.L. & Frances Bendall/A.L. Bendall Father
M. Brooks/C/F/Sept/Old Age/70y/Not Known/Sarah Brooks Friend
Susanna Bibb/W/F/__/Heart Disease/50y/Garrett & Sophia Hackett/Sarah Brooks Friend
Jno Carlton/W/M/June/Old Age/70y/Unknown/A Carlton Son
Sallie Grubbs/W/F/Nov/Erysipelas/61y/Thos Grubbs Husband/Thos Southworth Friend
M[illeg] Goodwin/W/M/July 24/Typhoid Fever/20y/L. & Caroline Goodwin/Single/M.A. Goodwin
H.F. Gant/W/F/May 22/Typhoid Fever/40y/C. Gant Husband
E[illeg] Gallery/C/F/March/Measles/4y/__/__/Jno Gallery Father
No Name Gregory/C/M/Oct/Still born/[illeg]
Rachel W. Head/W/F/Aug/Disentary/3y/Marcena W. & Elizabeth J. Head/M.W. Head Father
Mary Hurt/W/F/July 14/Not Known/7d/[illeg]
Jno Hackett/C/M/Mar 10/Congestive Chill/2y/[illeg]
No Name Jackson/C/F/Aug/Still born/Jno & Jane Jackson/Jno Jackson Father
Georgiana Lewis/C/F/__/Unknown/13y/__/R. Lewis Father
Emily Morris/W/F/Jan 10/Catarrh Fever/83y/__/Widow/Mary A. Morris Friend
Jos Michie/C/M/June 12/Heart Disease/80y/__/Middlesex Co/Laborer/Single/Moses Brown Friend
No Name Mines/C/M/Aug 10/d.Spotsylvania/Killed by R.R. Car/ 40y/Husband of [illeg]
No Name Stover/C/M/July/Still born/__/__/Wm Stover Father
Saml Morris/C/M/Aug/Congestive Chill/30y/__/Laborer/Married/Jos Gray Friend
__ Moren/W/M/Aug 25/Not Known/18m/__/Jno Moren Father

1873

Chas Allen/C/M/Apr 2/Not Known/26y/Henry & Clary Allen/Henry Allen Father
John Ayres/W/M/Mar 30/Paralized/67y/Not Known/A.L. Ayres Relation
Jos E. Barlow/W/M/July/Not Known/9y/Ro D. & Bettie L. Barlow/Ro D. Barlow Father
No Name Brooks/W/F/__/Not Known/__/Wm & Lucy A. Brooks/Wm Brooks Father
Butler Beazley/W/M/March/Brain Fever/7y/Mad. & Mary Beazley/Mad Beazley Father
Eliza P. Beazley/W/F/Nov/Bronchitis/56y/Phebe Beazley/Thos H. Beazley Husband
Peyton Brown/C/M/Dec/__/27d/P.B. & Lucy A. Brown/P.B. Brown Father
Alfred Boznell/C/M/Sept/Brain Fever/5y/Seth & Susan Boznell/ Seth Boznell Father
No Name/C/F/Nov 2/Not Known/1m/Taliaferro & Judy A. Baylor/Taliaferro Baylor Father
Matthew Chenault/W/M/Nov 2/Pneumonia/26y/Jas & Susan Chenault/James Chenault Father
Not Known/W/M/Nov 2/Not Known/5m 1d/Wm L. & Mollie Cecil/Jas R. Richerson Neighbor
Jane Carter/C/F/Nov 2/Not Known/70y/Not Known/Ambrose Carter Grand child
Dacey Elliott/W/M/Dec/Carbunkle/65y/Not Known/b.Essex Co/Mechanic/Mary W. Elliott wife/
  Thos B. Pavey Neighbor
James Wright/W/M/Jan/Consumption/60y/Ro& Eliza Wright/Merchant/Mary S. Wright wife/Jas E.
  Ennis Bro-in-Law
Muscoe Garnett/C/M/Dec 26/Pneumonia/37y/Not Known/Farmer/Susan Garnett wife
Jno R. Gatewood/W/M/Oct 16/__/1y 2m/G.R. & M.E. Gatewood/G.R. Gatewood Father
Phil J. Henson/W/M/June/Not Known/39y/Not Known/Unmarried/J.H. James Neighbor
Maria Loving/W/F/Aug 15/Old Age/85y/Not Known/Thos Loving Husband/Thos Loving Jr Son
Saml G. Motley/W/M/Aug 15/Brain Fever/14y/Thos & H.G. Motley/ Hannah Motley Mother
Harry Morton/C/M/Aug 15/Not Known/__ /__ & Sophia Morton/ Rachel Morton Grand Mother
Susan Noel/W/F/Dec 31/Heart Disease/27y/John & Ann Noel/Jas A. Noel Husband
Blanch Bruce/W/F/July 19/Bilious Fever/17y/Dallas & Alice Bruce/Dallas Bruce Father

Willie Jones/C/M/Dec 25/__/8y/Not Known/Wm A. Norman Relative
No Name/W/F/Dec/__/20d/Chester N. & B.S. Pitts/Ches A. Pitts Father
Margt Shepherd/C/F/Apr 26/__/42y/Lewis & Margt Shepherd/Lewis Shepherd Father
M.E. Gresham/W/M/__/Congestive Brain/9y/B.F. & Mary Gresham/B.J. Saunders Uncle
Mary Taylor/W/F/June 12/Old Age/70y/Tho Taylor/Jno C. Taylor Relative
Mary S. Vincent/W/F/Sept/Congestive Chill/2y/R.B. & Mary Vincent/R.B. Vincent Father
__Thompson/C/F/Nov/Not Known/70y/Not Known/b.Hanover/Buck Thompson Husband
__ Taylor/C/M/Jan/Not Known/3y/H. & Amanda Taylor/A. Taylor Mother
__ Washington/C/F/__/Whooping Cough/2y/J.& F. Washington/J. Washington Father
__ Washington/C/F/Mar 28/Dropsy/60y/Not Known/J. Washington Husband/__ Son
__ Young/W/F/Jan 25/Measles/92y/Not Known/Jas Young Husband/Lindsay Young Son
Jno L. Burnett/W/M/Apr 23/d.West Va/Injury from R.R. Car/23y/B.C. & A Burnett/R.R. Agent/B.C. Burnett Father
Wm Bensen/C/M/__/Not Known/20y/G. & Frances Bensen/Laborer/G. Bensen Father
Sarah E. Ball/W/F/July 1/Womb disease/28y/A. & Lucy F. Taliaferro/Dandridge Ball Husband/ Philip Taliaferro Brother
C[illeg] Boulware/C/M/__/Dropsy/70y/Unknown/Pauper/E. Lunsford Friend
Geo T. Collins/W/M/Dec/Pneumonia/71y/Not Known/Farmer/Widower/W.J. Collins Son
Alvira B. Cobb/W/F/__/Measles/1y/W.L. & B.C. Cobb/W.L. Cobb Father
No Name Carter/C/M/Aug/Still born/1d/Jas & Sallie Carter/Sallie Carter Mother
No Name Clear/C/M/Mar/Still born/1d/Jno & Sarah Clear/Jno Clear Father
Deane Davis/C/M/Dec 12/Old Age/99y/Not Known/Henry Davis Son
Eliza Day/C/F/Aug 11/Heart Disease/48y/Not Known/E. Lunsford Friend
John Ferguson/C/M/Feb/__/14y/A. & C. Ferguson/A. Ferguson Father
No Name Gatewood/2C/2M/Still Born/1d/Daniel & F. Gatewood/D. Gatewood Father
Rebecca Hill/W/F/__/Consumption/50y/Jas & E. Duval/Robt G. Hill Husband
Betsey Hiter/C/F/Dec 15/Consumption/30y/Not Known/__/A. Rawlings Friend
R.H. Johnson/C/M/Sept/Spasms/8d/H. & J.A. Johnson/H. Johnson Father
Jas B. Murray/W/M/__/Whooping Cough/3m/W.H. & M.A. Murray/W.H. Murray Father
Sarah E. Mason/W/F/Nov 27/Liver Disease/63y/R. & A. Peatross/Will M. Mason Husband
Emily E. Minor/C/F/Oct 9/Measles/8y/W. & H. Minor/Hannah Minor Mother
Beaufort Minor/C/M/Aug/Measles/29y/W. Minor & Nancy Jones/N. Jones Mother
Moses Napper/C/M/Jan 7/Shot accidently/6y/Moses & __ Napper/ Moses Napper
Julia O. Pemberton/W/F/Mar 25/Croup/2m/G.M. & M.J. Pemberton/ G.M. Pemberton Father
No Name Backs/C/M/Dec 6/Chills/8d/H. & G. Backs/H.B. Backs Father
Sallie Smithers/C/F/Aug 18/Spasms/8d/Tho & M. Smithers/Tho Smithers Father
No Name Gyles/C/F/Mar 8/Smothered/8d/H. & J. Gyles/H. Gyles Father
Susanna Gyles/C/F/Apr/Heart Disease/6y/H. & J. Gyles/H. Gyles Father
Wm Turner/C/M/Dec/Heart Disease/38y/H. & E. Turner/H. Turner Father
Mildred Terry/W/F/__/Not Known/83y/Not Known/Richard Terry Husband/[illeg] Friend
Ellen Taylor/C/F/Aug 18/Consumption/Not Known/A. & T. Taylor/T. Taylor Mother
Addison Taylor/C/M/Dec/__/68y/G. & G. Taylor/[illeg] Friend
No Name Turner/W/M/Still Born/1d/Jno L. & M. Turner/J.L. Turner Father
[illeg] E. Tunstall/W/M/June/Consumption/27y/B.A. & J.C. Tunstall/B.A. Tunstall Father
[illeg]/C/M/Nov/Burnt/80y/__/Pauper/E. Lunsford Friend
Heland M. Adams/W/F/July 20/d.London [Car Co]/Cholera Infantum/ 6y/J.A. & Molly E. Adams/b.London /J.A. Adams Father
Frank Ashton/C/M/Oct/d.Rapph Acdmy/Unknown/2y/Jos & Mary Ashton/b.Rapph Acdmy [Car

Co]/Mary Ashton Mother

Charles E. Blaydes/W/M/Sept/d.Guinea [Car Co]/Drowned/1y 9 m/Jo & Augy Blaydes/Jo Blaydes Father

Kitty A. Broaddus/C/F/May/d."Cedar Creek"/Brain Fever/5y/Jackson & Kitty Broaddus/b."Cedar Creek"/J. Broaddus Father

Nancy Cain/W/F/Sept/Unknown/12y/Dennis & Nancy Cain/b.Ireland/Dennis Cain Father

David Chapman/C/M/July 1/d.Windsor/Unknown/75y/Laborer/Davy Chapman Son

Rachel Claytor/C/F/Sept/d."Hayfield"/Unknown/40y/Jno Walker/S. Taliaferro former master

Martha Dratt/W/F/July/d."White Hall"/Colic/5y/Jno & Harriett Dratt/b.North {New York]/Jno Dratt Father

Maria Farinholt/W/F/Dec 12/d.Port Royal/Unknown/75y/Jno W. Kearle/b.Baltimore/Jno K. Farinholt Son

Mary French/C/F/Oct/d."Chestnut Valley"/Rheumatism/50y/Ralph Borino/David Lucas Fellow Servant

Eugene Garnett/C/M/Oct/d.Ellis Garnett's/Unknown/50y/__/Ellen Garnett wife

Jo Harrison/C/M/Sept/d."Yew Spring"/Pneumonia/30y/__/Martha Harrison wife

Wm Jackson/C/M/Aug 4/d.Ware Creek [Car Co]/Consumption/3y/Jno A. & Jenny Jackson/b."Ware Creek"/Jno A. Jackson Father

Andrew Lucas/C/M/Sept/d."Chestnut Valley"/Unknown/12y/Fanny Lucas/b."Chestnut Valley"/ Fanny Lucas Mother

Dr Edgar McKenney/W/M/Oct/d.Guinea [Car Co]/Consumption/45y/Cham McKenney/Dentist/ Betty P. McKenney wife

Adelade Motley/W/F/March/d."Midway"/Consumption/35y/Charles T. & S. Jesse/b."Midway"/ Thos H. Motley Husband

Lou Pryor/C/F/May/d."Wood Yard"/Unknown/30y/Lucy Gatewood/ b."Wood Yard"/Chas Pryor Husband

Jno P. Pryor/C/M/May/d."Wood Yard"/Unknown/3y/Chas & Lou Pryor/b." Wood Yard/Chas Pryor Father

Chas Pryor/C/M/Aug/d."Wood Yard"/__/1y/Chas & Lou Pryor/d."Wood Yard"/ Chas Pryor Father

Coleman Redd/C/M/Dec 25/d.R.H.W. Buckner's/Measles/19y/Jane Redd/b.R.H.W.B. [Rev Richard Henry Washington Buckner]/Jane Redd Mother

Jno Rick/C/M/Oct/d."Catlett's Hill"/Unknown/5y/Stafford & Eliz Rick/b."Catlett's Hill"/S. Rick Father

Esther Thornton/C/F/Sept 6/d.at Mrs Bowie's/Unknown/4d 6m 10d/Bob & Eliza Thornton/Bob Thornton Father

Eli R. Taylor/C/M/Aug/d."Mount Pleasant"/Measles/8y/Catharine Taylor/Cath Taylor Mother

Ned Willis/C/M/July/d."Chestnut Valley"/Unknown/80y/David Lucas Fellow Servant

No Name/W/M/Nov 1/d."North Garden"/Unknown/14d/Joseph & Martha Smith/b."North Garden"/ Joseph Smith Father

Ada Catlett/W/F/Nov 7/d."Locust Hill"/Measles/1y 6m/William J. & Elvira Catlett/b."Locust Hill"/ Wm J. Catlett Father

Jaminy Durrett/W/F/Dec 6/Consumption/25y/Unknown/Ellen Durrett Mother

Melzer Carter/W/M/Nov 14/Consumption/70y/Unknown/May Carter Wife

Edward Allen/W/M/Nov 1/d.Golansville [Car Co]/Pneumonia/4y 6m/N.J. & Kate Allen/N.J. Allen Father

Nancy Robb/W/F/Mar 8/Unknown/71y/Unknown/b.New York/Widow/W.L. Lockwell Mother

Catherine Arnold/W/F/Apr 7/Unknown/67y/Unknown/Richard Arnold Husband

Elizabeth Blanton/W/F/May 8/Bilious Colic/70y/Unknown/b.Spotsylvania/Widow/Nancy Durrett Sister

[illeg]Chiles/C/F/May 18/Dropsy/35y/Peggy Chiles/b.Louisa Co/Cook/Unmarried/Joshua Kesler

Friend
[illeg]/C/F/Oct 8/Pneumonia/60y/Unknown/Midwife/unmarried/Henry [illeg] Son
[illeg] Jones/C/F/June 16/Unknown/33y/Allen & Julia Jones/b.Spotsy/Cook/Unmarried/Allen Jones Father
[illeg] Wright/C/M/June 8/Unknown/1y 6m/Maria Wright/Maria Wright Mother
[illeg]Rock/C/M/July 16/Chills/2y 6m/Mary & John Rock/John Rock Father

1874

Mary Anderson/W/F/Dec 14/Com of Diseases/26y/John & Susan Noel/Ezer D. Anderson Husband
Nancy L. Allport/W/F/Sept 5/Not Known/Geo W. & Lucy A. Allport/__
Martha Allport/W/F/Feb 15/Heart Disease/29y/S. & Lucy Houston/M.W.V. Allport Husband
Mary C. Andrews/W/F/Sept/Consumption/34y/Eldred & Saburna Green/John J. Andrews Husband
Mary A. Bagby/W/F/Oct 17/Com of Diseases/64y/John & Ann Kidd/Travis Bagby Son
Benjm O. Brooks/W/M/June 6/Hemorage/__/Not Known/Carpenter/M. Brooks Son
Mordecia Byrd/C/M/Nov/Com of Diseases/50y/Edward & Sophia Byrd/Farmer/Mary J. Byrd Wife
Richard Good/C/M/Apr/Pneumonia/53y/Paul & Sallie Good/Farmer/Unmarried/Mary J. Byrd Friend
Willie Rodney/C/M/June/Consumption/__/Julius & L. Rodney/Jerry Beverley Friend
__ Baker/C/M/Sept/Still born/Jno & E. Baker/John Baker Father
C.A. Chiles/W/F/June 12/Consumption/66y/Jno M. & E. Gray/Eldred Chiles Husband
Jos Cecil/W/M/Apr/Pneumonia/62y/Jno & Sallie Cecil/Elizth Cecil Wife
Wilton Chenault/W/M/Apr/Pneumonia/25/S. & Susan Chenault/Unmarried/Susan Chenault Mother
Salome Chenault/W/F/Dec 4/Not Known/7y 9m/Parkerson & S. Chenault/Parkerson Chenault Father
Willis W. Coleman/C/M/July 11/d.Bowling Green/Com of Dis/40y/Not Known/Mechanic/Margaret Coleman Wife
Eddie Dimue/W/M/June 23/Not Known/2m 6d/A.J. & Julia Dimue/A.J. Dimue Father
Blanch Farmer/W/F/Sept/Not Known/3y/Lewis & Mary Farmer/Lewis Farmer Father
Ceasar Corbin/C/M/Sept/d.Bowling Green/Asthma/38y/Not Known/Mechanic/Rebecca Corbin Wife
Emeline S. Tennant/W/F/June 30/d.Bowling Green/Com of Dis/67y/Jno & Elenora Tennant/Unmarried/ G.L. Frazier Friend
William Farmer/W/M/Oct/Pneumonia/40y/Not Known/Mechanic/ Elizabeth Farmer Wife
Geo Gouldman/W/M/June/Not Known/__/G. & Eliza Gouldman/Mollie T. Gouldman Wife
Sallie A. Green/W/F/May/Not Known/48y/Nathl & Lucy Motley/Farmer/Richard Green Husband
Mary J. Gray/W/F/__/Consumption/43y/Jno & Eliza Minor/b.Essex Co/W.E. Gray Husband
Saml G. Garnett/W/M/__/Old Age/77y/Ro & Lucy Garnett/R.B. Garnett Son
Jno R. Gatewood/W/M/Oct 13/Killed by accident/35y/W.M. & A.M. Gatewood/Ro Gatewood Uncle
__ Hill/C/F/__/Com of Dis/2y/Ro & Lucy Hill/Ro Hill Father
Matilda Johnson/C/F/June/Old Age/85y/Sallie Johnson/S. Johnson Son
Brooking Loving/W/M/Oct/Old Age/74y/Not Known/Geo Loving Son
Patric[sic] Lewis/C/M/Dec 15/Not Known/__/Not Known/Wilson Miller Friend
__ Lumpkin/W/M/Sept/Still born/Geo & R. Lumpkin/Geo Lumpkin Father
Thomas A. Mason/W/M/__/d.Bowling Green/Old Age/__/Not Known/b.New Kent Co/Tailor/Rebecca Mason Wife/L.R.Delanie Nephew
George Marshall/W/M/Oct 12/d.Bowling Green/Old Age/70y/R. & Sallie Marshall/Farmer/James H. Marshall Son
Emamuel Monroe/C/M/Dec/d.Bowling Green/Chills/__/Gabriel & Mary Monroe/Gabriel Monroe Father
Katy Gray/C/F/__/d.Bowling Green/Old Age/__/Not Known/Gabriel Gray Friend

Rebecca P. Noel/W/F/July 23/d.Bowling Green/Heart Disease/ 22y/R.L. & C.E. Noel/Unmarried/Cathd E. Noel Mother
Franklin Noel/W/M/Jan/d.Bowling Green/Consumption/40y/Alex & Lucy Noel/Ellen Noel Wife
Ida Noel/W/F/Jan 7/d.Bowling Green/Com of Dis/26y/Ro & Va Bruce/James N. Noel Husband
Robt Norman/C/M/June 3/d.Bowling Green/Whooping Cough/1y 3m/W.A. & L.N. Norman/W.A. Norman Father
Charles Norman/C/M/June 22/d.Bowling Green/Whooping Cough/2y/Willie Norman/W.A. Norman Father
Thomas Smith/W/M/June 8/Old Age/70y/Nellie Smith/Farmer/Unmarried/J.R. Penney Friend
William Pruett/W/M/July/Com of Dis/__/Not Known/Farmer/Unmarried/Jno D. Butler Physician
Henry Parr/C/M/Sept 18/Com of Dis/__/Not Known/Farmer/Widower/Henry Parr Son
Wm D. Page/W/M/Oct 14/Heart Dis/35y/Wm & E.R. Page/M.E. Page Wife
Andrew J. Pitts/W/M/Dec 12/Not Known/45y/Willis & Mahala Pitts/S.E. Pitts Wife
Pleasant Banks/C/M/Aug/Consumption/14y/W. & A. Banks Father
Emily Scott/W/F/July/Old Age/74y/Not Known/Unmarried/W.T. Chandler Friend
Allen McCray/C/M/Apr/Com of Dis/65y/Not Known/Unmarried/Phil Samuel Friend
William Southworth/W/M/Apr/Com of Dis/64y/Not Known/Widower/J.H. Taliaferro Friend
Fannie Shepherd/C/F/June/Com of Dis/60y/Not Known/Beufou Shepherd Husband
John C. Samuel/C/M/Aug/Not Known/__/Fannie Samuel/Fannie Samuel Mother
Sallie Taylor/W/F/Dec 27/Old Age/72y/Not Known/Widow/Hiram Taylor Son
__ Wright/W/M/Aug/Spasms/9d/G.W. & M.J. Wright/G.W. Wright Father
__ Wharton/W/M/May 24/Not Known/1m 26d/Festus & M.J. Wharton/Festus Wharton Father
__ White/W/M/July/Not Known/14d/J.E. & J. White/J.E. White Father
Peter White/C/M/Sept/Not Known/3y/Maj & Louisa White/Maj White Father
Mathew Ware/C/M/Aug/Not Known/75y/Not Known/Alice Ware Wife
Louisa Young/C/F/July 25/Heart Disease/75y/J.W. & Nelly Lee/Widow/Isaac White Friend
__ Jackson/C/M/Dec 24/Not Known/23d/Henry & M. Jackson/Henry Jackson Father
Mary Wright/W/F/__/Consumption/__/__ Longs/Ro B. Wright Husband
No Name Anderson/C/M/June/Still born/1d/G. & C. Anderson/G. Anderson Father
Thos H. Butler/W/M/Sept/d.Richmond/Typhoid Fever/17y/Jas & Elizt Butler/Jas T. Butler Father
Faney Banks/C/F/Feb/Old Age/70y/Unknown/Richard Banks Husband/Albert Banks Son
Gabriel Benson/C/M/Nov/Not Known/7y/Gabriel & Frances Benson/Gabriel Benson Father
No Name Barlow/W/F/Oct/d.Poor House/7y/Bettie Barlow/E. Lansford Friend
Jno Budd/C/M/Mar 11/d.Poor House/Dropsy/72y/Unknown/Pauper/E. Lunsford Friend
Susan Cauthorn/C/F/July/Not Known/58y/Unknown/Consort of C. Cauthorn/C. Cauthorn Husband
No Name Carter/C/M/July/Still born/Jas & Sallie Carter/Jas Carter Father
Wm J. Dyson/W/M/July 11/Drowned/2y/J.W. & O.A. Dyson/J.W. Dyson Father
Millie Gentry/W/F/Mar/d.Poor House/Dropsy/75y/Unknown/Pauper/E. Lunsford Friend
No Name Gatewood/C/M/Dec/Still born/__/D. & J.A. Gatewood/D. Gatewood Father
No Name Green/C/M/June/Not Known/1m/Edmund & Patsy Green/Edmund Green Father
Cynthia Jefferson/C/F/May/Unknown/25y/H. & E. Jefferson/Henry Jefferson Father
No Name Jackson/C/M/July/__/__/Frank & Susan Jackson/Frank Jackson Father
Jemima Lindsay/C/F/__/Cold/50y/__/Tyler Lindsay Husband
Robt Lindsay/C/M/Oct/Unknown/4m/Tyler & J. Lindsay/Tyler Lindsay Father
No Name Page/C/F/Oct/Unknown/1d/Watt & Sarah Page/Watt Page Father
Bettie L. Patterson/W/F/May 5/Unknown/2d/Jas & Martha Patterson/Martha Patterson Mother
E.A. Rossin/W/F/Apr 1/Chronic Diarrhea/24y/Thos B. & C.E. Grubbs/W.B. Rossin Husband
Martha S. Ricks/W/F/July 3/Not Known/39y 8m/B.K. & J.C. Whitlock/R.A. Ricks Husband

No Name Ricks/W/F/June 29/Still Born/R.A. & Martha S. Ricks/R.A. Ricks Father
Lindsay Rawlings/C/M/Apr/Unknown/34y/Robt & Jenie Rawlings/Ella Rawlings Wife
Sallie T. Samuel/W/F/Feb 15/Unknown/71y/Bob & Sallie Graham/John W. Samuel Husband/Philip Samuel Friend
Sallie T. Satterwhite/W/F/Oct 10/Whooping Cough/7m/B.F. & A. Satterwhite/B.F. Satterwhite Father
No Name Wash/W/M/June 2/Unknown/1d/Thos & Sallie Wash/Thos Wash Father
No Name West/C/F/June/Thrash/1m/Luciius & Alice West/Lucius West Father
Inft Payne/C/M/Nov 4/d."Hazelwood"/Unknown/1d/Lewis & Sarah Payne/b."Hazelwood"/Pres Payne Grand Mother
Lewis Payne/C/M/Apr 8/d."Hazelwood"/Heart Disease/31y/Bob & Precilla Payne/Sarah Payne Wife/Pres Payne Mother
James H. Peyton/C/M/Nov 12/d."LaGrange"/Unknown/1y/Jno H. & Angelica Peyton/b."LaGrange"/J.A. Peyton Father
[illeg] Purkes/W/F/May 3/d.Summit [Post Office]/Old Age/70y/__/Widow/Starks Purkes Son
Joseph Redd/C/M/Aug 5/d.R.H.W. Buckner's/Consumption/20y/Jane Spencer/Jane Spencer Mother
Maria Redd/C/F/Sept 8/R.H.W. Buckner's/Consumption/25y/Jane Spencer/Laborer/Unmarried/Jane Spencer Mother
Bartlett Redd/C/M/Sept 27/R.H.W. Buckner's/Concumption/10y/Jane Spencer/Jane Spencer Mother
Inf Redd/C/F/Aug 14/R.H.W. Buckner's/Consumption/1m/Maria Redd/Jane Spencer Grand Mother
Eliza Richerson/W/F/Feb 21/Consumption/33y/Geo & Theresa Marshall/George P. Richerson Husband
Cath Saunders/C/F/Nov 20/R.H.W. Buckner's/Old Age/80y/Susan Pendleton Daughter
M.E. Saunders/W/F/Sept 7/d.Summit [Post Office]/Dropsy/6y/Buck & Precilla Saunders/B. Saunders Father
Roberta Saunders/C/F/Aug/d.Ware Creek [Car Co]/Scrofula/35y/__/b.Essex Co/Ambrose Saunders Husband
S.A. Taylor/C/F/Dec 6/d.Vanfleets/Unknown/15y/Martha Montague/b.King & Queen Co/M. Montague Mother
Eliza Taylor/C/F/Dec 8/Unknown/__/Robin & Cathy Taylor/R. Taylor Father
Richard Wallace/C/M/Aug 20/d."HayMont"/Congestive Ague/50y/__/Mary Wallace Wife
Susan Adkins/W/F/June 14/d."Hayfield"/Congestive Fever/3y/Jno & Susan Adkins/Jno Adkins Father
Waller Askins/W/M/Oct 27/d.Port Royal/Abcess/2m/Wm C. & E.F. Askins/b.Port Royal/W.C. Askins Father
Inf Bartlett/C/M/Mar 25/d.Lyndon/Unknown/1/2d/Dana Bartlett/b.Lyndon/B.W. Bartlett Grand Father
Inf Braxton/C/M/May/b.Lyndon/Unknown/10d/Geo & Matilda Braxton/Geo Braxton Father
Kitty A. Broaddus/C/F/July 8/d."Cedar Creek"/Brain Fever/4d/Jackson & Fanny Broaddus/J. Broaddus Father
Elizabeth Dodson/C/F/Nov 6/d."Hazelwood"/Pneumonia/1y/Horace & Kitty Dodson/Hor Dodson Father
Wm Dickinson/C/M/Apr 10/d."Mill Hill"/Unknown/10m/Wm & Frances Dickinson/Frances Dickinson Mother
Armistead Dickinson/C/M/May 3/d."Mill Hill"/Unknown/1y/Queen Dickinson Mother
Inf Dishman/C/M/Dec 5/d.Dr. McKenney's/Unknown/1d/Wm & Silva Dishman/Wm Dishman Father
Inf Fortune/C/M/Oct 8/d."Clifton"/1/4d/Cam & Mary Fortune/d."Clifton"/C. Fortune Father
Mary Ann French/C/F/Oct 17/d."Chestnut Valley"/Consumption/54y/Laborer/Albert French Husband
Sarah Goodwin/C/F/Sept 10/d.Lyndon/Unknown/4y/Littleton & Ella Goodwin/Ella Goodwin Mother
Ellis Gravatt/W/M/Oct/Indigestion/70y/__/Farmer/Widower/B.A. Gravatt Son
Inft Hailstork/C/M/Sept 20/d.Farmer's Shop/Unknown/7d/Wm & Jenny Hailstork/b.Farmer's Shop/Jenny Hailstork Mother

Matilda Hays/C/F/July 8/Old Age/80y/__/Widow/Morton Jefferson Son
Moses Homes/C/M/May 29/d.Vanfleets/Erysepilas/3y/Mary Homes/b.Vanfleets/M. Homes Mother
Fanny Johnson/C/F/Aug 14/d."Hazelwood"/Pneumonia/5m/Woodford & Marcella Johnson/
  b."Hazelwood"/Wm Johnson Father
Helen Lindsay/C/F/Feb 21/Dropsy/26y/__/Wm Lindsay Husband
Inft Lucas/C/M/Sept 5/d.Lyndon/Unknown/10d/Albert & Lydia Lucas/b.Lyndon/A. Lucus Father
Julia Minor/C/F/Dec 1/d.Dr. Chandler's/Unknown/__/Zeb & Cath Minor/b.Dr. Chandler's/Zeb Minor
  Father
James T. Newton/W/M/July 10/d."Hay Mont"/Fever/4y/Robt & Lucy Newton/b."Hay Mont"/
  Robt Newton Father
Washington News/C/M/July 18/Unknown/58y/__/Farmer/Rose News Wife/Fred News Brother
Rose News/C/F/Aug 16/Unknown/60y/Husband/Wash News/Fred News Brother-in-Law

1875

No Name/C/F/Oct/Cause Not Known/1m/Alfred & Rosa Allen/Alfred Allen Father
Addison Ayres/W/M/May/Accidentlly Killed/56y/Parents Not Known/Farmer/Mary Ayres Wife
Benjm Anderson/W/M/Sept/Heart Dis/80y/Parents Not Known/Thos K. Chandler Son-in-Law
Susan Bozwell/C/F/Nov/Dropsy/50y/Jas & Elizabeth Coleman/Seth Bozwell Husband
Georgianna Baylor/C/F/Oct/Dropsy/21y/W. & Caroline Baylor/Walker Baylor Father
No Name/W/F/Mar/__/1d/Wm C. & Ann E. Beazley/Wm C. Beazley Father
No Name/W/M/July/__/1d/G.W. & Josephine Ball/Geo W. Ball Father
No Name/W/M/July/__/6d/G.W. & Josephine Ball/G.W. Ball Father
Martha Braxton/C/F/Nov/__/5y/G. & Matilda Braxton/Geo Braxton Father
Eliza Baker/C/F/Nov/Burnt to death/4y/Cato & Lucy Baker/Cato Baker Father
Elizabeth Brown/C/F/Mar/No Report/10y/J.H. & Dolly Brown/Jas H. Brown Father
Louisa Blagburn/C/F/Nov/Child Birth/25y/Parents Unknown/Jas Blagburn Husband
No Name/C/F/Nov/__/10d/Jas & Louisa Blagburn/Jas Blagburn Father
Sallie Baylor/C/F/Dec/Consumption/50y/Phil & Lucinda Johnson/Saml Baylor Relative
Burton Brooks/C/M/May/Gun Shot/45y/Parents Unknown/Nat B. Taliaferro Neighbor
Annie Chenault/W/F/March/Child Birth/55y/Jno & Annie Chenault/Jno Chenault Father
Randall Coleman/C/M/Oct/Old Age/90y/Parents Not Known/Farmer/Gilbert Sheperd Relative
Lucy A. Dickinson/C/F/Aug/Cause Unknown/49y/Parents Not Known/Richd Dickinson Relative
No Name/W/2F/Nov/__/1d/J.B. & Cordelia Dillard/Jas B. Dillard Father
Lewis Dishman/C/M/Dec/Cause Unknown/14y/Wm & Sylva Dishman/Wm Dishman Father
Walker Dennis/C/M/Dec/Pneumonia/35y/Richd & Annie Dennis/Jos Vesseles Neighbor
Clarence Fortune/C/M/Dec/Typhoid Fever/23y/Jas & Charlotte Fortune/Jas Fortune Father
Thomas Foy/C/M/Apr/Cause Unknown/30y/Parents Unknown/Jas A. Cash Neighbor
Mary Fields/W/F/Mar/Dropsy/65y/Jos & Risa Fields/Jacob Graves Relative
No Name/C/M/__/Spasms/16d/H & Martha Gravatt/Henry Gravatt Father
Edward Gray/W/M/March/Brain Fever/15y/H. & Bettie Gray/Henry Gray Father
Mary J. Gravatt/W/F/Jan/Child Birth/33y/Thos & Phebe Goldman/And [Andrew] J. Gravatt
  Husband
Elijah Griffin/W/M/July/Consumption/70y/Parents Unknown/Gus Farmer Relative
No Name/W/M/Nov/Spasms/5d/A.B. & A.E. Houston/Andr B. Houston Father
No Name/C/M/Sept/Unknown/7d/Wm & A. Hailstock/Wm Hailstock Father
Moses Holmes/C/M/Nov/Cause Unknown/40y/Parents Unknown/Lewis Gayle Neighbor
Susan Howard/C/F/Dec/Cause Unknown/36y/Richd & Caroline Thornton/Thos Howard Husband

Mary & Martha/2C/F/Dec/Cause Unknown/5m/Richd & Dolly Harring/Richd Harring Father
Thornton Jackson/C/M/Dec/Pneumonia/40y/Parents Unknown/Silas Holmes Neighbor
Anna Jackson/C/F/Dec/Cause Unknown/25y/Parents Unknown/Chas Jackson Relative
Thornton Jackson/C/M/Sept/Ague & Fever/60y/Parents Unknown/Jas Willis Relative
Ella Johnson/C/F/July/Cause Unknown/4y/Parents Unknown/Andr Jackson Relative
Sally Johnson/C/F/Dec/Consumption/40y/Dal & Fannie Rollins/Roger Johnson Relative
No Name/C/M/Jan/Cause Unknown/25d/Ro & Margt Beverley/Henry Jackson Relative
Not Named/2C/1M/1F/Apr/__/1d/Lewis & Millie Johnson/Lewis Johnson Father
Va A. Johnson/C/F/Burned to death/27y/Chas & Kitty Johnson/Jas R. Dishman Neighbor
Howard Jefferson/C/M/Sept/Cause Unknown/1y/Silas & Mary E. Jefferson/Silas Jefferson Father
Robt Jessie/W/M/June/Consumption/68y/Jno & Mary Jessie/Richd Jessie Brother
Wm B. Kidd/W/M/Dec/Consumption/46y/Wm & Margaret H. Kidd/Farmer/Attie M. Kidd wife
H.C. Lumpkin/W/F/Nov/Consumption/73y/Jack & Ann Miller/Jas B. Lumpkin Son
Not Named/C/F/Apr/__/3d/Wm & Emma Lomax/Wm Lomax Father
Willie Johnson/C/M/Oct/Cause Unknown/7y/Richd & Rodney Johnson/Wm Lomax Neighbor
Phebe Loven/W/F/Oct/Consumption/70y/Larkin & Sally Loven/Jessie Loven Relative
Adeline Lee/W/F/Mar/Scalled To Death/11m/Ed & Maria Lee/Edmd Lee Father
Ann M. Lee/C/F/Sept/Burned to death/Jos & Louisa Lee/Jos Lee Father
Julia Minor/C/F/Dec/Cause Unknown/15m/Zeb & Mary Minor/Zebalin Minor Father
Tamah Miller/C/F/May/Old Age/90y/Parents Unknown/Geo Mann Relative
Julius L. May/W/M/Nov/Consumption/36y/J.P. & Martha May/Jos C. Acors Relative
Jas Moore/C/M/Oct/Dropsy/11y/G. & Fanny Moore/Geo Moore Father
Not Names/C/M/Sept/__/1d/Jas H. & Ann Peyton/Jas H. Peyton Father
Samuel Parker/C/M/Sept/Old Age/90y/Parents Unknown/John Lomax Son-in-Law
Mary A. Proctor/W/F/Nov/Consumption/30y/Jas & Frances Proctor/Jas Proctor Father
Jno E. Pegg/W/M/Nov/Spasms/8d/Ed & Rebecca Pegg/Edward Pegg Father
Ray Richerson/C/M/July/Old Age/70y/Parents Unknown/Roy Richerson Relative
Mary E. Roy/C/F/Jan/Gun Wound/21y/Nace & Hannah Roy/Nace Roy Father
Wm Redd/C/M/Jan/Consumption/32y/Parents Unknown/Geo Richerson Relative
Jos Redd/C/M/Jan/Consumption/12m/Wm & Jane Redd/Geo Richerson Relative
Wm Redd/C/M/__/Cause Unknown/24y/Jas & Jane Redd/Jacob Robinson Relative
Ray Russell/C/M/Aug/Pneumonia/2y/Wm & Mary Russell/Geo Robinson Relative
Willie Rodney/C/M/Aug/Cause Unknown/10y/Julius & Lucy Rodney/Archd Samuel Neighbor
Elizth G. Samuel/W/F/July/Consumption/50y/Nath & Lucy Motley/G. Samuel Husband
Not Named/W/M/July/Cause Unknown/20d/R.E. & Jane E. Samuel/Ro C. Samuel Father
Montana Scott/C/M/Sept/Cause Unknown/15y/Jos & Milly Scott/Isaac Scott Father[sic]
No Name/C/M/Dec/Cause Unknown/8d/Aaron & Julia Smith/Aaron Smith Father
Richd H. Satterwhite/C/M/Oct/Cause Unknown/17y/Jno & Elizth Rollins/Geo Rollins Relative
Caroline Schools/C/F/Oct/Consumption/56y/Wm & Esther Bundy/Cephas M. Schools Son
Mary F. Schools/W/F/Oct/30y/Chas W. & Mary A. Moore/Mary A. Moore Mother
Lucy L. Taylor/W/F/Jan/Complication of Dis/22y/Jas & Sally A. Beazley/Hiram Taylor Husband
Geo Taylor/C/M/Mar/Consumption/40y/Parents Unknown/Richerson Loving Neighbor
Wiley Wright/W/M/Apr/Cancer/75y/Wiley & Caroline Wright/Caroline V. Wright Wife
Robt Washington/C/M/May/Cause Unknown/2m/Wm & Bettie Washington/Wm Washington Father
Henry Washington/C/M/May/Brain Fever/Wm & Bettie Washington/Wm Washington Father
No Name Wharton/W/M/Aug/Cause Unknown/__/Festus & Martha Wharton/Festus Wharton Father

Marcella Young/C/F/Dec/Child Birth/21y/Parents Unknown/Smith Young Relative
Lewis Jones/C/M/Dec/Unknown/1d/M. & E. Jones/M. Jones Father
No Name Lee/C/M/Sept/Unknown/3d/T. & C. Lee/Thornton Lee Father
Harry Manuel/C/M/__/Old Age/90y/Not Known/Pauper/E. Lunsford Friend
Robt Madison/W/M/Nov/__/4m/Robt & C. Madison/Robt Madison Father
No Name Mitchell/W/F/Jan 1/__/4d/J.P. & R. Mitchell/Rosanna Mitchell Mother
Richard C. Moren/W/M/Mar/Consumption/48y/G. & A. Moren/Merchant/M.J. Moren Wife
Giles Mont/C/M/__/70y/__/Shoemaker/Eliza Mont Wife
Frances Mines/C/F/__/Burnt/4y/N. & A. Mines/Nelson Mines Father
No Name Moore/W/F/Not Known/16d/__ & L. Moore/__ Friend
Jno Newton/W/M/__/__/43y/Jas & F. Newton/Carpenter/M.F. Newton Wife/Geo Newton Son
Jno M. Ramsay/W/M/__/Not Known/24y/W.C. & J.E. Ramsay/W.C. Ramsay Father
No Name Rawlings/C/F/__/5d/D. & J. Rawlings/Dungo Rawlings Father
Jno Robertson/C/M/__/Not Known/40y/__ & Nancy Robertson/Nellie Robertson Wife No Name
Reynolds/C/M/Not Known/1d/Jno & E. Reynolds/Jno Reynolds Father
Mary H. Stevens/W/F/May 12/Not Known/33y/Lewis & S. Proctor/W.E. Stevens Husband
Geo Smith/C/M/Jan/Not Known/17d/Jesse & C. Smith/J. Smith Father
Hannah Taylor/W/F/Feb/Dyptheria/7m/Geo Taylor/G. Taylor Father
Geo T. Terrel/W/M/Dec 29/Inflamation of Bowels/38y/J.W. & M.E. Terrel/S.E. Terrel Wife
Catharine Terry/W/F/June 15/Congestive Chill/43y/W. & B. Southworth/T.F. Terry Husband
Richardson Turner/W/M/July/Cancer/58y/Jno R. & E. Turner/Farmer/Widower/__ Friend
Anthony Thornton/C/M/__/Scrofula/50y/Not Known/b.Spotsyvania/Agnes Thornton Wife/__ Friend
No Name Temple/C/M/July/Not Known/1d/P. & B. Temple/Phillip Temple Father
No Name Taliaferro/C/M/Apr/Still born/W. H. Taliaferro/W. Taliaferro Father
Hugh R. White/W/M/Complication of diseases/63y/__/E. White Wife/H.R. White Son
Georgianna Wingfield/C/F/July/Consumption/20y/Jno & R. Wingfield/Jno Wingfield Father
Harriet Wright/C/F/Feb 6/Pneumonia/28y/R. & E. Yarborough/Jas & A. West/Jas West Father
Jno B. Wilshire/W/M/Heart disease/56y/Not Known/b.Orange Co/A. Wilshire wife/__Friend
Phillis White/C/F/__/Cold/68y/Not Known/Pauper/E. Lunsford Friend
No Name Williams/C/M/__/Not Known/1d/__/E. Lunsford Friend
Roberta Allen/W/F/Sept 1/Congestive Chill/37y/Overton & Clarissa Burruss/S.W. Allen Husband
M.W. Arnold/W/F/June/Cholera Infantum/6m/G.W. & A.M. Arnold/ M. Arnold Mother
W. Martin/W/M/__/Cholera Infantum/6m/G.W. & A.M. Arnold/M. Arnold Mother
Jas C. Arnold/W/M/July 14/Typhoid Fever/10y/G.W. & A.M. Arnold/M. Arnold Mother
W. Alexander/C/M/Feb 14/Pneumonia/12y/Jas & C. Alexander/Jas Alexander Father
No Name Buckner/C/M/__/Not Known/1d/__/__ Friend
No Name Beazley/C/F/Apr/__/3d/P.A. & M. Beazley/P.A. Beazley Father
A.C. Baughn/W/F/Mar 5/Dyptheria/5y/A. & E. Baughn/A. Baughn Father
No Name Buckner/C/F/Sept/Not Known/9d/Jack & C. Buckner/Jack Buckner Father
No Name Boulware/C/M/__/Not Known/1d/L. & F. Boulware/L. Boulware Father
Maria Boulware/C/F/__/Not Known/3y/Winston & M. Boulware/W. Boulware Father
No Name Barlow/W/F/Whooping Cough/14d/__ & Bettie Barlow/E. Lunsford Friend
Wm Boulware/C/M/Not Known/6y/Winston & M. Boulware/W. Boulware Father
No Name Buckner/C/M/Not Known/1y/__ & C. Buckner/__Friend
Bettie Barlow/W/F/__/Not Known/30y/Not Known/Pauper/E. Lunsford Friend
Edward Carneal/W/M. Aug 20/Spinal Mengitas/36y/Thos & Nancy Carneal/__
Emma Collins/W/F/__/Not Known/18m/W. & N. Collins/C. Collins G. Father

Wm Collins/W/M/__/Consumption/30y/Christopher & __Collins/Mary Collins Wife/C. Collins Father
Wm Carneal/W/M/Aug/Old Age/94y/Wm & Nancy Carneal/E.S. Carneal Wife/__ Friend
No Name Carneal/W/F/Aug/Still born/__/Josiah & E.G. Carneal/J. Carneal Father
Jemima Coleman/C/F/__/Not Known/40y/__ & Polly Freeman/Arch Coleman Husband
No Name Davis/W/M/Aug/Spasms/8d/M. & Lucy Davis/M. Davis Father
No Name Doggestt/W/M/July 2/Not Known/1d/H.W. & M.E. Doggett/H.W. Doggett Father
Sarah A. Dyson/W/F/__/Not Known/67y/Alfred Dyson Husband/S.H. Hart Friend
Rena J. Freeman/C/F/Nov/Croup/2y/Jas & Nancy Freeman/Jas Freeman Father
Eliz Ford/C/F/Pneumonia/40y/__/__Ford wife/R.S. Parr Brother
T.E. Goodloe/W/F/Consumption/59y/B. & E. Howard/W.T. Goodloe Husband/L.B. Goodloe Son
No Name Grant/W/F/Not Known/1d/C. & J. Grant/C. Grant Father
Mary C. Green/C/F/__/Brain Fever/5y/R. & C. Green/Robt Green Father
No Name Grimes/C/F/Aug/Not Known/8d/J.F. & L. Grimes/J.F. Grimes Father
No Name Gibbs/C/M/Oct/Not Known/28d/Chas & __ Gibbs/Chas Gibbs Father
Elizabeth Grubbs/W/F/Aug 4/Asthma/67y/J.& H. Seay/b.Louisa/W. Grubbs Husband/__ Friend
Mary A. Gray/W/F/Apr/Not Known/25y/__/Wm Gray Husband/__ Friend
No Name Hunter/C/M/Feb/__/2m/R.& R. Hunter/R. Hunter Father
No Name Jones/C/F/__/__/6d/R. & C. Jones/Robt Jones Father
__ Johnson/C/F/__/__/__/Thos Johnson Father

1876

Judson Ayers/W/M/Feb/Brain Fever/15d/Wm & E.G. Ayers/Wm Ayers Father
Ruffin E. Anderson/C/M/__/Spasms/24d/D. & A. Anderson/D. Anderson Father
Major Anderson/W/M/Nov/Consumption/15y/G. & J. Anderson/G. Anderson Father
__Butzner/W/M/Feb 24/Unknown/1d/J.H. & L.H. Butzner/J.H. Butzner Father
Maria Bromton/C/F/Sept/Unknown/75y/Unknown/Carter Bromton Friend
Bettie Barlow/W/F/Jan/Pneumonia/38y/Unknown/E. Lunsford Friend
Esther Chapman/C/F/June/Consumption/30y/__/Nancy Brown/b.Hanover Co/Nancy Brown Mother
Mary E. Carneal/W/F/23y/Jno & Mary Shackleford/R.H. Carneal Husband
No Name Cobb/W/M/July/Still born/W.L. & B.C. Cobb/W.L. Cobb Father
__Cox/W/M/Feb 1/Spasms/8d/J.W. & Susan Cox/J.W. Cox Father
Jas Carter/C/M/Dec/Typhoid Fever/70y/Jas & S. Carter/Laborer/Jas Carter Father
No Name Conway/C/M/Apr 5/Still born/T. & P. Conway/T. Conway Father
Not Known/C/M/Mar 10/Unknown/4y/G. & Sallie Coleman/G. Coleman Father
Frances Coleman/C/F/Mar 13/Unknown/57y/Unknown/b.Louisa Co/__ Friend
__Canday/C/M/Dec/Spasms/10d/J. & M. Canday/J. Canday Father
Martha Cole/C/F/Oct/Old Age/80y/Unknown/b.Louisa Co/__Friend
Robinson Carter/C/M/__/Heart Disease/63y/Unknown/Laborer/__ Friend
__ Dyson/W.F/__/Unknown/1d/H.H. & M.E. Dyson/H.H. Dyson Father
Daisey Ellis/C/F/Unknown/__/__/C. & N. Ellis/C. Ellis Father
Bennet Flippo/W/M/__/Unknown/1m/Jno G. & M.E. Flippo/Jno G. Flippo Father
Randal Harris/C/M/__/Unknown/__/A. & Lucy Harris/Sallie Harris Wife
Geo H. Hailstock/C/M/__/Unknown/10m/ J. & __/__
Nanna Jones/C/F/Oct/Scrofula/9y/Caroline Jones/Caroline Jones Mother
Thos B. Jesse/W/M/Apr 3/__/3m/J. & B.W. Jesse/J. Jesse Father

B.W. Jesse/W/F/Nov 7/Consumption/31y/T.J. & J. Burk/Jas Jesse Husband
__ Johnson/C/M/Jan 20/Still born/Thos & A. Johnson/Thos Johnson Father
__ Jackson/C/M/Nov 30/Infanticed/__/Sallie Jackson/J.E. Dickerson Friend
Martha Kelly/W/F/__/Paralysis/60y/Unknown/Ben Kelly Husband/R. Lunsford Friend
Martha E. Kelly/W/F/Sept/Killed by accident/3y/R. & S.E. Kelly/Robt S. Kelly Father
No Name Bennet/W/M/Nov/Unknown/13d/A.T. & L.C. Bennett/__
__ King/C/M/Oct/Spasms/8d/S. & E. King/S. King Father
Joel Luck/W/M/Sept/Cancer/72y/Unknown/b.Hanover Co/Farmer/N.S. Luck Wife/L. Luck Son
__ Lucus/C/M/Unknown/25d/J. & E. Lucas/Jesse Lucas Father
[Next two lines unable to read]
No Name Madison/W/F/July/Spasms/8d/J.W. & Nancy Madison/J.W. Madison Father
Thos H. Mont/C/M/Sept/brain fever/1y/J.A. & M. Mont/J.A. Mont Father
__ Mines/C/F/Sept/Still born/Dick & susan Mines/Dick Mines Father
Chas Mines/C/M/Oct/Pneumonia/20y/Unknown/__ Friend
Henry Monroe/C/M/__/Old Age/80y/Unknown/Widower/__ Friend
Lewis Minor/C/M/Jan/Old Age/90y/Unknown/__ Friend
Jno T. Norment/W/M/Sept 27/Consumption/23y/R. & T. Norment/W. Samuel Friend
Ella Payne/W/F/May/brain fever/11m/E.T. & H. Payne/E.T. Payne Father
William R. Peatross/W/M/Sept 14/Consumption/60y/R. & L. Peatross/Farmer/L.T. Peatross wife
Emily Rocks/C/F/Oct/Teething/2y/H. & S. Rocks/H. Rocks Father
Lucy Rock/C/F/Sept/Burnt/7y/G. & J. Rock/G. Rock Father
O.L. Rock/W/M/Sept/Unknown/70y/Jno & L. Rock/Jno Rock Father
Eliza Rock/C/F/Jul 22/Thphoid Pneumonia/68y/__ & Maria Pendleton/Ellis Rock Wife/__ Friend
Dianna Sutton/C/F/Mar 25/Consumption/28y/Ham Sutton Husband/__ Friend
C.E. Skinner/W/M/Aug 7/Unknown/10d/E. & G. Skinner/E. Skinner Father
N.B. Southworth/W/F/Feb/Burnt/4y/Thos & F. J. Southworth/Thos Southworth Father
Bettie Southworth/W/F/Dec 19/Unknown/7y/P. & S. Southworth/P. Southworth Father
Jas Scott/C/M/June/Unknown/3y/Frances Morton/Frances Morton Mother
Lucy Scott/C/F/June 10/Unknown/4y/D. & N. Scott/David Scott Father
Belle Thompson/C/F/July/Unknown/Ann Thompson/__ Friend
E.L. Terry/W/F/July 16/Unknown/20d/S. & S. Terry/S. Terry Father
S.A. Trainham/W/F/Aug 19/Whooping Cough/10m/T.F. & E. Trainham/T.F. Trainham Father
__ Terrel/C/M/June/Still born/A. & P. Terrel/A. Terrel Father
__ Taliaferro/C/M/Feb/Unknown/8d/W. & N. Taliaferro/W. Taliaferro Father
__ Turner/C/M/May/Colera/21d/G. & M. Turner/Geo Turner Father
Lucy Tyree/C/F/Oct/Consumption/11y/Jas & E. Tyree/Jas Tyree Father
Adam Taylor/C/M/__/Unknown/30y/Unknown/Laborer/Married/F.W. Campbell Friend
__ West/C/F/Mar/Thrash/7m/L. & a. West/Lewis West Father
Agnes Wingfield/C/F/Jan/Dropsy/50y/Unknown/J. Wingfield Husband
Wm Winston/W/M/Jan/Unknown/70y/__/Farmer/Jno Madison Friend
Peter Young/C/M/Nov/Not Known/60y/Not Known/Wm H. Young Relative
J.C. Bruce/W/F/Nov/Child Birth/18y/Geo F. & Mary T. Gouldman/Wallace Bruce Husband
Harriett Lindsey/C/F/Apr/Consumption/52y/Not Known/Jacob Lindsey Husband
Richd Mason/W/M/Aug/Old Age/82y/Jno & Mary Mason/Nancy Mason Wife
Frank Richerson/W/M/June/Cho Inft/6m/T.H. & Nannie B. Richerson/Thos H. Richerson Father
Willie T. Beazley/W/M/June/Burnt by fire/6y/Ad & Judith Ayres/Robt S. Pitts Neighbor
Not Named/W/M/Aug/Not Known/7d/G.L. & L.B. Frazier/G.L. Frazier Father
Not Named/W/F/Oct/Not Known/2d/L. L. & Laura A. Poates/L.L. Poates Father

No Name/C/M/May/Not Known/5d/Lucian & Frances Loney/Lucian Loney Father
Jas Eubanks/W/M/May/Old Age/70y/Not Known/Mechanic/Ellis Reynolds Relative
Lucy Upshaw/C/F/Feb/Not Known/1m/Tarlton & Jena Upshaw/Tarlton Upshaw Father
J.A. Jones/W/M/Oct/Bilious Fever/7y/Nichas & Mary J. Jones/Nicholas Jones Father
Nancy Baylor/C/F/Sept/Com of Dis/60y/Not Known/Warner Baylor Neighbor
Lucy E. Robb/C/F/July/Worms/6y/Frances Robb/Geo Robb Relative
Harriett Smith/C/F/Oct/Not Known/60y/Not Known/Caleb Smith Relative
Reney Taylor/C/F/Dec/Not Known/1m/Not Known/Lewis Taylor Relative
Mary S. Thornton/W/F/June/Consumption/54y/Thos B. & Mary Thornley/b.King Geo Co/
  Henry F. Thornton Husband
Wm J. Thomas/W/M/Dec/Dropsy/52y/Jas & Nancy Long/Sarah A. Thomas Relative
Lou Baylor/C/F/Aug/Cho Infantum/22d/Lewis & Bettie Baylor/Lewis Baylor Father
Jane Brown/C/F/Aug/Com of Dis/24y/Spencer & J.A. Brown/Spencer Brown Father
Julia A. Brown/C/M/Aug/Paralysis/75y/G. & Lucy Slaughter/Spencer Brown Relative
Amanda Carter/C/F/Nov/Com of Dis/40y/Not Reported/Davey Carter Relative
Mary W. Conway/C/F/Aug/Bilious Fever/18y/Wm H. & M. Conway/Wm H. Conway Father
Henry Carneal/W/M/May/Teething/1y/Jno C. & Susie Carneal/Jno C. Carneal Father
Isabella Coates/C/F/Apr/Not Known/17y/Chas & T.W. Coates/Lewis Coates Father[sic]
Virginia Jeter/C/F/Dec/Not Known/1m/Jas & Mary Jeter/Jas Jeter Father
John A. Holmes/C/M/Aug/Not Known/7m/A. & Nancy Holmes/Nathaniel Jones Relative
John J. Morton/C/M/May/Not Known/2m/Jas & Louisa Morton/Jas Morton Father
Milly Matthews/C/F/Oct/Old Age/100y/Not Known/Wm Matthews Relative
Sally Matthews/C/F/Mar/Asthma/40y/Not Known/Wm Matthews Relative
Not Named Pemberton/W/F/Apr/Asthma/__/Geo M. & Cla Pemberton/G.M. Pemberton Father
Not Named Parker/C/M/Apr/Asthma/__/Wm H. & __ Parker/Wm H. Parker Father
William Redd/C/M/Jan/Consumption/28y/E[illeg]/[illeg]
Ezekial Taylor/C/M/Apr/Com of Dis/70y/Simon [illeg]/[illeg]
Luke L. Brown/C/M/Jan/Not Known/8m/Andrew S. Brown/Andrew S. Brown Father
Richd Herring/C/M/Dec/Consumption/30y/Verkley & Dolly Herring/And S. Brown Relative
No Name/C/M/Dec/Not Known/5d/[illeg]/Jno Clatterbuck Neighbor
Lou Dabney/C/F/Nov/Not Known/4y/Jas & E.J. Dabney/Jas Dabney Father
Lewis Dishman/C/M/July/Not Known/1y/__/Wm Dishman Father
William Hoodlass/W/M/June/Teething/10m/Saml [illeg]/S.N. Hoodlass Father
Silas & Bettie Johnson/1C/1M/1F/Dec/Not Known/3d & 2d/Not Known/Chas Johnson Relative
Cath Reynolds/C/F/Mar/Not Known/12y/Geo [illeg]/Geo Reynolds Father
Rose Dandridge/C/F/Mar/Consumption/50y/__/Lewis Dandridge Husband
E.L. Sorrell/W/M/Sept/Com of Dis/42y/[illeg]/[illeg]Neighbor
Amanda Carter/W/F/Nov/Heart Dis/30y/Geo [illeg]/[illeg]Bibb Father
Sample Eubanks/W/M/Aug/Consumption/25y/[illeg]/[illeg]
Lucinda Wright/W/F/July/Old Age/77y/[illeg]/[illeg]
Mary Poates/W/F/May/Dropsy/60y/[illeg]/[illeg]
Frances Chiles/C/F/May/Dropsy/50y/Wm & M. Gouldman/Moses Chiles Relative
A.[Alice]B.[Broaddus] Collins/W/F/June/Consumption/24y/Thos B. & Elizth Sale/Wm J. Collins
  Husband
Lucy A. Johnson/C/F/July/Thrash/6m/__ & M.L. Johnson/Joe Lonesome Relative
Mary E. Shackleford/W/F/July/Com of Dis/40y/W.E. & Bettie T. Shackleford alias
  Rachel/Wm M. Shackleford Husband
Irvin Washington/C/M/May/Cho Infantum/3m/Wm & Bettie Washington/Wm Washington Father

Geo T. Burruss/W/M/Oct/Old Age/67y/Jacob & Mary Burruss/b.King Wm Co/Farmer/Jno G. Burruss Son

Brooking Chenault/W/M/May/Old Age/72y/Not Known/b.King & Queen Co/Wm Cecil Relative

Clara Chapman/C/F/Apr/Pneumonia/24y/Rob & Sophia Chapman/Robinson Chapman Father

William Robinson/C/M/Dec/Pneumonia/40y/Not Known/Jno Carter Neighbor

Cath S. Dillard/W/F/Sept/Consumption/51y/Archils & Cath Southworth/Geo W. Dillard Husband

Phil Gatewood/W/M/Jan/Old Age/90y/Jno & __ Gatewood/Jno T. Gatewood Son

O.M. Harris/W/M/Sept/Pneumonia/48y/Thos & F.O. Harris/S.L.A. Harris Wife

Eugene C. Lee/C/M/July/Cho Inft/2m/Geo & Delia Lee/Geo Lee Father

Matt Taylor/C/M/Dec/Teething/5m/__ & Caroline Taylor/Phil Taylor Relative

__ Ashton/C/F/June/Not Known/1d/Jno & Mary Lee Ashton/Jno Ashton Father

Lucy Chapman/C/F/Sept/Consumption/21y/Not Known/Thos Coghill Relative

Wellford Chapman/C/M/Aug/Not Known/3m/__ & Lucy Chapman/Thos Coghill Relative

Thos & Wilton Holmes/2C/2M/July/Not Known/13m/Thos & Rachel Holmes/Thos H. Holmes Father

John Pendleton/C/M/Dec/Old Age/74y/Robinson & Tinah Pendleton/Eliza Pemberton Wife

Beverly Shakesphere/C/M/July/Consumption/27y/Saukey & L. Shakesphere/Saukey Shakesphere Father

Cath Norman/C/F/Aug/Child Birth/40y/Geo & Helen Ellis/Geo Ellis Father

No Name/C/M/Aug/__/20d/Chas & L. Norman/Geo Ellis Grand Father

Albert Garnett/C/M/Apr/Consumption/50y/Not Known/Fannie Garnett wife

Clara Dodson/C/F/July/Old Age/70y/Not Known/Oliver Hopkins Relative

Jos Jones/W/M/Aug/Not Known/20d/W.M. & M.B. Jones/W.M. Jones Father

Rodney Johnson/C/M/Feb/Consumption/24y/Moses & B. Johnson/Wm Lomax Relative

Mary A. Richerson/W/F/May/Consumption/15y/Jos M. & G.A. Richerson/Jos M. Richerson Father

Isaac Richerson/C/M/Sept/Com of Dis/60y/Not Known/Ellen Richerson Wife

Harriett Sale/C/F/Feb/Not Known/28y/Peter & Matilda Gray/Hampton Sale Husband

Mary L. Williams/C/F/July/Brain Fever/5y/Byrd & Mary Williams/Byrd Williams Father

Not Named/W/2M/Mar/__/1d/Chas E. & F.A. Wiltshire/Chas E. Wiltshire Father

Chance Green/C/M/Apr/Deep Cold/3m/Silas & Elizth Green/Wilas Green Father

Not Named Gray/C/M/Dec/Not Known/6d/Peter & Ellen Gray/Peter Gray Father

Not Named Howard/W/M/Nov/Not Known/1m/Ed & Va Howard/Ed Howard Father

M. Belle Howard/W/F/Not Known/3d/Lunsford & M.S. Howard/Lunsford Howard Father

Emily S. Howard/W/F/Sept/11m/Lunsford & M.S. Howard/Lunsford Howard Father

Betsy Haile/C/F/June/Child Birth/30y/Math & Esther Eppes/William Haile Husband

Not Named/2C/2F/June/16d/Wm & Betsy Haile/William Haile Father

J.R. Richerson/C/M/Oct/Com of Dis/62y/Not Known/Harvey Holmes Neighbor

Burkett Saunders/C/M/Mar/Pneumonia/36y/Not Known/Mechanic/Willie Jackson Neighbor

Chas King/C/M/Nov/Pneumonia/70y/Not Known/Farmer/Willie Jackson Neighbor

1877

Lewis Williams/C/M/Oct/Brain Fever/42y/Parents Not Known/Farmer/Geo Blayburn Relative

Nancy Loving/W/F/Nov/Dropsy/60y/Larkin & Sally Loving/Jane Loving Relative

Ella Martin/W/F/Apr/Consumption/23y/Royal & Mary Eubanks/Geo T. Martin Husband

Ann S. Miller/W/F/Aug/Old Age/74y/Danl & Sarah Duvall/Jno H. James Relative

Fannie Miller/C/F/Feb/Not Known/7y/W.J. & Mary Miller/Wilson Miller Father

Chris Mathews/C/M/June/Not Reported/6m/Wm & Molly Mathews/William Mathews Father
Edward Mathews/C/M/July/Consumption/5y/Wm & Molly Mathews/ William Mathews Father
Georgia Micou/W/F/July/Child Bed/23y/Wm C. & Betsy Burruss/Jas R. Micou Husband
Geo L. Minor/C/M/Mar/Not Known/17d/L. & Judith Minor/Lewis Minor Father
Jack Monroe/C/M/Aug/Old Age/80y/Parents Not Known/Beverly Walker Relative
P.H. Pendleton/W/M/July/Kidney Dis/68y/Jno & Ann Pendleton/Merchant/__ Pemberton Wife
Chas Prior/C/M/__/Not Known/68y/parents Not Known/Farmer/Jas Prior Relative
Willis Pitts/W/M/June/Old Age/87y/Parents Not Known/Farmer/Mahala Pitts Wife
Geo W. Pitts/W/M/May/Not Known/6m/O.D. & Mary H. Pitts/O.D. Pitts Father
Nancy Redd/C/F/Apr/Consumption/28y/Geo & Margt Robinson/Geo Robinson Father
Arthur Robinson/C/M/Aug/Not Reported/22y/Wm & Sarah Robinson/Wm Robinson Father
Jos Robinson/C/M/Feb/Not Reported/1m/Thos & Ellen Robinson/Thos Robinson Father
Lucinda Roots/C/F/May/Consumption/30y/Walker & L. Beverly/Soloman Roots Husband
Walker Richerson/C/M/June/Consumption/37y/Roy & Phillis Richerson/Henry Washington Relative
Willie Richerson/C/M/Aug/Drowned/12y/W. & N.B. Richerson/Henry Washington Relative
Not Named/C/M/Jan/Not Known/5d/Jas & Eliza Jackson/Jas W. Jackson Father
Not Named/C/F/June/Not Known/3d/Wm H. & Cam Robb/Wm H. Robb Father
Not Named/W/M/Sept/Not Known/15d/R.F. & Va B. Farmer/R.F. Farmer Father
Not Named/C/M/Mar/Not Known/Parents Not Known/Washington Catlett Relative
Not Named/C/F/Oct/Not Known/20d/Ro & Charity Richerson/Robin Richerson Father
Not Named/W/F/Jan/Not Known/9m/E. & Mary Farmer/Eugene Farmer Father
Not Named/W/M/March/Not Known/9m/W.H. & Nancy Farmer/Wm H. Farmer Father
J. Ann Satterwhite/C/F/May/Consumption/64y/Wm & __ Hardiman/Jno Satterwhite Relative
Hyter Saunders/C/M/Dec/Dropsy/60y/Parents Not Known/Lewis Jones Neighbor
Not Named/C/M/May/Not Known/10d/F. & Lucy Carter/Fleming Carter Father
John Taylor/C/M/Sept/Consumption/60y/Parents Not Known/Jno Catlett Neighbor
Adeline Taylor/C/F/Jan/Not Known/60y/Jack & Eliza Freeman/Fleming Minor Father[sic]
Jack Taylor/C/M/Aug/Consumption/35y/Parents Not Known/Seth Bogwell Relative
Frances E. Thomas/W/F/Sept/Not Known/9y/J.R. & Georgia Thomas/Jas R. Thomas Father
S.P. Thornley/W/F/June/Heart Dis/65y/Mark & Lucy Boulware/H.G. Thornley Son
Mary F. Toombs/W/F/Dec/Not Known/60y/Ellis & Martha Gravatt/Wm H. Toombs Husband
Cathe Upshaw/C/F/Oct/Not Known/9y/R. & Mary Upshaw/Rich. Upshaw Father
Lewis Upshaw/C/M/Dec/Old Age/70y/Parents Not Known/F.D. Campbell Neighbor
James Vessells/C/M/Jan/Cause Not Known/12m/Jno & Rebecca Vessells/Jos Vessells Father
John Whitticoe/W/M/Dec/Consumption/66y/Parents Not Known/J.B. Stilling Neighbor
Jack Whitticoe/W/M/Nov/Consumption/66y/Parents Not Known/Lewis Jones Neighbor
Ulyses Washington/C/M/July/Unknown/2m/C.M. & L. Washington/C.M. Washington Father
Wharton/W/F/July/Cause Not Known/1d/A.B. & M.E. Wharton/A.B. Wharton Father
Betty A. Wallace/C/F/Apr/Burnt/5y/Wm & Margt Wallace/Wm Callawn Neighbor
Thomas West/C/M/July/Not Known/9y/Lew & Sarah West/Lewis West Father
James West/C/M/Sept/Not Known/2y/Lew & Sarah West/Lewis West Father
Lelia L. West/C/F/May/Not Known/6m/Lew & Sarah West/Lewis West Father
Addison Ayres/W/M/May/Killed Accidently/65y/Not Known/Farmer/Betey Ayres wife
Mary Ayres/W/F/Mar/Consumption/22y/Jas & Julia Sorrell/Betey Ayres Relative
Maria Brooks/C/F/Oct/Pneumonia/7m/Henry & Va Brooks/Henry Brooks Father
Nelly S. Blythe/W/F/Mar/Not Known/2m/B.G. & Carrie Blythe/B.G. Blythe Father
Luke Brown/C/M/Feb/Not Known/15d/And & Isabella Brown/An S. Brown Father

Sallie Bozwell/C/F/Dec/Not Known/14d/S. & Delia Bozwell/Seth Bozwell Father
Geo R. Bozwell/C/M/Oct/Not Known/7d/Lew & Kitty Bozwell/Lewis Bozwell Father
Margarett Baylor/C/F/Jan/Child Birth/36y/Not Known/Lewis Baylor Friend
Jas W. Beazley/W/M/Feb/Burnt accidently/2y/Jas K. & Molly S. Beazley/Jas K. Beazley Father
James Cullen/C/M/May/Heart Dis/62y/Not Known/W.J. Henderson Neighbor
Judith Campbell/W/F/May/Not Known/60y/Seth & Cathe Saunders/F.D. Campbell Husband
Moris A. Carter/W/M/July/Chol Infantum/18m/L.A. & L.M. Carter/Luther A. Carter Father
Jane Catlett/C/F/Mar/Child Bed/26y/Not Known/Washgt Catlett Relative
Peley Coleman/C/F/Dec/Not Known/40y/Not Known/Henry Coleman Father
Eldred Chiles/W/M/June/Old Age/74y/Saml & Patsy Chiles/Jno S. Chiles Son
Rose Dandridge/C/F/Mar/Not Known/35y/Not Known/Lew Dandridge Relative
M.S. Dickinson/C/F/Mar/Consumption/56y/Not Known/Jas Dickinson Relative
Lottie Ferguson/C/F/Aug/Old Age/70y/Jno & Sarah Sale/An S. Ferguson Son
Clementina Farish/W/F/June/Old Age/86y/Jno & Alice Dillard/___ Farish child
Roberta Fortune/C/F/Aug/Consumption/38y/Henry & Milly Clarke/Wm Fortune Relative
Betty Fortune/C/F/Nov/Consumption/40y/Abram & M. Clarke/Wm Fortune Relative
Jas H. Green/C/M/Oct/Not Reported/3m/Ro & Anna Green/Robt Green Father
Edward Goodwin/C/M/Oct/Congestive Chill/8y/Henry & __ Goodwin/Henry Goodwin Father
Elton Gatewood/W/F/Aug/Dysentery/7y/R.C. & __ Gatewood/R.C. Gatewood Father
Peter Grayson/C/M/Jan/Not Known/2m/B. & Ann Grayson/Barnett Grayson Father
Alice Gatewood/W/F/Sept/Consumption/30y/Thos & Mary E. Jones/L.E. Gatewood Husband
Louisa Goodwin/C/F/Oct/Child Bed/26y/Not Known/Thos Goodwin Relative
Isiah Grymes/C/M/Aug/Not Known/3m/H. & Fanny Grymes/Hiram Grymes Father
Elizabeth Grymes/W/F/Jan/Not Known/50y/Geo & Nancy Donahoe/Jno Grymes Husband
William Harris/C/M/Sept/Pneumonia/26y/O. & Dolly Harris/Overton Harris Father
Richard Herring/C/M/Jan/Consumption/45y/Parents Not Known/Chas Galory Neighbor
Penellope Howard/W/F/Feb/Dropsy/50y/Wm & Nancy Pickett/Jas B. Howard Husband
Wm Howard/W/M/Aug/Not Known/50y/Parents Not Known/Ed Howard Relative
Mildred Howard/W/F/June/Not Known/50y/Parents Not Known/Ed Howard Relative
Bettie Johnson/C/F/May/Pneumonia/2y/__ & Eliz Johnson/Chas Johnson Relative
Silas Johnson/C/M/June/Pneumonia/10y/__ & Eliz Johnson/Chas Johnson Relative
Cilla Johnson/C/F/Jan/Child Birth/27y/Danl & Polly Johnson/Wm Johnson Husband
Nannie Johnson/C/F/June/Consumption/11y/Jno & Polly Johnson/Jno Johnson Father
Spencer Jones/C/M/Dec/Not Known/80y/Parents Not Known/__Relative
Ralph Jones/C/M/Dec/Not Known/64y/Parents Not Known/__Neighbor
Milicent Jones/W/F/Aug/Consumption/70y/__/__Relative
Woolfolk Jones/W/M/Consumption/68y/__/__Relative
[Note: top of page missing for 31 names]
Overton Henderson/C/M/__/Dropsy/60y/__/__
No Name Johnson/W/F/Aug 12/Unknown/1d/L. & M. Johnson/L. Johnson Father
Jno Johnson/C/M/Sept 22/Scrofula/2y/Chas & a. Johnson/Chas Johnson Father
Moses Johnson/C/M/Whooping Cough/2y/Chas & A. Johnson/Chas Johnson Father
No Name John/C/M/May/Unknown/1m/Lewis & R Johnson/L. Johnson Father
Becca Jackson/C/F/Jan 2/Heart Dis/26y/Jno & A. Wingfield/Jno Wingfield Friend
Austin Jones/C/M/Mar 8/Unknown/4m/Jno & E. Jones/Jno Jones Father
__ Johnson/C/F/__/Still Born/__/Mona Johnson Mother
Edward Lunsford/W/M/July 7/Diarrhea/77y/Unknown/b.Nansmond/Farmer/Sarah Lunsford
   Wife/R.T. Lunsford Son

No Name Lewis/C/F/Apr 1/Unknown/__/C. & M. Lewis/C Lewis Father
No Name Lawson/C/M/Aug 2/Still Born/R. & T. Lawson/R. Lawson Father
Henry Minor/C/M/Jan 1/Old Age/84y/__/__ Friend
No Name Mills/C/M/Apr/Unknown/1m/Sallie Mills/Sallie Mills Mother
No Name Minor/C/M/Mar/Unknown/__/W. & C. Minor/Wm Minor Friend
Henry Minor/C/M/Dec/Old Age/84y/__/Wm Minor Friend [listed twice, but different death dates, see line 6 above]
W. Norment/W/M/Sept 8/Gravel/80y/Unknown/Mary W. Norment wife
Judson Ayers/W/M/Mar 19/Brain fever/13y/Wm & E.G. Ayers/Wm Ayers Father
Geo Ancarro[w]/W/M/Nov 30/Killed from fall of tree/18y/W. & Nancy Ancarro/W. Ancarro Father
No Name Ayers/W/M/Mar 12/Still born/Richd & M. Ayers/Richd Ayers Father
Billie Atkinson/W/__/Sept/d.Louisa Co/Consumption/30y/Unknown/Wm Atkinson Father
Sallie H. Blanton/W/F/May 25/Unknown/48y/A. & C. Goodloe/Geo W. Blanton Husband
Ida Branham/C/F/Sept 17/Unknown/3m/F. & Nancy Branham/Frank Branham Father
Cecil B. Baylor/C/M/Oct 26/Typhoid Fever/7y/W. & Mary Baylor/W. Baylor Father
Jas H. Bolley/C/M/May/Pneumonia/17y/Jas & M. Bolley/Jas Bolley Father
Clifton Boswell/C/M/Apr 3/Unknown/6m/Jas & H. Boswell/Jas Boswell Father
Affy Baylor/C/M/__/Unknown/65y/__/__ Friend
Jno Beverly/C/M/[rest illeg]
No Name Chewning/W/M/Oct 10/Still born/Jno & T.J. Chewning/Jno C. Chewning Father
Jas C. Cobb/W/M/Feb 27/Kidney Disease/61y/E. & __ Cobb/M.C. Cobb Wife
__ Carneal/W/M/Oct 11/Unknown/84y/W. Carneal/Martha Carneal Wife/W. Carneal
No Name Carneal/W/M/July/Brain fever/1y/Jas & __ Carneal/Jas Carneal Father
Margaret Chapman/C/F/__/Unknown/35yUnknown/R.T. Lunsford Friend
No Name Coleman/C/F/Lock Jaw/1y/Jane Beverly/R.T. Lunsford Friend
Jas Carter/C/M.Sept/Unknown/18y/Jas & S. Carter/Jas Carter Father
Jane Chiles/C/F/June 22/Fall from tree/45y/Unknown/Arch Chiles Husband/Rufus Chiles Friend
Ella J. Donahoe/W/F/Aug/Bilious Fever/4y/R. & A.T. Donahoe/R. Donahoe Father
Lucy Dyson/W/F/__/Congestion of bowels/22m/A.J. & L.A. Dyson/A. J. Dyson Father
No Name Dyson/W/M/__/Unknown/7m/H.H. & M. Dyson/H.H. Dyson Father
Anne E. Durrett/W/F/Oct 25/Unknown/__/Jno & Bettie Durrett/Jno Durrett Father
No Name Fox/C/F/Sept/Still born/T. & K. Fox/Thos Fox Father
A.C. Goodall/C/M/July 22/Unknown/19m/A. & Mary Goodall/M. Goodall Mother
Jim Gray/C/M/__/Unknown/__/Geo & V. Gray/__
D. Hall/C/M/May 19/Cancer/71y/Unknown/__
Mary H. Hart/W/F/Aug 4/Unknown/85y/A. & C. Carter/C. Hart Husband/[illeg] Son
Sallie Hailstork/C/F/May 20/Consumption/30y/G. & P. Todd/J. Hailstork Husband
Caroline Harrison/C/F/Oct/Whooping Cough/7y/__ & A. Harrison/[illeg] Friend
__ Nelson/C/F/__/__/A.J. & __ Addison/Jno Duval Friend
B.C. Rawlings/C/M/June 6/__/1y/S. & L.A. Rawlings/S. Rawlings Father
No Name Roots/C/M/Feb/Still born/__/Geo & J. Roots/Geo Roots Father
Nancy Rawlings/C/F/Oct/Old Age/90y/A. & A. Rawlings/Daniel Rawlings Husband/Wm Rawlings Son
W.A. Sutton/W/M/Oct 8/Scarlet Fever/4y/W.O. & M.E. Sutton/W.O. Sutton Father
Roland Samuel/W/M/Sept/9m/A. & L. Samuel/A. Samuel Father
Bettie B. Shooks/C/F/Aug/Typhoid Fever/18m/R. & S. Shooks/R. Shooks Father
H. Shooks/C/F/__/Whooping Cough/2y/R. & S. Shooks/R. Shooks Father

Henry Stevens/C/M/__/Unknown/75y/__/Lucy Stevens Wife/R. Shooks Friend
Geo Turner/C/M/Aug 16/Typhoid Pneumonia/48y/__/R. Shooks Friend
Jno Tiller/W/M/__/Old Age/80y/Wm & Sarah Tiller/Sarah Tiller wife/[illeg] Daughter
Jno T. Timberlake/W/M/__/Unknown/41y/W. & M. Timberlake/E.G. Timberlake wife/[illeg] Friend
Charlott Taylor/C/F/May 7/Heart dis/21y/Tom & Bell Taylor/Tom Taylor Father
Henry Thompson/C/M/Mar/Unknown/7y/H.S. Thompson/H. Thompson Father
No Name Taylor/C/M/Mar 10/Spasms/8d/J. & E. Taylor/Jas Taylor Father
Milither A. Tribble/W/M/__/83y/Unknown/Married/[illeg] Son
Richard Wright/W/M/July 19/Paralysis/70y/R. & B. Wright/E. Wright wife
Wm H. Wright/W/M/__/Liver Dis/60y/__/Ellen Wright wife/ R. Wright Son
Garnett Wright/W/M/Mar 23/Cronic Diptheria/65y/L.J. & Mary [illeg]/[illeg] Friend
No Name Welsh/C/M/__/Still born/D. & E. Welsh/D. Welsh Father
T. Wright/C/F/__/Whooping Cough/6m/[illeg] & Maria Wright/[illeg]/[illeg] Friend
Jacob Willis/C/M/June/Unknown/60y/[illeg]/[illeg] Friend
Mary E. Young/W/F/July 25/Unknown/35y/A. & J. Bendall/Timothy "Tim" Young Husband

1878

Rose Allen/C/F/Dec/Not Known/__/Addison & Polly Allen/Chas Allen Relative
William Allen/C/M/Dec/Pneumonia/7y/Jerry & Annie Allen/Jerry Allen Father
Kitty A. Broaddus/C/F/Feb/Not Known/3y/Jackson & Nancy Broaddus/Jackson Broaddus Father
Sarah Beazley/W/F/Feb/Not Known/58y/Chas & Polly Beazley/John Beazley Husband
Taliaferro Baylor/C/M/Aug/Consumption/50y/Billy & Nancy Baylor/Allen Baylor Relative
No Name/2C/2F/June 6/1d/Lewis & Betty Baylor/Lewis Baylor Father
Joanna Barlow/W/F/Feb/Congestive Chill/66y/Jno & Margt Seal/Jno W. Barlow Son
Not Named/W/M/Aug 18/Not Known/8d/J.A. & S.L. Cridlin/Jas A. Cridlin Father
Mark L. Boulware/W/M/June/Not Known/18y/M.L. & Rose Boulware/A.F. Carter Step Father
Richd Brown/C/M/Apr/Not Known/16y/Wm & Martha Upshaw/Dennis Upshaw Relative
Annie M. Covington/W/F/June/9m/J.H. & A.M. Covington/J.H. Covington Father
Mollie Clatterbuck/C/F/Oct/Not Known/40y/Jno & Mary Hailstock/Jno Clatterbuck Husband
Sally Conway/W/F/Dec/Congestive Chill/35y/Chas L. & H. Jesse/A.H. Conway Husband
Jeanie Chiles/C/F/Dec/Not Known/18y/Winston & F. Chiles/Winston Chiles Father
No Name/C/F/Mar/Not Known/__/Lindsay & L.A. Chiles/Winston Chiles Father
No Name/W/M/Mar/Not Known/17d/J.G. & Sally Carneal/J.G. Carneal Father
Jas R. Dishman/W/M/Oct/Not Known/68y/David & Margt Dishman/Eliza E. Dishman wife
Robt Dennis/C/M/June/Not Known/26y/Alex & Martha Dennis/b.Essex Co/Alex Dennis Father
Not Known/W/F/May Not Known/2m/___ & Elizth Clark/Robt Des Neighbor
Hattie Gouldin/W/F/July/6m/Jno & S.A. Gouldin/J.W. Gouldin Father
Silas S. Garrett/W/M/July/Consumption/70y/Wm & Clara Garrett/Rose A. Garrett wife
Richd H. Garrett/W/M/Feb/Not Known/67y/Wm & Clara Garrett/J.M. Garrett Son
Milly Grymes/C/F/Dec/Dropsy/30y/Not Known/Geo Grymes Relative
Sally Green/C/F/Dec/Not Known/2m/Silas & Elizabeth Green/Silas Green Father
Jno G. Gouldman/W/M/July/Not Known/16y/E.F. & M.S. Gouldman/M.S. Gouldman Mother
Nora Graves/C/F/June/Not Known/2y/Jacob & Mary Graves/Jacob Graves Father
Turner Grimes/C/M/Apr/Consumption/60y/Not Reported/Jno Hopkins Son-in-Law
S.R. Hoodlass/W/M/June/Dropsy/70y/Not Known/Wal W. Withers Bro-in-Law

Mary Hoomes/C/F/June/Not Known/62y/Ro & Franky Willis/Fredk Hoomes Relative
Infant Hoomes/C/M/Sept/Not Known/6y/Armistead & A. Hoomes/Armistead Hoomes Father
Hatty Hoomes/C/F/Apr/Not Known/2y/Armistead & A. Hoomes/Armistead Hoomes Father
Isaac Harris/C/M/Oct/Not Known/1m/Isaac & Lizie Harris/Isaac Harris Father
Wm Hardiman/C/M/Oct/Consumption/27y/Parents Not Known/Martha Hardiman wife
No Name/W/M/June/Not Known/1m 15d/W.G. & Cassie Hudgins/Wal G. Hudgins Father
Alfred Jackson/C/M/Dec/Not Known/__/Davey & Emma Jackson/Davey Jackson Father
Emily Jackson/C/F/Aug/Not Known/53y/Stephen & Charity Hoomes/Achill Jackson Husband
Sarah J. Jackson/C/F/Jan/Not Known/43y/Jno & M. Hailstock/Jas H. Jackson Husband
Aff Johnson/C/F/Apr/Not Known/60y/P. & J. Warren/Chas Johnson Husband
Polly Johnson/C/F/Aug/Not Known/62y/Carter & F. Nelson/Woodford Johnson Husband
Sally M. Johnson/C/F/Aug/Brain Fever/7d/__ & A.L. Johnson/Woodford Johnson Relative
Nicholas Jones/W/M/Oct/Consumption/55y/Parents Not Known/Wm Jones Relative
Va L. Jordan/W/F/Aug/Chol Infantum/1y 6m/J.L. & L.E. Jordan/J.L. Jordan Father
Samuel Loven/W/M/Oct/Not Known/32y/B. & Sally Loven/Farmer/Geo Loven Brother
Margt Marshall/W/F/Oct/Consumption/39y/Thos & Margt Taylor/Jas H. Marshall Husband
Lew G. Mahon/W/M/Jan/Hemerage/22y/Alex & C.A. Mahon/Alex Mahon Father
Silas Minor/C/M/Sept/Pneumonia/4m/Lew & Mary Minor/Lewis Minor Father
Molly Mathews/C/F/Feb/Not Reported/82y/Not Known/Wm H. Mathews Husband
Charles Morris/C/M/May/Pneumonia/1y/Jno & Mary Morris/John Morris Father
C.E. Noel/W/M/Aug/Cancer/53y/Mus & J.W. Noel/J.L. Taylor Relative
Julia W. Osborn/C/F/Dec/Not Known/29y/F. & H. Osborn/Frank Osborn Father
Willis Pitts/W/M/Apr/Old Age/84y/Not Known/Mahala Pitts wife
Willis Pitts Jr/W/M/June/Brain Fever/1m 16d/O.D. & Mary H. Pitts/Mahalda Pitts Grand Mother
Ellen R. Pearce/W/F/Jan/Cancer/32y/Jos & B. Penney/J.E. Pearce Husband
Robt F. Pavey/W/M/June/Cancer/1y/Jas S. & S.A. Pavey/Jas S. Pavey Father
William Robinson/C/M/Sept/Consumption/66y/Wm & P. Robinson/Elizth Robinson wife
William Robinson/C/M/May/Hung/32y/Robt & __ Semple/Robt Semple Father [sic]
Alfred Rooks/C/M/Dec/Consumption/20y/Robt & Agnes Rooks/Elizth Robinson Relative
Geo G. Richerson/W/M/Dec/Consumption/27y/A.S. & Mary Richerson/Polly Richerson Mother
Not Named/W/F/June/Not Known/2m/T.G. & Margt Ritchie/T.G. Ritchie Father
Addison Smith/W/M/Mar/Not Known/70y/Not Reported/R.C. Samuel Neighbor
Lucy Sterne/W/F/Oct/Old Age/84y/Not Reported/D.S. Cash Grand Son
Mary E. Saunders/W/F/Apr/Consumption/67y/Not Reported/b.King George Co/Robbie Broaddus Neighbor
Virginia Saunders/W/F/Apr/Consumption/55y/Geo & Carrie Thornton/R.C. Samuel Neighbor
Frances Saunders/W/F/Dec/Not Known/60y/Billy & P. Saunders/Geo W. Samuel Relative
Lillian Samuel/W/F/July/Not Known/11m/B.F. & R.A. Smoot/B.F. Smoot Father
J.A. Self/W/M/Aug/Consumption/27y/Job & Eliza Self/Job Self Father
Lucy A. Sale/W/F/Sept/Consumption/22y/R. & M.A. Eubanks/Wm J. Sale Husband
Kitty Taylor/C/F/July/Not Known/2m/A. & L. Taylor/Henry Taylor Father
Rebecca Taylor/W/F/May/Pneumonia/46y/Wm & Betsy Penney/Jno F. Taylor lHusband
Richd Upshaw/C/M/Sept/Consumption/70y/Not Known/Jane Upshaw Relative
Cathl Upshaw/C/F/Mar/Not Known/8y/R. & J. Upshaw/Jane Upshaw Relative
No Name/W/M/June/__/20d/G.L. & Helen Frazier/G.L. Frazier Father
Lewis Upshaw/C/M/Dec/Consumption/53y/Not Reported/Farmer/Jane Upshaw Relative
Henry Vaughan/W/M/July/Not Known/50y/Not Reported/Jas Vaughan Relative

Robt Wright/W/M/Sept/Consumption/70y/Not Reported/Farmer/Robt Fortune Neighbor
Julia Wise/C/F/Dec/Not Known/25y/Fr K. & Julia Osborn/Jeff Wise Husband
No Name/C/F/Feb/Not Known/20d/Wm & Lizie Woolfolk/Wm Woolfolk Father
John Willis/C/M/Dec/Consumption/44y/__ & M. Whiting/M.G. Ware Father
Willis Washington/C/M/Mar/Pneumonia/2y/Richd & __ Washington/Richd Washington Father
Sarah Self/W/M/Dec/Not Known/9d/Wm J. & Fanny Self/Wm J. Self Father
Henry T. Young/C/M/Sept/Typhoid Fever/14y/Henry & Matilda Young/Henry Young Father
No Name/C/M/June/Not Known/5d/Jno H. & Adeline Young/Jno H. Young Father
Jas T. Redd/W/M/Apr/Unknown/65y/Farmer/Married/[illeg] Friend
Emma Reynolds/C/F/Oct/Unknown/34y/Jno & E. Reynolds/Jno Reynolds Father
No Name Robinson/C/F/Feb 26/Still born/1d/S. & W. Robinson/S. Robinson Father
No Name Reynolds/W/M/Nov 3/Still born/1d/Thos & B. Reynolds/Thos Reynolds Father
Carson Rawlings/W/M/__/Heart Dis/Not Known/Not Known/b.Louisa Co/[illeg] Friend
Mary A. Southworth/W/F/Dec 28/Consumption/45y/Jas & B. Searls/Charles Southworth Husband
Lelia Stevens/C/F/July 3/Unknown/6d/__ & J.B. Swann/[illeg] Friend
Henry Stewart/C/M/June/Unknown/80y/Unknown/[illeg] Friend
No Name Shocks/C/F/Oct/__/1d/L. & Mary Shocks/Lewis Shocks Father
Patsy Samuel/C/F/June 4/Old Age/77y/Unknown/Thomas Samuel Husband/Henry Samuel Son
Saml Harrison/W/M/Feb/Paralysis/75y/[illeg]/[illeg]Friend
No Name Taliaferro/C/F/Dec/Unknown/1d/Walter & M. Taliaferro/W. Taliaferro Father
Allen J. Thomas/W/M/Diabetic/65y/J. & __ Thomas/D.A. Thomas Wife/Jas Thomas Son
Jas Thomas/W/M/__/Unknown/2m/W. & M. Thomas/Wm Thomas Father
M. Taylor/C/F/Spasms/3y/S. & M. Taylor/S/ Taylor Father
Wm R.B. Wyatt/W/M/__/Chronic Diarrhea/70y/W.L. & __ Wyatt/Isabella Wyatt Wife/Jim Wyatt Son
Thornmoy Moore/W/M/Mar 2/Old Age/82y/R. & S. Moore/Lucy Moore Wife/Jos B. Moore Son
No Name Wright/W/F/July/Unknown/1m/P. & Julia Wright/P. Wright Father
__ Wright/C/F/Sept/Unknown/5y/__/T.E. Wright Father
Rachel Williams/C/F/__/Consumption/23y/A. & B. Williams/A. Williams Father
E.T. Abrams/W/F/Not Known/Unknown/55y/Ben & Patsy Mason/Geo Abrams Husband
Overton Ayres/W/M/Jan 1/Unknown/80y/Unknown/R.T. Lunsford Friend
Maria Buchanan/W/F/Not Known/Disentary/57y/S. & __ Samuel/Willis Buchanan Husband
Robt R. Baber/C/M/Mar 25/Not Known/8m/J & M. Baber/J. Baber Father
No Name Baber/C/M/__/Not Known/8d/W. & M. Baber/W. Baber Father
Simon Clayborn/C/M/Oct 30/Not Known/8d/A.G. & D. Clayborn/A.G. Clayborn Father
No Name Coleman/C/M/Aug 27/Not Known/1d/G. & Sallie Coleman/G. Coleman Father
Jennie Carpenter/C/F/Unknown/Unknown/24y/Unknown/Betty Carpenter Wife
No Name Cox/W/M/Unknown/Not Known/1d/J.W. & S. Cox/J.W. Cox Father
No Name Carter/W/F/Aug/Not Known/4m/J.B. & R. Carter/J.B. Carter Father
Thos L. Catlett/W/M/Mar 2/Dropsy/58y/Not Known/N.S. Catlett Wife/[illeg] Son
Mary Dickinson/W/F/June 25/Unknown/90y/Jas Dickinson Husband/Jno Dickinson Son
Frances A. Doggett/W/F/May 10/Congestion of Liver/3y/H.T. & F.E. Doggett/H.T. Doggett Father
Mary Dickinson/C/F/Oct/Not Known/30y/Unknown/Pop Dickinson Husband
No Name Dudley/C/M/Not Known/Still born/1d/E. & S. Dudley/E. Dudley Father
Mary Fox/C/F/May/Unknown/1d/J. & D. Fox/J. Fox Father
No Name Fox/C/F/Aug/Unknown/1y/J.H. & Mary Fox/J.H. Fox Father
Stephen Hean/W/M/Sept 3/d.Albemarle Co/Consumption/46y/W. & T. Hean/Farmer/

b.Albemarle Co/E.E. Hean Wife
Arch Hean/W/M/Oct 6/b.Albemarle Co/Congestion of Brain/10m/M. & E.E. Hean/E.E. Hean Mother
P[illeg] Johnson/C/F/Feb/Unknown/2y/H. & E. Johnson/H. Johnson Father
No Name Lawson/C/F/Feb/Unknown/__/__/__/Lucy Lawson Mother
No Name Lawson/C/F/July/__/__/Lucy Lawson/L. Lawson Mother
No Name Marmaduke/W/M/June 25/__/3m/G. & M.E. Marmaduke/G. Marmaduke Father
No Name Mosby/C/M/Apr/__/1d/Wm & Sarah Mosby/Wm Mosby Father
Charlotte Moore/C/F/Dec 18/Consumption/100y/B. & C. York/b.North Carolina/A. Moore Husband
McCarthy/W/F/__/Unknown/74y/Not Known/b.Jefferson Co, Va/J.T. Butler Friend
Eliz Parr/W/F/June 20/Old Age/88y/__/b.Philadelphia/Jno Parr Husband/Jno Parr Son
__ Page/W/M/Aug 7/Unknown/1d/J.F. & S. Page/J.F. Page Father

1879

Henry Alsop/C/M/__/Kidney Disease/50y/__ & Rachel Alsop/Farmer/Rose Alsop Wife
Paucoats Burnett/W/M/Jan 10/Consumption/33y/Benj C. & Angelina Burnett/Salesman/ unmarried/Benj C. Burnett Father & Physician
Ann Boxley/W/F/Apr/Old Age/74y/Jas & Winnd Boxley/b.Louisa Co/Eldred Turner Bro- in-law
Walter Branham/W/M/July/Brain Fever/1y/Frank & Nancy Branham/Frank Branham Father
Rose Broaddus/C/F/Dec 22/Old Age/110y/Unknown/Jack Washington Son-in-Law
__/Baylor/C/M/Aug/Unknown/1d/Henry & Caroline Baylor/Henry Baylor Father
Stephen Beverly/C/M/Mar 10/Heart Disease/19y/Wm & Belle Beverly/Larorer/Wm Beverly Father
__ Beazley/W/F/Aug 20/Unknown/5d/James T. & Cornelia Beazley/Jas T. Beazley Father
Nicie Coleman/C/F/Aug 13/Congestive Chill/17y/Robt & Fannie Coleman/b.Spotsylvania Co/ Robt Coleman Father
__ Collins/W/M/Mar/Unknown/14d/Robt E. & Belle Collins/Robt E. Collins Father
__Cobb/W/M/July 15/Unknown/__/Wm L. & Bettie C. Cobb/W.L. Cobb Father
David T. Cobb/W/M/Feb 19/Old Age/74y/David & __ Cobb/Farmer/Jno S. Carpenter Friend
Lucy Crump/C/F/July 1/Cancer/35y/Unknown/Geo Crump Husband
__ Cannon/W/M/Jan 15/Unknown/8d/Jas R. & Mildred Cannon/Jas R. Cannon Father
__ Cannon/W/M/Jan 18/Unknown/11d/Jas R. & Mildred Cannon/Jas R. Cannon Father
__ Coleman/C/F/June 20/Unknown/1d/Gilbert & Sallie Coleman/Sallie Coleman Mother
__ Cox/W/M/Feb/Unknown/1d/James W. & Susan Cox/Jas W. Cox Father
__ Coghill/W/F/Sept/Unknown/3m/Lewis L. & Anna B. Coghill/Lewis L. Coghill Father
Mary L. Carneal/W/F/Oct 3/Croup/8y/E.G. & Mary E. Carneal/E.G. Carneal Father
Ann V. Duval/W/F/July 29/Spinal Affection/54y/Henry & Sarah Hill/James Duval Husband
Matilda Fountain/C/F/May 16/Unknown/40y/Saml & Nancy Taylor/b.Spotsylvania Co/Peter Fountain
Betsy Fries/C/F/Apr 3/Old Age/70y/Jack & Lizzie Riddle/Jno Fries Son
Burwell B.Gatewood/W/M/Apr 13/Dropsy/70y/__/Gatewood/Farmer/__/Lucy Barlow Friend
Saml Gibbs/C/M/May/Unknown/11y/Anthony & Martha Gibbs/Anthony Gibbs Father
__Gibson/C/M/Feb/Unknown/__/[illeg] & Nellie Gibson/Geo Gibson Grandfather
__ Gatewood/C/F/Nov 26/Unknown/__/Robt & Lucy Gatewood/Robt Gatewood Father
William Gravatt/W/M/Dec 16/Old Age/93y/[illeg] & Judie Gravatt/P.A. Gravatt Nephew
Robt G. Hill/W/M/Oct/Unknown/63y/Henry & Sarah Hill/R.G. Hill Jr Son

Sallie Hendricks/C/F/Aug/Unknown/45y/Saml & Jennie Harris/b.King Wm Co/Reuben Hendricks Husband/Jennie Harris Mother
Rosetta Hill/C/F/May 1/Pneumonia/76y/Unknown/Unknown/Jno Hill Son
Ann E. Holmes/C/F/Aug 21/Unknown/2y/Bartlett & Eliza Holmes/Bartlett Holmes Father
James S. Jerrell/W/M/Dec/Old Age/79y/Lucy Jerrell/Farmer/Rachel Jerrell Wife
Peggie James/C/F/Sept 27/Old Age/83y/Wm & Fannie Turner/Wm James Son
Lilian Luck/W/F/Apr 28/Intermittant Fever/3y/Silas M. & H.B. Luck/b.Tennessee/Robt S. Hargrave Cousin
__ Minor/C/M/Aug/Unknown/__/Wm & C. Minor/Wm Minor Father
John Monroe/C/M/Nov 20/Spasms/8d/Andrew & Rebecca Monroe/Andrew Monroe Father
Mallisa Madison/W/F/Mar/Dropsy/63y/Wm & Rebecca Carneal/Jno T. Madison Husband
Ned Minor/C/M/Apr/Old Age/70y/Unknown/b.Spotsylvania Co/Farmer/Unmarried/Timothy Temple Friend
Saml Page/C/M/Sept 2/Thrush/1m/Watt & S.E. Page/S.E. Page Mother
John Phillips/C/M/Sept 20/Unknown/1y/Tarlton & Margt Philips/Tarlton Philips Father
__ Reynolds/C/M/Jan 10/Unknown/1d/Jno & Sophia Reynolds/Jno Reynolds Father
Austin S. Richerson/W/M/June 29/Dropsy/40y/Jas & Lucy Richerson/Shoemaker/Martha Richerson Wife/Lucinda Richerson Sister
Nancy Richerson/W/F/May 7/Old Age/73y/Ditus & [illeg] Ould/Unmarried/Wm Richerson Nephew
Bertha B. Rosson/W/F/Mar 29/Diptheria/1y/Wm B. & P.A. Rosson/Wm B. Rosson Father
Alice Reynolds/C/F/Sept/Unknown/3y/Rachel Reynolds/Geo Reynolds Grandfather
__ Reynolds/C/F/June 25/Spasms/5d/Wm & Sarah Reynolds/Wm Reynolds Father
Sallie W. Smith/W/F/July 1/Unknown/26y/[illeg] Owen/b.Tennessee/A.G. Smith Husband
Mary Shocks/C/F/Mar 25/Heart Disease/30y/Unknown/Lewis Shocks Husband/J. Shocks Step Daughter
Angelina Satterwhite/W/F/Feb/Congestive Chill/42y/Thos & Sarah Thacker/Benj Satterwhite Husband
Maria Samuel/C/F/May/Enysypilas/60y/Spencer & Patsy Samuel/S. Samuel Husband/Jno Samuel Son
A.O. Saunders/W/M/Aug 18/Consumption/20y/Wren & Mary D. Saunders Father
Moses Turner/C/M/Apr 3/Apoplexy/80y/Unknown/b.King Wm Co/Farmer/Unmarried/ Jno Turner Friend
Daniel Turner/W/M/July 11/Kidney Disease/71y/Reuben & Clara Turner/Mary Turner Wife/ Frank Turner Son
__ Taylor/C/M/Dec/Spasms/3y/Jno F. & Eliza Taylor/Jno F. Taylor Friend
__ Taylor/C/M/Dec 1/Spasms/3y/Jno F. & Eliza Taylor/Jno F. Taylor Father
Audie S. Taylor/C/M/Sept/Teething/1y/Rachel Taylor/Rachel Taylor Mother
Mary Temple/C/F/June 5/Consumption/87y/Jas & Rena Scott/ b.Spotsylvania Co/James L. Temple Husband
Lewis Temple/C/M/June 15/Dropsy/75y/Gilbert & [illeg] Temple/Ditcher/James S. Temple Son
Mary W. Temple/C/F/Jan 5/Whooping Cough/2y/Timothy & Bettie Temple/b.Spotsylvania Co/Timothy Temple Father
Lewis Terry/C/M/July 1/Dysentery/83y/Unmarried/Chas Terry Friend
James T. Terry/W/M/Sept 2/Fall from a cart/39y/Jno W. & Elizb Terry/b.Hanover Co Va/Sec Master/Sallie A. Terry Wife
Stephen Terry/W/M/Sept/Liver Disease/50y/Roland & Mildred Terry/Farmer/Sally Terry Wife/

Thos T. Terry Brother
__ Terrell/W/F/Sept 29/Unknown/9d/Jno T. & Ella A. Terrell/Jno T. Terrell Father
__ Williams/C/F/Feb/Spasms/8d/Zack & Lucy Williams/Zack Williams Father
__ Walker/C/M/Apr 29/Unknown/__/Lewis & Martha Walker/Lewis Walker Father
Mary F. Kidd/W/F/Mar 20/Pneumonia/40y/Henry & Frances Kidd/Lew T. Kidd Brother
No Name/C/F/Oct/Not Known/2d/Chas & Amey Lindsay/Chas Lindsay Father
John Loving/W/M/Mar/Old Age/72y/Not Reported/Farmer/Baynham Loving Son
Lucy A. Loving/W/F/Mar/Not Known/4m/R.S. & Ceny V. Loving/R.S. Loving Father
Malinda Lee/C/F/May/Old Age/79y/P. & Susan Lee/Hugh Norman Son-in-Law
Albert Morton/C/M/Sept/Not Known/7m/Law & Mary Morton/Anthony Morton Relative
Joe Man/C/M/Dec/Pneumonia/60y/Not Known/Anthony Morton Relative
Selina J. Moore/W/F/Dec/Consumption/68y/Ed & Phoebe Jones/Wm S. Moore Son
Matilda Mathews/W/F/Old Age/70y/Not Known/Wm Mathews Relative
James Martin/W/M/Jan/Old Age/74y/Not Known/Dand [Dandridge] Pitts Neighbor
Fanny Noel/W/F/Mar/Com of Dis/18y/Alex & Molly Carter/Alex Carter Father
Jno R. Napier/W/M/Dec 28/Not Known/89y/Jas & Eliza Napier/Jas Napier Father
Hariet Osborn/C/F/June 7/Heart Disease/60y/A. & Catey Osborn/Alfred Osborn Father
No Name/C/F/Apr 24/Not Known/10m/J.D. & Rose V. Pendleton/Jas D. Pendleton Father
Ro F. Pavey/W/M/Jan/Pneumonia/4m/J.S. & Sarah A. Pavey/Jas A. Pavey Father
Lewis Picardatti/W/M/Jan/Old Age/70y/Not Known/A. Beazley Neighbor
Molly Parker/C/F/Mar/Consumption/22y/Jno & Jane Reynolds/Jas Parker Relative
Ann Poindexter/C/M/May/Com of Dis/65y/Not Known/Jas Parker Relative
Aggy Richards/C/F/May/Consumption/86y/Chas & Adeline Lindsay/Richd Richards Husband
Saberna Rouse/W/F/May/Com of Dis/40y/Not Known/Carter Loving Neighbor
Humphrey Roane/C/M/__/Consumption/60y/Not Known/Jas E. Pare Neighbor
Marshall Shepherd/C/M/Dec/Burnt/2m/Not Known/Ann Shepherd Mother
Gilbert Shepherd/C/M/Oct/Comb of Dis/70y/Benja & Mary Shepherd/Ann Shepherd Relative
Julia A. Sale/W/F/Dec/Paralized/45y/Not Known/Peyton Brown Neighbor
Fanny E. Tuck/W/F/May/Pneumonia/59y/Wm & Jane E. Chapman/A.C. Tuck Husband
No Name Self/W/M/Jany/Not Known/9d/Wm J. & Sarah Self/Wm J. Self Father
Kitty Taylor/W/F/June/Not Known/__/Henry & Louisa Taylor/Henry Taylor Father
Columbia Pare/W/F/Oct/Consumption/84y/R. & Lucy Carneal/Robt Carneal Father
James Vessells/C/M/Apr/Not Known/1m/Joe & Reb Vessells/Joe Vessells Father
Sarah E. Wright/W/F/Aug/Apoplexy/40y/S.W. & Mary Wright/J.W. Wright Relative
Eliza Walker/C/F/Dec/Old Age/70y/Ed & Phoebe Walker/Beverly Walker Relative
Betsy Williams/C/F/Sept/Old Age/80y/Not Known/Thos Gatewood Neighbor
Chastine Ayres/W/M/Aug/Not Known/28y/Not Known/Farmer/Unmarried/Julia Ayres Mother
No Name/C/F/June/Unknown/1m/Alfred & Sarah Allen/Alfred Allen Father
Chis Anderson/W/M/Sept/Not Known/50y/Not Known/Wm Anderson Relative
Wm Banks/C/M/May/Accidently Killed/5y/Esaw & Alice Banks/Esaw Banks Father
Sally Banks/C/F/July/Not Known/8d/Danl & Susan Banks/Danl Banks Father
No Name/W/F/Sept 6/Not Known/6d/Jno T. & Betty Carter/Jno T. Carter Father
Martha J. Broaddus/W/F/July/Comsumption/70y/Phil & Sarah Long/Jas J. Broaddus Son
Jack Banks/C/M/Sept/Old Age/80y/Not Known/Joe Lonesome Relative
Julie Berry/C/F/Dec/Cancer/55y/__/Lewis Minor Relative
Alex Chiles/C/M/Mar/Not Known/16y/Walker & Levina Chiles/Walker Chiles Father
Richard Chiles/C/M/May/Old Age/90y/Not Known/Walker Chiles Relative
Wm J. Campbell/W/M/Sept 27/Consumption/87y/[son of Cornelius C. & Emily Dulaney

Campbell]/Wm W. & Chris Broaddus [parents of the wife instead of Wm J. Campbell are listed in the register]/Lucy Broaddus Wife
F.G. Claiborn/W/M/May 1/Consumption/39y/Not Reported/E. Claiborn Mother
Thos L. Coates/C/M/Apr/Typhoid Fever/8y/Lewis & Fanny Coates/Lewis Coates Father
Charlotte Digges/C/F/Mar/Not Known/60y/Not Known/Wm Fleming Relative
Maggie O. Davis/W/F/Nov/Com of Dis/30y/Jas S. & Mary Davis/Jas S. Davis Father
No Name/W/F/Oct 20/Not Known/12d/A.C. & Frances Fugett/Albert Fugett Father
Mildred Garnett/C/F/July/Not Known/26y/Jas & Mary Fields/Jas Fields Relative
Fanny B. Garnett/C/F/Nov/Not Known/15y/Nelson & Eliza Garnett/Nelson Garnett Father
Betty Gatewood/W/F/Sept 8/Heart Disease/40y/Not Reported/Thos Gatewood Husband
Asah P. Gouldman/W/M/Nov 8/Not Known/20y/A.J. & Sally Gouldman/Albert J. Gouldman Father
Edie W. Grimsley/W/M/July/Chol Inft/18m/T.W. & Sally Grimsley/T.W. Grimsley Father
Robin H. Grimsley/W/F/July 17/Chol Inft/12m/T.W. & Sally A. Grimsley/T.W. Grimsley Father
Robt Howard/W/M/Nov/Congestive Chill/8y/Ro & Mary S. Howard/Robt Howard Father
Reubin Hill/C/M/Apr/Old Age/75y/Not Known/L.B. White Neighbor
Celey Hooper/C/F/Apr/Com of Dis/26y/Not Known/Spencer Sale Neighbor
Martha Jackson/C/F/Oct/Child Birth/30y/Archilles & Betsy Taliaferro/Robt Jackson Relative
No Name/C/M/Aug 7/Not Known/10y/Richd & Patsy Coleman/Jas McKenney Neighbor
No Name/C/M/Dec/Not Known/8d/Wm & Maria Jackson/Alex Jackson Relative
Sarah J. Jackson/C/F/Jan 6/Consumption/39y/J.H. & Sarah Jackson/Jas H. Jackson Father
James Jackson/C/M/Mar 26/Not Known/2y/J.H. & Sarah Jackson/Jas H. Jackson Father
Lizie D. Jackson/C/F/Mar 2/Not Known/2y/J.H. & Sarah Jackson/James H. Jackson Father
Nancy Jackson/C/F/Sept/Not Known/38y/R. & Mary Hopkins/Jas H. Jackson Relative
No Neme/C/M/Apt/Not Known/8d/Saml A. Johnson/C/M/Oct/Not Known/3y/W.T. & Cella Johnson/W.T. Johnson Father
Nancy Hoomes/C/F/Oct/Not Known/86y/N. & Amey Todd/Moses Homes Relative
No Name/C/M/Feb/Not Known/6m/Isaac & Lizie Harris/Isaac Harris Father
Thos Fortune/C/M/Oct/Old Age/80y/Not Known/Jas K. Micou Neighbor
Cain Fortune/C/M/Dec/Not Known/__/Thos & Sally Fortune/Jas K. Micou Neighbor

1880

Clara Allen/W/F/May 5/Typhoid Pneumonia/24y/Overton & Clara Burruss/Silas W. Allen Husband
Mary E. Allen/C/F/Mar 11/Spinal Affection/2y/Wilson T. & Hairett Allen/Wilson T. Allen Father
Albert S. Allen/W/M/Apr 1/Unknown/1m/Jno C. & Bettie G. Allen/Jno C. Allen Father
__ Anderson/C/M/Aug 18/Unknown/3d/Salada Anderson/Salada Anderson Mother
__ Ayres/W/F/May 17/Still Born/Richd & Mildred Ayres/Richd Ayres Father
William Baughn/W/M/Dec 9/Unknown/23y/Phil & [illeg] Baughn/b.Richmond/Laborer/ Unmarried/Patrick H. Jones Friend
Mary Baughn/W/F/Mar 16/Paralysis/60y/Phil & [illeg] Baughn/ Unmarried/Patrick H. Jones Friend
Roland Bowers/W/M/May/Unknown/6m/Wm S. & E.R. Bowers/Wm S. Bowers Father
Rachel Brown/C/F/Aug 11/Childbirth/22y/Jno & Matilda Thomas/Henry Brown Husband/ Wm Henderson Friend
__ Brown/C/M/Aug 11/Unknown/1d/Henry & Rachel Brown/Wm Henderson Friend

__ Brown/C/M/Aug 11/Unknown/1d/Henry & Rachel Brown/Wm Henderson Friend
Jno Bullock/W/M/June 11/Consumption/2y/Jas E. & Annie M. Bullock/Patrick R. Catlett Grandfather
__ Bullock/W/M.May 26/Still Born/Jas E. & Annie M. Bullock/Patrick R. Catlett Grandfather
Baylor Burton/C/M/Sept 3/Old Age/87y/Unknown/Laborer/Eleanor Burton Wife/T.J. Loyal - Friend
Lila Buckner/C/F/Apr 4/Rheumatism/60y/Unknown/Unmarried/Geo Boulware Friend
Seth Campbell/W/M/Dec 26/Pneumonia/79y/Zach & Nancy Campbell/Farmer/Felix W. Campbell Son
George Campbell/W/M/June 22/Brain Fever/3m/Felix W. & Ogenia Campbell/Felix W. Campbell Father
Henderson Carneal/W/M/Sept 1/Unknown/58y/Wm & Rebecca Carneal/Laborer/Ellen Carneal Wife/Martha Carneal Aunt
Patrick Carneal/W/M/Mar 4/Pneumonia/63y/Pleasant & Lucy Carneal/Farmer/Augusta Carneal Wife/Ed T. Thacker Neighbor
Jno W. Carneal/W/M/Feb/Unknown/19y/Jas J. & Frances Carneal/Jas J. Carneal Father
__ Carter/C/F/Mar/Unknown/1d/Betsy Carter/Betsy Carter Mother
Geo W. Carter/C/M/Dec 3/Pneumonia/7m/Henry & Anna Carter/Henry Carter Father
Louisa Chiles/C/F/Nov 8/Typhoid Fever/24y/Lewis & Jane Chiles/Lewis Chiles Father
Geo Chapman/C/M/Mar 21/Unknown/41y/Geo & Aggy Chapman/Laborer/Levinia Chapman/ Pitch [Pitchegru] Woolfolk Bro-in-Law
Emma Coates/C/F/June/Croup/11m/Jno & Mary Coates/Jno Coates Father
Harmonia Coates/C/F/Dec 1/Scrofula/3y/Jno & Mary Coates/Jno Coates Father
__ Cobb/W/M/Oct/Diptheria/2m/Wm L. & Bettie Cobb/W.L. Cobb Father
William G. Cobb/W/M/Apr 6/Consumption/40y/David & Nancy Cobb/Mechanic/ Mary Cobb Wife/Geo W. Amael Neighbor
Mary Coghill/W/F/Oct 12/Old Age/84y/[illeg] Samuel/E.R. Coghill Grandson
__ Coleman/C/M/Nov/Unknown/1d/Benj & Millie Coleman/Benj Coleman Father
Sallie S. Collins/W/F/July 16/Congestion of Brain/35y/Seth & Susan [Susannah] Campbell/Jno W. Collins Husband
Laura Dollins/W/F/Dec 1/Diptheria/3y/Alex & Sarah Dollins/Alex Dollins Father
James P. Farish/W/M/June 23/Typhoid Fever/35y/Stephen & Jane Farish/Farmer/Mollie N. Farish Wife/Jane Farish Mother
Victoria Farish/W/F/Oct/Unknown/39y/Stephen & Jane Farish/Unmarried/Jane Farish Mother
James Fells/C/M/Oct 23/Unknown/5d/Lewis & Belle Fells/Lewis Fells Father
Susan T. Flippo/W/F/Aug 17/Paralysis/60y/Wm & Eliza Burruss/ Albert R. Flippo Husband
Martha Fox/C/F/Nov/Diptheria/8y/Thos & Frances Fox/Thos Fox Father
Philip Fox/C/M/Nov/Burns/1y/Lollie & Dora Fox/Lollie Fox Father
Wm B. Gatewood/W/M/Oct 8/Paralysis/87y/Wm B. & Frances Gatewood/Farmer/ Henry W. Gatewood Son
__ Holmes/C/F/Sept 1/Unknown/1d/Bartlett & Eliza Holmes/Bartlett Holmes Father
Patsy Jackson/C/F/Apr 21/Bronchitis/40y/Jesse & Maria Claiborne/Henry Jackson Husband
Peggy James/C/F/Sept/Unknown/70y/Wm & Tama James/Unmarried/Moses Carter Friend
Gilbert Jamison/C/M/May/Brain Fever/6m/James & Jane Jamison/James Jamison Father
Alexander Lane/C/M/Oct 20/Unknown/65y/Reed & Jiana Lane/Laborer/N.M. Corbin Neighbor
Josie Lewis/C/F/Aug/Unknown/4y/Reuben & Courtney Lewis/Reuben Lewis Father
Elizabeth Long/W/F/May 30/Paralysis/97y/Chas & Letitia Blanton/Jno Long Husband

James C. Luck/W/M/Apr 14/Inflamation of Brain/74y/Wm & Judith Luck/Farmer/Sallie Luck Wife/Albert Luck Brother

Hauzie Marmaduke/W/F/May 26/Consumption/24y/Montreville & Ann F. Marmaduke Mother

Richd M. Marmaduke/W/M/July 29/Consumption/28y/Montreville & Ann F. Marmaduke/ Unmarried/Ann F. Marmaduke Mother

Joseph F. Mason/W/M/July 27/Typhoid Fever/8y/Joseph W. & Bettie Mason/Joseph W. Mason Father

Huldah McLaughlin/W/F/Feb 25/Pneumonia/80y/B. & Huldah Duke/b.Hanover Co/Geo M. McLaughlin Husband

Ella C. Murray/W/F/July 11/Unknown/10m/Wm H. & Mary A. Murray/Wm H. Murray Father

Nelson Minor/C/M/Sept/Unknown/56y/Jno & Easter Minor/b.Spotsylvania Co/Laborer/Mary Minor Wife

__ Monroe/C/M/Sept 20/Still Born/Andrew & Rebecca Monroe/Andrew Monroe Father

__ Newton/W/F/Aug 10/Unknown/12d/Jno W. & Elizabeth Newton/Jno W. Newton Father

Jane Nelson/C/F/June/Heart Disease/57y/Unity Webb/York Nelson Husband

Jesse Peatross/C/M/July 25/Unknown/20y/Jacob & Lucy Peatross/Jacob Peatross Father

Robt S. Peatross/W/M/Nov/Heart Disease/76y/Richd & Agnes Peatross/Ro O. Peatross Son

Fannie [Frances] A. Peatross/W/F/Oct 24/Consumption/51y/Seth & Susan [Susannah]Campbell/ Richd F. Blanton Neighbor

[Note: Page 3 of year 1880, following items 60-80 of the original, some smeared beyond reading]

Kate C. Redd/W/F/[illeg] 10/Childbirth/25y/Edmd & Mary Taylor/b.Hanover Co/James T. [Temple] Redd/Thomasia Redd Mother-in-Law

[illeg] Redd/W/M/Nov 18/Brain Fever/1m/James T. & Kate C. Redd/Thomasia Redd Grandmother

__ Rollins/C.M/Oct 1/Diptheria/2d/Dingo & Matilda Rollins/Dingo Rollins Father

[illeg] Shackelford/W/M/Feb 15/Brain Fever/11y/Jno L. & Pamedia Shackleford/Jno L. Shackleford Father

__ Samuel/W/F/Oct 1/Diptheria/4y/W.H. & Mattie Samuel/W.H. Samuel Father

William Smith/C/M/[illeg] 28/Unknown/1y/Richd & Sallie Smith/Richd Smith Father

Mary Smith/W/F/Nov 1/Diptheria/7y/Lewis H. & Jane Smith/Lewis H. Smith Father

__ Smith/W/M/Aug 20/Still Born/Robt S. & Hattie Smith/Ro S. Smith Father

[illeg] Stevenson/C/F/Sept 4/Unknown/6m/Wm H. & Maria L. Stevenson/Wm H. Stevenson Father

[illeg] Taylor/C/F/Apr/Spasms/1y/Chas & Susan Taylor/Susan Taylor Mother

William Terrell/W/M/Aug 23/Chronic Diarrhea/65y/Jas & Sallie Terrell/Farmer/Unmarried/Jas H. Terrell Nephew

[illeg] T. Thacker/W/M/Mar 5/Liver Disease/50y/Ben & Lucy Thacker/Ed T. Thacker Friend

[illeg] Wadlington/C/M/Sept/Unknown/5m/Gabriel & Ann Wadlington/Gabriel Wadlington Father

[illeg] Waller/W/M/Aug/Disease of Bladder/76y/Dabney & Elizabeth Waller/b.Spotsylvania Co/ Teacher/Dabney J. Waller Son

[illeg] Washington/C/F/Aug/Unknown/1y/Annie Washington/Annie Washington Mother

[illeg] Williams/C/F/June/Croup/5m/Geo & Elizh Williams/Geo Williams Father

Henry Williams/C/M/July/Stabbed/30y/Andrew & Lucy Williams/Laborer/Anderson Williams Brother

Olie R. Wingfield/C/F/Oct/Croup/1y/Wm & Lucinda Wingfield/Wm Wingfield Father

Robt T. Wortham/W/M/May 28/Heart Disease/58y/Saml & Tracy Wortham/Physician/Mary F. Wortham Wife

__ Wright/C/M/Apr/Still Born/Thos & Bettie Wright/Thos Wright Father

Susan Wyatt/W/F/May 11/Old Age/93y/Vivian & Elizb Minor/Jno G. Coleman Son-in-Law

1881

Elizth B. Garnett/W/F/Nov 5/Consumption/57y/Robt & Fannie Spindle/b.Essex Co/Widow/Jas B. Garnett Son

Virginia M. Gouldin/W/F/July 27/Consumption/43y/Nathl & M. Motley/ James F. Gouldin Husband

Jno L. Gouldin/W/M/Oct 21/Not Known/2d/Jno L. & Carry Gouldin/Jno L. Gouldin Father

Caroline V. Garrett/W/F/July 7/Com of Diseases/28y/Thos & Fannie Powers/Henry S. Garrett Husband

Richard Gouldman/W/M/Mar 10/Consumption/76/Richd & Phoeby Gouldman/Farmer/Ann E. Gouldman Wife/C.M. Gouldman Son

Bernie H. Gouldman/W/F/Sept 8/Com of Diseases/1y 1m/Henry P. & Bernie H. Gouldman/H.P. Gouldman Father

Robb Gravatt/C/M/Oct 10/Chills/11m/Henry & Catharine Gravatt/Henry Gravatt Father

No Name Gatewood/C/F/Jan 21/Not Known/2d/Thos & Nelly Gatewood/Thos Gatewood Father

James Gus/C/M/Mar 5/Not Known/7y/Thos & Hannah Gus/Thos Gus Father

No Name Gus/C/F/Apr 1/Not Known/1d/Thos & Hannah Gus/Thos Gus Father

William Graves/W/M/Dec 2/Old Age/75y/Not Known/Farmer/Mary Graves Wife

Zim Hoomes/C/M/Aug 10/Brain Fever/11y/Zim & Lucy Hoomes/Zim Hoomes Father

No Name Hoomes/C/M/Oct 5/Still Born/Wm & Emily Hoomes/Wm Hoomes Father

No Name Houston/W/M/Sept 5/Not Known/1d/Dewitt C. & Sallie Houston/D.C. Houston Father

Thomas Howard/C/M/Jan 5/Typhoid Fever/24y/Lindsey & Ellen Howard/Laborer/Unmarried/ Lindsey Howard Father

No Name Harris/W/M/Aug 10/Not Known/4d/Jno & Burton Harris/Jno Harris Father

No Name Jefferson/C/F/July 10/d.Port Royal/Still Born/Silas & Margarett Jefferson/Silas Jefferson Father

Catharine Jackson/C/F/July 15/d.Port Royal/Com of Diseases/ 22y/Edwd & Ellen Jackson/b.Port Royal/Edwd Jackson Father

Peachley Johnson/C/M/Sept 8/Not Known/8d/Mary Carter Mother

No Name Jackson/C/M/Oct 1/Not Known/Robinson & Rose Jackson/R. Jackson Father

No Name Jackson/C/M/July 3/Still Born/Davey & Emma Jackson/Davey Jackson Father

Annie Jeter/C/F/June 5/Consumption/25y/Washington & Patsy Jeter/Servant/Jno Jeter Brother

Millie Jones/W/F/June 10/Consumption/31y/NotKnown/b.Spotsylvania/Waller Jones Husband

No Name Jones/W/M/Dec 3/Still Born/C. Evans & Laura G. Jones/C.E. Jones Father

No Name Jones/W/M/Apr 30/Still Born/Charles L. & C. Mildred Jones/C.L. Jones Father

Thos Kidd/W/M/June 1/Hemmorage/55y/Willis & Lucy Kidd/Farmer/Mary Kidd Wife/Henry W. Kidd Brother

Mildred J. Kay/C/F/Sept 11/Cancer/58y/Geo & Elizth Cooper/Widow/R.V. Pendleton Daughter

William Lewis/C/M/May 10/Consumption/65y/Father & Mother Not Known/Laborer/Mary Lewis Wife/R.B. Richerson Friend

Negee Lee/C/M/Aug 13/Not Known/6d/Negee & Janice Lee/Negee Lee Father

No Name Latane/C/F/Jan 16/Not Known/5d/Tom & Ella Latane/Tom Latane Father

George Lee/W/M/Oct 5/Chills/5y/Lucy Lee/Lucy Lee Mother

Jennie Lomax/C/F/June/Not Known/11y/Albert & Bettie Lomax/Albert Lomax Father

Geo Lefoe/W/M/Oct 9/Not Known/6y/Jno W. & Annie Lefoe/Jno W. Lefoe Father

No Name Gray/W/M/Sept 4/Not Known/1d/Julia Gray/Julia Gray Mother

Victor Coats/C/F/May 3/Unknown/4y/Caty Coats/Cady Coats Mother

Lee Minor/C/M/May 5/Killed by Falling tree/36y/Lewis & Mary Minor/Laborer/Mary Minor Wife/Burley Walker Friend

Richd Moore/C/M/May 20/d.Port Royal/Croup/85y/Not Known/Lucy Moore Wife

No Name Osborn/C/M/May 11/Not Known/1d/Wesley & Maria Osborn/Wesley Osborn Father

[Note: First 2 columns faded beyond recognition]

[illeg] Anderson/C/M/July/Killed on Rail Road/28y/Page & Frances Anderson/Laborer/Mary Anderson Wife/Page Anderson Father

[illeg]/[illeg]/[illeg]/Apr/Cancer/50y/James & Mary Carneal/Widow/W.B. Anderson Friend

[illeg] Acors/[illeg]/[illeg]/Aug 10/Congestive Chill/65y/Wm & Mary Waller/H.D. Acors Husband

[illeg] Acors/[illeg]/[illeg]/Feb 5/d.Bowling Green/Consumption/45y/Jos T. & Maria May/Paul C. Acors Husband

[illeg] Beazley/Jan/Com of D/39y/Maria Croley Mother/James Beasley Husband

Etta T. Beasley/C/F/Feb 2/Brain Fever/54y/Jas & Louticia Beasley/James Beasley Father

[illeg] Broaddus/C/F/June 15/Not Known/5d/Davey & Frances Broaddus/Davey Broaddus Father

E[illeg] Broaddus/W/F/Oct/Brain Fever/8y/Geo W. & Lizzie R. Broaddus/__

[illeg] Baylor/C/F/Jan 10/Com of D/25y/F & M Not known/Warner Baylor Husband

W.E. Byrd/C/M/July 1/Not Known/6y/Mary Byrd Father Unknown/Mary Byrd Mother

No Name Bruce/W/M/Still Born/Ro S. & Lucy Bruce/Ro S. Bruce Father

James O. Byrd/C/M/Aug 5/Not Known/22y/James & Sallie Byrd/Laborer/James Byrd Father

No Name Bullock/W/M/Oct 11/Not Known/1d/David & Mary Bullock/D.T. Bullock Father

Frances Boulware/W/F/Oct 3/Consumption/49y/Martha & Jno Poats/b.King George/Mark Boulware Husband

__ Bique/W/M/Dec/Not Known/1d/David & Sallie Bique/David Bique Father

[illeg] Barlow/W/F/d.Bowling Green/Consumption/50y/Jno & Mary Gray/Widow/James Barlow Son

[illeg] Bullard/W/F/July 25/d.Bowling Green/Consumption/55y/Wm & Lucinda Bullard/Unmarried/ Wm E. Bullard Nephew

No Name Carter/__/__/Still Born/John & Sela Carter/John Carter Father

__ Chenault/__/__/Not Known/1d/Calvin & Emma Chenault/Calvin Chenault Father

[illeg] Chiles/C/__/__/Consumption/21y/Danl & Sallie Chiles/Unmarried/Danl Chiles Father

__ Coleman/C/__/__/Not Known/10d/Wm & Sallie Coleman/Wm Coleman Father

Mary E. Chandler/W/F/Feb/Com of Diseases/60y/Jno & Mary Frazier/b.Spotsylvania/Thos C. Chandler Husband

__ Chambers/C/M/Aug/Not Known/2d/Lee & Elizth Chambers/Lee Chambers Father

Daniel Coleman DeJarnette/W/M/Aug 20/Com of D/59y/D.C. & Hulda DeJarnette/Farmer/Louisa J. DeJarnette Wife

[illeg] Donaway/W/F/May/d.Bowling Green/Com of Dis/50y/J. & M. Kidd/A.B. Donaway Husband

[illeg] Franks/W/M/Nov/d.Bowling Green/Consumption/48y/Not Known/b.King George/Silversmith/ Lucy Franks Wife/J.S. Tracy Friend

[illeg] Farmer/W/M/May 10/Typhoid Fever/18y/Wm P & Sallie Farmer/Wm P. Farmer Father

[illeg]/C/M/Aug 19/Consumption/24y/No Father, Sarah Ferguson/Laborer/Sarah Ferguson Mother

[illeg] Fortune/C/M/Sept 8/Old Age/75y/Father & Mother Not Known/Laborer/Wm Fortune Son

James J. Gutridge/W/M/__/Com of Dis/38y/James & B. Gutridge/Farmer/Virginia Gutridge Wife

[illeg] Gibbs/W/M/__/d.Port Royal/Consumption/58y/Jno P. & Ann Gibbs/Farmer/Mary S. Gibbs Wife

[illeg] Gray/C/F/__/Child Birth/30y/F[ather] & M[other] Not Known/Archer Gray Husband

__ Gray/C/F/Aug 10/Not Known/2d/Archer & Veria Gray/Archer Gray Father

[illeg] Gray/C/F/__/Dropsy/40y/F & M Not Known/Archer Gray Friend

__ Gray/__/__/__/Not Known/2d/Charles & Isabella Gray/Charles Gray Father
[illeg] Gray/C/F/__/Consumption/50y/F & Mother Not Known/Lewis Gray Husband
[illeg] Garnett/C/F/__/Consumption/50y/Susan Corbin/Ben Garnett Husband
Rosa L. Prior/C/F/Oct 6/Not Known/__/James & Bettie Prior/James Prior Father
Moore Baylor/C/M/May 10/Consumption/44y/Andrew & Lelia Baylor/Farmer/Jos R.Penney Friend
Phil D. Pendleton/C/M/Feb 25/Consumption/31y/Phil & Emily Pendleton/b.Hanover/Merchant/
 Rose V. Pendleton Wife
Elizth Pendleton/C/F/Jan 31/Com of Dis/8m/Phil D. & Rose V. Pendleton/R.V. Pendleton Mother
Ellen P. Pavey/W/F/Nov 10/Teething/7m/James S. & Sarah A. Pavey/J.S. Pavey Father
Geo R. Wharton/C/M/May 18/Old Age/80y/Not Known/Laborer/P. Smith Friend
Lucy [illeg]/C/F/Oct 9/Consumption/50y/Not Known/Servant/Robt Crenshaw Friend
G [illeg] Rieves/C/M/May 25/Brain Fever/1y 3m/Martha Reeves/Martha Rieves Mother
Mary Richerson/C/F/Oct 5/Brain Fever/5y 6m 1d/Alex & Elizth Richerson/Alex Richerson Father
Nathl Robb/C/M/Aug 1/Teething/1y 6m/Wm & Caroline Robb/Wm Robb Father
Bettie A. Kelley/W/M/June 4/Cancer/38y/Dick & Alice D. Richards/Widow/Dick Richards Father
[illeg] Richards/C/M/May 3/Chills/5y/Jno & Sallie Richards/Jno Richards Father
[illeg] Smithey/C/F/Oct 5/Consumption/39y/Not Known/Latane Smithey Husband/Thornton Coleman
 Friend
[illeg] Sirles/W/F/Aug 10/Consumption/44y/James & Maria Cecil/Wesley Sirles Husband/Atwell
 Houston Friend
[illeg] Minor/C/F/Sept 3/Consumption/34y/Jessy & Mary Johnson/Samuel Minor Husband
M. Gertrude Samuel/W/F/Apr 4/Child Bed/28y/Edwd & Sarah Kay/b.Essex/Geo W. Samuel Husband
[illeg] Samuel/__/__/__/Still Born/Geo W. & M. Gertrude Samuel/Geo W. Samuel Father
[illeg] Smith/__/__/__/Pluracy/1y/Aaron & Julia Smith/Aaron Smith Father
[illeg] Sale/C/F/__/Consumption/65y/Not Known/Servant/James Sale Husband
[illeg] Self/W/M/__/Consumption/24y/Wm & Mary Self/Laborer/Unmarried/Jno Self Step Father
[illeg] Schooler/__/__/__/Dysentery/7m/Dan & Mary Schooler/Dan Schooler Father
[illeg] Sorrell/__/__/__/Still Born/Wm J. & Sarah Sorrell/Wm J. Sorrell Father
[illeg] Carneal/W/F/__/Consumption/54y/Wm & Mary Diggins/Housekeeper/Widow/J.D. Carneal Son
[illeg] Taylor?/C/F/Oct 18/__/85y/Not Known/Widow/Cathe Taylor Daughter
[illeg] Taylor/C/F/July 5/Dysentery/1y/Susan Taylor/Unmarried/Unmarried/Willis Taylor Uncle
No Name Taliaferro/C/F/Oct 10/Not Known/1d/Morton & Mary Taliaferro/Morton Taliaferro Father
No Name Turner/C/F/Sept 16/Still Born/Hazelwood & Susan Turner/H. Turner Father
Mary [illeg]/W/F/Dec 18/Consumption/40y/Charles & Nelly Howard/Widow/Wm Toombs Friend
Frances Vaughan/W/F/Dec 29/Com of D/70y/Jno & Lucy Baston/Eldred Vaughan Husband
Joe Vessels/C/M/Dec 18/Dysentery/5y/Joe & Rebecca Vessels/Joe Vessels Father
No Name Walker/C/M/Aug 19/Still Born/J.E. & Lavinia Walker/J.E. Walker Father
Lillie R. Wright/W/F/Nov 6/Killed by falling tree/22y/B. & Phoeby Smoot/Lulie T. Wright Husband
[illeg] Walker/C/F/Aug 29/Consumption/33y/Joe & Bettie Minor/Beverley Walker Husband
[illeg] Whittaco [Whittaker] /W/F/Jan 1/Child Birth/20y/Dick & Mary Chandler/R.D. Whittaco
 Husband
[illeg] Beasley/W/F/Dec 18/Paralysis/60y/Edwd & Anna Beasley/Midwife/Unmarried/Geo Whittaco
 Friend
[illeg] Washington/C/F/July 8/Not Known/1m/Monroe & Peggy Washington/M. Washington Father
[illeg] White/C/M/June 10/Dropsy/16y/Isaac & Ella White/Isaac White Father
[illeg] Ware/C/F/Sept 3/Consumption/60y/Betsy Ware/Widow/Charles Ware Son
[illeg] Allen/W/F/Dec 13/Unknown/1d/Jno T. & Bettie L. Allen/Jno T. Allen Father
Gracie M. Allen/W/F/Sept/Unknown/7m/Jno C. & Bettie G. Allen/Jno C. Allen Father

Washington Alexander/C/M/July 5/Saw Mill Explosion/21y/James & Elvira/Laborer/James Alexander Father
Emiline Adams/C/F/Nov 2/Consumption/30y/Marco & Dinah Moore/Peter Adams Husband/Dinah Moore Mother
Thomas Adams/C/M/May 13/Sarfula/2y/Peter & Emiline/Dinah Moore Grandmother
__ Atkinson/W/M/Aug 1/Unknown/3m/Jno J. & Eliza Atkinson/Jno J. Atkinson Father
Joseph Braxton/C/M/Mar 3/Unknown/13y/Carter & Ellen Carter Braxton/Carter Braxton Father
__ Baber/C/M/June/Still Born/Waller & Marter Baber/Waller Baber Father
__ Beazley/W/M/Oct/Unknown/6d/Phil A. & Mildred Beazley/Phil A. Beazley Father
Carrie B. Blanton/W/F/Sept 8/Congestive Chill/8y/Thos H. & Mary E. Blanton/Thos H. Blanton Father
__ Banks/C/M/Mar 5/Still Born/Jno H. & Laura Banks/Jno H. Banks Father
Rhoda Carter/C/F/Apr/Diptheria/21d/Thomas & Emma Carter/Thos Carter Father
Ellanora Carneal/W/F/Oct 15/Congestive Lungs/12y/E.G. & Mary E. Carneal/E.G. Carneal Father
Ida Carneal/W/F/Nov 20/Typhoid Fever/6y/E.G. & Mary E. Carneal/E.G. Carneal Father
__ Cammack/C/M/Apr/Still born/Chas & Margt Cammick/Chas Cammick
Chiles/C/M/Jan/Unknown/1d/Rufus & Georgianna Chiles/Rufus Chiles Father
Evert Chiles/W/M/July 20/Chol Infantum/6m/Jno E. & Alice C./Jno E. Chiles Father
Douglas A. Chisholm/W/M/Jan 15/Diptheria/5y/J.A. & Ada T. Chisholm/b.King William Co/J.A. Chisholm Father
Joseph Claiborne/C/M/Sept/Scrofula/37y/Jesse & Maria/Laborer/Evelyn Claiborne Wife
Mary J. Claytor/W/F/Apr 12/Dropsy/38y/Thos & Rebecca Madison/French Claytor Husband
__ Claytor/W/M/Apr 12/Still Born/French & Mary J. Claytor/French Claytor Father
Saml Coleman/C/M/Aug 31/Typhoid Fever/19y/Richd R. & Catherine Coleman/Richd R. Coleman Father
__ Coleman/C/F/Nov 9/Unknown/7d/Bug & Millie Coleman/Bug Coleman Father
Maria Coleman/C/F/Sept/Heart Disease/80y/Unknown/Geo Coleman Husband/Richd C. Friend
Bettie C. Cobb/W/F/Aug 30/Child birth/30y/Wm C. & Mildred Thomas/b.Louisa Co/Wm L. Cobb Husband
Nancy Cobb/W/F/Nov 16/Old Age/70y/Unknown/Jno S. Carpenter Friend
Mary Cobb/W/F/Sept/Consumption/43y/A.G. & Lucy Bendall/W.B. Bendall Brother
Rufus Courtney/C/M/Oct 25/Diptheria/13y/Wm J. & Eliza Courtney/Wm J. Courtney Father
Mary A Davis/C/F/Nov 14/Typhoid Pneumonia/__/Peter & Delia A. Davis/Peter Davis Father
__ Duracott/C/M/Aug 3/Still Born/Geo W. & Lucy J. Duracott/Geo W Duracott Father
Catharine E. Durrett/W/F/Apr 28/Measles/56y/Jno & Cath Martin/b.Hanover Co/Bettie Brooks Daughter
Jennie A. Dyson/W/F/Dec 20/Pleuricy/50y/Jos A. & Mary Mason/James W. Dyson Husband
Mary E. Dyson/W/F/Nov 16/Consumption/44y/Thos & Frances Young/Henry H. Dyson Husband
Jane Farish/W/F/Dec 11/Unknown/70y/Robert Wood/E.R. Coghill Friend
Jno J. Flippo/W/M/June 10/Wm E. & Rachel T. Flippo/Farmer/Elenora H. Flippo Wife
Rose Fells/C/F/Oct 8/__/3m/Coss & Lizzie Fells/Coss Fells Father
__ Freeman/W/F/May 26/__/__/Wm & Susan E. Freeman/Wm Freeman Father
Janet Giles/C/F/__/Burn/3y/L. & Eliza Giles/Mary Jackson Grandmother
Louisa Giles/C/F/__/Typhoid Fever/5y/L. & Eliza Giles/Mary Jackson Grandmother
Lafayette Grimes/C/F/__/Burns/2y/Robt & Betsy Grimes/Ro Grimes Father
Annie L. Hailstork/C/F/Unknown/7m/Josh & Mary Hailstork/Josh Hailstork Father
Wm M. Hutcheson/W/M/Cave of a well/33y/Jno & Parthenia Hutcheson/Farmer/J[illeg]C. Hutcheson Wife/Parthenia Hutcheson Mother

Alb[ert] S. Hundley/W/M/__/Fall/75y/Mathew P. & Lucy A. [Kidd] Hundley/Farmer/A.M. Hundley Son
Martha Jackson/C/F/__/Unknown/1y/Henry & Patsy Jackson/Henry Jackson Father
Eddie Jackson/C/M/__/Pneumonia/4y/Henry & Patsy Jackson/Henry Jackson Father
__ Johnson/C/F/__/Unknown/2m/Lewis & Rose Johnson/Lewis Johnson Father
Nelson Jones/C/M/__/Consumption/60y/Unknown/Laborer/W.H. McKenny Friend
Mary F. Kelly/W/F/__/Consumption/48y/Richd & Lucinda Kelly/Single/S.E. Kelly Sister
Josie Lawrence/C/F/__/Chol Infantum/11m/Ro & Frances Lawrence/Frances Lawrence Mother
Emuella Luck/W/F/__/Child birth/35y/R. Pemberton/Thos L. Luck Husband
Eliza Luck/W/F/__/Old Age/78y/Wm & Mary Luck/b.Hanover Co/Single/Thos L. Luck Nephew
Wm A. McKein/W/M/__/Congestive Chill/66y/Unknown/b.RichmondVa/Farmer/Lucy T. McKein Wife
Cotes Mines/C/M/__/Unknown/35y/Chas & Nancy Mines/Laborer/Betsy Mines wife
Clara Mines/C/F/__/Diptheria/4y/Richd & Frances Mines/Richd Mines Father
Richd Minor/C/M/__/Saw Mill Explosion/35y/Unknown/Single/Ed Weaver Friend
__ Minor/C/M/__/Unknown/1d/Fleming & Millie Minor/Fleming Minor Father
__ Minor/__/__/__/Unknown/15d/Wm & Sophia Minor/Wm Minor Father
Emily Montague/C/F/__/Typhoid Fever/48y/Unknown/Guy Montague Husband
Moracco Moore/__/__/__/d.Henrico Co/Drowned/23y/Moracco & Dinah Moore/Laborer/Single/ Dinah Moore Mother
__ Page/W/F/__/Convulsions/6y/Jos T. & Susan E. Page/Jos T. Page Father
Marshall Parker/C/M/__/Unknown/6y/Marshall & Bettie Parker/Mar Parker Father
Chas Pemberton/W/M/__/Killed by Horse/10y/Robt B. & Catharine Pemberton/R.B. Pemberton Father
__ Pemberton/C/F/__/Still born/Thos J. & Ann/Thos J. Pemberton Father
Geo F. Pickett/C/M/__/Typhoid Fever/28y/__ & Betsy Pickett/Laborer/Lucy Pickett Wife/Jno W. Satterwhite Friend
__ Quash/C/M/__/Still born/__ & Betsy Quash/Betsy Quash Mother
Kate Randal/C/F/__/Small Pox/43y/Unknown/Felix Randal Husband/T.H. Jones Friend
__ Robinson/C/M/__/Diarrhea/4d/Saml & Willie Ann Robinson/Saml Robinson Father
[illeg] Saunders/W/M/__/Typhoid Fever/61y/__ & Fannie Saunders/Farmer/Lucy A. Saunders Wife
[illeg] Satterwhite/W/M/__/Brain Fever/1y/J.E. & Bettie Satterwhite/J.E. Satterwhite Father
[illeg] Smith/W/F/__/Diarrhea/4y/R.L. & Hattie T. Smith/R.L. Smith Father
[illeg] Smith/C/M/__/Unknown/1y/Thornton & Dorothea Smith/Thornton Smith Father
[illeg] Smith/W/F/__/Unknown/3y/R.L. & Debbie Smith/R.L. Smith Father
[illeg] Smith/W/M/__/[illeg]/[illeg] & Mary Smith/Farmer/Julia Smith Wife
[illeg] Stevens/__/[illeg]/[illeg]/[illeg]/[illeg]/Ro Stevens Husband
[Note: This is the end of the fading in the original script]
Charles Taylor/C/M/Dec 18/Unknown/39y/Robinson & Phoebe Taylor/Hannah Taylor Wife/Tim Taylor Brother
Birksie Taylor/C/F/Nov/Unknown/3y/__ & Matilda Taylor/Matilda Taylor Mother
Ernest Taylor/C/M/July/Measles/1y/Spencer & Alberta Taylor/Spencer Taylor Father
Monahan Thacker/W/M/Mar/Congestion/9y/__ & Sarah Monahan/Ed Acors Friend
Mollie Thomas/C/F/Nov/Childbirth/29y/Thos Mima Freeman/Wm Thomas Husband
__ Thomas/C/M/Nov/Still born/Wm & Mollie Thomas/Wm Thomas Father
Caroline Todd/C/F/Feb/Unknown/5d/Peter & Josephine Todd/Peter Todd Father
Thos J. Tribble/W/M/Dec 15/Pneumonia/52y/__ & Patsy Tribble/Farmer/Lithiann Tribble Wife/ C.M. Tribble Son

__ Trainham/W/F/Apr/Still born/Thos J. & Ann E. Trainham/T.J. Trainham Father
Nancy Waller/C/F/Nov 5/Consumption/40y/Unknown/Henry Waller Husband
Cora Washington/W/F/Oct/Typhoid Fever/21y/Geo B. & Millie Washington/G.B. Washington Father
Mildred Washington/C/F/Nov/Unknown/45y/Unknown/Lewis Washington Husband
James Williams/C/M/Apr 16/Unknown/75y/Unknown/Hairet Williams Wife
William R. White/W/M/Sept/Croup/5y/Jno G. & Nannie White/Jno G. White - Father
Mathew Wright/C/M/Nov 25/Typhoid Fever/17y/James & Hairat [Harriett] Wright/James Wright Father
James F. Wright/C/M/Sept 20/Typhoid Fever/56y/__ & DandridgeWright/Preacher/Roxie Wright Wife/Thos P. Wright Son

1882

Mary S. Ayres/W/F/May 11/Pneumonia/25y/Geo & Elizabeth Askins/Wm Ayres Husband
[Note: last 3 columns on this page are faded and smeared and most are beyond recognition]
Wm F. Beall/W/M/Mar 12/Whooping Cough/1m/Saml O.W. & Mary E. Beall/[illeg]
Alphonze O. Blanton/W/M/June 20/Consumption/27y/Chas C. & Mary J. Blanton/Farmer/[illeg]
Jno E. Bowers/W/M/Mar 22/Old Age/83y/Wm & Fannie Bowers/Farmer/Mary Bowers [illeg]
Monroe Boxley/C/M/Sept 18/Fever/75y/Unknown/b.Spotsylvania/Blacksmith/Sarah Boxley [illeg]
Nathaniel Burruss/W/M/Sept 18/Bronchitis/10m/Pleas T. & Jane Burruss/[illeg]
Wm S. Burruss/W/M/May 17/Unknown/2m/Thos W. & Coptela Burruss/[illeg]
Bettie P. Burruss/W/F/Aug 15/Unknown/61y/Unknown/Married/[illeg]
John Burruss/W/M/May 21/Gangrene/75y/Henry & Sarah T. Burruss/Merchant/Married/[illeg]
Isabella Burke/W/F/Nov 20/Unknown/70y/James & Frances Garnett/b.Essex Co/Widow/[illeg]
__ Cammack/C/M/July/Still Born/Chas & Margt Cammack/[illeg]
Tomasia Carneal/W/F/Nov/Paralysis/50y/Pleasant & Lucy Carneal/[illeg]
Margt Carson/W/F/Nov 6/Old Age/85y/Wm & Jane McKee/b.August Co/Widow/[illeg]
Frederick Carter/W/M/Jan 2/Croup/2y/Jno A. & Sallie Carter/[illeg]
Sarah L. Coghill/W/F/Jan 3/Rheumatism/58y/Sym B. & Elizab Goodloe/b.Spotsylvania Co/Widow/[illeg]
William Coleman/C/M/June 20/Unknown/60y/Suny & Sarah Coleman/Farmer/Matilda Coleman Wife/[illeg]
__ Courtney/C/M/Apr 18/Unknown/1d/Tim G. & Mary J. Courtney/[illeg]
Charlotte Edwards/W/F/Apr 5/Consumption/36y/Barthelomew & Bertha Taylor/[;illeg]
Elizabeth T. Flippo/W/F/Sept 23/Typhoid Fever/82y/May & Elizb Flippo/Unmarried/[illeg]
__ Freeman/W/F/May 8/Unknown/8d/Wm & Susan Freeman/[illeg]
__ Gatewood/C/M/Oct 30/Still Born/Jonas & Maria Gatewood/[illeg]
Mary E. Gayle/W/F/Jan 19/Dysentary/50y/Thos A. & Mary Acors/[illeg]
Wm H. Goodloe/W/M/Apr 22/Chronic Diarrhea/60y/Aquilla & Elizb Goodloe/Farmer/[illeg]
Clara Goodwin/W/F/Apr/Unknown/60y/Chas & __ Goodwin/[illeg]
__ Green/C/M/Jan/Unknown/1m/Geo & Jennie Green/[illeg]
__ Hackett/C/F/May 17/Chol Infantum/2m/Montgomery & Alice Hackett/[illeg]
__ Hughes/W/F/Aug 20/Unknown/1d/Jno & Bettie Hughes/[illeg]
Alvis James/C/M/Mar 25/Unknown/11m/Peter & Emma James/[illeg]
Chas James/C/M/Mar 2/Drowned/21y/Randal & Mary James/Laborer/[illeg]
__ Jefferson/C/M/July/Whooping Cough/2m/Bennett & Lucy Jefferson/[illeg]
Andrew Johnson/W/M/June 25/Apoplexy/38y/Ben & Mary Johnson/Farmer/[illeg]

Jessie Johnson/C/F/Feb 15/Rising in head/7m/Chas & Elizh Johnson/[illeg]
[Note: end of faded section]
Frank Johnson/C/M/Mar 10/Unknown/10m/Henry & Etta Johnson/Henry Johnson Father
Mary Lewis/C/F/Apr 24/d.Washington D.C./Consumption/40y/Harry & Nancy Baylor/Edmond Lewis Husband
Andrew Lewis/C/M/Nov/d.Washington D.C./Mumps/10y/Edmond & Mary Lewis/Edmond Lewis Father
Dorothea Lewis/C/F/Nov/d.Washington D.C./Diarrhea/2y/Edmond & Mary Lewis/Edmond Lewis Father
__ Lewis/C/M/Apr/d.Washington D.C./Unknown/21d/Edmond & Mary Lewis/Edmond Lewis Father
Jno Lucas/C/M/Aug 12/Consumption/24y/Leonard & Fannie Lucas/Laborer/Unmarried/Leonard Lucas Father
Fannie E. Lumpkin/W/F/May 16/Unknown/67y/Jesse & __ Terrell/Widow/T.R. Lumpkin Son
Ann F. Marmaduke/W/F/Apr 13/Consumption/60y/Geo W. & __ Madison/Jno S. Marmaduke Son
Alex H. McKenny/W/M/Dec 23/Consumption/31y/Alex G. & Mar McKenny/Farmer/Sallie McKenny Wife/W.H. McKenny Bro
__ Minor/C/F/Mar/Unknown/1d/Wm & Sophia Minor/Wm Minor Father
Bettie Minor/C/F/Dec/Old Age/75y/Unknown/Widow/Wm G. Harris Friend
Wm M. Monroe/C/M/Jul 23/Scrofula/10m/And & Rebecca Monroe/Andrew Monroe Father
Ida Monroe/C/F/Dec 28/Bronchitis/1y/And & Rebecca Monroe/Andrew Monroe Father
__ Moore/C/M/Feb/Still born/Jacob & Mary E. Moore/Jacob Moore Father
__ Moren/W/F/Apr/Still born/Wm G. & Fannie E. Moren/Wm G. Moren Father
__ Morton/C/F/Jan/Unknown/8d/Eugene & Eudora Morton/Eugene Morton Father
Betsy Quash/C/F/Dec 21/Paralysis/33y/__ & Tama Terry/Joseph Quash Husband
Julian W. Ricks/W/M/June 29/Chol Infantum/3m/Richd A. & Catharine Ricks/R.A.Ricks Father
Joseph E. Robinson/W/M/June 20/Chol Infantum/4m/Jos B. & Mollie Robinson/J.B.Robinson Father
Matilda Rollins/C/F/June 27/Heart Disease/30y/Sancho & Lucinda Shakespheare/Dingo Rollins Husband
__ Ross/C/M/Nov/Unknown/5d/Redevio & Lucy J. Ross/Rod Ross Father
Wm E. Smith/W/M/May/Fits/41y/Ro L. & Debbie Smith/R.L. Smith Father
James T. Smith/W/M/Mar 15/Paralysis/63y/Wm & Fannie Smith/Farmer/Widower/M.N. Smith Son
Edwd J. Stevens/W/M/Dec 12/Pneumonia/59y/Ro & Susan Stevens/Farmer/Bettie Stevens Wife
Ellen Whiple/C/F/Apr/Paralysis/63y/Unknown/Widow/Watt Page Friend
Ro L. Terrell/W/M/Mar 17/Heart Disease/72y/Lun & __ Terrell/Farmer/Rachel T. Terrell Wife/Ro S. Hargrave Nephew
Rachel T. Terrell/W/F/Apr 5/Paralysis/61y/Garland & Lucy Hargrave/Widow/R.S. Hargrave Nephew
Jno Terry/C/M/Mar 15/Pneumonia/20y/Armistead & Patsy Terry/Laborer/Unmarried/Armistead Terry Father
Lydia Thomas/C/F/Oct 5/Chills/19m/Ro H. & Vicie A. Thomas/Ro H. Thomas Father
Bartholmew Thomas/W/M/Mar 5/Bronchitis/1y/Thos C. & Liberta Thomas/Thos C. Thomas Father
__ Thompson/C/M/Jan 20/Unknown/1d/Henry & Susan Thompson/Henry Thompson Father
__ Tunstall/W/F/Sept 9/Unknown/1d/Lewis H. & Mary E. Tunstall/L.H. Tunstall Father
Jane Tunstall/W/F/June 16/Disease of Liver/70y/Henry & __ Hill/Widow/L.H. Tunstall Son
__ Walker/C/M/Sept/Still born/Martha Walker/Martha Walker Mother
Nannie C. Watkins/W/F/May 9/Unknown/16y/Jno W. & Barbara E. Watkins/Jno W. Watkins Father

Mathew Willard/W/M/June 30/Dropsy/68y/Jas & Heuldak Willard/Farmer/Agnes Willard Wife
__ Wilson/C/M/Apr 9/Still born/Wm L. & Charlotte Wilson/W.L. Wilson Father
Geo Wingfield/C/M/Oct/b.Kentucky/Unknown/19y/Wm & Lucinda Wingfield/Wm Wingfield Father
Alice Wood/W/F/July 10/Consumption/26y/Jesse G.& M.A. Hewlett/b.Hanover Co/Frank Wood
  Husband/J.B. Wood Bro-in-Law
Frank Wood/W/M/Oct 11/Typhoid Fever/28y/Fleming & Lucy A. Wood/b.Spotsylvania/Widower/
  J.B. Wood Bro
Roxie Wright/C/F/Apr 28/Spinal Affection/60y/Thos & Matilda Wright/Thos P. Wright Son

1883

Arthur W. Alexander/C/M/Apr 10/Not Known/3m/Richard & Mary Alexander/Richd Alexander
  Father
Bloxum Acors/W/M/Feb 5/d.Bowling Green/Consumption/22y/P.C. Acors/Farmer/P.C. Acors Father
No Name Beazley/W/M/May 20/__/1d/Adam & Bettie Beasley/Adam Beasley Father
No Name Baylor/C/F/Dec 18/Still Born/Thos & Linda Baylor/Thos Baylor Father
Emma Broaddus/W/F/June 10/d.Bowling Green/Comsumption/33y/Cornelius & E. Campbell/S.W.
  Broaddus Husband
Ellen Brooks/C/F/Apr 10/Old Age/85y/Not Known/Servant/Unmarried/Lewis Banks Friend
Ro L. Bullock/W/M/Mar 8/Horse fell on him/23y/Geo W. & Martha L. Bullock/Farmer/Geo W.
  Bullock Father
Alfred Bullock/W/M/Feb 22/Not Known/2m/Thos S. & Eva Bullock/Thos S. Bullock Father
Abram Buckner/C/M/Sept 4/Not Known/2m/Abram & Isabell Buckner/A. Buckner Father
Jane Buckner/C/F/Sept 10/Womb/35y/Not Known/Servant/Geo Buckner Husband
Ellen Bates/C/F/Oct 3/Not Known/15y/Henry & Jane Bates/James Bates Brother
James Bates/C/M/Nov 5/Old Age/74y/Not Known/Farmer/Lawson Bates Son
James Bates/C/M/Feb 9/Not Known/2y/Nannie Bates/Nannie Bates Mother
Mary Bates/C/F/Jan 10/Not Known/4y/Nannie Bates/Nannie Bates Mother
No Name Clark/C/F/Aug 16/Not Known/15d/Jno L. & Martha Clark/Jno L. Clark Father
Turner Clayton/W/M/Aug 12/Old Age/76y/Not Known/Farmer/Susan Claytor Wife
Jim Frazier/W/M/May 10/Com of D/2y/G.L. & Helen Frazier/G.L. Frazier Father
Frank Farmer/W/M/June 3/Not Known/5m/R.F. & Va B. Farmer/R.F. Farmer Father
Jno L. Farmer/W/M/June 14/Old Age/79y/Lewis & Susan Farmer/Emily Farmer Wife/Ann C.
  Farmer Daughter
Emily Farmer/W/F/Dec 25/Not Known/68y/Ed & Amey Pruett/Jno L. Farmer Husband/
  Ann C. Farmer Daughter
Eugene Farish/W/M/Apr 1/Burned/K.R. & Alice Farish/K.R. Farish Father
Alice Farish/W/F/Apr/Apr 1/Burned/__/K.R. & Alice Farish/K.R. Farish Father
Ophice Fryes/C/F/June 2/Not Known/1d/W.L. & Anny Fryes/W.L. Fryes Father
Mary C. Gray/W/F/Aug 1/Not Known/5m/Smith & Matilda Gray/Smith Gray Father
No Name Gravatt/C/F/Dec 20/Not Known/20d/Henry & Rachel Gravatt/Henry Gravatt Father
Rachel Coleman/C/F/Dec 23/Com of Diseases/70y/Not Known/Servant/Henry Gravatt Son-in-Law
Ned Gaines/C/M/Mar 10/Consumption/25y/Morton & Felitia Gaines/Morton Gaines Father
Daisey Gaines/C/F/Sept 28/Not Known/1m/Wm & Fannie Gaines/Wm G. Gaines Father
Moses Green/C/M/Feb 12/Not Known/2d/Moses & Mary Green/Moses Green Father
No Name Gouldman/C/F/Dec 1/Still Born/__/Jno P. & Mary Gouldman/Jno P. Gouldman Father
Jno Greenstreet/W/M/Jan 3/Consumption/76y/Not Known/Farmer/Jno Greenstreet Friend
Lucy Harris/C/F/Apr 5/Consumption/16y/Wm & Louisa Louis/Servant/Geo H. Harris Uncle

Mary Hunter/C/F/Apr 15/Consumption/30y/James & Lucy Hunter/Servant/James Hunter Father
No Name Hopkins/C/F/Oct 2/Not Known/2d/Oliver & Fannie Hopkins/Oliver Hopkins Father
No Name Ham/C/M/Aug 5/Not Known/2d/Lomax & Sarah Ham/Lomax Ham Father
Martha James/W/F/Sept 18/Child Birth/35y/Joe & Susan Dillard/Joe James Husband
Mary Johnson/C/F/Dec 10/Not Known/5y/Edwd & Susan Johnson/Ed Johnson Father
No Name Johnson/C/M/Dec 10/Still Born/Arthur & Mary Johnson/Arthur Johnson Father
Robt J. Johnson/W/M/Dec 8/Not Known/__/Ro & Martha Johnson/Robt Johnson Father
No Name Jones/W/M/Jan 1/Still Born/A.L. & Ellen Jones/Alex L. Jones Father
Sallie Ashton/C/F/June 5/Consumption/50y/Edwd & Jane Redd/Servant/Josh Ashton Husband/
  Wm Lee Brother
Mary Lewis/C/F/Sept 5/Not Known/5m/J.H. & Mary Lewis/J.H. Lewis Father
Minnie Lumpkin/W/F/Sept/Not Known/9m/Jno & Lucy Lumpkin/Jno Lumpkin Father
Mary Lonesome/C/F/Oct 11/Not Known/4y/Jno & Mary Lonesome/Jno Lewis Uncle
Silas Lonesome/C/M/Nov 15/Not Known/3m/Frank & Sarah Lonesome/Frank Lonesome Father
No Name Lawson/C/F/Feb 3/Still Born/Edmd & Courtney Lawson/Edmd Lawson Father
No Name Lawson/C/M/July 6/Not Known/2d/Robt & Kitty Lawson/Robt Lawson Father
No Name Kay/W/M/Sept 3/Not Known/1d/H.B. & Emma Kay/H.B. Kay Father
No Name Moore/C/M/Dec/Still Born/Lindsay & Berta Moore/Lindsay Moore Father
Berta Moore/C/F/Dec 3/Child Birth/25y/Spencer & Mary Rollins/Lindsay Moore Husband
Rodney Garnett/C/F/Nov 10/Old Age/76y/Not Known/Servant/Zeb Minor Son-in-Law
Gracy Minor/C/F/July 5/Consumption/6m/Zeb & Mary Minor/Zeb Minor Father
No Name Minor/C/F/Dec 2/Still Born/Lewis & Judy Minor/Lewis Minor Father
No Name Marshall/C/F/Oct 10/Not Known/1d/Iverson & Bettie Marshall/Iverson Marshall Father
Kate Mathews/C/F/May 1/Not Known/10y/W.C. & Milly Mathews/W.C. Mathews Father
No Name McCauley/W/F/May 18/Still Born/Wm H. & Kate F. McCauley/Wm H. McCauley
  Father
Mattie McCauley/W/F/Apr 5/Not Known/1y 2m/Wm H. & Kate F. McCauley/Wm H.
  McCauley Father
Hugh Norman/C/M/Nov 10/Consumption/60y/Not Known/Laborer/Unmarried/Anderson Banks
  Friend
Henry Nelson/C/M/Apr 6/Not Known/3y/Adison & Mary Nelson/Adison Nelson Father
Frederick News/C/M/Mar 15/Consumption/65y/Maria News/Laborer/Jno Pendleton Friend
Carrie Osborne/C/F/Oct 18/Not Known/7m 7d/Alfred & Julia Osborne/Alfred Osborne Father
Harry Jackson/C/M/Dec 23/Unknown/60y/Not Known/Laborer/Alfred Osborne Friend
Jane Owens/C/F/July 10/Unknown/6d/Henry & Fannie Owens/Henry Owens Father
No Name Parker/C/F/Apr 11/Unknown/1d/Aaron & Emily Parker/Aaron Parker Father
Mary P. Pugh/W/F/June 17/Pneumonia/43y/Lewis & Mary Johnson/b.Albemarle/Wm H. Pugh Sr
  Husband
Eulah L. Pugh/W/F/Mar 10/Fever/12y/A.C. & Nancy Pugh/b.Albemarle/A.C. Pugh Father
John Pruett/W/M/Aug 30/Not Known/5m 4d/J.N. & Mary Pruett/J.N. Pruett Father
John Queen/C/M/May 15/Not Known/2d/Warner & Mary Queen/Warner Queen Father
Edmond Ennis/W/M/Aug 15/Old Age/84y/Not Known/Mail Driver/Judy Ennis Wife/J.E. Ennis Son
No Name Richerson/W/F/July 10/Still Born/Thos H. & N.E. Richerson/Thos H. Richerson Father
No Name Rollins/C/F/Aug 5/Still Born/Spencer & Smithey Rollins/Spencer Rollins Father
Walter Reynolds/C/M/May 5/Not Known/6m/Jno A. & Lucy Reynolds/Jno A. Reynolds Father
Jno W. Rice/W/M/Feb 3/Typhoid Fever/5y/J.B. & Sallie A. Rice/b.Albemarle/J.B. Rice Father
Eliza Samuel/C/F/Feb/Consumption/30y/Harry & Malinda Samuel/Servant/Unmarried/Harry Samuel
  Father

John Samuel/C/M/Feb/Consumption/24y/Harry & Malinda Samuel/Servant/Unmarried/Harry Samuel Father
Mary Samuel/C/F/Aug/Consumption/28y/Hary & Malinda Samuel/Servant/Unmarried/Harry Samuel Father
Julia Samuel/C/F/July 3/Typhoid Fever/7y/Eliz Samuel/Harry Samuel Grand Father
Malinda Samuel/C/F/Sept 9/Consumption/67y/Henry & Malinda Hopkins/Harry Samuel Husband
Harriett Stevens/W/F/Jan 10/Consumption/65y/Not Known/Unmarried/J.J. Gravatt Friend
Lucy Smith/C/F/Feb 9/Consumption/60y/Not Known/Jacob Smith Husband
Mamie Shepherd/C/F/May 10/Not Known/6y/Gilbert & Sallie Shepherd/Gilbert Shepherd Father
Saml Skinker/W/M/Apr 1/Not Known/2y/W.P. & Alice Skinker/W.P. Skinker Father
Reubin Sketton/C/M/Oct 5/Not Known/70y/Not Known/Farmer/Unmarried/Sallie Sketton Sister
Morton Sketton/C/M/Dec 6/Not Known/68y/Not Known/Unmarried/Sallie Sketton Sister
Rosa Webb/W/F/Nov 11/Not Known/1y 6m/C.S. & Ella Webb/C.S. Webb Father
Willis Taylor/C/M/Oct 10/H. Disease/55y/Not Known/Farmer/Ellen Taylor Wife
No Name Taliaferro/C/F/Sept 8/Still Born/Frances Taliaferro/Frances Taliaferro Mother
No Name Taylor/C/F/Sept 8/Still Born/Robt & Lucy Taylor/Robt Taylor Father
Eugene Thomas/W/M/Mar 1/Not Known/3m/J.S. & M.E. Thomas/J.S. Thomas Father
Ann Thornton/C/F/June 15/Typhoid Fever/15y/Robt & Eliza Thornton/Servant/Robt Thornton Father
Liddia Thornton/C/F/Mar 1/Typhoid Fever/18y/Robt & Eliza Thornton/Servant/Robt Taylor Father
Cephus Thornton/C/M/July 10/Typhoid Fever/16y/Robt & Eliza Taylor/Servant/Robt Taylor Father
No Name Vessels/C/M/Dec 18/Not Known/1m 8d/Joe & Rebecca Vessels/Joe Vessels Father
Emily Waits/C/F/Nov 5/Old Age/85y/Not Known/b.Albemarle Co/Servant/Unmarried/J.R. Baylor Friend
Beverley Walker/C/M/Apr 5/Drowned/25y/Not Known/Farmer/Dicey Waler Wife/J.R. Baylor Friend
No Name Williams/W/M/Sept/Not Known/1d/J.J. & Val Williams/J.J. Williams Father
Ammanda Yates/W/F/Aug 20/Not Known/59y/Charles & Lucy Phillips/R.W. Yates Husband/Reu Yates Son
Addie Nelson/C/F/Nov 25/Burnt/2y/Scott & Susan Nelson/Scott Nelson Father
Charles Lee Noel/W/M/June 26/Heart Disease/9y/Edward Noel/Edward Noel Father
A.G. Peatross/C/M/June 18/Measles/1y 7m/Jacob & Lucy Peatross/Jacob Peatross Father
Lucy Potter/C/F/Sept 27/Old Age/86y/Unknown/Married/Robt L. Brooks Friend
Tamer Quash/C/F/June 10/Unknown/2y/Jos & Bettie Quash/Jos Quash Father
Sophia Reynolds/C/F/Apr 17/Cholora Morbus/38y/Edmond & Patsy Green/Jno Reynolds Husband
No Name Reynolds/C/M/Apr 16/Unknown/13d/Jno S. & Sophia Reynolds/Jno Reynolds Father
Sallie A. Robinson/C/F/July 20/Dropsy/22y/Moses & Critta Robinson/Boswell Robinson Brother
Maria Smithers/C/F/June 26/Pneumonia/30y/E. & Hannah Dodson/Thos Smithers Husband
Sarah B. Smith/C/F/July 9/Burnt/6y/Wm & Rhoda Smith/Wm Smith Father
Martha A. Southworth/W/F/July 3/Brain Fever/2y/Thos & H.E. Southworth/Thos Southworth Father
E.J. Stevens/W/M/Mar 11/Heart Disease/59y/Robt & Caroline Stevens/Charles Stevens Son
Louisa Stevens/W/F/Apr 10/Pneumonia/70y/Unknown/J.L. Turner Friend
B.F. Taylor/W/M/Nov 18/Consumption/55y/Unknown/Farmer/Mary E. Taylor Wife
Gus Taylor/C/M/June 22/Chronic Diarrhea/3y/Wm & Eliza Taylor/William Taylor Father
Sallie Taylor/C/F/Aug 17/Unknown/2m/Wm & Eliza Taylor/William Taylor Father
No Name/C/F/Oct 10/Croup/1m/Wm & Ellen Tavner/Wm Tavner Father
Nelson Thornton/C/M/May 10/Croup/2y/Nelson & Bettie Thronton/Nelson Thornton Father
G.W. Thompson/W/M/Nov 5/Paralysis/66y/Unknown/Farmer/Mary A. Thompson Wife
Patsey Thompson/C/F/Oct 9/Heart Disease/45y/Unknown/Taylor Thompson Husband

Charles Todd/C/M/Dec 23/Consumption/41y/Geo & Phoebe Todd/Laborer/Josh Hailstork Friend
Flora A. Wilton/W/F/Apr 29/Inflamation of Bowels/55y/Timor & Sallie Mills/b.New York/W.J. Wilton Husband
Nelson White/C/M/Dec 15/Liver Disease/67y/Unknown/Farmer/Married/Jas Winkfield Friend
Tavner Winn/W/M/Apr 12/Heart Disease/78y/Tavner & Nancy Winn/Farmer/L.J. Winn Son
J.D. Wright/W/M/Aug 23/Typhoid Fever/26y/Jas B. & Mary Wright/Minister of Gospel/Jas D. Wright Father
Beauregard Wiglesworth/W/M/Nov 2/d.West Va/Accident/22y/Robt S. & Drucilla Wiglesworth/ b.Spotsylvania/Farmer/R.S. Wiglesworth Father
Sarah A. Pendleton/W/F/May 27/Old Age/79y/Unknown/Mary A. Morris Friend
Rosa L. Allen/W/F/Oct 2/Consumption/23y/Wm M. & Ann E. Pendleton/b.Spotsylvania/ W.L. Allen Husband
Mary A. Anderson/C/F/June 26/Croup/2m/Danl & June Anderson/Danl Anderson Father
No Name/C/M/June 11/Unknown/1d/Geo & Mattie Bowler/Geo Bowler Father
Nellie Berly/C/F/Apr 10/Measles/3y/Richd & Ava Berly/Frank Thomas Friend
William Brit/C/M/June 10/Dropsy/12y/Sizer & Milly Brit/b.Richmond/Robt Coleman Friend
John Brown/C/M/June 20/Scrofula/5y/Mac & Ella Brown/Mac Brown Father
Nathaniel Burruss/W/M/Aug/Bronchitis/11m/T.T. & J.F. Burruss/T.T. Burruss Father
Elizabeth Carneal/W/F/Oct 16/Dropsy/71y/Jas & Sarah Carneal/Jas Carneal Son
John Carneal/W/M/July 9/Brain Fever/11m/Wesley & Nancy Carneal/Wesley Carneal Father
Emily Carlton/W/F/Jan 10/Pneumonia/66y/Reuben & Nancy Truman/C.S. Wollard Friend
Agnes Chatman/C/F/Feb 14/Old Age/78y/Unknown/Peachea [Pichegru]Woolfolk Friend
J.L. Clayton/W/M/Mar 10/Measles/2y/J.W. Claytor/J.W. Claytor Father
Frank Coleman/C/M/Jan 15/Broken Leg/65y/Unknown/Farmer/Married/Sophia Coleman Friend
Andrew B. Dollings/W/M/June 20/Cholera Infantum/2m/A.A. & Sarah N. Dollings/Alex A. Dollings Father
Nancy Durrett/W/F/July 17/Old Age/85y/Harry & Nancy Hodges/b.Spotsylvania/Albert Durrett Husband
Mary Farley/C/F/June 10/Chronic Thrash/35y/Tom & Amanda Sludg/Jno W. Farley Husband
No Name/C/F/Mar 12/Unknown/2m/Lewis & Bell Fells/Lewis Fells Father
Doroghy Fox/C/F/July 10/Flux/1y/S.P. & Dinah Fox/Simon P. Fox Father
Nannie Freeman/C/F/Dec 10/Brain Fever/5m/Robt & Partheny Freeman/Robt Freeman Father
Mary S. Galery/C/F/Dec 9/Heart Disease/40y/Unknown/John Galery Husband
J.T. Goodwin/W/M/Feb 28/Unknown/65y/Littleton & Margaret Goodwin/Farmer/W.V. Goodwin Son
Sarah J. Gray/W/F/Jan/Childbirth/30y/Silas & Maria Gray/Silas Gray Father
James Green/C/M/Aug 10/Typhoid Fever/12y/Simon Green/Simon Green Father
Josephine Ham/C/F/June 7/Deep Cold/3y/Waller & Bettie Ham/Waller Ham Father
Sallie T. Harper/W/F/Jan 26/Paralysis/89y/Unknown/Married/Mary A. Morris Friend
Delia Harrison/C/F/Sept 1/Old Age/75y/Unknown/Married/Jos Flippo Friend
No Name/C/F/June 10/Unknown/3m/Abram & Charlotte Henry/Abram Henry Father
William D. Hope/W/M/Apr 23/d.Hanover Co/Accident/22y/Edmond & Mary Hope/Farmer/Edmond Hope Father
Mattie Johnson/W/F/Oct 9/Inflamation of Bowels/28y/Oswell & Elizabeth Gatewood/L.M. Johnson Husband
John Johnson/C/M/June 10/Cholera Morbus/6y/Edgar & Fannie Johnson/Edgar Johnson Father
Sarah J. Johnson/W/F/Apr 16/Heart Disease/76y/Edwd & Jennie Beazley/Robt B. Johnson Husband
Howard J. Kelley/C/M/Oct 20/Cholera Morbus/6m/Wm & Alice Kelley/Wm Kelley Father

Elizabeth King/W/F/May 5/Paralysis/80y/Unknown/married/Jno Richelson Friend
John Long/W/M/Oct 1/Paralysis/98y/Unknown/Farmer/Jno Long Son
Nellie Lumpkins/W/F/Dec 1/Typhoid Fever/27y/Wm & Jennie Taliaferro/b.New Kent/T.R. Lumpkins Husband
No Name/C/F/July 25/Unknown/5d/Wm & Catharine Minor/Wm Minor Father
Delila Mitchell/W/F/Jan 6/Old Age/76y/Wm & Elizabeth Wright/Married/Geo Arnold Friend
Americus Moore/C/F/Nov 21/Heart Disease/65y/Jno & Ailery Moore/gardener/Augustus Moore Relation
Wade Myers/C/M/July 1/Cholera/1y/Milly Myers/L.C. Pollard Friend

1884

E. Frans Anderson/W/F/July 6/Not Known/5m/Wm M. & Lilly Anderson/Wm M. Anderson Father
Wilton Alexander/C/M/Apr 10/Not Known/3m/R. & Lucy Alexander/R. Alexander Father
Judy Anderson/C/F/Dec 5/Heart Dea/46y/Tom & Hannah Monroe/Geo Anderson Husband
Thomas Bullock/W/M/Jan 9/Not Known/1y 6m/A. & Ella Bullock/A. Bullock Father
George Ellis/C/M/Oct 5/Dropsy/71y/Not Known/Farmer/Unmarried/Peter Buckner Friend
Cora Barlow/W/F/Sept 5/Not Known/9m/Jno W. & Eliz Barlow/Jno W. Barlow Father
Nannie S. Catlett/W/F/Dec 10/Heart Dea/60y/Rice F. Schooler/W.W. Catlett
Husband/Charles Bruce Son-[in-Law?]
Ben Covington/C/M/June 8/Killed/17y/Joe & Lucy Covington/Laborer/Anderson Brown Brother
L.M. George/W/M/Oct 28/Old Age/82y/Not Known/Farmer/B. George Wife
Lucy A. Carter/W/F/June 10/Child Birth/25y/Phil & Mary Carter/L.A. Carter Husband
No Name Carter/W/F/June 10/Still Born/L.A. & Lucy A. Carter/L.A. Carter Father
No Name Chiles/C/M/Dec 20/Still Born/Wm & Lucy Chiles/Wm Chiles Father
Queen Carneal/W/F/Sept 10/Worms/7y/Ro L. & Fannie Carneal/Ro L. Carneal Father
Cathy Clark/W/F/Nov 17/Child Birth/28y/M. & Mary Murray/Charles S. Clark Husband
No Name Clark/W/M/Nov 17/Still Born/Charles S. & Caty Clark/C.S. Clark Father
No Name Coghill/C/M/Dec 9/Still Born/Tom & Emma Coghill/Tom Coghill Father
No Name Caynor/W/F/Dec 20/Still Born/Jno & Mary Caynor/Jno Caynor Father
Emma B. Rowe/W/F/Aug 24/d.Bowling Green/Child Birth/38y/Frank & M. Scott/b.Bowling Green/E.H. Rowe Husband
Ella Jackson/C/F/Nov 3/d.Bowling Green/Still Born/Father Not Known/b.Bowling Green/Ella Jackson Mother
Effie Gouldin/C/F/Aug 5/d.Port Royal/Not Known/1y/Tom & Hessie Gouldin/b.Port Royal/Tom Gouldin Father
Eliza Vaughan/C/F/July 5/d.Port Royal/Consumption/40y/A. Montague Mother/b.Port Royal/Charles Vaughan Husband
Sarah J. Gray/W/F/Mar 15/Child Birth/30y/Silas & Maria Gray/W.M. Gray Husband
No Name Gray/W/F/Mar 15/Still Born/W.M. & Sarah J. Gray/W.M. Gray Father
No Name Gatewood/W/M/Sept 10/Still Born/Jos T. & Stella J. Gatewood/Jos T. Gatewood Father
Stella J. Gatewood/W/F/Sept 10/Child Birth/30y/James & Jane Skinker/Jos T. Gatewood Husband
Jno P. Gouldin/W/M/Dec 9/Still Born/Jno P. & Mary Gouldin/Jno P. Gouldin Father
Jno A. Grymes/C/M/Jan 10/Not Known/2y/Elliott & Allie Grymes/Ben Howard Grand Father
Sarah A. Hicks/W/F/June 19/Com of Dea/55y/W.E. & R. Flippo/B.H. Hicks Husband
No Name Johnson/C/M/Jan 9/Still Born/Moses & Susan Johnson/Moses Johnson Father
Mildred Fields/C/F/Nov 8/Not Known/50y/Not Known/Servant/Alex Johnson Friend
Davey Jackson/C/M/Oct 10/Not Known/1d/Davey & Emma Jackson/Davey Jackson Father

Julia E. Jones/W/F/Sept 20/Consumption/19y/Wm B. & Bettie Jones/Wm B. Jones Father
Jos W. Kay/W/M/Apr 30/Com of Dea/65y/Jno & Lucy Kay/b.Essex/Farmer/L.B. Kay Wife
George Keys/C/M/May 1/Not Known/3m/Lewis & Sarah Keys/Lewis Keys Father
No Name King/C/M/Oct/Still Born/Wm & Nancy King/Wm King Father
No Name Loving/W/M/Nov 30/Still Born/Ro F. & Emily Loving/Ro F. Loving Father
Emily Loving/W/F/Dec 4/Child Birth/25y/Julia Samuel Mother/Ro F. Loving Husband
No Name Lee/C/F/July 5/Not Known/1d/Joe & Louisa Lee/Joe Lee Father
Minnie Lumpkin/W/F/Sept 1/Not Known/8m/Jno & Lucy Lumpkin/Jno Lumpkin Father
Julia Lomax/C/F/Jul 20/Consumption/18y/Wm & Matilda Lomax/Wm Lomax Father
Nannie B. Lefoe/W/F/Sept 27/Com of Dea/7m/J.H. & Bettie B. Lefoe/J.H. Lefoe Father
Thos H. Motley/W/M/Feb 27/Still Born/Thos H. & Lizzie L. Motley/Thos H. Motley Father
Wm Moore/W/M/May 1/Not Known/6m/Wm S. & Susan Moore/Wm S. Moore Father
Carrie Moore/C/F/Sept/Not Known/2m/Isaac & Lucy Moore/Isaac Moore Father
Zeb Minor/C/M/Sept 10/Not Known/3m/Zeb & Mary Minor/Zeb Minor Father
Bertie Marshall/W/F/Aug 8/Not Known/5m/J. & Bettie Marshall/J[illeg] Marshall Father
Mattie McCauley/W/F/Dec 10/Brain Fever/1y 2m/Wm H. & Kate McCauley/Wm H. McCauley Father
James McCauley/W/M/Dec 20/Brain Fever/2y 8m/Wm H. & Kate McCauley/Wm H. McCauley Father
No Name Noel/W/M/Sept 12/Not Known/__/R.B. & Sarah F. Noel/R.B. Noel Father
Harry Osborne/C/M/Aug 18/Not Known/1y/Alfred & Julia Osborne/Alfred Osborne Father
Robt Owens/C/M/July 5/Not Known/4y/Henry & Fannie Owens/Henry Owens Father
Wm W. Pugh/W/M/Apr 21/Brain Fever/7m/Wm H. & C. Pugh/Wm H. Pugh Father
Geo Pendleton/C/M/June 16/Chof Inft/10m/Eugene & J.A. Pendleton/E. Pendleton Father
George Pendleton/C/M/July 28/Heart Dea/36y/Father Not Known - Rosetta/Farmer/Jno Pendleton Brother
Otho Reynolds/W/M/June 10/Not Known/9m/Thos & H. Reynolds/Thos Reynolds Father
No Name Randall/C/F/Apr 10/Still Born/Jeff & Nancy Randall/Jeff Randall Father
Fleming Carter/C/M/Dec/Drowned/30y/Father & Mother Not Known/Farmer/Lucy Carter Wife/ Lawson Smith Friend
Matilda Carter/C/F/Dec 10/Not Known/11m/Matilda Carter Mother/Lawson Friend
Jno Samuel/C/M/Aug/Drowned/12y/Minor & Lucy Samuel/Minor Samuel Father
No Name Saunders/C/F/Dec 21/Still Born/Wm & Betsy Saunders/Wm Saunders Father
No Name Syrles/W/M/July 10/Still born/W.P. & Lelia Syrles/W.P. Syrles Father
Mary Turner/C/F/Sept 11/Old Age/72y/Geo & Judy French/Jno H. Turner Husband
Inrod Turner/C/M/Oct 17/Liver Dea/2y 5m/Cornelius & Sarah Turner/Jno L. Turner Father[sic]
Mary P. Petross [Peatross]/W/F/Jan 10/Child Birth/22y/Wm & Lucy Toombs/Wm Ro Petross Husband/Wm Toombs Father
No Name Petross [Peatross]/W/M/Jan 10/Still Born/Ro & Mary Petross/Wm Toombs Grand Father
Esla Willis/C/F/May 18/Consumption/25y/Father & Mother Not Known/Jno Willis Father
John Willis/C/M/July 10/Not Known/3m/Jno & Esla Willis/Jno Willis Father
Louisa Willis/C/F/Sept/Not Known/3y/Jno & Esla Willis/Jno Willis Father
Robt Woolfolk/C/M/__/Unknown/3m/Wm & Eliza Woolfolk/Wm Woolfolk Father
__ Young/C/M/__/Still Born/Wm & Dolly Young/Wm Young Father
M.W. Young/C/F/Nov 10/Not Known/25y/Robt & Sallie Young/Servant/Unmarried/Robt Young Father
No Name/C/M/Nov 26/Unknown/16d/Jno & Mildred Mont/Jno A. Mont Father
No Name/C/M/Unknown/16d/Jno & Mildred Mont/Jno A. Mont Father

Annie L. Moore/C/F/Mar 16/Pneumonia/10d/Jeff & __ Moore/Jeff Moore Father
Reubin Page/C/M/Mar 19/Unknown/70y/Unknown/Farmer/Reubin Page Jr. Son
Lucy Ellen Pitcher/C/F/Feb 17/Consumption/26y/Thos & Maria Rolls/Thos Rolls Father
John Redd/C/M/Dec 10/Old Age/80y/Jno & Rachel Redd/Jack Toliver Friend
Betsy Scott/C/F/Apr 10/Whooping Cough/14m/Temple & Sallie Scott/Temple Scott Father
Clarence Shuman/W/M/July 10/Whooping Cough/18m/Frank & Nannie Shuman/Frank E. Shuman Father
Lee H. Smith/W/M/Jan/Croup/10m/Robt L. & D.N. Smith/Robt L. Smith Father
Adjutane Smithers/C/M/June 1/Whooping Cough/3y/Matt & Jennie Smithers/Matt Smithers Father
Granville Smithers/C/M/June 5/Whooping Cough/9m/Matt & Jennie Smithers/Matt Smithers Father
Wm T. Tate/W/M/Nov 6/Dropsy/30y/__/b.Louisa Co/Farmer/Jas H. Tate Relation
A.L. Taylor/W/M/Dec 6/Diptheria/20y/B.F. & Bettie Taylor/Benj F. Taylor Father
No Name/C/M/Sept 10/Brain Fever/2m 10d/Wm F. & Nannie Taylor/Wm F. Taylor Father
Mary Taylor/C/F/June 8/Unknown/10m/Wm & Rachel Taylor/Wm Taylor Father
Lucy R. Temple/W/F/May 9/Old Age/84y/Bennett & Elizabeth Tompkins/Jos F. Dabney Friend
Isaac Thompson/C/M/Mar 29/Scrofula/60y/Unknown/b.Hanover Co/Arch Coleman Friend
No Name/C/M/Dec 29/Croup/9d/Jno & Sicily Thompson/Jno Thompson Father
Charles Todd/C/M/Feb 10/Unknown/10m/Peter & Josephine Todd/Peter Todd Father
Agnes Todd/C/F/Mar 1/Croup/6m/Evy Todd/Peter Todd Relation
Henry H. Tunstall/W/M/June 10/Cholera/14y/L.H. & M.E. Tunstall/Lewis H. Tunstall Father
Wm A. Thomas/W/M/Dec 19/Unknown/8m/Jno H. & Maria Thomas/Jno H. Thomas Father
Virgil Walker/C/M/Sept 10/Croup/6m/Lewis & Emily Walker/Lewis Walker Father
Mary Williams/C/F/June 1/Burnt/14y/Henry & Judie Williams/Charles Hopkins Friend
Hattie A. Winston/C/F/June 26/Whooping Cough/5m/Alfred & Mary Winston/Alfred Winston Father
Mollie W. Woollard/W/F/Nov 23/Whooping Cough/15m/Charles S. Woollard/Chas S. Woollard Father
Martha A. Yates/C/F/Sept 2/Consumption/20y/Frank & Eliza Yates/Frank Yates Father
Frances A. Young/W/F/Mar 20/Malarial Fever/68y/Unknown/Married/Wm Claytor Friend
George Acors/W/M/Mar 16/Dropsy/64y/Thos A. & Nancy Acors/Farmer/Married/W.W. Butler Son-in-Law
Mary A. Adams/W/F/Apr 20/Heart Disease/69y/John & Sarah Myers/Andrew B. Adams Husband
Lelia V. Allen/W/F/July 10/Consumption/22y/Jas O. & Elizabeth Allen/J.O. Allen Father
James Armistead/C/M/June/Dropsy/3y/Wm & Alice Armistead/Wm Armistead Father
Robert Ayers/W/M/Dec 10/Whooping Cough/2y/Wm & Sarah Ayers/Wm Ayers Father
No Name/C/M/June 20/Unknown/10d/Waller & Martha Baber/Waller Baber Father
Mary Brooks/C/F/Jan 2/Consumption/29y/Don't Know/Married/Cuffy Coleman Friend
Mabel Burruss/W/F/Aug 9/Consumption/25y/Chas C. & Catharine Burruss/K.V. Burruss Relation
B.C. Burnett/W/M/July 5/Typhoid Fever/70y/Jos & Winifred Burnett/Physician/B.C. Burnett Jr Son
Thos R. Buchanan/W/M/Sept/Unknown/5m/Jno L. & Anna Buchanan/Jno L. Buchanan Father
Ann M. Coleman/C/F/Dec 10/Unknown/7m/Robt & Fannie Coleman/Wm Gaynor Relation
Robert Coleman/C/M/Oct 20/Consumption/23y/Richd & Maria Coleman/Laborer/Wm Gaynor Relation
Elizabeth Coleman/C/F/Sept/Heart Disease/60y/Maria Coleman/Lawrence Coleman Husband
Maria Coleman/C/F/__/Unknown/80y/Unknown/Lawrence Coleman Son-in-Law
Wm M. Courtney/C/M/Feb 10/Unknown/28y/Wm & Eliza Courtney/Wm J. Courtney Father
Jasper Davis/C/M/Sept 1/Dropsy/3y/Franklin & Emma Davis/Franklin Davis Father

Agnes Dyson/W/F/Sept 2/Unknown/70y/Jno E. & Betsy Long/H.H. Dyson Son
Rebecca England/W/F/Aug 19/Consumption/36y/Ed & Elizabeth M. Connell/Jno W. England
   Husband
Willie E. Gray/W/M/Aug 10/Cholera/7m/Henry & Mollie Gray/Silas Gray Grand Father
Rosa B. Hailstork/C/F/Apr 20/Croup/7m/Joshua & Mary Hailstork/Joshua Hailstork Father
Lewis Holmes/C/M/May 10/Croup/8m/Marcellus & Judie Holmes/Marcellus Holmes Father
Lansee Holmes/C/M/Mar 10/Unknown/2y/Bartlett & Eliza Holmes/Bartlett Holmes Father
Mattie Holmes/C/F/June 8/Whooping Cough/1y/Bartlett & Eliza Holmes/Bartlett Holmes Father
Rachel Jones/C/F/Mar 10/Old Age/80y/Unknown/Edwd Weaver Friend
Wm P. Jackson/C/M/Mar 18/Unknown/20y/Henry & A.M. Jackson/Henry Jackson Father
George H. Jackson/C/M/Dec 10/Unknown/23y/Henry & A.M. Jackson/Henry Jackson Father
Dianna Jackson/C/F/Mar 10/Old Age/85y/Unknown/Frank Jackson Son
Gracie A. Jefferson/C/F/Mar 20/Consumption/35y/Unknown/Wm Jefferson Husband
Bessie Jefferson/C/F/Feb 10/Consumption/15m/Wm & Gracie Jefferson/Wm Jefferson Father
No Name/C/M/Mar 20/Unknown/10d/Danl & Julia Jones/Daniel Jones Father
Maria Lewis/C/F/June 10/Whooping Cough/1y/Edmond & Lillie Lewis/Edmond Lewis Father
James F. Luck/W/M/Dec 20/Consumption/29y/Wm F. & Mary S. Luck/Wm F. Luck Father
Annie L. McDowell/W/F/Mar 17/Apoplexy/28y/Don't Know/Jas H. McDowell Husband
Clarence Mills/C/M/Feb 10/Croup/1y/Fleming & Lucy Mills/Fleming Mills Father

1885

Elias Acors/W/M/Dec 10/d.Bowling Green/Consumption/17y/Paul & Mary Acors/P.C. Acors
   Father & Telegraph Operator
J. Hunter Brooks/W/M/Nov 10/d.Bowling Green/Consumption/30y/Wm & Mary Brooks/Farmer/
   Unmarried/Jno W. Brooks Brother
Fannie E. Braxton/C/F/Sept 8/d.Bowling Green/Pluracy/7y/Geo & Va Braxton/Geo Braxton Father
Jno Baylor/C/M/Apr 3/d.Bowling Green/Not Known/75y/Not Known/Laborer/Fannie Baylor Wife
No Name Beasley/W/M/Oct 8/Not Known/1d/Luther & Leana Beasley/Luther Beasley Father
Every T. Bullock/W/F/Nov 22/Com of D/30y/Ed & M.E. Thornton/Thos S. Bullock Husband
No Name Bullock/W/M/Mar 10/Still Born/M & L. Boulware/M. Boulware Husband
Cato Baker/C/M/Aug 5/Brain Fever/56y/Not Known/Farmer/Lucy Baker Wife
Randall Baker/C/M/Nov 25/Not Known/5y/Jno & Sallie Baker/Jno Baker Father
John Ball/W/M/Feb 10/Plueracy/67y/Richd & Sarah Ball/Farmer/Widower/James Ball Son
Robt Blagburne/C/M/Nov 8/Whooping Cough/2y/Robt & Sally Blagburne/Robt Blagburne Father
Joe Black/C/M/May 3/Not Known/5m/Joe & Maria Black/Joe Blagburne [sic] Father
Oliva Campbell/W/F/July 8/Chol Inft/1y 6m/Ro L. & Fannie S. Campbell/R.L. Campbell Father
Ada R. Carter/W/F/Mar 29/Child Birth/24y/Philip & Emily Carter/E.F. Carter Husband
No Name Carter/W/M/Oct 12/Still born/T.J. & Hassie Carter/T.J. Carter Father
No Name Carter/W/M.Oct 12/Still Born/T.J. & Hassie Carter/T.J. Carter Father [Note: These were
   apparently twins]
Acubin Clattibuck/C/M/Dec 15/Com of D/25y/Wm & Lucy Clattibuck/Peter Carter Friend
James Clattibuck/C/M/Nov 10/Old Age/85y/Not Known/Widower/James Clattibuck Son
Catherine Chinault/W/F/May 17/Child Birth/26y/Not Known/T.J. Chinault Husband
Rosa Chinault/W/F/Nov 4/Old Age/75y/Unknown/T.J. Chenault Son
Sallie Carneal/W/F/Oct 3/Consumption/40y/Lindsay & Patsy Carneal/Robt Carneal Uncle
Malinda Chapman/C/F/Aug 5/Old Age/85y/Not Known/Davey Chapman Son
Jeff Catlett/C/M/Sept/Not Known/2m/Walter & America Catlett/Walter Catlett Father

Joe T. Collins/W/M/Mar 8/Diptheria/10m/C.[Charles]L. & Bettie L. Collins/C.L. Collins Father
Gracy L. Day/C/F/Aug 5/Not Known/4m/Ed & Lelia Day/Ed Day Father
Berryman Elliott/W/M/Nov 8/Paralized/79y/Martin & Phoeby Elliott/Jno L. Elliott Son
Walker Baylor/C/M/Mar 10/Consumption/75y/Not Known/Jeff Fortune Friend
Rebecca Flippo/W/M/Dec 1/Not Known/10m/W.P. & Elvira Flippo/W.P. Flippo Father
George Ellis/C/M/Nov 10/Dropsy/7y/Not Known/Peter Buckner Friend
Richmond Green/C/M/Oct 17/Consumption/70y/Not Known/Atwell Coleman Friend
No Name Garnett/W/M/Dec 27/Not Known/1d/Jno W. & Mary Garnett/Jno W. Garnett Father
Ben Garnett/C/M/Apr 11/Not Known/27y/Ben & Letta Garnett/Laborer/James Garnett Brother
Cathl Garnett/W/F/Sept 10/Old Age/73y/Jno & Judy Garnett/J.M. Garnett Husband
Laura Grymes/C/F/June 10/Brain Fever/9y/Keeling & Mary Grymes/Keeling Grimes Father
Lizzie Grymes/C/F/Oct 5/Brain Fever/1y 6m/Keeling & Mary Grymes/Keeling Grimes Father
Thomas Howard/C/M/Sept 10/Consumption/50y/Thos & Mary Howard/Farmer/Reuben Howard
   Husband
Peggy Howard/C/M/June 10/Consumption/20y/Thos & Mary Howard/Mary Howard Mother
No Name Hoomes [sic]/C/F/Nov 10/Still Born/Ed & Lucy Howard/Edmond Howard Father
Mary V. Holloway/W/F/June 10/Brain Fever/5y/A.G. & Eliza Holloway/R.G. Holloway
Martha Harris/C/F/Sept 8/Whooping Cough/2y/Overton & S. Harris/Overton Harris Father
Cornelius Harris/C/M/Dec 5/Not Known/8m/Alice Harris/Alice Harris Mother
Walter Hill/C/M/Nov 8/Not Known/4y/Sam & Mollie Hill/Sam Hill Father
Cora Ham/C/F/Dec 5/Not Known/11m/Lomax & Sarah Ham/Lomax Ham Father
Leroy Ham/C/M/Dec 5/Not Known/11m/Lomax & Sarah Ham/Lomax Ham Father
Mary F. Hopkins/C/F/June 10/Not Known/5m/Father Not Known & Mary Hopkins/James
   Hopkins Uncle
Lewis Haynes/W/M/May 24/Old Age/80y/Thos & Hannah Haynes/Geo L. Haynes Son
Mary Johnson/C/F/July 10/Billious Fever/25y/Phil & Bettie Johnson/Phil Johnson Father
Lee Johnson/C/M/Dec 30/Consumption/23y/Henry & Sallie Johnson/Laborer/Henry Johnson
   Father
No Name Johnson/C/M/Jan 1/Still Born/Moses & Susan Johnson/Moses Johnson Father
Felecia Johnson/C/F/Aug 10/Old Age/80y/Not Known/Widow/Abram Johnson Son
Martha Johnson/C/F/Mar 9/Not Known/5y/Thos & Martha Johnson/Thos Johnson Father
Willis Jackson/C/M/Aug 10/Not Known/21d/Willis & Rose Jackson/Willis Jackson Father
Danl Jackson/W/M/Apr 6/Not Known/23y/Wade & Sallie Jackson/Wade Jackson Father
John Jackson/C/M/Mar 6/Not Known/70y/Jno & Lucinda Jackson/Wade Jackson Father
R.S. Loving/W/M/Apr 25/Com of Dea/49y/Geo & Levenia Loving/Farmer/Wm H. Loving Son
Peggy Lomax/C/F/Sept 9/Consumption/60y/Patsy Young/Jno Lomax Husband
No Name Lomax/C/F/July 9/Still Born/Jo & Sallie Lomax/Joe Lomax Father
No Name Lomax/C/F/July 9/Still Born/Jo & Sallie Lomas/Joe Lomax Father [Note: Listed
   twice, apparently twins]
Annie Lucus/C/F/July 10/Chol Inft/9m/Smith & Sallie Lucas/Smith Lucas Father
No Name Latane/C/M/May 20/Not Known/5d/W.T. & Ella Latane/W.T. Latane Father
Rachel Lonesome/C/F/Oct 19/Consumption/62y/Not Known/Widow/Warner Lonesome Son
Polly Morton/C/F/Feb 4/Consumption/66y/Not Known/Servant/Widow/R.M. Morton Son
Luther Martin/W/M/July 10/Consumption/20y/Jno & Mary Martin/Farmer/Widower/R.F.
   Dillard Friend
Annie Morton/C/F/Sept 20/Old Age/80y/Not Known/Widow/Matt Morton Son
Isabella Monroe/C/F/Sept 23/Whooping Cough/3y/Horace & Lettie Monroe/Horace Monroe
   Father

Dennis Young/C/M/Jan 10/Old Age/90y/Not Known/Laborer/Widower/Wilson Miller Friend
Dan'l J. Young/C/M/Nov 5/Consumption/22y/Washington & Julia Young/Teacher/nmarried/
 Washington Young Father
No Name Farinholt/W/F/Oct 10/d.Port Royal/Still Born/E. & Emma G. Farinholt/b.Port Royal/
 E. Farinholt Father
Kitty Stocas/C/F/Nov 10/d.Port Royal/Old Age/80y/Not Known/Servant/Widow/James Jackson
 Son-in-Law
No Name Lucas/C/M/Oct 9/d.Port Royal/Still Born/Wm & Frances Lucas/Wm Lucas Father
Wilson Miller/C/M/Feb 25/Not Known/1d/Wilson & Mary Miller/Wilson Miller Father
Mary Miller/C/F/Feb 25/Child Birth/35y/Not Known/Wilson Miller Husband
Pearl B. Pitts/W/F/Sept 19/Not Known/1m 15d/P.B. & M.E. Pitts/P.B. Pitts Father
R.L. Parker/W/M/Feb 16/Still Born/R.L. & W. Parker/R.L. Parker Father
Thos A. Purkes/W/M/June 10/Still Born/Thos A. & Bettie Purkes/Thos A. Purkes Father
Maria Pratt/C/F/May 1/Com of Dea/50y/A. & Lottie Ferguson/Carry Pratt Husband
Ora Parr/W/F/June 9/Cancer/17y/J.E. & Elenora Parr/J.E. Parr Father
Ida Queen/C/F/Dec 18/Not Known/11m/W. & Emily Queen/Warner Queen Father
George Reynolds/C/M/Dec 10/Consumption/75y/Not Known/Farmer/Widower/A. Minor Friend
Nancy Robb/C/F/Nov 8/Old Age/80y/Not Known/Widow/Geo Robb Son
Wm H. Robb/C/M/Sept 1/Not Known/3d/Wm H. & Caroline Robb/Wm H. Robb Father
Nancy Johnson/C/F/Oct 8/Old Age/83y/Not Known/Widow/Wm H. Robb Friend
James Taylor/C/M/Nov 10/Whooping Cough/10m/Jeanette Taylor/Sam Robinson Friend
Butler Reynolds/W/M/Dec 5/Not Known/5m/Thos W. & Harriett Reynolds/Thos W. Reynolds
 Father
Jno A. Reynolds/C/F/Dec 30/Still Born/Jno A. & Lucy Reynolds/Jno A. Reynolds Father
Sophia Morrison/W/F/Dec 7/Old Age/80y/Not Known/Widow/Chastine Rouse Grand Son
Peter F. Ryerson/W/M/Aug 17/Com of Dia/68y/Not Known/b.New York/Farmer/Hattie A. Ryerson
 Wife
Spencer Sale/C/M/Dec 10/Old Age/80y/Not Known/Farmer/Widower/Seth Browell Friend
Martha Skinner/W/F/Apr 4/Whooping Cough/2y/Ro B. & Mary Skinner/Ro B. Skinner Father
Susan Skinner/W/F/July 3/Dropsy/68y/Wm & Millie Skinner/Henry Skinner Husband/A.B. Skinner
 Son
Henry Skinner/W/M/Nov 22/Old Age/75y/Wm & Millie Skinner/Farmer/Susan Skinner Wife/A.B.
 Skinner Son
Nancy Skinner/C/F/Jan 11/Old Age/89y/Unknown/Washington Skinner Husband
Amey Shepherd/C/F/Dec 11/Child Birth/16y/Jno & Harriett Shepherd/Servant/Jno Shepherd Father
Wm Maryweather/C/M/Mar 27/Old Age/80y/Not Known/Farmer/Mary Maryweather Wife/Jno L.
 Seal Friend
Henry Turner/C/M/Oct 20/Dropsy/60y/Ro & Maria Turner/Farmer/Tom Turner Son
Maria Taylor/C/F/Dec 9/Old Age/100y/Not Known/Servant/Widow/Geo Lonesome Grand Son
M.E. Thornton/W/F/July 10/Paralized/72y/Peter & M. Catlett/Widow/Thos Bullock Son-in-Law
Lucy Sale/C/F/Dec 20/Not Known/8m/Mary Sale/Mary Sale Mother
Cathl Rich/C/F/July 8/Paralized/35y/Andrew & Milly Rich/Servant/Unmarried/A. Rich Brother
Peter Taylor/W/M/Dec 20/Consumption/16y/Chris & Sarah Taylor/Chris Taylor Father
S.F. Rouse/W/M/Aug 5/Consumption/45y/Not Known/Farmer/Mary Rouse Wife/Robt Taylor
 Friend
Edmond Smith/C/M/May 10/Old Age/95y/Not Known/Laborer/Widower/Morton Taliaferro Friend
Eliza Thornton/C/F/Mar 11/Consumption/55y/Enoch & Sallie Johnson/Servant/Bob Thornton
 Husband

No Name Vessels/C/F/Nov 1/Not Known/16d/Joe & Rebecca Vessels/Joe Vessels Father
Martha S. Wright/W/F/Feb 10/Consumption/62y/Jno G. & M.R. Cole/Widow/A.F. Wright Son
Jos F. Whitticoe/W/M/July 10/Not Known/3d/Ben & Rose Whitticoe/Ben Whitticoe/Ben Whitticoe Father
Milton Cook/W/M/Dec 10/Not Known/25y/Not Known/b.King & Queen/Farmer/Married/Isaac White - Friend
No Name Wallace/C/M/Dec 9/Still Born/Wm & M. Wallace/Wm Wallace Father
Tillie B. Wallace/C/F/Feb 14/Not Known/1y/Not Known/Wm Wallace Grand Father
Leanna Alsop/C/F/Apr 15/Whooping Cough/9m/Moses & Venie Alsop/Moses Alsop Father
Lilian Arnold/W/F/June 14/Flux/6y/Robt B. & Lucy Arnold/Robt Arnold Father
No Name/C/M/Oct 11/Unknown/1d/Thos & Matilda Beazley/Thomas Beazley Father
Linwood Blanton/W/M/June 19/Unknown/2y/Archie & Lucy L. Blanton/Archie Blanton Father
No Name/W/F/July 8/Unknown/1d/W.W. & Edna Burruss/W.W. Burruss Father
Charles P. Burruss/W/M/Apr 19/Paralysis/72y/Henry & Sarah Burruss/Farmer/Mrs. Burruss Wife
No Name/W/M/July 10/Unknown/1d/Jos & Catharine Cannon/Jos L. Cannon Father
W.V. Carlton/W/M/July 7/Unknown/62y/Phil & Dollie Carlton/Mrs. Carlton Wife
N.H. Carter/W/M/Dec/Gravel/67y/Thompson & Mary Carter/Emily Carter Wife
Algern Chandler/C/M/Mar 20/Whooping Cough/2y/Henry & Millie Chandler/Henry Chandler Father
Zachry Clark/C/M/Apr 20/Consumption/25y/Woodson & MarthaClark/Laborer/Marcellus Clark Friend
Sophia Clayton/C/F/Apr 30/Burnt/10y/Richd & Joanna Clayton/Richd Clayton Father
Lewis D. Coghill/W/M/Oct 25/d.Penola [Post Office]/Diptheria/3y/L.L. Coghill/L.L. Coghill Father
Randall Coleman/C/M/Feb 20/Scrofula/27y/Robt & Fannie Coleman/Robt Coleman Father
No Name/C/M/July 25/Unknown/5d/Sallie Coleman/Sallie Coleman Mother
No Name/C/F/Aug 9/Unknown/1d/Dick & Margaret Coleman/Dick Coleman Father
Rachael Dabney/W/F/Dec 10/Old Age/86y/Unknown/James Dabney Son
Elander Farley/C/F/Aug 5/Heart Disease/63y/Unknown/Isaiah Farley Husband
Manny Fells/C/M/Feb 23/Whooping Cough/1y/Coss Fells/Coss Fells Father
James Fox/C/M/June 12/Whooping Cough/2y/Milly Fox/Milly Fox Mother
John M. Givings/C/M/Mar 10/Cold/17y/Robt & Fannie Givings/Robt Givings Father
Edmond Green/C/M/May 30/Bronchitis/65y/Unknown/Farmer/Mrs. Green Wife
Mary Green/C/F/Aug 30/Unknown/8y/Henry & Page Green/Henry Green Father
No Name/C/M/Feb 4/Unknown/6d/Joshua & Mary Hailstork/Jos Hailstork Father
Lucy E. Hart/W/F/Sept 2/Heart Disease/29y/John & Nancy Moren/ Philip Hart Husband
Lillie Harris/C/F/Feb 20/Whooping Cough/2y/James & Lucy Harris/James Harris Father
Jas L. Henderson/W/M/May 8/Unknown/2d 4m/Roy & Victoria Henderson/Roy Henderson Father
William Holmes/C/M/Dec 28/Unknown/3y/Wm & Anna Holmes/Wm Hoomes Father
Mary E. Hughes/W/F/Aug 14/Cancer/46y/Thos & Betsy Whively/John Hughes Husband
Walter Jackson/C/M/Apr 4/Dropsy/27y/Unknown/Lizzie Jackson Wife
Henry Johnson/C/M/June 10/Bowel Compliant/1y/Henry & Henrietta Johnson/Henry Johnson Father
Reuben Johnson/C/M/May 7/Old Age/85y/Unknown/A.G. Goodwin Friend
No Name/C/M/Jan 10/Croup/2m/Martha E. Johnson/Martha Johnson Mother
Lula T. Jones/C/F/Aug 19/Unknown/2m/C.B. & Anna M. Jones/C.B. Jones Father
Frank Jordan/C/M/May 14/Unknown/65y/Unknown/Married/Richd Blanton Friend
Normand Lewis/C/M/May 5/Unknown/1y/Annie Lewis/Annie Lewis Mother
James Lewis/C/M/Mar 6/Whooping Cough/5y/Edmond & Sallie Lewis/Edmond Lewis Father
Lucy Lewis/C/F/Mar 6/Whooping Cough/5y/Edmond & Sallie Lewis/Edmond Lewis Father

Henry L. Lively/W/M/Apr 16/Typhoid Fever/25y/Thos & Mary E. Lively/Farmer/Married/Alex Lively Brother
E.J. Long/W/F/Oct 28/Consumption/55y/T. & Frances M. Young/Woodford Long Husband
N.P. Luck/W/M/Sept 10/Consumption/64y/Samuel Luck/Mrs. Luck Wife
John Madison/W/M/Apr 23/Unknown/70y/John Madison/Farmer/Jack Madison Son
Maggie Mills/C/F/Aug 15/Whooping Cough/4m/Fleming & Lucy Mills/Fleming Mills Father
Polly Minor/C/F/Dec 10/Unknown/10m/Wm & Sophis Minor/William Minor Father
Ida Monroe/C/F/Aug 1/Unknown/3m/Andrew & Rebecca Monroe/Andrew Monroe Father
Sarah Mosby/C/F/Dec 10/Congestive Chill/30y/Chas & Ella Mosby/William Mosby Husband
Mary A. Moore/C/F/Nov 9/Unknown/25y/Unknown/John Moore Husband
E. Joseph Partlow/W/M/July 25/Old Age/72y/Eliza & Nancy Partlow/Farmer/Ella Dickinson Friend
Frances Parker/C/F/May 6/Unknown/6y/Saml & Eliza Parker/Saml Parker Father
Julia A.[Archibald] Peatross/W/F/May 12/Congestion of the Brain/50y/Col Archibald Samuel/R.O. Peatross Husband
Lucy Pitcher/C/F/Feb 10/Consumption/29y/Unknown/Cary Pitcher Husband
Nannie Pitcher/C/F/May 17/Unknown/3y/Cary & Lucy Pitcher/Cary Pitcher Father
Silas Pitcher/C/M/May 31/Unknown/6y/Cary & Lucy Pitcher/Cary Pitcher Father
Robert Pitcher/C/M/Sept 14/Unknown/2y/Cary & Lucy Pitcher/Cary Pitcher Father
Sarah Pierce/C/F/May 11/Paralized/88y/James & Mollie Bolding/Anthony Pierce Husband
George B[utler] Pollard/W/M/Feb 22/d."Oak Grove"/Hard Liver/74y/George & Hannah Pollard/ Farmer/Delia Pollard Wife
John Redd/C/M/May 10/Old Age/70y/Unknown/Farmer/Jack Toliver Son-in-Law
Willie A. Robinson/C/F/May 3/Heart Disease/43y/Elizabeth Dickinson/Saml Robinson Husband
No Name Robinson/C/F/Feb 23/Unknown/9d/Boswell & Venie Robinson/B. Robinson Father
Lucy E. Rolls/C/F/Dec 27/Unknown/1m 27d/Cornelius & Patsy Rolls/Cornelius Rolls Father
No Name Rolls/C/M/Sept 5/Unknown/4d/John & Matilda Rolls/John Rolls Father
Margaret Rolls/C/F/Aug 6/Consumption/56y/Unknown/Thos Rolls Husband
George Ross Sr/C/M/June 25/Heart Disease/73y/Unknown/George Ross Jr Son
No Name/C/F/July 27/Thrash/1m 13d/Allen & Ada Rollins/Allen Rollins Father
W.A. Samuel/W/M/Nov 8/Consumption/46y/John & Sallie Samuel/Farmer/Allie Samuel Son
George A. Seay/W/M/Aug 6/Unknown/7m/George & Sarah Seay/George Seay Father
Martha C. Sizer/W/F/June 20/Flux/60y/Unknown/G.A. Sizer Brother-in-Law
Cora Sizer/W/F/July 10/Flux/2y/G.A. & Credilla Sizer/G.A. Sizer Father
Osa Smith/C/M/May 17/Whooping Cough/2y/Wm & Sallie Smith/Wm Smith Father
Harriet Smith/C/F/Feb 28/Whooping Cough/2y/W.H. & R.E. Smith/W.H. Smith Father
Virginia Southworth/W/F/Apr 22/Unknown/56y/Unknown/Pitchegru Southworth Husband
Minor Stuart/C/M/Apr 9/Colic/70y/Unknown/Winston Stuart Son
Lou Taylor/C/F/June 4/Measles/2m/Wm & Rachael Taylor/Wm Taylor Father
Mary A. Toliver/C/F/June 9/Typhoid Fever/12y/John & Harriet Toliver/John Toliver Father
No Name/C/M/Oct 8/Unknown/1d/Thos & Susan Thomas/Thos Thomas Father
No Name/C/M/Apr 9/Unknown/9d/John & Emily Tompson/John Tompson Father
B.F. Trevillian/W/M/Aug 12/Hemorrhage/62y/Unknown/Mrs. B. Trevillian Wife
Mary T. Turner/W/F/May 29/Pneumonia/82y/Unknown/Frank Turner Son
Rosa Turner/W/F/Apr 15/Dropsy/2y/J.L. & M.E. Turner/J.L. Turner Father
Mary Tyree/C/F/Aug 8/Typhoid Fever/22y/Wm & Isabella Tyree/Wm Tyree Father
Nannie White/W/F/July 9/Typhoid Fever/32y/Ryland & Maria Jeter/George White Husband
D.M. Wiglesworth/W/F/Feb 10/Consumption/56y/John & Sallie Hewlett/H.S. Wiglesworth Son
Chas Williams/C/M/Mar 1/Unknown/1y/Ben & Mary Williams/Ben Williams Father

Ricey Wingfield/C/F/June 10/Burnt/2y/Minor Wingfield/Minor Wingfield Father
Isaac Wright/C/M/Mar 20/Pneumonia/22y/J.F. & Roxie A. Wright/John F. Wright Father
Anna G. Wright/W/F/July 22/Consumption/21y/Stephen & Ann Oliver/John V. Wright Husband
Oscar V. Wright/W/M/July 22/Unknown/7y/John V. & Anna Wright/John V. Wright Father

1886

Sallie Allen/C/F/Dec 8/Consumption/40y/Not Known/Jerry Allen Husband
Lizzie Brown [sic]/C/F/Oct 9/Not Known/9m/Maria Lewis/Maria Lewis Mother
Seth Boxwell/C/M/Dec 10/Consumption/60y/Not Known/Farmer/Unmarried/Henry Bates Friend
Judy Baylor/C/F/Dec 5/Consumption/55y/Tom & Mary Fray/W. Baylor Husband
Randall Beverley/C/M/Nov 10/Consumption/38y/Not Known/Laborer/Frances Beverley Wife
Jno Baker/C/M/Dec 8/Consumption/45y/Not Known/Laborer/Lucy Baker Wife
Ellen Braxton/C/F/Jan 10/Not Known/6y/Geo & Mary Braxton/Geo Braxton Father
James Carter/C/M/Feb 15/Consumption/60y/Not Known/Sallie Carter Wife
Mary Carter/C/F/Oct 10/Not Known/26y/Paul & Mary Carter/Unmarried/Paul Carter Father
Henry Carter/C/M/Sept 10/Still Born/Henry & Mary Carter/Henry Carter Father
A.C. Chenault/W/M/July 10/Not Known/3y/A.C. & Mary Chenault/A.C. Chenault Father
No Name Chenault/W/F/July 10/Still Born/J.B. & Lucy Chenault/J.B. Chenault Father
No Name Chiles/C/M/Nov 20/Still Born/Wm & Emma Chiles/Wm Chiles Father
Mary B. Clark/W/F/Jan 9/Child birth/35y/Not Known/b.Ireland/C.S. Clark Husband
Mary S. Collins/W/F/Sept 3/Typhoid Fever/65y/Not Known/b.Richmond/Widow/T.C. Chandler
  Son-in-Law
Ella Catlett/C/F/Oct 5/Not Known/2y/W. & A. Catlett/Walter Catlett Father
Luther Cole/W/M/June 10/Not Known/5m/H.J. & Lucy S. Cole/H.J. Cole Father
Mary Cosby/W/F/June 15/Consumption/50y/__/b.Chesterfield/N.D. Cosby Husband
Sallie Evans/C/F/June 10/Child Birth/20y/Charles & E. Brooks/Wm Evans Husband.
No Name Evans/C/F/June 10/Still born/Wm & Sallie Evans/Wm Evans Father
Newt Baylor/C/M/July 10/Consumption/70y/Not Known/Farmer/Tom Baylor Son
Nancy Grymes/W/F/June 5/Cancer/60y/Jacob & Patsy Seymour/Nellie Frawner [Fraughnaugh] Sister
Thompson Grymes/C/M/Oct 10/Old Age/82y/Not Known/Thos Grymes Son
No Name Graves/C/M/Aug 15/Still Born/Charles & Lucy Graves/Charles Graves Father
No Name Garnett/W/M/Jan 15/Still Born/Jno & E.C. Garnett/Jno Garnett Father
No Name Garnett/W/M/Aug 5/Not Known/2m/W.A. & Emily Garnett/W.A. Garnett Father
James Garnett/C/M/July 10/Not Known/2y/Abram & Fannie Garnett/A. Garnett Father
Jackson Gouldin/C/M/Sept 18/Not Known/2y 6m/Henry & Eulin Gouldin/Henry Gouldin Father
Henry L. Garrett/W/M/Aug 20/Fever/2y 8m/H.S. & Rose Garrett/H.S. Garrett Father
Mary Grymes/W/F/Dec 10/Pluracy/40y/Mark & S. Beasley/J.E. Grymes Husband
Caroline Grymes/C/F/July 20/Brain Fever/3y/Geo & Martha Grymes/Geo Grimes Father
No Name Gouldman/W/M/Aug 10/Still Born/Jno P. & M.T. Gouldman/J.P. Gouldman Father
Lottie Gus/C/F/June 5/Pluracy/2y/C. & Martha Gus/Claiborn Gus Father
Jeff Gus/C/M/Feb 6/Measles/3y/Thos & H. Gus/Thos Gus Father
Lindsey Howard/C/M/Aug 10/Old Age/80y/Not Known/Farmer/Jno Howard Son
Clarence Hoomes/C/M/June 9/Teething/1y/Thos & Mary Hoomes/Thos Hoomes Father
Lulie Hoomes/C/F/June 6/Pluracy/2y/Abram & Sarah Hoomes/Abram Hoomes Father
Joe Hoomes/C/M/Oct 5/Not Known/4y/Andrew & S. Hoomes/Andrew Hoomes Father
Cornelia Harris/C/F/May 10/Measles/2y/Alice Harris/Alice Harris Mother
Kennie Ham/C/M/Mar 10/Pluracy/3y 4m/Jack & Isabella Ham/Jack Ham Father

Polly Hawkins/C/F/Feb 3/Old Age/70y/Not Known/Farmer/Widow/Barnett Hawkins Son
Wm Hate [sic]/C/M/Dec 10/Consumption/37y/Not Known/Farmer/S.W. Hayes Wife
Henry Johnson/C/M/Feb 18/Measles/2y/Henry & Alice Johnson/Henry Johnson Father
No Name Jones/W/M/Aug 10/Still Born/C.L. & M. Jones/C.L. Jones Father
Cosmore Jones/C/Apr 19/Pluracy/3y/Arthur & Alice Jones/Arthur Jones Father
William Jackson/C/M/Mar 10/Pluracy/10y/Wm & Matilda Jackson/Wm Jackson Father
Jno Jackson/C/M/Dec 6/Not Known/6y/Andrew & A. Jackson/Andrew Jackson Father
Cor. S. Long/W/M/Dec 10/Consumption/65y/A.L. & Mary Long/Farmer/James Long Son
Isaac Lawson/C/M/July 10/Old Age/8y/Not Known/Ursley Lawson Wife
George Lindsey/C/M/Oct 19/Pluracy/2y/Charles & Anna Lindsey/Charles Lindsey Father
Mary Meyers/C/F/Dec 10/Burned/2y/Linden & Mary Myers/Linden Myers Father
Sallie Martin/W/F/June 9/Consumption/50y/Not Known/Jno Martin Husband
Ailsey Minor/C/F/Nov 6/Measles/5y/Nathan & Ann Minor/Nathan Minor Father
Cassie Minor/C/F/Oct 10/Pluracy/3y/Jno & Kate Minor/Jno Minor Father
Lidia A. Monroe/C/F/June 8/Pluracy/16y/Jno & Millie Monroe/Jno Monroe Father
Willard Pullman/W/M/Dec 10/Com of Dea/70y/Not Known/Mary Pullman Wife/Jno A. Chiles
    Friend
No Name Parker/C/M/Oct 30/Still Born/Phil & Mary Parker/Phil Parker Father
Bettie Pendleton/C/F/Jan 6/Com of Dia/60y/Not Known/Jno Pendleton Husband
No Name Puller/C/F/Oct 9/Still Born/Woodson & J. Puller/Woodson Puller Father
Jno F. Pierson/W/M/July 10/Com of Dea/46y/Not Known/b.England/Farmer/Unmarried/W.B.
    Dickinson Friend
No Name Richerson [sic]/C/M/Sept 30/Still Born/Phil & Maria Rollins/Phil Rollins Father
Louisa Randall/C/F/Nov 6/Pluracy/13y/Jef & Nancy Randall/Jeff Randall Father
No Name Samuel/C/F/July 8/Still Born/Leo Samuel/Leo Samuel Mother
No Name Samuel/W/M/July 8/Still Born/Arch & Julia Samuel/Arch Samuel Father
Mary Shackleford/W/F/July 5/Burned/20y/B.C. & Mary Shackleford/B.C. Shackleford Father
Joe Seal/W/F/Sept 9/Consumption/30y/P. & Mary Acors/Divorced/P.G. Acors Father
Wm Sale/W/M/Dec 10/Com of Dea/30y/Not Known/b.Essex/Farmer/Mary Sale Wife
Amey Shepherd/C/F/Apr 6/Child birth/16y/Jno & Mary Shepherd/Jno Shepherd Father
No Name Shepherd/C/F/Apr 6/Still Born/Not Known/Jno Shepherd Grandfather
Maria Taylor/C/F/Mar 5/Consumption/33y/Harry & L. Samuel/Cris Taylor Husband
Eldred Vaughan/W/M/Nov 18/Old Age/82y/Not Known/Widower/J.G. Farmer Son-in-Law
No Name Williams/C/M/July 26/Not Known/5m/J.R. & Matilda Williams/J.R. Williams Father
Jno J. Gravatt/W/M/Aug 10/d.Port Royal/Com of Dea/70y/No one to give parents name/Doctor/
    Married/D.B. Powers Friend
Louisa Carr/W/F/May 5/d.Port Royal/Old Age/80y/No one to give parents name/Widow/D.B.
    Powers Friend
Jno P. Downing/W/F/Dec 8/d.Bowling Green/Not Known/3d/Jno P. & __ Downing/b.Bowling
    Green/J.P. Downing Father
Geo Swain/W/M/Nov 8/d.Bowling Green/Not Known/1m/G.T. & M. Swain/b.Bowling Green/
    G.T. Swain Father
Flora Webb/W/F/Jan 20/d.Bowling Green/Diptheria/5y/C.S. & Ella Webb/b.Bowling Green/C.S.
    Webb Father
Daisy Allen/W/F/Nov 2/Unknown/4m/W.L. & S.H. Allen/Wm L. Allen Father
No Name/C/F/Oct 20/Unknown/10d/Josh & Lina Alsop/Josh Alsop Father
No Name/C/M/May 5/Unknown/5d/Lucy Anderson/Lucy Anderson Mother
Lucy P. Barlow/W/F/May 28/d."Hickory Grove"/Chronic Thrash/32y/C.B. & L. Fogg/Married/

W.H. Barlow Husband
Hannah Bazley/C/F/Aug 18/d."Prospect Hill"/Croup/2y/J. & H. Bazley/Jas Bazley Father
Geo B. Benum/C/M/July 4/Unknown/8m/Ben & L. Benum/Ben Benum Father
Howell Blank/W/M/Nov 18/d.Ruther Glen [Post Office]/Unknown/14d/H.S. & B.L. Blank/
  b.Ruther Glen/H.S. Blank Father
George Buckner/C/M/July 10/Old Age/90y/Unknown/Laborer/Mrs. Buckner Wife
Sallie C. Carter/C/F/Aug 10/Unknown/1m/R. & P. Carter/Robt Carter Father
Wm H. Carneal/W/M/Dec 15/Unknown/57y/Hay & Nancy Carneal/Farmer/T.A. Carneal Friend
Robt L. Cobb/W/M/Aug 10/Diarrhea/13y/Mary E. Cobb/Mary E. Cobb Mother
Luvenia Coleman/C/F/July 28/Unknown/20y/Frank & Sophia Coleman/Frank Coleman Father
Ruffin H. Coleman/W/M/Sept 29/Disease of the Brain/64y/Francis & Sallie Coleman/
  b.Spotsylvania/Bettie Coleman Wife
Maggie Davis/C/F/Nov 17/Bronchitis/4m 15d/Franklin & Emma Davis/Franklin Davis Father
John Dickinson/W/M/Apr 8/Dropsy/65y/Unknown/__ Friend
Robt A. Durrett/W/M/Nov 17/Pneumonia/66y/Unknown/Lewis Durrett Son
Jefferson Flippo/W/M/July 17/Old Age/89y/M. & Elizabeth Flippo/Thomas Flippo Son
Robt Fox/C/M/Dec 2/Unknown/7m/Henry & Susan Fox/Henry Fox Father
Isaac M. Fox/C/M/Nov 6/Unknown/4m 3d/Robt Fox/Robt Fox Father
Arthur Freeman/C/M/June 10/Unknown/3m/W. & J. Freeman/W. Freeman Father
John Gatewood/W/M/Aug 27/Old Age/80y/Unknown/Jno W. Stanley Friend
Mildred Gentry/W/F/Oct 21/Heart Disease/44y/Ben & Maria Sacra/W.J. Gentry Husband
Bettie Gray/C/F/July 6/Unknown/48y/Jack & Lucy Gray/Lucy Gray Mother
C.S. Haywood/W/F/Aug 2/Cancer/35y/Mick & Ann Young/T.R. Haywood Husband
Joanna Kelley/W/F/June 15/Old Age/80y/Unknown/__ Friend
Girtie V. Lively/W/F/Dec 5/Congestive Chill/4y/Henry & Fannie Lively/W.S. Flagg Friend
Aron Lewis/C/M/Feb 10/Unknown/1y/Reubin & Catesy Lewis/Reubin Lewis Father
Squire __/C/F/Apr 8/Consumption/54y/Unnknown/Laborer/Alvira Lewis Daughter
Mary A. Mitchell/W/F/Sept 25/Tumor/47y/Reuben & Elizabeth Donahoe/W.T. Mitchell Husband
Ella Mills/C/F/May 10/Unknown/1y/Henry & Eliza Mills/Henry Mills Father
T.K. Mills/C/F/Sept 9/Unknown/8m/Fleming & Lucy Mills/Fleming Mills Father
Polly Minor/C/F/July 10/Unknown/40y/Eliza Thompson/Steven Minor Husband
Agnes Morton/C/F/Oct 14/Unknown/21y/Elijah & Frances Morton/Elijah Morton Father
Sallie J. Moncure/W/F/Aug 17/Unknown/3m 15d/R.T. & A.J. Moncure/R.T. Moncure Father
Pinkey Marshall/C/F/May 1/Consumption/16y/Milly A. Myers/L.C. Pollard Friend
Frances A. Parr/W/F/Nov 11/d."Herring Bone"/Consumption/26y/R.L. & C.V. Parr/R.L. Parr Father
William Partlow/W/M/Sept 8/Unknown/60y/Unknown/Farmer/Ella Dickinson Friend
Sallie A. Page/C/F/May 21/Unknown/8y/E. & R. Page/E. Page Father
Callio D. Page/C/F/May 22/Unknown/2y/E. & R. Page/E. Page Father
James Pearce/W/M/Sept 15/Disease of Kidneys/75y/Unknown/b.England/C.M. Hunter Friend
No Name/C/M/May 11/Unknown/1d/Arthur & Lucy A. Quarles/Arthur Quarles Father
Sarah Redd/C/F/Oct 19/Dropsy/3y/Belle Redd/Belle Redd Mother
Arthur Reynolds/C/June 10/Drowned/13y/Thos & Bettie Reynolds/Thos Reynolds Father
Wm C. Rock/C/M/Oct/Whooping Cough/11m/Bettie Rock/Bettie Rock Mother
No Name/C/F/Mar 17/Unknown/9d/Boswell & L. Robinson/B.Robinson Father
Woodson Seay/W/M/Sept 1/Old Age/85y/Unknown/Herman Seay Son
James Scott/C/M/May 6/Unknown/24y/Cyrus & Christian Scott/Laborer/Cyrus Scott Father
Phoebe Samuel/W/F/Dec 19/Heart Disease/__/Mr. & Mrs. Farmer/S.C. Southworth Friend
Susan Slaughter/W/F/Nov 10/Old Age/80y/Unknown/J.L. Turner Friend

Nannie Smithers/C/F/Oct 20/Pneumonia/28y/E. & P. Fells/Richd Smithers Husband
Blanche Tate/W/F/Nov 30/Diptheria/2y/J.R. & Alice Tate/J.R. Tate Father
Barton Tate/W/M/Dec 15/Diptheria/3m/J.R. & Alice Tate/J.R. Tate Father
Isaac Tompson/C/M/Nov 12/Old Age/84y/Unknown/Major Tompson Son
Mary Tompson/C/F/Nov 18/Consumption/36y/Unknown/Major Tompson Husband
Inez Tompson/C/F/Dec 8/Unknown/__/Major & Mary Tompson/Major Tompkins Father
Lillie Turpin/C/F/Mar 1/Unknown/40y/Unknown/Major Tompson Friend
Annie C. Waller/W/F/Sept 6/Typhoid Fever/39y/Garland & Sophia Waddy/D.J. Waller Husband
William Waller/C/M/Feb 10/Cholera Infantum/3y/R. & H. Waller/Reubin Waller Father
Ellen White/C/F/Apr 1/Old Age/90y/Unknown/Richd Blanton Friend
Jno D. Wright/W/M/Sept 18/Suicide/57y/Vivian & Bettie Wright/Farmer/Jno V. Wright Son
Ernest Wright/W/M/Sept 18/Typhoid Fever/20y/Wm & Ellen Wright/Ellen Wright Mother
Dabney Wright/C/M/Aug 20/Unknown/8m/Dabney & Edie Wright/Dabney Wright Father
Humphrey Sale/C/M/Apr 20/Consumption/23y/Piney Sale/Laborer/Piney Sale Mother

1887

James Ferguson/C/M/Oct 10/Killed on R.R./23y/Wm & Patsy Ferguson/Laborer/Unmarried/Wm Ferguson Father
Andrew Fortune/C/M/Oct 30/Dropsy/2y/Joe & Mary Fortune/Joe Fortune Father
Lee F. Flemming/C/M/May 20/Not Known/1d/Wm H. & Mary Flemming/[illeg]
Lucy Garrett/W/F/Aug 10/Dysentery/2y 6m/C. & L. Garrett/C. Garrett Father
Tyler Gray/W/M/June 22/d.New York/Killed on R.R./40y/Not Known/Laborer/Mary Gray Wife
Mary Garnett/W/F/July 20/Dysentery/1y 6m/S. & Julia Garnett/Stafford Garnett Father
No Name Garnett/W/M/Dec 24/Not Known/3d/S. & Julia Garnett/Stafford Garnett Father
No Name Garnett/W/F/Dec 24/Not Known/3d/S. & Julia Garnett/Stafford Garnett Father
Bell Garnett/C/F/Nov 8/Not Known/7y/Dick & Ella Garnett/Dick Garnett Father
Rachel Grymes/C/F/Feb 10/Com of D/40y/Not Known/James Grymes Husband
Callie Gravatt/W/F/Oct 18/Not Known/1m/Thos J. & Sarah H. Gravatt/Thos J. Gravatt Father
Rose Howard/W/F/Sept 3/Not Known/27y/R.T. & C.C. Chandler/Jno Howard Husband
M.W. Howard/W/M/Dec 5/Apoplexy/52y/Robt & Hannah Howard/Shoe Maker/Mary Howard Wife
Lindsey Hoomes/C/M/Feb 4/Old Age/87y/Spencer & Amelia Holmes/Farmer/Lindsey Hoomes Son
Peter Harris/C/M/July 8/Pluracy/1m 2d/Jno & Rose Harris/Jno Harris Father
Ethel Hicks/C/Dec 10/Not Known/8m/Ben & Mary Hicks/Ben Hicks Father
Bettie T. Haynes/W/F/July 15/Dysentary/18y/Geo & Sarah Haynes/Geo Haynes Father
Mollie Hawkins/C/F/June 10/Pluracy/6m/P.[sic] & Emma Hawkins/B. Hawkins Father
Richd Jesse/W/M/Sept 8/Not Known/76y/Not Known/Farmer/Eugene Bowie Friend
Jos M. Jessie/W/M/Feb 9/Pluracy/50y/Joe & Mary Jessee/Married/W.R. Chewning Friend
No Name Jones/W/F/Aug 13/Not Known/6m/A. & L. Jones/A.L. Jones Father
Wm Jones/C/M/June 10/Dysentary/38y/Not Known/Married/Davey Young Friend
Wm S. Jones/C/M/June 15/Dysentary/4y/Wm & Emily Jones/Davey Young Friend
Emily Jones/C/F/June 16/Dysentery/26y/Not Known/Married/Davey Young Friend
Lottie Jackson/C/F/Nov 10/Diptheria/2y 6m/R. & Rose Jackson/R. Jackson Father
R.W. Jeter/W/M/Feb 9/Pluracy/33d/J.G. & B.W. Jeter/J.G. Jeter Father
Susan Humphreys/W/F/June 20/Dysentery/60y/Not Known/Married/D.B. Powers Friend
Ada B. Cecil/W/F/July 21/Dropsy/24y/W.H. & Lucy Loving/Married/W. H. Loving Father
Ollie Loving/W/F/July 4/Consumption/15y/Lindsay & Eliz Loving/R.E. Loving Father

Danl Lomax/C/M/Nov 5/Diptheria/11y/Adison & Lucy Lomax/Adison Lomax Father
Lucy Lomax/C/F/Nov 8/Diptheria/16y/Adison & Lucy Lomax/Adison Lomax Father
Fannie Lewis/C/F/Apr 10/Consumption/22y/Jno & Mary Lewis/Jno T. Lewis Father
W. Tom Latane/C/M/July 10/Not Known/6m/W.T. & Ella Latane/W.T. Latane Father
Ben Holmes/C/M/July 15/Old Age/80y/Not Known/Farmer/W.T. Latane Father
Humphrey Latane/C/M/Aug 10/Dysentery/60y/Not Known/Ella Latane Wife
__ Long/W/M/Mar 13/Consumption/35y/James & Nancy Long/James Long Son
Laura Allen/C/F/Jan 9/Not Known/40y/Not Known/Servant/Charles Allen Husband
America Allen/C/F/Mar 10/Consumption/25y/Jim & Betsy Brooks/Jerry Allen Husband
Harrison Armistead/C/M/Apr 10/Consumption/21y/Harriett Armistead/Laborer/Unmarried/H. Armistead Mother
No Name Beasley/W/M/Apr 9/Still Born/L.S. & Lena Beasley/L.S. Beasley Father
Robbin Broaddus/W/M/Nov 13/Cansor/40y/Wm & S.F. Murray/C.C. Broaddus Husband
S.A. Broaddus/W/F/Sept 20/Old Age/75y/Not Known/Widow/Jno P. Broaddus Son
Judy Baylor/C/F/Feb 10/Consumption/48y/Jack & Nancy Fry/Washington Baylor Husband
Josephine Baylor/C/F/Apr 8/Not Known/8m/L. & Annie Baylor/Lawrence Baylor Father
Lewis Banks/C/M/Dec 29/Apoplexy/60y/D. & Smithey Banks/Mary Banks Wife
No Name Banks/C/M/Dec 10/Still born/Joe & Sallie Banks/Joe Banks Father
Bettie Banks/C/F/July 5/Consumption/40y/Not Known/Joe Banks Husband
No Name Byrd/C/M/Nov 8/Still Born/Jno P. & Mary Byrd/J.P. Byrd Father
Lucy Beverly/C/F/Aug 10/Old Age/80y/Not Known/Widow/Madison Beverly Son
Rose Burnett/C/F/Apr 10/Consumption/29y/Not Known/Sam Burnett Husband
Fred Burnett/C/M/Apr 20/Measles/7m/Sam & Rose Burnett/Sam Burnett Father
Lucy Burruss/W/F/July 10/Com of Dea/22y/W.O. & Lucy Burruss/W.O. Burruss Father
No Name Broaddus/W/M/July 10/Still born/S.W. & __ Broaddus/S.W. Broaddus Father
No Name Campbell/C/F/May 15/Not Known/6d/Wm & Sue Campbell/Wm Campbell Father
Martha Carter/C/F/Feb 13/Consumption/32y/C. & L. Willis/Phil Carter Husband
Judy Carter/C/F/Jan 27/Old Age/80y/Lewis & Peggy Carter/Widow/Phil Carter Son
James Fields/C/M/March/Consumption/78y/Billy & Mary Fields/Widower/Ben Carter Friend
Mary F. Carter/C/F/July 12/Dropsy/18y/Jno & Sally Carter/Jno Carter Father
R.H. Carter/W/M/July 7/Pneumonia/72y/Phil & Bettie Carter/Emma Carter Wife
Robinett Clark/W/F/Oct 16/Dropsy/27y/Not Known/Chas S. Clark Husband
No Name Coleman/C/M/Feb 25/Still Born/Thornton & Ellen Coleman/Thornton Coleman Father
Jos Covington/C/M/Sept 27/Old Age/80y/Toler & Nancy Covington/Farmer/Andrew Covington Son
Rose Chandler/W/F/Sept 10/Not Known/20y/R.F. & Columbia Chandler/R.F. Chandler Father
James C. Catlett/C/M/Aug 10/Not Known/21y/Page & Mary Catlett/Walter Catlett Father
No Name Catlett/C/M/Dec 10/Still born/Walter & Mary Catlett/Walter Catlett Father
Martha Corbin/C/F/Aug 10/Dropsy/13y/Washington & Maria Corbin/__ Corbin Father
W.R. Chewning/W/M/Sept 10/Not Known/75y/Jos & Bettie Chewning/Widower/Farmer/W.S. Chewning Father
Henry Brown/C/M/Jan 10/Consumption/50y/Not Known/Farmer/Dennis Cain Friend
Pearl Cox/W/F/July 15/Disentery/1y 6m/Jno & Mary Cox/Jno Cox Father
Downing __/W/F/Jan 10/Not Known/8m/J.P. & Lelia Downing/J.P. Downing Father
Hattie Dratt/W/F/Nov 10/Cancer/28y/J. & Harriet Dratt/Harriett Dratt Mother
Caroline Elliott/W/F/Mar 10/Com of D/40y/Jno H. & Jane Pavey/Widow/J.L. Elliott Son
Sallie C. Samuel/W/F/Aug 15/Consumption/34y/J.J. & Mary Massey/Wm H. Samuel Husband
Nettie Saunders/C/F/July 15/Not Known/1y/Albert & Luvenia Saunders/Albert Saunders Father

__ Saunders/C/M/Mar 10/Still born/Wm & Betsy Saunders/Wm Saunders Father
__ Shepherd/C/M/Apr 10/Not Known/12d/Joe & Lucy Shepherd/Joe Shepherd Father
__ Shepherd/C/F/Apr 10/Not Known/12d/Joe & Lucy Shepherd/Joe Shepherd Father
H.F. Stevens/W/M/June 10/Accident/65y/James & Counthia? Stevens/Farmer/H.F. Stevens Son
Eugene Shaddock/W/M/Dec 17/Com of Dea/21y/James & Ann Shaddock/Farmer/James Shaddock Father
Sallie Thomas/W/F/June 25/Old Age/89y/Jno & Nancy Riggin/Widow/Alex Pugh Son
James Taylor/C/M/June 25/Dysentery/74y/Jack & Jennie Taylor/Farmer/Married/James Prier Friend
Thos C. Thornton/W/M/Jan 15/Consumption/46y/Edmd & C. Thornton/Farmer/Married/Edmd Thornton Father
Mary E. Taylor/W/F/Sept 10/Consumption/23y/J.T. & Sallie Taylor/Sallie Taylor Mother
Mary R. Taylor/W/F/Feb 25/Rheumatism/42y/Not Known/J.M. Taylor Husband
Lena Taliaferro/C/F/Jan 10/Consumption/32y/Matt & S. Taliaferro/Servant/Matt Taliaferro Father
F.H. Thornton/W/M/Aug 10/Old Age/84y/Clark & C. Rowe/R.C. Thornton Son
__ Tignor/W/F/Apr 10/Still Born/Jos H. & Louisa Tignor/J.H. Tignor Father
Wm S. Royston/W/M/Oct 2/Old Age/87y/Wm & Mary Royston/Farmer/Widower/C.W. Tompkins Son-in-Law
C.H. Tompkins/W/M/nov 20/Dysentery/4y/C.W. & Sallie Tompkins/C.W. Tompkins Father
Susan Upshaw/C/F/Aug 15/Not Known/5m/Taylor & Susan Upshaw/Taylor Upshaw Father
Martha Wright/W/F/Dec 10/Croup/2m/J.H. & S.F. Wright/J.H. Wright Father
__ Williams/C/M/July 26/Croup/5m 6d/James & M. Williams/James Williams Father
James T. White/W/M/Nov 18/Old Age/81y/A.C. White/Jno L. White Son
Jno Washington/W/M/Sept 25/Not Known/60y/Jno & Ann Washington/Atty at Law/J.B. Washington Son
Wm Ware/C/M/Aug 15/Not Known/6m/Jacob & Mary Ware/Jacob Ware Father
George Willis/C/M/June 10/Not Known/1y 6m/James & E. Willis/James Willis Father
Wm Woolfolk/C/M/Dec 8/Heart Dea/55y/Not Known/Farmer/Married/Harry Ward Son-in-Law
Robt Young/C/M/Jan 9/Not Known/18y/Robt & Sallie Young/Farmer/Robt Young Father
Delila Long/W/F/Jan 26/Consumption/53y/S. & Delila Sale/James Long Son
Thomas Monroe/C/M/June 25/Old Age/86y/Joe & Judy Minor/Lucian Loney Son
Martha A. Myers/C/F/Dec/Pneumonia/20y/W. & Lizzie Myers/W. Myers Father
Wm Matthews/C/M/June 5/Old Age/85y/Kellis & Milly Matthews/Farmer/Lucy Matthews Daughter
Stafford H. Morton/C/M/July 13/Dysentery/50y/Not Known/Farmer/Married/Geo Haynes Friend
Wm A. Baynham/W/M/June 17/Heart Dea/77y/Not Known/Minister/Unmarried/J.H. Martin Friend
Wm Hopkins/C/M/Nov 10/Consumption/60y/W. & T. Hopkins/Laborer/Unmarried/Geo Martin Friend
No Name Moore[sic]/C/F/Oct 11/Not Known/1d/Fannie Goodwin/Fannie Goodwin Mother
Jane Gray/C/F/Dec 10/Dysentery/3y/Lewis & Polly Gray/G. McGrudo Friend
Polly Gray/C/F/July 5/Dysentery/40y/Robt & Polly Warner/Married/G. McGrudo Friend
Wm A. Norman/C/M/Nov 10/Heart Disease/60y/Not Known/__Mason/Married/Peyton Brown Friend
Elizth Peyton/W/F/May 5/Old Age/85y/Champ & Sarah Broken-borough/Widow/Sarah J. Peyton Daughter
W.B. Quisenberry/W/M/Apr 24/Com of Deas/40y/Not Known/Merchant/Married/D.B. Bowers Friend
Catherine Parker/C/F/July 11/Dysentery/20y/Aaron & Emily Parker/Aaron Parker Father

Sanford Parker/C/M/Dec 20/Not Known/3m/J.E. & Zell Parker/J.E. Parker Father
Cassie M. Pugh/W/F/Aug 1/Not Known/4y/Jason F. & C.B. Pugh/Jason F. Pugh Father
__ Pugh/W/F/Feb 10/Not Known/6d/Wm H. & L.F. Pugh/Wm H. Pugh Father
Nannie Pendleton/C/F/Oct 20/Typhoid Fever/11y/Anthony & Margarett Pendleton/Anthony Pendleton Father
Julia Pleasants/C/F/Apr 10/Old Age/80y/Not Known/Sam Pleasants Husband
Henry Catlett/C/M/Dec 19/Pluracy/12m/Betsy Catlett/Wm Page Friend
Minnie L. Catlett/C/F/Aug 14/Pluracy/8m/Betsy Catlett/Wm Page Friend
James Roy/C/M/Oct 10/Consumption/40y/Not Known/Farmer/Married/Wm Bowie Friend
George Richerson/C/M/Sept 20/Dysentery/65y/George & Patsy Richerson/Farmer/Geo D. Richerson Son
Edmond Lee/C/M/May 10/Heart Deas/65y/Not Known/Soloman Rollins Friend
Cary Osborne/C/M/June 10/Consumption/6y/Cary & Emma Osborne/Isaac Roberson Friend
Caroline Roberson/C/F/May 10/Heart Deas/70y/Spencer & Peggy Reives/Sample Roberson Husband
Rubin Roberson/C/M/Dec 30/Not Known/1y/Jno & Eliza Roberson/Jno Roberson Father
T.U. Reynolds/W/M/Sept 10/Heart Deas/65y/Not Known/Farmer/James Reynolds Son
Bettie Roy/C/F/May 10/Com of Deas/60y/Bob & Martha Chapman/J. Roy Son
Mattie Rowe/W/F/Oct 15/Inf of Bowels/3m/E.C. & Mary L. Rowe/E.C. Rowe Father
L. Catherine Rouse/W/F/July 10/Dysentery/8y/F.W. & Emma Rouse/F.W. Rouse Father
Mary Roane/C/F/June 10/Consumption/40y/Not Known/Humphrey Roane Husband
Michell Smith/W/M/Nov 8/Erysipelas/54y/Andrew & B. Smith/Farmer/M.E. Smith Wife
__ Samuel/C/F/May 15/__/10d/Geo & Cata Samuel/George Samuel Father
__ Samuel/C/F/July 10/Still born/Arch & Julia Samuel/Arch Samuel Father
Thos W. Samuel/W/M/Mar 10/Pneumonia/18y/Phil & Elizth Samuel/Phil Samuel Father
John C. Allen/W/M/Nov 30/d."North Wales"/Neuralgia/60y/Unknown/Mrs. Allen Wife
Lenny Barlow/W/M/Aug 20/d."Arnolds Hills"/Unknown/2m/Robt & B.L. Barlow/Robt Barlow Father
No Name/C/M/Mar 4/Spasms/10d/Waller & Martha Baber/Waller Baber Father
Elliott Brooks/W/M/Sept/Killed in Saw Mill/25y/Unknown/Laborer/S.W. Allen Friend
Robt L. Brooks/W/M/Apr 20/d."Chestnut Grove"/Paralysis/67y/Jas & Frances Brooks/Farmer/ Mrs. Brooks Wife
Churchill Carter/W/M/Dec/Dropsy/60y/Thompson Carter/Miller/Page Carter Son
Cattie J. Carneal/W/F/June 20/d."Herring Bone"/Measles/17y/J.B. & L.C. Carneal/J.B. Carneal Father
Patsy Carneal/W/F/Dec 10/Old Age/81y/Jas & Sallie Carneal/Gid Carneal Nephew
Wm H. Carter/C/M/Sept 10/Consumption/9y/Moses & Peggy Carter/Moses Carter Father
Callis Carter/W/Dec 26/Consumption/27y/Tom & Almira Acors/W.B. Carter Husband
M.E. Carlton/W/F/July 18/Sun Stroke/29y/R.F. & J.A. Dyson/Zack Carlton Husband
Louisa Carthorne/C/F/July 10/Unknown/22y/W.H. & S.A. Carthorne/W.H. Carthorne Father
Catharine Collins/W/F/May 4/Old Age/77y/Unknown/R.E. Collins Son
Jordan Cooper/C/M/July 3/Old Age/70y/Unknown/Laborer/Jno Baylor Friend
Matt Dimue/W/M/May 31/Unknown/41y/Matt & Frances Dimue/Farmer/Bettie Dimue Wife
Wilton Durrett/W/M/Feb 20/Unknown/2y/W.S. & Mary Durrett/W.S. Durrett Father
Martha England/W/F/Mar 20/Old Age/75y/Wm Thacher & Lida Mason/Inadratus England Son
No Name/C/M/Apr 9/Unknown/9d/Kitty Fox/Kitty Fox Mother
Pearl Fox/C/F/Feb 5/Pneumonia/1y 6m/Henry & Martha Fox/Henry Fox Father
Ada Fox/C/F/May/Unknown/2m/Laura Fox/Laura Fox Mother
Susan Harris/C/F/May 4/d.New York/Dropsy/22y/Margarett Harris/Margarett Harris Mother

Frank Harper/W/M/Sept/Killed at Saw Mill/30y/Unknown/S.W. Allen Friend
Susie A. Hart/W/F/Apr 5/d.Richmond/Measles/16y/W.T. & B.W. Hart/W.T. Hart Father
Theo Holmes/C/M/June 7/Bronchitis/1y/Bartlett & Eliza Holmes/Bartlett Holmes Father
Gertie Holmes/C/F/July 9/Bronchitis/1y/Bartlett & Eliza Holmes/Bartlett Holmes Father
James Hunter/W/M/Apr 15/d."Elan Gowan"/Heart disease/74y/Taliaferro & Elizabeth Hunter/ b.Middlesex/Ellen D. Hunter Wife
Rich W. Hutcherson/W/M/Sept 2/d."Locust Grove"/Consumption/62y/Rich & M. Hutcherson/ F.A. Hutcherson Wife
Erminta Johnson/C/F/Feb 10/Consumption/21y/Edmond & Caroline Johnson/Edmond Johnson Father
Betsy Johnson/C/F/Aug 20/Consumption/22y/Edmond & Caroline Johnson/Edmond Johnson Father
Wylis Johnson/C/M/Nov 4/Consumption/18y/Edmund & Caroline Johnson/Edmund Johnson Father
Moses Jones/C/M/Mar 20/Old Age/80y/Unknown/Minor Jones Son
Wm B. Jones/C/M/Dec 30/Consumption/24y/Wm & Eliza Jones/Wm Jones Father
Hattie Kempt/C/F/June 1/Old Age/85y/Catherine Robinson/Cyrus Scott Friend
Bettie Minor/C/F/June 10/Consumption/24y/Sam & Nancy Alsop/Nelson Minor Husband
No Name/C/M/Aug 10/Unknown/1m/Jno & Mildred Mont/Jno Mont Father
Wm F. Pugh/W/M/Feb 28/Unknown/11y/Robt L. Pugh/Robt L. Pugh Father
Nancy Quarles/C/F/Aug 20/Consumption/25y/Jno & Nancy Quarles/Nancy Quarles Mother
Jno W. Quarles/C/M/Aug 10/Unknown/70y/Unknown/Blacksmith/Nancy Quarles Wife
John Redd/C/M/Aug 20/Unknown/22y/Geo & Maria Redd/Robt Smith Friend
Boswell Robinson/C/M/Aug 17/Consumption/28y/Moses & Woetta Robinson/Farmer/Luvenia Robinson Wife
No Name/C/M/June 9/Unknown/29d/Chas & Susan Sacra/Chas Sacra Father
No Name/C/M/Mar 18/Spasms/9d/Henry & Bettie Samuel/Henry Samuel Father
No Name/W/F/July 3/Unknown/3m/Jno L. & Sue Seay/Jno L. Seay Father
Sarah Seay/W/F/July 19/Consumption/65y/Thos & Sarah Buchanan/Jno L. Seay Son
Sarah F. Smith/W/F/Nov 11/Dispepsia/47y/Erasmus & Sarah Walton/Wilber Smith Son
Chester Smith/C/M/June 10/Unknown/6m/Emmett & K. Smith/Emmett Smith Father
Lucy S. Smith/C/F/Feb 2/Unknown/63y/Unknown/Jno Smith Husband
Louisa Stevens/W/F/Mar 27/Consumption/62y/Jno & E. Long/Theo Stevens Husband
Silvia Tompson/C/F/Apr 10/Old Age/75y/Unknown/D.J. Waller Friend
Susan Walker/C/F/Dec 8/Unknown/2y/Lewis & Fannie Walker/Lewis Walker Father
No Name/C/M/Aug 13/1m 10d/Isaac & Mary Wadkins/Isaac Watkins Father
Richd Williams/C/Dec 4/Unknown/3m/Rici & Charlotte Williams/Rici Williams Father
Sallie Wilson/C/F/Oct 10/Unknown/11m/Wm & Charlotte Wilson/Wm Wilson Father
C.S. Woolard/W/M/May 18/Unknown/32y/Thos & Eliza Woolard/Mrs. Woolard Wife
Jerry Wormley/C/M/Nov 16/Pneumonia/75y/Jerry & Selvina Wormley/Ben Thompson Friend
Virgie Wright/C/M/July 15/Unknown/6m/Dabney & Edie Wright/Dabney Wright Father
Lillie B. West/W/F/Dec 20/Unknown/3m/Geo & Bertie West/Geo West Father
Sarah West/W/F/Sept 20/Old Age/80y/Geo & Sarah Gaynes/Geo West Step Son

1888

Elizabeth Allen/W/F/Sept 20/Consumption/62y/Wm & Ann Blanton/Married/J.O. Allen
Mary E. Blanton//W/F/Mar 7/Cancer/47y/John H. & Mary Arnold/b.King George Co/Thos H. Blanton Husband
Alma Blanton/W/F/May 11/d.Centre[l] Point [Car Co/Pneumonia/2y/W.A. & Vandelia Blanton/

b.Centre Point/W.A. Blanton Father
Clarice R. Blanton/W/F/Aug 4/Unknown/1y 5m/Jas R. & Cora L. Blanton/J.R. Blanton Father
No Name/C/M/Feb 23/Unknown/__/10d/Waller & Martha Baber/Waller Baber Father
Richard Boulware/W/M/Apr 14/Old Age/84y/Wm & Mary Boulware/Farmer/M. Boulware Wife
Frank Braxton/C/M/Oct 10/Killed/21y/Elz Braxton/Henry Samuel Friend
Burnett Burruss/C/M/Mar 1/Burned/2y/Thos & Ida Burruss/Thos Burruss Father
Robert Carter/C/M/Aug 1/Malarial Fever/35y/Phillis & W. Carter/Mrs Carter Wife
Maria Carter/C/F/Sept 30/Unknown/22y/Peter & Eliza Mines/Samuel Carter Husband
Mary Clark/W/F/Dec/Consumption/60y/John & Sarah Dickinson/John Clark Husband
Susan Coleman/C/F/Apr 20/Dropsy/26y/E. & Martha Coleman/Erasmus Coleman Father
Frances Cooper/C/F/Dec 1/Unknown/25y/Jordan & Nancy Cooper/Geo Wormley Friend
W.G. Dandridge/W/M/Jan 11/Bladder disease/61y/Unknown/W.C. Flagg Son-in-Law
H.S. Dandridge/W/F/Apr 23/Cancer/45y/Jas Redd/W.C. Flagg Son-in-Law
Maria Davis/C/F/Mar 14/d."Goose Pond"/Child birth/23y/Henry & Judie Johnson/John Davis
  Husband
Elizabeth Fells/C/F/July 4/d."Centreville"/Unknown/36y/Jennie Morris/Coss Fells Husband
Theodore Fells/C/M/Feb 18/d.Centreville/Unknown/2y/Cos & Elizabeth Fells/Coss Fells Father
Peter Fells/C/M/July 1/Brain Fever/2y/Robt & Ellen Fells/Robt Fells Father
Anna E. Fells/C/F/July/Child birth/22y/James & S. James/Chas Fells Father
Mollie Fells/C/F/Nov 20/Child birth/23y/Thos & Addie Johnson/Thos Johnson Father
Albert R. Flippo/W/M/Dec 26/Old Age/80y/Joseph Flippo/T. Blanton Friend
Sarah Fkippo/W/F/Sept 5/Old Age/75y/Unknown/L. Flippo Husband
Emma Fountain/C/F/Sept 20/Consumption/23y/Peter & Matilda Fountain/Peter Fountain Father
James Freeman/C/M/June/Old Age/80y/Unknown/Mrs. Freeman Wife
Elvira Frawner/C/F/Apr 11/Old Age/75y/Fannie Twisdale/E. Moore Friend
W.B. Garnett/W/M/Dec 1/Malarial Fever/34y/Woodford & Caroline Garnett/J.H. Garnett Brother
Sam Garnett/C/M/Oct 6/Unknown/10y/Aaron & __ Garnett/Chas Terry Friend
Arthur Gatewood/C/M/Oct 10/d."Arnoldsville"/Congestive Chill/17y/Daniel & Frances Gatewood/
  Dan'l Gatewood Father
George Gibson/C/M/Nov 20/Unknown/60y/Unknown/Edmond Carter Friend
Chas B. Goldsby/W/M/Oct 8/Malarial Fever/14y/Jno & Nannie F. Goldsby/John Goldsby Father
James II. Goldsby/W/M/Aug 1/Malarial Fever/36y/Caleb & M.A. Goldsby/Martha A. Goldsby
  Mother
[illeg]retta Golden/C/F/Sept/Unknown/7m/Dingo & H. Golden/Dingo Golden Father
Margarett Golden/C/F/July 13/Old Age/79y/Levi & Minerva Minor/Married/Dingo Golden Son
__ Hart/W/M/Sept 11/Unknown/1d/B.J. & Bettie Hart/B.J. Hart Father
__/Holmes/C/F/June 16/Unknown/1d/Marcellus & Judie Holmes/Marcellus Holmes Father
Lucy M. Coughton/W/F/July 10/Paralysis/84y/Chas & Margarett Croughton/E.G. Seay Friend
Frank James/W/M/Mar 1/d."Palestine"/Pneumonia/72y/Unknown/Mrs. James Wife
Thains James/C/M/Feb 10/Bronchitis/3m/Peter & Emma James/Peter James Father
Jennie Johnson/C/F/Sept 18/Malarial Fever/15y/Edmond & Caroline Johnson/Edmond Johnson
  Father
A.E. Kelley/W/F/May 16/Miscarriage/38y/J.F. & Mary Lucord/R.F. Kelley Husband
Rose Lewis/C/F/Sept 8/Old Age/70y/Unknown/James Catlett Friend
No Name/C/M/Sept 6/Unknown/3d/Josephine Lewis/Josephine Lewis Mother
Martha Mahone/W/F/Aug 19/d.Hanover/Paralized/2y/J.B. & Martha Mahone/b.Hanover/J.B.
  Mahone Father
Oscar McKinney/W/M/Aug 15/Unknown/57y/Wm & Sallie McKinney/T.H. Blanton Friend

Charles Monroe/C/M/Jan 7/Consumption/30y/Toby & Delsey Monroe/Delsey Monroe Mother
Donia Moore/C/F/Mar 15/Child birth/37y/Elizabeth Robinson/Jeff Moore Husband
York Nelson Sr/C/M/Apr/Old Age/80y/Unknown/York Nelson Jr Son
Hardenia M. Pearce/W/F/Nov 20/d."Fair View"/Consumption/75y/W.D. & S.B. Taylor/C.M. Hunter Friend
George G. Prince/W/M/Mar 28/Asthma/52y/Jas H. & Elizabeth Prince/Sarah A. Prince Wife
Maria Redd/C/F/Feb 28/Unknown/44y/Unknown/Robt Smith Friend
Sallie Redd/C/F/May 10/Unknown/1y/Maria Redd/Robt Smith Friend
Harry Redd/C/M/July 20/Unknown/4y/Maria Redd/Robt Smith Friend
No Name/C/F/Feb 19/Unknown/4d/Simor & Ann Reynolds/Simon Reynolds Father
Ida Ross/C/F/June 30/Burned to death/2y/Sallie A. Ross/Roderick Ross Grandfather
Frank Rowzie/C/M/Aug 9/Consumption/55y/Edmond & Lucy Rowzie/Mrs. Rowzie Wife
Guy Roots/C/M/June 11/Old Age/75y/Unknown/George Tilman Friend
Harmond Seay/W/M/Sept 9/Malarial Fever/60y/Woodford & H. Seay/G.T. Seay Son
Eliza Shepherd/C/F/Aug 6/Brain Fever/23y/Not Known/John Shepherd Husband
Elizabeth M. Sizer/W/F/Nov 25/Old Age/93y/Wm & Clara Gatewood/Married/Jos H. Wiglesworth
Frances Smith/W/F/May 4/Old Age/90y/Unknown/Married/Wm Smith
Nelson Smith/C/M/Dec 6/Old Age/80y/Unknown/J.T. Hargrave Friend
Christine Smith/W/F/July 10/Unknown/1y 8m/Millard & Nannie Smith/Millard Smith Father
Emma Southworth/W/F/Apr 29/Unknown/40y/J.B. & Eliz Southworth/Chas Gordon
Harriett Spindle/C/F/Sept 15y/Unknown/80y/Winston & Harriett Spindle/Coss Fells
Annie Taylor/C/F/Nov 28/Unknown/24y/Chas & Nancy Mickens/Wm Taylor
Caroline Terry/W/F/Feb 15/Burned to death/28y/Geo & Matilda Arnold/Thos F. Terry
Eliza A. Terry/C/F/Sept 7/Malarial Fever/56y/Saml & Mary Braxton/Peter Mines
Martha Temple/C/F/Feb 15/Unknown/54y/Unknown/Fes Flippo Friend
Clayborn Tinsley/C/M/Dec 10/Unknown/70y/Unknown/M.F. Wortham
Henry Tompkins/C/M/Oct 20/Fits/28y/Walker Tompkins/ Laborer/G.W. Tompkins
Frances Washington/C/F/Apr 6/Dropsy/35y/Unknown/Jack Washington
Wm R. Williams/C/M/Apr 3/Unknown/4y/Rice & Charlotte Williams/Charlotte Williams
Susie Campbell/C/F/May 20/d.Port Royal/Not Known/8d/Wm & Susan Campbell/b.Port Royal/ Wm Campbell Father
Jno B. Lightfoot/W/M/July 10/d.Port Royal/Com of Dia/74y/Phil & R. Lightfoot
Lina Allen/C/F/Jan 4/Not Known/40y/Not Known/Charles Allen Husband
Otha Alexander/C/M/Mar 6/Not Known/7m/R. & S. Alexander/R. Alexander Father
Josaphine Baylor/C/F/Apr 8/Typhoid Fever/8m/L.A. Baylor/L. Baylor Father
Mary M. Brooks/C/F/Oct 1/Paralized/76y/Not Known/Widow/A. Brooks Son
Louisa Eppes/C/F/Mar 10/Old Age/70y/A. & L. Eppes/Widow/Joe Banks Son
No Name Brooks/C/M/Aug 9/Still born/Joe & S. Banks/Joe Banks Father
No Name Bruce/W/M/Aug 17/Not Known/2d/R. & Mary Bruce/R.S. Bruce Father
No Name Bundy/C/M/Aug 5/Not Known/4m/E. & S. Bundy/E. Bundy Father
Madison Byrd[sic]/C/M/Dec 9/Cansor/32y/M. & Lucy Beverley/ Bettie Beverley Wife
John Bell/W/M/Dec 26/Not Known/72y/Not Known/Farmer/R.H. Bell Son
No Name Bell/W/M/Feb 10/Not Known/14d/J. & Jenetta Bell/J.W. Bell Father
James E. Buckner/C/M/Oct 6/Not Known/4d/Peter & F. Buckner/Peter Buckner Father
Isabela Buckner/C/F/June 12/Heart Disease/45y/George & Helen Ellis/Abram Buckner Husband
Richd Bowie/W/M/Dec 9/Heart Disease/76y/Not Known/Farmer/Widower/C. Bowie Son
Fredie Bowie/C/M/Jan 10/Diptheria/6y/W. & Caroline Bowie/W.T. Bowie Father
Joseph Black/W/M/Aug 6/Not Known/1m/J. & Nannie Black/J.A. Black Father

No Name Bland/W/M/Feb 10/Not Known/1m/Jno & Allie Bland/John Bland Father
Polly Butcher/C/F/Aug 12/Old Age/80y/Not Known/Widow/W.F. Byers Friend
No Name Bennett/C/M/Mar 10/Measles/3d/Sam & Rose Bennett/S. Bennett Father
Rose Bennett/C/F/Mar 11/Measles/28d/Not Known/S. Bennett Husband
Henry Claytor/W/M/Aug 5/Dysentery/56y/Not Known/Farmer/Married/H. Whitticoe Friend
Sallie Claytor/W/F/July 10/Dysentery/15y/Henry & May Claytor/H. Whitticoe Friend
Bettie Claytor/W/F/July 20/Dysentery/13y/Henry & Mae Claytor/H. Whitticoe Friend
Martha Carter/C/F/Feb 13/Consumption/32y/C. & L. Willis/Phil Carter Son
Judy Carter/C/F/Jan 27/Old Age/80y/L. & P. Willis/Phil Carter Son
Lina Cater/C/F/Dec 6/Old Age/76y/Not Known/Ben Carter Son
Cora Carter/C/F/Dec 19/Burned/6y/Patrick & L. Carter/Patrick Carter Father
Charity Lewis/C/F/Jan 7/Old Age/82y/Ben & S. Shepherd/Widower/W.H. Carter Friend
Hattie Chiles/C/F/July 26/Not Known/11m/Steven & E. Chiles/Steven Chiles Father
Winston J. Chiles/C/M/Oct 25/Com of Dia/65y/Not Known/Laborer/Winston Chiles Son
Nancy Campbell/C/F/Mar 5/Heart Dis/20y/Robt Campbell/Unmarried/R. Campbell Father
Danl Covington/C/M/Jan 10/Dropsy/46y/Not Known/Farmer/Widower/A. Covington Son
Washington Corbin/C/M/Nov 7/Killed/19y/W. & Manal Corbin/Laborer/W. Corbin Father
No Name Cole/W/M/Feb 1/Not Known/1m/H. & Lucy Cole/H. Cole Father
Betsy Cook/C/F/May 29/Heart Dis/50y/Not Known/Married/R. Cook Husband
No Name Farmer/W/F/July 7/Not Known/3m/R. & Va Farmer/R. Farmer Father
Ben Flippo/W/M/July 15/Old Age/76y/Not Known/Widower/Wm Flippo Son
Bell Garnett/C/F/Nov 8/Not Known/7y/Dick Garnett/D. Garnett Father
Lena Gouldman/W/F/Aug 15/Child Birth/20y/Geo & M. Gouldman/G. Gouldman Husband
No Name Gouldman/W/M/Aug 15/Still born/Jno & Lina Gouldman/J. Gouldman Father
Nellie Gatewood/C/F/Aug 28/Child Birth/25y/Not Known/T. Gatewood Husband
Callie Gravatt/W/F/Oct 20/Not Known/1m/Thos & Sarah Gravatt/Thos Gravatt Father
Silas Gayle/W/M/Mar 16/Consumption/35y/M.J. & Va Gayle/Farmer/F. Gayle Father
Jno W. Gill/W/M/Oct 10/Com of Dea/56y/J. & M. Gill/Hotel etc/Lou Gill Wife
Thomas Hoomes/C/M/Aug 20/Not Known/2y/T. & B. Hoomes/T. Hoomes Father
Eliza Houston/W/F/Dec 5/Com of Dea/65y/Not Known/Geo Houston Husband
Ann Hopkins/C/F/Aug 10/Old Age/80y/Not Known/James Hopkins Husband
Bettie Haynes/W/F/July 15/Direah/18y/G.L. & Sarah Haynes/G.L. Haynes Father
Mollie Hawkins/C/F/June 6/Pneumonia/1y 1m/B. & Emma Hawkins/B. Hawkins Father
Wm T. Hailstalk/C/M/Nov 3/Paralysis/65y/John & S. Hailstalk/Laborer/Widower/W/Hailstalk
 Son
No Name Johnson/C/M/Feb 15/Still Born/Ned & Sarah Johnson/Ned Johnson Father
No Name Johnson/C/F/May 9/Still born/M. & Susan Johnson/Moses Johnson Father
Polly Johnson/C/F/Dec 24/Child Birth/46y/Not Known/John Johnson Husband
Willie Johnson/C/M/Oct 1/Not Known/10m/Phil & Lettie Johnson/Phil Johnson Father
No Name Jones/W/F/June 1/Still born/Chas & L. Jones/Chas Jones Father
Liza A. Jones/W/F/July 22/Not Known/6m/Wm & Sarah Jones/Wm Jones Father
James Jeter/C/M/July 10/Consumption/38y/Wash & Patsy Jeter/Laborer/John Jeter Brother
Patsy Jeter/C/F/Sept 1/Consumption/72y/Not Known/Wash Jeter Son
Wm James/W/M/Aug 16/Not Known/15m/Joe & Bettie James/Joe James Father
Annie Lewis/C/F/June 9/Not Known/18m/Robt & Eugenia Lewis/Robt Lewis Father
Fannie Lucas/C/F/Mar 15/Heart Dea/48y/Not Known/London Lucas Husband
Lucius Lonesome/C/M/Aug 10/Drowned/25y/Moses & Rachael Lonesome/Mr Lonesome Father
Thomas Martin/C/M/Jan 12/Pneumonia/59y/Nancy Martin/Laborer/Widower/Silas Martin Son

Elizth Minor/C/F/Oct 9/Old Age/84y/Not Known/E. Minor Husband
Ida B.Minor/C/F/Mar 22/Consumption/8m/Jonas & M. Minor/Jonas Minor Father
London Myers/C/M/Oct 10/Old Age/90y/Not Known/Farmer/Widower/L. Myers Son
Hannah Montague/C/F/June 3/Com of Dea/67y/Ben & Winnie Johnson/R. Montague Husband
Eliz Norman/C/F/Aug 17/Com of Dea/18y/Littleton & S. Norman/Unmarried/L. Norman Father
No Name News/C/F/Sept 30/Still born/Washington & J. News/W. News Father
Thomas Pugh/W/M/Oct 24/Old Age/89y/Lewis & Mary Pugh/Farmer/Widower/A.J. Pugh Son
Henrietta Puller/C/F/Aug 1/Not Known/18m/Woodson & Mary Puller/Unmarried/W. Puller Father
Timothy Puller/C/M/Sept 30/Not Known/8d/Woodson & Mary Puller/W. Puller Father
Mary Richerson/C/F/July 15/Consumption/30y/Geo & Patsy Richerson/G. Richerson Father
Ollie Richerson/C/F/Aug 1/Not Known/27y/Geo & Patsy Richerson/G. Richerson Father
Mary Richerson/C/F/Oct 10/Consumption/60y/Geo & Mary Richerson/E.M. Richerson Husband
George Robb/C/M/Aug 17/Dysentery/14m/James & Eliza Robb/James Robb Father
Precilla Paine/C/F/Oct 6/Consumption/70y/Not Known/Widow/Armistead Robb Friend
Aleorsha Robb/C/F/June 7/Not Known/10m/A. & Emma Robb/Armistead Robb Friend
Lucy Roots/C/F/Dec 22/Typhoid Fever/16y/S. & L. Roots/Soloman Roots Father
James Roots/C/M/Sept 25/Not Known/22y/S. & L. Roots/Soloman Roots Father
Richd Richard/C/M/Jan 11/Not Known/60y/Not Known/Widower/R. Richard Son
Mary Roane/C/F/Jan 1/Not Known/40y/Not Known/H. Roane Husband
Laura Smith/W/F/June 10/Consumption/30y/Phil & L. Samuel/Jno Smith Husband
Edmond Smith/C/M/July 18/Diriah/14y/Richd & Leticia Smith[sic]/Edmund Smith Father
Thos W. Samuel/C/M/Mar 10/Pneumonia/18y/Phil & Elizth Samuel/Phil Samuel Father
Jno Sale/C/M/Dec 1/Croup/2y/Butler & Sallie Sale/Butler Sale Father
No Name Saunders/C/M/Feb 16/Not Known/14d/Wm & Betsy Saunders/Wm Saunders Father
Caroline Street/C/F/May 1/Not Known/5y/Robt & Patsy Street/Robt Street Father
Robert Taylor/W/M/June 2/Heart Dea/75y/Not Known/Widower/W.L. Taylor Son
Pollie Taylor/C/F/Sept 15/Cansor/35y/Not Known/Phil Taylor Husband
Martha Taylor/W/F/Mar 15/Not Known/16m/W. & Sarah Taylor/W. Taylor Father
No Name Taliaferro/C/F/Jan 19/Not Known/14m/W. & Ellen Taliaferro/W. Taliaferro Father
Sam Wright/W/M/Sept 16/Diptheria/4y/Sam & Elizth Wright/Sam Wright Father
Nannie Wright/W/F/Sept 30/Not Known/36y/James & Mary Garrett/Sam Wright Husband
No Name Wright/W/F/May 23/Not Known/3d/Jno & Nancy Wright/John Wright Father
Emily Wright/C/F/Jan 5/Child birth/24y/Not Known/Robt Wright Husband
No Name Wright/C/M/Jan 4/Still born/Robt & Emily Wright/Robt Wright Father
No Name Wright/C/M/Jan 4/Still born/Robt & Emily Wright/Robt Wright Father
 [apparently twins]
Albert Williams/C/F/Nov 14/Not Known/3m/L. & Mary Williams/L. Williams Father
Fannie Grymes/C/F/Jan 1/Not Known/82y/Rob & Anne Grymes/Edmd Whitticoe Friend
Ellen Beazley/W/F/Sept/Not Known/49y/Jno & Polly Beasley/Unmarried/Edmd Whitticoe Friend
Muscoe Washington/C/M/Aug 25/Dysentery/50y/Not Known/Laborer/Widower/Ira White Friend
Bettie Washington/C/F/June 1/Com of Dea/45y/B. & M. Washington/Wm Washington Husband
Alberta Ware/C/F/Aug 6/Not Known/12y/Charles & A. Ware/Charles Ware Father
Wm H. Young/C/M/Sept 28/Not Known/1d/W.H. & N. Young/W.H. Young Father
Maggie H. Gayle/W/F/Aug 10/Not Known/5y/Lewis & Fannie Gayle/Lewis Gayle Father
No Name Broaddus/W/M/June 20/d.Bowling Green/Not Known/21d/S.W. & Emily Broaddus/
 b.Bowling Green/S.W. Broaddus Father
Sallie G. Sutton/W/F/Apr 20/d.Bowling Green/Cansor/50y/Robt & Sallie Hudgin/b.Bowling
 Green/Widow/R. Hudgin Father

No Name Jones/W/F/Aug 10/d.Bowling Green/Not Known/6m/A.L. & Ellen Jones/b.Bowling Green/Lee W. Jones Uncle
Robt Jones/W/M/May 9/d.Bowling Green/Consumption/23y/James J. & Nancy Jones/Mechanic/ Unmarried/Lee W. Jones Brother
Charlie Pegg/W/M/June 10/d.Bowling Green/Killed on Rail Road/20y/Ed & Rebecca Pegg/b.Bowling Green/Mechanic/Unmarried/E. Pegg Father
E.R. Pegg/W/M/Oct 5/d.Bowling Green/Dysentery/28y/Ed & Rebecca Pegg/b.Bowling Green/Clerk/ Unmarried/E. Pegg Father
A.M. Glassell/W/M/__/d.Bowling Green/Com of D/80y/J.M. & C. Glassell/b.Albemarle/Doctor/ Fannie Glassell Wife

1889

Grover Ayres/W/M/Feb 10/Not Known/6m/Wm & Indiana Ayres/Wm Ayres Father
Bettie Samuel/W/F/Sept 8/Dropsy/26y/Henry & Frans Whitticoe [Whittaker] /Married/Wm Ayres Friend
Kittie Armistead/C/F/Apr 28/Poisoned/2y 6m/Waller & Bettie Armistead/W. Armistead Father
Albin Brown/W/M/Apr 6/Typhoid Fever/28y/A.H. & Sarah Brown/A.H. Brown Father
Arthur Brown/W/M/May 10/Typhoid Fever/26y/A.H. & Sarah Brown/A.H. Brown Father
Rose Baylor/C/F/Aug 8/Dysentary/12m/Walker & Nannie Baylor/Walker Baylor Father
No Name Bowie/C/F/Sept 17//Not Known/7d/Wm & Caroline Bowie/Wm Bowie Father
Allie L. Beasley/C/W/July 6/Dysentary/2m/B.B. & Laura Beasley/B.B. Beasley Father
Susie Carter/W/F/Sept 10/Dysentary/3m/E.P. & Mary Carter/E.P. Carter Father
Thomas Chinault/W/M/Jan 15/Not Known/7y/H. & Mary S. Chinault/H. Chinault Father
No Name Covington/W/N/May 5/Not Known/3d/A. & L. Covington/A. Covington Father
Susan Catlett/W/F/Mar 30/Old Age/84y/Catlett & Mary Thomas/Widower/John H. Catlett Son
Annie L. Dillard/W/F/July 10/Dysentery/27y/Jno & Julia Wharton/Married/C.E. Dillard Husband
Bessie Dillard/W/F/July 11/Dysentery/6y/C.E. & A.L. Dillard/C.E. Dillard Father
Henry Epps/C/M/Oct 10/Old Age/86y/Henry & R. Epps/Unmarried/James Epps Son
Jos T. Farish/W/M/Oct 10/Blood Poison/49y/Hiter & L. Farish/Married/K.R. Farish Brother
Robt Fells/W/M/Nov 10/Shot/17y/M. & M. Fells/Marshall Fells Father
Ann Freeman/C/F/July 10/Cancer/70y/Jack & E. Freeman/Servant/Andrew Ferguson Friend
No Name Gray/W/F/Nov 15/Not Known/5d/Jno F. & Lelia M. Gray/Jno F. Gray Father
Liddie Gatewood/C/F/Dec 8/Old Age/85y/Not Known/Married/Lou Gatewood Daughter
Obey Gatewood/C/M/Dec 9/Old Age/90y/Not Known/Farmer/Married/Lou Gatewood Daughter
Luther S. Houston/W/M/Apr 6/Not Known/14y/C.A. & M. Houston/C.A. Houston Father
Mary Jordan/W/F/July 6/Consumption/65y/E. & M. Richerson/Married/Wm Jordan Husband
Ben Jones/W/M/Feb 5/Consumption/40y/C.W. & M. Jones/Henry Jones Brother
Hannah Muscoe/C/F/May 7/Old Age/80y/Tarlton & Ann Upshaw/Widow/Lucian Loney Son
Frank Osborne/C/M/July 6/Gravel/65y/Skinker & Tulip Osborne/Widower/Wesley Osborne Son
Cath Pendleton/C/F/Mar 8/Consumption/29y/Jno & Susan Pendleton/Jno Pendleton Father
No Name Pugh/W/M/Mar 1/Not Known/20d/W.C. & Susan Pugh/W.C. Pugh Father
Mary Richrson/W/F/May 7/Consumption/67y/Jno & Mary Kay/E.M. Richerson Husband
Jno W. Rains/W/M/June 28/Not Known/1y 6m/Jno & E.G. Rains/Jno J. Rains Father
Martha Robb/C/F/Aug 10/Not Known/12y/James & Eliza Robb/James Robb Father
Martha Shepherd/C/F/Sept 18/Typhoid Fever/22y/Sam & M. Shepherd/Sam Shepherd Father
No Name Shepherd/C/M/Dec 8/Still Born/Gilbert & Sallie Shepherd/Gilbert Shepherd Father
No Name Johnson/C/F/May 10/3m/Father Not Known/Mary Johnson Mother

Lucy Wingfield/C/F/May 20/Consumption/12y/Wm & Mary Wingfield/Arch Samuel Friend
Ann Wingfield/C/F/June 10/Cancer/65y/Eliza & Jack Freeman/Servant/Widow/Wm Samuel Son
Joe Skinner/W/M/Jan 5/Grip/38y/Joe & M. Skinner/Married/Thos Skinner Brother
Rowe Callis/W/M/Aug 25/Shot/15y/Walter & Ann Calliss/C.R. Thornton Friend
Louisa Tignor/W/F/Aug 4/Consumption/32y/Theo & Sallie Taylor/J.H. Tignor Husband
No Name Tignor/W/F/Sept 11/Not Known/1m 15d/J. H. & Louisa Tignor/J.H. Tignor Father
Frances Taliaferro/C/F/Sept 8/Consumption/32y/Matt & Agnes Taliaferro/Servant/Matt Taliaferro Father
Geo Whittico [Whittaker]/M/Mar 24/Killed in Well/45y/M. & S. Whittico/Farmer/Married/R.D. Whittico Brother
Mary Wright/W/F/Sept 10/Com of D/65y/B. & M. Wright/Unmarried/B.B. Wright Nephew
Geo W. Anderson/C/M/Aug 10/d.Bowling Green/Dropsy/75y/Not Known/Laborer/Unmarried/ Anderson Baylor Friend
Malinda Miller/C/F/July 15/d.Bowling Green/Com of D/70y/Servant/Married/H. Miller Husband
Henry Morton/C/M/Oct 10/Consumption/72y/Not Known/Farmer/Married/Henry Upshaw Son-in-Law
Edmd Thornton/W/M/Nov 18/Old Age/82y/Peter & M. Thornton/Widower/Wm Chewning Son-in-Law
James L. Coleman/W/M/July/d.Bowling Green/Blood Poison/49y/Clayton & H. Coleman/Merchant/ Married/A.M. Coleman Wife
No Name/W/F/Nov 12/Broncitis/6m/John T. & Bettie L. Allen/Jno T. Allen Father
No Name/C/F/Dec 31/Unknown/7d/Ben & Eliza Benson/Ben Benson Father
William Beverly/C/M/Jan 17/Old Age/70y/Unknown/Laborer/Mrs. Beverly Wife
Ernest Blanton/W/M/Oct 10/Unknown/2y 6m/A.G. & Lucy Blanton/A.G. Blanton Father
Harrie Bowers/W/M/July 18/Typhoid Fever/20y/W.S. Bowers/W.S. Bowers Father
Nicey Brown/C/F/Sept 15/Unknown/60y/Unknown/Henry Brown Husband
Ida Burnett/C/F/Mar 1/La Grippe/1y/Wm & Ida Burnett/Ida Burnett Mother
Nannie Burnett/C/F/May 10/La Grippe/2y/Wm & Ida Burnett/Ida Burnett Wife
William Burnett/C/M/Jan 8/La Grippe/25y/Unknown/Ida Burnett Wife
John Carter/C/M/Feb 21/Scalded/2y/Edmund & Bettie Carter/Edmund Carter Father
No Name/C/F/Mar 7/Unknown/1d/Jas & Sophia Carter/Jas Carter Father
Emily Carlton/W/F/Apr 11/Consumption/69y/Jno & Nannie Carlton/Ambrose Carlton Husband
Arch T. Carneal/W/M/Apr 21/Pneumonia/60y/Thos & Nancy Carneal/J.A. Carneal Mother
Goodyear Clayborn/C/M/Dec 10/Unknown/19y/Unknown/Lewis Sharks Friend
Mary F. Clark/W/F/Dec 1/Heart Disease/52y/Jas & Mary Dickinson/A.J. Clark Husband
Marcellus Clark/C/M/Aug 17/La Grippe/47y/Unknown/Farmer/Mrs. Clark Wife
Ben Cloy/C/M/Dec 1/Old Age/70y/Unknown/Frank Cloy Son
Mary Coleman/C/F/Apr 1/La Grippe/22y/Richd & Kittie Coleman/Richd Coleman Father
No Name/C/M/May 30/Smothered/1m/Ella Coleman/Ella Coleman Mother
No Name/W/M/Apr 20/Unknown/4m/Jas B. & Ella Dabney/Jas B. Dabney Father
Sarah Davis/C/F/May 2/Typhoid Fever/56y/Unknown/Peter Davis Husband
Ann J. Donahoe/W/F/June 2/Consumption/54y/Thos & Mary Mitchell/Jas Donahoe Husband
Albert Durrett/W/M/Sept 26/Old Age/84y/J.J. & Polly Durrett/b.Spotsylvania/C.A. Baker Grandson
Beverly L. Dyson/W/M/Apr 26/d.Richmond/Killed by Cars/21y/Jas & Virginia Dyson/Jas W. Dyson Father
Richmond Ellyson/W/M/July 12/Unknown/Unknown/Lucy J. Ellyson Wife
George Flippo/W/M/Dec 15/Unknown/19y/Jas & Harriett Flippo/Jas Flippo Father
Howard Freeman/C/M/June 17/Unknown/2y/W.L. & Georgia Freeman/W.L. Freeman Father

Henrietta Gay/C/F/May 28/Pneumonia/25y/Dicis Gay/Wm Randof Friend
Mollie B. Gibson/W/F/July 7/Cholera Infantum/2m/Jas N. & Emma Gibson/Jas N. Gibson Father
Jno G. Goodwin/W/M/Aug 15/Typhoid Fever/29y/A.G. & Maria Goodwin/A.G. Goodwin Father
Maria H. Goodwin/W/F/Sept 7/Typhoid Fever/67y/H. & Maria Coleman/A.G. Goodwin Husband
Harriett Hackett/C/F/Sept 8/Malaria/18y/Brice & Ella Hackett/Brice Hackett Father
Ella Hagan/W/F/May 1/Scrofula/26y/Unknown/Elijah Klock Friend
No Name/C/F/July 7/Unknown/1d/Marcellus & Julie Holmes/Mr. Holmes Father
No Name/C/F/Mar 12/La Grippe/2m/Bartlett & Eliza Holmes/Bartlett Holmes Father
Nathaniel Holmes/C/M/Sept 23/Unknown/9y/Jas & Nancy Holmes/Jas Holmes Father
Wm H. Johnson/W/M/June 14/Typhoid Fever/59y/Robt & Sarah Johnson/Married/Robt B. Johnson Son
No Name/C/M/June 5/Unknown/10d/Nannie Johnson/C.C. Blanton Friend
Heywood Johnson/C/M/July 4/Killed/23y/Isaac & Jane Johnson/Isaac Johnson Father
John Johnson/C/M/June 27/Drowned/6y/Jas & Adline Johnson/James Johnson Father
No Name Johnson/C/M/July 3/Unknown/8d/Jas & Adline Johnson/James Johnson Father
Melvina Jackson/C/F/Sept 20/Heart Disease/60y/Unknown/Lewis Washington Friend
Susan Jones/W/F/July 12/Old Age/99y/Jno & Susan Madison/Chas Jones Son
Dudley Jones/W/M.July 12/Unknown/3m/Lewis & Catharine Jones/Lewis Jones Father
Geo W. Madison/W/M/Feb 26/Unknown/64y/Geo & Sallie Madison/Mrs Madison Wife
Geo W. Madison Jr/W/M/July 13/Killed by cars/26y/Geo W. & Sarah Madison/Sarah Madison Mother
Frank Marshall/C/M/Jan 29/Consumption/26y/Sallie A. Marshall/L.C. Pollard Friend
No Name/C/M/Sept 10/Unknown/10d/Adam & Josephine Meades/Adam Meades Father
Louisa Meads/C/F/Dec 10/Consumption/17y/Nelson & Harriett Meades/Richd Jackson Friend
Eliza Mills/C/F/Apr 20/Consumption/40y/Unknown/__/__/
Sarah Mines/C/F/Aug 1/Malarial Fever/13y/Saml & Agnes Mines/Jno Terry Friend
Clara Mines/C/F/May 25/Malarial Fever/16y/Dick & Susan Mines/Dick Mines Father
Barbara H. Morris/W/F/Feb 4/Old Age/80y/Mary & Al Dickinson/Jas H. Morris Son
Thos E. Philips/W/M/Dec 18/Dropsy/75y/Lewis & Elizabeth Philips/Catharine Philips Wife
Joseph Quash/C/M/June 30/Asthma/48y/Isabella Quash/Jas Quash Son
Ciller Roane/C/F/Mar 25/Scrofula/12y/Jno & Mary Roane/Alex Dodson Friend
Mary Roane/C/F/Mar 10/Malarial Fever/__/Minerva Gaphney/Alex Didson Friend
Robert Roots/C/M/Apr 15/Consumption/17y/Robt & Lettie Roots/Robt Roots Father
Lula Sacra/W/F/Nov 25/Typhoid Fever/15y/Chas & Ann E. Sacra/Chas Sacra Father
Clarence Samuel/W/M/May 20/Mumps/2y/Eugene & Bettie Samuel/Eugene Samuel Father
Paul J. Seale/W/M/May 15/Unknown/9m/Jno & Sarah L. Seale/Jno Seale Father
Frances E. Seale/W/F/May 29/Consumption/66y/Unknown/Jno Seale Son
No Name/C/M/Feb 14/Unknown/30d/Mary Roane/Richd Smith Friend
Lucy S. Southworth/W/F/May 8/Unknown/72y/Jas & Elizabeth Handyman/O.W. Southworth Son
Mack Turpin/C/M/Oct 10/Paralysis/60y/Unknown/Gilbert Turpin Son
Waller T. Turpin/C/M/Feb 20/Unknown/18y/Unknown/Gilbert Turpin
Annie Taylor/W/F/May 31/Consumption/28y/Christopher & C. Collins/Woodford Taylor Husband
Ellen Taylor/C/F/June 1/Old Age/90y/Unknown/Isaac Taylor Son
James Thornton/C/M/Oct 9/Unknown/9m/Jas & Annie Thornton/Jas Thornton Father
Richd J. Tunstall/W/M/Dec 16/Liver Compliant/12y/L.H. & M.E. Tunstall/L.H. Tunstall Father
John Terry/C/M/July 16/Pneumonia/23y/James Terry/C. Carter Friend
Geo B. Washington/W/M/Aug 3/Unknown/60y/Jno & Ann Washington/Farmer/Mrs Washington

Wife
Delila Walker/C/F/Oct 20/Typhoid Fever/22y/Lewis & Martha Walker/Lewis Walker Father
W.J. Welton/W/M/Oct 12/Unknown/66y/Saml & Lucy Welton/b.New York/Farmer/Married/H.C. Welton Son
Robert Woolfolk/W/M/June 7/Old Age/82y/Unknown/Farmer/Married/W.A. Woolfolk Son
Carlton Woolfolk/W/M/Sept 14/Flux/11y/__/__/W.A. Woolfolk

1890

Stanley M. Brooks/W/M/Nov 29/Croup/3m 3d/Richd & Alice Brooks/Unmarried/Richd Brooks Father
Jos Barlow/W/M/June 10/Not Known/2y/John & Elizth Barlow/John Barlow Father
Mary Carter/W/F/May 16/Consumption/32y/R.E. & May Brooks/__ Husband
__ Covington/W/M/May 25/Not Known/6d/Albert & Lavenia Covington/Albert Covington Father
Susan Catlett/W/F/Mar 30/Old Age/84y/Catlett & Mary Thomas/Widow/__ Son
Mary Caynor/W/F/Nov 2/Not Known/16y/John & Mary Caynor/John Caynor Father
Edmond Dillard/W/M/June 4/Old Age/75y/Geo & Va Dillard/Farmer/Widower/__ Son
W.T. Dunn/W/M/June 12/Not Known/61y/Andrew & H. Dunn/Widower/__ Son
Saml Gordon/W/M/Aug 4/Old Age/86y/Sam & Susan Gordon/Widower/__ Son
Bettie Jordan/W/F/Aug 10/Cancer/40y/B.A. & B. Jordan/__ Husband
__ Pugh/W/M/Mar 30/Not Known/20d/W.C. & Susan Pugh/W.C. Pugh Father
T.H. Richerson/W/M/Sept 14/Consumption/55y/Reu B. & M. Richerson/Farmer/Unmarried/__ Brother
Lissie L. Syrles/W/F/June 10/Not Known/4m/L.L. & Lucy Syrles/L.L. Syrles Father
Oteria C. Shuman/W/F/June 24/Consumption/47y/Wm & Ellen R. Page/[C.A. Shuman]Husband
James Thomas/W/M/Aug 10/Old Age/80y/Not Known/Widower/__ Son
Saml Gordon/W/M/Aug 19/Old Age/86y/Not Known/Widower/__ Son
Ida Houston/W/F/Oct 19/Measssles/1y 2m/Geo S. & Mary Houston/Geo S. Houston Father
Geo White/W/M/Aug 20/Consumption/25y/L.B. & Eliza White/Unmarried/L.B. White Father
Ed Thornton/W/M/Nov 17/Com of Disease/82y/Peter & Mary Thornton/Widower/John W. Covington
Wm B. Carter/W/M/July 6/Com of Disease/71y/Wm Carter/Widower/__ Son
Elizth B. Peyton/W/F/Nov 16/Com of Disease/45y/Valentine & Elizth Peyton/Unmarried/__ Sister
Edmonia Ware/W/F/July 3/Not Known/9m/S.S. & Elizth Ware/S.S. Ware Father
Kittie Armistead/C/F/Apr 28/Not Known/2y/J.W. & Bettie Armistead/J.W. Armistead Father
Joe Bates/C/M/Feb 10/Grip/35y/Jim & Mary Bates/Laborer/Unmarried/Jim Bates Father
Martha Buckner/C/F/Aug 7/Not Known/45y/Miston M. Jackson/Married/__ Buckner Husband
Lillie B. Byrd/C/F/Sept 11/Not Known/8m/Tazewell & Anna Byrd/Tazewell Byrd Father
Jack Banks/C/M/Aug 2/Paralysis/55y/Jack & Va Banks/Laborer/__ Wife
Wise Green/C/M/Dec 18/Consumption/35y/Fannie Broaddus/Laborer/Unmarried/__ Sister
Laura Chiles/C/F/May 28/Not Known/8m/Steven & Liza Chiles/Steven Chiles Father
Geo W. Anderson/C/M/Sept 6/Consumption/75y/Not Known/Unmarried/Robt Carter
Lula Green/C/F/June 10/Not Known/1m/Silas & Eliza Green/Silas Green Father
Thomas Monroe/C/M/Feb 9/Not Known/4y/Festus & Jane Monroe/Festus Monroe Father
__ Parker/C/F/Mar 15/Unknown/1m 6d/J.E. & Zela Parker/J.E. Parker Father
Mary Robinson/C/F/Aug 4/Child birth/53y/Gabriel & Eliza Monroe/__ Husband
Chris Robinson/C/M/Dec 10/Burnt/8y/Sue Robinson/Sam Robinson Father

Dallas Saunders/C/M/Oct 16/Consumption/45y/Danl & Lucy Saunders/Unmarried/Danl Saunders Father
Wm Smith/C/M/July 4/Not Known/2m/Wm & Lucy Smith/Wm Smith Father
Bettie Ware/C/F/Oct 10/Not Known/1m/John & Bettie Ware/John Ware Father
Jack Washington/C/M/Aug 10/Consumption/60y/Not Known/__
Bettie Wright/C/F/Feb 10/Pneumonia/60y/Not Known/__ Husband
Thos N. Young/C/M/Sept 6/Croup/5y/Wm & Dolly Young/Wm Young Father
__ Robinson/C/M/Aug 4/Still born/John & Mary Robinson/John Robinson Father
Wm Clark/C/Oct 20/Not Known/14d/Wm & Sallie Clark/Wm Clark Father
__ Dodson/C/M/Nov 1/Not Known/21d/Robt & Sallie Dodson/Robt Dodson Father
Henry Epps/C/M/Oct 4/Paralysis/56y/Henry & Rebecca Epps/Widower/__ Son
Robt Flood/C/M/Dec 20/Not Known/10d/Allen & Mary Flood/Allen Flood Father
Taylor Gordon/C/M/Nov 3/Not Known/W. & Mary Gordon/W. Gordon Father
Danl Goode/C/M/Dec 20/Unknown/10m/Danl & Jane Goode/Danl Goode Father
John Hoomes/C/M/Dec 15/Not Known/9m/Lindsey & Sallie Hoomes/Lindsey Hoomes Father
Martha Robb/C/F/Aug/Not Known/12y/James & Eliza Robb/James Robb Father
Stafford Rich/C/M/Aug 17/Lock Jaw/50y/Mary Rich/Widower/__ Son
Wm Campbell/C/M/Jan 10/Not Known/55y/Not Known/Widower/__ Son
Mary Anderson/W/F/June 12/Unknown/60y/Jos R. & Rachel Dabney/Ben Anderson
Marcia Anderson/C/F/Aug 16/Child Birth/40y/Unknown/Thos Anderson Husband
Susan Austin/W/F/June 6/Cholera Infantum/3y/W.R. & Caroline Austin/W.R. Austin Father
Mary E. Baughn/W/F/June 10/Whooping Cough/5y/A.S. & Maria E. Baughn/A.S. Baughn Father
Callie Brown/C/F/June 5/Unknown/20y/Lewis & Mildred Washington/Sam Brown Husband
No Name/W/M/Feb 16/Unknown/1d/W.W. & Eddie Burruss/W.W. Burruss Father
No Name/W/M/Feb 16/Unknown/1d/W.W. & Eddie Burruss/W.W. Burruss Father [listed twice, apparently twins]
John T. Blanton/W/M/Sept 15/Unknown/68y/Richd & Mary Blanton/Farmer/A.G. Blanton Son
Marcellus Burnett/C/M/Mar 10/Unknown/5y/Wm & Ida Burnett/Wm Burnett Father
Ida Burnett/C/F/July 8/Unknown/35y/Unknown/Wm Burnett Husband
Lucy A. Chiles/W/F/Mar/Unknown/79y/Unknown/J.E. Chiles Son
A.C. Chiles/W/F/Mar/Unknown/40y/Unknown/J.E. Chiles Husband
E.W. Chiles/W/F/Mar/Unknown/23y/J.E. & A.C. Chiles/J.E. Chiles Father
Wm D. Chinault/W/M/May 9/Typhoid Dysentery/3y/J.C. & Emma Chinault/J.C. Chinault Father
Tena Coleman/C/F/Aug 3/Consumption/23y/Erasmus & Martha Coleman/Erasmus Coleman Father
Wm B. Coleman/C/M/Dec 26/Diptheria/3y/J. & Lincoln Coleman/Jack Coleman Father
No Name/W/F/Apr 27/Unknown/1m/S.A. & Julia Coleman/S.A. Coleman Father
Moses Coleman/C/M/Sept 1/Unknown/65y/Unknown/T.H. Blanton Friend
Charles Dangerfield/C/M/Feb 13/Consumption/22y/Chas & Rose Dangerfield/Chas Dangerfield Father
Russell H. Day/W/M/July 3/Malaria Fever/35y/Frank & Mary J. Day/Sam Day Brother
Susan Dickinson/W/F/May 8/Unknown/64y/Washington & E. Dickinson/Thos H. Jones Friend
Washington Derrycott/C/M/Dec 20/Consumptin/30y/Louisa Derrycott/Laborer/Thornton Dickinson Friend
Jane M. Donahoe/W/F/Dec 23/Pneumonia/62y/Unknown/George D. Miller Friend
Roland L. Dunn/W/M/Nov/Unknown/5m/Willie & Edmonia Dunn/Willie Dunn Father
No Name/W/M/Apr 26/Measles/13d/H.H. & A.M. Dyson/H.H. Dyson Father
No Name/W/M/June/Cholera Infantum/8m/C.L. & Nannie Durrett/C.L. Durrett Father
Emma G. DuVal/W/F/Nov 25/Pneumonia/43y/Montague & Elizabeth Abrams.James DuVal Husband

Joseph Fells/C/M/Dec 6/Unknown/6y/Sarah Fells/Lewis Fells
Albert Fergerson/C/M/Aug 2/Unknown/18y/Ben & Violet Fergerson/Ben Fergerson Father
E.F. Flagg/W/M/Dec 26/Unknown/57y/E.T. & E.T.[sic] Flagg/Farmer/Mrs. Flagg Wife
Littleton Flippo/W/M/July 20/Unknown/24y/Littleton & Sarah Flippo/Merchant/A.C. Flippo Brother
William Fox/C/M/July 1/Old Age/70y/Unknown/Farmer/Robt Fox Son
Cora D. Gayle/W/F/Feb 14/Unknown/1m/Jno T. & A. Gayle/John T. Gayle Father
Nancy Gaynes/C/F/Sept 7/Unknown/__/Lucy Cooper/Wm Gaynes Husband
Willie Green/C/M/Feb 10/Pneumonia/3m/Jordan & Sallie Green/Jordan Green Father
Tarleton Harris/W/M/June 13/Typhoid Fever/64y/Unknown/Mary E. Harris Wife
Sallie D. Hill/W/F/Aug 6/Heart Disease/38y/Wm P. & Ann E. Richerson/A.V. Hill Husband
L. Humphries/W/M/June 28/Teething/1y/S.J. & E.L. Humphries/S.J. Humphries Father
No Name/W/F/Aug 16/Unknown/1d/T. & Lizzie Hunter/Taliaferro Hunter Father
Amy Johnson/C/F/Mar 21/Scrofula/55y/Unknown/Chas Johnson Husband
Sam Lewis/C/M/May 10/Old Age/65y/Unknown/Fleming Lewis Son
Blanche Lewis/C/F/Nov 4/Unknown/12y/Temple & Sophia Lewis/Temple Lewis Father
Etta Madison/W/F/June 25/Cancer/45y/John & Mary Cox/Jas T. Madison Husband
George Mills/C/M/Dec 30/Typhoid Fever/12y/Pleasant Mills/Wm Dimue Friend
Wallis Moore/C/M/Feb 25/Pneumonia/11m/J.M. & Sallie Moore/J.M. Moore Father
Julia A. Mont/C/F/June 6/Unknown/1y/Jno & Mary Mont/Jno Mont Father
Alfred Paling/W/M/July 28/Mumps/21y/George & Caroline Paling/Geo Paling Father
Willie Parker/C/M/Apr 1/Brain Fever/8y/Marshall Parker/M. Parker Father
John Parr/W/M/Jan 10/Old Age/84y/Unknown/J.H. Parr Son
Mary F. Perkins/W/F/Apr 19/Typhoid Fever/24y/Montgomery & Margaret Cobb/Montgomery Cobb Father
Bristoe Robinson/C/M/Feb/Old Age/70y/Unknown/Wallis Robinson Son
Rachel Robinson/C/F/Feb 8/Typhoid Fever/32y/Bristoe & Bettie Robinson/Wallis Robinson Brother
Dollie Robinson/C/F/Feb 20/Typhoid Fever/31y/Bristoe & Bettie Robinson/Wallis Robinson Brother
Josephine Robinson/C/F/Sept 9/Consumption/20y/Lewis & Anna Robinson/Lewis Robinson Father
Moses Robinson/C/M/Dec 26/Accident/16y/Lewis & Anna Robinson/Lewis Robinson Father
Ella Robinson/C/F/Nov 20/Burnt to death/3y/Wm B. & Caroline Robinson/Wm B. Robinson Father
Louisa Rock/C/F/Apr 6/Cancer/67y/Unknown/John Rock Husband
James L. Sale/W/M/June/Cholera Infantum/8m/Wm T. & Etta Sale/Wm T. Sale Father
A.S. Samuel/W/M/Nov 26/Consumption/26y/Wm M. & Cornelia Samuel/Farmer/Robert Samuel Uncle
Frank Saunders/C/M/June 25/Old Age/80y/Unknown/Laborer/Mrs. Saunders Wife
Sallie Smith/C/F/Feb 29/La Grippe/28y/Moses & Minerva Gaphney/Rich Smith Husband
Margaret Smith/C/F/Sept 10/Unknown/24y/Jno & Leanna Smith/John Smith Father
No Name/W/M/Sept 3/Unknown/1d/Chas & Goldie Southworth/Chas Southworth Father
Mary Taliaferro/C/F/Apr 1/La Grippe/2y/Jas & Maria Taliaferro/James Taliaferro Father
Fannie Taliaferro/C/F/Apr 14/La Grippe/3m/Jas & Maria Taliaferro/Jas Taliaferro Father
Alice Taliaferro/C/F/Apr 12/Unknown/21d/Walker & Patsy Taliaferro/Walker Taliaferro Father
John Taliaferro/C/M/May 16/Dropsy/2y/Walker & Patsy Taliaferro/ Walker Taliaferro Father
Allie Taylor/C/M/Dec 10/Unknown/7m/Wm & Elizabeth Taylor/Wm Taylor Father
Lloyd P. Thompson/C/M/June 8/Cholera Infantum/1y/Elias & Silvia Thompson Father
Peter Todd/C/M/Dec 11/Burnt/5y/Peter & Josephine Todd/Peter Todd Father
Charles Weatheress/C/M/May 2/Teething/2y/Jno & E. Weatheress/John Weatheress Father

Jack Williams/C/M/Sept 8/Accident/14y/Ancel & Martha Williams/Ancel Williams Father
Margarett Williams/C/F/Dec 9/Cholera Infantum/5y/Ancel & Matilda Williams/Ancel Williams Father
Irene Wright/C/F/Sept 22/Unknown/10m/Jas & Mary Wright/James Wright Father
No Name/C/M/Feb 10/Unknown/1m/Thos P. & Bettie Wright/Thos P. Wright Father
No Name/W/M/Sept 3/Unknown/3d/Jno V. & Fannie Wright/John V. Wright Father
No Name/W/F/Aug 28/Unknown/24d/E.W. & S.L. Young/E.W. Young Father
John T. Fox/C/M/Sept 16/Unknown/40y/Unknown/W.E. Wright Friend

1891

A.B. Adams/W/M/Mar 28/Pneumonia/84y/Thos & Annie Adams/Farmer/Geo Adams Son
Sam Alsop/C/M/Dec 10/Old Age/90y/Unknown/Farmer/Josh Alsop
Olin Arnold/W/M/Sept 30/Shot/14y/Robt B. & Lucy Arnold/R.B. Arnold Father
Matilda Bazell/C/F/Jan 17/Congestion/45y/Unknown/John Bazell Husband
Lucy E. Beverly/C/F/May 8/Burnt/18y/Robt & Bettie Beverly/Robt Beverly Father
No Name/W/M/Aug 15/Unknown/1m 14d/J.H. & Maud Blackley/J.H. Blackley Father
No Name/W/F/Aug 30/Unknown/1m 21d/J.H. & Maud Blackley/J.H. Blackley Father
John J. Blanton/W/M/Sept 1/Dropsy/69y/Wm & Ann Blanton/J.A. Blanton Son
Sianna Brown/C/F/Jan 26/Child Birth/36y/Susan Brown/William Brown Husband
Mack Brown/C/M/May 10/Measles/5y/Geo & Sophia Brown/Geo Brown Father
Ida Burnett/C/F/Sept 9/Consumption/30y/Wm & Sarah Holmes/Wm Holmes Father
Ida May Carter/C/F/Nov 15/Unknown/10m/Robt & Addie Carter/Robt Carter Father
Lydia A. Carson/W/F/July 5/Blood Poison/62y/Unknown/Cyrus Carson Father
Jennette Carneal/W/F/Sept 21/Typhoid Fever/21y/A.T. & Mildred Carneal/Arch Carneal Father
Ida Cannon/W/F/Sept 9/Unknown/30y/Unknown/G.H. Cannon Husband
Mary E. Coleman/W/F/May 21/Unknown/77y/Unknown/Jno G. Coleman Husband
Kittie Coleman/C/F/Oct 26/Consumption/49y/Unknown/Richd Coleman Husband
T.S. Davenport/W/M/July 11/Old Age/80y/Unknown/b.Buckingham Co/J.H. Davenport Son
Washington Derrycott/C/M/Nov 10/Consumption/37y/Unknown/Ella Dickinson Friend
Joseph Dickinson/C/M/July 9/Unknown/4y/Thornton & Ella Dickinson/Ella Dickinson Mother
James Donahoe/W/M/July 5/d.Ruther Glen/Unknown/4m/Jas & Mary Donahoe/Jas Donahoe Father
No Name/W/F/Aug/Unknown/3m/Chas & Nannie Durrett/Chas Durrett Father
Charlie Durrett/W/M/Mar/Unknown/2y/Jno F. & Edna Durrett/Jno F. Durrett Father
Dora Fox/C/F/July 3/Dropsy/35y/Unknown/Lolly Fox Husband
Joseph Fox/C/M/Sept 20/Malaria Fever/20y/Kate & Peter Fox/Peter Fox Father
Abram Freeman/C/M/Feb 12/Consumption/24y/Chas & Jane Freeman/Danl Freeman Friend
No Name/C/F/Nov 10/Unknown/1m/Walker & Emma Foies/Walker Foies Father
No Name/W/F/Mar 20/Unknown/2d/Jas H. & M.D. Garnett/Jas H. Garnett Father
No Name/W/F/Dec 24/Unknown/9d/Jas B. & Dolly Gatewood/Jas B. Gatewood Father
No Name/C/M/Apr/Unknown/2m/Lucy Grascow/Warner Glascow Grandfather
Maria Goodwin/W/F/July 13/Inflamation of Bowels/2y/Wm W. & Bettie Goodwin/W.W. Goodwin Father
B. Green/C/F/June 1/Burnt/2y/Elaine Green/Warner Glascow Friend
R.C. Hackett/W/M/Sept/Unknown/70y/Unknown/Farmer/Married/F.T. Bibb Friend
Henry J. Holmes/C/M/Apr 9/Consumption/17y/Bartlett & Eliza Holmes/Farmer/Married/Bartlett Holmes Father

Charles Hopkins/C/M/Sept 10/Killed/65y/Unknown/Farmer/Kittie Hopkins Wife
C.M. Hunter/W/M/Sept 10/Consumption/__/Unknown/Farmer/L.B. Hunter Wife
Tina Johnson/C/F/Oct 15/Old Age/80y/Unknown/Married/Aron Godfrey Friend
Charlotte Jones/C/F/Aug 2/Consumption/28y/Daniel Jones/Danl Jones Father
Lena Jones/C/F/Sept 9/La Grippe/3y/Daniel Jones/Danl Jones Father
William Key/C/M/Feb 9/Unknown/9d/Pleasant & Mary Key/Pleasant Key Father
Eliza Lewis/C/F/July 15/Consumption/26y/Calvin Lewis Husband
Adison Lewis/C/M/Aug/Consumption/64y/Unknown/Louisa Co/Josh Alsop Brother
Lulie W. Long/W/F/Aug 18/Dysentery/1y/Jno L. & Isabella Long/Jno L. Long Father
Wm F. Luck/W/M/Aug/Consumption/68y/Sam & Maria Luck/Mrs. Luck Wife
Wm K. Luck/W/M/Apr 3/Measles/50y/J.T. & Nicey Luck/W.T. Luck Son
Elvira A. Luck/W/F/Nov 12/Typhoid Fever/51y/L.L. & Mary A. Terrell/W.T. Luck Son
Sophia J. Luck/W/F/July 16.Bronchitis/63y/Garland & Lucy Hargrave/Geo P. Luck Husband
Wm H. Mackay/W/M/June 16/Dysentery/1y 4m/Henry & Miriam Mackay/Henry Mackay Father
Frances Madison/W/F/Sept 16/Typhoid Fever/52y/Unknown/Jos S. Madison Son
Ida Madison/W/F/Sept 9/Typhoid Fever/35y/Geo & Frances Madison/Jos S. Madison Brother
Thomas Madison/W/M/Dec 15/Old Age/72y/Unknown/Wm Madison Son
John Meads/C/M/Feb 10/Dropsy/19y/Lewis & Kissie Meads/Lewis Meads Father
George Miles/C/M/Jan 1/Typhoid Disentery/13y/Pleasant Miles/Wm Dimue Friend
Judie Monroe/C/F/July 20/Consumption/21y/Violet Washington/Willis Monroe Husband
Percy Monroe/C/M/July 20/Unknown/3m/Willis & Judie Monroe/Willis Monroe Father
Willie C. Moore/C/F/[sic]Nov 2/Burnt/4y/J.M. & Sallie Moore/J.M. Moore Father
Mary E. Mosby/C/F/Feb 27/La Grippe/30y/Unknown/Henry Nelson Friend
Mary E. Noel/W/F/July 16/Unknown/30y?/B.F. & Emma Noel/B.F. Noel Father
Chas Pendleton/C/M/Aug 6/Typhoid Fever/21y/Jesse & Anna Pendleton/Jesse Pendleton Father
Jesse Pendleton/C/M/July 21/__/19y/Jesse & Anna Pendleton/Jesse Pendleton Father
No Name/C/F/June 10/Unknown/1d/Thornton & Mattie Roots/Thornton Roots Father
No Name/W/M/Aug 8/Cholera Infantum/3m/W.T. & Etta Sale/W.T. Sale Father
Russell A. Samuel/W/M/Jan 15/Consumption/22y/Noel & Cornelia Samuel/Farmer/Robt A. Samuel
   Uncle
Joseph M. Seay/W/M/Sept 30/Heart Disease/77y/F. & Elizabeth Seay/Farmer/E.Y. Seay Wife
Lizzie Scripture/W/F/Nov 20/Child Birth/75y/James & Fannie Ponton/Married/N.C. Scripture
   Father-in-Law
John Shackleford/W/M/Jan 9/Unknown/15y/Chas & Mary Shackleford/Chas Shackleford Father
Isla Taylor/C/F/Mar 9/La Grippe/5y/Wm & Rachel Taylor/Wm Taylor Father
No Name Taylor/C/M/Mar 3/Unknown/5d/Wm & Rachel Taylor/Wm Taylor Father
Anna Taylor/C/F/July 5/Unknown/5m/Chas & Susan Taylor/Chas Taylor Father
Alberta Taylor/C/F/Oct 9/Unknown/25y/Spencer Taylor/Spencer Taylor Father
T.F. Terry/W/M/May 12/Inflamation of Bowels/63y/Unknown/Mrs. Terry Wife
Annie Roots/C/F/Dec 4/Unknown/76y/Edmond & F. Banks/Geo Tilman Friend
Nannie H. Tribble/W/F/Dec 11/Unknown/2y/J.C. & E.T. Tribble/J.C. Tribble Father
Jack Williams/C/M/Sept 10/Killed at Mill/14y/Ans & Matilda Williams/Ans Williams Father
Margaret Williams/C/F/Jan 1/Measles/5y/Ans & Matilda Williams/Ans Williams Father
John Williams/C/M/Apr 10/Measles/3y/Ans & Matilda Williams/Ans Williams Father
No Name/C/M/Sept 9/Unknown/4m/Thos P. & Bettie Wright/Thos P. Wright Father
Rosa Wright/C/F/Aug 15/Unknown/2y/Martha E. Wright/M.E. Wright Mother
Fannie Young/W/F/Sept 4/Paralysis/15y/Jas & Nannie Young/Jas Southworth Friend
Geo W. Allport/W/M/Aug 10/Com of Disease/50y/__ Allport/Farmer/Lucy Allport Wife

V. Beazley/W/F/May 10/Not Known/50y/W. & M. Wright/W. Beazley Husband
Susan Caynor/W/F/Sept 10/Typhoid Fever/15y/Jno & M.F. Caynor/Jno Caynor Father
Martha Green/W/F/June 17/Consumption/41y/R. & M. Richards/T.W. Green Husband
Thos D. Kidd/W/M/Dec 10/Apoplexy/60y/Thos & H. Kidd/Farmer/Unmarried/M.L. Kidd Sister
Jno L. Motley/W/M/Mar 5/Consumption/60y/Nathl & R. Motley/Farmer/Maria L. Motley Wife
Mary Pitts/W/F/May 8/Consumption/40y/Thos & M. Gouldin/C.N. Pitts Husband
Dan Pitts/W/M/__/Com of Disease/58y/S. & M. Pitts/Merchant/S.E. Pitts Son
Mary Silva/W/F/May 10/Consumption/45y/N. & M. Pitts/Farmer/Frank Silva Husband
Lucy Sterne/W/F/Jan 15/Consumption/69y/Wm & A. Murray/Fran Sterne Husband
E.G. Thornton/W/M/Aug 20/Consumption/39y/Henry & M. Thornton/Farmer/E.L.Thornton Wife
L.T. Vaughan/W/F/Sept 16/Not Known/2m 1d/J.W. & E. Vaughan/J.W. Vaughan Father
No Name Vaughan/W/F/July 18/Still born/Robt & L. Vaughan/Robt Vaughan Father
Eva Wright/W/F/Dec 30/Not Known/14d/J.H. & Sallie Wright/J.H. Wright Father
Willie Wright/W/M/June 10/Not Known/__/J. Henry & Nora Wright/J.H. Wright Father
James Wright/W/M/Nov 10/Unknown/2m 20d/Sam & Ruth Wright/Sam Wright Father
Reu Whittico/W/M/Dec 20/Not Known/1m 4d/H. & A. Whittico/H. Whittico Father
Ellen Watts/W/F/Sept 1/Not Known/2m 14d/Wm & Elizth Watts/Wm Watts Father
Jno W. Woolfolk/W/M/June/Com of Disease/Jordan & Elizth Woolfolk/Farmer/Lucy Woolfolk Wife
Jno J. Tennent/W/M/June/Pluracy/69y/__/Unmarried/G.L. Frazier Brother-in-Law
Maude Taylor/W/F/May 18/Old Age/80y/Jordan & L. Taylor/Robt Taylor Husband/Geo Taylor Son
Lina Baker/W/F/__/d.Bowling Green/__/__/C.L. & L. Baker/C.L. Baker Father
Mollie Throm/W/F/Oct 18/Chills/20y/G.H. & M.E. Throm/G.H. Throm Father
Wm G. Coghill/W/M/June 10/d.Bowling Green/Com of Disease/9m/ M.G. & L.L. Coghill/W.G. Coghill Father
James A. Chapman/W/M/Apr/d.Bowling Green/Heart Disease/56y/Wm & Judy Chapman/Dentist/ Ida Chapman Wife
Martha Richerson/W/F/May 20/Com of Disease/75y/Not Known/Wm Richerson Husband/J.S. Pavey Son-in-Law
Mary Anderson/C/F/Nov 30/Com of Disease/65y/Not Known/Page Anderson Husband
Kitty Armistead/C/F/Apr 28/Com of Disease/2y/Geo & Kittie Armistead/Waller Armistead Father
J. Bates/C/M/Mar 15/Pluracy/33y/James & Mary Bates/Laborer/Henry Bates Brother
Sarah Byrd/C/F/Mar 10/Not Known/2m/Ottwa & Clara Byrd/Ottway Byrd Father
No Name Bundy/C/F/July 15/__/1m 5d/Burkett & Sue Bundy Burkett Bundy Father
Robt Banks/C/M/Sept 16/3m 1d/A. & L. Banks/A. Banks Father
Alex Brown/C/M/Dec 16/5m 1d/Alex & M. Brown/Alex Brown Father
Emma Coleman/C/F/Oct 22/__/5m 3d/D. & Judy Coleman/Dick Coleman Father
William Chiles/C/M/Dec 20/__/2m 10d/Wm & Pattie Chiles/Wm Chiles Father
Nora Fox/C/F/Dec 25/__/2m 9d/Folly & [illeg] Fox/Folly Fox Father
Sarah A. Fortune/C/F/June 20/Killed by Lightning/31y/James & V. Carter/A.B. Fortune Husband
Georgeanna Gaines/C/F/Apr 10/Com of Disease/55y/Not Known/Ned Gaines Husband
James Gouldin/C/M/Dec 20/Not Known/2m 25d/H. & E. Gouldin
Stephen Hill/C/M/Dec 25/Pluracy/4y/Padro & Rose Hill/Padro Hill Father
Henry Jeter/C/M/Nov 10/Not Known/50y/James & M. Jeter/Farmer/Married/James Jeter Father
Lucy Jackson/C/F/Dec 6/Pluracy/7m/Andrew & S. Jackson/Andrew Jackson Father
Susan Johnson/C/F/Dec 2/Not Known/2m 1d/Ned & Bertie Johnson/Ned Johnson Father

No Name Johnson/C/M/Dec 18/Not Known/8d/Sam & M. Johnson/Sam Johnson Father
Eva Lewis/C/F/Dec 14/Not Known/__/Hiter & Kate Lewis/Hiter Lewis Father
Isaac Lawson/C/M/Aug 10/Old Age/105y/Not Known/L. Leann Lawson Wife
William Moore/C/M/Dec 14/Not Known/14d/Not Known/Geo Moore Father
Alice Puller/C/F/Dec 10/Not Known/1y/W. & J. Puller/W. Puller Father
Geo T. Richerson/C/M/Oct 10/Pluracy/5y/G.T. & M. Richerson/Geo T. Richerson Father
Lewis Robinson/C/M/Oct 15/Pluracy/5m 10d/Nelson & L. Robinson/Nelson Robinson Father
Sam Roy/C/M/Aug 10/Not Known/3m/Naee & Bertie Roy/Naee Roy Father
James Stewart/C/M/July 17/Not Known/__/Ned & Ellen Stewart/Ned Stewart Father
Jno Schools/C/M/Oct 8/Pluracy/6m/Robt & Mary Schools/Robt Schools Father
Allen Turner/C/M/Sept 1/Not Known/5d/Allen & Sarah Turner/Allen Turner Father
Jno Young/C/M/Oct 5/Not Known/8y 6d/Wm & Dolly Young/Wm Young Father
Henry Young/C/M/June 10/Old Age/80y/Not Known/Farmer/Muir Young Son
Edwd Brooks/W/M/Oct 20/Not Known/1m 2d/C.H. & Ella Brooks/C.H. Brooks Father
Thos Chenault/W/M/Oct 25/Not Known/1m 10d/Thos & Sallie Chenault/Thos Chenault Father
James Carter/W/M/Dec 30/Not Known/1m 14d/Henry & Nora Carter/Henry Carter Father
H.S. Farish/W/M/June 15/Consumption/70y/G.B. & S. Farish/G.B. Farish Son
Alborn Gray/W/M/Aug 10/Not Known/4m/S.H. & M. Gray/S.H. Gray Father
Bazil Gordon/W/M/Dec 19/Cancer/84y/Bazil & S. Gordon/E.M. Gordon Wife
M.L. Kidd/W/F/Nov 6/Cancer/50y/A. & M. Kidd/L.T. Kidd Brother
No Name Mills/W/M/July 15/Still born/B.F. & Elizth Mills/B.F. Mills Father
No Name Parker/W/F/July 5/Still born/W.W. & Mollie Parker/W.W. Parker Father
E.M. Richerson/W/M/June 10/Com of Disease/65y/E.& M. Richerson/Widower/Ira Richerson
  Brother
Mary E. Throm/W/F/Dec 21/Paralysis/53y/Ben & M. Skinker/G.H. Throm Husband
No Name Sale/Aug 5/Still born/W.J. & M. Sale/W.J. Sale Father
Mary F. Owens/W/F/Nov 1/Kidney Disease/62y/Not Known/W.P. Owens Husband
Edmonia Ware/W/F/July 31/Teething/9m/S.S. & M. Ware/S.S. Ware Father
No Name Chiles/C/F/Aug 10/Still born/Wm & Ella Chiles/Wm Chiles Father
No Name Dodson/C/F/June 15/Still born/Robt & Sallie Dodson/Robt Dodson Father
No Name Johnson/C/M/Nov 8/Still born/Arthur & M. Johnson/A. Johnson Father
Jno Massey/C/M/Feb 10/Consumptin/60y/Not Known/Farmer/Mary Massey Wife
Wash Street/C/F/Mar 14/Not Known/4d/W. & A. Street/W. Street Father
No Name Thornton/C/M/Dec 28/Not Known/__/Wade & Sallie Thornton/Wade Thornton Father
Wm Campbell/C/M/Jan 10/d.Port Royal/Not Known/55y/Not Known/Laborer/Single/Wm Lucas
  Friend
Carrie P. Broaddus/W/F/July 7/d.Bowling Green/Consumption/36y/Fred B. Power/b.York County/
  Rev A. Broaddus Jr Husband

1892

Callie Shuman/W/F/Oct 19/__/8d/C.A. & M. Shuman/C.A. Shuman Father
Lucy Sylva/W/F/June 1/Old Age/76y/__/G.W. Sylva Husband
Lucy Sale/W/F/Dec 1/__/2y/W.J. & S. Sale/W.J. Sale Father
Catherine Saunders/W/F/Aug 4/Old Age/80y/__/Married/A.J. Saunders Son
Jack Samuel/C/M/Feb 20/__/3m/N.B. & F. Samuel/N.B. Samuel Father
Henry Smith/C/M/Aug 30/Consumption/29y/Richd & Laticia Smith/Farmer/R. Smith Father
__ Smith/C/F/Dec 2/__/12d/Liz Smith/Liz Smith Mother

Sallie Smith/C/F/Feb 10/Old Age/82y/__/W.L. Smith Husband
John Tennant/W/M/Mar 11/Old Age/70y/John Tennant/Gabe Frazier Son-in-Law
Chas Taliaferro/C/M/Apr 17/__/2d/W. & M.E. Taliaferro/Farmer/Wm Taliaferro Father
T.D. Taylor/W/M/Dec 6/Dropsy/14y/Worfield Taylor/W. Taylor Father
Bertha Vincent/W/F/June 20/6m 10d/R.D. & Fannie Vincent/R.D. Vincent Father
E.R. Vaughan/W/M/July 24/Flux/4m/J.T. & E. Vaughan/J.T. Vaughan Father
Ezer White/C/M/Oct 10/La Grip/60y/__White/Farmer/Married/Ellen Whittaker
A.R. Wright/W/F/Nov 18/Consumption/2y/J.B. Wright & wife/J.B. Wright Father
B. Taylor Wright/C/M/Apr 6/Consumption/9y/Robt Wright & wife/Robt Wright Father
Sallie Young/C/F/Dec 5/Heart Disease/__/Robt & Maria Young/Robt Young Husband
John Alsop/C/M/May 1/Liver/40y/John & Mary Alsop/Farmer/Married/Ellen Alsop Mother
__ Barnes/W/M/June 18/Not Known/1/12d/E. & Alice Barnes/E. Barnes - Father & Tel Operator
[Note: The next 24 entries are blank in the column where the names of the deceased should appear]
__/W/M/Feb 10/Cramp/2m/R.W. & M.F. Bell/R.W. Bell Father
__/W/F/Oct 11/Not Known/8d/J.M. & Ada Bruce/J.M. Bruce Father
__/W/F/Oct 19/Consumption/35y/B.W. & E. Bruce/Wife of __/B.W. Bruce Father
__/C/F/Aug 23/Flux/5m 15d/Mary J. Baylor/Susan Baylor GrandMother
__/C/M/Sept 28/Heart Disease/65y/Lewis Baylor/Married/Doctor/Doctor
[M.J. Broaddus]/W/M/July 21/Accident/49y/__ Broaddus/Mrs. M.J. Broaddus Wife
__/W/M/Mar 10/Not Known/1/12d/A.N. & L. Covington/Farmer/A.N. Covington Father
[Martha Ellen Houston]/W/F/July/31/Old Age/74y/__ Houston/Farmer/Mrs J.F. Covington Daughter
__/W/M/May 8/Spasms/8d/S.F. & A.L. Farmer/S.F. Farmer Father
__/W/F/May 24/Not Known/__/__/J.P. Gouldin Son
__/W/F/June 20/Weakness/1/12d/W.E. & J.B. Gray/Wm E. Gray Father
__/C/M/Aug 25/__/2y/Thos Guss/Thos Guss Father
__/C/F/Dec 25/Old Age/68y/John Hill/Joe Hill Husband
__/C/M/Feb 19/Old Age/76y/__ Hill/Mary Hill Wife
__/C/M/Aug 20/__/1m/John & Rose Harris/John Hill Father
__/W/F/Nov 10/__/2m/C.N. & C. Houston/C.N. Houston Father
[Robert Hudgin]/W/M/Apr 16/Old Age/88y/__ Hudgin/[Caroline Co[unty] Clerk/C.W. Downing Daughter
__/W/M/Apr 6/__/1d/J.T. & L.T. Jordan/J.L. Jordan Father & Lumber Dealer
__/C/F/Oct 20/Consumption/55y/Richard & M. Lightfoot/Married/R. Lightfoot Father
__/W/M.Feb 6/Burned/18m/A.S. & A.R. Lee/A.S. Lee Father
[T.H. Motley]/W/M/July 4/La Grip/56y/Thos Motley/Mrs. T.H. Motley Wife
__/C/M/Feb 22/Cramp/7y/Willis & M. Myers/Willis Myers Father
__/W/F/Apr 28/__/1d/W.A. & A. Pitts/W.A. Pitts Father
__/C/F/June 30/Killed {Train}/2y 6m/Woodson & M. Puller/W. Puller Father
[Mary Rosina Powers]/W/F/Oct 10/Heart Disease/40y/C.B. & Eliz Thornton/D.B. Powers Husband
[William Richerson]/W/M/July 20/Old Age/80y/Wm Richerson/Shoe Maker/[wife Martha]/B.T. Richerson Son
__/W/M/Sept 30/__/1m 20d/W.W. & Sallie Raines/W.W. Raines Father
__/C/M/July 6/Fever/14y/Milton & Mollie Sampson/M. Sampson Father
__/W/M/June 30/__/9m/Otho & Sallie Smoot/Otho Smoot Father
[Caroline O. Shuman]/W/F/Aug 30/[illeg]/[illeg]/C.A. & Oteria Shuman/C.A. Shuman Father
James O. Allen/W/M/Aug 15/Heart Disease/69y/Geo & Maria Allen/Farmer/Married/S.W. Allen Brother
Kate C. Allen/W/F/Jan 10/Consumption/40y/Mary & Saml Rice/b.Staunton Va/R.T. Allen Husband

Virgie Anderson/C/F/Aug 15.Whooping Cough/6m/Jack & Evelyn Anderson/Jack Anderson Father
Henry Armistead/C/M/July 9/Pneumonia/60y/Unknown/T.H. Blanton Friend
Nannie E. Blanton/W/F/July 16/Dysentery/7y/Thos H. & Mary E. Blanton Father
Forrest Blanton/W/M/July 7/Congestion of Brain/2y/J.A. & Georgeanna Blanton/J.A. Blanton Father
Charles C. Blanton/W/M/June 24/d."Marl Hill"/Heart Disease/67y/Jno & Lucy Blanton/M.J. Blanton Wife
Maude Blair/C/F/Aug 20/Whooping Cough/3y/Emma Blair/Emma Blair Mother
Garnett Beazley/W/M/Jan 15/Diptheria/4y/O.T. & Fannie Beazley/O.T. Beazley Father
Carroll Beazley/W/M/Jan 15/Diptheria/4y/O.T. & Fannie Beazley/O.T. Beazley Father
Lewis M. Bowers/W/M/July 27/Killed at Saw Mill/28y/Jno E. & Mary F. Bowers/Thos C. Bowers Brother
Henry Brown/C/M/Dec 25/Old Age/69y/Unknown/Judson Brown Son
Walker S. Carneal/W/M/May 24/Unknown/2y/A.D. & Minnie Carneal/A.D. Carneal Father
Clarence S. Carneal/W/M/July 2/Unknown/1y 4m/A.D. & Minnie Carneal/A.D. Carneal Father
Joseph Carneal/W/M/June 16/Unknown/4y/R.H. & Sallie Carneal/R.H. Carneal Father
Edmond Carter/C/M/Sept 20/La Grippe/60y/Unknown/E. Carter Wife
Henry Carter/C/F/Oct 17/Consumption/65y/Unknown/Mrs. Carter Wife
Emily Carlton/W/F/June 15/Paralysis/60y/Jos & Patsy Turner/Jno L. Turner Father
Charles Cash/C/M/Mar 10/Unknown/50y/Unknown/Mrs Cash Wife
Buckner Carter/C/F/Dec 10/Old Age/79y/Unknown/Geo Carter Son
Edward Christian/W/M/Feb 5/Heart Disease/74y/Catharine & Thos Christian/M.E. Christian Wife
Mattie Clark/W/F/July 15/Unknown/21y/Jno & Mary Clark/Jno J. Clark Brother
Emma L. Cobb/W/F/Oct/Diptheria/7y/W.L. & Lannie Cobb/W.L. Cobb Father
No Name/C/M/Oct 2/Unknown/1m/Sigh & Ella Coleman/Sigh Coleman Father
Eliza Coleman/C/F/Oct 10/Dysentery/3y/Wm & Sarah Coleman/Wm Coleman Father
Thomas Coleman/C/M/Aug 12/Typhoid Fever/24y/Erasmus & Martha Coleman/Erasmus Coleman Father
John Corr/W/M/Oct 8/Dropsy/79y/Unknown/Chas L. Corr Son
Martha E. Corr/W/F/Apr 6/Old Age/72y/Wm & Fannie Flippo/Chas L. Corr Son
Jno F. Enroughty/W/M/Dec 1/Old Age/70y/Unknown/J.T. Hargrave Friend
Saml Flippo/W/M/Aug 20/Unknown/1y/E.J. & Anna Flippo/E.J. Flippo Father
Bettie W. Flippo/W/F/July 9/Consumption/43y/A.G. & Alex McKenney/A.C. Flippo Husband
Wm S. Flippo/W/M/Nov 12/Paralysis/27y/Wm & Fannie Flippo/M.E. Flippo Wife
Robert Fox/C/M/Feb 16/Burned/1y/Henry & Sarah Fox/Henry Fox Father
Gertie Fox/C/F/Nov 8/Unknown/2m/Walker & Emma Fox/Walker Fox Father
Henry W. Gatewood/W/M/Aug 17/Cancer/69y/Wm & Peggy Gatewood/C.J. Gatewood Son
Josephine George/C/F/Apr 20/La Grippe/11m/Dick & Rosella George/Dick George Father
Susie C. Gibson/W/F/July 20/Unknown/2m/J.N. & Emma Gibson/Jas N. Gibson Father
Arthur Gibbs/C/M/Apr 10/Pneumonia/16y/Anthony Gibbs/Laborer/Anthony Gibbs Father
Lucy Gibbs/C/F/Jan 10/Consumption/20y/Oliver & Harriett Gibbs/Oliver Gibbs Father
Lizzie Gray/C/F/Aug 20/La Grippe/34y/Phil & Amelia Gray/Philip Gray Father
Bettie Harris/W/F/Apr 15/Tumor/66y/Jesse & Louise Winn/J.L. Durrett Son-in-Law
No Name/C/F/Dec 10/Unknown/1d/Mary Hopkins/Mary Hopkins Mother
No Name/C/M/Aug 17/Unknown/1m/Danl & Julia Howard/Danl Howard Father
Clarence Holmes/C/M/Aug 10/Consumption/40y/Unknown/T. Blanton Friend
Jane Holmes/C/F/Sept 9/Consumption/20y/Unknown/T. Blanton Friend
Lizzie Hunter/W/F/July 25/Unknown/30y/James Coleman/b.Alabama/Taliaferro Hunter Husband

Parthenia Hutcherson/W/F/May 8/Heart Disease/69y/Jno & Marla Wright/b.New Kent/Jno Hutcherson Husband
No Name/W/F/June 28/Unknown/11d/Jas & Mildred Jones/ Jas Jones Father
Chas E. Lewis/W/M/Sept 15/Malaria Fever/35y/Arthur & Cornelia Lewis/Cornelia Lewis Mother
Lizzie Lewis/C/F/Dec 15/Unknown/16y/Mary S. & Winston Lewis/Sam Lewis
Robert Lewis/C/M/Mar 5/La Grippe/18y/Wm & Bettie Lewis/Wm Lewis Father
Josephine Meads/C/F/Sept 4/Typhoid Fever/28y/Unknown/Adam Meads Husband
Emma Mills/C/F/July 3/Unknown/3y/Fleming & Lucy Mills/Fleming Mills Father
Amelia Minor/C/F/Jan 20/Pneumonia/60y/Unknown/Nelson Minor Son
George Pitts/W/M/Oct 11/Killed by Horse/50y/Willis & Susan Pitts/Bettie Pitts Wife
Frances B. Pollard/W/F/Jan 15/d."Oak Grove"/Heart Disease/73y/ Richard & G.A. Bridges/Delia F. Pollard Daughter
Henry Quash/C/M/Dec/Drowned/16y/Jas & Bettie Quash/Jas Quash Father
Thos W. Richerson/W/M/Mar 17/Unknown/55y/Jno & Lucy Richerson/R.S. Richerson Bro
Rachel Ross/C/F/June 15/Whooping Cough/6y/Nelson & Rachel Ross/Nelson Ross Father
Benj Satterwhite/W/M/Aug 10/Paralysis/60y/Edmond & Sallie Satterwhite/Edmond Satterwhite Father
Franklin Satterwhite/W/M/July 11/Paralysis/70y/Not Known/Farmer/Mrs. Satterwhite Wife
John Shackleford/W/M/Oct 6/Unknown/9y/Chas E.& Mary Shackleford/Chas E. Shackleford Father
Clara Shuman/W/F/July 1/Malaria Fever/9m/F.E. & N.J. Shuman/F.E. Shuman Father
No Name/W/F/May 20/Unknown/1d/A.L. & Mary Stanley/A.L. Stanley Father
Jesse Stanley/W/M/July 1/Unknown/7m/A.L. & Mary Stanley/A.L. Stanley Father
Jane Stevens/C/F/Aug 13/Malaria Fever/58y/Sallie Smithers/W.H. Stevens Husband
Robt Taylor/C/M/May 31/Unknown/1d/Chas & Susan Taylor/Chas Taylor Father
Silvia Thompson/C/F/Oct 28/Unknown/23y/Susan & Henry Thompson/Henry Thompson/Henry Thompson Father
James Thompson/C/M/July 29/Dysentery/1y/Ottoway & Mary Thompson/Ottoway Thompson Father
John West/C/M/June 6/Mashed/17y/Jerry & Denie West/Jerry West Father
No Name/W/F/Nov 24/Unknown/3d/H.S. & Joana Wiglesworth/H.S. Wiglesworth Father
No Name/C/M/July/Unknown/4m/Jennie Williams/Jennie Williams Mother
Isaiah Wright/C/M/Aug 12/Unknown/1y/Fountain & Sarah Wright/Fountain Wright Father
James Wright/C/M/July 15/Unknown/4m/J.J. & Liza Wright/J.J. Wright Father

1893

L.B. Lee/C/F/Mar 6/Not Known/42y/__/Geo Lee Husband
Edmond Monroe/C/M/Nov 20/Old Age/80y/Ed Monroe/Farmer/__ Wife
Humphrey Miller/C/M/__/Old Age/70y/John Miller/Laborer/M. Miller Wife/Annie Baylor
Sam Pleasant/C/M/Oct 5/Old Age/75y/__ Pleasant/Laborer/Married/___/__/
No Name Samuel/C/M/Dec 24/Not Known/3d/Geo & Estes Samuel/Geo Samuel Father
Matthew Taliaferro/C/M/Sept 6/Old Age/70y/__ Taliaferro/Agnes Taliafero Wife
Morc Ware/C/M/Sept 19/__/9m/Chas Ware/Morc Ware
Winnie Washington/C/F/Dec 1/Old Age/70y/__/Married/Geo Washington Son
Chas Washington/C/M/Feb 13/__/20y/Chas Washington/Laborer/A. Allen
Mamie D. Young/C/F/June 23/__/18y/Jno H. Young/Jno H. Young Father
L.B. Conway/W/M/Feb 6/__/15m/C.B. & B. Conway/C.B. Conway Father

No Name Gray/W/F/Jan 18/Not Known/1/4d/W.E. & F.R. Gray/W.E. Gray Father
No Name Gravatt/W/M/Dec 27/Not Known/6d/J.D. & E.H. Gravatt/J.D. Gravatt Father
Susan H. Oesterheld/W/F/July 10/__/50y/__/Married/__Oesterheld
W.L. Shackleford/W/M/Oct 10/Not Known/13m/Jno G. Shackleford/Jno G. Shackleford Father
Arthur Sale/W/M/Aug 12/Sc Fever/12m/J.B. Sale/J.B. Sale Father
Sarah J. Travis/W/F/Jan 23/Congestive Chill/73y/__/F.M. Travis Son
Battaile Thomas/W/M/July 20/__/18y/J.S. Thomas/J.S. Thomas Father
Peter Carter/C/M/Mar 28/Not Known/65y/__ Carter/Farmer/ M. Carter Wife
No Name Dishman/C/F/June 21/Not Known/2d/Wm & S. Dishman/Wm Dishman Father
Ellen & E. Harrison/2C/2F/Aug 6 & 4/Brain Fever/4y & 2y/Washington Harrison/W. Harrison
  Father
Not Named Jackson/C/M/Mar 2/Not Known/1d/Steven & Mattie Jackson/Steven Jackson Father
Malinda Jackson/C/F/Apr 27/Child Birth/35y/__/W.F. Jackson Husband
Frances Jones/C/F/Apr 1/__/20y/Wm Jones/Wm Jones Father
John Holmes/C/M/June 10/Fever/22y/__Holmes/Farmer/Wm Reives
Peter Lewis/C/M/Jan 1/Pneumonia/55y/__Lewis/Farmer/T. Saunders
Eliza Taliaferro/C/F/July 13/Old Age/72y/__Taliaferro/Morton Taliaferro Husband
Richard Taylor/C/M/Mar 28/Heart Trouble/47y/Richd Taylor/Farmer/__ Wife
Hesikiah Walker/C/M/Apr 10/Old Age/80y/__Walker/Farmer/__ Walker Wife
Henry Washington/C/M/July 17/Lightning/60y/__Washington/C.B. Washington Wife/__
  Commissioner
C.B. Washington/C/F/July 17/Lightning/19y/__/Henry Washington Husband/__ Commissioner
Monie Waugh/C/F/Oct 10/Dropsy/2y/Henry Waugh/H. Waugh Father
Walter Anderson/C/M/Nov 6/__/1m 27d/Martha Anderson/Martha Anderson Mother
Mary Anderson/W/F/July 29/Cancer/45y/E.D. Anderson Husband
M. Jane Broaddus/W/F/Mar 17/Heart Disease/73y/A. Broaddus Husband
Ethel Beasley/W/F/Apr 6/Burnt/1y/L.M. Beazley/L.M. Beazley Father
Armanda Claytor/W/F/Mar 5/Consumption/63y/__/__/
Seth Claytor/W/M/July 12/Old Age/74y/__Claytor/__ Wife
__ Gray/W/F/June 22/Not Known/1/2d/Jas & Bessie Gray/James Gray Father
Ace Gouldman/W/M/June 10/Old Age/87y/__Gouldman/__ Wife
Felitia Gaines/C/F/July 22/Cancer/75y/__/__ Husband
__Gray/W/F/Apr 10/Not Known/4d/Jno F. & L. Gray/Jno F. Gray Father
J.R.P. Houston/W/M/Aug 11/Old Age/76y/__Houston/[Elizabeth]/Houston Wife
Daniel Koles/W/M/May 10/Heart Disease/65y/__Koles/__Koles Wife
M. Lee Loving/W/F/July 18/Dysentery/3y/R.F. & Dora Loving/R.F. Loving Father
__Motley/W/M/Dec 7/__/2y 6m/J.N. & L.W. Motley/J.N. Motley Father
S.J. Pugh/W/F/June 9/Consumption/22y/E.L. Pugh/E.L. Pugh Father
Mary Eubank/W/F/June 21/__/68y/W.H. Pugh/W.H. Pugh Father
P.B. Pitts/W/M/Oct 1/Consumption/68y/P.B. Pitts/__Wife
__Sylva/W/F/June 15/Consumption/9d/W.T. & M.A. Sylva/W.T. Sylva Father
L.N. Self/W/F/July 24/Spasms/13m/D.C. & S.E. Self/D.C. Self Father
Charlie B. Seymour/W/M/Jan 7/Shot/15y/Jacob Seymour/Jacob Seymour Father
Albert Tignor/W/M/Oct 10/Heart Trouble/65y/__/__ Wife
S.J.R. White/W/M/May 23/Old Age/73y/__White/Merchant/Ann E. White Wife
Charles [Tod] Wright/W/M/Jan 17/Brain disease/61y/[Dr Burton B. & Ann Tod]Wright/Doctor/
  [Anne Elizabeth]Lizzie Wright Wife
Daisy Wright/W/F/June 10/Lung Disease/4y/J.B. Wright/J.B. Wright Father

Lucy E. Bates/C/F/July 10/__/8y/Jno H. Bates/Jno H. Bates Father
Thomas Butler/C/M/July 24/__/27y/Mary Butler/Mary Butler Mother
John Boswell/C/M/May 1/Pneumonia/24y/John Boswell/Single/Jno Boswell Father
Lewis Boswell/C/M/July 16/Consumption/55y/__Boswell/Married/Jno Boswell
L.L. Baylor/C/M/Mar 6/__/63y/Lewis Baylor/__Baylor Wife
George Corbin/C/M/Apr 10/Consumption/42y/Geo Corbin/Laborer/Single/__Commissioner
Sallie Green/C/F/Aug 10/Dropsy/50y/__/Single/__Sister
Jane Holmes/C/F/Mar 20/Child Birth/21y/R.C. Holmes/R.C. Holmes Father
Ben Hampton/C/M/May 6/Accident/65y/Benjm Hampton/Farmer/M. Hunter Wife
Kate Hill/C/F/Sept 6/Dropsy/50y/__/Madison Hill Husband
Sam Johnson/C/M/Nov 20/__/70y/Samuel Johnson/M.A. Johnson Wife
M. Jackson/C/M/__/__/__/G.J. & Lucy Jackson/G.J. Jackson
Robt Arnold/W/M/June 11/Shot Himself/11y/R.B. & Sarah Arnold/R.B. Arnold Father
Lavenia Baughn/W/F/May 29/Old Age/84y/Unknown/Married/Philip Baughn Son
Maude E. Blanton/W/F/Dec 30/d.Balty [Car Co]/Congestion of Brain/4y/J.R. & C.L.Blanton/
    b.Balty/J.R. Blanton Father
No Name/W/F/July 20/Unknown/5d/A.G. & L.L. Blanton/A.G. Blanton Father
No Name/C/M/July 25/Unknown/20d/E.L. & Eula Boxley/E.L. Boxley Father
Mabel Bullock/W/F/July 17//2y/Sidney & Rosa Bullock/Sidney Bullock Father
Julian Burruss/C/M/Apr 16/Unknown/2y/Thos & Ida Burruss/Thos Burruss Father
Rachel Branan/W/F/July 6/Old Age/80y/Jno & Winnie Branan/Thos Southworth Friend
Lillie Carneal/W/F/Dec 15/Unknown/6m/Geo & Minnie Carneal/Geo Carneal Father
Jane Coleman/W/F/July 10/Old Age/60y/Elijah & Mary Wiglesworth/J.A. Coleman Daughter
No Name/W/F/May 28/Unknown/14d/R.E. & G.B. Collins/R.E. Collins Father
No Name/W/F/June 10/Unknown/18d/R.J. & Lucy Corr/R.J. Corr Father
Moses Dangerfield/C/M/Apr 7/__/17y/Chas Dangerfield/Chas Dangerfield Father
Floyd Davis/C/M/Oct 10/Whooping Cough/2y/Jno & Clarissa Davis/Jno Davis Father
James C. Dejarnette/W/M/Mar 17/Old Age/77y/Unknown/J.E. Dejarnette Son
James Dejarnette/W/M/July 17/Unknown/2m/Jas & Anna Dejarnette/Jas Dejarnette Father
P.A. Dew/W/M/Sept 12/Unknown/54y/Philip & Lucy Dew/M.D./Fannie Dew Wife
Ann F. Donahoe/W/F/Apr 26/Unknown/43y/Not Known/Reubin Donahoe Husband
W.W. Durrett/W/M/Sept/Dropsy/60y/Clayborn & Fannie Durrett/__
Jos T. Dyson/W/M/Dec 12/Pneumonia/24y/H.H. & M.E. Dyson/H.H. Dyson Father
Maria England/W/F/Mar 3/Unknown/60y/Unknown/L. England Husband
Maria L. Flippo/W/F/Aug 25/Whooping Cough/7y/E.J. & A.B. Flippo/E.J. Flippo Father
Geo W. Fountain/C/M/Oct 1/Consumption/24y/Peter & Viola Fountain/Peter Fountain Father
Willie Fox/C/M/Dec 5/Consumption/27y/Kate Fox/Peter Fox Father
Florry Freeman/C/F/Jan 9/Unknown/1y/Robt & Susan Freeman/Robt Freeman Father
Susan E. Freeman/W/F/June 28/Unknown/44y/Geo W. & Mary Thompson/Wm Freeman Husband
Lee Gatewood/C/M/Aug 15/Unknown/2y/R.H. & Belle Gatewood/R.H. Gatewood Father
W.C. Gatewood/W/M/Jan 8/Unknown/60y/Bartlett & Frances Gatewood/Thos A. Gatewood Son
A.G. Goodwin/W/M/Aug 20/Inflamation of Bowels/75y/Unknown/Farmer/S.E. Goodwin Wife
George Hicks/C/M/Nov 20/Old Age/70y/Unknown/Laborer/Mrs. Hicks Wife
Jno H. Jackson/C/M/Dec/Consumption/23y/Frank & Susan Jackson/Frank Jackson Father
No Name/C/M/June 15/Unknown/2m/Jas & Lucy A. Jamison/Jas Jamison Father
William Mines/C/M/Aug 10/Pneumonia/21y/Moses & M. Mines/Moses Mines Father
John A. Mont/C/M/Nov 27/Erysipelas/58y/Jas & Betsy Mont/Jas Mont Father
Wm G. Moren/W/M/Sept 5/Consumption/37y/Jas & M. Moren/Jno T. Moren Brother

Clarence Moore/W/M/July 13/Cholera Infantum/15m/Oscar & Mildred Moore/Oscar Moore Father
Jno T. Newton/W/M/Mar 23/Unknown/53y/Henry & Mary Newton/Farmer/Ida Newton Wife
No Name/W/F/Aug 5/Unknown/1m/Richd & Florence Parker/R.H. Parker Father
Julia Payne/W/F/Feb 15/Unknown/33y/Unknown/A.L. Payne Husband
Mary Pemberton/W/F/May 24/Unknown/5m/Jas & Mary Pemberton/Jas Pemberton Father
Courtney Pendleton/C/F/Apr 15/Consumption/40y/Jas & Catharine Pendleton/Jas Pendleton Husband
No Name/C/F/June 16/Unknown/8m/Jos & Lucy Randol/Jos Randol Father
No Name/C/M/Feb 8/Unknown/1m/Thos & Bettie Reynolds/Thos Reynolds Father
Anna Rollins/C/F/Oct 15/Unknown/20y/Dingo & Matilda Rollins/Dingo Rollins Father
Tom Saunders/W/M/Jan 21/Unknown/2d/W.W. & Martha Saunders/W.W. Saunders Father
No Name/C/M/Nov 26/Unknown/1d/Saml & Lottie Seams/Saml Seams Father
No Name/C/M/Dec 5/__/1m/Lewis & Lottie Shooks/Lewis Shooks Father
R.P. Smith/W/M/May 26/Old Age/81y/Not Known/Lee J. Smith Father
Millie J. Smith/W/F/June 9/Unknown/50y/Not Known/L.C. Smith Husband
Patsy Smith/W/F/May 15/Old Age/82y/Not Known/M.A. Smith Son
E.J. Spindle/W/M/Aug 21/Old Age/72y/Not Known/Alice Spindle Wife
No Name/W/F/May 21/Unknown/1d/Lewis & Alice Stanley/Lewis Stanley Father
Margarett Stern/C/F/Aug 13/Consumption/46y/Unknown/Peter Stern Husband
Margarett Stern/C/F/Jan 9/Cancer/52y/Unknown/Ben Jackson Friend
Lavina Taylor/C/F/Oct 10/Old Age/81y/Unknown/W.J. Courtney Friend
Moyle Taylor/C/M/Apr 8/Unknown/6m/Wm & Nannie Taylor/Wm Taylor Father
Sallie Tribble/W/F/Apr/Unknown/2y/John C. & Ella Tribble/J.C. Tribble Father
Clara B. Watkins/W/F/Oct 15/Typhoid Fever/55y/Hasting & C. Watkins/C.T.Watkins Father
Mary Webster/C/F/Aug 8/Unknown/60y/Unknown/Danl Webster Husband
A.E. Waller/W/F/July 19/Old Age/75y/William & J. Dabney/H.B. White Friend
Arch Williams/C/M/Nov 12/Whooping Cough/7d/Arch & Charlotte Williams/Arch Williams Father
Frank Williams/C/M/July 5/Unknown/1m/Antny & Matilda Williams/Antny [Anthony]Williams Father
Angelina Wiltshire/W/F/Mar 17/Not Known/74y/Unknown/Reubin Donahoe Friend
Jane Wormley/C/F/Jan 5/Not Known/__/Mary Wormley/Geo Wormley Friend
No Name/C/M/Mar 14/Unknown/1d/Thos & Margarett Wright/Thos Wright Father
Margaret Wright/C/F/Mar 7/Unknown/43y/Unknown/Thos Wright Husband
Emma M. Wright/W/F/Jan 28/Old Age/84y/Unknown/R.A. Wright Husband

1894

Sarah J. Acors/W/F/Dec 24/__/60y/Henry Acors Husband
Ellen V. Beasley/W/F/Jan 26/Cancer/54y/T.H. Beasley Husband
Ida Beasley/W/F/Oct 4/Consumption/35y/E.T. Beasley Husband
Martha J. Broaddus/W/F/Mar 17/Heart Disease/73y/Wm & Jane Pitts/A. Broaddus Husband
__Brooks/W/F/July 11/Not Known/1m 1d/A. & H.E. Brooks/A. Brooks Father
Thomas Eubank/W/M/Apr 2/Not Known/57y/__Eubank/__Eubank Wife
Peyton W. Farmer/W/M/Sept 1/Not Known/24y/Lewis & Mary Farmer/Lewis Farmer Father
__Gray/W/F/Jan 20/10d/G.W. & M.C/ Gray/G.W. Gray Father
T.M. Harris/W/M/Apr 29/Copnsumption/35y/__Harris/Farmer/__Harris Wife
Jno Loving/W/M/June 6/Brain Fever/3y/Jno Loving & wife/Jno R. Loving Father

__Loving/W/M/Nov 13/__/6d/F. & P. Loving/Frank Loving Father
M.G. Martin/W/F/Nov 2/Old Age/75y/__/Married/__Daughter
Olive E. Monday/W/F/Sept 15/Heart Trouble/40y/Martha W. Monday/M.W. Monday Mother
Kate Peatross/W/F/Feb 10/Old Age/74y/__Peatross/Single/__ Peatross
R.E. Pitts/W/F/Sept 23/Cholera Infantum/4m 26d/E.G. & M.V. Pitts/E.G. Pitts Father
C.[Callie]O. Pollard/W/F/Sept 27/Croup/2y/W.L.K. Pollard [& Alice Gray Pollard]/W.L.K. [Willie Lee Kidd] Pollard Father
Paul Self/W/M/Feb 3/Consumption/56y/__Self/Farmer/Married/__
__Self/2W/1M/1F/Nov 18/12d/W.H. & F. Self/W.H. Self Father
Bertie Taylor/W/F/Oct 25/Heart Trouble/80y/__/Bartholomew Taylor Husband
__Beasley/C/M/Apr 8/__/8d/B.B. Beasley/B.B. Beasley Father
Lucy Beverley/C/F/June 6/__/3y/__Beverley/__Beverley
Moses Christoper/C/M/Nov 14/Hung/17y/D. & C. Christopher/Laborer/D. Christopher Father
__Coleman/C/M/Feb 16/Not Known/3d/R. & C. Coleman/Rolph Coleman Father
Jerry Taylor/C/M/Mar 25/Old Age/82y/__Taylor/Married/W.H. Coleman Friend
Albert Fortune/C/M/July 11/Old Age/75y/__Fortune/Farmer/__
Nancy Goodwin/C/F/Nov 12/Dropsy/40y/__/Henry Goodwin Husband
__Gray/C/M/Oct 10/Not Known/1/2d/C. & L.L. Gray/Chas Gray Father
Rose Jackson/C/F/Oct 10/Consumption/35y/__/Willis Jackson Husband
__Jackson/C/F/June 26/__/26d/Law & Lea Jackson/Law Jackson Father
Philip Johnson Jr/C/M/Nov 9/Consumption/30y/Phillip Johnson/Farmer/Married/__
J.E. Johnson/C/M/Oct 17/Dropsy/42y/__/Farmer/Married/__
D.W. Johnson/C/M/May 16/__/__/E.A. & E.F. Johnson/Single/E.A. Johnson Father
Lucy Lewis/C/F/July 2/Old Age/70y/__Lewis/Single/Eliz Garrett Niece
Ben Lewis/C/M/June 12/Old Age/70y/__Lewis/Farmer/Married/Delia Lewis Daughter
M.E. Lomax/C/F/July 7/Not Known/27y/Joe Lomax Husband
John Morton/C/M/July 10/Dropsy/60y/__Morton/Farmer/Married/__/__
Lucy Morton/C/F/Dec 5/Not Known/42y/__/Law Morton Husband
Fannie Myers/C/F/Apr 10/Cancer/40y/__/Phil Myers Husband
Hammie Richerson/C/M/Sept 25/__/4y/Geo & A. Richerson/Geo Richerson Father
Harry Samuel/C/M/Dec 29/Old Age/96y/__Samuel/Carpenter/Arch Samuel Son
__Waite/C/F/Nov 20/Spasms/19d/Paul & Anna Waite/Farmer/Paul Waite Father
Fannie Ware/C/F/June 28/Whooping Cough/6m/Nelson Ware/Nelson Ware Father
Bertha Washington/C/F/Dec 15/Burned/3y/__/Sallie Washington Mother
Luther Williams/C/M/Oct 10/Not Known/28y/__Williams/Laborer/__Williams Wife
Tener Young/C/F/Apr 5/Not Known/65y/__/Jas C. Young Husband
G.W. Carter/W/M/Mar 29/Not Known/50y/__Carter/Farmer/Married/__/__
Almo Carter/W/M/Oct 12/Typhoid/16y/R.R. & M.A. Carter/Single/R.R. Carter Father
Gracie Toombs/C/F/Nov 6/Burned/3y/F. & Alice Toombs/F. Toombs Father
Sallie B. Gray/C/F/Nov 27/__/31y/__/Archie Gray Husband
Dollie Guss/C/F/Nov 10/Consumption/2y/Claiborn Guss/C. Guss Father
Hannah Guss/C/F/June 10/__/30y/__/Thomas Guss Husband
John Hill/C/M/Nov 10/Typhoid Fever/24y/Sam & F. Hill/Laborer/Single/Sam Hill Father
Lewis Jackson/C/M/Mar 20/Consumption/25y/Alexander Jackson/A. Jackson Father
__Jackson/C/F/Sept/Not Known/1d/__/Margaret Jackson Mother
__Lewis/C/M/Feb 25/__/1d/Robt & E/ Lewis/Robt Lewis Father
Jane Rieves/C/M/Mar 1/Old Age/60y/__/Wm R. Rieves Husband
__Rieves/C/M/Aug 10/__/8d/T.L. & L.V. Rieves/T.L. Rieves Father

__Shelton/C/F/June 29/Spasms/8d/Ro & M.L. Shelton/Robt Shelton
Rich Smith/C/M/May 20/__/65y/__Smith/Married/__/__
Jas Ware/C/M/July 10/__/3y/C. & Mary E. Ware/Jacob Ware Relation
Farmer Young/C/F/Feb 22/Dropsy/60y/__/Married/__
William Young/C/M/June 2/Gravel/65y/__ Young/Farmer/Married/__/__
Cecil W. Baker/W/M/__/Bronchitis/__/C.L. & M.L. Baker/C.L. Baker Father & Lumber Dealer
Carrie M. Broaddus/W/F/Apr 13/Consumptin/11y/S.W. & Emma Broaddus/S.W. Broaddus Father & Merchant
Bessie G. Davis/W/F/Oct 23/Cholera Infantum/8m/J.P. & M.S. Davis/J.P. Davis Father
Sarah Ellen Digges/W/F/Apr/Consumption/70y/C. & E. Coleman/Wm S. Digges Husband/Wm C. Digges Son
Earl R. Smoot/W/M/Sept 25/__/14m/O.P. & S.H. Smoot/O.P. Smoot Father
H.D. Acors/W/M/June 17/Dysentary/26y/Thos A. & Nancy Acors/Farmer/Elizabeth Acors Wife/ P.C. Acors Brother
Catherine Acors/W/F/Apr 4/Change of Life/49y/Wm & Mary Pruett/Paul C. Acors Husband
Edmond Anderson/C/M/Nov 22/Accidental/65y/Not Known/Laborer/Married/Mrs. Anderson Wife
M. Maude Blanton/W/F/Nov 27/Cramp/7y/N.A. & Vandelia Blanton/N.A. Blanton Father
Wm H. Burruss/W/M/Dec 24/Heart Disease/77y/Wm & Sarah Burruss/Farmer/E.E. Burruss Son
Robt H. Chapman/C/M/July 15/Hemorhage/39y/Henry & Eliza Chapman/Farmer/Married/Eliz Chapman Mother
Rufus Chiles/C/M/Aug 9/Consumption/39y/Not Known/Laborer/Married/Dennis Chiles Brother
James R. Chiles/W/M/Apr 15/Not Known/23y/Jno E. Chiles/Jno E. Chiles Father
Jim F. Courtney/C/M/Apr 10/Rheumatism/70y/Unknown/Laborer/Jane Courtney Wife
No Name/W/M/June 7/Not Known/14d/Ryland & Nettie Dillard/Ryland Dillard Father
M.A. Dimue/W/F/June 7/Appoplexy/42y/Alfred & Ann Dyson/Wm Dimue Husband
Sallie E. Dunn/W/F/June 20/Cancer/5y/Jno & Priscilla Burruss/E.S. Dunn Husband
Maria England/W/F/Mar 6/Paralysis/60y/Geo & Martha England/L. England Brother
Irene Foster/C/F/July 2/Not Known/8y/Jno & Sallie Foster/John Foster Father
Katie Fox/C/F/Apr/Heart Disease/63y/Unknown/Peter Fox Husband
No Name/C/M/Dec 28/Not Known/21d/Henry & Martha Fox/Henry Fox Father
Charles Freeman/C/M/Oct 10/Consumption/17y/Nelson & Casandria Freeman/Nelson Freeman Father
Parthena Freeman/C/F/Dec 18/Consumption/20y/Rich & Joannna Freeman/Richd Freeman Father
Wm C. Gatewood/W/M/Jan 10/Pneumonia/60y/Bartell & Fannie Gatewood/Farmer/Tom Blanton Friend
W.W. Hancock/W/M/Sept 24/Heart Disease/62y/Wm & Lucy Hancock/Farmer/Jno W. Hancock Son
Judie Holmes/C/F/Sept 10/Dropsy/45y/Not Known/M. Holmes Husband
Rachel Jerrell/W/F/May 22/Old Age/83y 10m/Wm & Frances Wright/C.V. Jerrell Daughter
Edward Johnson/C/M/June 3/Not Known/3m/Melvin & Gracie Johnson/Melvin Johnson Father
Warner M. Jones/C/M/May 9/Consumptin/56y/Not Known/Isaac Johnson Friend
Sallie Lewis/C/F/Oct 16/Not Known/5m/Reuben & Mollie Lewis/Reuben Lewis Father
Rebecca L. Luck/W/F/Sept 23/Inflamation of Stomach/41y/Elliott & May Lucy/b.Texas/S.A. Luck Brother
Sammie Mines/C/M/Sept 30/Not Known/1m/Nelson & Lizzie Mines/Nelson Mines Father
Smith Mason/W/M/Sept 2/Not Known/69y/Not Known/Jno Mason Son
No Name/C/M/Sept 22/Not Known/__/Wm & Mary Montague/Wm Montague Father
Eliza B. Moore/W/F/Apr 2/Old Age/80y/Not Known/Jas F. Moore Husband
Melvina Peatross/C/F/June 3/Heart Failure/70y/Not Known/Tom Blanton Friend

Robert Rollins/C/M/Apr 10/Old Age/70y/Roger Rollins/W. Bouldin Friend
Patsy Rolls/C/F/July 20/Consumption/29y/Not Known/Cornelius Rolls Husband
Ada Ragland/C/F/June 8/Consumption/21y/Stephen & Lucy Ragland/Lucy Ann Ross Friend
John Ryland/C/M/Aug 20/Typhoid Fever/60y/Not Known/Geo Ross Friend
Willis Roots/C/M/Mar 2/Consumption/27y/Robt & Maria Roots/Robt Roots Father
Frederick Smithers/C/M/Sept 1/Consumption/18y/Matt & Jennie Smithers/Matt Smithers Father
Margaret Stern/C/F/Jan 10/Cancer/52y/Not Known/Peter Stern Husband
No Name/C/M/May 8/Not Known/2d/W.H. & Maria Stevenson/W.H. Stevenson Father
Willie A. Swann/W/F/Sept 20/Gastric Fever/63y/Enoch & Ann Edwards/S.E. Swann Husband
Georgeanna Taylor/C/F/Mar 21/Brain Affection/29y/America Taylor/America Taylor Mother
Eldred Turner/W/M/July 28/Not Known/72y/Not Known/E. Turner Son
Susan Turner/C/F/Dec 29/Old Age/71y/Not Known/Sandy Turner Son
M.A. Wiglesworth/W/F/Oct 5/Old Age/75y/Jno & Betsy Sizer/ Jos Wiglesworth Husband
No Name/W/F/Nov 1/Not Known/2m/H.S. & Iona Wiglesworth/H.S. Wiglesworth Father
Arch Williams/C/M/Apr 10/Whooping Cough/1y 8m/Arch & Charlotte Williams/Arch Williams Father
Emily M. Wright/W/F/Jan 28/Old Age/84y/Robt H. Wiglesworth/R.A. Wright Son

1895

Sarah J. Acors/W/F/Dec 24/Old Age/60y/Henry Acors Husband
Jas B. Andrews/W/M/Sept 15/Cancer/67y/__Andrews/Farmer/Mary E. Andrews Wife
S.F. Bullock/W/F/Sept 18/Colic/65y/W.G. Bullock Husband
Richd T. Chandler/W/M/Aug 25/Blood Poison/65y/__Chandler/Farmer/Married/__ Wife
Rachel K. Farish/W/F/Dec 20/Old Age/78y/Keeling & Rebecca Rowe/Widow/K.R. Farish Brother
J. Waller Gouldin/W/M/Aug 2/Diseased Liver/76y/Farmer/Anna Gouldin Wife
__Gouldman/W/F/June 2/Not Known/2y/J.P. & F.E. Gouldman/Jno P. Gouldman Father
John Hart/W/M/July 21/Disease of Kidney/68y/Jno & Eliz Hart/b.Louisa Co/Teacher/Sallie Hart Wife/John Hart Jr Son
Sarah M. Haynes/W/F/Mar 10/Heart Disease/85y/G.L. Haynes Husband
V.E. Houston/W/F/Mar 20/Consumption/60y/Jas W. Houston Husband
Mary Beasley/W/F/Jan 9/Old Age/85y/Wm [illeg]/J.H. Murrow Husband
William Pugh/W/M/Sept 1/Old Age/90y/Wm Pugh/Farmer/A. Reynolds Daughter
Cally Upshaw/W/F/Oct 7/Consumption/35y/Jno T. Vaughan/T.E. Upshaw Husband
Emma E. Vaughan/W/F/Oct 10/Not Known/14y 6m/Jno T. Vaughan/J.T. Vaughan Father
Edna White/W/F/Aug 6/Cholera Infantum/12m/L.B. White/L.B. White Father
Juliett Wharton/W/F/Feb 14/__/65y/__/Jno Wharton Husband
Rich Alexander/C/M/Apr 1/__/1m/R. & Sallie Alexander/Richd Alexander Father
Jerry Allen/C/M/Nov 2/__/59y/__Allen/Laborer/__Wife
__Baylor/C/M/Nov 13/__/8d/A.W. & L.A. Baylor/A.W. Baylor Father
L.A. Beasley/C/M/Dec 30/Consumption/45y/__/P.B. Beasley Husband
__Beasley/C/F/Aug 25/__/17d/B.B. & L.A. Beasley/B.B. Beasley Father
Caroline Bowie/C/F/Feb 10/Child Birth/35y/__/W.T. Bowie Husband
James Bowie/C/M/Aug 20/__/3y/W.T. & Caroline Bowie/W.T. Bowie Father
Peyton Brown/C/M/June 15/Diseased Bladder/65y/__Brown/Laborer/Lucy A. Brown Wife
C. Bundy/C/M/Aug 12/Not Known/9y/R.T. Bundy/R.T. Bundy Father
J.H. Moore/C/M/Oct 11/Typhoid Fever/13y/Andrew & T. Moore/J.L. Courtney Neighbor
Eliz Dollins/C/F/June 10/Dropsy/73y/__/Betty Dollins Daughter

Wm L. Fry/C/M/May 6/Consumption/40y/Wm Fry/Laborer/Ann Fry Wife
M.S.B. Fortune/C/F/May 28/Not Known/65y/R.B. Fortune Husband
Lizzie Freeman/C/F/June 14/Consumption/28y/Willis Freeman Husband
Katherine Gravatt/C/F/Dec 20/Heart Disease/40y/Henry Gravatt Husband
Lillie Jackson/C/F/Jan 17/Consumption/11y/Willis Jackson/Willis Jackson Father
Ella Johnson/C/F/July 6/Colic/26d/J.F. & Bettie Johnson/J.F. Johnson Father
Simon Johnson/C/M/Oct 17/Consumption/73y/__Johnson/Married/Commissioner
James Jeter/C/M/June 30/Old Age/81y/Martha Jeter Wife
Robt E. Lomax/C/M/Sept 13/__/8d/W.R. & [illeg] Lomax/W.R. Lomax Father
Maria Lee/C/F/Apr 10/Pneumonia/50y/__/Nelson Lee Husband
Taliaferro Parker/C/M/Apr 18/Old Age/90y/Parker Farmer/Jas E. Parker Son
Elizth Monroe/C/F/May 20/__/76y/__/Married/A. Pendleton Friend
G.C. Pitts/C/M/Aug 26/Dropsy/39y/__/Blacksmith/Sallie Pitts Wife/Commissioner
Sallie Rollins/C/F/Sept 22/Heart Disease/70y/__/David Rollins Husband
J.D. Samuel/C/M/Apr 10/Pneumonia/13y/George Samuel/Geo Samuel Father
Peter Thomas/C/M/Dec 17/__/65y/__Thomas/Farmer/Mahaley Thomas Wife
Wm L. Turner/C/M/Sept 28/Horse Kick/5y/Allen Turner/Allen Turner Father
Fannie Waite/C/F/Mar 18/Consumption/55y/__/Paul Waite Husband
Luther Williams/C/M/Dec 20/Heart Disease/29y/__Williams/Laborer/Married/__
Martha Tyler/C/F/Aug 5/Old Age/70y/__/S. Anderson
Nat Jones/C/M/Aug 25/Old Age/74y/Married/__
William Minor/C/M/Jan 24/Not Known/28y/__Minor/Laborer/Married/__
Jno A. Dodson/C/M/Sept 20/Cholera Infantum/2y/Robt Dodson/Robt Dodson Father
Chas Grimes/C/M/Dec 24/__/2y/__Grimes/Chas Gray
Thomas Guss/C/M/Dec 20/Not Known/__/__/Married/__
V.A. Hailstock/C/F/Sept 29/Old Age/70y/Wm H. Hailstock Husband
S. Walker/C/M/Oct 12/Old Age/83y/__ Walker/Abraham Holmes
Mary E. Johnson/C/F/July 10/__/3y/Harry & Alice Johnson/Harry Johnson Father
Edna Johnson/C/F/June 27/__/[illeg]/M.C. & A. Johnson/M.C. Johnson Father
__King/C/M/July 15/__/5d/Wm & N. King/Wm King Father
Chastine Lewis/C/F/Dec 6/1y 1m/Robt E. Lewis/Robt Lewis Father
__Lucus/2C/1M/1F/June 7/2d/Len & Lucy Lucus/Len Lucus Father
Alli Minor/C/F/Jan 5/__/1d/Jno & K.C. Minor/Jno Minor Father
__Morton/C/F/Sept 6/__/1/8d/Wm & Mag Morton/Wm Morton Father
Aaron Parker/C/M/May 10/Old Age/75y/__Parker/Laborer/Married/__/__
Henry Robertson/C/M/Sept 10/Typhoid/11y/R. & B. Robertson/Robt Robertson Father
Ben Williams/C/M/Mar 10/Pneumonia/20y/Byrd Williams/Laborer/Byrd Williams Father
Geo W. Catlett/W/M/May 28/80y/__Catlett/Married/Commissioner
Oline L. Carter/W/F/Sept 29/Typhoid/21y/Mary F. Carter/Unmarried/Mary F. Carter Mother
Lucy C. Clarke/W/F/May 31/Not Known/45y/__/Joseph Clarke Husband
James M. Dillard/W/M/Nov 12/Consumption/71y/__Dillard/Farmer/Alma L. Dillard Wife
J.B. Howard/W/M/May 1/__/60y/__Howard/Virginia Howard Wife
L.H. Jeter/W/M/Feb 17/Whooping Cough/9m/J.G. & W. Jeter/J.G. Jeter Father
C.L. Jones/W/M/Oct 26/Rheumatism/48y/Wm F. & Sallie Jones/Farmer/Mrs. C.L. Jones Wife
Ethel McQuirt/W/F/Sept 20/Liver/5m/J.W. McQuirt/J.W. McQuirt Father
R.H.W.[Richard Henry Washington] Buckner/W/M/Feb 25/85y/__Buckner/Farmer/Married/
  W.L. Wright Relation

1896

Maggie L. Anderson/W/F/June 21/Typhoid Fever/17y/A.A. & M.L. Anderson/Single/A.A. Anderson Father
Sarah E. George/W/F/June 5/__/81y/A. & A.K. Samuel/L.M. George Husband/L.M. Baker Daughter
L.A. Gay/W/F/July 28/Bilious Fever/28y/__/R.L. Gay Husband
Sarah E. Gray/W/F/Aug 10/Cholera Infantum/3m/R.M. & E.P. Gray/R.M. Gray Father
Frans Moore/W/F/Sept/Fever/1y/F.E. & M.R. Moore/E.C. Moncure Grand Father
William Wright/W/M/Aug 20/Bowel Trouble/78y/__Wright/b.Goochland Co/Carriage Mfr/C.J. Wright Wife/W.W. Wright Son
Mattie Beasley/W/F/Mar 20/Typhoid Fever/18y/Wm & Bell Beasley/Farmer/W. Beasley Father
Nancy Baldwin/W/F/Mar 1/Heart disease/6y/G.B. Baldwin/G.B. Father
R.L. Baldwin/W/F/July 9/Measles/6m/J.B. & S.B. Baldwin/J.B. Baldwin Father
Virginia Beasley/W/F/Apr 4/Pneumonia/40y/__/A.M. Beasley Husband
Bettie W. Beasley/W/F/Mar 11/__/51y/__/J.A. Beasley Husband
__Bell/W/F/June 14/__/8d/R.W.& M.L. Bell/R.W. Bell Father
James A. Chash/W/M/Sept 5/Kidney Trouble/74y/__/Farmer/G.W. Boulware Son-in-Law
Lucy C. Broaddus/W/F/June 16/Heart Trouble/65y/__/W.W. Broaddus Husband
Alice M. Brooks/W/F/Aug 18/Typhoid Fever/50y/__/R.E. Brooks Husband
D. [Dallas] C. Bruce/W/M/June 14/Murdered/54y/__Bruce/Farmer/Married/P.W. Bruce Bro
__Bruce/W/M/Nov 18/__/1h/M.J. & L.C. Bruce/M.J. Bruce Father
H.L. Thornton/W/M/June 17/76y/__/Farmer/Married/Noraly Carter Daughter
Julia A. Gatewood/W/F/June 6/__/72y/__/Married/W.P. Chapman
M.B. Gatewood/W/F/Aug 15/__/59y/__/Married/W.P. Chapman
Younger Chinault/W/M/Sept 6/Croup/12m/Mary A. Chinault/M.A. Chinault Mother
Mary Seal/W/F/Oct 10/__/80y/__/Married/Sam Chinault
Rachel K. Farish/W/F/Dec 20/__/78y/Keeling & Rebecca Rowe/Married/K.R. Farish
Geo W. Garnett/W/M/May 2/__/21y/W.A. & E.A. Garnett/Farmer/Single/__/__
John Greenstreet/W/M/Jan 23/Heart Trouble/60y/Jno & M.S. Greenstreet/Farmer/Robt Greenstreet
Jessee Loving/W/M/Nov 6/40y/__Loving/Married/Barbee Loving
__Loving/W/M/Aug 10/__/1h/L.H. & Matilda Loving/L.H. Loving Father
__Martin/2W/2M/15 & 19 Dec/4 & 9d/Chas & R.A. Martin/Chas Martin Father
Russell Martin/W/M/Aug 23/__/1y 6m/Law & R.A. Martin/Law Martin Father
Kate Minir/W/F/Oct 20/__/1y/Jno C. & B.H. Minir/Jno C. Minir Father
Martha W. Monday/W/F/Sept 17/Paralysis/72y/__/Married/J.W. Monday Son
R.S. Parr/W/M/Dec 11/Suicide/56y/__Parr/Farmer/Sallie B. Parr Wife
Carry Pitts/W/F/Mar 11/Child Birth/22y/Married/F.H. Pitts Husband
Lucy E. Puller/W/F/Apr 6/Fever/24y/W.S. & S.E. Puller/J.E. Puller Husband
M.E. Rolph/W/F/Apr 3/Pneumonia/68y/__/Phillips Rolph Son
Jno M. Self/W/M/Aug 29/Consumption/54y/__Self/Married/J.F. Self
__Sylva/W/F/June 25/1m 20d/W.T. & M.A. Sylva/W.T. Sylva Father
Roland Taylor/W/M/Aug 10/Heart Trouble/21y/R.L. & T.J. Taylor/Farmer/R.L. Taylor Father
__Shepherd/C/F/Sept/__/3m/Laura Shepherd/L. Shepherd Mother
__Alexander/C/F/Dec 26/__/6d/J.E. & M.L. Alexander/J.E. Alexander Father
Willie & Rose Alexander/2C/1M/1F/8 & 22 May/28d & 4d/R. & Sally Alexander/Richard Alexander Father

O.G. Allen/C/F/Aug 10/Brain Fever/8m/R. & E. Allen/R. Allen Father
Charles Baylor/C/M/Jan 10/Shot/__/Mary Baylor/Mary Baylor Mother
Geo Brown/C/M/Mar 10/Bladder/21y/Peyton & L. Brown/Laborer/Lucy Brown Mother
Robt Brown/C/M/Jan 10/__/76y/__Brown/Laborer/Commissioner
__Brown/C/F/Sept 10/__/2m/Walker & Ella Brown/Walker Brown Father
Ella Brown/C/F/Aug 2/Heart Trouble/30y/__/Walker Brown Husband
Kate Ware/C/F/Sept 4/__/30y/__Ware/Single/Jas L. Byrd
D.M. Byrd/C/F/Oct 7/__/3y/J.W. & N.T. Byrd/J.W. Byrd Father
__Carter/C/M/Feb 26/Spasms/1m 2d/P.H. & Lucy Carter/P.H. Carter Father
C.T. Coleman/C/M/Feb 26/Bowel Trouble/60y/__Coleman/Laborer/Malinda Coleman Wife
__Davis/2C/2F/Feb 10/__/8d/L. & M.L. Davis/Lewis Davis Father
Nannie Gouldin/C/F/July 2/Burnt/9y/W.L. & Ella Gouldin/W.L. Gouldin Father
J.P. Green/C/M/July 12/Brain Fever/19y/Mary Green/Mary Green Mother
Calvin Green/C/M/Nov 27/Consumption/24y/J.T. & C. Green/J.T. Green Father
Mary Rollins/C/F/June 12/Hurt/37y/Spencer & S. Rollins/Ben Hicks
Columbia Ross/C/F/Oct 10/Consumption/58y/__/Married/L.D. Hudson
__Jackson/C/M/Nov 10/__/1m/Geo & Fanny Jackson/Geo Jackson Father
William Jeter/C/M/Aug 28/Dropsy/15y/Sam & M.E. Jeter/Sam Jeter Father
Robt M. Johnson/C/M/Mar 2/Heart Trouble/49y/__Johnson/Mary L. Johnson Wife
L.D. Lee/C/F/Sept 11/Cholera/20y/Nelson & Elsie Lee/Nelson Lee Father
Flossie Lee/C/F/Sept 11/Cholera/11y/Nelson & Elsie Lee/Nelson Lee Father
Tom Lee/C/M/Sept 11/Cholera/15y/Nelson & Elsie Lee/Nelson Lee Father
Hattie Lee/C/F/Sept ll/Cholera/12y/Nelson & Elsie Lee/Nelson Lee Father
Lizzie M. Lomax/C/F/Dec 10/__/1m 10d/Joe & Veria Lomax/Joe Lomax Father
Lottie Ludley/C/F/July 2/__/21y/Wm & Veria Ludley/Wm Ludley Father
Cath Merriweather/C/F/Nov 27/__/79y/Jno & Clara Harper/Wm Merriweather Husband
Clarence Walker/C/M/Mar 15/__/4m/Annie Walker/Annie Walker Mother
Alfred Moore/C/M/Oct 11/__/2m 28d/Mary Moore/Mary Moore Mother
M.M. Parker/C/F/May 10/Consumption/25y/__/Jas E. Parker Husband
Eliz & __Parker/2C/1M/1F/June 1 & Aug 2/__/2m & 1d/P.B. & A.W. Parker/P.B. Parker Father
John Pearson/C/M/Sept/Burnt/9m/C.L. & Lucy B. Parker/C.L. Parker Father
__Queen/C/M/June 17/__/7d/Polly Queen/Polly Queen Mother
Naee Roy/C/M/Apr 11/Pneumonia/45y/Naee & Hannah Roy/Farmer/A.B. Roy Wife
Isaac Brown/C/M/July 26/__/60y/J. Brown/Farmer/Luther Scott
Harriett Taylor/C/F/June 20/__/28y/Abram Taylor Husband
Thomas Whiting/C/M/July 27/__/77y/Tom Whiting/Albert Whiting Son
Maria Willis/C/F/Mar 10/Hemoridge/60y/__/B.G. Willis Husband
H.M. Young/C/M/Dec 8/Consumption/22y/J. & A.E. Young/Laborer/Jas Young Father
Sarah Brown/W/F/June 9/Cholera Infantum/4m/R.M. & Carry Brown/R.M. Brown Father
Fanny Coleman/W/F/June 17/__/72y/__/Married/__/__
Catlett Conway/W/M/July 13/__/74y/J.C. Conway/Farmer/M.F. Conway Wife
B.H. Hicks/W/M/June 22/Bladder/72y/Jno Hicks/Farmer/Married/C.F. Hicks Son
Laura Motley/W/F/June 18/Fever/2y/F.H. & L.L. Motley/T.H. Motley Father
Wm H. Samuel/W/M/Nov 10/Consumption/48y/__Samuel/J.J. Raines
G.G. Samuel/W/F/Sept 6/__/4m/J.L. & P.C. Samuel/J.L. Samuel Father
__Saunders/W/M/July 10/1m 20d/W.W. & M.J. Saunders/W.W. Saunders Father
Geo M. Harris/C/M/Aug 5/Fever/18y/Jno F. & Rose Harris/Jno F. Harris Father

Jno T. Ware/C/M/July 25/__/4y/Jacob & M.E. Ware/Jacob Ware Father
Lula Banks/C/F/Nov 25/Typhoid Fever/17y/W. & Emma Banks/Wm Banks Father
Estelle Banks/C/F/Dec 23/Typhoid Fever/13y/Wm & Emma Banks/Wm Banks Father
Rachel Jones/C/F/May 29/__/60y/__/Willie Banks
J.B. Young/C/M/Jan 23/__/25y/__Young/Laborer/Warner Baylor
Tom Coghill/C/M/Dec 8/84y/__Coghill/Farmer/__/__
Wm Ferguson/C/M/June 20/Typhoid Fever/__/Wm Ferguson/__
Temple Grymes/C/M/Sept 25/84y/Temple Grymes/Farmer/Jane Grymes Wife
Ann Howard/C/F/Feb 20/__/17y/Jane Howard/Jane Howard Mother
Thos Guss/C/M/Apr 10/Pneumonia/21y/__Guss/__/__
Julian Ham/C/M/Oct 16/__/19y/Sarah Ham/Sarah Ham Mother
Reuben Ellis/C/M/July 10/__/75y/__Ellis/James Hopkins
Reuben Johnson/C/M/Apr 9/Scrofula/55y/__Johnson/__
James Parker/C/M/Nov 15/__/74y/__Parker/Married/__
Jacob Robertson/C/M/May 10/Heart/50y/__Robertson/__
L.B. Robertson/C/F/Feb 10/Typhoid Fever/16y/Robt & Bettie Robertson/Robt Robertson Father
Julia Robertson/C/M/Sept 15/Typhoid Fever/14y/Robt & Bettie Robertson/Robt Robertson Father
Robt Roy/C/M/Feb 10/Pneumonia/45y/__Roy/Married/Jerry Roy
Ellen Ware/C/F/Oct 10/__/72y/__/Geo Ware Husband
A.L. McKenney/W/F/Feb 29/Consumption/75y/Chas & Malinda Beasley/Widow/M.E. Sutton Aunt
__Thomas/C/F/Mar 17/__/__/Fanny Thomas/M.E. Sutton Employer
No Name/W/M/July 26/Unknown/10d/Jno T. & Bettie Allen/Jno T. Allen Father
Ella L. Ancarrow/W/F/Nov 26/Child Birth/38y/Lewis & Martha Sirles/Married/R.P. Ancarrow Husband
Waller Baber/C/M/Dec 10/Rheumatism/40y/Not Known/Farmer/Mrs Baber Wife
Linwood Blanton/W/M/Nov 23/Croup/3y/Geo & Blanche Blanton/Geo G. Blanton Father
No Name/W/M/Mar 6/Unknown/3d/Geo & Blanche Blanton
J. Alvin Blanton/W/M/June 16/Congestion of Brain/7m/J.A. & Callie Blanton/J.A. Blanton Father
Ruby Blanton/W/F/June 13/Flux/3y/R.A. & Kate Blanton/R.A. Blanton Father
Henry S. Blank/W/M/June 8/Suicide/50y/William & Virginia Blank/Merchant/B.J. Blank Wife
Ann Brown/C/F/Mar 12/Unknown/2y/Geo & Sophia Brown/Geo Brown Father
Lillian B. Burruss/W/F/July 5/Unknown/9y/W.W. & Eddie Burruss/W.W. Burruss Father
George W. Bush/W/M/Oct 20/Gravel/68y/Unknown/Farmer/Mrs. Bush Wife
Mary Carter/C/F/May 5/Unknown/11y/Albert & Barbara Carter/Albert Carter Father
Sam Carter/C/M/Sept 20/Spinal Affection/1y/Thos & Emma Carter/Thos Carter Father
Sallie B. Carter/W/F/Apr 4/Unknown/13y/Jno & Sallie Carter/Jno Carter Father
Martha R.E. Cannon/W/F/Apr 5/Heart Disease/63y/Thos & Mary Grubbs/C.R. Cannon Daughter
Mary Catlett/W/F/Aug 21/Old Age/82y/Lawrence & Mary Catlett/T.H. Blanton Friend
No Name/W/M/Apr 11/Unknown/1d/Arch & Lucy J. Clark/Arch Clark Father
Lettie Cooper/C/F/Feb 3/Consumption/6y/Jas & Bettie Cooper/James Cooper Father
Emma Cooper/C/F/Feb 17/Consumption/5y/Jas & Bettie Cooper/James Cooper Father
Bettie Cooper/C/F/May 1/Consumption/27y/Not Known/James Cooper Husband
John Cooper/C/M/May 8/Consumption/2y/Jas & Bettie Cooper/Jas Cooper Father
Bettie Cooper/C/F/May 9/Consumption/4m/Jas & Betty Cooper/James Cooper Father
No Name/W/F/Apr 15/Unknown/1d/R.T. & Nellie Dillard/R.T. Dillard Father
Horace Dodson/C/M/Nov 5/Whooping Cough/2m/Alex & Clemmie Dodson/Alex Dodson Father

Emma Durrett/W/F/Oct 6/Child Birth/30y/Lafayette & Jennie Young/b.Spottsylvania/E.V. Durrett Husband

A.C. Flippo/W/M/July 11/Unknown/50y/Littleton & Sarah Flippo/Farmer/T.J. Flippo Cousin

Jos A. Flippo/W/M/Apr 5/Cancer of Stomach/74y/Jos P. & Fannie Flippo/Physician/Mary E. Flippo Wife

Robert Fox/C/M/Jan/Unknown/5y/Robt & Rose Fox/Robt Fox Father

Warner Glasco/C/M/Apr 30/Consumption/60y/Unknown/Laborer/Mary Glasco Daughter

Patrick Gouldin/W/M/Nov 1/Suicide/22y/Silas & Lucy Gouldin/Silas Gouldin Father

Lucy Ann Holmes/C/F/Oct/Unknown/48y 10d/Unknown/Cornelius Holmes Husband

No Name/C/M/May 14/Unknown/1d/Danl & Martha James/Danl James Father

Alice Johnson/C/F/Apr 4/Lagrippe/36y/Margarett Washington/Chas Johnson Husband

Martha Johnson/C/F/Jan 6/Unknown/17y/Lewis & Rose Johnson/Lewis Johnson Father

T.H. Jones/W/M/May 19/Paralysis/66y/Unknown/Farmer/E.C. Jones Wife

Isaac King/C/M/June 12/Consumption/42y/Unknown/Lewis King Son

Sallie King/C/F/Mar 15/Child Birth/38y/Lewis King Son

Julia Lewis/C/F/Dec 6/Burnt/5y/Jesse & Matilda Lewis/Jesse Lewis Father

Lucy Lewis/C/F/Oct 6/Whooping Cough/11y/Mollie Lewis/Mollie Lewis Mother

Temple Lewis/C/M/May 11/Consumption/65y/Unknown/Sophia Lewis Wife

Theodore Mason/W/M/June 12/Unknown/17y/J.D. & Mary Mason/J.D. Mason Father

Cassandria Minor/C/F/June 29/Paralysis/49y/Unknown/Jas Coleman Friend

Mary Mont/C/F/Apr 10/Consumption/22y/Willie & Maria Jones/Jiles Mont Husband

Wm M. Moore/C/M/Nov 6/Whooping Cough/2m/Jas M. & Sallie Moore/Jas M. Moore Father

W.L. Moore/C/F/Nov 15/Whooping Cough/2y/Jeff & Elizabeth Moore/Jeff Moore Father

W.J. Moore/C/F/Nov 14/Child Birth/17y/F.C. & Nancy Bowman/Burton Moore Husband

No Name/C/M/Nov 16/Unknown/6d/Burton & W.J. Moore/Burton Moore Father

No Name/W/F/Feb 6/Unknown/6d/R.J. & Mary Payne/R.J. Payne Father

Thos H. Reynolds/W/M/Feb 10/Pneumonia/35y/Tazewell & Amanda Reynolds/Bettie S. Reynolds Wife

Matilda Rolls/C/F/Dec 20/Unknown/31y/Wesley & Maria Jones/Maria Jones Mother

Cora Lee Sacra/W/F/May 15/Burnt/6y/Jas T. & Clemmie Sacra/Jas T. Sacra Father

Joseph Shuman/W/M/Nov 8/Membranious Croup/3y/F.E. & N.J. Shuman/F.E. Shuman Father

James D. Smith/W/M/July 10/Old Age/83y/Mary & J.R. Smith/Millard A. Smith Son

Minnie B. Southworth/W/F/Oct 5/Cholera Infantum/11m/Jas N. & M.F. Southworth/Jas N. Southworth Father

Taylor Stuart/C/M/Aug 15/Fever/9y/Winston & Mary Stuart/Winston Stuart Father

John Swann/C/M/Mar 18/Consumption/14y/Minor & Lucy Swann/Minor Swann Father

Edmond Taylor/C/M/June 10/Drowned/22y/Jas & Jennie Taylor/James Taylor Father

James Temple/C/M/Mar 16/Consumption/65y/Jas & Mary Temple/Jas Temple Father

Alice Thompson/C/F/Oct 10/Unknown/30y/Danl & Eliza Webster/Byrd Thompson Husband

Almira Williams/C/F/Mar 18/Consumption/60y/Geo & Mary Williams/Oliver Williams Son

J.H. Winn/W/M/Dec 28/Old Age/70y/Jesse Winn/Kitty Winn Wife

F.A. Woolfolk/W/F/Jan 6/Congestion of Brain/41y/Wm H. & Rachel Farish/W.A. Woolfolk Husband

Eliza Hill/W/F/Sept 10/Old Age/86y/Unknown/L.H. Tunstall Friend

SURNAME INDEX

ABRAHAM, 10 43
ABRAMS, 113 155
ACORS, 44 49 53 56 79 102 121 124 127 133-134 140 145 166 168-169
ACRES, 73
ADAMS, 13 19 81 96 123 133 157
ADDISON, 110
ADKINS, 100
ALEXANDER, 30 89 103 123 127 131 148 169 171
ALLEN, 1 13 19 22 25 29-30 36 41 44 49 54 59 61 68-69 75 79 81 83 87 89-92 94-95 97 101 103 111 116-117 122 130 133 139-140 143 145-146 148 152 161 163 169 172-173
ALLPORT, 32 90 98 158
ALPORT, 54
ALSOP, 46 63 78-79 85 92 114 137 140 146 157-158 161
AMAEL, 118
AMBROSE, 30
ANCARRO, 110
ANCARROW, 173
ANDERSON, 1 5 7 10 21 23 25 27 29 32 38-39 41-42 44 46 48 54 56-57 64-65 68 85 89 98-99 101 104 116-117 121 130-131 140 152 154-155 159 162 164 168 170-171
ANDREW, 47
ANDREWS, 5 31 33 38 43 47 61-62 65 76 78 83-85 90 98 169
ARMISTEAD, 133 143 151 154 159 162
ARNALL, 87
ARNOLD, 49 97 103 131 137 146 148 157 165
ASHTON, 96-97 107 128
ASKINS, 100 125
ASKO, 88
ATKINS, 21 35 40 49-50
ATKINSON, 8 27 49 59 70 87 110 123
AUSTIN, 155
AYERS, 104 110 133
AYRES, 17 22 95 101 105 108 113 116-117 125 151
BABER, 113 123 133 145 147 173
BACKS, 96

BAGBY, 16 53 56 98
BAKER, 46 63 98 101 134 139 152 159 168 171
BALDWIN, 22 90 171
BALL, 9 44 47 60 96 101 134
BANDER, 31
BANKS, 82 85 99 116 123 127-128 143 148 154 159 173
BARBEE, 1 5 17 32-33 47 55 66
BARLOW, 1 8 46 55 66 77 79 84 95 99 103-104 111 114 121 131 140-141 145 154
BARNES, 161
BARRUSS, 29
BARTLETT, 100 153
BASTON, 122
BATES, 1 5 127 154 159 165
BATTAILE, 11 16 25 33-34 37 45 63 80
BATTAILES, 93
BAUGHAN, 8 11
BAUGHN, 21 26-27 50 60 103 117 155 165
BAYHAN, 8
BAYLOR, 5 46 49 54-55 64 79 83 90 93 95 101 106 109-111 114 121-122 126-127 129 134-135 139 139 143 145 148 151 161 163 165 169 172-173
BAYNHAM, 82 144
BAZELL, 36 157
BAZLEY, 141
BEALL, 125
BEASLEY, 121-122 127 134 139 143 150-151 164 166-167 169 171 173
BEAZLEY, 12-13 16 22-23 28 31 39-40 46 51 60 65 67 73 79 84-85 87 95 101-103 105 109 111 114 116 121 123 127 130 137 150 159 162 164
BELL, 4-5 38 148 161 171
BENDALL, 76 95 123
BENDELL, 3
BENNET, 105
BENNETT, 74 79 105 149
BENSEN, 96
BENSON, 99 152
BENUM, 141
BERKLEY, 12

BERLY, 130
BERNARD, 1 5 15 24 33 39 49 66
BERRY, 44 116
BEVERLEY, 98 102 139 148 167
BEVERLY, 108 110 114 143 152 157
BIBB, 4 7 10-11 41 69 95 106 157
BIBBS, 50
BIQUE, 121
BIRD, 1 24 55 78
BLACK, 134 148
BLACKLEY, 157
BLAGBURN, 101
BLAGBURNE, 134
BLAIR, 162
BLAKE, 15
BLAND, 89 149
BLANK, 141 173
BLANTON, 3-4 8 10 17 29 36 41-42 50 53 69 75-76 79 81 83 87-88 90 95 97 110 118-119 123 125 137 142 146-147 152-153 155 157 162 165 168 173
BLAYBURN, 107
BLAYDES, 9 27 50 97
BLUNT, 29 36 52 69 79 87 89
BLYTHE, 108
BOGWELL, 108
BOLLEY, 110
BORINO, 97
BOSWELL, 110 165
BOULDIN, 169
BOULWARE, 1 3 5 12 14 19 23-24 32-34 36 39-41 43-45 49-50 53 55 61-62 64 67 82 85 87 89-90 96 103 108 111 118 121 134 147 171
BOUTWELL, 5 15 23 31 40 45-47 56 65 86
BOWERS, 7 53 82 93 117 125 144 152 162
BOWIE, 24 48 54 93 142 145 148 151 169
BOWLER, 130
BOXLEY, 114 125 165
BOXWELL, 139
BOZNELL, 95
BOZWELL, 101 109
BRANAN, 165
BRANHAM, 110 114
BRAXTON, 8 74 100-101 123 134 139 147-148
BRAYNHAM, 40
BRIDGES, 69 163
BRIT, 130
BRITZIN, 74
BROADDUS, 1-2 5 15-16 22-23 30 32-34 38-39 43-44 46-49 54-55 61 66 76-77 79 84 97 100 111-112 114 116-117 121 127 143 150 154 160-161 164 166 168 171

BROADUS, 53
BROKEN, 144
BROMTON, 104
BROOKE, 15 79
BROOKS, 1 3 17 22 30 44 46-47 54 62 66 76-77 89 95 98 101 108 123 127 129 133-134 143 145 148 154 160 166 171
BROWELL, 136
BROWN, 16 25 42 78 83-84 90 95 101 104 106 108 111 116-118 130-131 139 143-144 151-152 155 157 159 162 169 172-173
BRUCE, 1 40 95 99 105 121 131 148 161 171
BUCHANAN, 113 133 146
BUCKLEY, 50 74
BUCKNER, 1 5 14-15 25 33-34 49 57 63 66 78 85 87 97 100 103 118 127 131 135 141 148 154 170
BUDD, 99
BULLARD, 50 121
BULLOCK, 1 47 87 89 118 121 127 131 134 136 165 169
BUNDY, 69 102 148 159 169
BURK, 20 57 105
BURKE, 4 10 13 27 40 69 79 125
BURKINS, 87
BURKLEY, 42 58
BURNARD, 5 15
BURNETT, 36 89 96 114 133 143 152 155 157
BURRUS, 37
BURRUSS, 4 7 9-11 13 18 21 23 27 30 32 35-36 40 47 50 57 60 67 69 76 79 87 103 107-108 118 125 130 133 137 143 147 155 165 168 173
BURSLEY, 78
BURTON, 45 118
BURUSS, 18 32
BUSH, 173
BUTCHER, 149
BUTLER, 5 25 38 55 67 69 77 88 99 114 133 165
BUTTS, 87
BUTZNER, 104
BYERS, 149
BYRD, 98 121 143 148 154 159 172
CAIN, 97 143
CALLAWN, 108
CALLIS, 77 152
CALLISS, 24 152
CAMMACK, 123 125
CAMMICK, 123
CAMPBELL, 3-4 7 9 13 17 20 26 29 32 38 43-44 48 53 56-57 60 65 69 75 84 91 93 105 108-109 116-119 127 134 143 148-149 155 160
CANADY, 88
CANDAY, 104

CANNON, 37 75 83 114 137 157 173
CANNOR, 88
CARATER, 87
CARE, 84
CARLTON, 50 69-70 95 130 137 145 152 162
CARNAL, 3 7 10 13 19 29 37-38
CARNALL, 3 10
CARNEAL, 1 3 5 11 19 24 28-29 36 43-44 47 49 65-68 79-80 87 92 103-104 106 110-111 114-116 118 121-123 125 130-131 134 141 145 152 157 162 165
CARPENTER, 58 113-114 123
CARR, 68 140
CARRICK, 49
CARRISON, 88
CARSON, 50 125 157
CARTER, 1 5 8-9 17 19 21 26-27 30 39-40 43-44 48 50 52 58-60 62 67-69 72-73 78 80-83 87-89 91 95-97 99 104 106-111 113 116 118 120-121 123 125 131-132 134 137 139 141 143 145 147 149 151-154 157 159-160 162 164 167 170-173
CARTHORNE, 145
CASE, 17
CASH, 52 88 101 112 162
CATER, 149
CATLETT, 5 11 16-17 24 29 32 34 37 41 45 47-48 53 57 68 79 85 91 93 97 108-109 113 118 131 134 136 139 143 145 147 151 154 170 173
CATTLETT, 57
CAUTHORN, 83 99
CAYNOR, 131 154 159
CECIL, 1 15-16 30 43 47 53 76 95 98 107 122 142
CHAMBERS, 121
CHANDLER, 1 3-5 7 9-11 13-14 17 19 21 24 33-35 40 42-45 48 50 53 56 58-59 62 65 68 74-75 82 84 90 99 101 121-122 137 139 142-143 169
CHAPMAN, 1 5 16 22 30 38 53 63 79 85 97 104 107 110 116 118 134 145 159 168 171
CHARLTON, 34
CHASH, 171
CHATMAN, 130
CHENAULT, 1 15 46-47 49 54 76 84 95 98 101 107 121 134 139 160
CHEWNING, 91 110 142-143 152
CHILES, 12 34 53 60-61 68 79-80 82 88 92 97-98 106 109-111 116 118 121 123 131 139-140 149 154-155 159-160 168
CHINAULT, 33 46 91 134 151 155 171
CHISHOLM, 123
CHRISIAN, 74
CHRISTIAN, 19 74 85 162
CHRISTOPHER, 167
CLAIBORN, 117
CLAIBORNE, 92 118 123
CLARK, 28 44 62 127 131 137 139 143 147 155 162 173
CLARKE, 2 4 16 25 34-35 44 48 84-85 109 170
CLATTERBUCK, 106 111
CLATTIBUCK, 134
CLAYBORN, 113 152
CLAYTON, 55 127 130 137
CLAYTOR, 26 83-84 89 97 123 127 130 133 149 164
CLEAR, 96
CLOE, 57
CLORE, 52
CLOY, 152
COALTER, 49
COATE, 80
COATES, 9 106 117-118
COATS, 36 40 50 68 88-89 92 120
COATTER, 54
COBB, 67-68 72 80 88 92 96 104 110 114 118 123 141 156 162
COBBS, 8-12 17 19 29 38 40 50 58-59 82
COGHILL, 1 13 16 22 37 40-41 53 60 64-65 68 91 107 114 118 123 125 131 137 159 173
COLE, 5 15 46 54 61 76-77 91 104 137 139 149
COLEMAN, 3-4 7 9-10 12-13 15-16 19-22 28-29 32 35-37 40-43 52-53 57-60 68-69 80-82 84 87-89 92 98 101 104 109-110 113-114 117-119 121-123 125 127 130 133 135 137 141 143 147 152-153 155 157 159 162 165 167-168 172 174
COLLAWN, 1 5 14-15 24 33 55
COLLINS, 12 15 17-19 28-29 36 40-41 43 50 59 68-69 75 80-81 92 96 103-104 106 114 118 135 139 145 153 165
CONDUIT, 6 84
CONNELL, 134
CONNER, 82 88
CONWAY, 1 24-25 30 45 49 56 63 79 84 86 104 106 111 163 172
COOK, 74 137 149
COOKE, 91
COOPER, 17 35 82 88 120 145 147 156 173
COOR, 37
COOTES, 60
COR, 37
CORBIN, 12 14 25 34 46 49 56 68 98 118 122 143 149 165
CORR, 82 88 162 165
CORSE, 55
COSBY, 139
COUGHTON, 147

COURTNEY, 42 73 88 123 125 133 166 168-169
COVINGTON, 13 16 30-31 74 78 84 111 131 143 149 151 154 161
COWEN, 6 16
COX, 1 34-35 38 68 104 113-114 143 156
CRANIE, 22
CRENSHAW, 82 88 122
CRIDLIN, 111
CROLEY, 121
CRONIE, 5 16
CROUGHTON, 147
CROWLEY, 25 48-49
CRUMP, 23 31 114
CULLEN, 109
DABNEY, 40 87 106 133 137 152 166
DANDRIDGE, 89 106 109 147
DANGERFIELD, 155 165
DAPREE, 55
DAVENPORT, 157
DAVIES, 90
DAVIS, 48 96 104 117 123 133 141 147 152 165 168 172
DAY, 96 135 155
DEJARNETT, 40 57 67 84 88
DEJARNETTE, 1 9 21-23 30 43 45-47 49 57 86 121 165
DEJARNETTTE, 49
DELANIE, 98
DELONGAN, 28
DENNIS, 101 111
DERRYCOTT, 155 157
DES, 111
DEW, 1 14 22-23 31 34 38-39 44 46 67-68 165
DICK, 3 29 60 75
DICKENS, 88
DICKERSON, 105
DICKINS, 18 50
DICKINSON, 3-4 7 9 12-13 17 20-21 25 28-29 34-37 49-50 55 59 65 69-70 87 92 100-101 109 113 138 140-141 147 152-153 155 157
DIDLAKE, 16
DIEHL, 13
DIGGES, 117 168
DIGGINS, 122
DIGGS, 59 69
DILLARD, 1-2 45 101 107 109 128 135 151 154 168 170 173
DIMMUE, 18
DIMUE, 98 145 156 158 168
DISHAGO, 77
DISHAYS, 24
DISHMAN, 91 100-102 106 111 164

DODSON, 89 100 107 129 153 155 160 170 173
DOGGESTT, 104
DOGGETT, 10-11 19 37-38 43 52 69 79-80 82 104 113
DOLLINGS, 130
DOLLINS, 32 47 62 77 118 169
DONAHOE, 12 17 22-23 25 69 74 109-110 141 152 155 157 165-166
DONAWAY, 121
DORSEY, 92
DOUGLACE, 88
DOWNING, 2 5 17 32 34 44 48 55-56 140 143 161
DRATT, 97 143
DUDLEY, 113
DUKE, 57 119
DULANEY, 116
DULING, 32 39
DUN, 54
DUNN, 54 82 85 154-155 168
DUNNARANT, 85
DURACOTT, 123
DURETT, 87
DURRETT, 10 20-21 28 37 42 50 59-60 68 70 73 81 97 110 123 130 141 145 152 155 157 162 165 174
DURVIN, 37 80
DURVINE, 75
DUSTIN, 68
DUTTON, 72
DUVAL, 5 11 32 110 114 155
DUVALL, 38 60 69 107
DYSON, 8 12 35 42 58-59 68 70 72 74-75 99 104 110 123 134 145 152 155 165 168
EDMONDSON, 30 67
EDMUNDSON, 76
EDWARDS, 12 66 84 125
ELLERSON, 32
ELLIOTT, 62 95 135 143
ELLIS, 89 104 107 131 135 148 173
ELLYSON, 152
ENGLAND, 29 57 134 145 165 168
ENNIS, 61 66 85 94 128
EPPES, 107 148
EPPS, 151 155
ESTES, 1 6 36 50
ESTIS, 8
EUBANK, 22 29 50 70 164 166
EUBANKS, 66 106-107 112
EVANS, 27 36 58 70 139
FARINHOLD, 94
FARINHOLT, 23 31 39 64 66 94 97 136
FARISH, 4 20 24 41 44 50 55 58-59 75 91 109 118

FARISH (Cont.) 123 127 151 160 171 174
FARLEY, 130 137
FARMER, 3 5-6 35 45-46 48 63 65 78 85 98 101 108 121 127 140 149 161 166
FARRINGTON, 82
FELL, 87
FELLS, 118 123 130 137 142 147-148 151 156
FERGERSON, 156
FERGUSON, 88 96 109 121 136 142 151 173
FIELDS, 16 78 101 117 131 143
FISE, 81
FITZHUGH, 1 34 39 45 47 53-54 57 61 66
FKIPPO, 147
FLAGG, 36 80-82 141 147 156
FLEMING, 88 117
FLEMMING, 142
FLIPPO, 4 9 11 19-20 28 35 41 53 58 70 76 80 88 92 104 118 123 125 130-131 135 141 147-149 152 156 162 165 174
FLOOD, 155
FOGG, 140
FOIES, 157
FORD, 104
FORTUNE, 44 66 78 93-94 100-101 109 113 117 121 135 142 159 167 170
FOSE, 81 88
FOSTER, 168
FOUNTAIN, 47 114 147 165
FOUNTLOE, 6
FOUNTTON, 47
FOX, 4 28 57 80-81 89 92 110 113 118 130 137 141 145 156-157 159 162 165 168 174
FOY, 101
FRANKS, 121
FRAUGHNAUGH, 139
FRAWNER, 139 147
FRAZIER, 44 55 82 98 105 112 127 159 161
FREEMAN, 11 23 25 27 36 89 104 108 123 125 130 141 147 151-152 157 165 168 170
FRENCH, 97 100 132
FRIES, 74 114
FRY, 143 170
FRYES, 127
FUGETT, 117
GAINES, 127 159 164
GALERY, 88 130
GALLERY, 82 84 95
GALLORY, 79
GALORY, 109
GANT, 70 95
GAPHNEY, 153 156

GARNETT, 3 6 8 11 15 17 19 22-25 35 39 45 48 77-78 84-85 95 97-98 107 117 120 122 128 135 139 142 147 149 157 171
GARNETTE, 80
GARRET, 54
GARRETT, 6 22 47 57 64-67 111 120 139 142 150 167
GATES, 54
GATEWOOD, 10-11 19 21 29 31-32 37 39 41 53-54 62 66-67 75-76 79-80 84 91 95-98 107 109 114 116-118 120 125 130-131 141 147-149 151 157 162 165 168 171
GAY, 153 171
GAYLE, 15 30 101 125 149-150 156
GAYNES, 146 149 156
GAYNOR, 133
GENTRY, 99 141
GEORGE, 5 7 10 13 18-19 25-26 35 41 50 57 70 131 162 171
GIBBS, 31 39 45 48 89 93-94 104 114 121 162
GIBSON, 41 114 147 153 162
GILES, 123
GILL, 149
GIVINGS, 137
GLASCO, 174
GLASCOE, 92-93
GLASSEL, 32
GLASSELL, 6 15 24 32 44 48-49 151
GLEN, 141
GODFREY, 158
GOLDBERRY, 36 74
GOLDBERY, 51
GOLDEN, 147
GOLDMAN, 101
GOLDSBERRY, 9 74
GOLDSBURY, 73
GOLDSBY, 9 51 73 88 147
GOOD, 98
GOODALL, 110
GOODE, 30 155
GOODLOE, 4 18 37 70 74 104 110 125
GOODWIN, 4-6 10 12-13 16-17 20 27-29 36 43 50-51 53 57 61 73 95 100 109 125 130 137 144 153 157 165 167
GORDAN, 91
GORDON, 2 6 13 34 46 49 66 85 148 154-155 160
GOULDIN, 1-2 6 24 30 33 38-39 44-47 49 54-55 57 64-66 76-77 79 85 91 94 111 120 131 139 159 161 169 172 174
GOULDMAN, 6 16 39 45 48 53-54 66 85 98 105-106 111 117 120 127 139 149 164 169
GRAHAM, 100

GRAND, 131 134
GRANNELL, 52
GRANT, 104
GRASCOW, 157
GRAVATT, 16 20 24 31-32 34 41 44 47 49 56 61 66 73 76 85 88 100-101 108 114 120 127 129 140 142 149 164 170
GRAVATTE, 79
GRAVES, 12 85 101 111 120 139
GRAY, 14 24 31 38 40 46-47 55 65-66 77 91-92 95 98 101 104 107 110 120-122 127 130-131 134 141-142 144 151 160-162 164 166-167 170-171
GRAYSON, 109
GREEN, 2 6 14-16 22 39 43-46 54 61-63 78 80-82 84 94 98-99 104 107 109 111 125 127 129-130 135 137 154 156-157 159 165
GREENSTREET, 66 84 127 171
GREGORY, 88 95
GREN, 172
GRESHAM, 96
GRIFFIN, 33 101
GRIMES, 5 19 23-24 44 88 104 111 123 135 139 170
GRIMSLEY, 117
GRUBBS, 10 73 95 99 104 173
GRUNDY, 89
GRYMES, 109 111 131 135 139 142 150 173
GURST, 62
GUS, 120 139
GUSS, 161 167 170 173
GUTHRIDGE, 49 53 85
GUTHRIGHT, 62
GUTRIDGE, 121
GYLES, 96
HACKETT, 3 3 7 11 51 70 95 125 153 157
HACKNEY, 21
HAGAN, 90 153
HAIDEN, 79 85
HAILE, 107
HAILSTALK, 149
HAILSTOCK, 45 88 93 101 104 111-112 170
HAILSTORK, 100 110 123 130 134 137
HAINES, 80
HALEY, 3
HALL, 80 110
HAM, 128 130 135 139 173
HAMPTON, 165
HANCOCK, 4 9 29 41 51 168
HANCOCKE, 80
HANDYMAN, 153
HARDIMAN, 48 108 112
HARGRAVE, 11 60 71 76 115 126 148 158
HARPER, 75 130 146
HARRING, 102
HARRIS, 4 11 20 36 41 43 49 51 56 59 61 70 88 90 104 107 109 112 115 117 120 126-127 135 137 139 142 145 156 161-162 166 172
HARRISON, 2 6 15 23 30 32 55 97 110 113 130 164
HART, 58-59 75 80 104 110 137 146-147 169
HARVEY, 65
HATE, 140
HATTON, 52
HAUNES, 142
HAWKINS, 140 142 149
HAYDEN, 79 85 94
HAYES, 80 140
HAYNES, 91 135 144 169
HAYS, 80 101
HAYWOOD, 88 141
HEAD, 95
HEAN, 113-114
HENDERSON, 28 36 57 88 109 117-118 137
HENDRICKS, 115
HENRY, 40 130
HENSON, 95
HERRING, 106 109
HEWLETT, 127 138
HEYWOOD, 78
HICKS, 64 131 142 165 172
HILL, 3 7 26 41-42 46 51 75 80 85 87 96 98 114-115 117 126 135 156 159 161 165 167 174
HITER, 96
HODGES, 130
HOLLOWAY, 2 6 14 23-24 32 40 45 49 55 66 94 135
HOLMES, 88 101-102 106-107 115 118 134 137 142-143 146-147 153 157 162 164-165 168 170 174
HOLT, 14
HOMES, 93-94 101
HOODLASS, 106 111
HOOMES, 112 117 120 135 139 142 149 155
HOOPER, 117
HOPE, 130
HOPKIINS, 94
HOPKINS, 94 107 111 117 128-129 133 135 144 149 158 162 173
HORD, 52
HOUSTON, 22 25 30 32 39 46-47 55 61-62 64 66 76-77 90 98 101 120 122 149 151 154 161 164 169
HOWARD, 6 22 30 33 44 101 104 107 109 117 120 122 135 139 142 162 170 173
HUDGIN, 2 14 34 150 161

HUDGINS, 58 112
HUDSON, 2 172
HUGHES, 10 18 26 59 125 137
HUMPHREYS, 82 142
HUMPHRIES, 46 62 156
HUNDLEY, 7 10-11 19 60 70 75 87 124
HUNTER, 9 11 13 19 29 90 94 104 128 141 146 148 156 158 162 165
HURT, 13 21 27 37-38 41 70 74 88 95
HUTCHERSON, 54 146 163
HUTCHESON, 7 19 37 51 71 80 123
JACKSON, 57 70 80 84-85 87 94-95 97 99 102 105 107-109 112 117-118 120 123-124 128 131 134-137 140 142 153-154 159 164-167 170 172
JAMES, 35 47 59 84 88 95 107 115 118 125 128 147 149 174
JAMISON, 82 118 165
JARVIS, 86
JEFFERSON, 87 91 99 101-102 120 125 134
JENKINS, 62
JERRALL, 74
JERRELL, 26 74 115 168
JERROLD, 12
JESSE, 6 14 24-25 34 44-45 48 55-56 63-64 97 104-105 111 142
JESSEE, 142
JESSIE, 102
JETER, 2-3 6 9-10 15 22 24 42 44-45 47 57 74 78 84 106 120 138 142 149 159 170 172
JOHN, 109
JOHNSON, 37 41 44-45 48 53 58 63 74 76-77 79 82 84-86 90 94 96 98 101-102 104-107 109 112 114 117 120 122 124-126 128 130-131 135-137 140 146-147 149-151 153 156 158-160 165 167-168 170 172-174
JONES, 2 6 14-15 22 24 30 34 44 49 51-55 62 66 76 78 82 84 86-87 90-91 93-94 96 98 103-104 106-109 112 116-117 120 124 128 132 134 137 140 142 146 149 151 153 155 158 163-164 168 170 173-174
JORDAN, 6 18 22 32 44 48 56 77 112 137 151 154 161
JORDON, 6
JUNNY, 65
KANE, 75
KAY, 2 24 31-32 47 77 85 120 122 128 132 151
KEAN, 9 19 29 42
KEANE, 59 70
KEARLE, 97
KEESCE, 30
KEESER, 6
KEEZER, 30

KELLEY, 8 17 26 70 74 90-91 122 130 141 147
KELLY, 2-3 27 42 53 86 105 124
KELSO, 30
KEMP, 6
KEMPT, 146
KERSY, 21
KESLER, 97
KEY, 158
KEYS, 132
KIDD, 6 16 23 25 31-32 39 44 53-54 56 64 67 79 98 102 116 120-121 124 159-160 167
KIMBROUGH, 4
KING, 63 82 93 105 107 131-132 170 174
KINGSLY, 67
KLOCK, 153
KNOT, 27
KNOTE, 27
KOLES, 164
KRASS, 38
KRAUSS, 56
LACOST, 89
LACY, 90
LAFOE, 14 84
LAMBERT, 3 7
LANDRUM, 84
LANE, 118
LATANE, 120 135 143
LATHAM, 24
LAWRENCE, 124
LAWSON, 82 110 114 128 132 140 160
LEACOCK, 2
LEE, 41 91 99 102-103 107 116 120 128 132 145 161 163 170 172
LEFOE, 120 132
LETANY, 77
LEWCORD, 8 58
LEWIS, 23 28 36 39 43-44 51 71 76 80 86 88 90 95 98 110 118 120 126 128 134 137 139 141 143 147 149 156 158 160 163-164 167-168 170 174
LIGHTFOOT, 6 17 23 31 39 46-48 79 148 161
LINDSAY, 91 99 101 116
LINDSEY, 105 140
LIPSCOMB, 87
LITCHFIELD, 15 36
LIVELY, 138 141
LIVING, 85
LOCKLEY, 94
LOCKWELL, 97
LOMAX, 94 102 107 120 132 135 143 167 170 172
LONESOME, 106 116 128 135-136 149
LONEY, 106 144 151
LONG, 8 10 12 18 32 41 51 73 76 78-79 83 106 116

LONG (Cont.)
    118 131 134 138 140 143-144 146 158
LONGDON, 18
LONGEST, 2
LOREN, 61
LOUIS, 127
LOURIE, 45 56
LOURY, 65
LOVE, 32
LOVEN, 1-2 23 25 40 46 48 62-63 84 102 112
LOVIN, 77 79 91
LOVING, 11 25 62 85 91 95 98 102 107 116 132
    135 142 164 166-167 171
LOVIS, 73
LOWERY, 19
LOWRY, 10
LUCAS, 97 101 105 126 135-136 149 160
LUCK, 4 7-10 20 27 29 37 42-43 45 51 58-60 70-71
    73-74 80-81 87 89 93 105 115 119 124 134 138
    158 168
LUCORD, 147
LUCUS, 105 170
LUDLEY, 172
LUMPKIN, 20 23 26 36 43 63 70-71 74 91 98 102
    126 128 132
LUMPKINS, 131
LUNSFORD, 24 39 54 96 99 103-105 109-110 113
LYALL, 55 61
MABILE, 58
MACKAY, 158
MADISON, 4 10-11 18 21 25-28 36 80-81 90-91
    103 105 115 123 126 138 153 156 158
MAGRUDER, 44
MAHON, 6 14 54 62-63 76 112
MAHONE, 147
MALLORY, 8 21 29 40
MAN, 116
MANN, 102
MANUEL, 103
MARINOR, 2
MARMADUKE, 46 114 119 126
MARSHALL, 9 15 43 48 54 61 64 72 76 80 85 98
    100 112 128 132 141 153
MARTIN, 15 19 23 29-30 34 39 44-45 48 51 54 58
    61 65 76 78 87 91 103 107 116 123 135 140 144
    149 167 171
MARYWEATHER, 136
MASON, 7-8 10 12 15 18 58 60 70-72 96 98 105
    113 119 123 144-145 168 174
MASSEY, 143 160
MASSIE, 49
MATHEWS, 108 112 116 128
MATTHEWS, 106 144
MAURY, 2 16 22 30 44 49
MAY, 37 71 102 121
MCCALLEY, 24 33 84
MCCALLY, 66 78
MCCARTHY, 114
MCCAULEY, 128 132
MCCHALLEY, 14
MCCHESNEY, 6
MCCRAY, 99
MCDANIEL, 65
MCDOWELL, 134
MCGEE, 89
MCGRUDO, 144
MCKEE, 125
MCKEIN, 124
MCKENNEY, 28 34 51 54 97 117 173
MCKENNY, 16 124 126
MCKINNEY, 147
MCLAUGHLIN, 8 11 57 119
MCLOCKLAND, 28
MCLOCLINE, 28
MCMULLIN, 47
MCQUIRT, 170
MEADES, 153
MEADS, 153 158 163
MERRIWEATHER, 172
MERRYMAN, 44 54
MEYERS, 78 140
MICHIE, 95
MICKELBERRY, 35
MICKENS, 148
MICOU, 2 78 108 117
MILES, 158
MILLER, 24 29 40 48 51 65 71 73-74 86 98 102 107
    136 152 155 163
MILLS, 7-8 18 26 35 42 58 81 110 130 134 138 141
    153 156 160 163
MINER, 81-82 86
MINES, 80 95 103 105 124 147-148 153 165 168
MINIR, 171
MINOR, 82-83 86-87 90 93 96 98 101-102 105 108
    110 112 115-116 119 121-122 124 126 128 131-
    132 136 138 140-141 146-147 150 163 170 174
MINTER, 2
MITCHELL, 9 42 51 74 87 103 131 141 152
MITLER, 82
MOBILE, 35
MOMREN, 53
MONAHAN, 124
MONCURE, 21 59 73 75 141 171
MONDAY, 6 39 67 85 167 171

MONROE, 84 98 105 108 115 119 126 131 135 138 140 144 148 154 158 163 170
MONT, 103 105 132 146 156 165 174
MONTAGUE, 100 124 131 150 168
MONTH, 93
MOOR, 35-36 42 50 58 69 80
MOORE, 11-12 26 47 85 90 102-103 113-114 116 121 123-124 126 128 131-133 138 144 147-148 156 158 160 166 168-169 171-172 174
MORAN, 36
MOREN, 3 36 81 95 103 126 137 165
MORGAN, 8
MORIS, 79
MORR, 51
MORRIS, 4 8-9 19 24 36 51 71 80 82-83 95 112 130 147 153
MORRISON, 136
MORTON, 16 78 94-95 105-106 116 126 135 141 144 152 167 170
MOSBY, 114 138 158
MOSES, 59
MOTLEY, 2 6 14 22 24 26 30 38 44 46 48 56 61 63-64 84-85 95 97 102 120 132 159 161 164 172
MOUNT, 73 80 82
MUNDAY, 26 78
MURRAY, 49 96 119 131 143
MURROW, 6 15 24 33 169
MUSCOE, 151
MYERS, 3 78 86 131 133 140-141 144 150 161 167
NAPIER, 8 32 45 58 84 116
NAPPER, 96
NELSON, 10 110 112 119 128-129 148 158
NEWS, 101 128 150
NEWTON, 10-12 28 36-37 51 71 80 87 101 103 119 166
NOEL, 1 15-16 18 28 30 34 51 65 71 95 98-99 112 116 129 132 158
NORMAN, 94 96 99 107 116 128 144 150
NORMENT, 15 22-23 35 40 51 55 57 71 73 105 110
OESTERHELD, 164
OLIVER, 4 9 29 40 57 73 90 139
OSBORN, 93 112-113 116
OSBORNE, 128 132 145 151
OSGOOD, 18
OULD, 115
OWEN, 23
OWENS, 128 132 160
PAGE, 6 30 40 65 77 90 99 114-115 124 126 133 141 145 154
PAINE, 150
PALING, 156
PARE, 13 18 28 74 116

PARISH, 44
PARKER, 39 53 55 64 78-79 106 116 124 128 136 138 140 144-145 154 156 160 166 170 172-173
PARR, 18 74 93 99 104 114 136 141 156 171
PARTLOW, 29 41 58 138 141
PARTT, 46
PATTERSON, 81 99
PAVEY, 54 91 95 112 116 122 143 159
PAVY, 6 24 38 54 77 85
PAYNE, 93 100 105 166 174
PEARCE, 112 141 148
PEARSON, 172
PEATROSS, 3 10 19 41-42 51 60 68 71 75 82-83 89 96 105 119 129 132 138 167-168
PEGG, 102 151
PEMBERTON, 80-81 96 106-108 124 166
PENDLETON, 34 47 78 81 86 93 100 105 107-108 116 120 122 128 130 132 140 145 151 158 166 170
PENNEY, 24 51 57 99 112 122
PENNY, 72 80 85
PEREGORY, 46
PERKINS, 156
PETROSS, 132
PETTIS, 89
PEYTON, 2 32-33 65 67 91 100 102 144 154
PHILIPS, 115 153
PHILLIPS, 15 23 35 54 115 129
PICARDATTI, 116
PICARDETT, 22
PICARDETTE, 43
PICKETT, 40 48 109 124
PIERCE, 138
PIERSON, 93 140
PITCHER, 133 138
PITMAN, 33
PITTIS, 22 38 53
PITTMAN, 6 25
PITTS, 1-2 15 30 54 57 65-66 76-78 91 96 99 105 108 112 116 136 159 161 163-164 166-167 170-171
PLEASANT, 163
PLEASANTS, 82 145
POARKER, 102
POATES, 31 105-106
POATS, 31 121
POINDEXTER, 116
POLLARD, 3 8 12 18 42-43 51 53 60 71 86 131 138 141 153 163 167
PONTON, 158
POPE, 82
POTTER, 129

POWER, 160
POWERS, 2 34 45 62 120 140 142 161
PRATT, 14 31 39 46 48 136
PRICE, 49
PRIER, 144
PRINCE, 148
PRIOR, 14 108 122
PRITCHETT, 58
PROCTOR, 40 102-103
PRUETT, 56 91 99 127-128 168
PRYOR, 97
PUGH, 22-23 34 93 128 132 144-146 150-151 154 164 169
PULLEN, 63
PULLER, 1-2 23 30 38-40 43 46-47 63 66 76-78 91 140 150 160-161 171
PULLMAN, 140
PURKE, 1
PURKES, 14 77 93 100 136
PURKS, 33 82
QUARLES, 3 8-9 21 27 36 40 42 71 76 141 146
QUASH, 83 124 126 129 153 163
QUEEN, 128 136 172
QUESENBERRY, 10
QUISENBERRY, 15 20 77 144
RAGLAND, 169
RAINES, 93 161 172
RAINS, 151
RALWINGS, 100
RAMSAY, 103
RAMSEY, 53 59-60 74
RANDAL, 124
RANDALL, 132 140
RANDOF, 153
RANDOL, 166
RAPAPORT, 84
RARISH, 169
RAWLINGS, 94 96 103 110 113
RAY, 61 78
REDD, 10 21 29 38 42 53 75 81-83 93 97 100 102 106 108 113 119 128 133 138 141 146 148
REEVES, 33
REIVES, 164
REYNOLDS, 18 21-22 26 78 83 93 106 113 115-116 128-129 132 136 141 145 148 166 169 174
RICE, 128 161
RICH, 136 155
RICHARD, 150
RICHARDS, 3 7 11 18 35 42 76 81 91 116 122 159
RICHARDSON, 43
RICHELSON, 131
RICHERSON, 2 6 9 16 31 33 41 46-47 54 56 67 77

RICHERSON (Cont.)
   85-86 91 95 100 102 105 107-108 112 115 122 128 140 145 150-151 154 156 159-161 163 167
RICHESON, 53 71
RICHRSON, 151
RICK, 97
RICKS, 13 37 99-100 126
RIDDLE, 55 65 114
RIEVES, 122 167
RIGGIN, 144
RITCHIE, 112
RIX, 13
RIXEY, 2 24 32 63 79
ROANE, 2 6 14 45 116 145 150 153
ROBB, 79 97 106 108 122 136 150-151 155
ROBERSON, 93 145
ROBERTS, 17
ROBERTSON, 43 103 170 173
ROBINOSN, 91
ROBINSON, 10-11 79 81 83 86 90-91 94 107-108 112-113 124 126 129 136 138 141 146 148 154-156 160
ROCK, 21 81 87 93 98 105 141 156
ROCKS, 105
RODNEY, 98 102
ROLLINS, 2 14 66 78 83 102 119 126 128 138 140 145 166 169-170 172
ROLLS, 133 138 169 174
ROLPH, 171
ROOKS, 112
ROOTS, 77 108 110 148 150 153 158 169
ROPER, 2 17 48 62 84
ROSE, 22-23 44 78
ROSETTA, 132
ROSS, 126 138 148 163 169 172
ROSSIN, 99
ROSSON, 115
ROUSE, 2 35 77 116 136 145
ROWE, 15 25 31 46 63 72 78-79 131 144-145 171
ROWZIE, 78 148
ROY, 102 145 160 172-173
ROYSTON, 30-31 40 44 48 56 144
RUSSELL, 102
RYERSON, 136
RYLAND, 169
SACRA, 52 141 146 153 174
SALE, 2 14 16-17 22 29-30 34 38 49 54-55 63 76 84 86 93 106-107 109 112 116-117 122 136 140 142 144 150 156 158 160 164
SALES, 90
SALIE, 64
SAMPSON, 161

SAMUEL, 1-2 4 10 16 18-20 22-23 26 28-29 33 35 39-40 45 48 51-53 57-58 63 65-67 71 73 78 80 83 99-100 102 105 110 112-113 115 119 122 128-129 132 138 140-141 143 145-147 150-153 156 158 160 163 167 170-172
SAMUELL, 57
SATTERWHITE, 7 11 14 75 81 86 90 100 102 108 115 124 163
SATURWHITE, 93
SAUNDERS, 2 10 16 26 30 43 48 51 57 65-67 77 86 91 96 100 107-109 112 115 124 132 143-144 150 155-156 160 164 166 172
SAVAGE, 67
SCHOOLER, 4 10 20 28 37 53 57 122 131
SCHOOLS, 102 160
SCOTT, 11-12 18 25 28 35-37 41 52 57 71 81 90 93 99 102 105 131 133 141 146 172
SCRANGE, 23
SCRIPTURE, 158
SEAL, 35 46 76 86 111 136 140 171
SEALE, 153
SEAMER, 67
SEAMS, 166
SEARLS, 113
SEAY, 13 25 71 81 138 141 146-148 158
SELF, 6 22 47 54 64 66 77 112-113 116 122 164 167 171
SEMPLE, 112
SERINAGE, 48
SEYMOUR, 139 164
SHACKELFORD, 119
SHACKLEFORD, 35 43 104 106 119 140 158 163-164
SHADDOCK, 2 6 24 39-40 43 45 49 56 62 64 76 144
SHADOCK, 67
SHAKESPHEARE, 126
SHAKESPHERE, 107
SHARKS, 152
SHELTON, 168
SHENAULT, 10
SHEPERD, 101
SHEPHERD, 60 71 77 94 96 99 116 129 136 140 144 148-149 151 171
SHIP, 52 81
SHOCKS, 113 115
SHOOKS, 110-111 166
SHUMAN, 19 133 154 160-161 163 174
SILVA, 159
SIRLE, 84
SIRLES, 84 122 173
SIRLS, 31 91

SIZER, 21 41 52 81 87 138 148 169
SKETTON, 129
SKINKER, 2 14 129 131
SKINNER, 25 34 105 136 152
SLAUGHTER, 78 106 141
SLAVE, Aaron 56 60 Abba 75 Abraham 15 37-38 48 51 54 60 68 Abram 2 12 47 49 Achiles 41 Ada 2 Adalade 29 Adaline 27-28 Adam 5 17 31 36 50 58 72 Adelina 36 Adeline 6 25 65 75 Adison 28 62 Adrianna 21 Afferiah 40 Aggy 42 58 60 Agnes 2 34 51 70 Agness 34 Alace 73 75 Albert 10-11 14-15 37 41 54 56 62 Alexander 8 20 22 34 50 Aley 17 67 Aley Minor 57 Alfarria 75 Alfred 27 30 32-33 38 52 64 Alice 22 34 Allah 3 Allen 52 54 Allice 10 Almeda 2 Alpheus 32 Amanda 3 40 59 68 Amelia 10 25 Americus 25 Amey 24 30 Amos 26 Amy 12 17 Anderson 29 52 Andrew 5 17 32 49 63 72 Andrew Broaddus 4 Andrew Jackson 8 Angelina 11 Angelo 9 Ann 18 27 29 46 53-54 63 66-67 Ann Fortune 8 Anna 3 8 21 27-28 33 36 40 58 63 Anna Marie 39 Annie 61 Anth0ny 8 Anthony 3 7 22 24 Archie 14 62 72 Archy 75 Argyle 71 Arin 13 Arthur 13 32 68 Aureliius Garland 3 Austin 44 Baceni 75 Bankhead 23 Barnett 10 66 Bartlett 13 Bassett 3 Battaillel 61 Baughm 2 Becky 8 Belfield 70 Ben 11 20 41 52-53 55 71 Benjamin 31 43 Bennett 70 Bennette 55 Bernice 31 Betsey 56 Betsy 3 30 39 41 51 69 Betsy Fox 10 Bettie 1-2 4 25 46 49 54-55 64 Betty 20 25-26 42 55 Beverley 5 34 Beverly 67 72 Billy 3 9 19 21 23 59 63-64 Bob 1 12 38 66 69 72 Bobby 65 Bonie 65 Bristoe 6 Brutus 57-58 Buckner 59 Bumerage 35 Burtie 16 Burton 22 62 Camilla 12 Caroline 2 8 17-18 20 24 27 35 37 55 69 73 Cary 27 Cath 67 Catharine 26 61 Catherine 58-59 Cathl 14 Caty 12 15 24 Celia 10 Ceophas 53 Chana 7 Chaney 23 31 Chany 47 Chaplis 36 Charity 36 61 Charles 2 9 19 65 75 Charlott 9 47 Charlotte 24-25 32 34-36 46 55 62 Chas 14 30 33 55 64-65 Chas Harrey 6 Chauncy 14 China 19 Christine 34 Ciley 39 Cintha 16 Claiborne 13 Claibourne 60 Clara 12-13 Clarah 41 50 Clary 16 Clem Cooper 3 Clement 38 Clementine 68 Clemenza 7 Clemmy 42 Clemy 52 Cloe 46 Coleman 64 Comadorc 4 Cornclia 9 37 Cornelius 14 69-70 Cost 70 Courtney 32 38 Cupid 18 Cynthia 32 67 Cyrus 49 Dabney 37 Dallas 27 61 Daniel 11 15 38 44 47 Danl 23 49 Davey 46 55 David 36 62 Davy 4 29 59 Delia 9 18 65 Delilah 31 Delpey 36 Delpha 39 Delphia 4 56 Delphy 73 Dennis 9 32 46 Dick 11-12 21 Dick Clayton 60 Dinah 22 54 58 Dolly 18 35 Dunmore 64 Eda 64

SLAVE (Cont.)

Edmond 2 7 Edmund 8 11 38 48 52 Edward 1 4 23 Edy 32 47 Eli 5 Elijah 29 Eliz 40 46 Eliz Ann 58 Eliza 5 17 32 37 42 45-47 49 53 65 Elizabeth 2 11-12 18 59 63 Elizth 20 Ella 8 11 38 Ellar 72 Ellen 14 37 39 41 50 53 62-63 65 70 Ellett 41 Elliott 19 27 37 48 Ellis 19 Elmira 67 Elmore 28 Elvira 41 Elzer 31 Emanuell 56 Emelina 33 Emenual 49 Emily 8 11 39 46 61 64-65 Emma 10 14 63 70 Ephraim 57 Esaw 25 Esteller 70 Esther 18 46 Etta 5 30 Etter 75 Eva 56 Eve 14 27 Evelena 60 Evelina 57 61 66 Eveline 10 Fannie 25 Fanny 3 6-7 9 23 26 33-34 43 51 74 Festus 34 Fleming 35 Fletah 53 Frances 12 17 34 38 43-44 51 60 Francis 30 Frank 4 24 38 46 66 Frankey 12 Franklin 68 Franky 37 59 69 Fred 37 66 Frederick 69 Gabriel 13 34 58 63 66 Gardener 4 Garland 8 57 Gay 52 Gen'l Stuart 76 Geo 15 17 48 63-65 Georganna 25 George 1 3 6-7 10 15-16 21 26 29 31 33 36 39 42-43 46-47 56 60 62 68 George Anna 10 George Carter 74 George Washington 28 George-anna 62 Georgia 75 Ginay 17 Ginney 2 69 Ginny 28 45 68 Grace 74 Granville 5 Gregory 46 Gricie 64 Griffin 67 Gus 57 Hannah 12 25 33 41 43 45 59 69 74 Harriet 6 Harriett 3 14 23-24 26 31 36 44 52 55 57 64 68 Harry 2 15 17 19 22 36 45 53 57 Hartsey 4 Hattie 67 Hausey 31 Hellen 13 64 Henretta 45 Henrietta 72 Henry 5-6 9 11-13 16 25 28-29 31 33 43 47 50 53 56 58-59 64 66 71 Henry Davis 51 Hetta 53 Hezekiah 32 Hillgard 65 Hillyard 14 Horace 6 57 68 74 Howard 44 Humphrey 10 14 41 47-48 Humphrey Mills 7 Ida 29 Isaac 36 54 56-57 65 70-71 Isaac Anderson 4 Isabella 20-21 56 72 Jack 13 22 47 52 Jackson 5 40 Jacob 3 25 59 Jacobs 67 James 3 8 10-11 14 16-17 20 24 28 44-45 49 57 60-61 64 67 70 76 Jane 2 12-14 19 23 25 33 35-36 39 47 69 76 Jane Dabney 4 Jarod 6 Jarrett 51 Jas 16 34 47 Jefferson 20 29 Jemima 4 Jenny 43 Jerry 5 7 21 27 35 46 60 71 Jesse 10 16 23 29 Jeter George 37 Jim 4 9 13 31 33 39 54 56-57 61 63 66-67 Jinney 4 Jno 3 14 16 25 33-34 45 Jno Malin 45 Joe 9 21 27-29 31 47 55 60 70 73 Joe Minor 69 John 5-6 8-9 11-12 15 23 25 35 37 39 41-43 48-50 52 55-57 63 65-66 70-71 75 John Gaush 69 John Henry 21 John James 69 John Miller 43 John Minor 73 John Thomas 28 37 John Washington 10 John Wm 59 Jolly 16 30 Jonny 12 Jordan 19 31-32 Jos 43 Joseph 5 26-28 42 59 72 Juda 3 Judith 23 45-46 Judson 58 Judy 5 16 20 23 28-29 39 68 Julia 7 20 37 52-53 71 Juliett 43 June 53 Kannaki 69 Katy 45 Kennie 38 Keziah 6 22 Kilate 37 Kisiah 73

SLAVE (Cont.)

Kissy 60 Kitt 30 Kitty 2 11 39 61 Laberta 70 Lacy 39 Lamer 60 Lanah 58 Landon 69 Lavenia 27 Lawson 67 Leanna 52 Lee 8 Leland 26 Lepnober 2 Letitia 14 Letty 6 Letty Jane 29 Lewis 2 10 16 20 22 24 28 30 30 33-35 37-38 45 51 63 68 Lillyann 71 Linder 11 Lindsey 4 71 Littleton 4 Lizza 7 Lizzy 29 68 Lorane 37 Louis 24 Louisa 4 6 12-15 28 33 38 45 48 52 65 Louise 55 Lucinda 14 30 37 41 49 53 62 70 72 Lucius 30 Lucy 3 5-6 9 11 13 15-17 19-20 24-25 27-28 30-31 38-40 45 48 50 52 56-57 59 62-63 66-67 75 Lucy Ann 20 43 62 Lydia 17 29 44 Lydia Goodwin 10 M 22 Madison 15 Major 18 28 41 50 Malinda 11 32 34 56 61 Malissa 70 Manuel 9 Marcellus 72 Marcus 20 Margaret 34 Margarett 15 27 30 70 75 Margaretta 65 Margt 56 Maria 1 3-5 7-8 11-12 15-16 22-23 26 33 38 44 47-48 53 59 62-63 67 69 75 Maria Bet 40 Mariah 21 40 70 Mariah Page 35 Mark 32 Marsha 7 Marshall 27 Martha 12 18 20 26 28 33 35-36 38 41 52 54-55 62-63 71 73 Martha Ann 41 Martin 19 24 Mary 2 4-6 8 12 14-15 17-19 24 29-30 38 40 44-46 48 50 55 57 59-60 65 70 74 Mary Ann 34 37 42 52 54 68 Mary Frances 68 Mary Jane 37 66 Mary Louisa 7 57 Mary Warwick 45 Matilda 2 6 13 19 23-24 57 66 Matilda Ann 37 Matthew 14 16 Mattie 34 Matty 57 Mckensie 55 64 Mehala 74 Melvina 19 Michel 32 Mildred Ann 53 Millgard 48 Milly 9-10 12 17 21 24 28-30 34 43 54-55 71 75 Miltin 70 Milton 44 Minova 28 Mira 6 Missey 32 Molly 21 26 30 42 69 Moses 14 32 38 48 Nancy 12 19 22 26 28 30 36 40-42 49-50 71 74 Nancy Sale 46 Nathan 21 Ned 21 66 Nelly 14 28 39 Nelson 37 Newton 17 Nicey 6 Nimrod 60 Nissa 23 Norman 72 Olive 24 Oliver 48 55 63 Oscar 4 Oteria 51 Overton 40 Palace 9 Paster 59 Patience 14 Patrick 16 Patrick Washington 4 Patsey 7 Patsy 15 18 20 34-35 56 68 Pattie 46 Paty 2 Paul 15 40 Peggy 25 27 41 Pendleton 75 Penny 14 Peter 13 25 28 31 33 41-42 48 50 56-57 64-66 70 Petro 18 26 Phebe 17 32 Phil 39 44 49 Philicia 34 Philip 1 33 43 58 60 Philis 27 Phill 67 Phillip 57 68 Phillis 9 15 31 35 46 48 Piney 64 Pleasant 11 48 51 Pollux 46 Polly 4 6-7 11 14 26-27 31 41 54 65 Porter 68 Preston 71 Prince 25 Purity 38 Rachel 16 21 39-40 61 Randal 3 9 11-12 35 Randolph 51 54 64 66 Reana 24 Rebecca 6 31-32 67 Reuben 1 9 18 25 30 37 57 68 Rhoda 23 Richard 5 8 33 43 48-49 58 69 Richd 33 Rina 2 Risey 19 Robert 10 12 31 55-56 58-60 Robert Edmund 42 Roberta 56 Robin 32 39 54 Robinson 35 43 Robt 6 22 48-49 64-65

SLAVE (Cont.)
  Roburta 28 Roderick 12 Rosa 36 Rose 2 12 41 45 54 56 70 Rosena 59 Rosetta 36 49 Rosey Lee 70 Rudy 21 Ruffin 67 Salena 47 Salina 9 Sallie 2 31 34 38 48 Sally 5 13 16-17 23 27-28 32 50 55-56 58 62-63 69-70 Sam 7-8 13 15 19 21 33-35 40 49 55 72 Saml 14 Sampson 26 58 67 Samuel 54 64 Sandy 11 52 60 Sanford 33 Sara L 33 Sarah 4 6-7 18 21 24 28 34 39 43 45 49 Sarah Ann 4 Sarah Jane 36 Sazelson 21 Schnook 36 Scott 1 23 Sela 5 Selah 35 Selina 13 Shakespear 34 41 Sibrena 58 Silas 29 40 47 53 Silby 59 Silva 8 21 Silvia 60 Simon 45 52 59 Sinah 52 Siras 9 Soloman 6 46 56 69 Sophia 40 65 Spencer 10 45 70 Stafford 2 Stephen 14 57 Steven 1 47 Strother 6 Sukey 20 Sulky 37 Susan 6 9-10 13 16 18 32-33 45 47 66 72 Susan Farish 48 Susannah 26 Tabitia 43 Taliaferro 30 Taylor 21 Temple 17 46-47 Terissa 15 Terror 32 Thomas 5 9 11 15 17 26 35 40 48 50 53 55 61 69 Thomas Kemp 19 Thornton 56 63-64 70 Thos 15 33 39 Tinah 59 Titus 67 Tom 4 12 18 28 38 41-42 69 Tony 9 Tulip 2 19 23-24 Tunstall 55 Turner 24 Ursley 63 Venice 71 Victoria 12 29 Vilett 1-2 47 Vina 73 Violet 69 Vira 11 Virginia 6 25 38 44 Wahala 64 Walinda 64 Walker 1 13 15 20 28 31 38 56 61-62 64 73 Waller 64 Wallis 15 Walter 24 57 Walton 16 Warner 11 27 29 Warren 64 Washington 9 31 45 49 56 65 Wesley 12 68 William 2-5 9 11 13-15 17-20 22 25 28-29 31-35 38 41-42 45 50 52-54 56-57 59-61 63-64 67 69-70 Willie 63 Willis 8 13 17 56 60 64 Willy Ann 70 Willyann 70 Wilson 51 67 Wilton 60 Winney 11 15 28 30 Winston 17 41-42 63 Wm 9 15 Wm Allen 42 Wm Henry 9 Wm Minor 37 Woodson 57 Worter 72 York 50 Zachariah 57
SLE, 84
SLUDG, 130
SMITH, 4 9-10 14 23 29 36 41 45 56 59 71 73 75 77 90 97 99 102-103 106 112 115 119 122 124 126 129 132-133 136 138 145-146 148 150 153 155-156 160-161 166 168 174
SMITHER, 33
SMITHERS, 96 129 133 142 163 169
SMITHEY, 122
SMITHY, 77
SMOOT, 30 84 112 122 161 168
SORRELL, 46 67 76 106 108 122
SOUTHWORTH, 3-4 6 8 12 18 23 38-39 42 44 50-51 53 57-59 61 76 81 86 91 94-95 99 103 105 107 113 129 138 141 148 153 156 158 165 174
SPENCER, 100
SPICER, 83
SPIER, 52
SPINDLE, 2 53 90 120 148 166
STANLEY, 83 90 141 163 166
STERN, 16 166 169
STERNE, 91 112 159
STERNES, 62
STERNS, 80
STEVENS, 7-8 10 18 20 52 74 81 85-87 89 103 111 113 124 126 129 144 146 163
STEVENSON, 119 169
STEWART, 4 84 113 160
STILL, 81 86
STILLING, 108
STOCAS, 136
STOVER, 95
STREET, 150 160
STRESHLEY, 16 23 67 78
STUART, 57 138 174
SUGAR, 90
SUTTON, 3 5 11 60-61 71 73 76 94 105 110 150 173
SWAIN, 140
SWANN, 9 11 19-20 27 29 37 42 50 52 71 86 113 169 174
SWIFT, 84
SYLVA, 2 160 164 171
SYRLES, 132 154
TALIAFERO, 163
TALIAFERRO, 10 12 19 43 57 84 86 90 93 96-97 99 101 103 105 113 117 122 129 131 136 144 150 152 156 161 163-164
TARAPENCE, 81
TATE, 81 133 142
TAVNER, 129
TAYLOR, 2 4 6-7 14-15 22 24-25 32-35 38-39 42-46 49 54 56 62-63 65-67 75 77-81 83 87 89-90 93-94 96-97 99-100 102-103 105-108 111-116 119 122 124-125 129 133 136 138 140 144 148 150 152-153 156 158-159 161 163-164 166-167 169 171-172 174
TEMPLE, 27 59 103 115 119 133 148 174
TENNANT, 16 27 98 161
TENNENT, 159
TERREL, 103 105
TERRELL, 7 13 15 38 41 52 58-60 68 72 81 83 116 119 126 158
TERRY, 21 36 87 94 96 103 105 115-116 126 126 147-148 153 158
THACHER, 145
THACKER, 36 76 115 118-119 124
THOMAS, 8 12 16 18 26 30 32 34 36 58 58 67 72 74 77-78 81 83 106 108 113 117 123-124 126

THOMAS (Cont.)
    129-130 133 138 144 151 154 164 170 173
THOMPKINS, 9
THOMPSON, 8 81 83 94 96 105 111 126 129 133
    138 146 156 163 165 174
THORNLEY, 13 24 40 45 55 106 108
THORNTON, 2-3 6-7 14 17 24-25 30 32 34 44-46
    56 83-86 97 101 103 106 112 129 134 136 144
    152-154 159-161 171
THROM, 159-160
THRONTON, 64
TIBBS, 83
TIGNOR, 144 152 164
TILLER, 36 38 111
TILMAN, 148 158
TIMBERLAKE, 9 111
TINSLEY, 6 148
TOD, 33 117 156
TODD, 15 21 26 36 49 124 130 133
TOLIVER, 133 138
TOMPKINS, 11 13 29 41 51 72 75 93 133 142 144
    148
TOMPSON, 142 146
TOOMBS, 16 24 39 49 56 93 108 122 132 167
TRACY, 121
TRAINHAM, 18-19 83 105 125
TRAVILLIAN, 21
TRAVIS, 22 164
TRAYNHAM, 22
TREVILIAN, 3
TREVILLIAN, 138
TRIBBLE, 42 72 83 111 124 158 166
TRIBLE, 2 7
TRICE, 3 24 62 78 80 83 86-87 91
TRUMAN, 82 130
TUCK, 22 43 46 78 116
TUNSTALL, 16 22 30 44 48 65 72 91 94 96 126
    133 153 174
TURNER, 7 13 19-21 26 35 44 46-47 54 57 64 72
    74 81 87 89 91 96 103 105 111 114-115 122 132
    136 138 141 160 162 169-170
TURPIN, 142 153
TWISDALE, 8 147
TYLER, 4 10 20 27 38 40 72 170
TYREE, 36-37 72 105 138
UPSHAW, 38 56 61 78 106 108 111-112 144 151-
    152 169
URGUHART, 31 56
URQUHART, 17
VAUGHAN, 23 39 43 45 57 61 91 112 122 131 140
    159 161 169
VESSELES, 101

VESSELLS, 55 84 108 116
VESSELS, 122 129 137
VINCENT, 96 161
WADDY, 142
WADKINS, 146
WADLINGTON, 119
WAITE, 167 170
WAITS, 129
WALDRESS, 52
WALDROSS, 52-53
WALKER, 6 13 23-25 63 81 108 116 121-122 126
    129 133 146 154 164 170 172
WALLACE, 100 108 137
WALLER, 4 20 29 52 58 81 83 119 125 142 146 166
WALTON, 146
WARD, 93 144
WARE, 4 8 12 18 27 35 37 43 58-59 73 75 84 99
    113 122 144 150 154-155 160 163 167-168 172-
    173
WARWICK, 22-23
WASH, 100
WASHINGTON, 4 9 13 20 28 36 41 45-46 52 56 66
    72-73 77-78 86 96 102 106 108 113-114 119 122
    125 144 148 150 153 155 158 163-164 167 174
WATKINS, 10 21 29 52 61 126 146 166
WATTS, 79 159
WAUGH, 164
WEASNER, 3 7
WEATHERESS, 156
WEATHERS, 87
WEAVER, 82 124 134
WEBB, 119 129 140
WEBSTER, 166 174
WELCH, 21 41 58 67-68
WELSH, 36 111
WELTON, 154
WEST, 7-8 12 52 60 72 83 89 100 103 105 108 146
    163
WHARTON, 31 55 86 99 102 108 122 169
WHIPLE, 126
WHITE, 3 7 9 11 13-14 16-18 20 22 24 29 32-34 38
    41-42 44-45 48-49 52 55-56 58 81 83-84 91 99
    103 103 117 122 125 130 137-138 142 144 150
    154 161 164 169
WHITEL, 61 64-65
WHITICOE, 17 46 54 63
WHITIE, 54
WHITING, 113 172
WHITLOCK, 99
WHITTACO, 122
WHITTACOE, 35
WHITTAKER, 151-152 161

WHITTICO, 152 159
WHITTICOE, 35 108 137 149-151
WHIVELY, 137
WHTE, 166
WIGGLESWORTH, 42
WIGLESWORTH, 9 130 138 148 163 165 169
WILLARD, 127
WILLIAMS, 103 107 113 116 119 125 129 133 138 140 144 146 148 150 157-158 163 166-167 169-170 174
WILLIAMSON, 3 43
WILLIS, 18 97 102 111-113 132 144 149 172
WILSHIRE, 103
WILSON, 14 33 81 127 146
WILTON, 130
WILTSHIRE, 59 107 166
WINGFIELD, 89 103 105 109 119 127 139 152
WINKFIELD, 130
WINN, 4 9 11 17 20 29 37 42 52 72 74 81 89 130 162 174
WINSTON, 3 7 20 38 83 105 133
WISE, 113
WITHERS, 3 111
WITTAKIRE, 21
WOLLARD, 130 133
WOOD, 3 10 12 29 35 42 52 60 72 74-75 123 127
WOODSON, 161
WOOLARD, 74 146
WOOLFOLK, 7 10 13 15-16 19-20 22-24 27-28 32 37 39-40 43-46 48 52 60 64 72 84 91 93 113 118 130 132 144 154 159 174
WORMLEY, 146-147 166
WORTHAM, 3 7 18-19 27 35-36 57 72 75 94 119 148
WRIGHT, 3-5 7-11 13 16-17 19-20 22-23 26 28-32 34-43 45-47 52-55 57 60 62-63 72-73 75 79 81 83 85-87 89 91 93 95 98-99 102-103 106 111 113 116 119 122 125 127 130 137 139 142 144 146 150 152 155 157-159 161 163-164 166 168-171
WYATT, 8 20 35 52 72 83 86-87 89 113 119
YARBOROUGH, 103
YARBROUGH, 8 12 19 26 73
YATES, 3 65 87 129 133
YORK, 114
YOUNG, 4 7-8 12-13 18-19 21 23 26 28 35 37 42 50 58 68 73-75 81 83 89 96 99 103 105 111 113 123 132-133 136 138 141-142 144 150 155 157-158 160-161 163 167-168 172-174

www.ingramcontent.com/pod-product-compliance
Lightning Source LLC
Chambersburg PA
CBHW081203240426
43669CB00039B/2784